Photo: Jean Doresse

THE SITE OF THE DISCOVERY

The south-east flank of the Gebel et-Tarif, near the hamlet of Hamra-Dûm:
at the foot of this wall of rock, on the right, are the entrances to the tombs of the
princes of the sixth dynasty. The overturned earth in front of the cliff marks the
site of the ancient cemetery where the jar containing the manuscripts was buried.

Jean Doresse

THE SECRET BOOKS
OF THE
EGYPTIAN GNOSTICS

An Introduction to the Gnostic Coptic
manuscripts discovered at Chenoboskion

With an English Translation and critical evaluation of
THE GOSPEL ACCORDING TO THOMAS

MJF BOOKS
NEW YORK

Published by MJF Books
Fine Communications
322 Eighth Avenue
New York, NY 10001

Library of Congress Catalog Card Number 97-72760
ISBN 1-56731-227-6

The Secret Books of the Egyptian Gnostics
First U.S. edition 1986 by Inner Traditions International
Copyright © 1958 by Librairie Plon. First published in French
under the title, *Les livres secrets des Gnostiques d'Egypt*
by Librairie Plon, Paris, 1958.
The original text was revised and augmented by the author for the
English edition and published in the United Kingdom by
Hollis & Carter Ltd., 1960. English translation copyright © 1960
by Hollis & Carter Ltd.
Copyright © 1986 by Inner Traditions International
This edition published by arrangement with
Inner Traditions International.

Manufactured in the United States of America on acid-free paper ∞

MJF Books and the MJF colophon are trademarks of Fine Creative Media, Inc.

BG   10 9 8 7 6 5 4

CONTENTS

page

INTRODUCTION xi

I. THE PROBLEM OF GNOSTICISM: ITS EARLIEST KNOWN
ELEMENTS 1
   The Discovery and the Critical Study of Gnosticism 1
   Its ancient adversaries. 4
   The Sects as their enemies depict them . . 10
   The great Gnostic doctors (Nicolas, Simon and
     Helen, Menander, Satornil, Basilides, Carpocra-
     tes, Valentinus, Marcus, Justin) . . . 13
   The great sects: St Irenaeus on the Cainites,
     Barbelo-Gnostics; Ophites 35
   St Epiphanius on the Great Gnostics; Ophites;
     Cainites; Archontici, Audians and Mel-
     chizedekians 40
   The *Philosophumena* on the Naassenes, Peratae
     and Sethians 47
   Plotinus on Gnosticism 53
   Theodore Bar-Konaï, in the *Book of Scholia*, on
     the Audians, John of Apamea, the Kukeans,
     Kanteans and Battaï 55
   Some outstanding questions 61

II. ORIGINAL TEXTS AND MONUMENTS . . . 64
   The *Books of Pistis-Sophia* 64
   The *Books of the Saviour* 72
   The *Books of Jêou* 73
   The untitled and anonymous treatise of the Bruce
     Codex 76
   The Gnostic Manuscript of Berlin . . . 86
   Various fragments 88
   Gnostic monuments and paintings . . . 89

Remains of Gnosticism in the related literature of its times 94
The Main Features of Gnostic Doctrine . . 110

III. THE STORY OF A DISCOVERY 116
How the manuscripts came to light . . . 116
In the Egyptian Countryside 127

IV. THIRTEEN CODICES OF PAPYRUS 137
Paleographic aspects 141
List of Texts contained in the Codices . . . 142

V. FORTY-FOUR SECRET (AND HITHERTO UNKNOWN) BOOKS 146
The *Revelations* of the great prophets of Gnosticism, from Seth to Zoroaster 146
The *Paraphrase of Seth* and its Iranian models . 147
The *Apocalypses* of Zoroaster, Zostrian, Messos and *Allogenes* 156
The *Hypostasis of the Archons* or *Book of Nôrea* . 159
Writing No. 40: Eros in Gnostic mythology . 165
The *Sacred Book of the invisible Great Spirit* . 177
The *Treatise on the Triple Protennoïa* . . . 181
The *Revelations of Adam to Seth*, and writing No. 24 182
The *Apocalypse of Dositheus* 188
The *Exegesis upon the Soul* 190
The *Epistle of Eugnostos the Blessed* . . . 192
Gnostics disguised as Christians 197
The *Sophia of Jesus* 198
The *Secret Book of John* 201
The Gospels of Christianized Gnosticism . . 218
The anonymous writing No. 19 . . . 219
The *Gospels of Philip* and of *Matthias* . . 221
The *Gospel of Thomas* and the *Logia Iesou* . . 227
The *Acts* and *Revelations* of *Peter* and of *James* . 235
The *Apocalypse of Paul* 237
The *Gospel of Truth* 239
Hermes Trismegistus as an ally of Gnosticism . 241

VI. The Sethians According to their Writings . 249
    Literary Problems and Problems of Mythology . 250
    Origins and near Relations of Gnosticism . . 263
        Hellenic Thought and Gnosticism . . . 263
        The contribution from Astrology . . . 266
        What did Egypt contribute? 272
        Hermetic elements in Gnosticism . . . 275
        The Influence of the Iranian dualism . . 279
        India and Gnosticism 284
        Jewish Gnosticism and the Kabbala . . . 285
        Gnosticism and the sectaries of Qumrân . . 295
        Gnosticism and Christianity 300
VII. The Survival of Gnosticism: From Manichaeism
    to the Islamic Sects 310
Epilogue 324
Notes on Plates 5 and 11 327

Appendix I
The Teaching of Simon Magus in the Chenoboskion
Manuscripts 329

Appendix II
The Gospel According to Thomas

Introduction 333
Preliminary Note 353
Translation 355
Notes 370
Index of References to the Canonical Gospels . . 378

General Index 387

ILLUSTRATIONS

1. The site of the discovery . . . . . *Frontispiece*

facing page

2. Toga Mina and the author deciphering the first manuscript 110

3. Cast of a carved gem representing the demiurge Iaô. 111

4. Medal in lead representing on one side the demiurge
Iaô and on the other the spheres of the seven heavens 111

5. The Coptic manuscript of the *Pistis-Sophia*, page 143 126

6. The magic papyrus of Oslo No. 1, Column 1 . . 127

7. The Deir Anba-Palamun 222

8. The site of St Pachomius's principal monastery . . 222

9. The coptic priest David 223

10. The manuscripts of Chenoboskion 238

11. Codex X, pages 32 and 33, showing the beginning of
the *Gospel according to Thomas* 239

Ialdabaôth—also called Ariael: an engraved gnostic
gem 166

"See, Father," said Jesus, "how, pursued by evil, (the soul) is wandering far from thy spirit over the earth. She tries to flee from hateful chaos; she knows not how to emerge from it. To that end, Father, send me! I will descend, bearing the seals. I will pass through all the aeons; I will unveil every mystery; I will denounce the appearances of the gods and, under the name of Gnosis, I will transmit the secrets of the holy way."

(Hymn of the Soul, attributed to the Naassene Gnostics in the *Philosophumena*, V, 10, 2).

INTRODUCTION

AM I perhaps a little inclined to underrate the interest of those much-admired manuscripts discovered near the Dead Sea? By this I do not mean that I grudge them any of the importance that all the most competent specialists agree in ascribing to them. But neither do I go so far as to think that that discovery was the most extraordinary that could possibly have been made of the vanished world in which the Christian religion was born and bred. For this I have a personal but sufficient reason—I know of some other writings, a little less ancient (by some centuries) than the texts of Qumran, but richer; and they illuminate with the greatest abundance of detail one of the most obscure movements in the earliest centuries of our era. It is of these Coptic manuscripts found in Upper Egypt, and of the circumstances in which they were brought to light, that I propose to give a general account in this first book. Let it not be thought, however, that I am concerned to extol this discovery above anything that has been found elsewhere. I do think it important, because the texts recovered are indeed more numerous, far more revealing and perhaps also of greater historic consequence than those from the Judaean desert. But I do not at all want to defend this judgement in the spirit of a sports competition, which is out of place in scientific enquiries. I am well aware that, if I am wrong, other specialists will be only too pleased to put me right. Moreover, as soon as it becomes possible to make an exhaustive study of the fifty or so Gnostic documents lately recovered from the sands of Egypt and when the Qumran scrolls have yielded their last secret, we, may even discover some more or less tenuous relation between the histories of the two religious movements to which these two finds of manuscripts belonged; and the existence of such a link may enhance the interest of both.

As in the case of the manuscripts from the Judaean desert, the discovery of these in Upper Egypt was not in the least like one of those dramatic exhumations to which officials, journalists and sight-seers flock like crowds drawn to the scene of some notorious crime. Nearly everything took place behind curtains of discretion. It is owing to this circumstance that almost all the details of the story, as well as the actual nature of the manuscripts in question, are still practically unknown to the general public.

It was about 1945 or 1946 that a few peasants from a hamlet in Upper Egypt, who had at the time no particularly elevated aims, happened to unearth a jar filled with the finest batch of writings on religious subjects that even the soil of Egypt, rich as it is in relics, has yet restored to us. In 1946 the lamented Togo Mina, then Director of the Coptic Museum at Cairo, had the good luck to spot one of these manuscripts in the hands of a dealer, and bought it. Two years elapsed before Togo Mina and I, by our united efforts and powerfully assisted by the Canon Étienne Drioton—then Director-General of the Service of Antiquities—managed to get on the track of the rest of the contents of the jar, brought the manuscripts to light, and had them retained for purchase by the Council of the Cairo Coptic Museum. The Egyptian press, inured as it is to the most fantastic archaeological finds, then published, very simply, the brief communications that we put in its way.

A summary account of the first stage of this discovery which was given at Paris to the Académie des Inscriptions et Belles-Lettres, and to which Professor H. C. Puech willingly lent his authority, aroused a moderate degree of interest. This can be pretty well measured by the few lines allotted to our communication in the ever-accurate *Le Monde* on 23 February 1948—"Discovery of a papyrus of the fourth century. The Academy has been informed of the discovery, recently made in Egypt, of a collection on papyrus, of 152 pages, dating from the sixth century of our era. It contains in Coptic translation five unpublished Gnostic books. They furnish interesting information about the beliefs of that time." The report made to the Académie des Inscriptions was, at least, a good deal more accurate than this notice would lead one to suppose.

It is true that a year later, the far richer information I was able to give, this time about the manuscripts as a whole, not only one of them, aroused a legitimate interest in the press which extended, for example, from the *Nouvelles Littéraires* to the American reviews *Archeology* and *Newsweek*, besides appearing across the Channel in the *Manchester Guardian*. But there was no wave of excitement, either among specialists or the public.

Meanwhile, at Cairo, the formalities that had to be gone through before the valuable documents could become the undoubted property of the Egyptian government and be made available for systematic study, dragged on and on for years. Why such interminable delays? Well do I remember Togo Mina's anguish on the day when he realized that the competent authorities, whose decision had become essential to conclude a matter of such importance, were doing nothing about it. Togo Mina, who took the fate of the discovery all too much to heart, was to die long before any solution was in sight. And even after his decease an obstinate ill-luck beset every effort connected with the acquisition and projected publication of these documents. Was this due to the maledictions that the Egyptian Gnostics had written out in full upon their works, against anyone gaining unlawful knowledge of them? Or was it rather a consequence of all the covetousness, commercial and scientific, converging upon such a promising affair? If it were all to be gone through again, I confess that—although for my own part I received every possible assistance from the able scientific persons concerned, to whom I am profoundly grateful—I would probably think twice before I would again embroil myself for the sake of a discovery liable to arouse so many envies and jealousies.

Today the public is awakening to the interest offered by these newly-found writings. Primarily this is because the manuscripts have at last become the property of the Egyptian government, and are to be published under an international committee. At the same time, unofficial disclosures from one source and another have given some glimpses of the importance of their contents. One of the manuscripts was taken out of Egypt, and reached Europe where it was acquired by the Jung Foundation: various articles have already been published about this, and one of the writings it contains has just been carefully edited. On the other hand, some Gnostic treatises in Coptic, contained in a papyrus in the Berlin Museum where they had been awaiting publication for more than fifty years, have now at last been published: it has been possible to complete them from the variant readings of parallel texts among those now recovered in Egypt, which the authorities of the Coptic Museum have been willing to release for publication in this indirect manner. Finally, the Coptic Museum has begun to publish a photographic edition of the finest codices, and of this the first volume has appeared. It is therefore becoming possible for specialists to break the silence. Professor H. C. Puech, for instance, has been able to put forward the remarkable solution to the problem of the *Sayings of Jesus*—the *Logia*—at which he arrived thanks to one of the new-found documents. And for the same reasons it is now possible for me, at last, to say what this prodigious collection of sacred books really is, and how it was found. It is all the more desirable to make this known now, for since the death of Togo Mina I am the only first-hand witness of all the events that led up to the discovery and all the difficult transactions by which the treasure was secured. It is surely best, from now onward, to put a stop to such a cluster of fables as has been too often allowed to grow around other discoveries, merely to give them a fantastic garb and draw attention to them.

Admittedly, the introduction I offer in this volume cannot— except for the few texts to which I have been able to give thorough study—amount to more than a rapid outline. It is not based upon a complete reading of all the texts: for many of them, its essential foundation consists of the incomplete decipherments that I made in 1948, when my task was to find out the number, the nature and the importance of all that was comprised in the collection— taking the utmost care of the fragile pages of papyrus, many of which were broken and had yet to be put into a condition that would make them legible. I may even, faced with some of the imprecisions in my analyses, feel somewhat ashamed. But I am encouraged by the knowledge that some others, who were never in a position to read a single line of these writings, and whose information was limited precisely to the details disclosed in the first articles published by Togo Mina, H. C. Puech or myself, have not hesitated to produce pretentious summaries of the discovery which, although readers who are ill-informed may take them to have some weight, are in fact mere works of imagination! What value can one place upon "conclusions" which are no more than hazardous guesses at what these documents may eventually prove to contain? Such manoeuvres were in one respect clever enough, since the few persons who were reasonably well informed about the discovery were obliged, for reasons of administrative discretion, to keep silent about the exact nature of its content.

One would much like to know what precise status will be attributed to a discovery like this of Chenoboskion after another fifty years. The interest attached to any archaeological find— except in the case of objects of such undoubted and immediately sensible beauty that they lose nothing with the passage of time—is subject to great vicissitudes, especially when the interest is historical or religious. When first made known, such a find is greeted with an enthusiasm which even the most weighty criticism is for a time unable to moderate. Its importance is thus magnified; and the climate is favourable for false and exaggerated estimates. Then, the interest subsides more or less rapidly; and a day comes when nobody except the specialists remembers the existence of the documents which made such a stir when they were first discovered. And at last they sink into an oblivion almost as absolute as that which, at the same time, descends upon the names of the men who found them. This sequence of events is sometimes due to the fact that a discovery, however real its importance, may fade in the light of further scientific advances made because of it. But this can also happen because, when the excitement is over, we find that the great discovery had nothing like the importance at first attached to it.

I do not believe that the interest of such a discovery as this of Chenoboskion, rich as it is in texts which until then had been completely lost (there have indeed been very few finds even distantly comparable in this respect), will ever be forgotten, or even much diminished in comparison with present estimates of its value. I am even persuaded that when the texts are made completely and directly available, their literary, historical and religious interest will steadily increase—that again and again it will become necessary to refer to them, and to search them for further revelations.

Like the manuscripts of Qumran, they give us information about an age which, for the development of the human conscience, remains of paramount importance. This was the period in which the individual found himself most critically confronted by the problems of his personal destiny, and of the destiny of the empires and civilizations he had hoped to establish in perpetuity. The central moment of these ages is that of the Cross. But ages of darkness stretch before and after this; and long before our era, spiritual men were repudiating the optimism of antiquity as vain and irreconcilable with the moral problems of an unstable universe: they were torn by profound anxiety. For more than a thousand years after the coming of Christianity this anxiety still presents itself in almost the same terms. But what the Gnostic documents reveal to us is the spiritual attitude of those who were the most tragically sensitive to the problems of human destiny— "Whence do I come?" "Who am I?" "What is this material world?" "Where shall I go after the end of this life?" However dark is the imagery in which these speculations are enveloped, they help us to understand the depths at which Christianity had to deal, gradually but comprehensively, with the most poignant problems vexing the souls of the antique world in those centuries of crisis. Their anguish—which touched not only the élite but the masses too—is not without its grandeur: those centuries were doubtless infinitely more wretched, but also far more *conscious* than our own. Of the solutions that men tried to find for their disquietude two are still present among us; for one was Christianity, and the other, arriving later and from other races, was Islam. A third response, related to Christianity more in appearance than reality, was a dualist mysticism—that of the Gnostics and the Manichaeans, nourished by myths and conceptions which seem ineradicable and sometimes invade even the modern mind. That religious ferment of the Gnoses and the various forms of Manichaeism lingered on for nearly fifteen centuries, certain ramifications extending even into Asia and our Western world.

From the earliest, which were also the most decisive periods of this great movement there remained but a few vestiges and a dim memory of trouble and disquiet. It is only today that the origins of the Gnosis and its first religious fervour are suddenly disclosed to us by the library of Chenoboskion, with a wealth of detail far beyond the ordinary hopes and expectations of historians.

27 *June,* 1957.

Jean Doresse

THE SECRET BOOKS
OF THE
EGYPTIAN GNOSTICS

*An Introduction to the Gnostic Coptic
manuscripts discovered at Chenoboskion*

CHAPTER I

THE PROBLEM OF GNOSTICISM:
ITS EARLIEST KNOWN ELEMENTS

THE words Gnosis ($\gamma\nu\hat{\omega}\sigma\iota\varsigma$ = Knowledge) and Gnosticism relate
to certain sects which, during the first centuries in which Christi-
anity was developing, competed with it upon its own grounds.[1]
The most famous episode of this rivalry is the one about Simon
Magus recorded in Acts VIII—not, in itself, a very informative
event, although its place in apostolic history has assured it of
greater fame than many others of later date that are better known.[2]
    This is because, in reality, the memory of the Gnostic sects,
after the days when they had been eliminated by orthodox
Christianity, did not attract much attention. Thenceforth these
heresies were dismissed by historians of the Church as fantastic
dreams which a little light had been enough to dispel. It was not
until the eighteenth century, that epoch of universal curiosity—an
epoch in which, moreover, there were mystics, occultists and
hermetists searching for spiritual food in all the most ancient and
peculiar places—that the Gnosticism of antiquity began to be
thought less unworthy of interest.[3] Mosheim was the first to open
up the subject with his *Institutiones historiae Christianae majores*
(1739). The doctrine previously known by the name of Gnosis

---

[1] The name of Gnosis has been quite legitimately attached to the religion of
these sects. But other mystical movements and philosophies, unrelated to these
which competed with Christianity at its beginning, also laid claim to a doctrine
of salvation—to a gnosis based upon very different myths. It is therefore to the
distinctive myths which constituted the "knowledge" of our Gnostics, and not to
the general concept of "gnosis", that we shall have to refer for their more exact
definition.

[2] For legends and iconography (mediaeval) relating to Simon Magus, see
E. Male, *L'Art religieux en France au XIII*[e] *Siècle*, pp. 298-9, and L. Thorndike,
A History of Magic and Experimental Science, vol. I, New York 1947, chap. XVII,
especially p. 427.

[3] See L. Cerfaux, "Gnose préchrétienne et biblique", in the *Dictionnaire de la
Bible*, Supplement t. III, 1938, pp. 659-702.

had been, in his opinion, an "oriental philosophy" which had
spread fairly widely from Persia and Chaldea to Egypt, which the
Jews also had accepted, and which invaded our Mediterranean
world in opposition to Greek philosophy. Although this idea of
an oriental philosophy did not then convince all of the learned,
after 1805 Horn,[4] and after 1818 Lewald[5] looked for the source of
this "philosophy" in Zoroastrian dualism. A work which, after
theirs, was much appreciated was Matter's *Histoire critique du
Gnosticisme* (1828). Matter defined Gnosticism as "the introduction into the bosom of Christianity of all the cosmological and
theosophical speculations which had formed the most considerable part of the ancient religions of the Orient and had also been
adopted by the Neo-platonists of the West". In this teaching,
therefore, were combined the philosophies of Plato and Philo,
the Avesta and the Kabbala, the mysteries of Samothrace, Eleusis
and of Orphism. This treatise of Matter's was addressed to a
generation which was as attracted to mystical marvels as those
of the previous centuries had been allergic to them: it went far to
make Gnosticism fashionable. For a proof of this one need only
look again at the *Tentation de saint Antoine* where Flaubert so
vividly depicts all the strangely-attired sects in procession before
the hermit. A little later Barrès, in his "Turquoises gravées",[6]
drew with consummate art upon the same source of curious
inspiration, over which he had brooded during his travels in the
East.[7] Unfortunately, the popularity of Gnosticism tended to
influence the researches of certain archaeologists, too susceptible
to the taste of the public: for instance, a number of monuments
and relics dug up from the soil of Roman and Byzantine Egypt
were labelled "Gnostic" by the archaeologist Gayet when they
were lacking in any distinct character.

We need not here enumerate all the many works which, from
the time of Matter until recent years, have dealt with the subject
of Gnosticism. In 1851, such speculations were stimulated by the

---

[4] J. Horn, *Ueber die biblische Gnosis*, Hanover, 1805.
[5] Lewald, *Commentatio ad historiam religionum veterum illustrandum pertinens de
doctrina gnostica*, Heidelberg, 1818.   [6] In *Le Mystère en pleine Lumière*.
[7] See Barrès, *Cahiers*, XIV, p. 110 and J. Doresse, " Barrès et l'Orient" in *La
Table Ronde*, No. 111, March 1957.

discovery of a precious document—the *Philosophumena*, which is a refutation of heresies, inaccurately attributed to Hippolytus of Rome. The scope for learned controversy was also enlarged by the publication of rare original Gnostic documents. Harnack and de Faye put forward theories about the exact nature of these strange currents of religious thought, particularly in relation to ecclesiastical history. To these hypotheses was added another interpretation of Gnosticism conceived, this time, as a product of the main religious movements of the Orient. By 1897 Anz had already published the first hypothesis of this kind.[8] And in 1904 Reitzenstein in his *Poimandres* suggested Egyptian origins for certain themes of Gnosticism and of Hermeticism. Bousset, in *The Principal Problems of Gnosticism*,[9] pointed to other origins that the Gnostic sects might have had, and with greater likelihood, in the realm of Iranian and Babylonian doctrine, traces of which are apparent in Mandaeanism and Manichaeism. R. Reitzenstein, rallying to this idea, developed the principal implications of it with a sometimes exaggerated enthusiasm. For a summary account of the state at which these researches had lately attained one may turn, on the one hand, to the article by L. Cerfaux on "Pre-Christian and Biblical Gnosis",[10] and on the other to the very careful exposition "Where are we now with the Problem of Gnosticism?" by Prof. H. C. Puech[11]—an account which, though it is already twenty years old, has lost nothing of its reliability. One may also consult the two volumes by Jonas on "Gnosis and the Spirit of Late Antiquity".[12]

During the progress of researches bearing directly upon the history of Gnosticism, other related problems were becoming more clearly defined, thanks to certain discoveries of great importance about other religious movements closely connected

[8] W. Anz, "Zur Frage nach dem Ursprung des Gnostizismus" in *Texte und Untersuchungen*, vol. XV, fasc. 4, Leipzig, 1897.

[9] W. Bousset, *Hauptprobleme der Gnosis*, Göttingen, 1907.

[10] In the *Dictionnaire de la Bible*, Supplément, t. III.

[11] H. C. Puech, "Où en est le problème du Gnosticisme" in the *Revue de l'Université de Bruxelles*, 1934-5, pp. 137–158 and 295–314: to this one should add the explanations given in a study by the same author—"La Gnose et le temps" in the *Eranos Jahrbuch*, vol. XX, 1952, pp. 57ff.

[12] Hans Jonas, *Gnosis und spätantiker Geist*: 1. *Die mythologische Gnosis*; 2. *Von der Mythologie zur mystischen Philosophie*, Göttingen, 1934 and 1955.

with Gnosticism—firstly about Hermeticism and the vast output
of astrological and magical literature. Light was shed, at the same
time, upon the many separate fragments preserved in Greek, and
also in several Oriental languages, attributed to the magi Zoroaster, Ostanes and Hystaspes.[13] The importance of the *Chaldaean
Oracles* whose philosophy had strongly influenced Neo-Platonists from the time of Iamblichus, was also recognized.[14] Above
all, an enormous—and particularly informative—access of new
material was that of the Manichaean writings that were coming
to light everywhere from Africa to Central Asia—writings which
already enabled us to guess how much of the religion of Manes
had been a systematized form of the most typical Gnostic myths.[15]
Finally the sacred books of the Mandaeans, though they
did not yet divulge the secret history of this baptist sect—which
still survives in Mesopotamia—presented the clear picture of a
religion that was largely Gnostic.[16]

Yet in spite of all this new knowledge, Gnosticism itself continued to present the religious historian with an appalling number
of problems to which it was all the harder to find answers because
the documentation for the authentically Gnostic sects consisted
hardly at all of original texts (only the smallest fragments of
which survived) but almost entirely of works written against
these sects by their contemporary opponents. How unsatisfactory
such documentation can be for the historian will be seen from
the following summary of what was known about Gnosticism
before the Chenoboskion manuscripts were found.

*   *   *

Essentially, all that we knew about Gnosticism was what we
had learned from texts—most of them Christian—denouncing
these sects as heretical.[17] These refutations do, indeed, tell us

---

[13] See below, chap. II, p. 102, and chap. VI, pp. 280–1.
[14] Cf. J. Bidez, *La vie de l'empereur Julien*, Paris, 1930, part I, chap. XII. Cf. also
below, pp. 85, 102.
[15] See below, p. 98 and chap. VII.   [16] See below, p. 98 and chap. VII.
[17] H. C. Puech, "Où en est le problème du Gnosticisme?" and, more especially,
M. Friedländer, *Der vorchristliche Gnosis*, Göttingen, 1898, pp. 14ff, and J. Lebreton,
Histoire du dogme de la Trinité, 1927, II, pp. 81–2. Collections of the essential texts
in W. Völker, *Quellen zur Geschichte der christlichen Gnosis*, 1932; also E. de Faye,
Gnostiques et Gnosticisme, 2nd edn. 1925 (out-of-date).

something about the Gnostic teachers, books, systems and procedures, but only from a very limited point of view, since they are concerned only with portions of the teachings of the Gnostics, which, moreover, they take every opportunity to subject to sarcastic indictments and brutal mockery. "When you have learnt by heart all your books by Basilides, Manes, Barbelos and Leusiboras", writes St Jerome, apostrophizing his adversary Vigilantius, "go sing them in the weaving-women's workshops, or offer to read them to the unlearned in the taverns that you frequent; such twaddle will make them drink more deeply!"[18] What kind of impartiality can we expect from such impassioned polemics?

The earliest of these refutations known to us—the *Syntagma* of Justin,[19] written about A.D. 140—is lost, with the exception of a few passages quoted by his successors. Between A.D. 180 and 185 Irenaeus of Lyons composed a huge work entitled *The so-called Gnosis unmasked and overthrown*, in which he bore witness against a number of teachers of Gnostic sects, of whose sacred books this author had some knowledge.[20] Hegesippus, after travels which made him remarkably well informed (he went far into the Orient), produced five books of memoirs dealing with the history of the Church, arguing fervidly against the Gnostics: he presents them as the inheritors of various Jewish sects, Baptist and Judeo-Christian, which had grown up in Trans-Jordan or Lower Babylonia. The original of this work is lost, but we have fragments of it quoted, a little later, by the historian Eusebius.[21] Tertullian, too, attacked heretics.[22] And to Clement of Alexandria —who died before A.D. 215—we owe the preservation of quotations from several of them; Valentinus, Theodotus[23] and even Basilides.

---

[18] Jerome, *Liber contra Vigilantium*, § 6.
[19] Justin was a Samaritan, as were the earliest masters of Gnosis, and may have had particularly reliable information.
[20] See, e.g., his chapter XXIX.
[21] In Eusebius, *Kirchengeschichte*, herausg. von Ed. Schwartz (Gk. text), Leipzig, 1952.
[22] In the *De praesciptione haereticorum*, the *Adversus Valentinianos* and the *Scorpiace* (remedy against the scorpion's sting!).
[23] Clement of Alexandria, *Extraits de Théodote*, edn. F. Sagnard, 1948.

A particularly instructive work rediscovered about a century ago is the *Elenchos,* usually but incorrectly known as the *Philosophumena,*[24] and attributed to Hippolytus, though it was in fact composed about A.D. 230 by quite another author. This is a veritable encyclopaedia of religious history, which starts from the classical philosophies, gives expositions of the beliefs of the Brahmans and the Druids, of the astrologers and magicians, and then devotes all the remaining half of the work to an analysis of Gnostic doctrines which purports to be based upon fundamental works of the various sects. The value of this book, which is indeed a picturesque and engaging one, has sometimes been disputed. The Rev. Fr Festugière[25] thought it prudent to relegate the chapters dealing with the Brahmans to that class of romanticized reporting of exotic cults which was in vogue during the first centuries of our era; but twelve years ago Prof. J. Filiozat was able to show that many of the details about the Brahmans furnished by the pseudo-Hippolytus were correct.[26] If, then, the author of the *Elenchos* wished, and was able, to be so well informed upon so recondite a subject as the doctrines of India, one may reasonably suppose he could much more easily satisfy his curiosity about the beliefs of the Gnostics living all around him, and that he would be no less scrupulous in describing them to us.

It is to Origen, who died about A.D. 253 or 254, that we owe our knowledge of fragments of the writings of the Gnostic Heracleon, preserved in the former's *Commentary upon the gospel of St John.*[27] In another of his works Origen replied to the pagan Celsus, an opponent of Christianity.[28] This Celsus is perhaps the man to whom the philosopher Lucian dedicated the satire he wrote under the title of *Alexander, or the false Prophet.* Lucian's shafts were aimed at the pagan magi. Celsus had been attacking both the

[24] Hippolytus, *Werke,* Band III, *Refutatio omnium haeresium* (edition P. Wendland), 1916; translations of the essential chaps. and Hippolyte de Rome, *Philosophumena,* French trans. annotated by A. Siouville, 2 vols., Paris, 1928.
[25] Festugière, O. P., *La Révélation d'Hermès Trismégiste,* t. I, *L'Astrologie et les sciences occultes,* Paris, 1944, p. 35.
[26] J. Filliozat, "Les Doctrines des Brahmanes d'après saint Hippolyte" in the *Revue de l'Histoire des Religions,* t. CXXX, pp. 59ff.
[27] See Fr Sagnard, *La Gnose valentinienne et le témoignage de St Irénée,* 1947, pp. 48off. Texts quoted in Völker, *Quellen,* pp. 63ff.
[28] The work of Celsus dates from about A.D. 180.

Christians and the Gnostics, about whom he was pretty well informed. In reply to him, Origen pillories numerous details of this work of Celsus, the original of which is lost to us. It is here, in the *Contra Celse*, that we find the transcription of that very peculiar Ophite document, the *Diagram*.

The historian Eusebius, who died in A.D. 339, has left us some brief but particularly informative passages about what he knew of the most ancient sects, in his *Ecclestiastical History*. Some of these passages, as we have already said, are extracts from the lost work of Hegesippus, according to whom the principal sects—he enumerates those of Simon, Dositheus, Cleobios, Gothaïos, Menander, Carpocrates, Valentinus, Basilides and Satornil—are descended from various Jewish or Baptist sects, such as the Essenes, Galileans, Ebionites, Samaritans, Nazarenes, Osseans, Sampseans, Elkesaites, Hemerobaptists and Masbutheans. Eusebius also mentions a certain number of works, now lost, which had been written in order to refute the Gnostics and other heretics of the same kidney. Such, for instance, were the books of Agrippa Castor against Basilides; those of Philip of Gortyna and of Modestus against Marcion; of Musanus against the Encratites; of Rhodon against Apelles, Tatian and Marcion.[29]

From the first quarter of the fourth century dates one of the principal polemics launched by the Christians against Manichaeism—*The Acts of Archelaus*, which describes a controversy that had taken place between Manes himself and the Bishop of Kashqar in Mesopotamia. At the end of these discussions the Bishop relates the life of Manes and gives an account of his writings: in this part of the book there is a very precise statement about the Persian doctrines which, as well as those of Manes, had influenced the Gnostic Basilides, one of whose works is here quoted.[30]

We must also mention the anti-heretical writings of Serapion of Thmuis, of Didymus the Blind, of Philaster and others. They are all eclipsed by a voluminous treatise called the *Panarion*—meaning literally, the *medicine-chest against heresies*—which was

[29] Eusebius, *History*, IV, 7, 25, and V, 23.
[30] For text quoted, see Völker, *Quellen*, pp. 38–40.

compiled by St Epiphanius, chiefly by drawing upon previous works (those of Irenaeus especially) but also making use of a fine documentation of his own, hardly to be accounted for unless he had had direct experience in the Gnostic sects. Epiphanius' work is highly detailed, abounding in vivid—even journalistic—statements, and enhanced by the polemical aim which animates the whole.[31]

To what extent was Epiphanius really able to know and judge his adversaries? He himself tells us in his Chapter XXVI—which for good reason is one of the longest, devoted to the great "Gnostics"—that he frequented, in Egypt, a sect which was of a peculiar perversity.[32] Had he made contact with these heretics on purpose to learn about their teaching and be able to combat it? Or was there something in it which, for a time, allured him? He admits that he was almost involved more deeply than he had intended. And thus, as he assures us, it was out of the very mouths of its own practitioners that he learned the details of the heresy he describes in this chapter. It was indeed women, themselves misled into these errors, who tried to draw him into them also, by disclosing to him the myths in which they believed. Epiphanius was then quite young; and, like Potiphar's wife trying to seduce Joseph, they sought to inveigle him into the practices of the sect. "If I escaped from their claws", declares Epiphanius, "it was not by my personal virtue, but by the divine help vouchsafed in answer to my prayers." For these perverse ladies shrank from no guile. "The poor boy!" they would say one to another, "we have been unable to save him. But how can we leave him to perdition in the power of the Archon?"—meaning by this that if Epiphanius did not undergo their initiation he would be unable to escape from the evil Power who governs this base world. In accordance with the tactics of this group, the most seductive of the Gnostic women offered themselves to him as enticements, giving him to understand that whoever yielded to their charms would by no means be lost, but saved indeed. This practice was

---

[31] Epiphanius, *Panarion*, in the Holl. edn. Cf. R. A. Lipsius, *Die Quellenkritik des Epiphanius*, Vienna, 1865.

[32] For Epiphanius's sojourn in Egypt, see O. Bardenhewer, *Patrologie*, III, 1912, p. 293.

so customary among members of the sect that the prettiest of the initiated women used to snub those less favoured by nature, by saying "I am a vessel of election, and I can save those who are in error, which thou hast not the means to do."

Epiphanius makes no secret of it, that those who made him the most alluring offers were very well formed in face and figure, in spite of the demonic deformity of their adulterous souls. As soon as he had gained sufficient knowledge of their secret books Epiphanius escaped, made haste to the Church and the bishop of the city in which these adventures had taken place, and denounced eighty sectaries, men and women, who were forthwith excommunicated and banished.

Epiphanius catalogues the sects with the meticulousness of a naturalist. But after his time, first-hand information about these heretics becomes more scarce—perhaps because the rise of Manichaeism confronted the Church with more urgent problems. Those writers who deal with the Gnostics do little more than repeat what has been said by the heresiologists of the preceding centuries. We know, however, of the continued existence of the sects from such testimonies as those of John of Parallos in the sixth century and the Syrian Theodore Bar-Konai at the end of the eighth.[33]

These sects, under such violent attack from the Christians, were at the same time in conflict with the pagan defenders of the Hellenic philosophy: that fact alone shows how far the teaching of these Gnostics was removed—and that in the eyes of contemporaries better placed than we are to judge it—from the Hellenic doctrines to which some have supposed they were related. We have already mentioned that Origen has preserved for us some portions of a work by the pagan Celsus, written against both the Christians and the Gnostic Ophites. A still livelier struggle must have been carried on by the great Plotinus and his disciples. Plotinus himself wrote against the Gnostics between the years 263 and 267, in the ninth chapter of his second Ennead.[34]

[33] A. Van Lantschoot, "Fragments coptes d'une homélie de Jean de Parallos, in *Miscellanea Giovanni Mercati*, vol. I, *Studi e Testi* 121, Città del Vaticano, 1946.

[34] Plotinus, *Ennéades*, text revised in French translation by E. Bréhier, Paris, 1924, *seq.*

He gives no name or place to the adversaries he is seeking to refute, but a hint·as to who they were can be gleaned from a passage in the *Life of Plotinus*, written afterwards by his disciple Porphyry.[35] They were "Christians" such as the Adelphius and Aquilinus who are named here as having "departed from the ancient philosophy", and having supplemented the authentically philosophic writings of Alexander of Libya, of Philocomus and Demostratus of Libya, by adding some *Apocalypses* attributed to *Zoroaster, Zostrian, Nicotheus, Allogenes, Mesos* and other magi. We shall learn from what follows that the works in question were specifically Gnostic, in spite of the names under which they took cover. Moreover, Porphyry himself seconded Plotinus' efforts to refute these people by producing a very severe criticism of the *Book* put out under the name of *Zoroaster*, which he had shown— he tells us—to be a recent apocryphon. At the same time his co-disciple Amelius seems to have refuted the *Book of Zostrian*. Unluckily, these refutations written by Porphyry and Amelius have not been handed down to us.

*   *   *

If only we were not so uncertain of the accuracy of the testimony borne by these enemies, the history of the Gnostic sects that emerges from it would be, for the variety of its personalities, the colour of the doctrines, the strangeness of passions and customs, as animated and fantastic a scene as one could imagine. The broad outlines of that history, unfortunately more or less fictitious, have been well summarized in various works;[36] I need not, therefore, give more than a brief impression of it here.

First of all it is necessary to say something of the kind of universe in which the Gnostic doctrines were born and developed— presumably but a very little after the advent of Christianity. How mystical forces abounded during those centuries! All the pagan religions of the Near East and the Mediterranean had adapted their creeds to the great myths of astrology, which was accorded

---

[35] "Life of Plotinus", in Plotin, *Ennéades*, vol. I, p. 17. Quoted also in J. Bides and Franz Cumont, *Les Mages hellénisés*, Paris, 1938, vol. II, p. 249.
[36] H. Leisegang, *La Gnose* (trans. J. Gouillard), Paris, 1951; W. Bousset, article on "Gnosticism" in the *Enc. Britt.*, 14th edn.

the status of a science, and according to which man was subject to the planets and constellations from before birth until death, shackled to the wheel of Fate. Philosophy too was changing; like the religions, it was yielding more or less, in its conceptions, to the influence of the celestial powers. Meanwhile its thinking, moulded by the Greek thinkers, was sustaining also the irresistible impact of Oriental mysticisms. We need mention only Philo (20 B.C.– A.D. 40), who so remarkably exemplifies this evolution, since he assimilates to Judaism the allegorical interpretations of the Homeric poems which the Greeks had been elaborating; and because one can see, from various aspects of his thought, that though the ideas which were about to engender Gnosticism had not yet ripened, they were at least beginning to germinate. Philo does not yet know the anxiety which will underlie the speculations of the Gnostics. But several of the themes they were to develop are already virtually represented by him; the notion of a transcendent deity; and above all the idea that not only the earth but the heavens above it are in darkness.

It is in the second and third centuries that Gnosticism itself is to be found in full flower—centuries in which men's minds were specially prepared to welcome such beliefs. The great Gnostic myths harmonize well with the mystical propensities of this time when a crowd of other Oriental cults were invading the Latin world. This is the epoch in which exotic sanctuaries multiplied upon the Aventine hill; when the altars of Mithraism were spreading not only in the quarters of Rome but throughout the Romanized world. The case of Alexander Severus, who set up an effigy of Jesus in his domestic sanctuary side by side with those of the other spiritual masters he venerated—Alexander, Abraham, Orpheus, Apollonius of Tyana—is eminently symbolic. Even the art of Rome takes on a mystic manner unknown before; and with this spiritual urge is combined a taste for the colossal, in, for example, the gigantic basilica of Septimus Severus at Leptis Magna. The religious energy of the age was so powerful that, by the fourth century, epicureanism and atheism, formerly served by numerous "devotees", had been swept away and vanished.

The few facts that we can glean about the birth and the early expansion of the Gnostic sects have been summarized by H. C. Puech with great clarity in his study, "Where are we now with the Problem of Gnosticism?" Let us review, then, the main outlines of his exposition. Gnosticism appeared originally in Syria. It is in Samaria and the valley of the Lycos that we trace it for the first time.[37] Simon is a man of Gitta in Samaria; Menander is originally of Capparetia—again in Samaria; Satornil is of Antioch; Cerdon is a Syrian; Cerinthus comes from Asia Minor. "To this Syrian Gnosis", writes Prof. Puech, "a multitude of systems, anonymous and of a primitive tendency, are probably related, notably the Ophites' and all those grouped under the name of 'Adepts of the Mother' on account of the part played in their theories by this feminine entity. . . ."

In the time of Hadrian (A.D. 110–38), Gnosticism passes over from Syria into Egypt: it is in Alexandria that the greatest doctors of the heresy are flourishing—Basilides, Carpocrates, Valentinus. Then it reaches Rome; and this is the moment when the Christian doctors suddenly realize the importance of heresies which, in the East, had been incubating for a considerable time. How were the Gnostics able to establish themselves in Rome at the very moment when the authorities were banishing from that city the "Chaldean" astrologers and the devotees of Sabazios—a god who, they claimed, was identical with Iahweh Sabaôth?[38] That is a problem. For this was just the moment when Valentinus established himself in the city where, at first, he distinguished himself; but after being defeated in his candidature for the bishopric he broke with the Church and withdrew to Cyprus, so that the school which he founded was split into two branches, Italian and Oriental. About the same time a woman, Marcellina, brought to Rome, together with the icons of the Christ, of Paul, of Homer and of Pythagoras (to which she burnt incense), the impure teachings of Carpocrates. And before her had come Cerdon, of whom

---

[37] H. C. Puech, "Où en est le problème . . .", pp. 143 ff. For the Palestinian origins of Gnosticism, see O. Cullman, *Le Problème littéraire des écrits pseudoclémentins.*

[38] Fr. Cumont, *Lux Perpetua,* p. 253; *Religions orientales dans le paganisme romain,* 4th edn., pp. 152 and 285, Note 8.

Marcion was perhaps a disciple, for Marcion was in Rome from 140, and thence expelled by the Church in 144, being excommunicated by his own father, the Bishop of Sinope. A little later Marcus and his adepts were preaching not only in Asia Minor, but well into Gaul, as far as Lyons, a Valentinianism replete with magic. The Gnostics even found themselves reinforced by other sects such as the Nazarenes and the Elkesaïtes, also by that of Alcibiades, who came from Apamea at the end of the second century.[39]

Thenceforth Gnosticism, with its multiform and more or less secret sects, infested the whole of the Mediterranean world. It is unfortunate for the modern historian that it is just from this time onward that its traces become most obscured. The only sect to show itself in public is the Manichaean, which the authorities are beginning to proceed against. But these persecutions seem never to have been aimed directly at Gnosticism. One loses track of it, and, though it continues actively to spread from the West into Mesopotamia, Armenia and Egypt, one finds hardly any evidences of it that are of any historical or geographical precision.

*   *   *

To this historical outline, let us fill in some details. Surviving traditions about the origins of Gnosticism give prominence to two personalities who doubtless really lived, but who, owing to their prestige as founders, have been adorned with legendary characteristics until their historical physiognomy is effaced. These are Nicolas and Simon.

Nicolas had been one of the first deacons ordained by the Apostles. He came originally from Antioch.[40] It is against his doctrine that the Johannine *Apocalypse* (II, 6 and 15-16) warns the churches of Ephesus and Pergamos. But what this teaching was has only come down to us, unfortunately, from later sources and must be accepted with reserve. Eusebius, in his *Ecclesiastical History* (III, 29), tells us that Nicolas had a very beautiful wife, and that he gave a highly licentious interpretation to certain precepts about holding the flesh in contempt. Epiphanius adds that it was

---

[39] *Philosophumena*, IX, 13-17.
[40] See W. Bousset, *Hauptprobleme* . . . , chap. VII.

from the sectaries of Nicolas that the groups of the great "Gnostics" were derived, the Phibionite, the Stratiotic, the Levitical and others—that is, the principal Oriental sects. The Nicolaïtans, it seems, taught that in the beginning, before the face of the unbegotten, primordial Spirit, there were the Darkness, an abyss and the waters, which the Spirit had cast out, far from itself. Therefore the Darkness, in anger against the Spirit, surged up to attack it. It was then that a sort of womb was produced, which, from the Spirit, gave birth to four aeons,[41] which in turn engendered fourteen others; and this was followed by the formation of "the right" and "the left", the light and the darkness. . . .[42] One of the higher powers emanated from the supreme Spirit was, according to the Gnostics, Barbelô[43] the celestial Mother. She unfortunately gave birth to the entity who was to become the creator of this lower world—Ialdabaôth or Sabaôth. Barbelô had then, by her repentance, brought about the first stage of the salvation of the lower world. Taking advantage of her beauty, she showed herself to the Archons—the powers of the lower heavens —thus seducing them and depriving them, through voluptuousness,

[41] The term "aeon" or "age" was used by the Gnostics to signify the hierarchies of being in the universe. One cannot explain this nebulous term better than by quoting these lines from H. C. Puech; Gnosticism "is incapable of rational thinking by concepts or of concretely apprehending the persons or the events of history in their singularity. Concepts, for the Gnostic, become schemata, ill-defined in form—entities which are half-abstract, half-concrete, semi-personal, semi-impersonal—that is, 'aeons' . . . fragments of duration or periods of time spatialized and hypostatized, the elements or personages of a mythological drama; and, beside these, historic persons and facts are sublimated half-way between the real and the symbolic" (from "La Gnose et le Temps", *Eranos Jahrbuch*, vol. XX, 1952, pp. 110–11).

[42] The Gnostic systems assign the higher and lower elements, the psychic and the material, to the "right" and the "left" respectively. See Sagnard, *Gnose valentinienne*, pp. 544–5. See also p. 270 below.

[43] This mysterious name is found again not only among the "Barbelognostics", who constituted a distinct sect, but in most of the major myths of those whom historians regard as "the adepts of the Mother". It occurs also in the form of Berbali in a text of ordinary Hermeticism—the *Kosmopoiia* quoted in Festugière, *Révélation*, pp. 302–3. This is the entity, without doubt, which St Jerome calls the Gnostic "Barbelus" (Cf. Note 18 *ante* and the text cited). Attempts have been made to equate this name with the Egyptian for "seed"—in Coptic, BLBILE. It is more logical to connect it with a Semitic expression—B'arb'é Eloha—meaning approximately "God in four (powers)" and designating the four supreme entities, the Tetrad. Cf. Leisegang, *loc. cit.*, p. 129. Cf. also Bousset, *Hauptprobleme* . . . , p. 14.

of those portions of the light (that is, of the spiritual seed) which had descended into them.[44] Others among these Gnostics gave this seductive being the cruder Greek name of *Prounikos*—the "lascivious".

Even more than Nicolas the deacon, Simon the Samaritan was held to have founded Gnosticism. This myth was especially developed in the third century, in the long romantic and apocryphal writings known by the names of the *Recognitions* and the *Clementine Homilies*. The master—or the rival?—of Simon Magus had been a certain Dositheus,[45] who is sometimes presented as the founder of the Jewish sect of the Sadducees.[46] The groups under Dositheus and Simon would have been founded in Samaria after John the Baptist had been put to death. It is noteworthy that the traditions collected by Hegesippus, and transmitted also by Epiphanius, suggest that in a more general sense the Gnostic schools were related to that spiritual ferment in which the Essenian, Samaritan, Gorthynian and other sects arose. . . . If one is to believe the Clementine *Recognitions*, the sect of Dositheus consisted of thirty disciples—a number equal to that of the days in the month—and one woman, Helenê, identified however with Selenê—that is, with the Moon. Dositheus was designated "He who is upright"—an epithet we shall find again in the myths of Simon, which is meant to signify the supreme divinity.

Simon himself was a native of Gitta in Samaria : his existence is, as everyone knows, confirmed by the *Acts of the Apostles* (VIII, 9-13), which mentions his meeting with the Apostle Philip : "There was a man named Simon who had previously practised magic in the city and amazed the nation of Samaria, saying that he himself was somebody great. They all gave heed to him from the smallest to the greatest, saying 'This man is that power of God

[44] Cf. of the same myth of the "seduction of the Archons" in Manichaeism : Franz Cumont, *Recherches sur le Manichéisme*, fasc. I, Brussels, 1908, pp. 54ff.; see also below, chap. II, note 15.

[45] Eusebius, *History*, IV, 22, 5, mentions him among the heretics who had seceded from the first Christian community after the death of James. Concerning this hypothetical personality, cf. R. McL. Wilson, "Simon, Dositheus and the Dead Sea Scrolls" in *Zeitschr. für Religions u. Geistesgeschichte*, vol. IX, 1957, pp. 21ff. The Samaritans also number among their legendary doctors a Dunstan, assigned by them to a very ancient epoch.

[46] According to the *Clementine Recognitions*, I, 54 : cf. R. McL. Wilson, *loc. cit.*, note 27.

which is called Great.'" Simon had wished also to become a Christian, according to the *Acts*: "Even Simon himself believed, and after being baptized he continued with Philip. And seeing signs and great miracles performed he was amazed. . . ."

To find out what the personal teaching of the Magus can have been, one is obliged to turn to much less reliable sources.[47] Like Dositheus, Simon too had his Helen; who, according to both Irenaeus and the *Philosophumena*,[48] was a prostitute girl, a slave he had taken out of a brothel in Tyre. He had ransomed her for a sum of money, declaring that the primary purpose of his coming into the world (for he announced himself as the Great Power come down from the heavens, as "he who is upright") was to seek "the lost sheep" and to save it. He introduced Helen as the "First Thought" of his Spirit, the Mother of all things by whom, in the beginning, the angels and archangels had been created. This was, moreover, the same Helen for whose sake the war of Troy had been fought; for she had passed from one body to another by metempsychoses, seducing men at each new incarnation, up to this moment when she had taken on the form of the courtesan of Tyre.

In imitation of their master, Simon's disciples seem to have repeated, in their wilder moments, that one ought to give oneself up to carnal intercourse without limit: "All earth is earth, it matters little where one sows provided that one does sow." It was in this, they proclaimed, that "perfect love" consisted. The same adepts practised magic; they used incantations, concocted love-potions, made use of dreams and pretended to refer to familiar spirits. They installed, in their dwelling-places, images representing Simon with the features of Zeus, and Helen impersonating Athena.

Different legends are known to have been current about Simon's end. According to the apocryphal *Acts of Peter*[49] Simon

---

[47] For Simon, see Jonas, *Gnosis*, vol. I, pp. 353-8; L. Cerfaux, "La Gnose Simonienne" in *Recherches des Sciences religieuses*, 1926, pp. 279-85. H. J. Schoeps, "Simon Magus in der Haggada" in *Aus Frühchristliche Zeit*, pp. 239-54.
[48] L. Vincent, "Le Culte d'Hélène a Samaria", in *Revue biblique*, vol. XLV, pp. 221-34.
[49] M. R. James, *Apocryphal New Testament*, pp. 331-2.

offered, at Rome, to give proof of his divine power and was lifted up into the sky in view of all the people, but was then cast down from on high by the winds. Another tradition has it that, when he was on the point of being caught out as an impostor, and could not face the disgrace of exposure, he extricated himself by declaring that if he were buried alive he would revive on the third day after: upon which he submitted himself to this ordeal, and hid from his defeat in the tomb in which his life terminated.

Of his doctrine, even if we keep within the accounts of Irenaeus and the *Philosophumena*, there is a good deal to be said, although we do not know how much of their information was correct. The *Philosophumena* attributes to Simon a work entitled the *Great Revelation*,[50] which proclaimed itself in the following terms: "This is the writing of the *Revelation of the Voice and of the Name*, proceeding from the Thought and from the infinitely Great Power; therefore it shall be sealed, hidden, shut up in the abode wherein the root of the All has its foundations." The myth expounded in this work—authentic or apocryphal?—postulated the existence of one supreme god, alien and superior to the wicked universe. The Wisdom, the Mother of All, had come down through the heavens from the higher universe into this base world created by the god of *Genesis*, the wicked god. What is clear is that Simon, by his deeds quite as much as his writings, may well have been pretending to fulfil this myth in proclaiming himself as the Power of God, and his Helen as the Wisdom from on high.

Among the lengthy passages from the *Revelation* quoted or analysed in the *Philosophumena*, let us note the following, which is concerned with the very roots of the cosmic creation: judged by its style, it may perhaps have been the preamble to the work. . . . "To you then, I say what I say and write what I write! And what I write is this. Among the totality of the Aeons, two emanations there are that have neither beginning nor end. They spring from the one and only root which is a power: the Silence invisible and incomprehensible. One of these is manifested on high, the Spirit of the All which governs everything; it is masculine. The other is

---

[50] *Philosophumena*, VI, 7-20. Text quoted from the *Great Revelation* in Völker, *Quellen*, pp. 3-11.

from below; it is a great thought, feminine, which gives birth to all things. Thenceforth these two contrary emanations copulate, and bring about the principle which is their intermediator, the intangible space which has no origin and no end. In this resides the Father who sustains and nourishes everything that has a beginning and an end. This is 'He that is upright, he who has stood and who shall stand upright'. He is a power who is both male and female, as is the infinite pre-existent power which has neither beginning nor end, and exists in isolation. And it is from this that has come forth the one Thought which has turned into two. . . ."

In Simon much more than in Nicolas, we see the emergence of one of the pseudo-prophets of Gnosticism, analogous to those who had already been known in paganism and Judaism; personalities of a kind against which the Gospels and the Epistles were already warning the faithful to be on guard.[51] The pagan Celsus has sketched us portraits of such personalities, and into their mouths he puts these words: "I am God, or the Son of God, or the divine Spirit. I have come because the end of the world is at hand, and, because of your own faults, your end has come. But my will is to save you; you shall see me rise again with the Power of heaven. Happy then will be he who has adored me! Over all the others I shall hurl the everlasting fire, over their towns and their countries. In vain will the men who did not know to what chastisement they were destined [then] change their opinions and complain; only those who will follow me shall I preserve for ever."[52]

As for the indirect methods by which adepts of these doctrines used to beguile the minds of orthodox Christians, other contemporaries were sufficiently impressed to have recorded them. Tertullian tells us that, in the presence of the faithful, they would begin by "expounding the regular doctrine in equivocal terms",[53] to induce them into error. "When the Valentinians meet people of the great Church [as Irenaeus himself records] they attract them by speaking as we speak to one another. They complain to

[51] See below, pp. 302–3.
[52] Quoted by Origen, *Contra Celsum.* VII, 8; cf. Reitzenstein, *Poimandres,* pp. 222–3.
[53] *Adversus Valentinianos,* 1.

us that we are treating them as excommunicated when, in this or that respect, the doctrines are the same, and thus, they unsettle our faith little by little by their questions. Those who do not resist they make into their disciples: they take them aside to unveil before them the unspeakable mystery of their Pleroma." Thus tempted, many Christians must have resisted the seduction of ambiguous teachings less ardently than did Epiphanius.[54]

The theories of Simon seem also to have been preached by one of his disciples, Menander. He too was a Samaritan, from the town of Capparetia; but the chief centre of his activity was Antioch. He also claimed to be the Saviour sent by the invisible powers.[55]

It was in the same town of Antioch that Satornil must have preached. He claimed—if one is to believe the *Philosophumena*[56]—that a supreme, unbegotten, unknown Father had created the angels, the powers and aeons of the higher world, but that the lower world had been made by seven inferior angels (the planets), the greatest of whom was identical with the God of the Jews, the creator in *Genesis*. These seven Archons had undertaken to fashion man, in consequence of their having had a sudden revelation—that of a dazzling image which came from the supreme Power, and which the angels alone perceived, but could not recollect. It was then that they exhorted one another, saying, "Let us make man according to the image and likeness"—words which *Genesis* I, 26 had preserved only in an inaccurate form. But, because of the incompetence of the seven who made him, the terrestrial Adam at first crawled like a worm and could not stand upright. Then Virtue from on high took pity on him, because he had been made in her likeness; she sent him a spark of Life, which raised him up and enabled him to live. It is that spark of Life—so Satornil taught—which, after death, reascends from terrestrial man towards the higher beings to whom it is related.

---

[54] Irenaeus, *Contra Haereses*, III, xv, 2, in the translation of Lebreton, *Histoire de l'Église*, vol. II, p. 15.

[55] Irenaeus, I, xxiii, 5; *Philosophumena*, VII, 4; Tertullian, *De Anima*, 50.

[56] H. C. Puech emphasizes in his study "Où en est le Problème . . .", p. 142, that Satornil, in the time of Trajan, was apparently the first Gnostic to have mentioned Christ. For Satornil, see also *Philosophumena*, VIII, 28.

Satornil also taught that marriage and generation were of the devil—which does not mean that he preached continence. It must be noted, however, that his disciples abstained scrupulously from any nutriment that had had life.

Like Satornil, Basilides had been a disciple of Menander, and would in that way have inherited some of Simon's theories. So much is recorded by, for instance, the historian Eusebius. Basilides set up his school in Egypt, in Alexandria, in the days of the Emperors Hadrian and Antonine the Pious. The numerous writings that he composed are now lost; but he seems to have based his doctrine upon the pseudo-prophecies (written by himself) known under the names of *Cham*,[57] of *Barcabbas* and of *Barcoph* (or *Parchor*?). Not only did he write twenty-four books of *Commentaries* on the Gospels, but he also compiled an additional gospel, a sort of collection of the sayings of Christ, the style of which recalls those that are found in *St Luke*. He claimed (perhaps upon this subject) to have received by way of Matthias some secret doctrines which the Saviour had made known to that Apostle in private conversations. Basilides also bequeathed to his disciples some *Odes*, and some *Prayers* and *Incantations*.[58] His son Isidore completed this literature by compiling a collection of moral treatises, a work *On the Additional Soul* and the *Commentaries on the Prophet Parchor*.[59] The principal writings of Basilides were refuted by a Christian, Agrippa Castor, in an *Elenchos* which has also unfortunately disappeared.[60]

A passage in the anti-Manichaean work known as *The Acts of Archelaus*[61] makes reference to the 13th book of Basilides's *Commentary* on the Gospels. This text seems to have dealt with the problem of the origin of evil, which the Gnostic doctor treated in connection with the parable of Lazarus and the rich man in hell (*Luke* XVI, 19–31). This same chapter was entitled, "How

---

[57] A passage in the *Commentary on the Prophet Parchor* preserved by Clement of Alexandria (*Stromates*, VI, 6, 53–4) shows that Basilides' son Isidore combined, in his teaching, the prophecies of Cham and the classical mythology of Pherecydes. This Cham has been more or less confused with Zoroaster (see Bidez-Cumont, *Les Mages hellénisés*, vol. I, p. 43 and vol. II, p. 64, fragment B.54).

[58] Referred to in P. Alfaric, *Les Ecritures manichéennes*, vol. I, 1918, pp. 11–12.

[59] Alfaric, *loc. cit.*, p. 12.   [60] Cf. Eusebius, *Ecclesiastical History*, IV, 7.

[61] Quoted in Völker, *Quellen*, p. 38.

nature, without root and without reason, has developed into things". We must quote from this work the passage preserved in *The Acts of Archelaus*. Basilides is contrasting Greek philosophy with the theories of the Persians about good and evil: which proves that, if he did not altogether accept them, he at least knew them well and attached great importance to them: "Some among them have said that the principles of all things are two in number; and it is to these that they ascribe good and evil, saying that these principles are without beginning and unbegotten. More precisely, in the beginning there were the light and the darkness which had arisen out of themselves. . . . While each (of these principles) was (shut up) in itself, each of them led the life that was proper and suitable to it. . . . But after each principle had arrived at the knowledge of the other, the darkness, having beheld the light, was seized with desire for it as for something better, pursued it and wanted to mingle with, and to take part in it. Such was the behaviour of the darkness, whilst the light would not admit into itself anything of the darkness whatsoever, or even of desire for it. For all that, the light was seized with a desire to look at the darkness and, as it were in a mirror, did look at it: and thus, upon the darkness was projected only a reflection—something like a single colour of the light—although the light had done no more than to look and then withdraw, without having taken up the smallest portion of the darkness. But the darkness, itself, seized upon this look from the light. . . .[62]

As for the main body of the doctrines of Basilides, it is just as well analysed by Irenaeus as by the *Philosophumena*.[63] Irenaeus reproaches Basilides with having developed and elaborated his theory to infinity, in order to give it an appearance of profundity. From the unbegotten Father—according to this Gnostic—were engendered five aeons, of those hypostases which may be conceived as either spatial or temporal, as either the divine "abodes" or as "ages". The first of these was the Nous—Mind; from

[62] See p. 14 *ante*, on the dualism of the Nicolaïtans, which, it seems, knows no intermediate principle, whilst the two opposite principles of the Simonian Gnosis copulate to produce the intangible space which is intermediary to them, p. 17.
[63] *Philosophumena*, VII, 13–27. This account, and the information given by Irenaeus about Basilides, seem difficult to reconcile upon a number of points.

which proceeded the Word; from the Word, Reflection; from Reflection, Wisdom and Force; from Wisdom and Force, the Virtues, powers and angels by which, from emanation to emanation, the heavens above were created; and so on, even to the fourth of these heavens, which has its principalities, its angels . . . and three hundred and sixty-five firmaments, the number according to which the year was made.

This last heaven—the one we see—is filled with the angels who have themselves created all that is in the world here below. For their lord, they have the god whom the Jews recognize as the Creator of the universe and of the Law. But the inferior powers have become so corrupt that the unbegotten Father has sent his only Son—the Nous, also called the Christ—to liberate, from the domination of those powers, all who believe in him. It is by means of secret names, passwords, etc., that the elect will be able to re-ascend through the lower heavens, eluding their archons. Upon earth, the Christ who was manifested had nothing of man except the appearance: indeed, it was not he who suffered in the Passion: Simon of Cyrene, after having been made to bear the Cross, was metamorphized by the Saviour, so that the Jews took him for Jesus and nailed him to the wood instead; whilst Jesus, who meanwhile had taken on the appearance of Simon, remained close to Calvary and, before reascending to heaven, derided his enemies for their vain mistake!

This same notion of a crucifixion that was fictive and a miscarriage appears again in Manichaeism, where, according to the testimony of Evodius (*De Fide* 28), an *Epistle of the Foundation* taught that the Enemy, who was hoping to have the Saviour crucified, himself fell victim to that crucifixion! The Prince of Darkness was nailed to the Cross: it was even he who, before that, was tortured by the crown of thorns and arrayed for derision in the purple robe.[64]

[64] Cf. my article, "Le refus de la Croix . . ." in *La Table Ronde*, no. 120, Dec., 1957, pp. 89–97; also Antonio Orbe, *Los primeros herejes ante la persecucion* (quoted below in note 72), pp. 160 ff. This theme of a crucifixion that failed occurs again in the apocryphal *Acts of John*, § 98 (vision of the cross of light). Finally, it is strikingly illustrated, in the Middle Ages, by the illuminated designs in certain Ethiopian evangelistaries. See J. Doresse, *L'Empire du Prêtre-Jean*, II: *L'Ethiopie médiévale*, Paris, 1957, pp. 154–60.

More precise than that of Irenaeus, the text of the *Philosophu-mena* explains in particular how, according to Basilides, the god of this lower world was created. Once engendered, he lifted himself up into the firmament which, in his ignorance, he took to be the upper limit of everything in existence. Persuaded that there was nothing above this, he behaved without perversity, but even with goodness. Element by element he built up and or-ganized this lower world, and he began by begetting a Son still better and wiser than himself. This Son he seated beside him in the Ogdoad, that is, in the eighth heaven, which is that of the fixed stars above all the seven heavens of the planets, but is nevertheless lower than the highest world, from which it is separated. One detail, which is confirmed by a passage in St Jerome, is that the great creator-archon had been given, by Basilides, the name of Abraxas, a word which, if one adds up the numerical values of all the letters it is composed of, has the peculiarity of giving the total of 365, equal to the number of the heavens over which Abraxas reigned.[65]

One of the most original portions, it seems, of the teaching of Basilides dealt with the causes of the passions and the conditions for the salvation of the soul. His doctrine upon this point was further elucidated by his son Isidore in his treatise *On the Addi-tional Soul*. The passions, being lower, constituted as it were a second soul, which was added by the lower powers to that which man received from on high. This second soul was made up of spirits external to the former—of bestial or ferocious instincts which, producing desires in their own image, weigh man down and drag him into sin.[66]

A contemporary of Basilides, Carpocrates, gave rise to a sect explicitly called by the name "Gnostic"—if we are to believe Irenaeus.[67] His disciples, reports Epiphanius, had icons painted in colours and embellished with gold and silver, which represented Jesus, Pythagoras, Plato, Aristotle. . . . This Carpocrates had a son, another Epiphanius, who added to the teaching he held

[65] Cf. Leisegang, *loc. cit.*, pp. 107–71, and Campbell Bonner, *Studies in magical amulets*, Ann Arbor, 1950, pp. 133–5 and p. 192.
[66] Cf. below, pp. 72, 215 and chap. v, note 109.
[67] Irenaeus, I, xxv.

2*

from his father some other doctrines he had taken from Secundus, himself a disciple of the great Valentinus whom we shall mention later. This Epiphanius died at the age of seventeen. In the isle of Samos his disciples established divine honours in his memory, and it is even said that the inhabitants built a temple to him.

Doubts have been cast upon the Gnostic character of the doctrines of Marcion.[68] One can certainly recognize in that teaching an interpretation of the Pauline doctrines carried to extremes. (Marcion availed himself of, above all, the *Epistle to the Galatians.*) It is equally certain that the best account of Marcion's teaching that we have—the refutation by Tertullian, who had that heretic's *Antitheses* and *New Testament* in his hands—justifies us in treating the more or less Gnostic character of that theology with some reserve.

History tells us thàt Marcion, who arrived in Rome about A.D. 140, first entered into controversy with the elders of the Church upon *Luke* V, 36: "No man putteth a piece of a new garment upon an old . . . and no man putteth new wine into old bottles", and upon *Luke* VI, 43: "For a good tree bringeth not forth corrupt fruit, neither doth a corrupt tree bring forth good fruit." These discussions could not shake his conviction that the Gospel came forth, in Jesus, from a new God superior to that of the Old Testament. Tradition adds that it was then that Marcion broke with the Church and followed the Gnostic teaching of an otherwise little-known doctor named Cerdon. Thence Marcion came to elaborate his dualistic doctrine, tending at the same time to a rigorous asceticism.

More important for our subject than the personal teaching of Marcion is, in any case, Marcionism as succeeding generations developed and vulgarized it—thanks especially to some heretics

[68] For Marcion, see—Ad. Von Harnack, *Marcion*, Leipzig, 1921; and *Neue Studien zu Marcion*, Leipzig, 1923; W. Bousset, *Hauptprobleme der Gnosis*, pp. 109–13; Eug. de Faye, *Gnostiques et Gnosticisme*, pp. 142–88. On the refutation of Marcionism by Eznik of Kolb: J. M. Schmid, *Des Wardapet Eznik von Kolb* "Wider die Sekten", Vienna, 1900 (translation), and—for the history of that work—L. Mariès, *Le De Deo D'Eznik de Kolb connu sous le nom de "Contre les Sectes"*, Paris, 1925, taken from the *Revue des Études arméniennes*). See also *S. Ephraim's prose refutations of Mani, Marcion and Bardaisan*, vol. I, 1912 (published by C. W. Mitchell); vol. II, 1921 (published by C. W. Mitchell, completed by A. A. Bevan and F. C. Burkitt).

like Apelles. These secondary forms of the Marcionite teaching, which are undeniably Gnostic, were to attain such success that by the end of the fourth century there were Marcionites not only in Rome and in Italy, but as far afield as the Thebaïd, Palestine, Syria and even Persia. It was in that epoch that the doctrine was refuted, first by St Epiphanius and then, later, by the Armenian theologian Eznik of Kolb, who had the advantage of access to earlier documents no longer extant. From the treatise *Against the Sects* composed by this last-named author between 441 and 448, let us borrow a few details.

This later Marcionism did not confine itself to contrasting the supreme God (till then unknowable but whom the Christ had just revealed) with God the Creator of the physical universe and of the Mosaic Law. It fitted both the Old and the New Testaments into the framework of a mythology, the basis of which was the notion of *three* principles or three "heavens".

The first heaven, highest and inaccessible, was the habitation of the unknown God from whom salvation was to come, but whom humanity could not know until after the revelation of the New Testament. In the second heaven was the God of *Genesis* and of the Law, whose visage was more like a devil's. The third world was that of Matter, of the Earth and their powers. It is by associating himself with Matter that the God of the Law accomplishes the Creation described in *Genesis*; he fashions the universe and then, out of the Earth which Matter allows him, he fabricates Adam, into whom he breathes a living spirit. He places Adam in Paradise and then, seeing that he is noble and capable of serving him, wishes to steal him wholly away from Matter. To this end he admonishes man: "Adam, I am God and there is none beside me. If you serve any other God but me, know that you will die the death!" Adam keeps himself, thenceforth, away from Matter. But Matter, perceiving this, and in order to prevent his giving himself up to the service of the one Creator, distracts man by multiplying gods innumerable around him: and these he adores because he is unable to recognize which of them is his master. Incensed at this, the

Lord of the Creation then thrusts primitive mankind down into hell.

The good God, the Unknown, is troubled: he sends his Son who, by means of the Cross, takes on the likeness of death and goes down into hell, to deliver the captives and raise up into the third heaven—that of his Father—the souls who are imprisoned there. In his anger, the Lord of the Law tears his garments, rends in twain the veil of the Temple and covers the sun with darkness. But Jesus descends a second time—now in divine form—towards the Lord of the Law, and demands from him justice for the death that he has suffered. It is only then that the Creator, realizing at last the divinity of Jesus, learns that there is another God above himself. Jesus decrees that henceforth whoever will believe in him shall belong to him and be saved. Eznik adds to this, that Jesus then takes St Paul, reveals to him the conditions and the price of salvation, and sends him forth to preach the redemption.

After Simon and Basilides, and after Marcion, the most famous of the great heresiarchs is Valentinus. His career had begun at Alexandria in the time of Hadrian. He taught at Rome from A.D. 136 to 165, after which he removed his school into the isle of Cyprus. The adversaries of the Gnostics accuse him above all of having stolen doctrines from Pythagoras and still more from Plato. Beyond all doubt Valentinus is the most philosophic of the Gnostics and perhaps, for that reason, his over-scholastic speculations contain dilutions of the essential myths of these fluid religions.[69] He seems to have composed for himself a special gospel called the *Gospel of Truth*, and to have written homilies, epistles, hymns, a *Treatise of the Three Natures* and perhaps also some *Revelations* or *Visions*.[70] His doctrine is known to us mainly by the analyses of some of his writings by the heresiologists, who do not disclose their titles—and by some fragments of works by his disciples Ptolemy, Theodotus, Heracleon . . . e.g., the *Epistle of Ptolemy to Flora*, of which Epiphanius has even

[69] The Valentinian school was an offshoot of the sect of the Ophites, according to Irenaeus, I, xxx, 14; concerning the latter, see pp. 44, 47f.

[70] Cf. P. Alfaric, *loc. cit.*, pp. 12–13.

preserved the text. It retraces some essential lines of Valentinus's doctrine, but in very moderate fashion, so as not to shock those who are not yet attracted to Gnosticism.[71]

The system of Valentinus was characterized—if we are to believe its enemies—by its description, in the explanation it gives of the higher, primordial world, of a multiple series of emanations issuing from the supreme and invisible Father in successive couples. The summaries of this myth given by Irenaeus and in the *Philosophumena* agree pretty closely in all their details.[72]

The origin of all things, according to Valentinus, is a perfect aeon bearing the name of pro-Father, described also as the abyss. It is incomprehensible, intangible, invisible, eternal, unbegotten, and it dwells in profound repose. Here one can recognize a doctrine of the divine transcendence which was no invention of the Gnostics but had already been an object of Greek philosophic contemplation. Co-existent with this pro-Father is a Thought which is also Silence. From the primordial *union* of the pro-Father with his Thought emanate the pairs of aeons to the number of eight (the ogdoad) as follows: Father and Thought; Intelligence and Truth (or the only Son); Word and Life; primordial Man and the Church.

The Word and the Life emanate ten more aeons; primordial Man and the Church emanate another twelve. Thus is produced, together with the first eight, a total of thirty aeons—the Pleroma, or Plenitude.

But a drama is now enacted in this supernal and perfect world. The thirtieth and last of the aeons—Wisdom, or Sophia—tries to

---

[71] "Epistle of Ptolemy to Flora", analysed by Sagnard, in *Gnose valentinienne*, pp. 451–79; G. Quispel, "La lettre de Ptolémée á Flora" in *Vigiliae Christianae*, vol. II, pp. 17–56. *Fragments of Heracleon*, cf. Sagnard, *loc. cit.*, pp. 480–520.

[72] For Valentinus, see Sagnard, *loc. cit.*; Ant. Orbe, *En aurora de la exegesis del IV Evangelio* (Ioh. I, 3), (*Estudios Valentinianos*, II)=Analecta Gregoriana, vol. LXV, Rome, 1955; and, by the same author, *Los Primeros herejes ante la persecucion* (*Estudios Valentinianos*, V), *ibidem*, vol. LXXXIII, Rome, 1956; Quispel, *The Original Doctrine of Valentine*, in *Vigiliae Christianae*, vol. I, pp. 43–73; W. Foerster, "Von Valentin zu Herakleon" in *Beihefte zur Zeitschrift f. die neutestamentl. Wiss.*, 7, 1928. This last proves that Valentinus's Gnosis was more heavily charged with oriental, mythological elements than was the teaching of his disciples. Cf. H. C. Puech, "Problème . . . ", p. 156.

imitate the pro-Father by giving birth from herself, exactly as he did, that is, without a partner. She does not know, indeed, that this privilege of bringing forth *alone* is reserved for the one un-begotten being, the root of the All. Sophia therefore produces, not another perfect being, but a deformed substance, an abortion, at which she is seized with disgust and remorse. Thereupon the aeons pray to the pro-Father on behalf of Sophia, and the supreme Power commands Intelligence and Truth to engender a new pair or couple—that of the Christ and the Holy Spirit, which Spirit is feminine. At the same time he himself emanates a new aeon which is the Cross (Stauros) and the Limit (Horos): by this Cross and this Limit the Pleroma is strengthened and, by the same means, separated from the imperfect and inferior Creation of which Sophia has produced the first element.[73] When the Pleroma is thus consolidated, the aeons join in singing hymns to the pro-Father; and then, with one accord, the Pleroma emanates the Perfect Fruit who is Jesus the Saviour.

Being responsible for the imperfect creation that it has evoked, the Intention (Enthymesis) of the Wisdom has been excluded from the higher world and its light. This Intention is itself a wisdom which henceforth is also known by the Hebrew name of Akhamôth. It is whirling about in dark and empty places. But the Christ has pity upon it;[74] he gives form to its substance, and then withdraws toward the higher realms. Sophia, having in this way become conscious of her suffering, springs up in search of the light that has departed from her: but Horos—the Limit—prevents

[73] The notions of "the limit" and of "intersection" are, among others, ex-plained by the passage in the Timaeus (35a–36d), in which Plato imagines the creation by the Demiurge of the circles of "the same" and of "the other"—i.e., of the celestial equator and of the ecliptic intersecting in the form of a cross. Taking over this notion, the Gnostics saw this imaginary cross, traced upon the celestial vault which is the utmost bound of our eyesight, as "the limit" separating the higher universe from the material world in which we are confined. A Christian interpretation of this idea, analogous to that which Valentinus develops, is already to be found in the *Apology* of St Justin (I. 60) who puts it in this way—"Plato has said that the power which comes next to the highest God has been marked with a cross upon the universe". It is this image, again, which is developed in the vision of the Cross of Light described in the apocryphal *Acts of John*, §§ 97–101 (cf. M. R. James, *The Apocryphal New Testament*, pp. 254f.). See also above, references given in note 64 and, below, in note 124.

[74] Cf. Sagnard, *loc. cit.*, pp. 159ff.

her from reaching the Pleroma. Sophia then falls into fear, sadness and anxiety; her prayers go up towards him who has abandoned her; and out of this supplication and these emotions there comes the substance of the matter of which our world is to be formed. Akhamôth, this fallen Sophia, is also alluded to, in the myth, by the names of holy Spirit, of Earth, of heavenly Jerusalem, and of Mother. . . .

The Christ and the aeons then have pity upon her: they send her the Saviour in order that he—so says the *Philosophumena*—may be her spouse and allay the passions she has suffered. It is by Gnosis that the Saviour corrects these passions and drives them out of her. Thus espoused, the lower wisdom gives birth to angels. And from the main lines of this creation proceed the three principles—material, psychic and spiritual (pneumatic) which will interweave in the composition of the lower world, and to which will correspond three races of men with their higher and lower destinies. To these three principles also correspond three different planes in the lower world, the highest being the Ogdoad, also described as the "intermediate" plane (the *mesotēs*, because it lies immediately below the world of light) which is the dwelling of the Mother who generates the spiritual substance. Below the Ogdoad is the Hebdomad—the seventh heaven—inhabited by the Demiurge, creator of the visible heavens and the earth. Still lower, in our own base world, is the Cosmocrator, the devil, created by the Demiurge.

Under an impulse that he receives from the Mother, but of which he himself has no consciousness, the Demiurge—who is here called the Mêtropatôr (meaning the Mother-father)—forms the seven heavens and the celestial and terrestrial beings over whom he reigns. Having produced all these, he thinks, in his ignorance, that he is the only God, and cries out, through the mouths of the Biblical prophets,[75] "It is I alone who am God. and there is no other beside me!" Then he creates terrestrial man, into whom he breathes the psychic element: but besides this, the Mother has endowed man with a spiritual element, unknown to the Demiurge; and thus, in spite of himself, he has

[75] Cf. *Isaiah* XLV, 5–6; XLVI, 9.

sown in the soul of the first man on earth the higher spiritual quality. Thus man, when once he is created, unites in himself all three elements; the hylic—that of the *left*—which will perish inevitably; the psychic—that of the *right*—which can either assimilate itself to higher things and become immortal, or become like matter and perish in corruption; and, thirdly, the spiritual element which should be formed and perfected through Gnosis so that, when the ultimate consummation of the universe is attained, all the spiritual elements of this order may have been saved.[76]

This doctrine was translated into ceremonies and formulas by which the Valentinians believed they could render themselves invisible, after death, to the powers of heaven that their souls would have to encounter on their ascent towards the Light. To the lower powers these souls were supposed to answer, "I am a son of the Father, of the pre-existent Father. . . . I have come to see all things, those that are mine and those that are foreign to me, or rather, not totally alien to me but belonging to Akhamôth . . . who has made them. Thus I have my origin in the pre-existent, and am returning to my own essence from which I came."

Afterwards, to the powers of the Demiurge, these souls had to say, "I am a precious vessel, worthier than the feminine creature who made you. Your Mother knows not her origin, but I know myself; I know whence I come, and I call upon the incorruptible Sophia who is in the Father, who is also the Mother of your mother and who has neither father nor husband. That which has made you, knowing not who was its mother and believing itself alone to exist, this is a power both male and female, and it is the Mother of this that I invoke!" (Irenaeus, *Adversus Haereses* I, XXI, 5.)

It was to reform this world here below, the world of men, that Jesus was born "by means of Mary". The *Philosophumena* notes that, upon this point, two schools of thought arose among the inheritors of the Valentinian Gnosis. "The Italian school, to which Heracleon and Ptolemy belong, maintain that the body of

---

[76] Concerning the difference between the psychic and the "pneumatic" (spiritual) cf. Sagnard, *La Gnose valentinienne* . . . , pp. 387-415 and H. C. Puech, *Le Manichéisme, son fondateur, sa doctrine*, p. 186, note 374.

Jesus is *psychic*: that is why, at the moment of the Baptism, the Spirit—that is, the Word of the Mother from on high, of Sophia—descended upon Jesus in the form of a dove, cried out to the psychic element and awakened it from among the dead. . . . The Oriental school, on the contrary, to which Axionicos and Bardesan belong,[77] teach that the body of the Saviour was *spiritual*, for (already) the holy Spirit, namely Sophia, had descended upon Mary. . . ." Of the teachings of this Oriental school we still have the testimony of excerpts from the works of the Gnostic Theodotus, preserved by Clement of Alexandria.[78]

It is noteworthy that, according to the expositions of the Valentinian doctrine that we have summarized, the Demiurge, despite its fundamental ignorance, is not presented as an entirely evil god. Irenaeus even writes that, according to Valentinus, "when the Saviour came, the Demiurge learned everything from him, hastening joyfully to him with his whole army of angels". It is the Demiurge who, pending the final consummation of this lower world, is directing the "economy" of our universe. The reference in Irenaeus specifies what this consummation will be: it will be achieved when all the spiritual seed dispersed among beings will have attained to perfection. Then the Wisdom will leave the intermediate plane to enter into the Pleroma, where she will be espoused to the Saviour and finally united with him—a union for which the Pleroma will be, as it were, the bridal chamber. The pneumatic beings, having become pure intelligences and cleansed of the psychic elements which cannot, in any case, raise themselves above the Limit, will mount through the lower heavens without being molested or even seen by their archons, and will go right up into the Pleroma, where they will be the "brides" of the angels who surround the Saviour. As for the Demiurge, he will succeed to the position on the intermediate

[77] Axionicos (known to us only through Tertullian's treatise *Adv. Valent.*, IV) must have taught the doctrines of Valentinus at Antioch. Bardesan of Edessa (154–222) is the famous founder of Syrian poetry. In the second half of his life he abandoned Gnosticism. Nevertheless, it is believed to be partly in the form he had imparted to it that the doctrine was adopted by Mani. For the differences between the Italian and Oriental schools, see Sagnard, *loc. cit.*, pp. 524–5 and 547ff.
[78] Cf. note 23 *ante* and Sagnard, *Gnose valentinienne*, pp. 521–61

plane, previously occupied by Sophia his mother, where the souls—
the psychic elements—will find their rest. This done, the latent
heat hidden in the earth will flame forth, and, destroying matter
altogether, will be consumed with it and pass into nothingness.

The three human races—earthly, psychic and spiritual—are
prefigured by Cain, Abel and Seth (this last endowed with the
spiritual seed) and their respective descendants.

Irenaeus treats the Valentinian teaching with unrestrained
sarcasm. He goes so far as to parody it, in these terms: "There is
nothing to prevent some other inventor (than Valentinus), in the
same sort of exposition, from defining his terms thus: 'There is
a certain royal pro-principle, pro-intelligible, pro-denuded of
substance, a pro-rotundity. With this principle dwells a Virtue
that I call Cucurbitacy. With this Cucurbitacy is a virtue which,
for its part, I call Absolutely-empty. This Cucurbitacy and this
Absolutely-empty, which make but one, have emanated without
emanating a fruit visible on all sides, edible and savoury, a fruit
which language names Gourd. With this Gourd there is a virtue
of the same power as itself which I also call Melon. These virtues:
Cucurbitacy and Absolutely-empty, Gourd and Melon, have
emanated the whole multitude of the raving melons of Valentine. . . .'"[79]

One of the closest personal disciples of Valentinus was without
doubt Marcus, who carried on his apostolate in Asia Minor.
Irenaeus gives him a very bad reputation: he seems to have
seduced many of the faithful—men and women—in every sense
of the word. A deacon in Asia, for instance, who had welcomed
Marcus into his house and who had a very comely wife, had
reason to rue it. The doctor seduced the beauty, body and soul.
For a long time she followed him in his wanderings. Only in the
end, did some true Christians manage to open her eyes and bring
her back to the right path. Then she condemned herself to a
perpetual penance, weeping hot tears over the outrage that the
magian had put upon her.[80]

[79] Quoted by Sagnard, *loc. cit.*, p. 287. Irenaeus also ridiculed the aeons which
engender without having to unite one with another—"like hens without cocks"
(Irenaeus, II, xii, 4).
[80] Irenaeus, I, xii, 4.

Marcus claimed that the Gnosis he taught was a revelation that the Silence had deposited in him. According to the *Philosophumena* this Silence—the primordial and complete Tetrad (*colorbas* in Aramaic)—had come to visit him in feminine guise, had disclosed to him who she was, and had then explained to him the generation of the All, a matter which the Tetrad had never until then disclosed to anyone, either of the gods or of mankind.[81]

In its general lines the teaching of Marcus looks more like a mere amplification of the Valentinian Gnosis. It is, however, distinguished by one original feature: Marcus comments upon each entity of the supernal universe in function with the numerical values he derives from the letters composing each of their names—values of which he analyses the relations and harmonies according to a method which will be familiar to students of the Kabbala.[82]

Another originality of Marcus—although other Gnostics may have instituted similar rites without the heresiologists' knowledge —is to have codified a whole liturgy, which included baptisms, eucharists and an extreme unction. . . . Irenaeus records the principal formulas of these sacraments.[83]

To conclude our enumeration of the great Gnostic personalities mentioned, or rather ridiculed, by the heresiologists, we must not omit Justin. It is not known where or when he flourished: he is known to us only from the *Philosophumena*.[84]

Very different from all the Gnostic systems we have reviewed thus far, the myth that he taught had been expounded by him in a book called *Baruch*,[85] which a Greek account by the pseudo-Hippolytus tries to summarize. According to this revelation, the universe proceeded from *three* uncreated principles: a supreme

[81] The Tetrad—the first four aeons—reminds one also of Barbelô: cf. note 43; also Sagnard, *Gnose valentinienne*, chap. IX.

[82] Upon this numerology and its Pythagorean origins see Sagnard, *loc. cit.*, chap. X.

[83] The formulas of these sacraments—certain passages were in Aramaic—are translated in Leisegang, *loc. cit.*, chap. XI; text; Völker, *Quellen*, pp. 136ff.

[84] *Philosophumena*, V, 23–8; cf. Völker, *Quellen*, 27ff.; cf. upon Justin, Jonas, *loc. cit.*, vol. I, pp. 335–40.

[85] The prophet Baruch had acquired a mysterious prestige, and was sometimes likened to Zoroaster: see Bidez-Cumont, *Mages hellénisés*, vol. I, p. 49; vol. II, p. 129.

Father called "the Good"; a second principle, masculine, father of all born beings but destitute of any foreknowledge of the future—Elohim. And thirdly, a feminine principle equally deficient in prescience—Eden, also called Israel. From the love between Elohim and Eden, who in the beginning dwelt in the lower regions, were born the angels of the lower heavens, angels who together constituted the Paradise in which one of them, Baruch, was the tree of Life; whilst the tree of knowledge of good and evil was the angel Naas, the Serpent. The angels of Elohim took, from the upper half of the body of Eden, the good earth[86] of which Adam was made; whilst from the lower half of Eden they took the matter from which they fashioned the wild beasts and other animals.

But Elohim, after having constructed and ordered the world by his amours with Eden, had wanted to ascend into higher regions to see whether there was any defect in this creation. Attaining to a great height, he beheld a light more perfect than that which he had created. He invoked it; and then the supreme God, the Good, whom Elohim had never known till then, allowed him to attain to his presence where he kept him beside him. But Eden, seeking vengeance for his desertion of her, began to inflict suffering upon those portions of the spirit of Elohim which he had imparted to men. She even charged her angel Naas, the Serpent, to visit mankind with every possible chastisement. Naas obeyed her behest: he approached Eve and committed adultery with her; and then he made Adam his minion.

Thereupon Elohim sent the angel Baruch to give instruction to men, to the Jews, that they might turn towards the God on high, towards the Good. To the uncircumcised, the pagans, he also sent Hercules, to deliver them from the evil angels of Eden's

---

[86] Cf. this passage with a verse of the *Psalms of Solomon* (XIV, 2–3, in the edn. of J. Viteau, 1911). "The Paradise of the Lord, the trees of Life, these are his saints. Their plantation is rooted for eternity, for the portion and the heritage of God, that is Israel." Concerning Eden, confused with *adamâ* and thus becoming a mythic personification of the Earth, cf. K. Rudolph, "Ein Grundtyp gnostischer Urmensch-Adam Spekulation", in *Zeitschrift f. Relig. u. Geistesgeschichte*, LX, 1957, pp. 16–17 and note 94; also here, pp. 100–1 and chap. II, note 84

creation, by slaying one after another the Nemean lion, the boar of Erymanthus, the Lernean hydra . . . who are those angels.[87] At last, in the days of King Herod, Baruch was once more sent here below by Elohim: he came to Nazareth, where he found Jesus who was then twelve years old. Baruch revealed to him all the history, from the beginning, of Eden and Elohim; foretold him, moreover, the events of the future and encouraged him to preach the God from on high, the Good. Naas tried to prevent the fulfilment of this prophecy by having Jesus crucified; but Jesus abandoned the carnal body that he had from Eden's creation, left it on the Cross and ascended up into the highest heavens.

One has a yet more complete idea of the complexity of this system, if one notes how the supreme god in question is also identified with Priapus, who had been created "before anything was" and of whom, for that reason, images were set up in all the temples.[88] Similarly, the union of the swan with Leda, and the story of Danae appear as images of the loves of Elohim and Eden, whilst Ganymede and the eagle represent Adam at grips with Naas.

The author of the *Philosophumena* adds: "I have seen a great many heresies, my well-beloved; I never met with any, however, that was worse than this. Truly, we must imitate the Hercules of Justin in cleaning out these Augean stables—or rather sewers."

THE MAIN GNOSTIC SECTS

Even more than these leading teachers, adversaries of their heresies describe and stigmatize the sects which, like poisonous fungi, had sprung up in direct succession from the earliest, most mythical founders of Gnosticism—from Simon of Samaria, as

[87] Such allegorical interpretations of the myth of Hercules had already, long before this, been familiar to the Stoics, who regarded the hero as, in the words of the orator Heraclitus, a spirit "initiated in the heavenly wisdom". Heraclitus and Cleanthes have given a symbolic or moral exegesis of the twelve labours of Hercules. (Cf. Fél. Buffiére, *Les Mythes d'Homère et la pensée grecque*, 1956, pp. 376–7.) Nicomachus, too, compared Hercules to the Sun passing through the twelve signs of the Zodiac, each sign symbolizing one of the twelve labours (Buffiére, *loc. cit.*, pp. 144 and 296; note 84).We read in Eusebius, *Eccles. Hist.*, VI, 19, 8, how Origen, for example, knew and interpreted these allegories.

[88] For the phallic element in the Gnostic mysteries (?) cf. Tertullian, *Advers, Valent.*, I.

some said; from Nicolas, as was claimed by others. Was it from these sects that such as Basilides or Valentinus or Carpocrates derived the teachings that they rendered ever more subtle? Or was it, on the contrary, these groups which were simply popularizing the teachings of the great doctors? The question is most confusing! According to Irenaeus (I, xxxv, 6) the largest of the sects— the one that expressly called itself Gnostic—had not appeared at Rome until the time of Pope Anicetus (155-166); it had arisen from the sectaries of Carpocrates. Elsewhere (I, xxx, 14), Irenaeus suggests that the doctrine of Valentinus had its source in the myths of a group which seems to be that of the Ophites. What emerges as noteworthy is that the heretical "churches", contradictory though they are in spirit, some ascetic in tendency and others licentious in practice, appear almost all to be using the *same* myths, the *same* writings, whilst the great masters themselves disseminate more varied teachings of a relatively philosophic character.

*   *   *

The three sects which St Irenaeus knew best were: the Caïnites (I, xxxi); a group to which he gives no name but which his successors have identified as Ophite or Sethian; and, thirdly, the "Gnostics" also described as Barbelognostics (I, xxix).

Irenaeus knew only a little about the Cainites. They included among their prophets, Cain, Esau, Korah and the Sodomites. . . . They used a *Gospel of Judas*.[89] Some later authors, such as Epiphanius, also tell us that these sectaries had a book, *Against the Hystera*—that is, against "the womb", a name which they gave to the evil creator of the lower universe: they also read a fantastic *Ascension of Paul*.[90]

The passage devoted to the Barbelognostics gives no details about the sect itself and is limited to an account of its higher

---

[89] Upon this exaltation of the "accurst" by some of the Gnostics, see Puech, *La Gnose et le Temps*, note 32. Concerning the title of the *Gospel of Judas*, there is room for doubt whether it may not refer to Judas Didymus—i.e. to the Apostle Thomas. See below, p. 225.

[90] Apparently this work cannot be identical with the apocryphal *Apocalypse of St Paul* which has been preserved, and which contributed to the inspiration of the *Divina Commedia*.

cosmogony and of the generation by Sophia of the evil Demiurge, as these heretics taught those things. They owed their name to the fact that, in their system, the feminine power which emanates from the primordial Father, and which plays the part of the Word, was named Barbelô.[91] This text of Irenaeus is especially valuable to us since the discovery, half a century ago, of one of the very few original Gnostic scriptures so far available—the *Secret Book of John*[92]—has enabled us to see that Irenaeus, in this case, has followed sometimes word for word the text of a revelation undoubtedly in use by the Gnostics.

This passage in Irenaeus (I, xxx) refers apparently to the Ophites,[93] a sect which had been known to the pagan Celsus before A.D. 180; he had even been able to refer to one of their writings—the *Diagram*. Their cosmological and anthropological myths are fully expounded by Irenaeus; and it is noteworthy that they appear to have been closely analogous to those of the Barbelognostics, faithfully summarized by the saintly Bishop of Lyons in the preceding chapter of his book.

In the beginning, in the infinite abyss, there had been a Light, blissful, incorruptible and infinite, the Father of all, the First Man. His thought, proceeding from him, became the Son of Man. Then, underneath both of these, there arose a feminine principle, the holy Spirit, the First Woman, Mother of the Living. In the far depths, confronting these beings, were only the elements of chaos and the abyss, the waters and the darkness above which the Feminine Spirit[94] was upborne. From the three first and highest powers was born the Christ who, together with them, finally instituted the incorruptible aeon, namely the "Church".

It was then that, from the Woman, as out of waters in ebullition, there arose a dew of light—the androgyne being called

[91] Upon the Barbelognostics, see Jonas, *Gnosis*, vol. I, p. 361; upon the name Barbelô, cf. our note 43.

[92] Cf. C. Schmidt, *Irenäus und seine Quelle in Adv. Haeres.*, I, 29, in *Philotesia, Paul Kleinert zum LXX. Geburtstag dargebracht*, 1907, pp. 315–36.

[93] Upon the Ophites: Jonas, *loc. cit.*, vol. I, p. 360; Amann, article; "Ophites" in *Dict. de Théol. Cathol.*, XI, col. 1063–75; R. Liechtenhan; article "Ophiten" in *Herzog-Haupt*, XIV, 404–13. Reitzenstein u. Schaeder: *Studien zum antiken Synkretismus aus Iran u. Griechenland*, 1926, 1st part, chap. IV.

[94] *Genesis* I, 2.

Sophia or Prunikos. She falls down as far as the waters beneath, where Matter clings to her person, weighs it down and prevents it from rising up towards the light, without, however, being able to overwhelm it. Thanks to the strength of the light that she has received, Sophia raises herself and, from her outstretched body, she forms the visible heaven. Then she separates herself from this body. She gives birth to a son, from whom six others are born one after another, constituting the seven planets and their respective heavens—the Hebdomad, above which Sophia dwells in the eighth sphere, which is Ogdoad. The names of the seven are, in ascending order, Ialdabaôth, Iao, Sabaôth the Great, Adonaios, Eloaios, Horaios, Astaphaios. Ialdabaôth, having completed the heavens, the archangels, etc., by his desire for Matter produces a son who is the Serpent. Now he exclaims "I am the Father and God, and there is no one above me!"[95] But the Mother, over-hearing him, cries out to him, "Do not lie, Ialdabaôth; over and above thee there are the Father of all, the First Man, and the Son of Man!" This voice, the source of which is hidden by Ialdabaôth, troubles the powers below. It is then that the Demi-urge says to them, "Come, and let us make man in our image". At the same time the Mother, in order to incite them to this creation, through which she means to rob them of the power within them, reveals to them the heavenly image of the First Man. Together, the six powers of Ialdabaôth—the Archons—construct a man, who is immense but powerless: they cannot stand him upright. Then Sophia, in order to deprive the Demi-urge of the portion of light that is within him, inspires him to breathe his own spirit of life into terrestrial man. Man stands up erect and resplendent. But Ialdabaôth is seized with jealousy and, in order to take away the luminous power from Adam, he fabricates woman. The other Archons, beholding her, fall in love with her beauty and beget sons upon her who are angels. Then the Mother, by means of the Serpent, or perhaps even by taking on its appearance herself, induces Eve and Adam to eat of the fruit which Ialdabaôth has forbidden them. In this way Adam and Eve begin to acquire knowledge of the Virtue which is above

[95] *Isaiah* XLV, 5-6 and XLVI, 9.

all things, and turn away from their creator. Meanwhile Ialdabaôth, because of his ignorance and forgetfulness, knows nothing of the mystery enacted by our first parents, and he expels them from Paradise. The myth declares that Ialdabaôth would have liked, then, himself to beget sons by Eve,[96] but he could not, because his Mother had secretly deprived the human pair of the light-dew which was their strength, so that it should not be defiled by the Demiurge. Thus it was that the first man and the first woman were emptied of divine substance when Ialdabaôth cast them out of the heavens, which contained Paradise, down into this base world. Ialdabaôth also cast his son the Serpent down to earth: the latter took the lower angels into his charge and, in imitation of his father, gave himself six sons who, together with himself, make up the seven devils ceaselessly at war with the human race.

In the world here below Adam and Eve now had their gross bodies only, without light. Prunikos had pity upon them and gave them back the resplendent dew. Then were born to them Cain and Abel, between whom discord was sown by the Serpent, which had become the enemy of the human race, on whose account its father had chastised it. After this were born Seth[97] and Norea, who were of a superior race, and from whom the multitude of the Perfect were to descend.

Irritated because men no longer worshipped him, Ialdabaôth unleashed the deluge upon them. But Sophia saved Noah and his family by means of the Ark. And when the world re-emerged and was repeopled, Ialdabaôth chose Abraham from among men,

[96] Cf. *Genesis* IV, 1. "I have gotten a man with the help of the Lord", cries Eve after the birth of Cain; an exclamation which the Gnostic myth misinterprets by excessive literalism.

[97] The Valentinians, too, regarded Seth as the first of the race of the perfect ones, the spiritual in opposition to the material (Cain) and Abel (the psychic). Seth was, no doubt, well suited to become the great prophet of the Gnostic race, various attributes of prestige being ascribed to him in apocryphal traditions about the Old Testament: image of God, heir of Adam, inventor of astronomy. His sons were to be the "Sons of God" who, upon Mount Hermon, led a pious and secluded life cherishing the nostalgia for Paradise. Cf. Gruenbaum, "Beiträge zur vergleichende Mythologie aus der Haggada" in *Zeitschr. d. Deutsche Morgenl. Gesellsch.*, 1877, p. 247. H. C. Puech, "Fragments retrouvés de l'Apocalypse d'Allogène", in *Mélanges Cumont*, p. 949. Cf. also below, pp. 149 and 182-8.

making a covenant with him that, if the patriarch's descendants continued to serve him, he would give them the earth for their heritage. Later, by means of Moses, he led these descendants out of Egypt and gave them the Law. All the great prophets of the Old Testament, also, have been his servants. And yet, through the ingenuity of Sophia, they allowed certain words to slip into their prophecies which refer to the First Man, to the incorruptible Aeon and to the Christ. For Sophia was even contriving, without the knowledge of Ialdabaôth, to bring about the births of John the Baptist and of Jesus.

Since Sophia Prounikos had no rest either in heaven or earth, in her affliction she invoked the aid of the supreme Mother, who, taking pity on her repentance, besought the First Man to send the Christ to her assistance. Thus the Christ came down towards his sister the dew of light. Such, in outline, is the myth of salvation; which rises to its most dramatic climax at the incarnation of the Christ in the man Jesus. The mission of Christ is attacked by Ialdabaôth who, together with the Archons, plans the drama of Calvary. From the Cross, the Christ withdraws, ascending to the aeon: he sends down to the crucified Jesus a power which re-animates within him all that is capable of living again. And Jesus, after this resurrection, remains among his disciples for eighteen months, in order to teach the Mysteries to those who are worthy of knowing them. The Christ himself, having reascended into heaven, is seated at the right hand of Ialdabaôth, where—unknown to the latter, who does not see it—he receives the souls of the Perfect, enabling them to escape from the Demiurge's domain.

The consummation of this world—so the myth concludes—will be attained when all the dew of light that is scattered here below will have been brought together again on high, in the Aeon of incorruptibility.

*   *   *

These sects, described by Irenaeus, are those which Epiphanius came to know, with several others, at a later date. We have already seen the importance that Epiphanius attached to the Nicolaïtans[98] and the system that he attributed to them. Let us now turn to the picture that he gives us of the sect which is entitled above all to be called "Gnostic" and to whose perverse seductions he was exposed, in Egypt, during the years of his youth[99]—the ordeal through which he gained his own knowledge of their secret books.

We cannot be sure whether the school of thought which so explicitly assumed the name "Gnostic" was continuing the doctrine of Carpocrates, although the disciples of that teacher also chose to call themselves by that name. What is certain, however, is that some very different groups were connected with the same family of great Gnostics; among them, the Coddians, the Stratiotici, the Phibionites and the Zacchaeans, even the Barbeliotes. . . . The names were multiplied as the cults spread to different countries, or, perhaps, in function with more or less select initiations, creating a confusion in which the modern historian can easily lose his way.

But let Epiphanius describe them, and, in particular, their writings. It is noteworthy that they attributed some of their myths to the prophet *Barcabbas*—the name under which Basilides had composed some alleged revelations. Some of their great apocalypses were attributed to *Adam*. They had also various writings headed by the name of Seth, discussing, among other subjects, the Demiurge Ialdabaôth. They made use of a book called *The Interrogations of Mary*: and another of their books, entitled *On the Generation of Mary* contained, Epiphanius tells us, some horrible stories such as an account of the vision by which Zacharias was struck dumb in the Temple at Jerusalem;[100] which is interpreted as follows: Zacharias, as he was about to burn incense, saw a mysterious being with a human body and the head of an ass. At first, so that he should not make this apparition known, his throat was miraculously paralysed; and when his voice was restored to him, he addressed the congregation and

98 Cf. above, p. 14.
99 Cf. above, pp. 8ff.
100 The episode thus travestied is that of Zacharias's aphasia after seeing a vision of angel, in *Luke* I, 11-12.

reproached them for worshipping such a monstrous god: it was for this that the Jews put him to death.[101]

These sectaries had also a *Gospel of Perfection*, and referred to a *Gospel of Philip*—works which today are lost. Epiphanius quotes the preamble to an apocryphon which they called *The Gospel of Eve* containing these words—"I was standing upon a high mountain, when lo! I saw one person of tall stature and another who was lame.[102] Then I heard a voice like thunder. . . . I drew near . . . and the vision addressed me in these words: 'I am identical with thee, and thou art identical with me; wherever thou art, there am I, for I am sown in all things; wherever thou wilt thou reapest me; but in reaping me it is thyself that thou reapest.'"

One of their great myths was called by the name of Norea, that of a supposed sister of Seth and wife of Noah, which name, they said, was the equivalent in Semitic parlance to what was

[101] The god with the head of an ass is the image of the Demiurge Ialdabaôth, the "god of the Jews", cf. pp. 43 and 79. It is upon certain monuments of Egypt that we find the most ancient proofs of the attribution of a donkey's head to a god, who was to become progressively identified with the god of the Jews. This originated from the Asiatic god Sutekh, whom the Egyptians assimilated to one of their own greatest gods: Seth, the adversary of Osiris. They represented Seth also, after the period of the Persian invasions, with a human body and an ass's head. Afterwards, this god Seth was definitely regarded by the Egyptians—in accordance with a late myth mentioned by Plutarch in his *De Iside*, § 31—as the father of the legendary heroes Hierosolymus and Judaeus—that is, as the ancestor of the Jews! (Cf. P. Montet, *Le drame d'Avaris, essai sur la pénétration des Sémites en Égypte*, Paris, 1940, pp. 47-62; Marianne Guentch-Oglouceff, "Noms propres imprécatoires", in the *Bulletin, de l'Institut français d'Archéologie orientale du Caire*, XL, 1941, pp. 117-33.

It was therefore not without precedent that, in the first centuries of our era, the detractors of the Christians and the Jews, and some of our Gnostics also, vulgarized, generally in an offensive sense, a tradition that the god of the Jews had an ass's head: thence also the carving on the Palatine (of the third cent.) which represents a worshipper before a crucified figure with a donkey's head, with the ironical legend "Alexamenos worships God". Minucius Felix, at the same epoch, puts an allusion to this pagan calumny into the mouth of one of the speakers of his dialogue *Octavius*—"I have heard that, by I know not what fanatical aberration, they religiously adore the head of that most ugly animal, the ass!" Concerning this calumny and its origins, cf. P. de Labriolle, *La Réaction païenne*, pp. 193-9.

[102] The crippled being would symbolize the supreme power by whose mistake the material world was engendered. Upon the meaning of the words "I am I and thou art I", which suggest the recovery of our authentic being and the return to divinity, cf. Puech, *La Gnose et le temps*, p. 104 and note 65.

meant by Pyrrha, the wife of Deucalion.[103] We have already mentioned this Norea and the myth according to which she seduced the Archons, by the lust that she aroused in them, in order to deprive them of their potency of light.

Epiphanius, who gives yet further details of the principal myths of these "Gnostics", enumerates for examples the names of the beings who dwell in the heavens of our universe: in the eighth heaven, Barbelô and the Christ; in the seventh Ialdabaôth, or, in the opinion of other sectaries of the same group, Sabaôth; in the sixth Elilaios, Daden, Setheus, Sacla (who is addicted to impure delights) and finally Iaô. Amongst these, Sabaôth is distinguished by having a pig's or an ass's head;[104] it is he who is supposed to have created heaven and the earth.

The sexual practices of these heretics—if Epiphanius, who had pretty intimate knowledge of them, is not systematically trying to vilify them—were of the most frightful. What are we to think, for instance, of the Phibionites who dedicated their carnal unions in succession to the names of three hundred and sixty-five different powers? "Unite thyself to me", they said to their partners, invoking the name of one of these numerous powers, "so that I may lead thee towards the Prince!" And whilst using this singular method of spiritual aspiration, they refused to procreate, or, if their efforts to remain sterile were unsuccessful, they practised abortion. Even this operation was accompanied by abominable rites and practices.[105]

As for the salvation of the "race of the Perfect" to which they thought they belonged, they taught that the wicked Prince of this lower world prevented souls who were without Gnosis from reascending into the higher regions. This demon had the form of a serpent, or dragon. He swallowed up the imperfect souls which, passing through his body, were sent through his tail into

[103] *Norea* means "fiery", like the Greek name *Pyrrha*: the Gnostics found in this yet another reason for connecting Noah with Deucalion, already comparable because of the parts they played at the Deluge.
[104] Cf. note 101 above.
[105] Translated in Leisegang, *loc. cit.*, pp. 132–3. The "licentious" practices appeared less shocking to the ancients than to the Christians. Cf. the case of the mystics of Sabazios (identified with Jahweh) in Franz Cumont, *Lux Perpetua*, p. 257.

the terrestrial universe, where they were transferred into the souls of various animals. But the souls protected from him by Gnosis attained, first, to Sabaôth and then, higher still, to Barbelô, the Mother of the living.

Epiphanius also describes the sect of the Ophites.[106] These were successors to the great Gnostics and to several analogous groups; and their doctrines as a whole, which Epiphanius summarizes in somewhat the same terms as Irenaeus, fairly closely resemble those we have noted in the other sects. But to these they added a cult of the serpent (whence their name) which they explained thus: "We venerate the Serpent", they said, "because God has made it the cause of Gnosis for mankind. Ialdabaôth did not wish men to have any recollection of the Mother or of the Father on high. It was the Serpent, who by tempting them, brought them Gnosis; who taught the man and the woman the complete knowledge of the mysteries from on high. That is why [its] father Ialdabaôth, mad with fury, cast it down from the heavens." This image of the Serpent was ever afterwards to be found in the nature of man. "Our bowels, thanks to which we nourish ourselves and live, do they not reproduce the form of the serpent?" These Gnostics, moreover, made a very practical cult of these reptiles: they kept and fed them in baskets; they held their meetings close to the holes in which they lived. They arranged loaves of bread upon a table, and then, by means of incantations, they allured the snake until it came coiling its way among these offerings; and only then did they partake of the bread, each one kissing the muzzle of the reptile they had charmed. This, they claimed, was the perfect sacrifice, the true Eucharist.

Where is it—in the Dionysiac orgies, in the cult of Asclepios, or in the mysteries of Sabazios which, according to Arnobius (*Adversus nationes*, V, 21), also made use of the image of the serpent—that one must look for the origins of such practices? Or do they not remind one even more of the cults of certain pagan sects which made a special cult of the serpent of the constellation Ophiuchus (if we are to believe the *Astronomica* of Manilius, 5; 389–93)? Like our Ophites, these adepts held the reptiles to their

---

[106] Cf. references in note 93, above.

breasts and caressed them, as living symbols of the celestial image that they worshipped.

Epiphanius knew of the Cainites, also;[107] but what he tells us about them adds hardly anything to what Irenaeus had already said. On the other hand he is very well informed concerning the beliefs of the Sethians. The part played by Seth, prophet of Gnosticism and first of the race of the Perfect,[108] was already known, no doubt, to most of the sects. The Valentinians were not unaware of it; and if we are to credit, for instance, Tertullian (*Adversus Valentinianos*, XXIX), the spiritual essence was represented, for them too, by the great Seth. Epiphanius believes he remembers having come across some heretics in Egypt who presented their teaching under the special invocation of this son of Adam, whom they also called by the name of Christ.

The writings that they used included, above all, seven revelations attributed to Seth himself; then certain books called *allogeneous*, that is, from a *foreign* origin above this base world. They also had an alleged *Apocalypse of Abraham*; another attributed to Moses;[109] and lastly, some books written under the name of *Hôrea*, the wife of Seth—in whom we plainly recognize Nôrea. In his time, says Epiphanius, this heresy had become rare.

In the same stream of thought to which the leading Gnostics, the Ophites, the Sethians and even the Cainites belonged, we find also the Archontici and the Audians.

The Archontici[110] may have taken their name from the particular knowledge they claimed to have about the Archons—that is, the seven planets—and about methods of invoking their powers. Among the first propagandists of this doctrine was a man named Peter, a priest in Palestine who was expelled from the Church by

[107] Epiphanius, *Heresy*, XXXVIII.   [108] Cf. note 97.

[109] The *Apocalypse of Abraham* may have been the source of some of the Gnostic features which appear in a work of the same title which is now extant only in Slavonic: cf. Frey, article on "Abraham (Apocalypse of,)", in *Dict. de la Bible, Supplément*, vol. I, col. 28–33. Under the title of *Apocalypse of Moses*, there is known to be a version of the apocryphal work commonly called *The Life of Adam and Eve*. Preuschen, who wanted this recognized as a Sethian writing, has not managed to get his opinion accepted: cf. Frey, in *Dict. de la Bible, ibid.*, col. 102–6.

[110] Cf. H. C. Puech's article "Archontiker" in *Reallexikon für Antike und Christentum*, vol. I, 634–43.

the Bishop Aetius about the year 347. Peter at first took refuge in Kaukaban in Arabia, but returned, in his old age, to live as a hermit three miles from Hebron, in a cave near the village of Caphar-Barusha. Epiphanius, who at that time was the head of a monastery near the town of Eleutheropolis, had a bone to pick with him. In 361, this Peter had an opportunity to indoctrinate with his myths a person of the name of Eutactes, who propagated them in Greater Armenia.

As for the actual content of these doctrines, it seems clear that the Archontici can hardly have been more than a ramification of the Sethians.[111] Epiphanius connects them also with a secondary group of the Severians (XLV, 2, 1). Among their sacred books they had some *Symphonia*, treatises which dealt, perhaps, with such subjects as the harmony of the celestial spheres.[112] They also read the *Allogeneous* books which, as we saw, were used by the Sethians; an *Ascension of Isaiah*; and, finally, the revelations of the prophets *Martiades and Marsanes* who, caught up into heaven, had explored its secrets for three days. Who were these visionaries? Some have tried to connect the name of Marsanes with that of a certain Marcianus mentioned by Serapion of Antioch, and of whom we know only that he was a heretic.[113] But would it not be better to recall the two prophetesses Martos and Martana who, of the same family as Elkesaï, had been adored as goddesses by the baptist sect of the Sampseans?[114]

Epiphanius also mentions, among other minor sects, that of the Melchizedekians.[115] Melchizedek, invested with an immense sacerdotal prestige, and born, according to *Genesis*, without father or mother, already held a very special position in the Jewish traditions of the first centuries of our era and also among the Samaritans. The latter went so far as to identify him with Shem, to whom they ascribed somewhat the same prophetic

---

[111] Puech, *loc. cit.*, col. 635.   [112] Puech, *loc. cit.*, col. 636–7.

[113] In Eusebius, *Eccles. Hist.*, VI, 12.

[114] According to Theodore Bar-Konai, translated in Pognon's *Inscriptions Mandaïtes des coupes de Khouabir*, p. 176. But the names of Martianes and Martiades recall, no less, Mashya and Mashyanê (marṭya and marṭânî), names given in the Iranian language to the first man and the first woman. Cf. Reitzenstein-Schaeder, *Studien zum Antiken Synkretismus*, p. 226, note 1.

[115] Epiphanius, *Adversus Haereses*, LV.

reputation as to the great Seth.[116] We know, too, the mystical part that he plays in the *Epistle to the Hebrews*. The sect mentioned by Epiphanius made Melchizedek into a Virtue of the higher world, by transferring to him the functions which the other sects ascribed to Seth. This doctrine was adopted and propagated by the Egyptian Hierakas (Epiphanius, LXVII), a brilliant author of writings and hymns—which he composed equally well in Coptic as in Greek—whose theories seduced a number of monks in the Christian community of the Nile Valley.

★   ★   ★

To avoid separating Epiphanius' information about the sects from that of Irenaeus—and we were entitled to keep them together, since these two critics write from analogous points of view—we have left over until now the very precious, but highly personal accounts given in the *Philosophumena*. In this we find, above all, three exceptionally long and valuable chapters dealing with the Naassenes, the Peratae and the Sethians. One's first impression—purely affective and literary—of these chapters is that they analyse the Gnostic doctrines more profoundly, and with more sympathy and less hostility than Epiphanius and Irenaeus in their studies of Gnostic writings.

The account of the Naassenes[117] begins with these words: "The priests and leaders of this doctrine were those who were first called Naassenes, from the Hebrew word *naas*, which means

[116] According to Jerome, *ad Evagrium*, epist. 26; Epiphanius, *Adv. Haereses, Haer.* LV, 6. These speculations take their point of departure from Psalm CX., 4, and the *Epistle to the Hebrews*, VII, 3. Concerning the controversies over Melchizedek which arose in the second and third centuries, cf. Tertullian, *De Praescript.*, LIII (*Patrologia Latina*, vol. II, cols. 72–4); Philastrius, *de Haer*, LII and CVIII (*P. L.*, vol. XII, cols. 1168 and 1282–5); St Jerome, *Epistul*, LXXIII, ad Ev. Presb. (*P. L.*, vol. XXIII, col. 678–81) which seems to refute the opuscule preserved in St Augustine's *Quaest. ex utroque Test. mixtim*, CIX (*P. L.*, vol. XXXV, cols. 2324–30); Praedestinatus, XXXIV (*P. L.*, vol. LIII, col. 598). One finds them again in the apocryphal literature about Adam: the *Cave of Treasures* (cf. Bezold, *Die Schatzhöle*, p. 36); the *Book of the Bee* by Solomon of Basra, and the Ethiopian pseudo-Clementine literature (cf. S. Grebaut in the *Revue de l'Orient chrétien*, 1912, p. 136. Cf. also Eutychius in *Patrologia Graeca*, vol. CXI, col. 923); Cedrenus (in *P. G.*, vol. CXXI, col. 77); Glykas (in *P. G.*, vol. CLVIII, col. 265). See also D. Calmet, *Dissertation sur Melchisédech*; *Commentaire littéral aux Epîtres de S. Paul*, vol. II, Paris, 1730, pp. 575–91.

[117] *Philosophumena*, V, 6–11; Reitzenstein, *Poimandres*, pp. 83ff.; Reitzenstein-Schaeder, *loc. cit.*, part I, chap. IV; Jonas, vol. I, pp. 343 and 348.

'Serpent'. Later on, they themselves assumed the name of 'Gnostics', claiming to be unique in their knowledge of the deepest things." They divided themselves into a number of sects which, fundamentally, amounted to only one heresy, for, under various formulations, it was the same doctrine that they professed. Their teachings had been, first of all, passed on by James, brother of the Lord, to Mariamne. They recognized a *Gospel according to the Egyptians*, and they also made use of a *Gospel according to Thomas* which contained, among others, this saying attributed to the Christ: "He who seeks me will find me among the children of seven years of age, for it is there, in the fourteenth aeon, after having remained hidden, that I reveal myself."[118]

Nevertheless, in spite of their recourse to these Christian texts—apocryphal, it is true—they borrowed chiefly, according to this account, from the myths of Hellenic and Oriental paganism. In their teaching, the Hermes of Cyllene, thanks to a mystical interpretation of the *Odyssey*, is enabled to play the part of the Word. The Naassenes also availed themselves of the Mysteries—those of the Great Mother, of Eleusis and also of the Phrygians (from which they borrowed the comparison of the Father of the Universe to an almond kernel, existing before all things and containing within itself the perfect fruit from which was to come forth an invisible child, nameless and ineffable). They believed it was necessary to become initiated, first into the "lesser Mysteries" —those of "carnal generation"—and then into the "greater Mysteries", the heavenly mysteries through which the gates of heaven were opened to the Perfect—gates at which the Spiritual, when they enter, must put on the apparel prepared for them, and straightway become "husbands rendered more masculine by the virginal Spirit". Among the Gnostics, the myth of the Leucadian rock, itself derived from speculations about the *Odyssey*,[119] was jumbled up with images of the heavenly Jerusalem who is the Mother of the Living, and with the symbol of the Jordan which, flowing down to the deep, prevented the children of

---

[118] The *Gospel of the Egyptians* and the *Gospel of Thomas*; cf. M. R. James, *The Apocryphal New Testament*, pp. 10 and 14; Amann, in the *Dict. de la Bible*, vol. I, cols. 476 and 478.

[119] Cf. chap. v, p. 191.

Israel from going out of Egypt—that is, extricating themselves from involvement in matter—whereas Jesus (Joshua in the Bible, *Joshua* III, 14–17) made the river flow back towards its source and thus delivered the chosen people.[120]

At the beginning of the universe, as the Naassenes imagined, there had been a Man and a Son of Man, both androgynous. To the honour of that primordial Adam they composed numerous hymns. Among the great powers of the higher world, they took particular account of Kaulakau, Saulasau and Zeasar: "Kaulakau is related to the Man on high, Adamas; Saulasau, to the mortal man here below, Zeasar, to the Jordan flowing up-stream." In their anthropological speculations, the brain corresponds to Eden; the membranes enveloping the brain, to the heavens; the head of man, to Paradise, etc. Epiphanius notes some similar speculations among the Ophites, and we find them among the Sethians.[121] The *Philosophumena* recounts these beliefs to us from documents said to be original: "This river, flowing out of Eden [i.e., out of the brain], divides into four branches. The first river is called Phison; it is this which flows around the whole land of Evilat, where gold is found . . .[122] it is there also that one finds the carbuncle and the emerald; this refers to the eye, as the value and the colours of these precious stones suggest. The second river is called the Geon, it is this which surrounds the whole land of Ethiopia; that river is the ear, for it resembles a labyrinth. The third river is called the Tigris; it is that which flows near Syria; a river of the most impetuous current, which is the nostrils. It flows over against Syria because, in our respiration, the air breathed in from without rushes in with violent impetuosity to replace that which has just been breathed out . . ." and so forth.

[120] Egypt, the ideal image of the "land of bondage" in the Biblical *Genesis*, was thus changed into the symbol of the evil of matter: one finds it used again in this sense in Hymn of the Pearl in the *Acts of Thomas* (see below, pp. 95 and 191). Cf. also Andreas-Henning, *Mitteliranische Manichaïca*, III, p. 18: at his death, Mani is said to "leave Egypt", i.e., matter. The Jordan which flows from north to south becomes, in similar fashion, the mystic symbol of every stream of purifying waters: cf. E. S. Drower, *The Mandaeans*, 1937, p. xxiv; L. Tondelli, "Il Mandeismo e le origini cristiane" *Orientalia*, no. 33, 1928, p. 60. To flow to the right or to reascend towards the source are symbolically equivalent. Cf. here, p. 66 and p. 270.

[121] Cf. p. 44 and p. 52.   [122] Cf. *Genesis* II, 10–14.

These sectaries were against carnal intercourse, which they looked upon as a defilement for the race of the elect—the "race without a king", also called "the mysterious race of the perfect men". They knew of a baptism, the aim of which, they said, was to "bring into imperishable pleasure the man who has been washed in living water and anointed with an ineffable ointment".

Did the sect of the Peratae really differ from that of the Naassenes? It had been founded by Euphrates the Peratic and by Celbes of Carystia,[123] personalities otherwise unknown, unless by an allusion of Origen's to that Euphrates whom he took to be the founder of the Ophite sect. The Peratae were very specially addicted to astrology—that of the Chaldaeans, chiefly—and they had taken over from this a good deal of their system "by changing only the words".

One of their books was most oddly entitled *The Heads of the town up to the aether*. It seems to have been, essentially, a description and enumeration of the powers of the lower heavens, which makes us think also of the Archontici. It may be to this same work that we owe the content of the account in the *Philosophumena*, which purports to quote it upon several points. According to the Peratae, "the universe is composed of the Father, the Son and of Matter. Each of these *three* principles possesses within itself an infinity of powers. Between Matter and the Father resides the Son—Word and Spirit—a median principle always in movement, either towards the immobile Father or towards Matter, which is moved.[124] Sometimes it turns towards the Father and, in its own person, takes on his powers; sometimes, having taken these

[123] Cf. Jonas, vol. I, p. 341. Carystia, the homeland of Celbes, was in the isle of Euboea, which is also called Peran—the country "beyond" the sea—perhaps it was from this name that the sect acquired its name of Peratae? But the sectaries themselves pretended that they owed it to their being the only people whose knowledge enabled them to "pass beyond" (in Greek περᾶ) corruption: cf. Bunsen, *Hippolyt and his Age*, 2nd edn., vol. I, p. 347.

[124] Cf. the other forms of this intermediate element in the cosmogonies of Simon, of Marcion and of the Sethians . . . where it appears as antecedent to all creation, pp. 18, 25, 33, 52. Upon this curious celestial function attributed to the Christ, see my article, "Le refus de la Croix; Gnostiques et Manichéens" in *La Table Ronde*, no. 120, Dec. 1957, pp. 89–97: also Antonio Orbe, *Los Primeros Herejes ante la persecucion*, pp. 160ff.; finally, we may recall the passage of the *Philosophumena*, IV, 48, 7 (edn. Wendland, p. 71, 23–6) which compares the Logos—the Christ—to the celestial image of Ophiuchus mastering the serpent!

powers, it returns towards Matter: and Matter, being without form or quality, receives from the Son the imprint of the forms of which the Son himself has received the imprints from the Father." If we are to believe the summary given in the *Philosophumena*, these sectaries had built up a whole pattern of correspondences between the different powers of the lower heavens, such as those known to the other Gnostic systems and, at the same time, between those of the classic mythology and the celestial powers whose names the Ptolemaic astrology had multiplied. Thus the work of the Peratae quoted in this account enumerates: "Ariel, ruler of the winds, in whose image were made Aeolus and Briareus. The ruler of the twelve hours of the night is Soclan (or Sacla) whom the ignorant call Osiris;[125] in his image were Admetus, Medea, Hellen. . . . The ruler of the twelve hours of the day is Euno; it is he who is in charge of the ascendant of the first vault of heaven; the ignorant have called him Isis; his sign is the constellation of the Dog,[126] and he was the model for Ptolemy son of Arsinoe, Didymus, Cleopatra, Olympias. . . ."

It appears still more likely that the Peratae were no more than a branch of the Ophites, when we read such passages as this which follows: "Anyone", say the Peratae, "whose eyes are so favoured, will see, on looking up into the sky, the beautiful form of the Serpent coiled up at the grand beginning of the heavens and becoming, for all born beings, the principle of all movement."[127] Then he will understand that no being, either in heaven or on earth, was formed without the Serpent. . . ."

[125] The name of Sacla represents, perhaps, a deformation of that of *Sokar*, also called Sokaris, god of the necropolis of Memphis, who in Egyptian belief was assimilated sometimes to Ptah, and sometimes, in effect, to Osiris: the sounds *l* and *r* are confused together in Egyptian. Osiris, for his part, was identified with the constellation of Orion. Concerning the diverse names of Sacla, who becomes one of the forms of the evil Demiurge Ialdabaôth, see below, chap. v, note 30.

[126] The Egyptian religion related Venus, by the name of Sothis, to Isis.

[127] The constellation of the Dragon, next to the Great Bear, was in antiquity more or less identified with the axis of the world, from the fact that, four thousand years ago, its star *alpha* represented the North Pole. The effect of the combination of the movements of precession and nutation upon the axis of the earth have, since that epoch, shifted the celestial pole towards the star *alpha* of the Little Bear—our present Pole Star. Cf. here, chap. II, note 12.

Of a still more important interest is the *Philosophumena's* account of the Sethians.[128] Their essential doctrine, we are told, was contained in a book entitled the *Paraphrase of Seth*. According to this sect—which, like the one last mentioned, mixed some Hellenic myths with its doctrines—the universe had been made by the action of *three* distinct principles, each of which possessed, from the beginning, an infinite potency. These were the Light, the Darkness, and the pure Breath (the Spirit) dwelling between these two. But the Light and the Spirit have been attracted by the formidable waters of the Darkness, whence they have taken on the nature of that element. The consequence of this first encounter between the three principles was the formation of the heaven and the earth.

The Sethians imagined that the entire heaven and earth was like a pregnant woman's belly, with the navel in the middle. "Let anyone", they said, "examine the belly of any being soever when it is pregnant, and there they will discover the imprint of heaven, of the earth, and of all that is situated immovably in the midst."[129] They also said that the first principle to be engendered was a strong and impetuous wind, born from water, and in itself the cause of all vegetation. Agitating the waters, this wind stirred up waves; and the movement of waves—so they argued—is comparable to the efforts of the full womb to bring forth. The wind which blew so impetuously also resembled, as they thought, the Serpent by its hissing. It was, then, from the Serpent that generation first began. And when the Light and the Spirit from above entered into contact with the dark and disorderly Matter, then the Serpent (the wind issuing from the waters of the abyss) penetrated it and begot man. The Serpent, they said, is indeed the only form that is known and loved by this impure Womb. For that reason, the perfect Word of the Light from on high, when he wished to come down into the material world, took on the frightful form

---

[128] *Philosophumena*, V, 19–22; Jonas, vol. I, p. 342.
[129] The symbol of the womb commonly occurs on the engraved gems which are of a more or less Gnostic character. Cf. Campbell Bonner, *Studies in Magical Amulets*, 1950, chap. III and Plates VI–VII—which, however, too systematically ascribes a medical signification to these figures. C. G. Jung has commented upon this symbol in his *Psychological Types*, London, 1924, p. 289.

of the Serpent in order to enter into this impure Womb under that deceptive appearance. Such was the necessity that obliged the Word of God to come down into the body of a virgin. But, they added, it was not enough that the Perfect Man, the Word, should thus have penetrated the body of a virgin, and relieved the anguish that prevails in the Darkness: after having entered into the shameful mysteries of the womb, he cleansed himself, and drank of the cup of living water that must imperatively be drunk by whosoever wills to divest himself of the servile form and put on a heavenly garment.

The *Philosophumena* explains, in its own way, the doctrine of the Sethians: they had borrowed it from the ancient "theologians", Musaeus, Linus, Orpheus . . . for they speak of the womb as Orpheus did, and moreover, what they say about the phallus, symbol of virility, could have been read before in the Bacchics attributed to Orpheus.[130]

★   ★   ★

If we take account of what Porphyry says of them, the Gnostics whom Plotinus refuted made use, together with the revelations of Zoroaster, Zostrian, Mesos and Nicotheus, of an *Apocalypse of Allogenes*: they were therefore more or less related to the sects which, as we have seen, venerated the books written under the name of the great *Seth* and of his "sons", who are called *Allogenes*, though we have no means of identifying them more exactly. However, Plotinus' criticisms of them in the ninth chapter of his second *Ennead* call for consideration here; they give us glimpses of a system similar to those we have already reviewed. True, it is evident that the great doctor has paid attention only to certain points in the teaching of his adversaries: he may even have purposely disregarded one or another of the fundamental principles of their dualist myths which would have tended to make the doctrine he was refuting look less absurd.

According to these Gnostics, both the soul itself and a certain wisdom had a downward tendency—either the soul from the first

[130] Cf. note 88.

was so inclined, or the wisdom caused that inclination of the soul; or else the soul was identical with the wisdom. The other souls who were partakers in wisdom went down together and clothed themselves with bodies—human bodies, for instance— whilst she, who was the cause of the descent of souls, did not herself go down but only shed light in the darkness. From this illumination an image came to birth in matter. That is how these Gnostics conceived the generation of the lower being whom they called the Demiurge; they said that, once created, he was removed far from his Mother. Then, "in order to heap abuse upon the demiurge who made them" they pictured the world as proceeding from this demiurge, from reflection of reflection to the ultimate degree. Plotinus has no patience with people who can thus picture the celestial regions as soulless whilst they themselves, whose hearts are filled with vice, desire and anger, pretend to be capable of contact with an intelligibility higher than the heavens! He also condemns, as strange, their doctrine that the soul is composed of diverse elements,[131] and their belief in a "new Earth" higher than this world, where these mediocre elect are to go after their deaths. He reproves, finally, their use of incantations addressed to the heavenly powers in order to bewitch or charm them. "Do they think, then, that these beings obey their voice or are carried away by it, if one only has a good enough knowledge of the art of singing according to rules, or of prayer or of breathing or sibilant cries? After all, they have no teaching about virtue, and profess an absurd hatred of our physical nature."

Plotinus also ridicules the artificial and pretentious vocabulary of these sectaries . . . their "exiles", "imprints" and "repentances". . . . All that, he concludes, is from first to last "an invention of people who are not true to the ancient Hellenic culture, though they may have taken certain details from Plato".[132]

*   *   *

[131] Cf. the theory of Basilides and his son Isidore, p. 23.

[132] H. C. Puech ("Les nouveaux écrits gnostiques . . ." in *Coptic Studies in Honour of W. E. Crum*, 1950, p. 131) has summed up the data of the problem posed by this passage and the conclusions of the authors who have tried to resolve it: the content of Plotinus' criticism makes one think, at first sight, of the Valenti-

We cannot complete this picture of the sects without quoting one very late testimony—that of the *Book of Scholia* which Theodore Bar-Konaï wrote in Syriac at the end of the eighth century. The heresies he describes must have been, by that time, almost extinct or very degenerate. Nevertheless this work is distinguished by its vivid and precise accounts of several Gnostics, and of the curious character of certain heresies which it has helped to save from oblivion.

We can reassure ourselves as to the value of Theodore Bar-Konaï's information by comparing the testimony he offers about the sect of the Audians with the much poorer information upon the same subject collected by Epiphanius himself. Epiphanius did not show us these Audians as virulent heretics, but only as a schismatic church whose founder Audius was a Syrian of Mesopotamia.[133] He separated from the Church after the Council of Nicaea, rejecting its decrees about the celebration of Easter— and this, when he had already gained a great reputation by his asceticism. Some anchorites rallied round him: he founded monasteries and fought against the loose conduct of the clergy . . . his propagation of a schismatic belief cost him an exile among the Scythians; but there he made converts enough to set up a new Church with an episcopate and monasteries of its own. Of his disciples, the best known were the Mesopotamian Uranius and the Goth Silvanus. Persecuted by a pagan king, the Audians soon had to return to the Levant, where their monasteries reappeared in the Taurus, in Palestine and in Arabia. Many of the members of this movement then came back into the orthodox Church, so that when Epiphanius wrote (376–7), there were only

nians; but what Porphyry writes in his biography of the philosopher suggests the Archontici or the Sethians. To this last hypothesis one may relate that of some critics who have supposed that the Gnostics in question may have been connected with both the Naassenes and the Hermetists. The contents of the newly-discovered writings will show to what extent these suppositions approach the truth. Cf. C. Schmidt, "Plotinus Stellung zum Gnostizismus" in *Texte und Untersuchungen* II, 4a, 1901; R. Reitzenstein, *Poimandrès*, pp. 102–16 and 306–8; W. Bousset, *Hauptprobleme der Gnosis*, pp. 186–94.

[133] The sect of the Audians has attracted attention ever since the beginning of the eighteenth century: see J. G. Krafft, *De Haeresi Audianorum*, Dissert. Marburg, 1716. For the state of the question, see H. C. Puech's article "Audianer" in *Reallexikon für Antike und Christentum*, vol. I, pp. 910–15.

3*

little groups of the schismatics in the region of Damascus, around Antioch and in Mesopotamia.

But this, which Epiphanius took to be a merely schismatic Church, was, to the eyes of other critics, an undeniably Gnostic sect. Since before the year 373, St Ephraim had pointed to it as such; and it was clearly under this heretical aspect that the teaching of the Audians was gaining ground in the region of Edessa during the fifth century and still later. . . . The principal witness for the beliefs that they professed is precisely that of Theodore Bar-Konaï. He tells us that Audius admitted, in addition to the books of the Old and New Testaments, some apocryphal works: that he pretended that the light and the darkness were not created by God; and taught that God was composed of members and had, in all, the appearance of a man. This he deduced from the text, "Let us make man in our image, after our likeness". To expose a few of the impious opinions of Audius: "He writes, in his *Apocalypse* which bears the name of *Abraham*, ascribing the words to one of the creators: 'The world and the creation were made, by the darkness, from six other powers'. He also says: 'They saw by how many gods the soul is purified, and by how many gods the body is created'. He says, again, 'They asked, who compelled the angels and the powers to create the body?' In the *Apocalypse* which bears the name of *John*, it is said that 'These Powers[134] that I have seen, it is from them that my body has come'. He recounts the names of these five creators in the following sentence: 'My Wisdom has made the hair; the Intelligence has made the skin; Elohim has made the bones; my Royalty has made the blood; Adonaï has made the nerves; Zeal has made the flesh, and Thought has made the marrow.' He borrowed all that from the Chaldaeans. In the *Book of Strangers* he makes God speak as follows: 'God said to Eve, Conceive by me, so that the creators of Adam come not nigh thee'. He makes the aeons speak thus, in the *Book of Requests*: 'Come, let us cover Eve, so that what is born (of her) may belong to us'. And again—'The aeons took care of Eve, and covered her

---

[134] More exactly, "These aeons" . . . the term being used to denote the inferior powers; cf. above, note 41.

so that she should not come near Adam'. In the *Apocalypse of the Strangers* he makes the aeons say: 'Come, let us cast our seed into her and look after her (?) in the first place, so that what is born of her may be in our power'. He says, again, 'They led Eve away from the face of Adam and knew her'. Such were the impurities and the impieties that the perverse Audius imagined against God, against the angels and against the world."

We recognize here the myths of the creation of Adam by the Archons, and then of the defilement of Eve by the creator and his powers; these were not invented by Audius, but taken over by him from the principal Gnostic sects; among whom these doctrines were already known from the *Apocalypse of Abraham*, and from the *Books of the Strangers*, or *Allogeneous* books,[135] mentioned above. The *Book of Requests* alone may perhaps have been invented by Audius. . . .[136]

Theodore Bar-Konaï writes against some other more or less fantastic sects such as, for example, the Lampetians.[137] Also against John of Apamea,[138] a sectary who is named again by Bar-Hebraeus (1226–86), who states that he lived in the sixth century. According to Bar-Konaï this personage had been to Alexandria to get instruction from the magicians there, in some of the more or less occult sciences. On returning home to the monastery of St Simon he divulged, discreetly, the Gnostic teachings he had received. He believed in an unbegotten father who had produced seven sons, from whom many more were born. These seven primordial powers had composed, all together, the "Glorification of Melchizedek, the Chief of Priests". Abraham was to have been one of these seven powers but, having neglected to offer praises to the Father—the appropriate "glorifications"—he had fallen into improper "suspicions", from which arose all the hostile powers called devils and demons. Melchizedek had then prayed to the Father of Greatness to send

[135] Cf. H. C. Puech, "Fragments retrouvés de l'apocalypse d'Allogène" in *Mélanges Franz Cumont*, 1936, pp. 935ff.
[136] Unless it be identical with the *Interrogations of Mary*, in use, according to Epiphanius (*Panarion*, XXXIX, v, 1), among the leading Gnostics: cf. H. C. Puech, "Les Nouveaux écrits," p. 130, note 1.
[137] Translated in Pognon, *loc. cit.*, p. 206.
[138] Translated in Pognon, *loc. cit.*, p. 207.

his grace to Abraham, and to lead his thoughts back towards the good. Abraham, having then repented, reascended into the heavenly place whence he had come down.

John of Apamea also composed a book called *The Foundations*, and he had several disciples, named John, Zachaeus, Zura and Habib. The Gnosticism of John of Apamea diverged from the main lines of the most classic systems, in assigning to Melchizedek and to Abraham the parts usually played by the Mother and Sophia.

Stranger still was the sect of the Kukeans;[139] St Ephraim had heard of them; so they were already in existence in the middle of the fourth century. Bar-Konaï sums up their teaching as follows: "They say that God was born from the sea situated in the World of Light, which they call the Awakened Sea; and this Sea of Light and the world are more ancient than God. [They also say] that when God was born of the awakened Sea, he seated himself above the waters, looked into them, and saw his own image. He held out his hand, took [this image] to be his companion, had relations with it and thus engendered a multitude of gods and goddesses. They called this the Mother of Life, and said that she had made seventy worlds and twelve aeons. They added that, at a certain distance from the god who was born of the Awakened Sea, there was a sort of dead image like a statue without movement, without life, without thought or intelligence. The god, who found this hateful, evil and ugly . . ., thought to take it up and cast it far from his presence. But then he said, 'since it has neither the life, the intelligence nor the thought to make war against me, and seeing that I have no fault to find with it, it would be unjust of me to cast it out: I will therefore give it some of my own strength, of my own mobility and intelligence, and then it will declare war upon me'. They pretend that God issued an order to his worlds, which boiled over with heat, made a portion of their life overflow, and poured it into this ugly statue; and that the latter applied all its soul and all its intelligence to making war upon the beings on the side of the good, who withstood it in forty-two battles, and the oftener they fought the more the

---

[139] Translated in Pognon, *loc. cit.*, pp. 290ff.

carnal forces—that is, the animals, beasts and reptiles of the earth—multiplied."

"One day", they said, "the Mother of Life came down to it, accompanied by seven virgins. When she came near [this statue], the latter stood up and breathed upon the Mother of Life; its breath penetrated even to the sexual organs of the Mother and defiled her; she could not go into the dwelling of the gods her companions, and remained for seven days in a state of impurity. She then threw the seven virgins who were with her into the mouth of this great 'Gurha', which sucked them in during the seven days of the defilement of the Mother of Life, for she threw him one each day; so that the gods were obliged to come to the rescue of the seven virgins whom the Mother of Life had thrown into the mouth of this great 'Gurha'.

"They say that the beings on the side of evil join, from time to time, in a festivity; they bring forth these virgins, give them to their sons, and adorn themselves with the light proceeding from these [virgins]; while the beings on the side of the good— the betrothed of these [virgins]—come down on the festive day and each of them takes away his own betrothed. They affirm also that the coming of our Saviour into this world had no other motive but the rescue of his affianced lover here below: he took her up; he ascended from the Jordan, and he made the daughter of the Mother of Life. . . . [?] . . . of Egypt. They assert that the other virgins are, the one at Hetra, another at Mabbog, another at Harra; that their betrothed look on, and, when the moment comes, take them away."

Bar-Konaï mentions yet other and more astonishing sects— for instance that of the Kantaeans who claim that their doctrine is derived from Abel.[140] In the Sassanid Empire, this sect had persisted up to the time of the king Yezdegerd II (442-57). An old slave named Battaï introduced additional abominations into it during the reign of Peroz (459-84). This Battaï, who had formerly lived among certain Manichaeans, had pretended to submit to a

---

[140] Trans. in Pognon, loc. cit., pp. 220ff.; a sect half-way between the Mandaeans and the Manichaeans. Cf. Reitzenstein, Das mandäische Buch des Herrn der Grösse . . . , Heidelberg, 1919, pp. 28ff.

decree of king Peroz proscribing all religions other than that of the Magi. But he then propagated a somewhat composite doctrine, of which here are some extracts from Bar-Konaï: "Before the beginning of all things, there had been a divinity who divided himself into two, and from whom the Good and the Evil came to be. The Good gathered-together the lights, and the Evil the darkness. Then, the Evil gained understanding, and arose to make war upon the Father of Greatness. The Father of Greatness pronounced a word, from which the Lord God was created. The Lord God in his turn uttered seven words from which were born seven powers. But seven demons set themselves up against the Lord God and against the Powers he had engendered: after having shackled these adversaries, they stole from the Father of Greatness the principle of the soul. The demons then began to cleanse and scour Adam, the first man. But the Lord God came, and destroyed Adam and remade him.

The cosmogony of Battaï assigns the rôle of Saviour to the Son of the Light, to whom are attributed, for instance, the following words: "I advanced, and made my way towards the souls. When they saw me, they joined together . . . and greeted me with a thousand greetings. They sighed and said to me, 'Son of the Light, go and say to our Father, When will the captives be freed, and when will rest be granted to tortured and suffering beings? When will rest be granted to the souls who suffer the persecution of the world?' I replied to them, 'When the Euphrates will be dried up from its estuary, and when the Tigris will flow outside its bed; when all the rivers will be dry and the torrents will overflow, then will rest be granted to souls.'"

Another feature of their teaching reflects one of the most classic Gnostic doctrines; they believed that "the Cross is the secret of the Limit, between the Father of Greatness and the lower Earth".[141]

This glimpse of the history of the Kantaeans and of the prophet Battaï is confirmed by some details reported during the twelfth century in the *Chronicle* of Michael the Syrian. There it is said that this Battaï, after his conversion to Manichaeism, took the

[141] Cf. Horos-Stauros of the Valentinians, above p. 28.

name of Yazdani or Yazwani; and the sacred writings of the Mandaeans (for instance, the *Ginzâ of the first* or *"right" part,* Book IX, 1) make some definite allusions to the sect of the Yazuqeans, derived from both Judaism and Christianity, a sect which worshipped fire, whose members used the name of Jesus, and who carried their *barsum*—the Persians' sacramental bundle of branches—on the left shoulder, "in the manner of a cross".

★   ★   ★

From all the texts written about Gnosticism by its enemies I have made no more than a selection, moreover a rather cursory one. A more thorough exploration of the references would, no doubt, show that in touching upon some of the sects named, I had already, without being aware of it, overstepped the boundaries of authentic Gnosticism and strayed into the obscure regions of Manichaeism and, still more, of that Mandaeanism whose earliest adepts (if we can trust, for example, Theodore Bar-Konaï) gave themselves the name of Dosthaeans—that is, of Dositheans.[142]

From the historical point of view, the details we have gleaned about the first founders, the great doctors, and about the sects appear, for the most part, uncertain if not mythical. The sects knew how to hide from their enemies a great deal of their mysteries. We have glimpses, here and there, of ideas and myths, we have the titles, and even summaries, of "secret" writings of which one longs to know whether they really existed, were imagined, or misreported by certain enemies of the Gnostics. We wish we had proofs as convincing as many of the accounts seem to be contradictory; for the same sects, the same teachers may appear in a considerably different light according to whether we see them through the eyes of Irenaeus, of Epiphanius, of the anonymous author of the *Philosophumena* or of Theodore Bar-Konaï. True, the principal myths have a number of well-marked features in common; outstanding among these are the primordial figure of the invisible Father, of his Thought which becomes the

---

[142] These "Dositheans" do not, upon present information, appear to have been related to the Gnostic Dositheus; cf. R. McL. Wilson, "Simon, Dositheus . . . ," p. 27, note 39.

Mother and, in various guises, falls into the Matter from which she has afterwards to be rescued. We also find the creation of this base world described as the sensual, sinister work of the lower, wicked powers, to whose activity is ascribed the whole Creation recorded in *Genesis*, systematically twisted to the opposite of its customary meaning. But how are we to explain the extreme licentiousness of certain sects and the no less strict asceticism of other groups, who nevertheless make as much use as do the others —so we are told—of the same myths, contained in the same secret books? Are we to suspect that the worst abominations laid to the charge of certain heretics were merely imagined by malevolent critics? And how are we to define the position of our sectaries in relation to Christianity, from which they borrow much of their figure of the Saviour and several other features? And further— was Gnosticism really such a shapeless conglomeration of different religions, disparate philosophies, of astrology and magic as is here been painted for us, perhaps in forced colours? We may quite possibly be dealing with hasty interpretations built up by commentators who knew all too little about this religion; so that what they took to be its foundational tenets were really but the glosses or commentaries of over-literary members of the sects. To show how far the learned writers of those days might go, in ascribing just such a complicated physiognomy to mystics whom they set out to criticize, we can point to an example which has nothing to do with the Gnostics; namely, the indictment that Celsus drew up against Christianity itself. In this he asserts that the teaching of the Gospel derives, in part, from Plato, from Heraclitus, from the Stoics, the Jews, from the Egyptians and Persian myths and the Cabiri! The tone of such an attack recalls, as does even its style, the closely analogous criticisms directed against the Gnostics by the Christian heresiologists.[143] And what historian of today would entertain, in respect of Christianity, any hypotheses so excessive as those of Celsus? Must we not therefore suspect that the author of the *Philosophumena*, and the other adversaries of Gnosticism, who accused it of mixing its myths with Greek philosophy and the Mysteries, may often

[143] Cf. P. de Labriolle, *La Réaction païenne* . . . , 1934, pp. 118 and *passim*.

have done so by mere rhetorical artifice and with hardly any real justification?

However abundant, therefore, might be the information about Gnosticism that its enemies had collected, it could only be taken into consideration—this must be admitted—in so far as we could compare it with original, indubitable documents from which it could be verified. And it is just this which, until the last few years, has presented the most insoluble problem to the historian of Gnosticism. For of documents handed down directly and authentically from the Gnostics, we possessed almost none; and such fragments as there were had to be treated with so much reserve that they could hardly answer the great questions we wanted to put to them.

CHAPTER II

ORIGINAL TEXTS AND MONUMENTS

WITH regard to original documents, it is as though Fate had been trying to poke fun at the learned, for had she not bequeathed them, of all possible texts, the most complicated and surely the most incoherent that Gnosticism ever produced? Placed side by side with such documentation as the heresiologists have made known to us, the latter is made to look almost . . . eulogistic, almost benevolent towards the sects which the Fathers took so kindly and seriously as to do them the honour of refutation.

These relics of Gnostic literature consist, essentially, of three manuscripts obtained from Egypt, all three written in the Coptic language.[1] But it must not be inferred from this that Egypt played a greater part in the history of Gnosticism than other countries. These are writings very probably translated from the Greek; and if only these translations escaped destruction it is because the sands and ruins of the Nile valley offer conditions more favourable to the preservation of ancient manuscripts, as of all other remains, than those enjoyed by any other country.

The most widely known of these manuscripts is generally called by the name of *Pistis-Sophia*, though the title is appropriate to only a part of the contents. It is a book written on parchment, dating apparently from the fourth century, which was presumably brought to Europe in the second half of the eighteenth century. It first belonged to the library of a Dr Askew—whence

---

[1] *Coptic* is a vernacular form of the Egyptian language, no longer written in hieroglyphs but by means of the Greek alphabet, supplemented by certain signs meant to represent certain special sounds. After a few preliminary gropings, the most ancient Coptic texts appeared in the first centuries of our era. Making use of this writing, to which various Egyptian dialects were being adapted, the Christians of the Nile Valley produced an abundant literature. It was not until the tenth century that the Coptic language began to disappear, giving way to Arabic in common usage. It is still in use, however, in the liturgy of the Egyptian Church.

it is catalogued as the *Codex Askewianus*—and then was acquired by the British Museum in 1785. This parchment manuscript originally consisted, according to the pagination, of 356 pages of two columns each, of which only a few leaves have been lost. Of the five texts it contains, written in a Thebam dialect of Coptic—in Sahïdic—a first translation was published in 1851.[2]

One would hardly be able to understand anything at all in a summary account of these documents, unless we began by retracing, in broad outline, the fantastic universe which served as a setting for their speculations.

At the summit of this universe is an ineffable and infinite god, who is at once a light enclosed within himself and a power from which all things have emanated. This god develops thus into innumerable entities, until the whole is something like a gigantic primordial man of whom the powers of the higher world are the members. Was it like this, perhaps (as H. Leisegang suggests), that the Ophites imagined the Anthropos they placed at the head of their system?[3] Out of this ineffable god came forth the First Mystery, an entity which plays somewhat the same part as the Word does in other Gnostic mythologies. This First Mystery is surrounded by a crowd of beings—Apatôres or "fatherless"; super-triple-spirits; pro-triple-spirits, etc. . . . and beneath it are established twenty-four other mysteries. Further below is the Treasury of Light, with twelve saviours and nine guardians at its three portals. . . . It is this Treasury of Light which is finally attained by those human souls who have received the mysteries of Gnosticism. The higher world is separated from the lower heavens

---

[2] M. G. Schwartze, *Pistis Sophis: Opus gnosticum Valentino adiudicatum . . . latine vertit M. G. Schwartze. Edidit J. H. Petermann*, Berlin 1851-3. The edition of the Coptic text now in use is C. Schmidt, *Pistis-Sophia*, Hauniae, 1925. Eng. translation: G. Horner, *Pistis-Sophia*, 1924; German: C. Schmidt, *Pistis-Sophia*, 1925, this last has been revised and published by W. Till, *Koptische-Gnostische Schriften*, 1st Volume: *Die Pistis-Sophia, Die Beiden Bücher des Jeû, Unbekanntes Altgnostisches Werk, herausg. von C. Schmidt*, 2nd edn., 1954. Concerning the name *Pistis-Sophia*, which for long remained a mystery (in 1847 Dulaurier translated it *Fidèle Sagesse*=Faithful Wisdom), we know from certain passages in more recently-discovered texts (see the *Sophia of Jesus*, in the Gnostic Codex of Berlin) that it refers to a Sophia "whom some also called Pistis".

[3] Leisegang, *loc. cit.*, pp. 243ff.

by veils; and in some of these veils there is a "left-hand door" which will open when the Three Times[4] have been completed, and when Sophia and the lower beings will have been liberated from Matter. The Place of the Just is appointed at a certain distance from the Treasury; it is the residence of Jêou; of the Guardian of the Great Light; the two Great Governors; Melchizedek and the Sabaôth called the Good. The function of these powers is to collect together all the portions of Light that have been lost throughout the aeons and in the cosmos and to bring them up again into the Treasury. More specifically, Sabaôth guards the "Portal of Life" which opens upon a lower zone—the intermediate region. Over this intermediate place reigns Iaô the great, who is good, assisted by Little Iaô the good and the Little Sabaôth the Good with his angels. There, also, is the great Virgin of Light who judges the souls, decides whether they shall go up to the Light or to damnation, and distributes the seals, the mysteries and the baptisms that are indispensable for a journey into the higher realms.

Beneath this Intermediary is the Place of the Left; where one finds, first, the Thirteenth Aeon, ruled over by the Great Invisible or Propatôr, with Barbelô and the Triple-Powers. With his wings, the Propatôr covers the *kerasmos* beneath— the world which is a mixture of light and of matter. The highest degree of this mixed world is constituted by the Twelve Aeons. The sphere of the Heimarmene (of Fatality) separates the Twelve aeons from the visible heavens and the terrestrial world.

Leisegang, who has catalogued very exactly the different parts of this universe,[5] points out that a distinction is introduced here, between the Right and the Left, the heavenly spheres being constrained, in certain cases, to turn in the one direction or the other. He recalls that, according to the Ophites—as described in the *Philosophumena*—"when the Ocean goes down [i.e., flows towards the Left], that is the birth of men; when it rises [flows to

[4] H. C. Puech, *Le Manichéisme, son fondateur, sa doctrine*, 1949, note 284; cf. pp. 113–14.
[5] Leisegang, *loc. cit.*, p. 245.

the right], towards the rampart and fortress of the Leucadian rock, then is the birth of the gods". Analogously, in the *Pistis-Sophia*, the soul that is making its way towards the right is mounting upward and escaping the destiny prefigured for it in the celestial sphere of Fatality. . . .

The *Codex Askewianus* consists, first, of the two *Books of Pistis-Sophia*. The somewhat theatrical preamble to the former of these writings leads us straight into the realm of pure fiction with an account of how Jesus, returning to earth during the first eleven years after his Resurrection (!) had as yet taught his disciples only a portion of the mysteries. It remains for him to instruct them in the highest of all: the Treasury of the Light. The scene is enacted on the Mount of Olives, the disciples seated in a group, Jesus keeping himself a little apart from them. Suddenly a light descends from above, envelops him and carries him away to a fantastic heaven.[6] Later on, Jesus comes down again, enrobed now in three different lights. Of these luminous vestments that he has received in the higher heavens, one is shining with the glory of all the higher mysteries—those of the First Commandment, of the Five Seals . . . , and those of the Treasury of the Light, with all its Saviours, the Seven Amens, the Seven Voices, the Five Trees, the Three Amens, the Twin Saviour also called the Child of the Child, the mystery of the Nine Guardians of the Three gates of the Treasury, etc. . . .

Jesus then tells his disciples how, reapparelled in this resplendent vesture, he has just overthrown the evil powers of the celestial spheres—more especially those of the Sphere of Fatality—thus preluding the salvation of the Perfect and consummation of the lower universe. Up to this time, indeed, the powers of the twelve aeons, the powers of Adamas the Tyrant, the planets and the zodiacal signs, had dominated the created world! And Adamas and his followers have done their best, even since this visitation by the Light, to wage disorderly war against it. But Jesus then stripped them of a third part of their power; he abolished the

[6] See the accounts of the Transfiguration in *Math.* XVII, 2; *Mark* IX, 2; *Luke* IX, 29; "And his face shone like the sun and his garments became white as light . . . ."

course of Fate;[7] he changed the regular movement of the spheres into an alternating movement, so that the planets could no longer exert their malign influence upon men, and that even the conjurations of the astrologers—hitherto regarded as all-powerful—became meaningless.[8] Upon these points, Mary and Philip question the Saviour; and Jesus explains to them the effects of the changes thus brought about. Then Mary gives praise for this defeat of astrology, which, until then, had left mankind exposed to malign Fatality. Recalling an oracle of the prophet Isaiah (*Isaiah* XIX, 3-12) she cries, "Egypt, where are now thy interpreters and thy casters of horoscopes, and those who are diviners by the earth and by the entrails? Let them tell thee, henceforth, the works that the Lord Sabaôth will accomplish! So prophesied, even before thou camest, the power that was in Isaiah the prophet! It prophesied of thee, that thou would'st take away their power

---

[7] Cf. Puech, *La Gnose et le Temps*, pp. 84-5 and note 28; Jonas, *loc. cit.*, vol. I, pp. 193-4. Cf. also Tertullian, *De idol.*, 9.

[8] What is the phenomenon alluded to in this episode of the upsetting of the rotation of the spheres? To understand it, one must look back to, for instance, the seventh letter of the pseudo-Dionysius the Areopagite, speculating upon *Joshua* X, 12 and 13, "And the sun stood still, and the moon stayed", upon II *Kings* XX, 9-11; and *Isaiah* XXXVIII, 8; "So the sun turned back on the dial the ten steps by which it had declined"; and upon the eclipse which occurred at the time of the Crucifixion, recorded in *Matt.* XXVII, 45; *Mark* XV, 33 and *Luke* XXIII, 44. Here is what the pseudo-Dionysius writes about each of these episodes respectively:—"Is it not thanks to (the Divine Power) that the sun and the moon . . . stood quite still, as did the entire heavens, and that all the heavenly bodies stood motionless a whole day in the same signs of the zodiac, unless—a still more marvellous prodigy—the higher spheres which surround the others continued to complete their entire revolution, although the lower spheres did not follow them in their circular motion?" "Another miracle: this day, which was prolonged to almost three times its normal length, so that, for twenty hours, either the whole heaven was stopped in its course by an impulse in the opposite direction, and reversed its motion by the most prodigious of retrogressions; or else it is the sun which, in its own path, reduced its time of revolution to ten hours by five stages, and then, reversing its motion for another space of ten hours, went over the whole path again backwards". "We saw this strange phenomenon; the moon occulting the sun when the time had not arrived for their conjunction; then, from the ninth hour until the evening, this same moon keeping itself miraculously in opposition with the sun. Remind him again of this other circumstance; we also saw the moon beginning its occultation of the sun, and then going back in its path, so that the occultation and the return of the light did not occur on the same side, but on the two opposite margins of the solar disc. Such were the wonders that took place at that juncture, and that the Christ alone could have produced." (Migne, *Patrologia Graeca*, vol. III, 1080-1; Maurice de Gandillac, *Oeuvres complètes du pseudo-Denys l'Aréopagite*, 1943, pp. 333-4.

from the Archons of the aeons, that thou wouldst overturn their sphere and their fatality; that they should no longer know anything. It is also concerning this, that (that power) has said, 'You shall no longer know that which the Lord Sabaôth will do'— that is to say, that no one among the Archons shall any more know what thou art about to do—which Archons here are Egypt, for it is they who are matter. . . . ''[9]

The salvaging of the portions of light dispersed throughout the cosmos is then discussed. It is Jêou, the "receivers" of the Moon and of the Sun, and Melchizedek . . . , who have to gather up the strength of the celestial powers—that is, the breath of their mouths, their tears and sweat. Out of the light that they extract from these they will either make souls of men and of animals or, on the other hand, will place it finally in the Treasury of the Light after having completely purified it.[10]

But Jesus, in his journey through the regions on high, came to the Thirteenth aeon (which corresponds to the Ogdoad in most of the Gnostic systems). Here he found Pistis-Sophia, sorrowing because she had not been reinstated in the Pleroma from which she had fallen, and grieving over the attacks to which she was still subjected by her greatest enemy, the *Authades*—the "self-willed" or the "ambitious". To a question that Mary now puts to him, Jesus answers by relating what happened at the fall of Sophia. Formerly this "Wisdom" had been numbered among the emanations of the Invisible in the higher regions. She had had a glimpse, above her, of the Veil of the Treasury of the Light, and was filled with longing to attain to it. But the Twelve aeons below were seized with hatred of her, and one of these wicked ones—the Authades—now produced a power with the face of a lion, Ialdabaôth, and peopled Chaos with a number of other emanations of matter. Then he made to glow, in the abyss, on purpose to allure Sophia, an apparition of light towards which she let herself be attracted. Immediately her own light-power was

[9] Cf. chap. I, note 120 and chap. VI, note 35.
[10] This same myth survived in Manichaeism: cf. Cumont, *Recherches sur le Manichéisme*, I, p. 55, Puech, *Manichéisme*, p. 80; the theme of the ascent of souls by way of the moon and the sun is of common occurrence: cf. Plutarch, *De facie in orbe lunae*, 28–30 (edn. Raingeard, 1935, pp. 43–8). Cf. below, note 24.

taken from her by Ialdabaôth, whilst the other powers of matter took possession of her.

Jesus then recites to the disciples the twelve prayers in which Sophia, from the depths of the abyss, offered up her repentance towards the Light on high. One after another, each of these prayers is commented upon by one of his listeners, who reply to Jesus, "Thou hast already announced these things by the mouth of the Prophet David", and quote to him, each in turn, one or another of the *Psalms* of the Old Testament appropriate to the sentiments expressed in each prayer of Sophia. But Jesus tells them, at the same time, how the repentance of Pistis-Sophia had been received on high; how he himself came down to take away from the lion-faced power that light which it had stolen, and to bring Sophia out of Chaos. Then he recites some more of the hymns of Sophia, which are again explained by the disciples, this time by comparing them with five of the apocryphal *Odes of Solomon.*[11]

It is at the end of this book that we find the insertion of a curious apocryphal episode in the life of Jesus, narrated by Mary, of which this is the translation:

"When thou wert quite little, before the spirit had come upon thee, whilst thou wert in the vineyard with Joseph, the Spirit came out of the height and came to me in my house, like unto thee; so that I did not know him, but I thought at first it was thou. And the Spirit said unto me: 'Where is Jesus, my brother, that I may go and meet him?' And when he had said this unto me, I was at a loss, and thought it was a phantom come to try me. So I seized him and bound him to the foot of the bed in my house, whilst I went forth to you, to thee and Joseph in the field; and I found you in the vineyard, to which Joseph was making a fence. It came to pass therefore when thou didst hear me speak unto Joseph, that thou didst understand what I said; thou wert joyful, and saidst: 'Where is he? I will go to see him rather than wait for

[11] The *Odes of Solomon* were known also to Lactantius, who quotes them in his *Inst.* 4, 12, 3; forty-one others, making a total of forty-two, have been recovered in Syriac and published by J. R. Harris in 1909. They date from the second century. There is still some dispute about the more or less Gnostic character of these hymns, which are inspired partly by the teaching of St John.

him here.' And when Joseph had heard thee say this he was startled. We went down together, we entered the house and found the Spirit bound to the bed. And we saw, looking on thee and on him, that he was like unto thee. But then he who was bound to the bed was unloosed; he took thee in his arms and kissed thee, and thou also didst kiss him; and ye became as one."

The *Second Book of Pistis-Sophia* (it is expressly so entitled, and begins at page 114 of the manuscript) recounts the rest of the struggle between the Authades and the powers (Michael and Gabriel above all) who bring Sophia out of Chaos, to reinstate her at the lower limit of the Thirteenth aeon. However, the story of Pistis-Sophia is completed—at page 169—and the Saviour then passes on to discuss such different subjects that we wonder whether we are not now in another text, distinct from the preceding one.

Replying to a question from Mary Magdalene, Jesus describes the celestial world, explaining how the light that has been dispersed among the things of the lower world is collected again and purified. Then he reveals, to his own, the Mystery of the Ineffable—the mystery whose words are of an extraordinary power, and thanks to which each of the Perfect ones will be absorbed, in the end, into the person of Jesus himself; "He is I, and I am he." Jesus also mentions some less exalted mysteries which are set forth, he says, in the two great *Books of Jêou*.

It is, perhaps, in this exposition that we are enabled to grasp, most completely, the mythical structure that our Gnostics ascribe to the higher world. Above our terrestrial world are ranged the heavenly spheres, one enveloping another, higher and higher and of vaster extent. Here, in succession, are: the Place of the Rulers of Destiny (the planets); then the twelve aeons (the Zodiac?); then the Place of the Midst—in which are the holy baptisms and the seals; then the Places of the Right; then the World of Light or the Treasury of the Light with its twelve Saviours, with the emanations of the seven Voices and of the five Trees and the Amens. Still higher, there is the Place of those who have received the inheritance and the mysteries. . . . A fantastic cosmology, upon which a whole apocalyptic teaching is developed, on the supposition that the return of the universe to its perfection will be signalized by the reascent of the Perfect ones throughout these stages, up to the highest degrees of all!

This treatise also outlines, in the form of questions left un-answered, the scheme of an extraordinary encyclopaedia, as much scientific and metaphysical as it is theological—Why do animals exist, or birds, or mountains, or precious stones, gold or silver? How were the seas created? Why should there be times of famine and of abundance? To what end were hatred and love created, etc. . . . .

At the end of this exposition (on page 233 of the manuscript) we find that the title is no longer the *Book of Pistis-Sophia* nor the *Second Book of Pistis-Sophia*, but is given as: *A part of the Books of the Saviour*. This confirms our impression that, on page 169 of the manuscript where the story of Pistis-Sophia ended, we had come to the commencement of a different work.

What follows, moreover, carries on a treatise which is mani-festly a continuation of the one just concluded, before the appearance of the formula, *A part of the Books of the Saviour*. In this text, the disciples question the Saviour about various problems touching the salvation of those souls which, whether they have or have not received the Mysteries—namely, the several baptisms and sacraments instituted by the sect—commit more or less serious sins. One great interest of this text, is that it shows us the human soul as made up of three parts—of spirit, of matter and, also, of a "counterfeiting spirit", which reminds one of the doctrines attributed to Basilides and his son Isidore. The counter-feiting spirit is that which the Archons of Fatality put into man, at his creation, to make him sin. Once it is established in the child, it nourishes itself and grows in strength by the carnal nourishment that it absorbs. It contradicts the motions of the spirit derived from on high, which lives in the same body. A passage in the Coptic text even compares its presence in the soul to that of the copper which, mixed with silver, was present as an alloy in the piece of money that served to illustrate the saying: "Render unto Caesar the things that are Caesar's and unto God the things that are God's." (*Matthew* XXII, 15-22). After death, this counterfeiting spirit bears witness against the soul of all the sins which he has made it commit.

The same treatise shows how the souls are then tried, by order of Jêou, before the Virgin of Light who is their judge. This Virgin of Light seals the perfect souls, and sends them to receive the anointings and baptisms without which none can ascend towards the powers of the Treasury. She sends the others back into the rotations of the celestial sphere, and even down into the infernal abodes peopled with fantastic demons, the long procession of which forms the body of the dragon of the outer "Darkness".[12] "In order to escape these punishments," says Jesus, "it is necessary for men to gain knowledge of the mysteries which are in the *Books of Jêou*, those that I caused to be written by Enoch in Paradise, when I spoke to him from the Tree of Knowledge and the Tree of Life. And I caused him to place them upon the rock of Ararat; and I set Kalapataurôth—the archon who is above Gemmut, him who is under the feet of Jêou and who makes all aeons and all destinies to revolve—that same archon I set to watch over the *Books of Jêou*, to [protect them] from the flood and [also] that no archon, seized with jealousy about them, might destroy them."

It should be noted, with regard to the two *Books of Pistis-Sophia* which constitute the first part of this compilation, that Harnack wanted, without very strong proofs but because of its dialogue form, to have it recognized as the lost book of the *Little Interrogations of Mary* which (according to Epiphanius, XXVI) was in use among the great Gnostics.

After these various texts comes an untitled portion (pp. 318

---

[12] Cf. the myth of the great Gnostics, described by Epiphanius (see above, chap. I, p. 43); the Leviathan of the *Diagram* of the Ophites: Leisegang, *loc. cit.*, Plate VII; Boll, article "Finsternisse" in *Realenzyklopädie* of Pauly-Wissowa; *Catal. Codic. Astrol. Graec.*, vol. VIII, 1, p. 194. We read in the *Acts of Thomas*, § 31, a few lines which indicate pretty clearly the mythical parentage and meaning of the fantastic dragons met with in these beliefs: the serpent which the Apostle is in the act of punishing describes himself thus: "I am the son of him who reigns over all the earth. I am the son of him who encircles the globe. I am related to him who is beyond the Ocean and whose tail is in his own mouth. It is I who stole into Paradise to speak to Eve and tell her that which my father had bidden me let her know. . . ." Cf., again, G. Furlani, "Tre trattati astrologici siriaci sulle eclisse solare e lunare" in *Atti dell' Accademia Nazionale dei Lincei*, 1947, *Classe di Scienze morali* . . ., vol. 2, fasc. 11/12, Nov.–Dec., 1948, Rome, pp. 569–606. Cf. also here below, pp. 225–6. This figure also appears later, as the serpent *ouroboros* in the alchemists' writings.

to 336 of the manuscript) beginning with a most extraordinary scene. It is soon after the Resurrection. Jesus—"who is Aberamenthô"[13]—is standing near the shore of the Ocean, upright upon an altar around which are ranged his disciples. He pronounces a mysterious prayer, in which there are some of the Kabbalistic names that we find also on those curious engraved gems which are commonly—though arbitrarily—described as "Gnostic", as well as in the formulas written on magic papyri, Greek and Coptic. Under the impact of these words the heavens are suddenly opened: Jesus and his followers are transported into intermediate space and in front of them, steering amid the winds, they behold the ships of the sun and the moon, manned by fantastic beings.[14] In one of these ships they can even distinguish the dragons whose function it is to wrest from the Archons the light that they have stolen.[15] Jesus then tells how the powers of Sabaôth the Adamas,[16]

[13] Cf. C. Bonner, *Studies in Magical Amulets*, p. 203, which suggests that this name, commonly found on the engraved gems, was borrowed by the Gnostics from the repertory of magic (?). It does occur in the magical texts: cf. S. Eitrem, *Papyri Osloenses*, fasc. I, Plate III, which shows a personage with the head of a cock, and with this name attached.

[14] The ritual of the opening of the heavens, by which Jesus transports his disciples into the upper spaces and makes the heavenly ships appear, may well derive from Pharaonic Egypt; the gods, in their celestial barks, are thus represented in their sanctuaries; cf. J. Doresse, "Un rituel magique des Gnostiques d'Egypte" in *La Tour Saint-Jacques*, Nos. 11–12, July–December, 1957, pp. 65–75. We find other magical formulas for opening the heavens in a demotic ritual; see *The Demotic Magical Papyrus of London and Leiden*, edited by F. Ll. Griffith and Herbert Thompson, London, 1904, cols. X, ll. 23–35, and col. XXVII, ll. 1–12. Such ships occur again in the myths of the Mandaeans: cf. G. Furlani, "I pianeti e lo zodiaco nella religione dei Mandei" in *Atti Accad. Naz. dei Lincei*, Series 8, vol. II, fasc. 3, 1948, pp. 128–31, where it appears, among other details, that the moon has a black face like that of a cat. Mandaean pictures showing such ships are reproduced in Drower, *The Mandaeans*, pp. 77 and 79.

[15] Cumont, *Recherches* . . ., pp. 54ff.; Puech *Manichéisme* . . ., pp. 79–80 and notes 321–24. According to the Manichaean myth recorded by St Augustine, *De Nat. Boni*, 44 and *Contra Faustum*, XX, 6, and by Evodius, *De Fide*, these powers came out of the ships of the sun and moon to go and seduce the Archons by taking the forms of young men and women stripped of all raiment. . . . Since this conception would have put the sun and moon among the benefic powers, they were replaced, in the list of the seven perverse "planets", by the Head and Tail of the Dragon—that is, by the two nodes of the lunar orbit —invisible points, made manifest only by the eclipses they were supposed to cause, and between which the body of the fabulous monster itself could be traced, in that constellation of the Dragon whose star *alpha* corresponded, in antiquity, to the Pole.

[16] Adamas the "indomitable": cf. the term *Authades* in the *Pistis-Sophia*.

who had at first persisted in procreating angels, decans and other powers, had been bound by Jêou, "Father of my Father", to the celestial sphere of Fatality—that is, to the wheel of time. One of these powers, Iabraôth, became converted and was instated higher up, whilst Sabaôth the Adamas remained obstinately attached to his lower works and was bound to the sphere. To the five planets—already entrusted with three hundred and sixty-five powers—certain forces drawn from the Triple-powers were subjected; for instance, the little Sabaôth, the Good, was linked in this way with Zeus, for the government of the sphere. Then Jêou regulated the movements of the heavens.

Underneath the sphere, in the Ways of the Midst, Jêou established three hundred and sixty-five of the powers of the Adamas, ruled by five great demons, those who torment mankind. Here, in a novel manner, is described the fate of the souls that are thrown into the continual circling of the heavens. At certain particular conjunctions of the zodiacal signs and of the planets—aspects which belong to an old, rather fantastic astrology[17]—the various sectors of the heavens, each under the rule of its demoniac power, are periodically annulled, and the souls they contain are set free by Sabaôth the Good.

After this exposition Jesus conjured up, before the eyes of his disciples, apparitions of fire and water, of wine and of blood, derived from the Treasury of the Light and from Barbelô respectively, to show what the elements of the Gnostic "baptisms" will be. Then, at a word from the Saviour, the heavens are closed, and they find themselves again upon the Mountain in Galilee.

The Christ now begins to celebrate, upon an altar, a mysterious sacrifice: he recites a magical prayer; and then comes a sign from heaven. Thus is accomplished the Baptism of the First Oblation, to which the faithful have yet to add the baptism of Fire, and then the baptism of the Spirit, which is a spiritual anointing.

The conclusion of this book is missing: it consisted of eight pages of manuscript which have been lost; and when the text continues after this lacuna we are manifestly in the beginning of

[17] Cf. chap. vi, note 33.

another work (pp. 345 to 354 of the codex), for the dialogue is framed in formulas that are quite different in style. This last treatise, of which the commencement is lacking, is a conversation between Jesus and his disciples about the different categories of sinners and the torments in store for them. According to a complicated classification, the guilty souls will be put through a series of degrees of infernal purification, at the end of which some will be irrevocably abandoned to the demons, who will torture and destroy them, whilst others will be returned to the torments of this base world, after having been made to drink the draught of oblivion. It is noteworthy that, among the greatest sinners to be punished, mention is made of the Gnostics who call themselves the heirs of Esau and of Jacob, sectaries addicted to such licentious practices as those which the heresiologists ascribe to the great Gnostics.[18]

The whole collection of texts contained in this codex is evidently somewhat muddled. We first remarked upon this at the abrupt change of subject on page 169 of the manuscript, most probably because this belongs to another work which the compiler had tacked on to the former without any transitional passage. Another example of this disorder occurs on pages 233–4 (between the end of the first *Book of the Saviour* and the beginning of the second treatise of the same title), where two pages are inserted, the contents of which do not belong to the second of these books, but should undoubtedly be placed earlier, among the last pages of the previous treatise. Finally, the last page of the manuscript, numbered 355, is written by another hand than the rest of the book, and gives the last lines of some apocryphal gospel of which nothing else has survived.

★   ★   ★

Another Gnostic manuscript is the *Bruce Codex*. This was bought at Thebes in 1769 by the famous Scottish traveller when he was on his way to the Sudan and Ethiopia. No doubt this book had been discovered in some hiding-place in the vast necropolis of the Thebaid which, after the decay of the old

[18] Cf. chap. I, pp. 36 and 43.

paganism, was a refuge for all sorts of magicians. It is a question—
the two manuscripts having come to light about the same time—
whether the *Codex Askewianus* may not have come from the same
Theban source: by their contents alone the two collections present
a family likeness that suggests this hypothesis. The *Bruce Codex* is
now in the Bodleian Library; its contents were not rightly estimated until 1872, by Eugène Revillout; and Amélineau published
it prematurely about 1891.[19]

The manuscript, which is of papyrus, comprises seventy-eight
pages written by several different hands, and consists essentially
of two parts. The first of these contains the two books of a *Great
Treatise according to the Mystery*, and may date from the fifth
century. The second contains a work whose title is missing and
its writing may go back to the end of the fourth century.

The two parts of the *Book of the great treatise according to the
Mystery* seem, by their contents, to be identifiable with the
two Books of Jêou mentioned in the *Pistis-Sophia*. The preamble
presents a conversation between Jesus and his disciples; but a
lacuna soon interrupts this part of the work. When the manuscript resumes this conversation, it is beginning the description of
sixty powers or emanations which surround Jêou in the Treasury
of Light. Of each of these the book gives an account complete
with the name, the sign, the seals, the veils and the mystic number
of the power in question. But after the description of the twenty-
eighth of these entities, a second lacuna interrupts the codex.
Upon the leaves that follow, we find ourselves travelling with
Jesus and his followers among the sixty "Treasures". Then the
Christ intones a hymn to the glory of the Father, the disciples
making responses to him after each verse.

After the preamble to the second *Book of the Treatise according
to the Mystery*, Jesus continues his revelations about the Treasury

---

[19] Amélineau, *Notice sur le papyrus gnostique Bruce, texte et traduction*, 1891
(out-of-date). For the text, one prefers C. Schmidt, "Gnostische Schriften in
koptischer Sprache aus dem Codex Brucianus" in *Texte und Untersuchungen*,
8, 1892; for the translation, C. Schmidt, *Koptisch-gnostische Schriften*, vol. I;
*Die Pistis Sophia, Die Beiden Bücher von Jehû, Unbekanntes alt-gnostischer Werk
. . . , berarbeitet von W. Till*, 1954. Cf. especially the edition with full commentary and translation by Charlotte Baynes, *A Coptic Gnostic Treatise contained
in the Codex Brucianus*, 1933.

of the Light. He describes how the "receivers" of the Treasury, at the death of a man, pilot the soul out of the body, through all the aeons of the invisible regions, and lead it as far as the Treasury; how they release it from sins and turn the soul into a pure light; how they bring it into the Three Amens, the Triple-Powers, the Five Trees and the Seven Voices . . . ; how, finally, they entrust it with their seals and their mysteries. "These mysteries I am revealing to you", Jesus now adds; "take care not to tell them to any man unworthy of them. Do not give them away to father or mother, nor to brother or sister nor to any relatives; disclose them not for food or drink nor for [the gift of] a woman; neither for gold nor silver. . . . Transmit them to no woman, to no man who is found acting upon any belief in the seventy-two Archons, or who is serving them; never reveal them [either] to those who worship the eight powers of the great Archons"— which refers, as the text makes clear, to certain sectaries who practised, upon such pretexts, veritable orgies and impure rituals while pretending to possess the true Gnosis and to adore the true God. For, Jesus continues, "their god is evil; he is the Triple-Power of the Great Archon, and his name is Taricheas, the son of Sabaôth the Adamas. He is the enemy of the Heavenly kingdom; he has the face of a wild-boar, his tusks project from his mouth; and from behind he has another face which is that of a lion."

After these exhortations to keep the secret, more especially from other Gnostics, Jesus announces to his disciples that he is about to administer three baptisms to them, those of water, fire and of the spirit; after which he will disclose to them the mystery of the spiritual anointing and the secrets of the Treasury of the Light. He has sent some of the disciples for cruets of wine and some vine-branches; the altar is made ready with the vessels of wine, the branches, with plants and aromatics, all precisely indicated. The disciples are clothed in linen, and in their hands, which are marked with the mystic number of the Seven Voices, they hold certain appropriate plants. The magical prayer which is then offered up by the Saviour ends with these words: "May these powers come, and may they baptize my disciples with the water of the Life of the Seven Virgins of Light; and may their sins be forgiven, and may they be cleansed from their iniquities, that they may be numbered among the inheritors of the Kingdom of the Light . . . then let a sign be given,[20] and let Zorokothora [Melchizedek] come and bring the water of the baptism of Life in one of these vessels." The sign prayed for is vouchsafed: the wine in the cruet on the right changes into water, and the disciples approach Jesus, who baptizes them. Then, by means of analogous rites, Jesus administers, one after another, the baptisms of Fire and of the Holy Spirit. Finally, he teaches them the "apologies"—that is, the pass-words and the signs by which they will have to make themselves known to each of the powers, when they are ascending through the heavens: this is a lengthy ritual which cannot well be summarized.

To this treatise are adjoined the fragments of two prayers, and then one leaf of a test describing the ascension of souls through the Ways of the Midst which are ruled by the perverse Archons. Amongst these mention is made of Typhon, "the great and powerful archon with the face of an ass".[21] The astrological ideas disclosed in this fragment are evidently of the same origin as those in the last treatise but one in the Codex Askewianus.

From the point of view of the doctrine they expound, these two writings are very close to the *Pistis-Sophia*, in which, moreover, they are twice quoted. One cannot decide to what Gnostic group they belong. They diverge upon too many points of detail from all those which the heresiologists have described to us. This sect professed a rigorous asceticism, and abominated, as we have seen, those Gnostics who worshipped either the seventy-two aeons or the eight archons[22] and meanwhile gave themselves up to unspeakable practices supposedly permitted by authority of Esau and Jacob. What most clearly distinguishes the authors of these writings is their description of the Treasury of the Light, peopled by such entities as the Three Amens, the Seven Amens,

[20] Cf. in the *Avesta, Yaçna, Gatha Ahunavaiti*, XXXIV, 6, an analogous formula for the offering to Ahura-Mazda: "If you really exist . . . , give me a sign of it!"

[21] Cf. chap. I, note 101, and p. 104.

[22] We do not know whether to lay this charge to the account of the Gnostic Archontici, whom we have already mentioned on pp. 45-6 when citing St Epiphanius.

4

the Five Trees,[23] the Seven Voices . . . ; also the celestial status they assign to Melchizedek; the very special character of the Virgin of Light; the "receivers" of the moon and the sun, by whom the light of the archons gathered up:[24] it is also that migration of souls through the circling spheres, a migration by which at last they are either completely purified or else returned to the cosmos, or even destroyed; it is, lastly, their precise allusion to the Three Moments.[25] All this shows that we are here upon the very verge of Manichaeism.

The second part of the Bruce Codex—said to be, from its writing, distinct from the rest of the manuscript—contains a text without a title (the beginning and the end of it are missing) which is of a different character. Unfortunately its leaves are considerably out of order, and the recent efforts of Charlotte Baynes to find out the correct order have not met with complete success.[26]

From what we have left of this work, the beginning seems to be

[23] The symbolic meaning of the "Trees" in these myths is pretty variable. We saw the trees of Paradise likened by Justin to angels. The *Psalms of Solomon* treat them as saints (cf. above, note 86, p. 34); the Manichaean *Kephalaion* VI gives us five "trees", but these belong to the world of darkness (cf. H. C. Puech, "Le Prince des Ténèbres" . . . , in the volume of *Études carmélitaines* devoted to *Satan*, 1948, p. 151). Just as, in Manichaeism, the five trees of the Tree of Death, the five trees of light in our Gnostic treatise may stand for abstract emanations of the Tree of Life. For example—as is doubtless the case with the "Voices" the "Amens" and other entities of that kind— the sources of the seals, the sacraments by which the Perfect attain to the Treasury of the Light.

These metaphorical *trees* were originally borrowed from the Gospel *Matt.* VII, 17–19 and XII, 33; *Luke* VI, 43–4), and they make use also of the fact that the Greek *hyle* (matter) has also the primary meaning of "wood". Cf. in Puech, *Le Manichéisme*, note 285 on pp. 159–61. For the survival of the symbolism of the Trees of Life and of Death, see e.g., a double page in a manuscript of the *Liber Floridus* of Lambert de Saint Omer dating from before A.D. 1120, which displays, face to face, pictures of the Tree of Good and the Tree of Evil—reduced, it is true, to the simply moral signification (cf. the reproduction given on p. 159 of A. Grabar and Carl Nordenfalk, *La peinture romane*, Skira, Geneva, 1958).

[24] The figure of the Virgin of Light presented in Manichaean texts is analysed by Cumont, *Recherches*, pp. 64–5, as "a very high Virtue dwelling in the Moon"; she recalls the Iranian divinity Anâhita, mistress "of the waters that flow from a heavenly source in the region of the stars" to whom the seed of Zoroaster is entrusted. Cf. the references given by Cumont with the *Vendidad*, with the *Boundahishn* and with the other Iranian treatises. Cf. also G. Widengren, *The Great Vohu Manah* . . . , 1945, pp. 24 and 28. Upon the ships of the sun and moon, see above notes 14 and 15.

[25] Cf. p. 114.

[26] Charlotte Baynes, *A Coptic Gnostic Treatise*, p. xviii.

a description of the supreme God, Father of the Universe, ineffable and invisible. His first Thought causes a Son to issue from him, a fantastic Anthropos in whom, it is said, he has depicted all the universes. This primordial man is described, detail by detail, and each part of his body reproduces, on a different scale, the entities that compose the higher universe. He is perfect and complete, and therefore androgyne. One advantage of our being given this long description of him is that we can deduce from this the mythical pattern of the higher world that it reflects. At the summit of this universe was the Setheus[27] who is again the primordial god, but this time in his aspect as Creator: and in the Setheus were contained the Monad and the Monogene.[28]

Some hymns of benediction are inserted here, and a eulogy of the Father of the Universe, which calls him the "first source, whose voice reaches into every place, the first sound".

Then, from the creation of the primordial Son, we pass on to the formation of the Second Place, called the second Creator, reason, source, etc. . . . The epithets applied to him, although obscure and confused, are not without beauty: he is called the support, the guardian, the father of the universe; "the light of his eyes pierces the spaces outside the Pleroma, the Word that goes out of his mouth reaches into the infinite heights and the abysses, the hairs of his head are of the number of the hidden worlds, the circumference of his countenance is the pattern of the aeons . . ., the extending of his hands is the manifestation of the Stauros;[29] he is the brimming source of the Silence." By his edict all things have received Gnosis, Life, Hope and Rest. In him are twelve

[27] Cf. Charlotte Baynes, *op. cit.*, pp. 19–21. Setheus, the Earth-Shaker, can probably be regarded as a form of the great Seth, the son of Adam, who is his earthly reflection.

[28] The Monad is perhaps assimilable to Barbelô, both of these, in the myths in which they appear, being the first image of the Father and the seed of the Cosmos—which would support the doubtful derivation of the name Barbelô from the Egyptian BLBILE, "seed" (see Baynes, *op. cit.*, pp. 49–50). As for the Monogene, it is identified with the Word. Its function may be better understood if one refers back to Irenaeus's *Adversus haereses*, I, XXIX, and to its Coptic parallel explained by C. Schmidt in his *Philotesia*; cf. above chap. I, note 92 on p. 37. Barbelô's gazing profoundly into the pure light causes her production of the Monogene, the first and only *begotten*. Whereas the Father is *unbegotten*: cf. Baynes, pp. 66–8, 78–80, 87–8.

[29] Cf. Horos-Stauros of the Valentinians, p. 28, above.

abysses; by him the Pleroma has been made, with its portals, its monads, its guardians and its powers; and there dwells Aphredon with the twelve Just ones, there is the Adam-Light with three hundred and sixty-five aeons; there is an abyss in which the Only-begotten is hidden. In another of these abysses there are three Paternities: one is that of the hidden God; the second contains the Five Trees; the third encloses a Silence and a Source in which the twelve Just ones behold themselves . . . in this are the Five Seals.

After this we are given a description of the universal Mother from whom the Ennead proceeds: its nine powers are enumerated by names, the last of which is Iouël. In another region there is an abyss in which there is a table, around which there are three great powers called Peaceful, Inconceivable and Infinite, and in the midst of them is a sonhood called Christ the assayer, for it is he who, with the seal of the Father, seals all those whom he sends on to that primordial Parent.

Yet further on we come to the abyss of Setheus himself, surrounded by twelve powers, each of whom has three aspects. And above these again are twelve more Paternities surrounding the mouth of the abyss; their diadems radiate light as far as to the universe of light which emanates from the Monogene hidden in the depth of this abyss. The author of the treatise now allows himself a digression, in order to tell us how this supreme entity who is the Monogene (the Only-begotten) is ineffable, and how few teachers have any knowledge of it. This is a very precious passage, for it makes definite allusions to the great Gnostic prophets and their lost revelations: "To speak of him [i.e., the Monogene] as he is, with the tongue of flesh is impossible." However, the text goes on, there have been some specially favoured men who have been able to know this mystery. "That is why the powers of the great aeons paid homage to the power that was in Marsanes, saying 'Who is this man, who has seen such things face to face? . . .' And Nicotheus (he too) spoke about this, for he saw who this being was, and he said, 'The Father exists, superior to every perfect thing'. He has revealed the Triple-Power, perfect and invisible. Every one of the perfect men saw him, they spoke of him and glorified him. . . . He is the Monogene who is hidden in the Setheus, and it is he whom they called 'obscurity of light' because in his excess of light they themselves appeared dim. . . ." It was through this Monogene that the Setheus gave himself the powers over which he reigns. The entities that surround him form, as it were, a crown from which his light radiates over the aeons and everything external to him finds itself under his feet. Incidentally, this glittering and complex vision is also likened to that of the divine chariot which, as we have seen elsewhere, was the favourite image in Jewish mysticism.[30] The Coptic treatise gives another quotation from another Gnostic teacher of whom even the name had been lost: "It is of him [the Monogene] that Phosilampes spoke, saying 'He exists "before the universe" . . .' and when Phosilampes understood this, he expressed himself in these terms, 'By him those things are that really and verily exist, and those things that verily do not exist. It is by him that exist even the hidden things—which verily *are*, and the things manifest which verily *are not at all*.'"

After a hymn of the powers to the Monogene, the myth is resumed. The Setheus projects into the Indivisible that lies beneath him a spark of light, which the powers welcome with thanksgiving, and out of which they form a man of light and truth. This man is then sent down below. Before him, the veils which separate the lower regions from the worlds on high open of themselves. Thus the Light descends even into matter, and, of the creatures who dwell there, some take on the form of the Light and rejoice, whilst others rebel and are mortified. At the same time, in order to help those who have had faith in the spark of light, guardians are despatched towards the aeons; their names are Gamaliel, Strempsuchos[31] and Agramas.

At this point the codex—but is not this because the leaves are again in disorder?—resumes its description of the various Places; it is now describing the Indivisible into which the spark of light has just been thrown. This region shows itself no less richly furnished with abysses, powers, sources and paternities

[30] Cf. chap. VI, p. 290-1.   [31] Cf. chap. VI, note 73.

than were the higher aeons. Aphredôn and Musanios rule it, with twelve Just ones. And hither the Setheus, from on high, sends a creative Word escorted by a multitude of crowned powers. This Word becomes a potent god, lord and saviour, father of those who have believed. At the same time the Virgin (is she the same as Sophia in the other systems?) receives the spark of light and establishes, upon the lower world, three powers— Propatôr, Autopatôr and Protogenitor. Out of matter the Protogenitor makes a world, and a city which is called Incorruptible, Jerusalem, the New Earth. . . . And then perversity is separated from matter; veils are set up in order to effect this. The Propatôr, placed in the aeon of the Mother, is endowed with multiple powers, angels and servitors. He even creates his own aeon, with a great Pleroma and a great sanctuary; he also lends himself obligingly to the designs of the higher world and conceives the will to change and convert the lower universe to the service of the hidden Father in the highest. At this the Mother expresses her gratification by some strange exclamations: "Three times born", she says, meaning that he has been brought to birth three times, for she repeats, "Thrice-engendered", adding "Hermes!" Must we not take this to be an allusion to the "Thrice-great" Hermes—to the Trismegistus?[32] The *Philosophumena* has already told us that, among the Naassenes, "Hermes is the Word who has expressed and fashioned the things that have been, that are and that will be."[33]

The Autopatôr is endowed in his turn: he is entrusted with the hidden things that are reserved for the race of the Perfect. And, lastly, the Mother establishes the Progenitor: he it was who extended himself over matter as a bird spreads its wings, to hatch out of it powers of every kind, to whom he will now give the law that they love one another and worship the most high God. The Mother and her three sons then send up a hymn towards the Light. The supreme Power answers this by sending them a wonderful flash of light; and, finally, in a sort of Last Judgment, the Lord of Glory comes to divide up matter, assigning some to life and the Light, and the rest to death and the Darkness. There

---

[32] Cf. Baynes, p. 156.   [33] Cf. *Philosophumena*, V, 7.

follows an outburst of joy from those who, born of matter, have caught a gleam of the hidden mystery, and now offer to the incorruptible Father a prayer which is full of grandeur. Perhaps in their own devotions the sectaries repeated this prayer, of which we will quote the final lines: "Hear our prayer and send to us incorporeal spirits to dwell with us. Let them teach us the things that thou hast promised us, and let them dwell in us that we may embody them. Since it is thy will that this be so, it will be done. And thou wilt give precepts for our work, and thou wilt establish it according to thy will, and according to the precept of the hidden aeons. And thou wilt guide us, for we are thine."

After this, the Father sends to the Perfect certain powers whose function it will be to guide them. In a sort of spiritual hierarchy, of grades rising from below to above—from those who have "progressed" to those who are still in penitence—are enumerated the powers put in charge of the spring of the Waters of Life—the source for the baptisms?—and their names are as follows: Mikhar and Mikheus; Barpharanges;[34] the aeons of the Sophia; Jesus as before the Resurrection; the celestial beings and the twelve aeons. In this region were placed also Seldao[35] and Eleïnos, Zôgenethles, Selmelkhe, and the aeons that were self-engendered. And here there were four luminaries: Heleleth, Daueithe, Oroïael and Harmozel.[36] It is during this evocation of the powers in charge of the salvation of the Perfect that our manuscript abruptly ends.

With its astonishing assemblage of Silences and Abysses, of sources and generative Wombs this treatise recalls, to a misleading degree, the obscure phraseology of the *Chaldean Oracles*

[34] The power here called Barpharanges is also named in Coptic magical texts and on the engraved gems, as Sesenges-Barpharanges: see C. Bonner, *op. cit.*, p. 201 and A. M. Kropp, *Ausgewählte Koptische Zaubertexte*, vol. III, 1930, p. 126.

[35] Baynes read this as Sellaô, which should be corrected to Seldao; cf. J. Doresse, "Hermès et la Gnose" in *Novum Testamentum*, I, 1956, pp. 66–7. The *Philosophumena*, VII, 30, quotes (in reference to a Gnostic *Gospel of the Egyptians*) Esaldaiô, which would be a name of the Demiurge. However, one of the newly-found texts mentions this entity, not as the demiurge, but rather as a power in charge of the heavenly baptisms: cf. below, p. 254. We may guess that the author of the *Philosophumena*, embarrassed by the multiplicity of names in the text he was summarizing, wrote Esaldaiô here in mistake for Sacla!

[36] Cf. A. M. Kropp, *op. cit.*, vol. III, §§ 36, 43–6, 51, 133, 137.

(which date from the second half of the second century) where one finds the same abundance of Wombs containing all things and of Sources of the blessed spirits conceiving in ineffable Silences. One can also compare it with a Greek hymn of the same nature which Porphyry translates in his *Philosophy of the Oracles*. In terms which, it is true, are devoid of any dualism, this poem invokes the beneficent Lord enthroned upon the ethereal zenith, the pole around which the celestial spheres revolve.[37]

In what it says about Marsianes and Nicotheus, the anonymous treatise of the Bruce Codex compares much more closely than do the Coptic texts previously mentioned, with what the heresiologists told us of the Gnostics. The *Apocalypse of Nicotheus* is one of those which the disciples of Porphyry refuted; it is also named in certain alchemical writings, and even by the Manichaeans.[38] Marsanes and Martiades have already been mentioned, as prophets who were caught up into heaven for three days, and who wrote *Revelations* in use among the Archontici.[39]

*   *   *

A third manuscript of Gnostic content is the *Codex Berolensis* 8502. No one knows what has now become of it: at the end of the last war it disappeared, taken to an unknown destination after the fall of Berlin. This again is a Coptic collection, written on papyrus and dating, doubtless, from the fifth century. It had been acquired in Cairo by Dr Rheinhardt, in 1896. The learned Carl Schmidt, to whom Coptic studies are indebted for many other discoveries,[40] at once drew attention to this find,[41] underlining

[37] Cf. Hans Lewy, *Chaldaean Oracles and Theurgy* . . . , Cairo, 1956, chap. II and—for the hymn preserved by Porphyry (which the lamented H. Lewy has the merit of having added to the collection of the *Oracles* already made by Kroll)—pp. 9–10. This last text appears also in the *Anthologia Palatina*, ed. Didot, vol. III, pp. 519, no. 261.

[38] Cf. below, p. 159; Nicotheus was counted among the number of the prophets by the Manichaeans: see H. C. Puech, *Manichéisme*, pp. 145 and 151.

[39] Cf. here, chap. I, note 114.

[40] More particularly by the identification and salvage of Coptic Manichaean texts unearthed in the Fayum about 1930; see C. Schmidt and J. Polotsky, *Ein Mani-Fund in Aegypten*, 1932.

[41] C. Schmidt, "Ein vorirenäisches gnostisches Originalwerk . . .", in *Sitzungsber. d. kgl. preussischen Akademie d. Wiss.*, 1896, pp. 839–47; and, by the same author, *Irenäus u. seine Quelle in Adv. Haereses*, I, 29, quoted above chap. I, note 92; cf. Sagnard, *Gnose valentinienne*, pp. 439ff.

the special interest attaching to one of the works it included, the *Secret Book of John*. Indeed, a part of this work corresponded exactly—in some sentences word for word—with the text of the passage in Irenaeus dealing with the Barbelo-gnostics (I, XXIX)—a proof of the reliability of the information Irenaeus had at his disposal when he wrote that chapter. It was also, conversely, a proof that the part of this Gnostic work which lent itself to his purpose existed before A.D. 180, the date when Irenaeus composed his treatise. The learned world had hopes of learning the details of this important text without further delay; but its publication was attended with incredible ill-luck, and was twice held up by chance. The second time, the type had already been set up when it was accidentally destroyed. It was only after the death of Carl Schmidt that the work undertaken was brought to completion by Professor Walter Till, who had it published in 1955[42]—that is, at a time when the rich find of texts from Chenoboskion had already provided us with other versions, and so deprived Carl Schmidt's manuscript of its uniqueness.

This manuscript contained a *Gospel of Mary*, a *Secret Book of John*, a *Sophia of Jesus Christ* and, lastly, some *Acts of Peter* which, however, are not Gnostic at all. We are dealing here with writings translated from the Greek; a fact of which we have formal proof, for a short passage in the *Gospel of Mary* exactly repeats part of a Greek papyrus attributed to the third century;[43] moreover, quite recently, in the course of a preliminary study of the Chenoboskion manuscripts, which also include a text of the *Sophia of Jesus*, Professor H. C. Puech was able to recognize a Greek fragment of the same work in the papyrus Oxyrhynchus 1081.[44]

---

[42] The beginning of the *Sophia of Jesus* has been translated by R. Liechtenhan in *Zeitschrift für die Neutestamentliche Wissenschaft*, III, 1902, p. 229; articles on the *Secret Book of John* and on the *Sophia of Jesus* in E. Hennecke, *Neutestamentliche Apokryphen*, 2nd edn., 1924, pp. 70–1; cf. also W. Till, "The Gnostic Apocryphon of John" in *Journal of Ecclesiastical History*, vol. III, No. 1, 1952, pp. 14–22; edition of the text with German translation: *Die gnostischen Schriften des koptischen Papyrus Berolinensis 8502*, Berlin, 1955. Some passages of the *Gospel of Mary* had already been quoted in translation by C. Schmidt in the preface to his version of the *Pistis-Sophia* published in 1925.

[43] Cf. Till, *Die gnostischen Schriften des Papyrus Berolinensis 8502*, pp. 24–5.

[44] H. C. Puech, Communication to the VIth International congress of Papyrology, Paris, 1949.

4*

I shall not attempt to summarize the *Secret Book of John* or the *Sophia of Jesus* in this chapter, for I shall have a better opportunity to describe them later, with the whole of the library from Chenoboskion—where other copies of the same text were found before the previously-found versions were even published![45]

The first pages of the *Gospel of Mary* are missing. This work is a conversation between the disciples and Mary (Magdalene?) revealing to them certain sayings which she alone had heard from the Saviour. The questions raised—"What is the sin of the world?" "How are we to preach the Gospel of the Kingdom of the Son of Man?"—are rather ordinary ones. Mary replies to the disciples with a good will. She describes, among other things, how the soul, during its ascension from heaven to heaven, is questioned by such powers as Darkness, Concupiscence, Ignorance . . . which try to detain her. But Peter loses his temper: he suggests that Mary has herself imagined what she is relating; at which she bursts into tears. Levi interposes to defend her. Then the disciples separate, in order to go and preach the Gospel to all peoples; and the text ends with their departure.

To complete this inventory of the Gnostic remains previously in our possession, we must mention a few more Coptic fragments, although they are not very informative. First, there are a few remnants of a manuscript on papyrus dating from the fourth century, which had been used in the binding of a more recent book.[46] They are written in Theban Coptic with some admixture of the dialect of Middle Egypt. We can see that they come from a work in which the names of Ialdabaôth and Sophia occur, and where the Seven powers and the lower heavens are mentioned.

We have also, of a book written on parchment, one complete page and some fragments of two others.[47] These are from a codex of rather small format, and came from Deir-Bala'izah, anciently the site of a particularly important monastery, some

[45] Cf. chap. v, below, pp. 197ff.

[46] British Museum Or. 4920 (1), edited in W. E. Crum, *Catalogue of the Coptic Manuscripts in the British Mus.*, 1905, p. 251, No. 522.

[47] First published by Crum in the *J.T.S.*, XLIV, 1943, pp. 176–9; cf. the new edition by P. Kahle, *Bala'izah*, vol. I, 1954, No. 52, pp. 473ff.

twelve miles south of Assiut.[48] These leaflets are usually assigned to the fourth century; but they seem to us later. The text is in Sahidic Coptic; and we give here a translation of the little that remains legible: "(. . .) the spiritual force, before it had been manifested, its name was not this at all, but it was: Silence. For everything that was in the heavenly Paradise was sealed in silence. Those who participate in this will become spiritual and will know the Whole. Thus, then, I have explained (everything?) to thee, John, of that which concerns Adam, Paradise and the Five Trees,[49] by an intelligible allegory. When I, John, heard that, I said, 'I have begun with a good beginning; encouraged by thy love, I have attained to a secret knowledge and a mystery, and some symbols of truth. Now I would again ask thee to explain to me, if it please thee, about Cain and Abel; in what way Cain killed Abel; and then also how he [Cain] was questioned in these words, by Him who asked him "Where is Abel thy brother?" whilst Cain denied, saying "Am I the guardian of [my brother] . . ." '" After this, the text is in tatters: from what remains on the following page one can only say that the explanations of the Saviour (?) that follow are about Noah and the Ark, and that John is now questioning him about Melchizedek, "without father or mother, of no known generation . . . without end of life . . . priest for eternity. . . ."

Finally, and this time far from Egypt, we possess one very intimate text—the funerary epitaph of an initiate, Flavia Sophe, who died in Rome about the year 300. She received the Gnostic sacraments, in order to escape from the planets, to return to her heavenly origin and, in becoming perfect, to assume masculinity.[50]

GNOSTIC MONUMENTS AND PAINTINGS

Is this really all? It would be less than just to forget to make mention here of a few relics which, though less eloquent than

[48] Concerning the monasteries of this region, see J. Doresse, "Recherches d'archéologie copte: les monastères de Moyenne-Egypte" in *Comptes rendus de l'Académie des Inscriptions et Belles-Lettres*, July, 1952.

[49] Cf. above, note 23.

[50] G. Quispel, "L'Inscription funéraire de Flava Sophe" in *Mélanges de Ghellinck*, Louvain, 1951.

the texts, are evocative in other ways—that is, certain monuments and other objects.

The most curious is an alabaster bowl covered with figures sculptured in relief. Did this big cup, some eight inches in diameter, come from Syria or Anatolia? We do not know; it is usually supposed to be Orphic. Inside it, at the centre, is a serpent with its coils ranged one above another, and around this are nude figures lying on their backs with their feet towards the centre of the bowl and their heads towards the rim. Their hands are up-raised in vague gestures or else concealing, but only casually, this or that part of the body. The outside of the cup is decorated with arcading in front of which, at the four diametrically opposite points, stand four personages symbolizing the four winds or the four cardinal points; and at their feet four Greek inscriptions are engraved around the base of the cup. Three of these are quotations from Orphic hymns to the Sun; the last is a passage from Euripides' *Melanippus* which dealt with the creation of the world from the cosmic egg. If one took these quotations alone into consideration, one would certainly class this vessel as Orphic. But it evokes, in highly realistic fashion, a ritual that one can hardly think any but Gnostics would celebrate. Certain sects did make such free use of themes from the Greek mysteries—as the *Philosophumena* tells us—that we may well suppose, with H. Leisegang, that this singular vase had some connection with the sect of the Ophites.[51]

Some more important monuments exist which in different degrees evoke the history of Gnosticism. Subterranean Rome, in its innumerable tombs, preserves the traces of many strange cults that history has forgotten. Do we not find there, even in the Vatican necropolis, the sepulchres of initiates who were wor-shippers of Isis and Bacchus at the same time?[52] Have they not found also, in the catacombs of Pretextat, the tomb of Vibia, an adept of that Phrygian Dionysos, Sabazios—who was identi-fied with the Lord Sabaôth?[53] The Gnostic sects were well enough

[51] Cf. Leisegang, in *Eranos Jahrbuch*, 1939 (published 1940), pp. 151–251. For some curious mediaeval representations of an analogous cult, see Jos. de Hammer, *Mémoire sur deux coffrets gnostiques du moyen âge*, Paris, 1832.

[52] J. Carcopino, *Études d'histoire Chrétienne* . . . , pp. 164–5.

[53] Cumont, *Les Religions orientales dans le paganisme romain*, 4th edn., 1929, p. 61 and p. 228, note 62.

represented in the Eternal City to encourage the hope of finding therein the tomb of some Naassene or Valentinian!

In old Rome, the purlieus of the church of St Sebastian were the first to be known by the name of catacombs (*catacumbas*), and here the name denoted simply a depression of the ground.[54] This served as a cemetery, and thence the name of "catacomb" came into general use for other burial-places. To return to the original Catacumbas—at first it was the Jewish, or near-Jewish graves that were dug in this place. Later on, the bodies of the Apostles Peter and Paul were preserved there for some time; and there, too, the holy martyr Sebastian was interred. A basilica of the Apostles was erected on the site and, while building it, the Christians condemned some of the funerary chapels of the earliest occupants. But recent excavations have brought some of these ancient sepulchres to light. One of these belonged to some people who particularly liked to call themselves the *Innocentii*, or Innocents. This tomb was adorned with paintings of a somewhat unusual character—with scenes of initiation and of funerals, which attracted the attention of archaeologists.[55] One symbol in particular, the *ascia*, or masons' trowel, which was an emblem much used by the Essenians and Pythagoreans,[56] was represented there. From his personal studies on the site, of these decoration and some inscriptions that were readable, Jerome Carcopino concluded that the owners of this tomb must have been Nazarenes or Ebionites. If we are to believe Epiphanius, these sects, originally Jewish, professed a special reverence for the Apostle James, who was regarded with the same favour in Gnostic traditions.[57] Moreover, among the names of the deceased incised upon this tomb under the church of St Sebastian, we find that of Hermes several times—Titus Flavius Hermes, Marcus Ulpius Hermes, Hermesianus . . . ; was it indeed some conception of the Word, the Logos, adopted by these semi-Gnostics, which gave them such a preference for the name of Hermes of Cyllene, to

[54] Carcopino, *De Pythagore aux Apôtres*, pp. 227 and 339ff.
[55] Carcopino, *loc. cit.*, pp. 361ff. A would-be archaeologist lately tried to explain some analogous scenes as representations of the dissection of a corpse (news in *Le Figaro*, 12 April, 1955).
[56] Carcopino, *Le Mystère d'un symbole chrétien.*
[57] Cf. chap. v, pp. 236–7.

whom the Naassenes also gave a special place in their speculations?[58]

Another Roman tomb has sometimes been thought to be Gnostic—that of Trebius Iustus, which bore the mystic name—the *signum*—of Asellus. I will do no more than refer the reader to what Ceccheli has published about this.[59]

Finally, there is a tomb which belonged to some authentic Gnostics, although to which of their sects cannot be determined with certainty. This is the sepulchre of the Aurelii in the Viale Manzoni, which was discovered some thirty years ago.[60] Of the part of this edifice which in ancient days was at the ground level, no more than the funerary chamber remains; but of what was underground two rooms have been preserved. According to Jerome Carcopino, the earliest date for this monument would fall in the reign of Caracalla (211–17), the latest in that of Alexander Severus[61] (122–35). The rich decoration of the sepulchre has unhappily been much damaged since its discovery: but the interpretation of the paintings, about which various experts had formed provisional hypotheses, has been the subject of a substantial recent study by Jerome Carcopino.[62] Among the figures that adorn these vaults we seem to recognize the triad of the Pleroma, and the Good Shepherd in a frame decorated with almonds—almonds, which for the Naassenes, inheriting that idea from the Phrygians, symbolized the Father of the Universe. There is also a scene which may represent the creation of man, watched over by someone with a rueful countenance (is this Ialdabaôth?), and elsewhere, Adam and Eve are receiving the revelation of Gnosis from the Serpent. Here, too, we find the Stauros—the Cross—which is also Horos, the limit of the Pleroma; and there stand the figures of Mariamne, of Sophia, of

[58] *Philosophumena*, V, 7.
[59] Ceccheli, *Monumenti cristiano-eretici di Roma*, 1944, pp. 135–46.
[60] G. Bendinelli, "Il monumento sepolcrale degli Aureli" in *Monumenti Antichi* published by the Academia dei Lincei XXVIII, 1922, pp. 290–514 and Mgr Wilpert, "Le pitture dell'ipogeo . . . presso il viale Manzoni . . ." in the *Memorie* of the Pontifical Academy of Archeology, I, part 2, pp. 1–42.
[61] Date established by J. Carcopino, *De Pythagore . . .* , p. 88.
[62] Ch. Picard, "La Grande peinture de l'hypogée funéraire du Viale Manzoni" in *Comptes rendus de l'Académie des Inscriptions et Belles-Lettres*, 1945, pp. 26–51.

the Apostles John and James and of Matthew (unless, as I think more likely, this last is Matthias, better known to the Gnostic sects). Here, again, is the Last Supper, and there the heavenly Jerusalem within its walls; and lastly—showing to what an extent this iconography corresponds with what the *Philosophumena* tells us of Gnosticism and utilization of the *Odyssey*—here are Ulysses, Penelope and the Suitors; or (if you prefer the explanation offered by Jérôme Carcopino) Ulysses and Circe the enchantress.[63] Some students may still question some of these identifications; but even allowing in advance for the possibility of somewhat different hypotheses, it is certain that they will not change the main lines of this interpretation, which has already caused the tomb of the Aurelii to be recognized as one of the most remarkable monuments of its kind.

One would like to find some more concrete relics of the beliefs of these sects: some there are, no doubt, among the curious figures and Kabbalistic signs of those engraved gems which were all, until lately, much too uncritically supposed to be Gnostic.[64] These display demoniac figures, with the head of a cock, with serpents in the place of legs, etc., accompanied by the inscribed names of Iaô, or of Abraxas. Another figure bears the name of Chnubis, inherited from an Egyptian divinity—the god Khnum of Elephantine or, rather, the Theban Kem-âtef.[65] He is given the appearance of a serpent whose head—which is that of a lion—is surrounded by rays; reminding us, surely, of the god who, according to the astrological treatises, was also a celestial sign—namely, Ialdabaôth the evil power with the face of a *lion*?

It is true that one could find, in the iconography of Oriental cults known to the Roman world, images analogous to this monstrous Gnostic entity, and of still more impressive aspect. There is, above all, the fantastic relic which was found at the Janiculum in Rome, in the ruins of a temple dedicated to some

[63] Under the titles "Le Pythagorisme des Gnostiques" and "Le Tombeau du Viale Manzoni" in his *De Pythagore aux Apôtres*, pp. 85ff.

[64] C. Bonner, *Studies in Magical Amulets, chiefly Greco-Egyptian*, Ann Arbor, 1950; an excellent inventory of the engraved figures, but the interpretation needs revision in the light of the Gnostic mythology.

[65] According to my Communication (unpublished) to the Institute of Egypt, *Chnoubis, figure d'un dieu gnostique*, Dec. 1951.

Syrian gods.[66] This figurine represents a masculine personage with the arms held straight down its stiffened body, enveloped in a shroud leaving the face alone visible: a serpent is coiled seven times around the legs and torso of this pseudo-mummy, its head rising just above the figure's cranium. Seven eggs were found, in position, just where they had been deposited upon this statuette, precisely between each of the reptile's coils. As Franz Cumont has observed, the seven coils of this serpent suggest the seven barriers of the planetary spheres which the soul must successfully pass through to attain to immortality. Another, much more widely current religious image evokes the fantastic characteristics that the Gnostics ascribed to Ialdabaôth, the serpent with a lion's face—namely, that of Chronos, the master of infinite time, statues of whom have been found in the remains of various Mithraic sanctuaries.[67] The most impressive of these comes from Ostia and is now in the Vatican Library. I know of one of them in France, in the lapidary museum at Arles. This master of the heavens of the Mithraic religion, this Aïôn, presents the terrifying aspect of a being with a human body and a lion's head, standing in the grip of six or seven coils of a serpent whose head has just come into view above the monster's mane. If the Gnostics ever had a less edulcorate iconography than we see in the vault of the Aurelii, it doubtless included figures comparable to these monstrosities of the talismanic stones, the statuette of the Janiculum and the Mithraic Aïôn. In any case—if we are to go by their texts—it was just such images of divinities that haunted their imaginations.

REMAINS OF GNOSTICISM IN THE
RELATED LITERATURE OF ITS TIMES

To what we learn about Gnosticism from the literature of its adversaries, fragments of its own books and relics of its monuments, must be added the witness of various religious literatures more or less contiguous in time and place.

---

[66] Cumont, *Religions orientales* . . . , plate XI, fig. 3.

[67] R. Pettazzoni, "La figura monstruosa del Tempo nella Religione mitriaca" in *Accademia Naz. dei Lincei*, Anno CCCXLVI, Quaderno no. 15, 1950.

We cannot here enumerate the numerous apocrypha of the Old Testament, some of which contributed to the formation of Gnosticism, whilst others were perhaps authentically Gnostic or Manichaean. Of the latter, there are some that survived in versions that were toned down or mutilated, of which it is not very easy to make use. Among such writings, the most interesting is the *Acts of Thomas*, Manichaean in tendency, in which there are three very beautiful hymns: one of the nuptial banquet, glorifying the union of the soul with the Wisdom, "The Virgin is the Daughter of the Light . . . "; then, the invocation supposedly pronounced by the Apostle Thomas at the baptism of the Persian king Gundaphor: "Come, holy name of Christ . . . Come, Mother of the seven dwellings . . . !" and above all, the admirable Hymn of the Soul, "When I was a little child in the palace of my Father, . . ." where the quest of the wonderful Pearl, guarded by a dragon in the land of Egypt, is taken as a symbol of the descent of the Saviour into Matter in search of the soul.[68] Similarly, one finds in the apocryphal *Acts of John* a strange hymn, to the words of which the Saviour and his disciples dance a roundelay.[69] Later on in this apocryphon, the Christ reveals to the same Apostle that it was only in appearance that he had undergone the Crucifixion; and directs his gaze to the true Cross, shining in the heavens, which is not the wooden one of Golgotha but the wonderful "cross of light".[70]

Other mythical elements can be gleaned from the narratives of the descent of the Christ into hell—for example, from that of the *Gospel of Nicodemus*, also called the *Acts of Pilate*, which recount great revelations which Seth the son of Adam is supposed to have received at the gates of Paradise in the earliest age of mankind:[71] and, still more, from that of the *Book of the Resurrection of Christ*, fallaciously attributed to the Apostle Bartholomew.[72] One should

[68] Cf. G. Bornkamm, *Mythos und legende in den apokryphen Thomasakten*, 1933; G. Widengren, "Der iranische Hintergrund der Gnosis" in *Zeitschrifte f. Relig, und Geistesgeschichte*, 1952, pp. 97ff.; Jonas, *loc. cit.*, pp. 320–8.

[69] Quoted in M. R. James, *The Apocryphal New Testament*, p. 253.

[70] See above, chap. I, note 73.   [71] See M. R. James, *loc. cit.*, pp. 94ff.

[72] "The Book of the Resurrection of Jesus Christ by the Apostle Bartholomew"; Coptic text and English translation by W. Budge, in *Coptic Apocrypha in the Dialect of Upper Egypt*, 1913; cf. also M. R. James, *loc. cit.*, pp. 181ff.

also re-read the celestial visions in an *Apocalypse of St Paul*.[73]
Other survivals of Gnostic themes can be gleaned from the
episodes of the fall of Satan, shorn of his angelic power, such as
were included in certain Coptic homilies *Upon the investiture of
Saint Michael*. Some of these even put an account of the creation
of man into the mouth of Adam.[74] With no less profit one may
look through the many writings directly inspired by the legendary
history of Adam, of which the most famous is the *Cave of
Treasures*, a compilation of some of the earliest apocrypha; some
details have also been preserved from a *Scriptura nomine Seth*, a

[73] Cf. M. R. James, *loc. cit.*, pp. 525ff.
[74] *The Book of the Investiture of the Archangel Michael*, fictively attributed to
St John, figures among the Pierpont Morgan Coptic MSS. (Manuscripts of
Hamouli, XVIII and XIX); they are unpublished. An *Eulogium of St Michael
Archangel* attributed to Theodosus of Alexandria is given, in text and translation,
by W. Budge, *Miscellaneous Coptic Texts in the Dialect of Upper Egypt*, 1915.
These writings are well analysed in Caspar Detlef G. Müller, *Die alte koptische
Predigt*, 1954, pp. 106ff. To these must be added an unpublished text contained in
the Brit. Museum Oriental MSS. no. 6782: it is an alleged discourse of Gregory
of Nazianzus replying to Eusebius, a monk of Mount Ararat, who had questioned
him about a Manichaean teaching to the effect that St Michael had been substituted for Satan. Cf. Budge, *Coptic Apocrypha in the Dialect of Upper Egypt*,
1913, pp. xxix–xxx. Upon the survival of these themes among the Bogomils and
the Cathars, see H. C. Puech and A. Vaillant, *Le traité contre les Bogomiles de Cosmas
le prêtre*, Paris, 1945, p. 96, note 1. These books were known to be sufficiently
heretical for John de Parallos, in the sixth century, to have thought fit to put
them on the Index, together with a number of other, definitely Gnostic works:
cf. A. Van Lantschoot, article mentioned above in chap. 1, note 33.
    To these fragments of Gnostic myths preserved in various Coptic MSS, we
have reason to add here the contents of a parchment leaflet (ninth or tenth
century) kept at Naples in the Borgia Collection. It is listed no. CCLXXVII,
by Zoëga, *Catalogus Codicum copticorum* . . . , Romae, 1810, p. 625; but this
author translated only a few lines of it. I owe to the courtesy of the Rev. Canon
Arn. van Lantschoot the communication of the whole text of this unpublished
fragment. We do not know the author nor the age of the treatise it comes from:
we can only be sure that it belongs to a discourse against the reading of certain
apocrypha which are abundantly quoted in it—perhaps this was a homily con-
demning Gnostic books which was pronounced at the end of the fourth century
by Theodore of Tabennisi (which we refer to later, on p. 135).
    Here is a translation of some passages from the Borgia leaflet, in which the
orator quotes several passages of a heretical writing: ". . . that I have created
at the command of the Father" . . . "All things that are seen in heaven and
on the earth, it is I who created them all at the command of the Father." And
again, "It is to me that belong the body and the soul; to my Father belong the
breath and the spirit" . . . "We have taken from Heaven, a portion, we have
mixed and melted it with a portion of the Earth, and we have made Man"
. . . "Listen and learn how blind are they who write apocrypha, and how blind
are they who accept the same, who believe in them and thereby fall into great

book which had a special prestige because of its supposed authorization by Seth.[75]

One needs also to look through a Coptic homily, the *Discourse upon Abbatôn* attributed to the Patriarch Timotheus of Alexandria, and to compare it with a mediaeval Ethiopian writing, the *Commandments of the Sabbath* (the *Te'ezaza Sanbât*) still in use today among the autochtonous Jews of that country, the Falashas. There one finds the exposition of a myth according to which the Creator sent his angels to rob the Earth of the pure dust of Eden, or Dudalem,[76] from which he wants to fashion Adam—matter which the Earth refuses him with loud cries, until one angel, bolder than the rest, makes away with it. Is this not clearly derived—though it leaves out the supreme figure of the alien God—from one of those speculations we have seen among the Marcionites, in which the Creator of this lower world, and Matter, were two rival principles? Ethiopia would also furnish us with some more, though mutilated, survivals of Gnostic mythology: have not these same Falashas another curious apocalypse, preserved under the name of a mysterious Gorgorios

depths" . . . The same text goes on, "The Son said, 'When the Father had finished creating the twelve universes that none of the angels knew, then he created seven other universes'". And, "In the midst of the twelve universes are the ineffable good things", and "Outside these seven [universes] he created five universes more; the Spirits of the Power are in them. Then, exterior to the five, he created three more universes, which are those called the Dwellings of the Angels. These twenty-seven universes are all outside this heaven and this earth."

[75] Upon the apocryphal books written in the name of Adam, cf. the notice by J. B. Frey in *Dictionnaire de la Bible: Supplément*, vol. I, cols. 101-34; for the *Cave of Treasures*, see the Bezold edn. *Die Schatzhöle* . . . , 1883; see also Bidez-Cumont, *op. cit.*, vol. I, p. 46 and vol. II, p. 119; also Monneret deVillard, *op. cit.*, pp. 20ff.

[76] On Dudalem, cf. *Enoch* X, 4, where the Lord commands Raphael to put the rebellious angel Azazel in chains and cast him into the darkness of "the desert that is in Dudael", a place which (according to Geiger, in the *Jüdische Zeitschrift*, vol. III, 1864-5, p. 200), would be identical with that Bethkhaduda into which the scape-goat was driven according to the *Targum Ierushalemi*. Cf., yet again, fragments of the *Book of Noah* included in the *Book of Enoch* (chap. LX, 7-9), where mention is made of the desert called Duidaïn occupied by Behemoth "to the east of the garden wherein dwell the elect and the just, and from which God took away my grandfather [Noah]". Kohut and Charles tried (but upon insufficient grounds) to identify Duidaïn with the Land of Nod, which *Genesis* situates to the east of Eden. See P. Grelot, "La géographie mythique d'Hénoch" in *Revue biblique*, LXV, 1958, p. 44.

"who saw the hidden things"?—an attribute hardly to be understood unless it applied to some Gnostic prophet.[77]

However, these numerous texts can as yet teach us little about
the Gnosticism of which they preserve such traces; we shall need
to know rather more than we do about Gnosticism and its
literature before we can exactly estimate the nature and the
interest of the various vestiges they contain.

Meanwhile, we have at our disposal two rich literatures produced by two religions of certainly Gnostic derivation—Manichaeism[78] and Mandaeanism, about which modern erudition has
been able to enlighten us to a fairly satisfactory extent. Mani
(215–76) first acquired his doctrine from some of the teachings of
baptist sects which were then active in Mesopotamia; from
mythical elements that were originally Iranian and also, for the
greatest and most important part, from direct acquaintance with
Gnostic thought. Hence there are many family likenesses between
the scriptures of the Manichaean Church which have been rediscovered, and what we know, directly or indirectly, of Gnostic
doctrines. This makes us better able to reconstruct the leading
myths of the latter.

Mandaeanism—a baptist religion which is followed to this day
in Mesopotamia by some who call themselves "Christians of St
John" (an unmerited title, for they shame the very face of
Christ)[79]—also has an abundant literature in the Syriac language;
of which many texts have been edited by the learned. Here we
mention only: the *Ginza* (or "Treasure"), also called the *Great
Book*; the *Book of John*; the liturgical chants of the *Book of Souls*
(or *Qolastâ*); the *Diwan Abatur*, dealing with the journey through
the Purgatories; the *Haran Gawaïta*, precious for its traces of the
highly mythical history of the sect's origins; the *Book of the Signs
of the Zodiac*, and, lastly, the *Book of the Baptism of Hibil-Ziwa*.

[77] Cf. the "Discourse on Abbatôn by Timothy, Archbp. of Alexandria",
published by A. E. W. Budge, *Coptic Martyrdoms in the dialect of Upper Egypt*,
London, 1914, pp. 225–49 and 474–96. Translations of the *Te'ezâza Sanbat* and
of the *Apocalypse of Gorgorios* are given by W. Leslau in his *Falasha Anthology*,
Yale U.P., 1951. Upon these texts see J. Doresse, *L'Empire du Prêtre Jean*, vol. II
(*L'Ethiopie médiévale*), 1957, pp. 187ff.
[78] On Manichaeism, cf. below, chap. VII, note 7.
[79] On Mandaeanism, cf. below, chap. VII, note 15.

The teaching of the Mandaeans seems to be a late Gnosticism, doubtless systematized after the rise of Manichaeism, for it shows that influence. But the history of Mandaeanism is almost wholly unknown, and from comparisons between this cult and our obscure knowledge of Gnosticism it is difficult to draw reliable conclusions—at least for the present.

With the great mystical teaching—as much a philosophy as a religion—of the Hermetic books, Gnosticism, as we know it from the heresiologists and from direct remains of the sects, is thought to have had little relation. The corpus of Greek writings assembled under the name of Hermes Trismegistus is, on the whole (for one finds two divergent doctrines in it), illuminated by a clear and tranquil Hellenic philosophy quite unlike the doctrines of our heretics. The one feature in common with Gnosticism to be found in these books—written in the first centuries of our era, and therefore about the same period as the Gnostic literature—is that the supreme knowledge is defined, here also, as a means of spiritual elevation, as a "gnosis".[80]

On the other hand, Gnosticism seems to have been on very good terms with the rather different, popular Hermetism which inspired the works of alchemy, magic and astrology.[81] It is noteworthy that one Greek alchemical text which may date from the end of the third century or the beginning of the fourth, is indebted, by precise references, to the heretical literature and mythology: this is the opusculum of the pseudo-Zosimos *Upon the letter Omega.* If refers to the *Revelations* of Nicotheus, the prophet who is mentioned in one of the Coptic treatises in the Bruce Codex, and whose apocalypse figures among the writings combated by Plotinus and his disciples. It quotes, moreover, from the writings of Hesiod and Homer, and some Hebrew myths about Adam—a list which reminds us of the eclecticism ascribed to the Gnostics by the *Philosophumena.* The value of this little treatise may be better appreciated if we give a few quotations:

[80] Hermetism indeed defined itself as a "gnosis"; cf. Cerfaux, in *Dictionnaire de la Bible, Supplément,* vol. III, cols. 676–9.

[81] See, for the essentials, Reitzenstein, *Poimandres*; and Festugière, *Révélation d'Hermès Trismegiste,* vol. I, "L'Astrologie et les sciences occultes".

"The letter Omega . . . formed of two parts belonging to the seventh zone—that of Chronos according to the corporeal sense—is, according to the incorporeal sense something other, inexplicable, which only Nicotheus the Hidden has known. . . . Zoroaster asserts too boldly that, by the knowledge of all the higher things, and by the magical virtue of the corporeal sense, one averts from oneself all the evils of Fate, particular or universal. Hermes, on the contrary, in his treatise *On the Immaterial* attacks magic, for he says that the spiritual man ought not to seek redress for anything whatever by magic . . . nor do any violence against Fate; [he must] progress solely by striving to know himself, remaining firm in the knowledge of God, the Triad ineffable, and let Fatality do what it will to the mud that is attached to him—that is, to his body.[82] Thus, he says, by this manner of thinking and of living, thou shalt see the Son of God becoming all things, for the good of pious souls, to draw the soul out of the realm of Fatality and raise it up to the incorporeal. . . . Penetrating through all bodies, illuminating the intellect of everyone, he gives them the urge to ascend towards the blessed region in which the intellect dwelt before becoming corporeal. . . ." Upon the subject of the First Man, this Zosimos writes: "The Chaldeans, the Parthians, the Medes and the Hebrews named him Adam, which, being interpreted, is virgin soil, earth red like blood, earth of flesh; one finds all that in the libraries of the Ptolemies, and they have made collections of these books in every temple, particularly in the Serapeum when they asked the high priest of Jerusalem to send them an interpreter,[83] who translated all the Hebrew texts into Greek and Egyptian. . . . Thus it is that the first man, who amongst us is called Thoth, has been called Adam by those people, a name taken from the language of angels. Moreover, those people named him thus for

[82] Festugière points out that this passage in the text of Zosimos (of which he gives a translation and analysis) gives forth a Christian sound; see his *Révélation*, p. 266, note 6; the text of Zosimos is also commented upon in Reitzenstein, *Poimandres*, pp. 192ff.

[83] This legend contradicts the well-known tradition that the High Priest Eleazar (and not Anesas) sent seventy interpreters to translate the Old Testament into Greek. It is in any case certain that the O.T. was well known in Egypt as early as the age of the Ptolemies.

the symbolic value of the *four* letters, that is, elements, drawn from the totality of the sphere." Zosimos then explains that the letters A–D–A–M correspond to the four cardinal points and the four elements.[84] "Therefore the carnal Adam is named Thoth as regards his external shape; as for the man who dwells within Adam—the spiritual man—he has both a proper name and a common name. His proper name is still unknown to me today; indeed, only Nicotheus the Undiscoverable has known it. His common name is Phôs."[85] Zosimos then quotes a myth which may well have been taken from a Gnostic treatise: "When Phôs [that is, Light] was taking a walk in Paradise, the Archons persuaded him, at the instigation of Fate—by pretending it was all without malice or much importance—to put on the body of Adam which they had just completed, a body born of Fatality and formed of the *four elements*. Phôs, being himself without malice, did not refuse, and they preened themselves upon the thought that they would henceforth hold him in bondage." But after thus enslaving the Light-man, continues Zosimos, Zeus sent to the Light another bond—Pandora, "she whom the Hebrews call Eve".

We must not underestimate the significance of the references to writings of Zoroaster so frankly included in this little work, which in itself constitutes an admirable little anthology of a Gnostic literature that we have lost, but that was doubtless the most important. Plotinus and his disciples—to cite them yet again—also discovered, together with the *Allogeneous* writings used by the Gnostics whom they combated, certain *Revelations*, one under the name of Zoroaster, and the other under that of Zostrian, another Persian magus from whom, according to some

[84] Cf. the paraphrase of the same myth, as it appears in the commentary on Zosimos' treatise *Upon Action* by Olympiodorus of Alexandria, in Berthelot and Ruelle, *Collection des anciens alchimistes grecs*, *Textes*, p. 89, and *Traductions*, p. 95. In Olympiodorus already appears the alchemical interpretation of this theme, which was destined, through him, to be propagated in mediaeval Latin. Cf. such indications as "Adam, red earth, mercury of the wise, sulphur, soul, natural fire; Eve, white earth, living earth, philosopher's mercury, root of moisture, spirit", pointed out in the *Bibliothèque des Philosophes chimistes*, vol. IV, 1754, pp. 570–8.

[85] The Greek word *phôs* signifies, according to its accentuation, either "light" or "man".

traditions, Zoroaster was descended.[86] Porphyry and Amelius even showed proofs that their adversaries had either composed or, more probably, compiled these alleged revelations at an epoch which might have been quite recent. Manichaean literature, too, numbers Zoroaster among its prophets, on the same level with Jesus.

These allusions to Zoroaster, for us evocative of the lost Gnostic writings, moreover tempt us to suppose that Gnosticism borrowed something from another very singular literature of which, unfortunately, only some fragments remain: these are writings composed in Greek and headed with the names of the Magi Zoroaster, Ostanes, Hystaspes. J. Bidez and Franz Cumont have systematically reassembled the scattered fragments of this which survive,[87] and often, in the myths that they retell, we can see that the beliefs inspiring them were authentically Iranian. Some of the myths are about the formation of the universe by two opposite principles, Light and Darkness: others recall the sending-down into this lower world of a Saviour born of the seed of Zoroaster. Furthermore, from this literature there proceeded a number of more and more confused traditions to the effect that Zoroaster, when necessary, changed his appearance in order to identify himself with the prophet Seth, the son of Adam, and that his descendant Saoshyant became a representation of Jesus.[88] This was found to justify—rather needlessly—the journey made by the Magi whom the star guided to the stable at Bethlehem. It also helps to explain why the Gnostics labelled some of their writings, that are now lost, with the names of Zoroaster and Zostrian, as well as of Seth and Adam.

Let us not forget that the *Chaldaean Oracles*, from some of the ways in which they speak of the supreme God, of the sources and of the abysses of the world of light, seem to be inspired by the same ideas as those developed in the last part of the Bruce Codex.

[86] Cf. Arnobius, *Adversus nationes*, I, 52: Armenius Zostriani nepos. . . .
[87] J. Bidez and Franz Cumont, *Les Mages hellénisés*; *Zoroastre, Ostanes et Hystaspe d'après la tradition grecque*, vols. I and II, 1938.
[88] Bidez–Cumont, *op. cit.*, vol. II, pp. 128 and 130; U. Monneret de Villard, *op. cit.*, chaps. I and II.

Perhaps the *Oracles* were influenced by Gnostic literature; they date from a period when the latter was in full bloom . . . but one would have to know more about the conditions in which they were composed.[89]

From these same centuries have come down to us a quantity of magical, alchemical and astrological texts whose origin and history elude us almost completely. They survive in Greek, in Coptic, in Arabic and even in Latin translations. The majority of these writings borrow myths, divine personages and rituals from one another quite regardless of religious frontiers: it follows that they are considerably entangled. The interest attaching to some of these manuscripts has not escaped the historians of Gnosticism, for the entities mentioned in them are often, indeed, those of the great Gnostic speculations (and did not Gnosticism, in return, include a great many of the practices and prayers of the magicians and astrologers?). For instance, one long formulary[90] elaborates a vision of fourteen heavens, the lowest of which is borne up by four angels. The Father is enthroned on high, robed in white, a crown of pearls upon his venerable head. Before him is a cloud of light, in which he dwelt before undertaking the Creation, a cloud that is called Marmarô and Marmarôth; it is the abode of the Spirits of the All-Powerful; it is also the worshipped Virgin in whom, at the beginning, the Father hid himself. . . . Reitzenstein has justly pointed out the contributions from Gnosticism, and also from Judaism, in this composition.

Often, too, in these rituals, great entities intervene who derive still more directly from Gnostic myths—Harmozel, Oroïael, Daueithe, Heleleth; and also the seven powers of the planets. Like the Gnostic speculations, these rituals incorporate innumerable hierarchies of angels, archangels and dominations who, with their rustling wings and their chanting, surround the Lord Iaô-Sabaôth on his heavenly throne. At the same time

---

[89] Hans Lewy, *Chaldaean Oracles and Theurgy*, Cairo, 1956; W. Kroll, *De oraculis Chaldaicis*, Breslau, 1894; Franz Cumont, in *Lux Perpetua*, pp. 273-4.

[90] The allegedly Gnostic treatise "Rossi" (so called from the name of its first editor). Translation in M. Kropp, *Ausgewählte koptische Zaubertexte*, vol. II, pp. 175ff; for its Gnostic elements see Reitzenstein-Schaeder, *Studien* . . . , p. 109.

there is an admixture of gods and demons from other origins, of whom the most characteristic is Seth, originally an Egyptian god.

In the Pharaonic religion Seth was the great enemy of the other principal gods; of Osiris, of Isis and of Horus. In this character he was ritually cursed in the great myths and in ceremonies held in the great temples.[91] However, he also had his own cult, in some places officially: some of the Pharaohs—the Sethi— even claimed him as the patron god of their dynasty. We can read, in Plutarch's treatise on *Isis and Osiris* (§§ 30–33 and 49–50), an exegesis of the mythical relations between Seth and Osiris, derived from sources which seem to have been quite authentically Egyptian, in which we find what is almost a Gnostic dualism. In the magic of the later period Seth is identified with the monstrous Greek genie Typhon, son of Tartarus, who has a serpent's body. He is supposed to have an ass's head, a feature which recalls the elongated snout and long ears of some African animal, with which Seth is sometimes represented in Pharaonic iconography. More often he seems to be identified with a sort of headless demon whose eyes are placed in his shoulders, the Akephalos.[92]

In the Gnostic myths which transform the God of *Genesis* into an evil god, and similarly turn various other values of Biblical doctrine upside down, this Seth—the enemy of the chief Egyptian gods—acquires a definite position.[93] One may even wonder whether, perchance, some of these myths did not bring him into such contact with his homonym, Seth the son of Adam, as to

[91] Cf. the article "Seth" in Bonnet, *Reallexikon der ägyptischen Religionsgeschichte*, 1952; P. Montet, *Le Drame d'Avaris, Essai sur la pénétration des Sémites en Égypte*, 1940; S. Schott, *Bücher und Sprüche gegen den Gott Seth*, fasc. 1 and 2, 1929 and 1939 (in *Urkunden des Aegypt. Altertums, Sechste Abteilung*); figures of Seth with an ass's head: Marianne Guentch-Ogloueff, "Noms propres imprécatoires" in *Bulletin de l'Institut français d'Archéologie*, Cairo, vol. XL, 1941, pp. 127ff.

[92] K. Preisendanz, *Akephalos, der kopflose Gott*, Leipzig, 1926.

[93] Thus, in these syncretic conceptions, the Egyptian myths had undergone the same inversion as had the traditional values of *Genesis*; the originally "good" god Osiris, of whom Seth was the enemy, became identified with Sacla-Ialdabaôth the wicked demiurge. Cf. above p. 51, citing the *Philosophumena's* account of the Peratae.

create some confusion between them. That is not impossible; we shall find later some curious traces of a cult of this Seth-Typhon presiding over Judeo-Gnostic rituals in which Adam plays the leading part. That this cult came to be actually codified is attested by the existence of Egyptian figurines of the god Seth, cast in bronze, which are perfectly appropriate to it. The most significant represent the god walking with the hieratic gait, his body girt with a loin-cloth and surmounted by a head which has not, now, the muzzle of the mythic "Sethian" animal commonly assigned to Seth in the Pharaonic tradition, but the ass's head much more rarely met with. There is no doubt about the identification of the god worshipped in this guise, as one of the great figures of Gnosticism: the pedestal is engraved with the name Aberamenthô, which denoted Jesus.[94]

To show what relations already existed between Gnosticism and the more confused magical literature in which this fantastic demon appears, let us read, for instance, an incantation entitled "The stele of Jêou the Painter",[95] the text of which is preserved in a Greek papyrus. The "headless" god is there referred to as creator of earth and heaven, of the night and the day . . . , he is identified with Osiris-Onnophris, the Egyptian god of the other world. It is said that he judges the just and the unjust; that he created all that is masculine and all that is feminine. And then the magician, identifying himself with Moses, invokes the god Osoronnophris, saying to him, "This is thy true name, which thou hast bequeathed to the prophets of Israel"; afterwards calling upon him by the names of Arbathiaô, Seth, Iaô, Sabaôth and Abrasax. . . .

Are we amazed at this mixture of Jewish and Egyptian elements? But did not the Greek historian Manetho say that Moses had been a priest of Osiris in Egypt?—which shows that such a belief was current in fairly early times.[96] And does not the Talmud also suggest that in the second century of our era there were Biblical manuscripts in "demotic" writing—that is, in the latest,

[94] G. Roeder, *Bronzefiguren*, 1957; § 99c and Pl. 72g.
[95] Reitzenstein, *Poimandres*, p. 184. For another example of these Sethian rituals, see S. Eitrem, *Papyri Osloenses*, fasc. I, Oslo, 1925.
[96] Quoted by Reitzenstein, *Poimandres*, p. 185.

most popular form of the old hieroglyphic script?[97] Moreover, one can point to some *Ptolemaic Books* in Greek, which combined the Egyptian theology with the Jewish.[98]

With this, let us take our leave of the Seth of the magic formulas—the Seth of those handbooks of incantation which carried his name and his cult throughout the Roman world[99]—and, rising above this category of somewhat barbarous writings, let us turn our attention to some texts of a higher kind of magic which disclose facts of more importance for the history of Gnosticism.

We were able to note, in our survey of the authentic Gnostic writings (particularly in the case of the *Pistis-Sophia*), that Biblical elements were associated with several Egyptian figures, some of infernal beings; but there was also, for instance, that fantastic opening of the heavens through which the Saviour and his disciples behold the ships of the sun and the moon, which belongs to a mystic conception inherited from the most ancient Pharaonic beliefs.[100] In the world to which these writings transport us there were two impressive Wisdoms which claimed to eclipse all the others: one had to endeavour systematically to connect, with one or the other of these, any myth whatever upon which one wanted to confer prestige. Thus, we find an alchemical manuscript entitled *A genuine Discourse by Sophe* [that is, Cheops] *the Egyptian, and by the god of the Hebrews, The Lord of Powers Sabaôth*; "for there are two sciences and two wisdoms: that of the Egyptians and that of the Hebrews".[101] One can clearly discern, in all this

---

[97] Reitzenstein, *Poimandres*, pp. 185–6; since this book was written, an Aramaic text transcribed into Egyptian script (demotic) has been discovered; and some quotations from the *Psalms* appear in the hieroglyphic texts on the Temple of Petosiris at Hermopolis (G. Lefebvre, *Le Tombeau de Petosiris*, Part I, Cairo, 1934, pp. 37ff. An influence from the Biblical *Genesis* is discernible in the cosmogonic texts incised on the portal of the sanctuary of the primordial gods (the little Temple of Medinet Habu) in the Theban necropolis; see below, chap. VI, note 38. Lastly there are more and more numerous evidences that the Coptic language served in the first place for Egyptian translations of the Old and not the New Testament.

[98] Reitzenstein, *op. cit.*, p. 186.

[99] R. Wunsch, *Sethianische Verflûchungstafeln aus Rom*, 1898; A. Audollent, *Defixionum Tabellae*, 1904.

[100] Cf. above, notes 14 and 15.

[101] Reitzenstein, *op. cit.*, p. 187.

magical, alchemical and astrological literature, a competition between two rival currents of thought, one Judaizing and the other Egyptianizing. Fr Festugière, in his *Revelation of Hermes Trismegistus*,[102] quotes the following sentence from a magical text full of salty sayings: "It is this very book which Hermes plagiarized when he named the seven perfumes of sacrifice in his sacred book entitled *The Wing*." But the book which Hermes— herald of the doctrines attributed to the Egyptian Thoth—is accused of having stolen, is a magical writing entitled the *Book of Moses*. Here we are observers of the active competition between two rival schools, one of them authentically Jewish, whilst the other persistently steals the myths propagated by the former group and stamps them with the name of Hermes Trismegistus, thereby claiming them as Egyptian. One could find many other proofs of such plagiarism in the sometimes closely parallel traditions handed down under the names of Enoch, of Seth, sometimes of Hermes.

One good example is furnished by two parallel versions, only slightly different, of a mystical prayer preserved on some Greek magical papyri. E. Peterson was able to compare and analyse these texts with excellent insight: in the Judaizing version (the older of the two) he discovered the outlines of an archaic Gnosticism which calls for a few words of description.

This is a prayer for salvation—of the kind called a "stele" in one of the most widely-used terminologies—and seems to be taken from a more important, secret work of which we have no knowledge.[103] From its liturgical form it should belong to a rather curious cult of Seth-Typhon in which, it appears, all kinds of mysteries were celebrated[104]. The celebrant who recites this particular incantation identifies himself, mythically, by the words that he pronounces, with Man, "the most beautiful creation of the god who is in heaven", who is said to be "made of spirit, of dew and of earth"; and who must therefore be Adam. From the terms of this prayer, man is longing to escape from Fate and

[102] Festugière, *op. cit.*, p. 288.
[103] E. Peterson, "La libération d'Adam de l'Aνάγκη" in *Revue biblique*, 1948, pp. 199ff.
[104] Peterson, *loc. cit.*, p. 200 and note 3.

return to his original form and to the spiritual state from which he has fallen. The Gnostic character of the text is still more evident when we find that the god who is invoked is named the Propatôr, the Pro-Father, the Aïôn who dwells in the zenith of heaven; he is described as the master of the Pole enthroned upon the constellation of the Chariot—points that identify him with the Biblical Sabaôth upon his throne and in his chariot. He is served by myriads of angels, and near beside him is the aeon Sophia. Adam is proclaiming, in this invocation, that he knows the divine name of salvation from the Demon of the air, and from Fate.

The interpretation of this prayer that Peterson was able to arrive at helps us to understand two other and more obscure texts. It explains why, in the Greek magical papyrus Mimaut (III, 145, 147), a prayer addressed to Helios is also phrased as though it were spoken by Adam. Similarly, in the famous Greek formulary commonly referred to as the *Mithraic Liturgy*,[105] it enables us to identify the mythical being from whose mouth its incantations are supposed to proceed; we can recognize him from certain details—he is "a perfect body", he has been made by the *right hand* of the divinity, in short, he is Adam. Born of the impure Womb, he is lamenting over his misfortune, and still expressing the hope that psychic power will be restored to him when the Fatality dispensed by the spheres will have been abolished. Then he will recover his immortal nature!

E. Peterson has, moreover, the great merit of having replaced these beliefs in the specific mystical system from which they come. Its constantly recurring theme is that of the ascent of Man towards heaven,[106] and is analogous to that of the ascension into Paradise which is one of the essential features of a mystical conception of Adam well known in the ancient Rabbinical literature. It was so widely believed in Judaism that some perfect teachers,

[105] The text speculatively described as a Mithraic liturgy or ritual has nothing to do with the Mithraic mysteries, according to Franz Cumont. Fr Festugière, who has more happily called it *Recette d'Immortalité* (Prescription for Immortality), translates it in his *Révélation* . . . , vol. I, pp. 303ff. This "liturgy" has some family resemblances to the Jewish mysticism of the great Hekhaloth (see our chap. VII, p. 290).

[106] Concerning these visions, see Festugière, *La Révélation d'Hermès Trismégiste*, vol. II, *Le dieu cosmique*, Paris, 1949, pp. 442ff.

identifying themselves with Adam, had been caught up into heaven, that an echo of this doctrine can even be found in the second *Epistle to the Corinthians* (XII, 2-4): "I know a man in Christ who, fourteen years ago, was caught up to the third heaven—whether in the body or out of the body I do not know, God knows. And I know that this man was caught up into Paradise . . . and he knew things that cannot be told, which man may not utter." This mysticism is still more in evidence in the *Book of Enoch*. At the same time, it is specially well represented among our Gnostics: Seth, Marsanes and Martiades, Nicotheus and other prophets were said to have been similarly caught up into heaven. Mere coincidence? It cannot be: we have proof that the Coptic Gnostics had a precise knowledge of these theories. As Peterson reminds us, the Rabbinical literature teaches that the Perfect one at the completion of his ascension becomes a little Iaô; and this teaching about the little Iaô, which appears in the Hebrew *Enoch*,[107] is found also in the first book of the *Pistis-Sophia*.[108]

According to Peterson, the earliest traces of this mysticism date back to the beginning of the Hellenistic age; they already appear[109] in the Biblical *Book of Wisdom* dating from about a century before our era. It is, moreover, noteworthy that in the prayers analysed by Peterson, certain Iranian elements are discernible, one of which is of a cosmological order—namely, the notion of an intermediary principle separating the Light from the Darkness; this is Air—Vayu—which is here assimilated to Fatality.

The presence of this mysticism about Adam in a text, certain details of which evoke the Gnostic myths, is of the highest interest. Something of the real nature and origins of Gnosticism is at last looming through the mists of the past, thanks to the searching exegesis we have just summarized.

[107] Cf. Scholem, *Les Grands courants de mystique juive*, pp. 82-3 and p. 379, note 105: and Odeberg, *Introduction to 3. Enoch*, p. 189.

[108] In the translation by W. Till, p. 7, 1, 35, and p. 8, 1, 11.

[109] Cf. Dupont-Sommer, "Adam, père du monde . . ." in *Revue de l'Histoire des Religions*, 1939, pp. 18ff.; and Peterson, *loc. cit.*, p. 211; the passage in question from the *Wisdom of Solomon* is as follows: "She preserved the first formed father of the world, that was created alone, and brought him out of his fall, and gave him the power to rule all things" (X, 1-2).

THE MAIN FEATURES OF GNOSTIC DOCTRINE

I would like to complete this picture of what was known about Gnosticism before the discovery of the manuscripts at Chenoboskion by outlining, in a few words, the main features of the Gnostic religion so far as one can define them from study of the previously known documents and of the heresiologists. For this we must take account of a study by Professor Puech, which sums up the most positive conclusions that a historian of the Gnostic problem could then arrive at. I refer to the article on "Gnosticism and Time" which appeared in 1952.[110]

There have been broadly two hypotheses about the origin of Gnosticism. Many historians have thought that this religion was merely a heresy that arose and developed within Christianity; but this theory has the defect of being hardly compatible with the facts—such as, for example, the existence of a Gnostic sect like that of the Mandaeans with their essentially anti-Christian attitude.[111] That is why other historians, seeing that there are some myths of characteristically Gnostic content which were equally well developed in both Judaism and Islam, have supposed that these various doctrines were all derived from the same stock of myth and imagery inherited from some identical source before the beginning of our era. To find this source they have looked to Egypt, to Babylonia and Persia, sometimes even to India. To admit this second hypothesis would amount to believing that the Gnosticisms which claimed to be Christian, far from being heresies generated within the religion of the New Testament, were in fact alien cults that crept into it as a result of more or less fortuitous contacts.

Now, if we find that the notion of Time is used as the basis of Professor Puech's analysis, this is because it enables him to identify, better than could the historians who first sought to ascribe independence and originality to Gnosticism, the basic elements that distinguish it from the chief surrounding currents of thought—with which others, again, had confused it. The

[110] H. C. Puech, "La Gnose et le Temps" in *Eranos-Jahrbuch*, XX, 1952, pp. 57ff.
[111] According to the Mandaeans, Jesus was a prophet of falsehood, whose imposture had been exposed by Anôsh-Uthra.

Photo: *Jean Doresse*

TOGO MINA AND THE AUTHOR DECIPHERING THE FIRST
MANUSCRIPT, OCTOBER 1947

CAST OF A CARVED GEM REPRESENTING THE DEMIURGE IAÔ,
MASTER OF THE SEVEN HEAVENS

(Twice actual size.)

The Demiurge is shown as a monstrous being with the head of a cock and limbs
in the form of serpents. The inscription is the formula ABRASAX. In the circle
of the shield held by the Demiurge is engraved a magic sequence of voyels.

MEDAL IN LEAD REPRESENTING ON ONE SIDE THE DEMIURGE
IAÔ, AND ON THE OTHER THE SPHERES OF THE SEVEN HEAVENS

(Actual size.)

The Demiurge is shown under the same aspect as in the gem above.

Collection du Musée Guimet, Paris.
Photos: Jean Doresse.

attitude of the Gnostic towards Time was in function with his beliefs; it reflected his conception of the world and all the myths unfolding within it. By analysing his notion of Time, therefore, it was possible to go farther than we had yet managed to do in the understanding of this doctrine for which the documents were so few and contradictory. In fact, Professor Puech showed that by its notion of Time, Gnosticism is absolutely distinct from both Hellenism and Christianity. Hellenism was characterized by a notion of Time that was cyclic, circular, "perpetually repeating itself . . . under the influence of the astronomical movements which decide and regulate . . . its course".[112] But in Christian thought, Time is rectilinear, it is a scroll unrolling itself irreversibly from the Creation straight on to the end of the universe. Whereas Gnosticism, taking its conceptions as a whole, never adapted its outlook to either of these two notions of Time.

Among the essential features of Gnostic doctrine, one of the most important is the opposition that it affirms between the created world and the supreme God. The entire universe of sensory experience is condemned as evil; the good, the perfect divinity is foreign to it. The power which rules over the cosmos is a god who is weak, ignorant, even perverse—a monstrous Prince of Darkness. What a gulf lies between this misshapen world and the Greek conception of a beautiful, good and ordered universe to which a Plotinus, for example, was devoted! In this base world, dominated by Fatality, where Fate is determined by great celestial figures and above all by the planets (the Archons), man is a slave, imprisoned and in chains. He is suffering, shut up in the flesh. That is why one of the stages of salvation is to be the deed by which Jesus—as we read in the *Pistis-Sophia*—will one day abolish Fatality by reversing the rotation of the spheres, thus counteracting their effects. For Fatality is inherent in cyclic Time—the time belonging to this base world, to what is created; whereas the higher world is timeless. Between the one and the other there is a limit, a frontier, which is in principle absolute and unpassable. Hence the anxious fear of the Gnostic, Mandaean or

[112] Puech, "La Gnose et le Temps" (*loc. cit.*), p. 59.

Manichaean, confronted with duration: this finds unusually powerful expression in a text quoted by Hans Jonas, which we mention here although it belongs to one of the great Mandaean books: "In this world (of Darkness) I was living for a thousand myriads of years, no one knowing that I was there . . . the years followed the years, the generations the generations: there was I, and they knew not that I was dwelling here in their world!"[113]

When the Saviour, under whatever name he presents himself, brings the revelation of the higher world to his elect, he first discloses to them the utter depravity of their bodies and of the creation in which they are prisoners: by the same token he reveals to them the falsity of the god of the Old Testament and of the Law to which the latter has subjected them. This complete over-turning of the values proclaimed by tradition even led certain sectaries to venerate those who in the Old Testament were accursed—the Serpent, Cain, the Sodomites. . . . Another moral consequence was that actions forbidden by the wicked demiurge became either indifferent or even means to salvation. Quoting some terms he found in St Irenaeus, Professor Puech writes, upon this point, "the Gnostic attitude led to a *contrarietas et dissolutio praeteritorum*".[114] The Gnostic myths led, indeed, to the conception of a man serving two gods—one good and one evil—and having two souls; one heavenly, the other a material soul put into him by the demons to make him sin. It follows, similarly, that the purpose of Gnosticism is the uplifting of a being who is good, but fallen—i.e., salvation.

The point of departure for mystical thinking is, to a Gnostic adept, the sense of Evil that is persecuting him: "Whence comes evil?" "Why does it exist?" Hence the Gnostic wishes to escape from Time which is also, to him, a defilement. He longs to free the spirit and the light within him from this "mixture". But the eschatology contained in the texts we have read is rather pessimistic: man has to pass through successive births, to undergo

[113] Puech, *loc. cit.*, pp. 92–3; also his *Manichéisme* . . . , p. 152, note 272; Jonas, *loc. cit.*, pp. 109–13.
[114] Irenaeus, *Adversus Haereses*, IV, XIII, 1.

reincarnation—which, in some of the Manichaean texts, becomes a sort of "decanting" process reminiscent of the Buddhists' *samsara*.[115] This eternal, or almost eternal, recurrence becomes indeed a "dance of death".

However, this universe, though its existence is the product of a degradation, is nevertheless destined to a still more supernatural salvation. By her own fault Sophia has made herself responsible for the creation of the lower world; she herself had felt attracted towards Matter and the depths. The salvation corresponding to her fall will be an intervention of the Timeless into the temporal. The Gnostics, in their exile here below, ask themselves: "Who am I, and where am I? Whence have I come, and why did I come hither?" In response to their anxiety, they are vouchsafed, in secret, a revelation of the higher world—the "gnosis". This "gnosis", moreover, is to be not so much a "knowing" as a remembering; it is to awaken the neophyte, to recall him to what was his original nature, superior to matter: finally, it is to restore to him the everlasting part of his being and put him beyond all danger from the spheres and from their powers. The Saviours themselves who bring this revelation remain strangers in the world of Time: when the Gnostics assign this character to Jesus they make him into a kind of phantom who never puts on real flesh and blood; who escapes from the Passion.[116]

Some scholars, such as W. Bousset and R. Reitzenstein, had already emphasized (somewhat hastily) what the Gnostic doc-

[115] Puech, "La Gnose et le Temps", p. 90 and note 39; *Le Manichéisme* . . . , p. 179, note 360. The theme of reincarnation appears also among the disciples of Simon, of Basilides, and of Carpocrates.

[116] The Christ of the Gnostics is distinguished primarily by the part he plays in the higher universe as an *aeon*. His incarnation is expounded in, for instance, the *Pistis-Sophia*, where Jesus explains that it was he who visited the Virgin under the guise of the angel Gabriel, and how he implanted in her, to be made into a body for him, a power he had received from Barbelô; and, for the formation of his soul, another power he had derived from Sabaôth the Good. After the birth of Jesus on earth, whilst he was still a child, the Holy Spirit came to visit him in Mary's house and mysteriously merged with him. At the baptism—according to Basilides and the Manichaeans also—the Christ was substituted for Jesus. The Saviour escaped the Cross, upon which Simon of Cyrene was crucified instead of him (q.v. Basilides). Lastly it is from the resurrected Christ that the Gnostics claim to have received their teachings; and to him they ascribe a sojourn upon earth lasting from eighteen months to twelve years.

trines might owe to Iran. In view of the notion of Time within which these myths have developed, we are enabled to say something more about this. We know that the Manichaeans had a theory of Three Phases in the history of the universe: firstly, the anterior phase when the two opposing principles—the light filled with wisdom and the darkness of stupidity—exist separately; then a middle phase in which the light is attacked by the darkness and the "muddle" is produced; and, thirdly, the conclusive phase, which is that of a definitive restoration of the primordial separation.[117] This notion of Three Phases, derived from Iranian myths, underlies all the Gnostic systems we have been surveying, and this, even more than the idea of a γνωσις (of a supersensible and secret knowledge) is an element of originality in them.

It is indeed remarkable how Professor Puech, with a documentation so contradictory and so poor in authentic elements, has been able to make such clever use of the Gnostics' doctrine of Time, applying it as a criterion and thereby bringing to light the leading characteristics of their thought and beliefs so much more successfully than those who had previously attacked the problem by different methods. The notion of Time upon which a religion is built up is, indeed, one of those which its original texts disclose unknowingly, and which adverse critics never attempt to distort to their purposes.

There remain, however, many essential problems to which the historian sees no solution. To describe Gnosticism by outlining its general tenets is one thing: to estimate its impact and evolution is another, and more important. Even of the precise content of the Gnostic myths we are still in some doubt; none of the texts that Gnosticism has directly bequeathed to us deal with its fundamental subjects. Concerning the sects, their prophets, the authors of their sacred books and their daily religious life, we know next to nothing. The allusions to Nicotheus, Marsanes, Phosilampes, Strempsuchos, only reveal to us . . . our ignorance of the real persons hidden behind those great names. The adversaries of the

---

[117] The Three Phases which provide the framework of the Manichaean cosmology are clearly implicit in Gnosticism, and are indeed explicitly referred to in, for example, the *Pistis-Sophia* (see above, pp. 65–6). Cf. Puech, *Le Manichéisme* . . . , pp. 157–9, note 284.

Gnostics describe abominable practices, to which the sectaries themselves indeed refer—but only to denounce rival groups, whom they despised for being addicted to them.[118] What was the reality behind this? Were there indeed some sordid rituals which, however, were expressive of the myths about the "gathering-in" of the seed of light scattered among all beings? Or were these merely orgies signifying an utter contempt for the physical nature created by an "evil" god?—or more simply still, were the accusations vulgar calumnies? Of this we are still just as ignorant as we are about the possible origins of this religious movement—whether they were in Jewry, Egypt, Babylonia, Iran, the Hellenic mysteries or elsewhere. . . . And what were the actual contacts between our Gnostics and, for instance, the baptist or Judeo-Christian groups which preceded them, with Christianity and—which is also important—with Hermetism? In short, we still lack the data for a direct presentation of Gnosticism, its authentic founders and its great Revelations—which were, no doubt, those given out under the names of Nicotheus, of Zoroaster and Zostrian, of Seth and Adam, much more probably than those of Valentinus and Basilides.

[118] Cf. Fendt, *Gnostische Mysterien*, 1922, pp. 3–29.

CHAPTER III

THE STORY OF A DISCOVERY

IN September 1947 I arrived in Egypt for the first time, upon a brief mission undertaken at the behest of the French Institute of Archaeology at Cairo. My researches were aimed at elucidating the history of the ancient Coptic monasteries whose ruins are scattered over the Theban countryside; and I was filled with eager desire to steep myself in the life of this country towards which my vocation had been drawing me for many years past. Unhappily, this was the moment at which an epidemic of cholera had just begun: the administrative measures immediately taken in order to check the progress of this scourge complicated our plans and postponed my departure for Upper Egypt, with which all communications were severed. During the consequent delay, I was able to make leisurely acquaintance with the collections of the Coptic Museum, whose quite modern buildings are established in Old Cairo; that is, in the setting that is the most evocative of the ancient days from which their contents come. The Old City extends beyond the crumbling vestiges of Fustât, right to the south of the present capital: with its many ancient churches and a no less archaic synagogue, this suburb fills up what remains of a fortified enclosure which was constructed on the strand of the Nile by the Romans.

In this autumn of 1947, the Director of the Coptic Museum was Togo Mina, whose most dependable knowledge and judgment were evident in the arrangement of the textiles, sculptures, paintings and manuscripts entrusted to him.[1] Togo Mina knew his Christian Egypt well, and how to make it live again in memory. One morning, he opened a drawer of his desk, took out of it a voluminous packet, opened it, and showed me, in a book-cover

[1] J. Doresse, "Togo Mina, 1906–1949" in *Chronique d'Égypte*, XXV, 1950, p. 389.

of soft leather, some pages of papyrus filled with large, fine Coptic writing which might date from the third or fourth century of our era. He asked me if I could identify the contents of these pages. From the first few words I could see that these were Gnostic texts, one of which bore the title of *The Sacred Book of the invisible Great Spirit*, whilst further on was the title of a *Secret Book of John*. I warmly congratulated Togo Mina upon his extraordinary discovery, and immediately undertook, with his help, the task of putting these leaves in order, for they had become considerably muddled. In the end, I was able to recognize five distinct writings, of which—strange to say—two were of substantially the same treatise, written in the one case in the form of an epistle under the name of Eugnostos, and in the other transformed into a sort of gospel—an imaginary dialogue between Jesus and his disciples. The contents of such documents appeared at the first glance to be of even greater interest than the treatises in the Bruce Codex and the *Pistis-Sophia* of the Codex Askewianus. At the same time, two of the books thus coming to light were new versions of texts in the Gnostic codex in Berlin, for the publication of which we had been waiting in vain for the last fifty years.[2]

How had this strange document come into the hands of Togo Mina? It had been previously offered, by a dealer, to an eminent Coptic scholar in Cairo, a Dr G. Sobhy. He had the happy thought of sending the seller to the Coptic Museum, where Togo Mina, seeing that these pages were something out of the ordinary, took care not to let them go anywhere else.

With Togo Mina's permission, I at once made these interesting texts known to Canon Etienne Drioton on the one hand, and on the other to Professor Puech, whom Togo agreed to invite to join with us in a committee for their publication. Because of the fact that the new manuscript contained two texts of which parallel versions existed in the unpublished Berlin codex, we also thought it fitting to co-opt, for the production of an edition as definitive as possible, the competent aid of Professor W. Till, whom the German Academy had just commissioned to publish the Gnostic Manuscripts at Berlin.

[2] Cf. chap. II, pp. 86ff.

But it was essential to know where the new papyri came from. The site where it had been disinterred might of itself reveal particularly interesting information about the sects which had used these scriptures. One might also, perhaps, find some other and similar writings there. The most we could learn, from various persons who were well informed about everything to do with the trade in antiquities, was less than satisfying. They spoke mysteriously of a large find of manuscripts having been made near a hamlet called Hamra-Dûm, well to the north of Luxor: unfortunately, they said, the peasants had burnt some of them to brew their tea. Of the alleged existence of these other documents, one tangible proof did emerge: an antiquary, Albert Eid, had acquired a number of pages rather similar to those in Togo Mina's keeping at the Coptic Museum. Apparently of later date, and more badly defaced, these pages contained undoubtedly Gnostic writings—a *Gospel of Truth*, an *Address to Reginos upon the Resurrection* and some other treatises new to us—less attractive, however, than the manuscript we had.[3] This second discovery had nevertheless its value. Togo Mina decided to advise the Council of the Coptic Museum to acquire this codex, and informed the holders of it that he would in no case be authorized to send a document of such interest out of Egypt.

But for this happy surprise, our enquiries led to no discovery of further information.[4] I went away to Upper Egypt; and had first to travel to Assiut by plane, the railway service from Cairo being still suspended. At Luxor I spent long weeks rambling over the ruins of Coptic monasteries, meanwhile making acquaintance

---

[3] Togo Mina, H. C. Puech and I have, since 1948, made known the contents of this manuscript: cf. Togo Mina, "Le Papyrus gnostique due Musée copte" in *Vigiliae Christianae*, II, 1948, p. 130; H. C. Puech and J. Doresse, "Nouveaux écrits gnostiques . . ." in *Comptes rendus de l'Académie des Inscriptions et Belles-Lettres*, 1948, p. 89; completed by J. Doresse and Togo Mina, "Nouveaux textes gnostiques coptes découverts en Haute-Egypte . . ." in *Vigiliae Christianae*, III, 1949, pp. 132-3 and 137, etc.

[4] With the exception of some fragments of pages written in the akhmimic dialect, possibly derived from the same find. Only by infinite patience has Mgr Lefort been able to restore some form to these vestiges, and thereby to reveal a few pages of the *Shepherd of Hermas*: cf. L. Th. Lefort, *Les Pères apostoliques en copte*, text and translation in the *C.S.C.O.*, vols. 135 and 136, Louvain, 1952.

with their neighbours, the great pharaonic monuments. In this region I ought to have been well placed to overhear any rumours about the circumstances in which our Gnostic manuscripts had been found, but no more precise information came my way. The silence that invariably hides the real circumstances surrounding great finds—and which we had thought we might break—was again impenetrable.

I did not get back to Cairo until shortly before the date of our return to Europe. Togo Mina was now definitely persuaded that there was nothing more to be discovered. The veil was therefore lifted, to disclose to public interest the manuscript acquired by the Coptic Museum; and on 11 and 12 January 1948 the Egyptian press briefly announced this new discovery, which made no great stir in a country so inured to archaeological marvels. When I had come back to Paris, Professor Puech and I made a report to the Académie des Inscriptions et Belles-Lettres, both upon the codex at the Coptic Museum and upon that of the antiquary Albert Eid. At the same time, Togo Mina published the same information at the Institute of Egypt.[5]

What we did not know was that other manuscripts *had* been discovered at the same time as those we had already secured. But they had remained hidden—why? Chiefly because of the intervention of a learned person, to whom three of these other manuscripts had been offered at a ridiculously low price—one hundred and ten pounds (Egyptian). On that occasion one of our colleagues had also had an opportunity of seeing them, and he was afterwards able to testify that these were indeed the documents that we should have been so delighted to discover. But this expert to whom they were offered refused them as of no interest, and mentioned them to no one else. It was a misjudgment like that which occurred in the case of the famous Manichaean manuscripts of Fayum twenty years earlier: these too, were carelessly rejected by another expert, who took them for Biblical texts of no interest,

[5] H. C. Puech and J. Doresse, "Nouveaux écrits gnostiques découverts en Egypte" in the *Comptes rendus de l'Académie des Inscriptions, Séance du 20 Fevr. 1948*, pp. 87–95. Togo Mina, "Le Papyrus gnostique du Musée Copte" in *Vigiliae Christianae*, II, 1948, pp. 129–36; J. Doresse, "Trois livres gnostiques inédits", *ibid.*, pp. 137–60.

5*

and were only recovered *in extremis* by the late Carl Schmidt, who was more intuitive—or less miserly.

As it happened, the Gnostic manuscripts which had been thus refused had not left Cairo. Perhaps because of what we had at last revealed about the value of the codex at the Coptic Museum, a highly cultured personage guessed what these writings were, and bought up all that she could lay hands upon. Less than a year after returning from my first journey to Egypt, I received from this person, in confidence, some photographs of manuscripts upon which my advice was solicited. The texts of which some passages were legible were such that my departure for Egypt was immediately arranged and organized by the competent authorities to whom I explained the situation. R. Dussaud and C. F. A. Schaeffer united in the effort to get me to Cairo without delay; and what I found there confirmed the hopes that these photographs had reawakened. It was not now a few isolated manuscripts that were shown to me, but half a score, almost all complete in their bindings of pliable leather. I was allowed to make no more than a rapid inspection of them—given just time enough to identify, to my personal satisfaction, the principal works they contained and to take notes of a few characteristic passages. Egypt was then at war with Israel, and on several occasions air-raid warnings (sounded on the slightest justification) cut short the few evenings upon which I was allowed access to the documents. However, I went on, from surprise to astonishment, until I had soon enumerated some forty new writings, some of them announced under sensationally attractive titles such as: the *Revelation of Adam to his son Seth*; a *Gospel of Thomas*; a *Paraphrase of Shem*; the *Interpretation of the Gnosis* . . . and the contents of some other treatises, of which the titles were lacking, afforded glimpses of still more impressive works. What was now reappearing, for the first time, was nothing less than the sacred library of an ancient sect, to all appearances complete. Pharaonic literature had never bequeathed to us a whole set of books so rich and homogeneous. The Manichaeans of the Fayum had transmitted to us only a few of their writings.[6] It is only the rich mediaeval libraries

[6] Cf. chap. II, note 40.

of Tuen Huang in Central Asia that have left us longer "runs" of their literature—and these treat of less forgotten subjects.[7] It was becoming important to steer this treasure-trove, not towards some foreign library, but into some purely Egyptian scientific institution, which, however, had to be one capable of putting the manuscripts into condition, of looking after them and arranging for their scrupulous publication. Consulted confidentially about this, Canon Drioton, Director-General of the Service of Antiquities, declared that such a treasure could not, in principle, go anywhere but to the Coptic Museum—unless, indeed, the authorities committed the unpardonable blunder of withholding the necessary funds, in which case it would be legitimate to authorize the export of the documents from Egypt, if the owner so desired. This business was all the more difficult to transact because, in the matter of antiquities, the Egyptian government has sometimes a tendency to exercise its right of confiscation, to avoid paying a fair price for certain treasures. However, this is an inconvenience that is so well known that no one in possession, however legitimately, of a valuable antiquity in that country dares to offer it to the authorities, but prefers to dispose of it in the clandestine market, whence it is exported.

Canon Drioton was very willing to take charge of the negotiations, in which I could play only a strictly scientific part, conforming strictly to his wishes in every other respect. It was not difficult to convince the owner that she ought not to keep the precious manuscripts to herself, nor offer them to foreign collections, but submit them to the competent authorities. This Miss Dattari—whose father had been a well-known numismatist—thus became willing to release the treasure she had withheld, and in the spring of 1949 she submitted the whole collection of documents to Togo Mina, who advised the Council of the Coptic Museum to acquire it. The Council then willingly commissioned

[7] The sands of Chinese Turkestan alone have preserved, as perfectly as those of Egypt, the written remains of ancient civilizations. At Tuen Huang, from caves that were walled up about A.D. 1035, P. Pelliot and Aurel Stein, separately, obtained more than 15,000 manuscripts dating between the sixth and seventh centuries. At Gilgit, a ruined Buddhist tower also contained a great number of manuscripts, some dating perhaps from the fourth century (seen by Jos. Hackin, then of the Citroën Mission).

me forthwith to draw up an expert description, more detailed than the first notes I had been able to make, and this second description remains, up to the present, *the only complete and direct inventory of the documents* that has been made: no other title of any work has yet been added to the list that I then prepared. Basing its case upon this report, which Canon Drioton and Togo Mina countersigned, the Council decided to acquire the manuscripts, and took the necessary steps to obtain from the Egyptian government a sum of money sufficient to disinterest Miss Dattari. I ought to add that this lady gave proof of the utmost goodwill, for, from the very day on which the Council decided in principle to buy the manuscripts, she kindly authorized me, with the approval of the Egyptian authorities, to make the discovery known to the Académie des Inscriptions et Belles-Lettres, and to other important learned societies, in the form of a summary of the report I had drawn up.[8]

Once they had been inventoried, the manuscripts themselves were provisionally put in order by me, and then placed, under seal, in a travelling-bag which their owner and Togo Mina agreed to entrust to the care of Canon Drioton. Already the specialists, lured by the first news we had allowed to be published, were waiting impatiently for further information. Already, indeed, thanks to the permission of the Egyptian authorities and also to the support given me on the French side by the Commission des Fouilles Archéologiques, the first pages of a critical edition of the

[8] J. Doresse, "Nouveaux documents gnostiques coptes découverts en Haute-Egypte" in *Comptes rendus de l'Académie des Inscriptions* . . . Paris, 1949, pp. 176–80; J. Doresse, "Une bibliothèque gnostique copte . . ." in *Bulletin de la Cl. des Lettres et des Sciences morales* of the Académie royale de Belgique, 5th series, 35, 1949, pp. 435–49; J. Doresse and Togo Mina, "Nouveaux textes gnostiques . . .": "La Bibliothèque de Chénoboskion" in *Vigiliae Christianae*, III, 1949, pp. 129–41; J. Doresse, "Une bibliothèque gnostique copte" in *La Nouvelle Clio*, I, 1949, pp. 59–70; J. Doresse, "A Gnostic Library from Upper Egypt" in *Archaeology*, III, New York, 1950, pp. 69–73; J. Doresse, "Douze volumes dans une jarre" in *Les Nouvelles Littéraires*, No. 1139, Paris, 30 June, 1949; J. Doresse, "Nouveaux aperçus historiques sur les gnostiques coptes: Ophites et Séthiens" in *Bulletin de l'Institut d'Egypte*, XXXI, 1948–9, pp. 409–19; J. Doresse, "Les Gnostiques d'Egypte" in *La Table Ronde*, No. 107, November, 1956, pp. 85–96; J. Doresse, "Le Roman d'une grande découverte" in *Les Nouvelles littéraires*, No. 1560, 25 July 1957. The first volume of a photographic edition of the original manuscripts has just been published by Dr Pahor Labib, *Coptic Gnostic Papyri in the Coptic Museum* . . . , vol. I, Cairo.

first codex, acquired in 1947 by the Coptic Museum, were being set up—a masterpiece of typography—in the press of the Imprimerie Nationale in Paris. That the study of the texts was, after this, delayed and postponed to the Greek calends was due to a series of calamities which had nothing to do with science, but which for seven whole years prevented the definite acquisition of the essential documents, and held up the publication of the codex that was already in the press. First, there was the assassination of Nokrashi Pasha the Prime Minister, which for long months kept all important business suspended. A new government having been constituted, it took the matter in hand, but unfortunately it then fell, at the critical moment when the excellent Ali Ayyub, minister of public instruction, was at last about to put at the disposal of the Coptic Museum a sum of fifty thousand Egyptian pounds, which would doubtless have sufficed to purchase the codices. Then, in October 1949, Togo Mina—who had taken all these delays too much to heart—died, after many months of illness: for a long while it was difficult to find a successor who would be competent to direct the Museum he had so much loved. Meanwhile, the incomplete but very precious manuscript in the possession of Albert Eid, which, through neglect, had not been sequestrated so rigorously as Miss Dattari's treasure, yielded to appeals emanating from abroad and escaped to Europe, where it was acquired by the Jung Institute at Zürich.[9]

The energetic and learned Taha Hussein, who in turn now became minister of public instruction, tried to hasten matters. He took the liveliest interest in the contents of these manuscripts, which I often had the pleasure of discussing with him; and he was hoping to put them at the disposal of the learned world as soon as possible. He decided to obtain a requisition for the documents, which would permit the study of them to be undertaken without waiting for the settlement of the financial question. But, like his predecessors, Taha Hussein had a run of ill-luck. In order to seize the manuscripts he had to have a new law controlling antiquities, which he accordingly drafted; but this was deferred

[9] Its "discovery" was then spoken of inaccurately, for we had called attention to this codex long before; cf. above, note 3.

again and again, and was promulgated only in the early summer of 1952. Only then did the handbag which had imprisoned the precious manuscripts since 1949, at last leave the Service of Antiquities for the Coptic Museum, to which a director had at last been nominated—Dr Pahor Labib. Did they now mean to open the priceless package, study its contents in detail, and all this regardless of the lawsuit which Miss Dattari, despoiled and indeed doubtless regarding herself as swindled, was bringing against the government? Yes, but this solution was so sudden and unexpected, that it came just as I had given up hope and was returning to France for the summer. Nor could I get back to Egypt before autumn.

The ensuing weeks were unexpectedly filled by the fateful events of the Egyptian revolution. Perhaps that occurrence can be justified from many points of view of more importance than that of the rchaeologists. But in this matter of the Gnostic papyri it had the most tiresome consequences. The great administration of pharaonic antiquities, which had been under the direction of French savants from the days of Mariette until those of Canon Drioton, was now entrusted to an Egyptian director—incidentally a remarkable man—Dr Mustapha Amer. Advantage was taken of the circumstances entirely to reorganize the Service, and to combine, under that one central authority, the hitherto independent administrations of the Coptic Museum, the Arabic Museum and the Arab Antiquities. In consequence, it was not until 1956, in spite of all the goodwill shown on one side and the other, that Dr Pahor Labib could see his way to deal with the problems of the Coptic Museum, which he now directed, or attend to the precious manuscripts entrusted to his care. At last, he was able to set up a new committee for their publication—different from the one previously mooted—which was to meet at Cairo in October 1956; but only two of the five European specialists invited by the Egyptian authorities could reply to this invitation in time; I myself received it too late to make the journey. The Committee met just before the outbreak of hostilities over the Suez Canal at the end of October; since which time it has not been possible to put the work of publication upon a sound footing. Must the scientific examination of the manuscripts once again be exposed to the storms and disorders of an uncertain future—a prospect all the more disquieting since the fragile leaves of papyrus are in great danger of deteriorating with time? In the above account I have passed in silence over a number of other annoyances which had to be endured. To make acquaintance with the rapacities and jealousies of the learned, which come growling obscurely around a discovery of this kind is anything but a soothing experience.

Does all this mean, then, that from 1947 until today the discovery of these invaluable writings has remained sterile? Far from it: we shall see, in this book, how much has already been done. Knowledge of some parallel texts from Chenoboskion, details of which I was able to give to Professor W. Till by agreement with the Egyptian authorities, helped him to complete the critical edition of the Gnostic manuscripts in Berlin, a publication for which the world had been waiting sixty years.[10] I have myself amplified, in various preliminary studies, the notes furnished by my initial inventory; I have drawn attention to the identity of an *Apocalypse of Zoroaster and Zostrian*, whose imposing title raises some significant problems;[11] and given some first glimpses of the contents of the *Gospel of the Egyptians*, of those of the *Epistle of Eugnostos*, and of the relation between this last text and the *Sophia of Jesus* where we find it in another form.[12] I have tried to give a better account of the exact nature of some Hermetic writings included in this vast collection of manuscripts;[13] and, lastly, my critical edition of the first codex—that which Togo Mina so happily acquired—has been ready for several years, and is only awaiting the good pleasure of the Egyptian authorities to be sent to the press.

[10] C. Schmidt and W. Till, *Die gnostischen Schriften des koptischen Papyru Berolinensis 8502*, Berlin, 1955.
[11] "Les Apocalypses de Zoroastre, de Zostrien, de Nicothée . . ." (Porphyre, Vie de Plotin, § 16), in "Coptic Studies in honor of W. E. Crum", *Bulletin of the Byzantine Institute*, II, 1950, pp. 255–63.
[12] "Trois livres gnostiques inédits . . .", *Vigiliae Christianae*, 1948, pp. 137–60.
[13] "Hermès et la Gnose: A propos de l'Asclepius copte" in *Novum Testamentum*, I, 1956, pp. 54–69.

Professor H. C. Puech also, from what I was able to impart to him of the original texts, has been able to make some discoveries of the greatest interest, particularly in respect of the *Gospel of Thomas*, which, by completing the impressive collection of them, has at last resolved the chief mystery of those "Sayings of Jesus" (*Logia Iesou*) which are not included in the canonical Gospels, but of which stray examples are to be found in all primitive Christian literature.[14] Professor Puech's recent report upon this subject to the Académie des Inscriptions et Belles-Lettres on 24 May 1957 has made that date lastingly memorable in the history of patristic studies.

Finally, from the Eid Codex, since known as the "Jung Codex", one of the contents has been published—the *Gospel of Truth*, which dates back, perhaps, (?) to the Gnostic Valentinus.[15]

Having listed these various writings, we prefer to be silent about a number of those published by various authors who—except in the case of the Jung Codex, to which several experts have given direct and enlightened attention—have been wholly dependent upon the studies that I published myself (though in many cases this was not acknowledged). The fact that it was impossible for me, so long as the documents had not been definitely "acquired" by the Egyptian authorities, to make known more than a small part of the discovery, certainly favoured the appearance, in certain quarters, of rash hypotheses about the new manuscripts and their bearing upon the history of Gnosticism. One fact in particular may well have misled interpreters in too much of a hurry—that is, the special attention given to one of the writings, the *Secret Book of John*; which we were more free to publicize, simply because another version of the same text, which happened to be in the Berlin Codex, had already been partly analysed in several articles by C. Schmidt and, as he had shown, it describes a cosmogony in close accord with a well-known

[14] H. C. Puech, "Un logion de Jésus sur bandelette funéraire" in *Bulletin de la Société Ernest Renan*, No. 3, 1954, pp. 126–9; and above all the report upon the *Gospel according to Thomas*, read to the Académie des Inscriptions et Belles-Lettres, 24 May 1957.
[15] *Evangelium Veritatis*, from the Jung Codex, edited by M. Malinine, H. C. Puech and G. Quispel.

THE COPTIC MANUSCRIPT OF THE *PISTIS-SOPHIA*, p. 143

(For translation, see page 327)

THE MAGIC PAPYRUS OF OSLO No. I, Column I

This shows the figure of Seth-Typhon-Aberamenthô, to be engraved on lead with a bronze stylus (as indicated by the Greek instruction above it) to accompany certain magic formulae. Fourth century, A.D.

Reproduced from *Papyri Osloenses*, fasc. I, S. Eitrem: *Magical papyri*, Oslo, 1925

description in St Irenaeus's treatise *Against Heretics.* The myths in question were also similar to those in the *Sacred Book of the invisible Great Spirit,* or *Gospel of the Egyptians,* and with those set forth in the *Sophia of Jesus*—writings which are also included in the first manuscript obtained by the Coptic Museum in 1946, and of which, therefore, we had been able since 1948 to furnish exact summaries. But all this amounted to no more than a few writings selected from a collection containing many others of which we were not authorized to publish anything except the titles. Certain authors, eager to have the glory of reporting what the Chenoboskion find might reveal, did not wait to learn more about it, but rushed into print with nothing to go upon beyond what had been published of the *Secret Book of John* and the other treatises in the first codex.[16] Omitting to emphasize the fact that as yet they knew *nothing* about some forty other texts beyond the titles, they built up theories that will not always survive the complete and integral disclosure of the documents as a whole.[17]

IN THE EGYPTIAN COUNTRYSIDE

One question with which we were concerned when dealing with that first manuscript at the Coptic Museum became still more important when we confronted the impressive mass of documents discovered soon afterwards. Did there exist, unknown to us, still more codices, or at least any stray leaves (two of our bundles were unbound and very incomplete), belonging to the same find? On this point, even today, one had better reserve judgment. Prudent collectors may well have been able to acquire portions of volumes and keep quiet about them. Above all, caution is necessary: some clever dealers may well take advantage of the prestige of the Chenoboskion discovery to obtain high prices for manuscripts supposedly derived therefrom, which are

[16] Cf. chap. II above, notes 43 and 44. I repeat that the Berlin Codex was accessible only after 1955.

[17] G. Quispel, to whom I had privately reported some details of the contents of the new texts, has since written, in his note "Die Reue des Schöpfers" (*Theologische Zeitschr.,* 5, 1949, p. 157), "Ich habe den koptischen Text unter Augen gehabt, kann ich aber natürlich vor der endgültigen Ausgabe nicht publizieren" ("I have had sight of the Coptic text, but naturally cannot publish it in advance of the authoritative edition"). This assertion is quite inaccurate.

really of different origin and of much less interest. Actually, although there have been a few more recent Egyptian discoveries of fairly valuable Coptic manuscripts, the supply from our strange library of Gnostic papyri seems, for the moment, to have dried up.[18]

Whence, precisely, did these documents come, and in what circumstances were they found? As we have mentioned, the information we collected in one way and another led us to believe that they were dug up near Hamra-Dûm, in the vicinity of Naga Hamadi, some sixty-odd miles from Luxor. They had been found buried in an earthenware pot near the site of the ancient townlet of Chenoboskion, at the foot of the mountain called Gebel et-Tarif. The discovery had taken place about 1945. Rumour added—as we have said—that two of these volumes had been used by the fellahs as fuel for making their tea, and that the rest had been sold for a trifling sum to the dealers who had taken them to Cairo. All this was mere indirect information, lacking precision or proof. Two main questions were worrying us: what was the exact nature of the place of discovery—was it a tomb, pagan or Christian, the ruins of a house or monastic building—and of what age? And then, under what circumstances could these documents have been buried?

The information I had obtained, during my journeys about Upper Egypt in 1947 and in the two following years, was rather vague. So at the end of January 1950 I visited the locality in question, to find out all that could be known about the conditions under which the find was made.[19] I was rewarded by the close acquaintance I made with one of the least known but most gorgeous of Egyptian landscapes; and also, when returning from Naga Hamadi to the Theban necropolis through the desert of

---

[18] Worthy of note, however, is the recent find of a codex of the fourth or fifth century, which contains, in archaic bohairic dialect, the *Gospel of John* and *Genesis* I–IV, 2, presenting some features which may be Gnostic . . . unless these peculiarities be due simply to the excessive literalism of a Coptic translator! (Papyrus Bodmer III, edited by R. Kasser in the *C.S.C.O.*, vol. 177, Louvain, 1958, cf. the Introduction, pp. xii–xiii.)

[19] J. Doresse, "Sur les traces des papyrus gnostiques": Recherches à Chenoboskion" in *Bulletin de l'Académie royale de Belgique, Classe des Lettres* . . . ., 5th series, 36, 1950, pp. 432ff.

Denderah, by a bite from a dog which, though it proved non-malignant, made me spend four weeks, as a docile patient, in the Anti-Rabies Institute of Cairo.

Too little known to archaeologists, the region of the present Naga Hamadi is by no means without interest. Its capital Hû—the Diospolis Parva of the Greeks—was for a few brief periods in antiquity, as also in the Middle Ages, a capital of Upper Egypt—of the Saʿid. It lost all its greatness after a plague, in the year 806 of the Hejira, had robbed it of more than fifteen thousand of its inhabitants. Hû is situated on the western bank of the river; but it was the neighbourhood around Chenoboskion on the eastern bank which became more particularly famous at about the epoch to which our papyri belong. Its celebrity is linked with the most ancient traditions of Christian monasticism. The Coptic name for the little town was Shenesit—the latest form of an Egyptian name which would signify "the acacias of (the god) Seth". The country would seem, therefore, to have been sacred to the divinity who, in pharaonic mythology, was opposed to Osiris, Horus and the other great gods. As for the Greek name of Chenoboskion, also borne by this locality about the beginning of our era, in translation this would refer to the "breeding of geese"; but it suggests some confusion; for an author of the first century—Alexander Polyhistor—tells us that there was no grass-land there for geese; and the inhabitants were said to have a great veneration for crocodiles, which were abundant.[20]

In the Roman period this town had been occupied by a military guard. Nevertheless, it became a wilderness, which was the fate of the neighbouring villages also, of Phbôu and Tabennisi. "Shenesit-Chenoboskion was then a desert village, grilling in the intense heat. There were not many inhabitants; only a few"—thus wrote a Coptic chronicler of the fourth century.[21] It was here, about the year 320, that the young Pachomius, liberated from a

[20] Fragment of the *Aigyptiaka* of Alexander Polyhistor, preserved by Stephen of Byzantium; published in the *Fragmenta Histor. Graec.*, III, fgt. 108.

[21] *Les Vies coptes de saint Pachôme et de ses premiers successeurs*; French translation by L. T. Lefort, Louvain, 1943, p. 83. The leading events in these biographies of Pachomius also appear in *Les Pères du désert*; texts selected and edited by R. Draguet, Paris (Plon), 1942.

Roman prison in the town of Antinopolis, became a professing Christian. He lived in a derelict brick-kiln a little way from the Nile; and they baptized him in a church near by. The earlier anchorites were there already—such as the aged Palamun, of whom Pachomius soon became a disciple, and the apa Ebonkh, who seems already to have been the director of some kind of community. Pachomius first received the tough instruction of Palamun, and then, instead of continuing to live as a hermit like his predecessors, he gathered other ascetics around him, for whom he drew up the first monastic rule. It was from this point that monasteries were soon to swarm far into the north—right to Alexandria—and far to the south, from communities created by Pachomius and his disciples.

The surroundings of Chenoboskion have been accurately described not very long ago by Mgr Lefort, who went there in search of traces of Palamun and Pachomius.[22] I may be excused, therefore, from describing them over again after my own search for mementoes of heretics and the hiding-place of their sacred books.

Below Luxor the Nile describes a wide curve westwards, in the neighbourhood of the town of Qenah and of the Temple of Dendera, for here it has to flow round the southern extremity of a lofty desert cliff known, at this point, as the Gebel et-Tarif. From thence it approaches the vicinity of Naga Hamadi by describing a complete semi-circle towards the south, before it resumes its course to the north-east. This second loop, nearly five miles in diameter, now encloses, between the river and the white cliff of the eastern desert, the dense, tall plantations of sugar-cane which have replaced the acacia plantations of former days. In this greenery are hidden the villages of el-Qasr, es-Sayyâd and ed-Dabba. Christians are very numerous here to this day.

Es-Sayyâd is almost on the site of the ancient Chenoboskion. Near to it, and not far from the Nile, a high, blank, massive wall surrounds a few churches and chapels clustered close together and surmounted by an enormous, fantastic bell-tower with latticed walls: this is the Deir anba-Palamun—the "monastery of the abbot Palamun". Further inland near Dabba rises a somewhat similar building, the Deir el-Malak, or "monastery of the Angel". Between these two "monasteries", now without any monks, stretches a little isolated desert which, according to the Coptic texts, was the site of the first monastic labours of Palamun and his disciples. A cave is still shown here, which is supposed by legend to have been a hermitage. To the north, far beyond the verdure of the tilled lands and past bushy orchards, which are enclosed by high walls still dominated by the square towers of great columbaries, there rises the enormous, abrupt cliff of Gebel et-Tarif, shutting off the whole horizon from west to east. On the railway that traverses this landscape, one passes for a few moments close to this rampart, formidable enough for André Gide to have recorded its mysterious aspect in his *Carnets d'Égypte*: ". . . walls of burning rock fissured with gorges into which Sinbad would have liked to adventure, and so would I."

But eastward the cliff suddenly curves back towards the north, and diminishes into the depths of the desert, farther and farther away from the Nile and its fertile plains. Upon that eastern slope of the mountain, near the ill-famed hamlet of Hamra-Dûm, are to be found the most ancient remains of the whole region. Half-way up the white cliffs are the openings to several galleries—pharaonic tombs of the princes who governed this district under the Sixth Dynasty. Two of these, at least, have rewarded the attentions of archaeologists: and even among seekers after the treasures of Coptic and Arab Egypt the place was once legendary. Here was "Ladamês the Great", wrote the mediaeval guides, doubtless distorting and magnifying an appellation which meant "the great grotto". "You will see, to the north-west, seven tombs set up on the side of the valley—four together, then two together, and the last by itself. Dig into this last, to the depth of one *qamah*: you will find the dead body, and beside it all its possessions. You will see also some high watch-towers around this same cemetery on the eastern side. Among these watch-towers there are five great tombs, each with a stone at the head and another stone at the feet, both implanted in the sand. Lift up the headstone and dig. . . ." In such terms as these did the *Book of buried Pearls and of the precious Mystery*, an Arab writing addressed to seekers after marvels, embellish this locality with remains which, perhaps, were never to be seen there.[23]

However, this was the place where, according to all we had gathered from our preliminary enquiries, one undeniable treasure had been found—that of our Gnostic library. Let us give a rather fuller description of the site. Midway up the flank of the cliff are the openings to the pharaonic tombs—seven, according to Arab tradition—that we have just mentioned. The first, approaching from the south, has no sculptures or hieroglyphic inscriptions; but on the wall some Coptic monk has painted in red, in his own language, the first words of Psalms LI to XCIII.[24] We shall find no other trace of Christianity anywhere in the neighbourhood: was it, then, to this place that St Pachomius sometimes withdrew, and here that he endured the temptation of which his biography tells us? "There were tombs in the vicinity of the place where the aged apa Palamun lived. Pachomius went away into one of these tombs and prayed. . . ." Actually, apart from these beginnings of Psalms, there is not a single graffito, none of those invocations that usually mark the places in which anchorites once lived. These Coptic graffiti, therefore, can hardly indicate more than the very temporary sojourn of some solitary ascetic.

More to the north, in the finest of the pharaonic tombs, a pagan pilgrim, at some date hardly more ancient than the period of the first Coptic monks, has inscribed a series of Greek invocations to Serapis. They show that this is a spot which, for reasons we cannot trace, was specially venerated in the Greek or Roman epoch. Even today, moreover, a small "sheikh"—a rustic holy place, indicated by some little votive cakes and a few big stones—

[23] *Livre des Perles enfouies et du Mystère précieux* . . . , translated and published by Ahmed Bey Kamal, vol. II, Cairo, 1907; translation p. 204; G. Daressy, "Indicateur topographique du Livre des Perle senfouies'", excerpt from the *Bulletin de l'Institut français d'Archéologie orientale*, Cairo, 1917, p. 48.
[24] P. Bucher, "Les commencements des Psaumes LI à XCIII, Inscription d'une tombe de Kasr es Saijâd" in *Kemi*, 4, 1931, pp. 157–60.

is to be seen at the bottom of the slope, showing that the place is still held in veneration.

Underneath the yawning entrances to the great tombs, the face of the cliff is pierced by many narrow, deep cavities in which bodies had been summarily interred. Sepulchres are scattered about to as far as a hundred yards from the base of the cliff, even into the sands of the desert, where a great number of excavations show how much they have been pillaged by the peasants, greedy for the natural manure which they call *sebakh*. Here, then, was the ancient cemetery, which served as such for the city of Diospolis Parva, and then for the little town of Chenoboskion; a vast but poor necropolis where bodies were deposited, each in its shroud, at the bottom of a hole. When was this cemetery abandoned? The numerous scraps of cloth one can obtain from the graves seem to be of the Greek or Roman epoch: it is to be noted too, that with the spread of Christianity the cemeteries of this region were removed to where the Copts are still buried today, in proximity to the churches; that is, to the Deir amba Palamun and the Deir el-Malak.

Was it in one of these tombs that the papyri were found? Certainly, one cannot, even if one searches very far around, see any other place—any ruin or sepulchre—from which they could have come. The peasants who accompanied us and who did not know the real object of our search (we had come here on the pretext of visiting the pharaonic tombs) guided us, of their own initiative, to the southern part of the cemetery and showed us a row of shapeless cavities. Not long since, they said, some peasants of Hamra-Dûm and of Dabba, in search of manure, found here a great *zir*—which means a jar—filled with leaves of papyrus; and these were bound like books. The vase was broken and nothing remains of it; the manuscripts were taken to Cairo and no one knows what then became of them. As to the exact location of the find, opinion differed by some few dozen yards; but everyone was sure that it was just about here. And from the ground itself we shall learn nothing more; it yields nothing but broken bones, fragments of cloth without interest and some potsherds.

Given as they were, quite spontaneously, I am sure that these testimonies related to our library: they agreed perfectly with the details we had been able to collect through different channels. Can one, however, control and clarify them further? After having thoroughly examined the site, we go back to the villages and their churches to gossip with sundry individuals who were concerned in the discovery. They all talk willingly about the find that was made four years ago and was no great matter of mystery here: the material profit was not for these peasants, whose total gain from it was doubtless no more than a few dozen piastres. Several remember having seen and handled the manuscripts. The Coptic *abuna* of the Deir al-Malak—a young priest named David—had even tried to read them, but in vain, since they were written in dialects other than the Bohaïric still used today in his liturgy. Was it he, then, who scribbled with his stylo those notes, in an obviously modern ink, which had so intrigued us on the margin of one of the pages? He mentions it himself, which shows us that he is not lying—or not much. True, one may have spoilt a few already damaged leaves; but one attached so little value to them! But all that remained intact was sold, for three Egyptian pounds, and no one has since thought any more about it. And there, in short, are all the particulars that one could collect on one side and another in Dabba, in es-Sayyâd, at Hamra-Dûm and even among the Bedouins who have settled as squatters right at the foot of Gebel.

However, we are now assured that it was not in the ruins of a building, either monastic or other, that the famous library was found, but that it was well buried in a tomb very far away from all the monasteries of the locality, in a cemetery which seems to have been no longer in use by the Christians. There is nothing surprising about these writings having been enclosed in a jar. It was in such receptacles, less costly than cupboards and coffers in this country with so little wood, that people usually stored their books and many other things.[25]

[25] Manuscripts of the pharaonic age as well as of the Roman epoch in Egypt, have fairly often been found in jars: cf. K. Preisendanz, *Papyrusfunde und Papyrusforschung*, 1934, p. 113; the jars in which the Dead Sea Scrolls were found are now famous enough; the custom is also alluded to in *Jeremiah* XXXII, 14, "Take these deeds . . . and put them in an earthenware vessel, that they may last for a long time".

Later on, we will show how we were able to date the manuscripts, from their calligraphy, and ascribe them to the third and fourth centuries. Already the contents of these Gnostic collections had led us to suppose that, whoever may have possessed them, they cannot have been monks. The spot where they were disinterred, moreover, would seem to prove that they were buried in pagan ground. But at what epoch? The place of discovery and the age of the manuscripts both lead us to believe that this library was hidden, at the latest, about the beginning of the fifth century, at the time when the Pachomian monasteries, which were distinguished throughout Egyptian monasticism by their strict orthodoxy of doctrine, finally extended their influence over the region. That they had to struggle against the Gnostics in these parts is shown by their writings. In 367 Theodore, who had just succeeded Pachomius as head of the monastery of Tabennisi, ordained that the thirty-ninth festal letter of St Athanasius should be translated into Coptic and read throughout the monasteries of the country: that letter was justly aimed against the books which were spuriously concocted by the heretics, and "to which they attribute antiquity and give the names of saints".[26] No doubt this is the same Theodore who, in a fragment of the most ancient Pachomian writing, denounces "one of those books that the heretics write; they have set it out under the names of the saints" —that is, of the Apostles—and it was written there that "after Eve was deceived and had eaten the fruit of the tree, it was of the devil that she gave birth to Cain".[27] This detail, as we shall see, agrees very closely with a myth that we read in some of the treatises of our new Gnostic library. Were such books indeed multiplying all around at this time, since they had to be so energetically combated? We know that, a few years earlier, some "philosophers" who may have been more or less Gnostic, came from the town of Akhmim to bait Pachomius about the interpretation of the Scriptures (so they cannot have been altogether pagan, but more probably heretics). Theodore gave

---

[26] *Les Vies coptes de saint Pachôme* . . . , p. 206, I, 17.
[27] *Ibid.*, pp. 370–1; cf. also the anonymous text that we mention in note 74 of chap. II above.

them a piece of his mind, and cleverly turned the tables on them in the course of a dialogue which his Coptic biographies have preserved in all the freshness of its savour, ". . . the philosopher said to him, 'You boast that you have knowledge of the Scriptures, as well as of their interpretation; well, then, teach me who was never born but is dead; who was born and did not die; and who died but never putrefied.' Theodore replied, 'O you, whose mind is like a leaky cask! . . . He who was never begotten and who is dead, that is Adam; he who was begotten and did not die, is Enoch; whilst he who was dead and did not putrefy, that is the wife of Lot, who became a statue of salt, wherewith to season anyone as foolish as you who so foolishly glorify yourselves.'"[28]

We are still discussing the provenance of many ancient manuscripts of which, for their better interpretation, it would be of the greatest value to know the origins. We have never been able to discover exactly where the Coptic Manichaean manuscripts came from, nor the *Pistis-Sophia*, nor the Bruce Codex. So it was well worth the trouble to find out, in a pagan cemetery a few miles from Chenoboskion, the exact site of one of the most voluminous finds of ancient literature; thus to be a little better able to place this library in the frame of history to which it belongs; and to support, with concordant details, the hypotheses that have been made about its antiquity.

[28] *Les Vies coptes* . . . , pp. 117–18.

CHAPTER IV

THIRTEEN CODICES OF PAPYRUS

THE manuscripts obtained from Chenoboskion are to be regarded as a whole, whether we are thinking of those held by the Coptic Museum, or of the Jung Codex—which, incidentally, had lost a certain number of pages that have been found among the mass of papyri conceded to the Museum by Miss Dattari. They amount, altogether, to thirteen manuscripts, eleven of which are complete with their bindings, while two are represented only by a few scattered leaves from each. In almost every case in which their arrangement could be verified, each codex constitutes a single big book of papyrus, bound to a leathern cover by a seam down the middle of the latter. One alone, No. 1 in the inventory, is indubitably an assemblage of booklets of eight pages each (quaternions) sewn in the same way as modern bindings.

Almost everything is written in the Coptic dialect of Upper Egypt—sahidic—which was the most important in the literary history of the Copts, and in which the other, previously-known Gnostic manuscripts are also written. In the Chenoboskion manuscripts this dialect is, however, sprinkled with archaisms which show it in an early stage of its development: one can also discern a strong influence from the dialects of Middle Egypt—akhmimic and subakhmimic. The vocabulary will supply a good many new words of the Coptic language, of which we have hitherto known little except in its latest forms. Only two writings, of the whole collection—the Jung Codex (No. XIII in the inventory) and the first text of Codex VIII—are written in the subakhmimic dialect.[1]

That these thirteen books, although written in different dialects and with some diversity of calligraphy, constituted a coherent

[1] The Coptic dialects (see chap. II, note 1) in which the new codices are written are: the sahidic, a dialect of Upper Egypt which some modern philologists also call Theban; the akhmimic and the subakhmimic (dialects closely related) of Middle Egypt.

whole, and were not a mere assemblage from unrelated origins, is confirmed by several facts. For example, the first treatise in the Codex VIII (which is a very thick volume of leaves of papyrus) is the *Interpretation of the Gnosis*, in the subakhmimic dialect and in a writing of the end of the third century. But the works which have been transcribed after it *in the same big book* are written in the dialect of Upper Egypt, which is that of the majority of all the manuscripts: they are transcribed, moreover, by a different hand, in writing of a rather later type. Do we want further evidence that this library shows us the work of copyists working in co-operation, even though their dialects differ? Here, in Codex VI, are some writings of a Hermetic nature, written in a fairly pure sahidic, no doubt after a Theban manuscript which was taken as a model: and between two of these treatises is inserted a long annotation by the copyist, excusing himself for not having transcribed, for those of his brethren who were collecting the Chenoboskion library, all of the writings he had in hand. But this copyist, when thus expressing himself personally, is not using altogether the same pure sahidic as in the treatises he has just been translating: he is now writing a sahidic mingled with akhmimic, similar in general to what we find in most of the other writings in our collection.

As for the precise period in which these manuscripts were recopied, we shall show that palaeography suggests some fairly exact dates. One peculiarity, apparently trivial, incidentally confirms the chronology that we shall put forward. In a page or two of Codex XIII, written in one of the latest styles of calligraphy that our collection exhibits, the ends of texts are decorated with small looped crosses—the hieroglyph ☥, a symbol of life, which the Copts inherited from their ancestors and use to this day as an equivalent of the Christian cross. But this sign does not appear to have been taken over from Egyptian paganism until the year 391. That, indeed, was the date when the Serapeum of Alexandria was destroyed by the mobs that the patriarch Theophilus had stirred up; when the famous statue of the god, sculptured by Bryaxis, was broken to pieces. Ecclesiastical tradition complaisantly records that, during these troubles, the Christians were astonished to discover, on the interior walls of the temple, this ancient sign so similar to the Cross, and were told that it was the symbol of "the life to come"; whilst the pagans, on their side, were stupefied when they saw the triumphant Cross painted upon the houses by their adversaries, so similar (for it was the Cross surmounted by a crown) to their hieroglyph of the "future life" [2] Certain ancient prophecies preserved by the remaining devotees of the Egyptian cults had foretold, it seems, that the manifestation of this sign would mark the advent of a new religion: thus many of the Alexandrian worshippers of Serapis became converts to the new faith, whilst the Christians, for their part, adopted this new form of the Cross, which had the advantage of having already signified, in their ancestral writing, the "life to come".

If we take account of this episode, it seems certain that Codex XIII, whose pages are adorned with the symbol in question, is later than the year 391, which is in accord with the presumable date of the writing represented in it.

The criteria of palaeography are, as we have said, the most reliable for the dating of manuscripts. They are all the more dependable here, where we can distinguish about nine styles of writing which represent, in continuous succession, clearly progressive degrees in the evolution of Coptic calligraphy—a sequence of stages that were already known.

We can group the successive varieties of writing into four principal types, according to which they are tabulated here on page 141.

In accordance with this evolution in the calligraphy, we have established a new classification of the manuscripts, different from the two which had been previously proposed—one by me, and the other, based upon my inventories, by Professor Puech.[3]

[2] Cf. the rather different accounts of this episode given, in their respective Histories, by Rufin (XI, 29); Sozomen (VII, 15); and Socrates. Cf. also J. Maspero, *Histoire des Patriarches d'Alexandrie*, 1923, p. 114.

[3] Cf. H. C. Puech, "Les nouveaux écrits gnostiques découverts en Haute-Égypte" in *Coptic Studies in honor of W. E. Crum* (The Byzantine Institute, Boston and Paris, 1950, pp. 91–154). An analysis of some of the Chenoboskion writings, also by Prof. Puech, has just appeared in the 3rd edn. of Edg. Hennecke . . ., *Neutestamentliche Apokryphen*.

This new classification of the various texts, the number of which has been re-verified,[4] has the advantage of presenting the manuscripts in nearly the same order as they were brought together, over about two centuries, to constitute the library of Chenoboskion.

In Codex I, we have the manuscript first acquired by Togo Mina for the Coptic Museum in 1946. Codex XIII is that of which by far the greater part was purchased for the Jung Foundation.

We have not in all cases been able to indicate the exact number of pages contained in each book. Most of the codices are still waiting to be completely reconditioned. Whilst I was making inventories, in 1948-9, of the major part of the whole collection, their fragile state made it impossible for me to turn over all the leaves of some of them. A word about their dimensions: The largest—which is also the finest—is No. X, which measures $10\frac{5}{8}$ by nearly 6 inches, with an average of 35 lines to a page. But most of the collection follow, with little variation, the format of Codex I, which measures $9\frac{3}{4}$ by $5\frac{1}{2}$ inches, and has an average of 26 lines per page. Codex XIII is distinguished by the height of its pages—nearly $11\frac{1}{2}$ by $5\frac{1}{2}$, with up to 37 lines per page.

---

[4] I had at first estimated that the total number of works would amount to 48 (cf. especially my article "Une bibliothèque gnostique copte" in *La Nouvelle Clio*, I, 1949, pp. 60-70; (note, however, a misprint that has crept into p. 62, last line of text, which should read VI, 2, not IV, 2). A more thorough examination of the group of Hermetic writings included in Codex VI has led me to think that this set of homogeneous texts was divided not into four, but five sections. Cf. J. Doresse, "Hermès et la Gnose" in *Novum Testamentum*, I, 1956, p. 57 and also, here below, pp. 241ff.

Note to opposite page.

  ★ In fact, it seems to me certain that this writing, which is used in Codex XIII, is by the *same hand* as the writing in Codex X, and that its accidental clumsiness is due to some physiological cause—failing sight, senility—by which the copyist was suddenly afflicted. One finds proof of this on p. 47 of Codex X, which begins making exactly the same blunders as occur in writing No. 8; but then it improves, is regularized and again becomes writing 6, in which all of Codex X is written, barring this single intermission.

PALAEOGRAPHY

CALLIGRAPHY OF THE CHENOBOSKION MSS.	TERMS OF COMPARISON

A.—Cursive writing, supple, unpretentious:

1.

2. This same hand is represented in five MSS. of our collection.

3. A little stiffer than the two previous writings, marked difference between thick and thin strokes.

See, as a model for comparison, the manuscript of *Ezechiel* in the Chester-Beatty collection (early third century); the papyrus Bodmer II—a *Gospel of John* in Greek; the Coptic fragment of *Ecclesiasticus*, Louvain, No. 9—rather more rigid and dating without doubt from the end of the third century.

B.—Stiffly calligraphic, down-strokes emphasized:

4.

5.

6. Flexible, without heaviness, this is the most beautiful hand that appears in our manuscripts.

7. Spare, stiff writing; down-strokes excessively thickened.

The transition from the cursive style A to the book-writing style of class B is said by palaeographic experts to have taken place during the fourth century.

C.—Written in stiff letters, thick, even impasted:

8. This hand is distinguished by its heaviness from the writing of No. 6. It is also marked, in certain pages, by irregularity in the lines and the dimensions of letters.*

Cf. the Coptic MS. of the *Ascension of Isaiah*, Louvain, No. 12; and the private letter in the John Rylands collection, which date from the late fourth century. *The Gospel of John* in sub-akhmimic dialect would be, more surely, from the second half of the fourth century. The Gnostic Berlin Codex, in still heavier writing than our No. 8, dates from the fifth century.

D.—Sloping writing, artificial, fulfilling in some sort the function of italic, for we find it in use concurrently with writing No. 4

9.   (in Codex VIII) and with writing No. 8 (in Codex XIII).

(*N.B.*—the numbers 1 to 9 enumerate the different "hands" we distinguish in our manuscripts).

TEXTS CONTAINED IN THE CODICES

A. *Manuscripts written in the Sahidic Dialect*

I. (MS. entered at the Coptic Museum in 1948. This originally comprised 152 pp., of which only 134 and some fragments remain).

Writing
1

(1) *Secret Book of John.*
(2) *Sacred Book of the invisible Great Spirit,* or *Gospel of the Egyptians.*
(3) *Epistle of Eugnostos the Blessed.*
(4) *The Sophia of Jesus.*
(5) *The Dialogue of the Saviour.*

II. (Originally of more than 70 pages, but much mutilated).

Writing
2

(6) *Secret Book of John* (the same work as No. 1).
(7) *Sacred Book of the invisible Great Spirit* (the same work as No. 2).

III. (88 pages).

Writing
2

(8) *Epistle of Eugnostos the Blessed* (the same work as No. 3).
(9) *Apocalypse of Paul.*
(10) *Apocalypse of James.*
(11) Another *Apocalypse of James.*
(12) *Apocalypse of Adam to his son Seth.*

IV. (140 pages).

Writing
2

(13) A Revelation, of which the title is lost.
(14) "*Discourse of Truth by Zostrian. God of Truth. Discourse of Zoroaster*". (Title given in cryptogram).
(15) *Epistle of Peter to Philip.*

V. (About 40 pages).

Writing
2

(16) A Revelation attributed to the Great Seth; title lost.

(17) An Epistle, chiefly concerned with the Father of the Universe and the primordial man Adamas.

(18) Treatise, in form of an epistle.

(19) Treatise, without title, against the Scribes and Pharisees, upon the baptism of John the Baptist, the water of Jordan, and Jesus.

VI. (About 80 pages. This manuscript was evidently very much in use. Some feathers served as bookmarks between certain pages).

Writing 2

(20) *Acts of Peter.*

(21) *"Authentic" discourse of Hermes to Tat.*

(22) *The Thought of the Great Power.*

(23) Hermetic treatise, without title.

(24) Sethian Revelation, title missing.

(25) Hermetic treatise, without title, ending with a prayer that we already know from the Greek papyrus Mimaut, and from the end of the *Asclepius*. The following note is added by the copyist:

> *This is the first discourse that I have copied for you. But there are many others that have come into my hands: I have not transcribed them, thinking that they have already reached you. For I hesitate to copy them for you, thinking that if they had already reached you, they would weary you. Indeed the discourses of Hermes that have come into my hands are very numerous.*

(26) Hermetic treatise, the essence of which is to be found in paragraphs 21–29 of the Latin *Asclepius*.

VII. (126 pages).

Writing 3

(27) *Paraphrase of Shem*, described at the end as the *Second Treatise of the Great Seth*.

6

(28) *Apocalypse of Peter.*
(29) *The Teachings of Silvanus.*
(30) *Revelation of Dositheus,* or *The Three Stelae of Seth.*

VIII.

Writings
9
and
4

(31) *The Interpretation of the Gnosis* (writing No. 9, and in the subakhmimic dialect).
(32) *The Supremes Allogenes* (writing No. 4).
(33) *Revelation of Messos* (judging by its content, the title being lost).

IX. (8 separate leaves, without binding).

Writing
5

(34) *The Triple discourse of the triple protennoïa,* a *Sacred Book written by the Father* (that is, by Seth).
(35) Sethian Revelation in form of an epistle. (Cf. No. 40.)

X. (The most beautiful as well as most voluminous of the manuscripts. Decorated binding—with Egyptian cross?—bands at top and at extremities. Format $10\frac{5}{8}$ by $8\frac{1}{4}$ ins., 175 pages of about 37 lines each.)

Writing
6

(36) *Secret Book of John* (a somewhat amplified version of this work, a simpler edition of which is given in Nos. 1 and 6).
(37) *Gospel of Thomas* (this contains the *Logia Iesou*).
(38) *Gospel of Philip.*
(39) *Hypostasis of the Archons* (this is the *Book of Nôrea*).
(40) Revelation without title, devoted especially to the *Pistis-Sophia.* (Same work as No. 35.)
(41) *The Exegesis upon the Soul.*

(42) *The Book of Thomas: secret sayings told by the Saviour to Jude Thomas and recorded by Matthew* (i.e. Matthias, see pp. 221 ff.). At the end of this volume the copyist has added the words: *O my brethren, remember me and (offer up) the prayer, 'Peace to the saints and to the Spiritual'.*

XI. (A few large pages of a lost volume).

Writing 7

(43) Fragments of works, dealing with, among other subjects, the influence of demons upon the soul.

XII (20 pages, with their binding, in sahidic dialect, marked by akhmimic influence).

Writing 8

(44) Fragments of a mystic treatise on the cosmos.

B. *Manuscripts written in Subakhmimic Dialect* (as is also text No. 31)

XIII. (Should contain 168 (?) pages. Most of its pages, formerly held by the antiquary Albert Eid, have been ceded to the Jung Foundation at Zurich: 23 pages are included in the lot acquired by the Coptic Museum).

Writings 8 and 9

(45) *Apocalypse of James* (different from Nos. 10 and 11).
(46) *Gospel of Truth.*
(47) *Discourse to Reginos upon the Resurrection.*
(48) Treatise without a title.
(49) *Prayer of the Apostle Peter.*

CHAPTER V

FORTY-FOUR SECRET (AND HITHERTO UNKNOWN) BOOKS

THE total number of works in this library is forty-nine. If we do not count those which are repetitions of the same work—but valuable nevertheless for the variant readings which they supply to one another—the number is reduced to forty-four. In estimating the novelty of the find, one may also subtract the two treatises that were already known in the Gnostic Codex of Berlin, and which since 1956 are no longer unpublished.

It is not yet possible to give equally complete or equally precise analyses of all the codices. Shall we perhaps find, one day, in this mass of writings still so difficult to inspect thoroughly, some work which has escaped our scrutiny? But the texts that have been identified show (in spite of the presence of a few deceptive titles which might falsely suggest writings we already knew, such as the *Apocalypse of Paul*, the *Acts of Peter*, etc.) that here we are dealing with books all previously unknown and new in content. We will divide them into four classes: first, that of the greatest, purely Gnostic revelations, with some commentaries expounding the myths that they contain; next, some revelations that are no less important but rather artificially veiled under Christian allusions; then, the authentically Christian apocrypha infiltrated by Gnostic speculations; and, lastly, some half-dozen treatises of which some belong properly to Hermetic literature while others exhibit a curious transition between Hermetism and Gnosticism.

REVELATIONS OF THE PROPHETS OF GNOSTICISM
FROM SETH TO ZOROASTER

In the forefront of the greatest "revelations" we will place the *Paraphrase of Shem* (No. 27). This is the longest and the most extraordinary of the apocalypses in our whole library. It is also, perhaps, one of the most important of all the writings that were in use among the Gnostics: we can see this from several characteristics of its contents.

The Coptic treatise begins with these words: "A paraphrase which was been made by the unbegotten spirit. I am Shem. These things have been revealed to me by Derdekea,[1] in conformity with the will of the Greatness. My intellect which is in my body has raised me above my generation; it has borne me away into the heights of the Creation, penetrating the light which radiates over all the universe. In that place I beheld no earthly appearances; yet it is light. Then my soul separated from my body of darkness: as though it had been in a dream, I heard a voice which said to me: Shem, since thou wast born from a pure power and art the first who has existed upon earth, hear and understand the things that I am about to tell thee, for the first time, about the great Powers. They existed in the beginning, before I had appeared. There was a Light and a Darkness, and between these there was a Spirit. . . . I will unveil to thee the truth about these Powers. The Light was a Thought filled with understanding and with logos, which were joined there into a single instrument. The Darkness was that of winds in water; it had a thought which was dwelling in a tumultuous fire. Lastly, the Spirit, which was between the one and the other, was pleasant and humble light. Such were the three roots.[2] They were reigning alone within themselves, yet enveloping one another mutually, each in its strength. The Light, since it possessed a great power,

[1] Perhaps one may connect this name with the Aramaic root DRDG, "to fall in droplets". The *Sophia of Jesus* (No. 4 of our collection which, at this point, needs completing by the parallel version contained in the Berlin Codex) alludes to the Drop as to a heavenly power descending from the Light and from the Spirit into the lower regions, for the salvation of created mankind (cf. C. Schmidt –W. Till, *Die gnostische Schriften des köpt. Papyr. Berolinensis* . . . , p. 103, l.13; p. 104, l. 15; p. 119, ll. 6–17). In its soteriological aspect, this "drop" may be compared with Barbelô, or the Tetrad—who, by the way, are supposed to have dictated other revelations, e.g., those transcribed by Marcus (see above, p. 33).

[2] The use of the term "root" to denote the primordial principles is common in the Manichaean writings: cf. the references collected by H. C. Puech in *Le Manichéisme* . . . , p. 160. This symbolic term cannot be dissociated from the symbolism of trees used by both Gnostics and Manichaeans to express the forces of life and of death: cf. above, chap. I, note 86; chap. II, note 23, and in chap. v, p. 197 and note III.

knew of the humility and the disorder of the Darkness, because
its root was vile. . . ." But now, behold! the Darkness wills
to raise itself up to the Light. Enveloped in its waters, it grows
agitated. By this tumult the Spirit is affrighted; it lifts itself up to
the height of the realms belonging to it, and from thence it sees,
on the one hand, a great dark water that fills it with loathing,
and on the other hand, the infinite Light. The Darkness mounts
up, "so that the Thought may spread throughout it", when the
Light suddenly appears to it. It is astounded, for it did not know
that any power existed higher than itself. And the Darkness,
seeing that its own appearance was so dim beside that of the
radiant Spirit, was distressed: by this distress, it lifted its thought
above the realms of darkness . . . and thus began the mingling
or mixture, which was the precondition for the Creation. The
Darkness, stupidly, wants to be equal to the unbegotten Spirit.
Its thought rears up and shines all over "hell" in a flash of fire,
but without being able to equal the Light from on high. And
this higher Light, for its part, now manifests itself from an infinite elevation, and shows its image to the unbegotten Spirit
(the intermediate principle?). The disclosure of these secrets
(so the treatise claims) had never before that time been granted,
except to some mysterious entities, to some prophets named
Elorkhaïos, Amoïas, Strophaeos, Kelkheak, Kelkhea, Aïleu. . . .

At the end of this long cosmogony, of which we have quoted
only the commencement, Shem recalls the splendours of the
heavenly regions as he had passed through them in his vision.
"I, Shem, on the day that I went out of my body [in ecstasy]
whilst my intellect remained in the body, I awoke as if after deep
sleep; and when I was awakened, as if from the heaviness of my
body, I said: Blessed are they who know, when they are asleep,
into what power their spirit will go to rest! And when the
Pleiades rose, I saw clouds that I had to pass through. Thus, the
cloud of the Pneuma is like a sacred beryl; the cloud of Hymen
is like a resplendent emerald; the cloud of Silence is like a delight-
ful amaranth; and the cloud of Mesotes is like a pure hyacinth."[3]

[3] The allusion to the Pleiades in this vision is perhaps to be explained by what
one reads in Book XII of the Syriac version of the treatises of Zosimos: this alludes

After this description of the ascent through the clouds of heaven, the Power who is communicating this vision to Shem speaks again to complete his instruction. He shows Shem the way through the lower heavens guarded by the Archons. From this point onward, the rest of the Gnostic cosmogony, just as one finds it almost uniformly in the other great revelations used by the sectaries of Chenoboskion, is developed at length. We are told about the creation of the cosmos by the evil god of the lower world who thinks that he alone exists and who cries out, swelling with pride: "I am God and there is no other God but I . . ." (cf. *Isaiah* XLV, 5–6, and XLVI, 9).

Finally, the treatise explicitly makes Shem into an appearance of Jesus Christ. "These things, it is I who have told them to you, I, Jesus Christ, son of the Man who is higher than the heavens, O ye Perfect and stainless . . . so that when we go out from the regions of this universe, we may receive there the symbols of incorruptibility, in spiritual Repose according to a Gnosis. For you know not that the cloud of the flesh is over you; whereas I am myself the companion of the unique Sophia. As for me, I am in the bosom of the Father from the beginning, in the Place of the Sons of the love of the truth and of the greatness. Take your rest with me, my spiritual friends and brethren, for ever."

This explanation ends upon this concluding title: *The Second Treatise of the Great Seth.* But I cannot be sure whether this applies to all of the long work that I have just described, or whether the treatise as a whole is divided into two sections, so that the whole represents both a *First* and a *Second Treatise of the Great Seth.*

This revelation, in which the prophet, upon his ascension into

to the seven heavens, the twelve dwellings (the Zodiac) and to "the Pleiades which are the world of the Thirteen" presumably meaning the Thirteenth aeon of the *Pistis-Sophia* (cf. above, pp. 66–67). This text of Zosimos is quoted in W. Scott, *Hermetica* vol. IV, 1936, p. 143.

As for the *hymen,* this allusion must be related to the teaching in the *Chaldaean Oracles* according to which a membrane (i.e., a hymen) separates the supernal, intellectual fire from the cosmic fire here below: cf. upon this "coverlet of Heaven", Bidez, in the *Revue de Philologie,* 1903, p. 80; Franz Cumont, in *Recherches* . . . , pp. 26–7, relates this myth to that of the flaying of the Archons, whose stretched-out skins, according to the Manichaeans, were used to form the sky.

heaven,[4] is welcomed by a "supreme Mother" called Derdekea, confirms the information given by Epiphanius (XL, 7), where he says that the Gnostic Archontici taught that Seth had been caught up into heaven for forty days by the supreme Power—the Mother—and by the angels of the good god, there to be instructed in the mysteries of the Pleroma and of the inferiority of the created world.[5] But we find a more exact echo of this treatise in the *Philosophumena* (V, 19-22). Our book is mentioned there under the title of *The Paraphrase of Seth*, and the critic writes that those who wish to make a complete study of the ideas of the Sethian Gnostics have only to read that work, in which all the ideas of those heretics are contained. It is certain that the treatise to which the author of the *Philosophumena* is alluding was identical, or nearly so, with the text of which we now have the Coptic version in our hands—only read the commentary he makes upon its preamble:

"The principles, according to the Sethians, are in essence the Light and the Darkness: in between is a pure Breath. This breath, which is between the Darkness which is below and the Light which is on high, is not a Breath like a gust of wind nor a gentle breeze . . . but it is like a perfume exhaled from an ointment, or a wisely-compounded incense. . . . The Light, as I said, is on high, the Darkness below, and the Breath between the two. The Light, like the rays of the sun, naturally sheds its qualities on the Darkness beneath it, and the Spirit which dwells in the midst sends out a good odour in every direction, as we see incense, thrown into the fire, exhale its perfumes. . . . Then, such is the power of the *three Principles*, that the power of the Light and that of the Breath find themselves, at the same time, in the Darkness situated underneath."

"The Darkness is a dreadful water; the Light and the Breath were attracted to it, and took on the nature of that element. The

---

[4] The Iranian literature describes analogous ascensions through the spheres: cf. Reitzenstein–Schaeder, *Studien* . . . , p. 13; cf. also Festugière, *La Révélation d'Hermès Trismégiste*, vol. II, *Le Dieu Cosmique*, pp. 441-59, which enables us to see just how far some classic visions such as *The Dream of Scipio* differ from these celestial ascensions of our Gnostics.

[5] Cf. Puech, *Fragments* . . . *de l'Apocalypse d'Allogène*, p. 950.

Darkness is not without intelligence; on the contrary, it is endowed with a consummate discretion, and it knows that if the Light were taken away from it, it would be left solitary, obscure, lustreless and weak. So it draws upon all the resources of its prudence and intelligence, forcibly to retain within itself the lustre and sparkle of the Light, with the good odour of the Pneuma. . . . As the Darkness aspires to clearness, to have the brilliance at its service and to see, so do the Light and the Breath desire to recover the forces that are their own. They are eager to withdraw these from the nether waters, dark and dreadful, with which they have become mingled, and to resume possession of them."

"The powers of the three Principles are infinite in number. They are reasonable and intelligent. So long as each remains isolated, they all remain quite tranquil; but if one power comes near to another, the dissimilarity of the Powers thus brought together sets up motion, and that motion produces an action, the form of which depends upon the concourse of the Powers thus met together. . . . "

This description of three primordial Principles—Light, Darkness and intermediate Spirit—and of their first movements fully confirms the Gnostic authenticity of one fundamental notion which the heresiologists all ascribe, more or less clearly, not only to the Sethian *Paraphrase* of which we have just found the original text, but also to Simon, to the Nicolaitans, to Basilides and to the Peratae. It is disclosed also in the teachings of Marcion and Bardesanes, then in the later Gnostic speculations of the Euchites, and finally in those of the Bogomils.[6]

No other text in the Chenoboskion library, it seems, describes this myth with as much detail as the *Paraphrase of Shem*. I have, however, found some other traces of it: for example, in the long version of the *Secret Book of John* (No. 36), there is an interpolation by a later scribe about the lower god—the demiurge

---

[6] Cf. above, pp. 17–18, 25, 33, 50; cf. Jonas, *loc. cit.*, vol. I, pp. 335–44. For the notion of "space" in Bardesanes, see Bidez-Cumont, vol. I, p. 62, note 4, and R. C. Zaehner, *Zurvan*, p. 202. For the Third Principle according to the Euchites and then the Bogomils, Puech and Vaillant, *Le Traité contre les Bogomiles* . . . , p. 186 and p. 314, note 2.

6*

Ialdabaôth—which adds this concise description: "The Light, when it reached the Darkness, made the Darkness to shine; whereas the Darkness, when it pursued the Light, darkened the Light and became neither Light nor Darkness, but found itself destitute. . . ." Still, this lacks any allusion to the intermediate principle.

At first sight, this exposition of the primordial war between Light and Darkness and of their intermingling recalls the Manichaean conceptions, according to which there was originally a Father of Greatness dwelling in the Light; over against him the evil empire of a king of Darkness; and then an attempt by the king of Darkness to mount up to the realm of Light whose splendours had excited his ambition, with the terrifying consequences of this devastating incursion.[7] But, here again, no more than two principles appear.[8]

To find the model or pattern for the system of our Gnostics, we have to go back to certain Iranian myths. Read, for instance, the opening paragraphs of one of their most important religious treatises, the *Bundahishn*:[9] "Thus is it revealed in the Good Religion. Ohrmazd was on high in omniscience and goodness: for infinite time he was ever in the Light. That Light is the Space

[7] Cumont, *Recherches sur le Manichéisme*, I, p. 13, II, pp. 120ff.; H. C. Puech, *Le Manichéisme, son fondateur, sa doctrine*, p. 76 and note 302; Flugel, *Mani*, p. 87.

[8] Concerning the disposition of these two principles, whether or not separated by a frontier or partition, in Manichaeism, cf. H. C. Puech, *Le Manichéisme* . . . , notes 293 and 299. A more specific notion is that the shadow penetrates into the domain of light like a wedge (St Augustine, *C. Faustum*, IV, 2, pp. 271, 2-3). May not this image be inspired by the simple fact that, in an area of illumination spreading all around a source of light, the zones of shadow projected outwards by objects enlarge into the distance, and thus resemble wedges driven into the area of light? (Cf. Bidez and Cumont, *Mages hellénisés*, vol. II, p. 78, note 25).

[9] Quoted from the translation by R. C. Zaehner, *Zurvan, a Zoroastrian Dilemma*, Oxford, 1955, pp. 312ff. Previously W. Bousset, in his *Hauptprobleme* . . . had drawn attention to the relationship between this myth of the *Bundahishn* and the *Philosophumena*'s account of the *Paraphrase of Seth* (the value of which account was not yet confirmed by our discovery of the original text); Bousset also compared the text of the *Bundahishn* with the passage in Plutarch's *De Iside* . . . 46 that describes the Persian belief in the two opposite principles Ohrmazd and Ahriman, and, as the third element between them, Mithra, also called *Mesites*— the "median". Upon this text—one of the most important that we have about the doctrine of the Magi—see Bidez and Cumont, vol. II, pp. 70ff.

Bousset had already been able to show relations between the doctrine in the *Pistis-Sophia* and the *Bundahish*, in his *Hauptprobleme* . . . , chap. v. For the discussions which this notion of the "void" was able to arouse, see, e.g., the treatise II B of the Hermetic writings, and §§ 33-4 of the *Asclepius*.

and place of Ohrmazd: some call it the Endless Light. Omniscience and goodness are the totality of Ohrmazd. . . . Ahriman, slow in knowledge, whose will is to smite, was deep down in the darkness: [he was] and is, yet will not be. The will to smite is his all, and darkness is his place: some call it the Endless Darkness. . . . Between them was the Void: some call it Vây in which the two Spirits mingle. Concerning the finite and the infinite: the heights which are called the Endless Light (since they have no end) and the depths which are the Endless Darkness, these are infinite. On the border, both are finite since between them is the Void and there is no contact between the two. Again, both spirits in themselves are finite. . . . Ohrmazd in his omniscience knew that the Destructive Spirit existed, that he would attack and, since his will is envy, would mingle with him. . . . The Destructive Spirit, ever slow to know, was unaware of the existence of Ohrmazd. Then he rose up from the depths and went to the border from whence the lights are seen. When he saw the Light of Ohrmazd intangible, he rushed forward. Because his will is to smite and his substance is envy, he made haste to destroy it. But seeing valour and supremacy superior to his own, he fled back to the darkness and fashioned many demons, a creation destructive and meet for battle. When Ohrmazd beheld the creation of the Destructive Spirit, it seemed not good to him—a frightful, putrid, bad and evil creation: and he revered it not. Then the Destructive Spirit beheld the creation of Ohrmazd and it seemed good to him—a creation most profound, victorious, informed of all; and he revered the creation of Ohrmazd."

Thus it is in the ancient myths, of which this version is given in the *Bundahishn*, that one must look for what served as a model for the system of our Gnostics.

The conception which is original in it—the existence of a *third* principle established between the Light and the Darkness—had already been known, before the development of Gnosticism, in some Greek writings of the Hellenistic age in which, pursuant to this idea, the Void is identified with Air and with Fate. Such is the case with several texts alleged to have been authorized by

Zoroaster.[10] J. Bidez and Franz Cumont had already pointed out that this peculiar principle[11]—which presents also some attributes of Mithra—was derived from an Iranian conception; indeed, from the one connected with Vây; namely, with the Spirit established between the Light of Ohrmuzd and the Darkness of Ahriman. Darmesteter[12] had already noted what this intermediate principle was: "All the cosmic motions take place in this Void; and thence the identity, or at least very close relation, of Vây with Time and with Destiny". E. Peterson, for his part, has recognized the existence of this same intermediary principle, identified with Fatality, in the two magical prayers in which he discovered a Gnostic substratum.[13] He has also shown it to be present in the mythology of the famous Mithraic Liturgy, where this principle is identified with Helios, with the god Mithra.

Another problem is presented by our manuscript: the prophet to whom this revelation is attributed is named indifferently Sêem (Shem), or Seth. The facts that the *Philosophumena* names this writing as the *Paraphrase of Seth*, and that in our text, too, the prophet is described as "the first who existed upon earth", would suggest that the name of Shem or Sêem might be due merely to the mistake of some copyist. Nevertheless, it may be that this writing was actually, in the first place, ascribed to Shem. Earlier, the Biblical apocryphon called the *Book of Jubilees* (X, 10, 15) said that Noah had received, from the angels, secrets which he transmitted to Shem. Certain Samaritans and—since the beginning of our era—the Jewish haggada, in their speculations, ascribed a position of importance to Shem, even making him into a figure of Melchizedek.[14] Some Gnostics—the Melchizedekians described in section LV of Epiphanius' treatise against heresies—preserved this identification. The Manichaeans counted Shem

---

[10] For example, in the treatise *Upon Nature* attributed to a Zoroaster who has been identified with the Er, son of Armenius, made famous by Plato. This text is cited by Proclus, *In Remp.* II: cf. Bidez–Cumont, *loc. cit.*, vol. II, p. 159.

[11] Bidez–Cumont, *op. cit.*, vol. II, p. 73, note 6; p. 159, note 14 and, above all, p. 160, note 3.

[12] *Zend Avesta*, II, p. 579.

[13] E. Peterson, "La Libération d'Adam . . .", pp. 211ff.

[14] M. Simon, "Melchisédech dans la polémique entre Juifs et Chrétiens et dans la légende" in *Revue d'Histoire et de Philos. relig.* 1937, pp. 59–93; cf. also *Pirqé Rabbi Eli'ezer*, XXI, 18; XXII, 19; Stein, *Philo und der Midrash*, p. 15.

among the "just" ones of old, to whom angels revealed the divine wisdom[15]—that is, among the great envoys of heaven who succeeded one another in the course of history, from Adam to Mani. The Mandaeans, also, attached the name of Shum-Kushta— i.e., Shem—to a part of one of their great sacred writings, the *Book of John*. Moreover, they attributed certain revelations in their books—one of them a heavenly vision which, like our Shem, he had had in a dream—to the mysterious scribe Dînânukht whose name, of Iranian origin, means simply "he who speaks according to religion". This personage had for wife Nuraïtha, sometimes presented as the wife of Noah, or else as the wife of Shem. Indeed, this Nuraïtha is assimilable to the figure of Nôrea, whom the Gnostics regarded as the wife of Seth and whose name they gave to a revelation mentioned by the heresiologists, the text of which—we shall be summarizing it later—turns up in the Chenoboskion library.[16] It is, finally, a remarkable fact that the wilful confusion between Seth, Melchizedek and Shem, thus attested in varying degrees, is found once more, right in the Mohammedan Middle Ages, among the sect of Ishmaelites which professes a Gnostic doctrine.[17]

After the *Paraphrase of Seth*—or rather *of Shem*—let us turn to some other writings giving rather different, or less complete, but still extremely important expositions of the Gnostic myths.

How can one resist the temptation to name here, in the first place, certain writings in the Chenoboskion library whose names

[15] Alfaric, *Les Écritures manichéennes*, II, pp. 155–6.
[16] Lidzbarski, *Das Johannesbuch der Mändaer*, 1915, pp. 58 and 64; *Ginzâ* . . . , edn. Lidzbarski, 1925, p. 205; G. Furlani, "I pianeti e lo zodiaco nella religione dei Mandei" in *Atti acc. Naz. dei Lincei, 1948, Memorie, Cl. di Sc. morali* . . . , ser. VIII, vol. II, fasc. 3, pp. 175 and 185. Finally, let us recall the curious traditions about Shem preserved in the Armenian writings of Moses of Khorene and of Thomas Ardzruni: Zervan is not a god but a divinized man; he is identical with Shem. Moses of Khorene claims to have got this myth from the *Sibylline Oracles*, III, 110; cf. Pr. Alfaric, *Zoroastre avant L'Avesta*, 1921, pp. 41–2.
[17] G. Vajda, "Melchisédech dans la mythologie ismaélienne" in *Journal Asiatique*, CCXXXIV, 1943–5, pp. 173ff. On the other hand, one reads in Tabarî that the Israelites once had a prophet of the name of Simî (Shem) who was sent for by the Iranian Bishtâsp (Hystaspe) with whom he entered into the capital of Balkh. Then he was joined by Zaradusht (Zoroaster) and the wise man Jâmâsp, son of Fashd. Simî spoke in Hebrew; Zoroaster understood this language, and wrote in Persian under his dictation. . . . (Tabarî, I, 681, 1–12; quoted by G. Messina, *I Magi a Betlemme E Una predizione di Zoroastro*, 1933, p. 57).

were known already by their being mentioned, among others, in Porphyry's life of his master Plotinus, who had personally combated (in his *Ennead*, II, 9), some sectaries using these apocrypha? To these visionaries Porphyry refers as Christians, among whom he denounces more particularly an Adelphius and an Aquilinus, who, he says, "had departed from the ancient philosophy and possessed a great number of works of Alexander of Libya, of Philocome, of Demostratus of Lydia. . . . They also made display of the *Revelations* of Zoroaster, of Zostrian, of Nicotheus, Allogenes, Mesos and others like them. They deceived many people . . . Plotinus often refuted them . . . but he left us more than enough to deal with. Amelius [a companion of Porphyry] wrote as many as forty chapters against the *Book of Zostrian*. For my part I have indited some searching criticisms of the *Book of Zoroaster*: I have proved it to be a recent apocryphon, made up by the founders of the sect to make people think that the dogmas they want to uphold are those of the ancient Zoroaster."

Of these writings, our collection restores to us the *Revelations of Zostrian and of Zoroaster* (No. 14), of the *Supreme Allogenes* (No. 32) and of *Messos* (No. 33).

Otherwise unknown, Zostrian is mentioned by the controversialist Arnobius (*Adversus Gentes*, I, 52) as having been the grandfather of "Zoroaster the Armenian"—that is, of the Zoroaster to whom has been attributed the apocalyptic narration of Er, reported by Plato in his *Republic*. He seems also to have been the author of a treatise in four books *Upon Nature*.[18] We note, however, that the colophon of our Coptic manuscript assimilates this discourse attributed to Zostrian to a *Discourse of Zoroaster*. That the lines which give this indication are written in a cryptogram (which is unique in our whole Gnostic library)

[18] Cf., above note 10. Upon the Gnostic prophecies which may have been set forth under the name of Zoroaster, cf. Bidez–Cumont, *op. cit.*, vol. I, pp. 153-7, and vol. II, fragments B.45 and Ost.9; see also G. Messina, *I Magi a Betlemme*; and U. Monneret de Villard, *Le leggende orientali sui Magi evangelici*. . . . According to Clement of Alexandria, the disciples of the Gnostic (?) Prodicos had used some books given under the name of Zoroaster (*Stromates*, 15, 69). As for the prophecies ascribed to *Zoroaster, grandson of Zostrian*, one would think, from the testimony of Arnobius, they were of a more or less Christian tendency.

shows what importance our sectaries attached to keeping this identification secret.[19]

The work in question is a revelation of the higher world in which are enumerated, for instance, the great aeons, Barbelô, the great luminaries Solmis, Doxomedon, Setheus. . . . Let us quote these words from it: "And I wrote three tablets: I left them for the information of those who will come after me, of the living elect. Then I ascended to the perceptible world". And do we not find another of our writings—the *Revelation of Dositheus*, apparently giving the text of three steles composed in this way by the great Seth!

As for *Messos*,[20] to judge by the beginning and by what is explicit in his revelation, he is reporting to his brethren, to be used by them in strict secrecy, a teaching which was revealed to him when he was caught up into the higher realms. More exactly, a celestial personage, or a prophet whose identity is obscure, reports to Messos in this vision what he himself had heard from some still higher entity, who had instructed him to hide these revelations upon a mountain: "And I", says this mysterious messenger, "was filled with joy; and I wrote this book which had been expounded to me, O my son Messos; and this, in order that I might reveal it to you."

In the *Supreme Allogenes* (No. 32) we again find a great vision of the creation of the higher world exalting, among others, Barbelô. What does this figure of Allogenes represent? The heresiologists who combated the Gnostics sometimes mention, indeed, as much in reference to the great Gnostics as to the Sethians,

[19] J. Doresse, "Les Apocalypse de Zoroastre, de Zostrien, de Nicothée . . ." in *Coptic Studies in honor of W. E. Crum*, 1950, pp. 256–63. Monneret de Villard, *op. cit.*, p. 138, note 6, has expressed his astonishment at the few lines in Coptic which have led us to propose, for Porphyry's text, the following translation: "The Apocalypses of *Zoroaster and Zostrian*, of Nicotheus, of Allogenes . . ." instead of the one currently accepted—"The Apocalypses of Zoroaster, of Zostrian, of Nicotheus, of Allogenes. . . ." I was the first to think the latter agreed ill with the fact that Porphyry and Amelius were able to share the task of refutation, one dealing with the book of Zoroaster and the other with the book of Zostrian. But the Coptic colophon in cryptography—showing the importance that the sectaries attached to keeping secrecy about the fictive origin of these contents—cannot be transcribed in any other way whatever.

[20] Concerning this name, see H. C. Puech, *Les Nouveaux écrits* . . . , p. 132.

the Archontici or the Audians,[21] an *Apocalypse of Allogenes*—
which is also cited by Porphyry—and sometimes seven *Allogeneous books* (while some Syriac writings name a *Book of
Foreigners*, thus literally translating the Greek ἀλλογενής). What
we are actually dealing with are revelations attributed to the great
Seth and his successors, and this title of "foreigner" or "alien"
given to the prophet and saviour of the Gnostic generation and
their descendants, means that Seth and his disciples are of a
particular race, separate from the rest of humanity and partici-
pating in the world of supreme powers—we must remember
here, the "Foreign God" of Marcion! Later on, this appellation of
"foreign" or "alien" is extended to include, for instance, the
Apostle Thomas preaching the new God.[22] As for Seth, the
description applies all the better to him, whom our cosmogonies
present as born of Eve and Adam but not of the same carnal and
inferior birth as Cain and Abel. Furthermore, certain traditions
well attested by St Epiphanius or collected later by George the
Syncellus[23] inform us, in effect, that Seth was taken up into heaven
by the Supreme Mother, who imparted the supreme secrets to
him. Finally he was identified with the Christ—a fact that we
shall find confirmed by several passages in our writings.

From certain allusions by the heresiologists of the early Middle
Ages—Theodore Bar-Konaï, Agapios of Membidj, and Gregory
bar-Hebraeus called Abu'l Faraj—Professor Puech saw how to
deduce the nature, if not the precise subjects, of the *Allogeneous
Books* a good while before the discovery at Chenoboskion
enabled us to verify the justice of his conclusions.[24] The title,
Apocalypse of Allogenes may correspond to that of the *Supreme
Allogenes* that we have now recovered. The description of *Allogeneous Books*, or *Books of Strangers* may itself apply, as will be

[21] H. C. Puech, *Fragments retrouvés de l'Apocalypse d'Allogène*, and articles
"Archontiker" and "Audianer".
[22] Cf. G. Widengren, *Muhammad, the Apostle of God, and his Ascension*, 1935,
p. 67; Jonas, *op. cit.*, vol. I, pp. 122–6. In a similar way, the appellation "alien"
is applied by Manichaeism to the luminous nature indwelling in man: cf. Ed.
Chavannes and P. Pelliot, "Un Traité manichéen retrouvé en Chine", reprint
from the *Journal Asiatique*, p. 50 (=546).
[23] Georges the Syncellus, *Chronographia*, pp. 16–17.
[24] Puech, *Fragments retrouvés de l'Apocalypse d'Allogène*.

seen, to various treatises put out under the name of Seth and of his followers which have turned up in the library of Chenoboskion.

One feels a lively hope, after rediscovering such writings in our collection, that we may yet find one of those texts which the school of Plotinus undertook to refute—that writing of *Nicotheus* "the hidden" which is mentioned not only by Porphyry but by Zosimos the alchemist in his treatise *On the Letter Omega*, and also (which proves its real importance) in a page of the treatise without a title in the Bruce Codex, and even in the Manichaean writings.[25] One would also like to recover the *Revelations of Marsianes and Martiades*—whose names are mentioned as those of two of the greatest teachers in the same treatise of the Bruce Codex, and by Epiphanius.[26] And the writings of Phôsilampes, also named in the Bruce Codex—ought not these to have been in our library? Certainly one or more of these precious treatises may yet be hidden among our Coptic books, perhaps under another title or, more simply, in one of those texts whose titles are missing, which we still need opportunity to examine.

In fact, like the impressive works that we have just catalogued, several other great revelations that we have still to enumerate represent—if we judge them by their contents—apocalypses supposedly inspired or written by Seth, by the Father of the incorruptible generation of the Perfect.

A system analogous to that of which we have already seen something in the *Pistis-Sophia*, is represented in our collection by two characteristic writings: on the one hand by the *Hypostasis of the Archons* (No. 39), and on the other by an untitled text (No. 40) of which some fragments are found a second time among the odd pages catalogued under No. 35.

The *Hypostasis of the Archons* begins in these terms: "Upon the subject of the hypostasis of the powers in the Spirit of the Father of the Truth. The great apostle has told us, concerning the powers of darkness: 'It is not against flesh and blood that you have to wrestle, but against the powers of the cosmos. . . .'" Starting from this quotation from St Paul's *Epistle to the Ephesians* (VI, 12),

[25] Cf. chap. II, p. 82.　　[26] Cf., above, p. 46; chap. I, notes 113 and 114.

the narrator tells us how the demiurge of this lower world, believing himself to be its sole god, became so swollen with pride as to exclaim: "There is no other god but I"; whereupon a voice from on high answered and said: "Thou art mistaken, Samael . . . !" From this point, the narrative goes on to tell us about the fabrication, by this arrogant god, of the material world. The powers of the lower universe decide to create man: "Come," they say, "let us make a man. . . ." The body of this man is fashioned from earth, in the image of the high God, a reflection of whom has just been seen by the Archons, in the waters below. This done, the demiurge breathes his strength into the mouth of this new creature, who immediately comes to life, but at first cannot stand upright on his feet. Afterwards, when Adam has been animated, the powers—the Archons—bring together the beasts and birds, for Adam to give them their names (cf. *Genesis* II, 19). They then place him in Paradise, while warning him never to eat of the tree of life. Out of his side they create Eve, his companion. Then the first man, from having been only material (hylic) becomes ensouled (psychic); Eve herself is spiritual (pneumic) and consequently it is she who gives life to him: that is why, when he sees Eve beside him, Adam names her "Mother of the Living". But the Archons themselves are dazzled at the sight of Eve; they fall in love with her: "Come, and let us send our seed into her." They pursue her, but she makes fun of their stupidity. But then comes the son of the demiurge, the Serpent, who suggests to the woman that she should taste of the Tree of life. Thereafter, this apocryphon follows fairly closely the outline of the Biblical *Genesis*. The Proto-archon, the Creator, calls Adam who, having sinned, knows that he is naked and hides himself; upon which the first couple are expelled from Paradise.

After the birth of Cain and Abel, engendered normally by Adam and Eve, and after the murder of Abel by his brother, the birth of Seth is, in this case, passed over in silence; nor does Seth play any notable part in the rest of the treatise.

But then our apocryphon diverges again from *Genesis*. The Creator of this base world, displeased with men who have greatly multiplied, orders Noah to build the Ark and prepares to unloose the Deluge. This episode takes place upon the mythic mountain of Seir.[27] Hôrea, daughter of Eve and of superior birth, wishes to go into the Ark, but Noah, inspired by the perverse creator, forbids her. She blows upon the hull in construction, at which it catches fire and is burnt up. Noah rebuilds the Ark. Meanwhile a violent quarrel breaks out between Hôrea—whose name is given also in the form of Nôrea[28]—and the lower archons. In response to the cries of Nôrea, the great angel Heleleth descends from before the holy Spirit; his aspect is like gold, his vesture like snow. To overcome and subdue the lower powers, Time is created, to which they are subjected, so that they may not again defile the incorruptible Generation.[29]

After this exposition of the earthly Genesis, the book recounts the history of Sophia, also called Pistis. Logically this second part of the treatise should have been placed at the beginning of the work, before what we have just summarized; for it describes the creation of the lower heavens.

Sophia—it tells us—desired to produce, without a partner, a creation modelled upon the heavenly pattern. She failed. There is a veil between the higher realms of light and the inferior aeons,

[27] Numerous traditions, relating as much to the Cave of Adam as to the Magi, locate the land of Shyr, or of Seir, beyond the inhabited world to the east, near the great Ocean. There rises the Mountain of Victories, or Mount of the Lord (a tradition already to be found in the *Avesta*). It is this, then, and not the Seir in the land of Edom (*Genesis* XXXVI) that is meant here by the term "Mountain of Seir". Here, it seems, was the Cave in which Adam deposited the treasures which the Magi were one day to carry to Bethlehem. He and his successors were buried there. Various identifications of this holy place have been proposed: perhaps it was at the Kuh-i-Khwâga which rises over the shores of Lake Hamun in the far east of Iran. Still to be seen there today are the ruins of a palace dating from the epoch of that king Gundophar whom tradition has made into the Magus Gaspar: an annual pilgrimage still marks the sacred character of the place. This identification is proposed by Herzfeld, *Archeological History of Iran*, 1935, pp. 58ff. and photograph, Pl. vii. It is also defended by Messina, *op. cit.*, pp. 82–83. U. Monneret de Villard criticizes it, apparently with reason, in his *Leggendi orientali sui Magi evangelici*, chaps. I and III; he suggests instead the mountain Sabalân, the highest peak in Azerbaijan (which would mean that the "eastern" Ocean was the Caspian Sea).

[28] Cf. above, chap. I, pp. 39 and 42–43, and note 103. Concerning the seduction of the Archons by Nôrea, and later development of that episode; cf. pp. 14–15.

[29] The "incorruptible Generation" means the race of the Perfect—of the Gnostics.

and darkness extends everywhere below that veil: the darkness becomes matter, and it is within matter that Sophia carries on her creative work—which is that of a monstrous being, shaped like a lion, male and female at the same time.[30] Opening its eyes, and seeing nothing around it but dark matter, this being, in its ignorance of the higher world, grows proud of its solitude and exclaims—in the words we have already found in the preamble of this writing—"I am God, and there is no other God but I"; thereby committing a grave sin. It is then that a voice from the higher worlds answers him: "Thou art mistaken Samael." "If anyone else has existed before me, let him show himself to me!" replies Samael. Sophia then comes down from the worlds above; she introduces light into matter, and then withdraws herself into the realms of Chaos. Then the evil Archon Samael (this is another name for Ialdabaôth) creates for himself seven sons, each both male and female, who are to preside over the seven planets; and he says

[30] This being is Ialdabaôth, whom the Gnostic myths identify with the God of *Genesis* and with the evil creator. Upon this same notion of the inferior god, cf. H. C. Puech, *La Gnose et le Temps*, note 26. Concerning his monstrous figure of a serpent with a lion's head, cf. Puech, "Le Prince des Ténèbres en son royaume" in *Satan: Études carmélitaines*, 1948, pp. 138–74. Ialdabaôth is sometimes also presented with the face of an ass or a pig. He is, moreover, known by several other names; sometimes he is called Samael, which assimilates him to the fallen angel, Satan, shown to us in, for example, the *Ascension of Isaiah*, warring against the armies of the higher heavens. He is also Ariel, the "lion of God" (cf. the engraved gem depicting Ialdabaôth-Ariel, C. Bonner, *op. cit.*, pp. 135–7, and pl. ix, no. 188). Above all, he is Sacla, whom one finds (albeit very rarely) identified with Osiris, for reasons which remain obscure; cf. above, chap. I, note 125). The Manichaeans knew him by this name: one of the *Kephalaia* found again in Coptic—the Chapter LVI—is even devoted to him. Sacla is also met with under the form of Eschakleo, in the myths of popular Hermetism: his birth is described (very differently from Gnostic descriptions of it) in the *Kosmopoiia*, a strange cosmogony preserved in a Greek papyrus at Leyden, in which some Jewish and Egyptian elements are intermingled: after the appearance of angels, of gods and of the light, the earth rises up in a round mass, the waters divide into three parts; and then it is that Eschakleo appears, and is given commandment over the abyss. (Festugière, *Révélation* . . . , vol. I, p. 301). F. Cumont, in his *Recherches* . . . , pp. 69ff., suggests an identity between the Omophore, the titanic entity who, according to the Manichaeans, holds up the earth, and Sacla. Perhaps this identification is too little in agreement with the part that is otherwise played by Sacla (also named Ashaqlun) in the Manichaean myths: on this point the study by Cumont brings together references that are equally valuable for the light they shed on the Sacla of the Gnostics.

to them, "I am the god of the Universe". But Zoë, the daughter of Sophia, reprimands him in her turn: "Thou art mistaken, Sacla!"—which name, adds the text, is translated Ialdabaôth.[31] Zoë breathes upon the creator, and her breath turns into an angel of fire who casts Ialdabaôth into the depths of Tartarus at the bottom of the abyss. Now Sabaôth, son of Ialdabaôth, seeing the power of the great angel engendered by the breath of Zoë, repents, realizes that his father and mother were matter, and offers up to Zoë the hymn of his repentance. Sophia and Zoë then install him in the seventh heaven, just below the veil which separates the lower world from the light. Sabaôth fashions for himself a great chariot, with four-faced cherubim and a multitude of angels, who sing psalms to the sound of harps.

The narrative closes upon the affliction of Ialdabaôth when he sees, from below, the glory of his repentant son.

Much of this treatise is manifestly an abridgement of a certain *Book of Nôrea*,[32] which Irenaeus tells us (in his *Adversus Haereses*, I, xxx), was in use among heretics whom we can identify surely enough with the Sethians and the Ophites. Epiphanius, when dealing with the great Gnostics in Chapter XXVI of his refutation, also cites this work as one of the most important. If we combine the information furnished by these two critics, we learn that Nôrea, or Hôrea, was born to Adam soon after Seth, and that the race of the Perfect is descended from both of them. After becoming Noah's wife, Nôrea set fire to the Ark as many as three times, because the demiurge, willing that she should perish with the rest of mankind, prevented her embarking in it. Her revolt against the Archons is also described.

In Chapter XXVI of Epiphanius, as also in Chapter XXV

[31] To this "translation" another is added by another of our Coptic texts (p. 174), which interprets the name Ialdabaôth as "the child who traverses places". Although somewhat obscure, this translation closely follows the Hebrew words that constitute the name of the evil god. Doubtless the passage in the *Hypostasis of the Archons* is intended only to mean that Sacla is identical with Ialdabaôth.

[32] Moreover, the Coptic writing which comes next after this one in our Codex No. 10, alludes, in two places, to the "preceding *Book of Nôrea*".

devoted to the Nicolaitans and XXI about the Simonians, an entity who is Nôrea in the first case, and who, in the other two cases, is identifiable either with Barbelô or else with Helen the companion of Simon Magus—is the heroine of a very peculiar myth: that of the "seduction of the Archons", whose impure passions are exploited by this feminine power in order to rob them of their seed. This myth is found again in Manichaeism.[33]

Under other names, Nôrea was equally well known to the Mandaeans, who called her Nuraïtha or Nhuraïta. Here she is usually, as among the Gnostics, wife of Noah and mother of Shem; sometimes, too, she is presented as the wife of the divine scribe Dinanukht.[34]

By its *title*, the Coptic treatise surely recalls, in the first place, the sect of the Archontici. It is the easier to regard it as one of the great books of that group because its contents as a whole correspond pretty closely with the myths generally attributed to them. Re-read, for example, the article devoted to them by Epiphanius in his Chapter XL against heresies: there we find one of the most original features of our Coptic writing very exactly reproduced—namely, the ambiguous part played by Sabaôth who, though he belongs to the lower heavens and is the father of the Serpent (that is, of "the devil"), is not here regarded as systematically evil. After his repentance, Sabaôth becomes lord of the seventh heaven, apparelled in the glory of the God of the Bible, Creator of this universe and of the Mosaic Law. The conception we knew before, from the Judeo-Gnostic invocations that have been analysed by Peterson.[35] These have shown us the

[33] Cf. Cumont, *Recherches* . . . , pp. 54ff. This myth has been as often told of Helen, Barbelô, Prunikos or Nôrea, as of the Virgin of Light who figures in the *Pistis-Sophia*, but above all in Manichaeism.

[34] Cf. Lidzbarski, *Das Johannesbuch der Mändaer*, p. 58; and the same author's *Ginzâ*, p. 205.

[35] Cf. above, chap. II, pp. 107ff. Here we must add that our Gnostics had a system of astrology, purely mythical, according to which each planet in turn ruled over the six others for a thousand years. Thus Kronos/Saturn (Ialdabaôth) was succeeded by Zeus/Jupiter (Sabaôth): this is in agreement with the myth that we have here (cf. pp. 75, 244–5 and 271). For their opposite characteristics—malefic for Saturn, benefic for Jupiter—which astrology ascribed to these planets and to which our myth conforms, see the references given by Nock and Festugière in vol. III of their edition of *Hermès Trismégiste*, p. cxcvi.

Propatôr, primordial Father, representing him as the aeon which stands motionless, the master of the Pole, upon the constellation of the Chariot—the constellation which, among our Gnostics, becomes like the divine Chariot in the vision of Ezechiel. The same prayers further prepare us for this identification, when they surround the god of the seventh heaven with archangels, decans and myriads of angels fashioned by him, and when they show just how this lord bears witness for Sophia, recalling the part played by her. In all this we find, in a more ancient guise, one of the essential myths of our Gnostic treatise.

The writing without a title which is No. 40 of our inventory, and of which our library contained another copy (the beginning of it is found on an odd leaf inventoried under No. 35), ought, by its contents, to be compared with the *Hypostasis of the Archons*. It is a treatise which is a didactic epistle, to which no name of a prophet, or author, or addressee is attached to define its nature.[36] It commences as follows:

"Though all the gods and men in the universe say, 'Nothing existed before the Chaos', I, for my part, will prove to you that they are all mistaken, for they never knew the nature of Chaos, nor its root. . . ." In terms not at all clear, and all too brief, the treatise goes on to say that even the darkness that existed before Chaos was the consequence of a primordial work (of the higher world?). In effect, at the beginning the Immortals alone existed, in a higher world the structure of which is not explained to us. And the treatise proceeds to describe—presumably in reference to this "primordial work"—the creation produced by "Pistis who is called Sophia". By her own initiative, her work develops between the Immortals and things here below; out of Darkness and Obscurity emerges the Chaos. This darkness feels that something exists stronger than itself; this feeling engenders Jealousy, and, from that moment, the abyss below is filled with a great mass of waters. Pistis beholds this darkness and these waters devoid of Spirit; she is dismayed that all this has been produced by her fault: the effect of her terror is to evoke the apparition,

---

[36] Cf. below, p. 195, our suggestion about possible relations between this writing No. 40 and the *Epistle of Eugnostos* (No. 3).

upon the waters, of a male-and-female archon with the face of a lion. Sophia speaks to it, calling it Ialdabaôth, the name that our author presumes to translate as "the child who is traversing places"; and a few lines further on our author adds: "The perfect call him Ariael, because he looks like a lion." Ialdabaôth, who as yet has seen only the reflection of Sophia in the waters, does not know of her power nor of the virtues which are above her. He therefore thinks that he alone exists. He creates for himself seven sons, one of whom is Sabaôth; and to these he adds yet other powers; the names and the strength of the male powers thus engendered are to be found—writes our compiler

Ialdabaôth — also called Ariael: an engraved gnostic gem.

—in the *Arkhangelikê of Moses the Prophet*; the names of the female in "the foregoing *Book of Nôrea*". After this Ialdabaôth builds heavens for each of his sons, habitations, great glories, thrones and temples; chariots and spirits escorted by innumerable armies of angels and archangels. The history of all these, adds our author, "thou wilt find it exactly stated in the preceding treatise of *Nôrea*". Ialdabaôth boasts about what he has just created: he exclaims, "I have no need of anyone! I am God and there is no other than I." Pistis hears the impious words of the great archon and cries: "Thou art mistaken, Samael" (meaning, our text says, "the blind god"). "An immortal man, a man of light existed before thee, who will be manifested in thy creation; he will trample thee underfoot as potters tread the clay, and thou wilt depart, thou and thine, down towards thy mother, the abyss of waters. . . ." Upon this, Pistis shows the reflection of her greatness on the water while she herself withdraws up into the light.

Hearing the voice of Pistis, Sabaôth sends up a hymn towards her: his invocation is accepted; Sabaôth receives honours and powers. He is called "the Lord of Armies". He begins to detest his Father the Darkness, and his Mother the abyss of waters; he is seized with loathing for his sister the Thought of Ialdabaôth.

But the powers of Chaos envy the glory which has now been given him; in the seventh heaven they prepare to wage a great war against him (cf. the Biblical *Revelation* XIII, 7). To the aid of Sabaôth Pistis-Sophia sends forth from her light, at first seven archangels, then three more, and then at last her daughter Zoë, who will help this god to create everything that is in the Ogdoad.

Our author expands at pleasure upon this creation. It comprises a glorious palace, a throne erected upon a chariot surrounded by cherubim with faces like those of a lion, a bull, a man and an eagle. The chariot, we are told, has been taken for a model by the seventy-two gods who govern the seventy-two languages of the peoples. There are also seraphim in the forms of dragons, who perpetually glorify their lord. Near to Sabaôth stands a first-born who is named Israel, "the man who sees God". Another is named Jesus the Christ, like to the Saviour who is in the highest heavens; he is seated at the right hand of Sabaôth. At the left of this Lord are enthroned the Virgin and the Holy Spirit. Before the throne a choir of virgins sing to the sound of the Psaltery and the trumpet.

Then Pistis separates the Darkness into two halves: the right, which is just, and the left, which is unjust.

Ialdabaôth, in the depths of the abyss, is tortured by jealousy. He creates death, which he establishes in the sixth heaven; this death is both male and female; it has seven sons and seven daughters whose names evoke evil passions and afflictions. The names and powers of the forty-nine demons who are subject to him are to be found, says our text, in the *Book of Solomon*. In response to this perverse creation of Ialdabaôth, Zoë provides Sabaôth with other powers which are good; powers which are enumerated, adds our author, in the *Schema of the Celestial Heimarmene*.[37]

It is not until this moment that Ialdabaôth recognizes, upon hearing her voice, that Sophia is the power who, in the beginning, cried out to him by name. Since he had then exclaimed, "There is no other God but I", he is afraid that at the advent of the Celestial Man, his own imposture will be exposed before the powers he governs. Hence his proclamation: "If anyone exists before me,

[37] *Heimarmene* means Fate.

let him show himself and let his light be seen!" From the height
of the Ogdoad there now descends through the heavens a shining
light in which is revealed a vision of Man. Seeing this, a Pronoïa
(i.e., a Prescience) who is associated with Ialdabaôth, falls in love
with the Man; but he hates her because she appears in the Darkness. She wishes to join with him, but in vain. Unable to appease
her amorous passion, she sheds her light (which is her blood?)
upon the earth. Ever since that day this angel has been called
Adam-Light, which means "the Man whose blood is light",
whilst the earth on which this was shed became the "holy,
Adamantine earth". Since that day, again, the Powers have
revered the blood of the Virgin. The earth has been purified by it
whilst the waters also were purified by the vision of Pistis-Sophia
which had been revealed in them.

Then suddenly Eros appears: he too is male and female; his
masculinity is made of the fire of the light, his femininity is a spirit
distilled from the blood of the Pronoïa. By his extreme beauty
Eros makes the gods and the angels fall in love with him and
becomes powerful over all the creatures of Chaos. He brings with
him the first-fruits of sensual pleasure and of carnal union. At the
same time, from the blood shed upon the earth, the vine is born
and some other trees grow up. It is then that Justice—one of the
powers of Sabaôth—creates a Paradise, remote from the cycles of
the Moon and the Sun, in a land of delights. There is found the
Tree of Life, which is to render immortal the souls of the Just who
are rising above matter. It grows up even to the sky; its beautiful
branches are like those of the cypress and its fruits are like bunches
of white grapes. The Tree of Knowledge grows here too: its
branches are like those of the fig tree, and its fruit similar to the
date.

Whilst the influence of Eros over the "daughters of the
Pronoïa" is developing, the plants, animals and birds make their
first appearance. A man is fashioned who is both male and female:
"This man", says our text, "the Greeks call Hermaphrodite; the
Hebrews call his mother, Eve from Zoë." Now also is created
"the beast"—that is, the Serpent destined to mislead the creatures.
"The meaning of the beast is, the Instructor"; he is wiser than all

other creatures. Lastly, the creation of Adam is described, in terms which recall those that we have already quoted and that we shall find again several times in our Coptic treatises. We will pass over the formation of Eve: once she has been created and is associated with Adam, she approaches "the tree", and the Dominations seize and defile her.

But the Archons, who have brought the various animals before Adam so that he might give them names, become troubled. "Look, here is Adam who has become like one of us, and knows the difference between the Light and the Darkness. Should he now approach the Tree of Life, and eat of it, he will also be immortal. Let us then throw him out of Paradise down to earth. . . ." They are afraid directly to attack the First Man on earth; so they surround the Tree of Life with animals of fire, to defend it from him: but their efforts are in vain. They then expel the first couple from Paradise: but Sophia and Zoë in their turn drive the Archons from the heavens. At this point our compiler has inserted a curious detail—the Phoenix, which periodically puts itself to death and resurrects, is said to have been created as a witness for the iniquitous judgment passed upon Adam by the Archons. On this subject allusion is made to a myth of "the three Phoenixes", then to "three water-hydria which are in Egypt", and the author even states there is something about the "third Phoenix" in the *Hierabiblos*—the *Sacred Book*. He then asks pardon for his digression and goes on; telling us how angels were created for the fallen archons, angels who proceeded to teach men various errors, drugs, magical practices, etc. . . . These are themes we shall find again in other treatises, and which need not detain us here.

The continuation of the narrative opens up an eschatological perspective. The salvation of the different categories of mankind is reviewed, and of the four classes enumerated one only, the Generation without a King—which means the Generation of the Perfect—will attain to the supreme Ogdoad, to the holy place of the Father in which these elect souls will come to rest in a glory and peace ineffable and everlasting. It is they, according to our writing, who are kings among the mortal, being themselves immortal. It is they who will judge and condemn the gods of Chaos and their powers.

The work we have just summarized is without any doubt a treatise of the highest importance, but one to which later commentaries and glosses have been added. Some of these annotations seem likely to be those of the compiler who put Codex X together: he has made similar additions both in the much amplified version that he gives of the *Secret Book of John* (No. 36, which we can compare with the shorter versions in two others of our manuscripts) and in the *Exegesis upon the Soul* (No. 41). For another proof that these annotations are the work of the compiler of the manuscript we have in our hands—two of them refer back to the "preceding" *Book of Nôrea*; that is, precisely to the work which, in Codex X, does come before the treatise in which these references occur. This Codex from the end of the fourth century thus provides a wonderfully living witness to the literary activity of the Gnostics.

Most of these interpolations are such as we can legitimately call "bibliographical references"—doubtless the most ancient in all literary history. One could find such references, though more imbedded in the text, in the little Greek treatise of the alchemist Zosimos which dates from about the same time and is partly inspired by the same mystical speculations.[38]

Can we identify the works named by our learned doctor? Which of the various works fictively attributed to Solomon in the literature of astrology and magic could we recognize as this *Book of Solomon* which, he says, enumerated the forty-nine demons here below? One that comes to mind is the *Epistle of Rehoboam* which was first noticed by Reitzenstein in his *Poimandres* and has been edited by Heeg in the *Catalogue of Greek Astrological Manuscripts*.[39] This text, which claims to be *The Key to Hydromancy*, describes the influences of the planets, of the angels and of the demons at each hour of each day of the week. It adds to this list some prayers to the planets and to the angels and,

[38] Cf. above, pp. 99ff, the analysis of this text.
[39] *Catalogus Codicum Astrologorum Graecorum*, VIII, fasc. 2, pp. 143ff; cf. Reitzenstein, *Poimandres*, pp. 186–7, and Festugière, *Révélation*, vol. I, pp. 399ff. Heeg says this text was composed in Egypt about the first century B.C.

finally, gives indications for the "characters" to be inscribed upon stone amulets and for the plants it is appropriate to associate with them. But may not the reference be—as seems more likely—to something in that vast collection entitled the *Testament of Solomon*, which enumerates a crowd of genies and mentions, for example, as rulers of this terrestrial world, Deception, Discord, Quarrelsomeness, violent Agitation, Error, Violence and Perversity.[40]

The *Arkhangelikê*, or *Book of the Archangels by Moses the Prophet*, is still more celebrated in astrological literature. We have it, well edited, in the *Poimandres* of Reitzenstein.[41] This brief treatise calls itself "a hymn of the archangels which the Lord gave to Moses upon Mount Sinai". In effect, the book is an enumeration of a multitude of powers, in order that he who is informed about them may protect himself against all demonic manifestations.

As for the title of *Sacred Book*, denoting a work in which there is some account of "three Phoenixes", it does not suggest any book that is known today. It surely cannot be the *Sacred Book of Hermes to Asclepius* published by Ruelle, which is concerned essentially with the thirty-six decans and the parts of the body governed by them.[42] Still less can we think it is the magical treatise entitled *Monad*, or *Eighth Book of Moses*, a work which gives itself this second title of *Sacred Book*. This formulary pretends—by a shocking anachronism!—that Moses revealed its contents "in the Temple of Jerusalem" to a disciple, making him swear to keep it carefully hidden. But it contains nothing of the tradition about the Phoenix to which our Coptic text alludes. What, then, are the myths referred to in these remarks about "three Phoenixes" and the "hydria that are in Egypt"? As for the Phoenix, any allusion to *three* of those fabulous birds is, in itself, of a certain originality. Indubitably all known traditions

---

[40] Cf. McCown, *The Testament of Solomon*, Chicado, 1922. Another edn. is published in A. Delatte, *Anecdota Graeca*, Brussels, 1927, pp. 212–27. Cf. also Fabricius, *Codex Pseudepigraphus*, I, 1047. Upon the apocryphal literature attributed to Solomon, see Wellman, *Der Physiologus*, p. 58, note 164 ; and Berthelot, *La Chimie au Moyen-âge*, vol. II, pp. 264–6.

[41] Reitzenstein, *Poimandres*, pp. 292ff.

[42] Cf. W. Gundel, *Dekane und Dekansternbilder*, 1936, pp. 374–9; and Festugière, *La Révélation d'Hermès Trismégiste*, vol. I, pp. 139–43.

about the Phoenix affirm that there was never more than the one which, periodically, died and was reborn. For that reason, indeed, its appearance in our texts is not surprising; for Christianity has willingly availed itself of this beautiful symbol of resurrections recurring at fixed periods.[43]

As for the myth of the "hydria that are in Egypt", this can refer only to the story of the demons which were banished by Solomon and imprisoned in seven bronze vases. Our commentator may have taken this, too, from the *Arkhangelikê*, which mentions it—unless he meant to allude to one of the writings put out under the name of Solomon which were known to Zosimos the alchemist and preserved in some later books. This work, now extant only in a Syriac version, says that the Egyptians used a book against the demons called *The Seven Heavens*, fictitiously ascribed to Solomon. It was concerned with the manner in which Solomon had made seven bottles of electrum (an alloy of silver and gold) in accordance with the number of the planets, and had engraved magical formulas upon them before imprisoning the genies in them. From Jerusalem, these vases had been taken to the priests of Egypt, in whose keeping they had remained.[44]

But we must compare these conjoined allusions to a plurality of Phoenixes and to the "hydria" in Egypt, with some curious passages in the *Book of the Secrets of Enoch*. This apocryphon dates from the first century of our era. Here we find, associated with the celestial powers, Phoenixes and "Khalkhydras" who accompany the chariot of the sun. Thus we read, in Chapter XII, that the chariot of the sun is escorted by a flight of Phoenixes and

---

[43] The myth of the Phoenix appears in Christian literature in the *First Epistle of Clement*; in the poem of Lactantius, *De Ave phoenice*; in the *Physiologus*, etc. A passage in the Coptic *Physiologus* mentions regular appearances of the phoenix, which sacrifices itself and is reborn upon every great event in Biblical history. (Cf. A. Van Lantschoot, "A propos du Physiologus" in *Coptic Studies in honor of W. E. Crum*, p. 357.) This is simply an adaptation of an ancient Egyptian tradition, that each new era was marked by a reappearance of the marvellous bird.

[44] Hydrion (ὑδρίον) was a word used by the Greeks in Egypt to denote a vessel to hold lustral water. Upon the text of Zosimos referring to Solomon and the "hydria" sent into Egypt, cf. Scott, *Hermetica*, vol. IV, pp. 140-1. In one line of the *Arkhangelikê of Moses*, the magician threatens the demons by reminding them how Solomon had once shut them up in hydria of bronze (cf. Reitzenstein, *Poimandres*, p. 295, text and note 2).

Khalkhydras; the latter being marvellous beings with the paws and tail of a lion and the head of a crocodile; their twelve wings are of all the colours of the rainbow. They accompany the sun as the bearers of its warmth and its dew. In Chapter xv we read that at the rising of the shining disc, the Phoenixes and Khalkhydras burst into song; and Chapter xix mentions six Phoenixes and six Khalkhydras in the midst of the angels of the sixth heaven, with six six-winged beasts, chanting unceasingly. Another and rather later apocryphon—the third *Book of Baruch*—gives us in its Chapters vi and vii some allusions to the unique Phoenix to add to this picture. This Phoenix flies round in circles in front of the chariot of the sun, with outspread wings shielding the human race from its too ardent rays. The bird feeds upon dew and manna; and an inscription in letters of gold adorns its wings.[45]

The myth of *one* Phoenix, or *several*, which appears in these two writings must have been fairly widely known, for it occurs again in Lactantius's poem *De Phoenice* at the end of the third century, which makes the Phoenix a companion of the sun (l. 33) and depicts the bird saluting the day-star at its rising by the beating of its wings (ll. 43–54).

But what are these strange Khalkhydras who, by their close association with the Phoenixes, remind us of the allusion of our Coptic text to "the water-hydria that are in Egypt"? Certainly the modern commentators on the *Book of the Secrets of Enoch*—the only text in which this curious term Khalkhydra had ever been found until now—have tried to explain it by supposing that "bronze hydria" were mythological animals who, they conjecture, may be equated with the serpents we find associated with the choir of Cherubim in a (no less highly exceptional) passage of the first *Enoch* (XX, 7).[46] But these "Khalkhydras"—our Coptic text allows no possible doubt—are indeed the bronze hydria in which Solomon shut up the demons, and which he afterwards entrusted to the care of the Egyptian priests.

How—we shall be asked—could these vessels possibly turn

---

[45] The passages quoted form the *Book of the Secrets of Enoch* and from the third *Book of Baruch*, are in R. H. Charles, *The Apocrypha and Pseudepigrapha of the Old Testament*, vol. II, pp. 436–8, 441 and 536–7.

[46] Cf. R. H. Charles, *op. cit.*, p. 436, notes.

into celestial beings with crocodiles' heads, accompanying the star of day with singing and the beating of wings? One can easily clear up this incredible muddle by turning back to the *Arkhangelikê of Moses.*[47] A passage in that ritual, after invoking the Cherubim, the Powers, the Dominations, Thrones, Lordships, and the "creatures with six wings" . . . proceeds to conjure up in similar fashion the evil spirits who, in the lower heavens, are correspondingly arrayed in hierarchies: these are the nine hundred and sixty spirits of the "church of perversity", who exercise their innumerable and malefic powers over the universe, and whom Solomon "when he had shut them up in the bronze hydria" compelled to swear fealty to him.

The close connection between Phoenixes and "Khalkhydras" in the *Book of the Secrets of Enoch* is, therefore, merely an allusion, deformed to the point of absurdity, to those inferior spirits, those fantastic and accursed creatures that Solomon had imprisoned for a time, according to the peculiar myth reported in the *Arkhangelikê*—a myth which our Coptic writer knew and referred to by his remarks about "three Phoenixes" and "bronze hydria in Egypt".

Finally, of the rare writings mentioned by our compiler, *The Schema of the heavenly Heimarmene* is completely unknown. It may well have been something like the *Book of the Seven Heavens* which we have just cited or like the *Diagram* used by the Ophites and mentioned by Celsus,[48] or, yet again, like the *Book of the Chiefs of the Towns up to the Aether* in use among the Peratae, which is summed up in Book V, § 14, of the *Philosophumena*.

The aim of the compiler, in enumerating all these writings, was to enlarge, even more than was directly possible in the pages at his disposal, the lists of celestial powers to which, for reasons of astrology or magic, such great importance was attributed. He had such a peculiar partiality for lists of this kind that he interpolated some of them even into his transcription of the *Secret Book of John.*

Another feature of our writing is that it tries to give explanations of the Semitic names of several of the powers—as, for instance, its translation of the name Ialdabaôth as "the child

---

[47] Quoted in Reitzenstein, *Poimandres*, pp. 294-5.   [48] See above, p. 7.

who traverses places" (?). Its gloss upon the name of Samael is "the blind god"—perhaps an allusion to the Jewish tradition that Moses made Samael blind when the latter, in discharge of his function as the angel of Death, came to fetch him away from this world.[49] Ariael, we are told, bears that name because he has the face of a lion; and, in fact, Ariael does mean in Hebrew "the lion of God". Noteworthy also is the speculation, based on the Semitic vocabulary, that the name of Adam signifies "blood" and "earth".[50] Such speculations about the name of Adam were common in Jewish mysticism. They were indeed so well known that a distinct echo of them still sounds in the treatise *On the Letter Omega*: "The Chaldaeans, the Parthians, the Medes and the Hebrews name him [i.e. the primordial man] Adam, which being interpreted is: virgin earth, earth the colour of blood, earth red as fire, earth of flesh".

As for the substance of the treatise itself, one would much like to know who exactly were the adversaries whom the author wanted to refute, and who said that the universe began with Chaos: were these, then, defenders of the Hellenic mythology? "Before anything was there was Chaos . . ." as Hesiod had written in his *Theogony* (line 116). We also wish we could better understand how the Gnostic doctor conceives the primordial principles of the universe, for he does not seem to have at all a good knowledge of the "three roots" so clearly set forth in the *Paraphrase of Shem*. Upon all the other subjects he expounds, this Coptic writing is particularly rich and clear. In the first place it develops the parts played by Sophia and by the Saviour—the primordial Adam; and into this great myth it introduces other

[49] Cf. *Debarim Rabbah*, XI; *Acts of Andrew and Matthias*, § 24 (in M. R. James, *Apocryphal New Testament*, p. 456); "Art thou not called Samael because thou art blind?" Theo. Bar-Konai, *Book of Scholia* in the edn. Pognon, p. 213; passage upon the Ophites, where Samael is again referred to as blind.

[50] We have already seen, in discussing Justin's Gnosticism, some speculations upon the supposed relations between the names of Eden (Edom in the Septuagint) and Adam: cf. above chap. I, note 87. Here, we have some further play upon words, starting from *dam* "blood" and *edom* "red". See also Josephus, *Jewish Antiquities*, I, 1, 2; and also the passage of Olympiodorus we have mentioned, p. 101 and note 84. As for the fictive relationship between each of the four letters of Adam's name and the Greek names for each of the cardinal points, cf. the *Sybilline Oracles* III, 24; and the Slavonic *Enoch*, chap. xxx.

7

speculations, the strangest being that intervention of Eros, the details of which are borrowed from Hellenic mythology. Let us reopen Hesiod at the passage we have just mentioned: "Before all things there was Chaos, then the broad-bosomed earth . . . and then Eros, the most beautiful among the immortal gods . . ." (*Theogony*, 116–20). It is to the advent of Eros that our Gnostic relates the birth of the trees, the plants and the animals: and in a passage of the *Danaids* of Aeschylus, Eros impels the sky to unite itself with the earth which, thus fecundated, brings forth for mortal beings "the grass, food for cattle and corn the nourishment of life. . . ."[51]

Thus our author's mind is still full of the classic myths even while he is refuting them in principle. This Coptic treatise is an authentic and admirable example of this particular syncretism to which certain sects were addicted, and of which we knew hardly anything until now, beyond what we could gather from portions of the *Philosophumena* devoted to heretics such as the Naassenes.[52]

The Jewish elements in our treatise are of the highest importance. Of these, certain features are already to be found in the best known of the Old Testament apocrypha, the *Book of Enoch* and the *Ascension of Isaiah*: such for example is the part played by Samael-Ialdabaôth, who, having at first been the highest of the "thrones", afterwards falls from his dignity and is cast into the abyss. Thus he becomes the "prince of this world"—of the world here below;[53] thus, also, he engages in battle against the

[51] Aeschylus, fragment 44 (Nauck). Cf. also the Orphic cosmogony expounded by Aristophanes in *The Birds*, 693–700.
[52] According to the *Philosophumena*, the Peratae in their book, *The Chiefs of the Towns up to the Aether* (more or less similar to the *Book of the Heavenly Heimarmene* mentioned in our Coptic text?) knew the figure of Eros, whom they made into a celestial power. "There is an androgyne power, a child forever . . . , cause of beauty, of pleasure . . . , of concupiscence: the ignorant called him Eros" (V, 14). Upon this syncretism see below pp. 263ff. Upon the cosmic Eros, creator of the world, see P. M. Schuhl, *Essai sur la formation de la pensée grecque*, 1934, p. 235.
[53] This episode of the deprivation of Ialdabaôth and his being supplanted in the seventh heaven by his son Sabaôth is also known—in another form—from the *First Book of Pistis-Sophia*, and from some fragments which are related to that text. Here we are told how Sabaôth the Adamas (now playing the same part as Ialdabaôth in our writing No. 40), having plunged into the disorders of procreation—himself and his archons—was deprived of his rank and shackled to a

Lord (who is now Sabaôth) in the firmament.[54] But we must
note above all, how the Gnostic account elaborates the description
of the divine throne, outlined before in the *Hypostasis of the
Archons* or *Book of Nôrea*. This vision originates in the originally
Jewish mysticism of the Merkaba—of the divine Chariot—
developed from the vision of Ezechiel and much amplified in a
whole Rabbinical literature describing the hidden glories of the
heavenly Majesty, the palaces (or Hekhalôth) where he resides,
and the Throne. "This throne", writes G. Scholem,[55] "is to the
Jewish mystic what the Pleroma, the plenitude, the shining
sphere of the divinity with all its powers, its aeons, archons and
dominations is to the Greek mystics and to the first Christian
mystics who appear in the history of religions under the names of
Gnostics and Hermetists." And it is in its Jewish form that this
mysticism reappears in Gnostic texts. But can it be introduced
here without contradictions? How is it compatible with the
intermediate position between the darkness and the abyss, in the
"middle ways" here occupied by Sabaôth?[56] Had Jewish mysticism ever known such a mixture of ideas? All these are problems
which it may take a long while yet to resolve.

A rather different account of the history of the higher world,
ending with an invocation taken from some ritual of spiritual
baptism, is given in the *Sacred Book of the invisible Great Spirit*,
or *Gospel of the Egyptians*,[57] of which there are two copies (No. 2

sphere of fate by the great power named Jêou, whilst his son Ibraôth (Sabaôth)
believed in the mysteries of the light and was elevated to heaven whence his
father had fallen.

[54] Cf. the battles fought in the heavens by the angels of Samael, mentioned in
the *Ascension of Isaiah* VII, 9 and X, 29, and in the Biblical *Revelation* XII, 7 et seq.
These combats between celestial spirits were known before in Mazdaism, and
then in classic astrology: cf. Cumont, *Lux Perpetua*, p. 299. We find them again
in the Muhammadan Gnosticisms: cf. H. Corbin, "De la Gnose antique à la
Gnose ismaélienne", p. 123, in Accademia Nazionale dei Lincei, Fondazione Al.
Volta, *Atti de Convegni*, 12=*Convegno di scienze morali, storiche e filologiche*, 1956,
Rome, 1957.

[55] G. G. Scholem, *Les Grands courants de la mystique juive*, p. 57; cf. ibid., p. 372,
note 9 and p. 374, note 24.

[56] Sabaôth here is perfectly assimilable to the Propatôr of the mystical text
analysed by Peterson (cf. here, p. 108). There the Propatôr is, indeed, represented
as the aeon which remains motionless on the constellation of the Chariot, master
of the Pole, surrounded by his decans and myriads of angels.

[57] J. Doresse, "Trois livres gnostiques inédits . . ."

and No. 7). This sacred book tells us how three great powers emerged from the invisible Great Spirit: the Father, the Mother and the Son, all "issuing from the living Silence, emanation of the everlasting Father". Then three Ogdoads formed themselves, among which one finds such names as Domedôn-Doxomedôn, the "aeon of aeons"; the Three male Children; Barbelon the Mother; the virgin Epititiôkh. . . . Emanation after emanation, we are shown, first how Mirôthea, mother of the incorruptible saints, engenders Adamas-light, born of the primordial Man; then how the great luminaries appears—Harmozel, Oroiael, Daueithe, Heleleth. With these are conjoined Grace, Sensibility, Comprehension and Reflection; then the great Gamaliel, Gabriel, Samlô and Abrasax; and then Memory, Charity, Peace and the Life everlasting. Here the incorruptible generation, seed of the Father on high, is called the "seed of the great Seth", from the name of the son of Adamas. At this moment, the great Christ, whose generation was expounded at the beginning of this catalogue of entities, but in a part of the manuscript which has been lost, establishes in the aeons the thrones, powers and glories which are to constitute the imperishable Church. This completes the first part of the book.

A following section then recounts how the great Seth returns thanks to the Invisible Spirit and to its surrounding entities—the male virgin Iouel, Hesephekh, Doxomedôn—beseeching them to grant him their seed. Thereupon they produce Plesithea, Mother of angels, a virgin "with four breasts, who brings forth the fruit from the source of Gomorrha and of Sodom", and this seed is established by the great Seth in the third of the luminaries, Daueithe. Five hundred years after this, Heleleth proclaims, "Let a king be [set up] over Chaos and over Hell!" Here, a mutilated page described the appearing of the demiurge Sacla, who creates for himself the heavens and twelve great angels charged with the rulership of the seven heavens and of the Amente (hell). As soon as this hebdomad is achieved, Sacla cries out, "I am a jealous god and there is no other beside me!" But a voice from on high answers him, "Man exists, and so does the Son of Man!" The image of the celestial Man is at once reflected in the waters. Sacla and his colleagues, in imitation of this, fashion the first human creature. The formation of this terrestrial Adam is only briefly indicated; the writer passes on quickly to the subject of the salvation of the human race of the Perfect, of the seed of Seth. He says that this seed is "planted in the aeons that have been engendered"—aeons of which "the number is the figure of Sodom", and about which this word has been uttered: "The great Seth has taken his seed from Gomorrha and has transplanted it into the second place which was called Sodom." Three divine visitations, including flood and fire, will come to persecute the great, incorruptible generation. But we are also told that the great Seth appealed to the great Invisible Spirit and to the other powers on high to obtain guardians for them—entities, no doubt supernatural, who are to protect his seed even to the end of this lower world. Moreover, the great Seth has had a holy baptism prepared, the five seals of which will enable his race to escape from the evil god—the god "of the thirteen aeons". Then are enumerated the mysterious entities put in charge of these sacraments, a few of whose names are already known to us from the anonymous treatise of the Bruce Codex: these are, besides Iessea Mazarea Iessedekea, the "great strategi" James the Great, Theopemptos, Isoauel, Mikhea, Mikhar, Mnesinous, Sessenggenpharaggen—a name often found also upon the magical gems!—Mikheus and others. These creatures preside over the "living water" at "the source of truth", at the "portals of the waters", on the "mountain of Seldaô" and on the Mount of Olives, upon the "way which leads to rest in the life everlasting". For the present, we are told, it will be given to the Perfect only to know these powers who are authorized to watch over them, and that, thanks to these beings, they will never taste of death. Later, for them, will come "the election of the five seals in the Baptism from the Source".

The third part of this mysterious text—though it is mixed with magical formulas made up of sequences of vowels devoid of meaning—recalls undoubtedly a baptismal liturgy, which makes it especially valuable. "I have known thee; I mingled myself with him who changes not; I armed myself in an armour of light.

. . . I took shape in the cycle of the riches of the light that is in my breast, giving form to that which is never begotten. . . . God of the Silence! thee I invoke, Thee altogether!"

This mystical text comes to its climax with the following declaration: "Here it is, the book written by the Great Seth. He left it in high mountains upon which the sun never rises, nor can it do so.[58] Since the days of the prophets, the apostles and the preachers, not even [its] name has ever appeared in men's hearts, nor could it do so. Their ears have never heard it. This book, the Great Seth wrote it in the writings of a hundred and thirty years: he left it in the mountain called Charax so that, in the last time and in the last instants, it might become manifest." And here is the title of this work, still better defined right at the end of it: "*The Gospel of the Egyptians*, a book written from God, sacred and hidden. . . . He who transcribed it is [I] Eugnostos the agapite, according to the spirit [i.e. his spiritual name]; in the flesh, my name is Goggessos. . . ."

Not only by its impressive attribution to Seth—which enables us to recognize it as one of the *Allogeneous Books* referred to by the heresiologists—but also by the very singular entities that it mentions, this apocryphon reflects the same doctrines as are expounded in the anonymous treatise of the Bruce Codex which was already known. The system in question will be further defined in several more of the great "Sethian" writings in our collection. But the *Book of the invisible Great Spirit* may well prove to be—taking into account the sobriety which is peculiar to it—one of the most ancient revelations of this class.

A *Gospel of the Egyptians* is mentioned in the *Philosophumena's* notice of the Naassenes; and what is there said about it, although

---

[58] Cf. above, note 27, concerning the country of Seir: we are again on the same inaccessible shores of the mythical Oriental Ocean. An alleged *Lapidary of Aristotle* has been preserved in Greek and Hebrew, and in the latter version it is stated explicitly that the stone Bâhit stands "on the coasts of the Ocean [speaking of the 'oriental' Ocean whither Alexander's expedition was marching to disaster], in a place where no light appears and where the sun does not rise". See J. Ruska, *Das Steinbuch des Aristoteles*, 1912, p. 12. It is hard to say, however, where to look for the Mountain of Charax named here. The only Charax we know of in that part of Asia was the town built on the Tigris in immediate proximity to the Persian Gulf (cf. below p. 256) and not in the mysterious regions near the oriental Ocean.

indefinite, suggests that it was a writing analogous to ours. . . . However, after gleaning from the other heresiologists all the few allusions they make to a *Gospel of the Egyptians*, we find that none of them coincide with any passage whatever in our Coptic text—which, moreover, is a treatise, whereas the work referred to in these refutations seems to have been in the form of a gospel. A no less peculiar phenomenon, showing how cautious one has to be, in identifying such and such a manuscript solely from indications furnished by the Gnostics' enemies, is that while our Coptic text contains nothing of what these critics say was in the *Gospel of the Egyptians*, it does, on the other hand, have a passage which Epiphanius (in his section XXVI), quotes as coming from . . . *The Gospel of Philip!*[59]

We will no more than mention No. 34, a *Treatise on the Triple Epiphany, on the Prôtennoïa in Threefold Form; a Sacred Writing from the Father in a perfect Gnosis.*[59a] In what poor pages remain of this manuscript, we have only some fragments of the end of the work thus entitled. This, again, is a cosmogony, where much is said of the Great Luminaries and of the celestial Virgin called Mirôthea. We find here the multiple figure of the evil demiurge, "the great demon who reigns over the abysses of Amente [of Hell] and Chaos, and who has no form at all and is in no way perfect, but has only the form of those who are engendered in the Darkness. They call him Sacla, which is to say Samael, Ialdabaôth, who has a power which is the Epinoïa of the light." The prophet into whose mouth this revelation is put lets us gather, from the last page, that he is identical with the Great Seth. In ending his prophecy, he recalls his reascent up from the lower heavens to the celestial world into which, later, he is to conduct the Perfect: "For myself, I have put on Jesus. I have led him out of the bitter tree [i.e., out of matter] and I have established him in the abode of the Father. And those who watch over their abode [that is, the lower angels described as "watchers"] did not recognize me, for I am an imperceptible, I and my seed that belong to me: I shall establish him in his holy light on high, in the Silence unattainable. Amen."

[59] Cf. p. 225.   [59a] On this work, cf. Appendix I.

Here, once more, is a great apocalypse; the *Revelation of Adam to his son Seth* (No. 12). "An apocalypse that Adam revealed to his son Seth in the seven hundreth year, saying this to him: Hear my words, my son Seth. When god [i.e. the Archon] created me from earth with Eve thy mother, I went with her into a glory. . . . She taught me one thing from the knowledge of the everlasting God: and that—it was the appearances of the eternal angels. For these were higher than the god who had created us, me and the powers who were with me. . . . Then the Archon, in anger, cut us off from the aeons of the powers. We then became two aeons, and the glory that was in us deserted us, me and thy mother Eve; and the primordial knowledge that had breathed in us also abandoned us. Because of that, I named thee with the name of the Man [i.e. Seth], who is the seed of the Great Generation proceeding from him. . . . After those same days, the eternal Gnosis of the God of Truth fled far from me and from thy mother Eve and, after that day, we learned mortal things like Men. It was then that we knew the gods who had created us, for we were not at all strangers to his power and we were serving him in fear and humility. . . ." Here Adam narrates, in a part of the manuscripts which unfortunately is damaged, how, while asleep, he dreamt that he saw "three men before me, of whom I could not bear the sight, because they were not of the powers of this [world]". And further on he tells us: "Because of that, the days of our life became few and I knew that I had passed into the power of Death. But now, Seth, I will reveal to you the things that have been unveiled to me. . . ."

Adam recalls the first proliferation of mankind over the earth, then the Flood, and the story of the Ark built by Noah, of which he says that it was also called Deucalion. Shem and Japhet are mentioned. Soon the exposition passes on to the promises that were made to the imperishable Generation, and for the future salvation of humanity. The great celestial powers Mikheus, Mikhar, Mnesinous, with Abraxas, Samlo and Gamaliel, are to draw the elect out of the fire up to heaven. And all the stages of a future devoted to the redemption of the Perfect are here in outline. The Enlighteners of Gnosticism will come down into this world. At the same epochs as various kingdoms, there is to be a succession of Saviours, whose births are predicted. Let us quote a few words from these prophecies: "The second royalty said to his subject: A great prophet has appeard. . . . A bird came; it took up the little child that had been born and carried him up to a high mountain where the birds of heaven fed him. An angel came and said to him, 'Rise up, God has glorified thee!' . . . The third royalty said to him, There has been a virgin mother; they banished him from his town, him and his mother; they took him out into a desert place. . . ." Then there is something about a Virgin bringing a child into the world and rearing it somewhere far away in the desert (cf. the *Revelation of St John* XII, 6). These revelations are continued as far as to a thirteenth royalty and perhaps still farther. The final words are: "These are the revelations that Adam disclosed to his son Seth, and this son has taught his descendants about them. Here it is, the Gnosis of the secrets of Adam which Seth has transmitted; it is the holy Perfection for those who know the Gnosis, eternally, by the [a number now illegible] incorruptible Enlighteners, begetters of the Word, who are born of the seed of [   ] Iesseus [   ] Mazareus [   ] Iessedekeus [   ] the *Revelation of Adam*."

Epiphanius (XXVI) said that the great Gnostics made use of a *Revelation of Adam*, with which, no doubt, our Coptic book may be identical. In the sixth century Bishop John of Parallos in Lower Egypt was still publicly denouncing these *Teachings of Adam* in the course of a homily against the reading of heresies.[60] Among the Manichaeans, the tenth chapter of their *Book of Mysteries* was devoted to the witness borne by Adam to the future advent of the Christ.[61] The Mandaeans, too, believed it was Adam to whom the first of the secret books were revealed, and named their great sacred book of the *Treasure*—the *Ginza Rba*—among these *Books of Adam*.

Our Coptic book is primarily distinguished by the fact that the powers which are named in it, Mikheus, Mikhar, Mnesinous, and

[60] Cf. Arn. Van Lantschoot, "Fragments coptes d'une homélie de Jean de Parallos . . ." in *Miscellanea Giovanni Mercati*, vol. I. Citta del Vaticano. 1946 (=*Studi e Testi*, 121).
[61] Ibn An-Nadim, *Fihrist*, translation of Flügel, p. 102.

7*

the salvational names of Iesseus Mazareus Iessedekeus are characteristic of a good many of the Sethian revelations—whether we are
thinking of the Gospel of the Egyptians or of the anonymous
treatise in the Bruce Codex. But the great prophecies which our
work puts into the mouth of Adam the father of Seth were in
themselves known before Gnosticism. Their original substance
appears in writings attributed to Zoroaster, and certainly goes
back to the *Avesta*.[62] Both Gnostics and Manichaeans—as we have
seen—liked to count Zoroaster in the number of their prophets.
In any case these revelations, in their earliest forms, recalled the
coming of saviours of whom the greatest must have been Saoshyant, of the line of this same Zoroaster. His myth was
popularized by a number of apocrypha, in which the great
saviour took on characteristics of the Christ, whilst Shem,
Melchizedek and Nimrod came into the story, and Zoroaster
was taken to be identical with the prophets Baruch and Balaam.[63]
At the same time, now mingling nascent Christianity with these
Iranian and Jewish myths, there were amplifications of the major
episode of the Magi keeping watch for the rising of the star that
was to guide them to Bethlehem for the adoration of the Messiah!

The principal work in which, after a long and obscure evolution, all these traditions became syncretized was the *Book of the
Cave of Treasures*, which enjoyed a prodigious diffusion. It puts
all these revelations into the mouth of Adam as the first of a long
series of prophets, who predicts how the Magi will await the
announcement of the Saviour, near this cave in which Adam
himself will have been interred by Seth, and where the Treasures
are concealed which the Magi will carry to Bethlehem.[64] With

[62] Cf. above, note 18.
[63] Cf. Bidez–Cumont, vol. I, part 1; upon the successive royalties and the
advent of the saviour, cf. also what is said in the same work about the *Apocalypse
of Hystaspes*, vol. I, pp. 217–22 and vol. II, pp. 364–76: see also Messina, *I Magi a
Betlemme*, pp. 74–82; cf. also above chap. II, note 72.
[64] Cf. Bezold, *Die Schatzhöhle* . . . , 1883; Frey, in the *Dictionnaire de la
Bible, Supplément*, vol. I, cols. 134ff. Monneret de Villard, *loc. cit.*; Preuschen,
Die Apokryphen gnostischen Adamschriften aus dem Armenischen übersetzt . . . ,
Giessen, 1900; A. Götze, "Die Schatzhöhle (Ueberlieferung und Quelle)" in
Sitzungsberichte der Heidelberger Akad. Philos.-Histor. Kl., 1922, No. 4. Preuschen
is perhaps mistaken in trying to assign a Gnostic origin to the writings on Adam
he has translated; more probable is Götze's suggestion that the first part of the
Book of the Cave may be founded on a Sethian book.

this book of the *Cave* we must class a great many other *Testaments* or *Books of Adam* preserved in Syriac, in Ethiopian, in Armenian or in Arabic.[65] . . . In the titles of these writings the name of Seth, as that of the supposed depositary of the loftiest secrets, soon tended, moreover, to eclipse that of his earthly father in prestige. Thus the pseudo-Chrysostom, in the *Unfinished Commentary on St Matthew*, refers expressly to a *Writing put under the name of Seth*.[66] In the Syriac *Chronicle* from the Zuqnîn monastery near Amida (finished about the year 774), the traditions about the Magi and the advent of the Saviour are summed up in terms that remind one chiefly of the narrative in the *Book of the Cave of Treasures*. However, let us quote from it these lines, supposedly spoken by the Magi, for they reflect the very general prestige that was attached to writings entitled, like our *Revelation of Adam*, with the name of Seth:

"Adam imparted revelations to his son Seth, and showed him his original greatness before the Transgression and his going out of Paradise. He recommended his son Seth never to fail in justice as he, Adam, had done. Seth welcomed the teaching of his father with a pure heart . . . it was given to him to inscribe this wisdom in a book and to teach it . . . and thanks to him, for the first time in this world, there was seen a book written in the name of the Most High. Seth bequeathed to his descendants the book thus written, and that book was handed down even to Noah. . . . In the time of the Flood, Noah took with him into the ark the books of these teachings, and when he came out of the ark, he ordained in his turn that the generations that came after him were to repeat the many things and the holy mysteries written in the books of Seth upon the Majesty of the Father and upon all the mysteries. Hence these books, these mysteries and this narrative were handed down even to our fathers, who welcomed them with joy and who passed them on to us . . .

[65] Upon the *Books of Adam*, cf. Frey, "Adam (apocrypha)" in the *Dictionnaire de la Bible, Supplément*, vol. I, cols. 101–34—particularly 119, 120 and 122. Cf. below, our chap. VIII, pp. 318ff. on the survival of one of these legends in an Arab MS. ascribed to Balinus (Apollonius of Tyana).

[66] Bidez–Cumont, *loc. cit.*, vol. I, p. 46; vol. II, pp. 118ff.; Monneret de Villard, *loc. cit.*, pp. 20ff.

and these books of the hidden mysteries were placed in the Mountain of Victories to the east of our country of Shyr, in a grotto: the Cave of Treasures of the Life of the Silence."[67]

Theodore Bar Konaï in the eighth century, and Solomon of Basra at the beginning of the thirteenth, still knew of such prophecies, not put into the mouth of Adam, but of Zoroaster—although the Saviour foretold in them was endowed with attributes of the Christ. Let us see how the one and the other of these compilers summarize a passage in these revelations:[68]

"Zaradusht, seated near the source of [living] water of Glosha of Hurîn [?] . . . , spoke thus to his disciples Sushtap, Sâsan and Mâhman [names which, though distorted, are of Iranian origin]. Listen, that I may reveal to you the prodigious mystery concerning the great king who must come into the world. At the end of times, at the moment of dissolution which will put an end to them, a child will be conceived and formed with its members in the womb of a virgin, without any man having approached her. He will be like a tree of lovely foliage and loaded with fruit, standing upon a parched soil. The inhabitants of that land will oppose his growing up and will strive to uproot him from the soil, but will not be able to do so. Then they will lay hands on him and will kill him on the gibbet; the earth and the heavens will wear mourning for his violent death and all the families of peoples will weep for him. He will open the descent into the depths of the earth and, from the depth, he will mount up on High. Then he will be seen coming with the army of the Light, for he is the Child of the Word that engenders all things. . . . He will arise from my family and from my line. I am He, and He is I. I am in Him and He is in Me. At the manifest commencement of this coming great prodigies will appear in the sky. A star will be seen shining in the midst of the sky: its light will outshine that of the sun. So then, my sons, you who are the Seed of Life issuing from the Treasury of the Light and of the Spirit, who have been sown in the soil of fire and of water, you

[67] Monneret de Villard, *loc. cit.*, pp. 27–8.
[68] Bidez–Cumont *loc. cit.*, vol. II, pp. 126ff.; Monneret de Villard, *loc. cit.*, pp. 129ff.; and more especially pp. 136–7.

must be on your guard and watch . . . for you will know beforehand of the coming of the great king for whom the captives are waiting to be freed. . . ."

In this passage the words of Zoroaster "I am He and He is I"[69] recall a passage in the notice that Epiphanius devotes to the Sethians (XXXIX, 3), in which it is said that Christ Jesus is of the line of Seth according to the seed and succession of the generations, but this in a miraculous fashion and without having been begotten. Identical with Seth even when he had become the Christ, he was sent by the Mother of heaven to dwell among mankind. This again confirms the identity of some of our myths given under the name of Seth with some of those ascribed to Zoroaster—an identity upon which the ancient writings were sometimes pleased to enlarge.[70]

Text No. 24 is another apocalypse, with no explicit title, but it is closely analogous to the *Revelation of Adam to Seth*. At the beginning it deals with the Creation, the Flood and the ark of Noah, as some others of our texts do more concisely. Later on, it presents some apocalyptic perspectives. We will cite a few passages from it:

". . . it is in that place that the word was made manifest at the beginning. Then the earth trembled and the towns were shaken; the birds fed to satiety upon their dead. The earth [became . . .] and the universe became a desert. Then, when the times were accomplished, perversity arose to extremity. . . . It was then that the Archon of the Occident and the Orient set to work to educate mankind in his malignity and to undo all the teachings and counsels of the Wisdom of truth. . . ." But this Archon fails.

"Then opened a new period, which altered the circumstances. For now came the time when the little child had grown up in its innocence. Then, the Archons sent to this man their Counterfeiter. . . . They were all looking to him [the perverse one]

---

[69] "I am identical with thee, and thou art identical with me: wherever thou art, I am, and I am sown throughout all things . . . ." says the *Gospel of Eve* of the Cainites, quoted by Epiphanius; see our chap. I, p. 42; cf. Puech, *La Gnose et le Temps*, p. 104.

[70] Cf. Bidez–Cumont, *loc. cit.*, vol. I, pp. 45ff.

to perform a prodigy: and he did bring about great prodigies: he reigned over the whole earth and over all that is in the sky: he set up his throne at the end of the earth, even as it has been said, 'I will deliver unto thee the kings of the Universe! . . .' He will work wonders and miracles, and thenceforth hearts will be hardened and those who follow him will be led into circumcision; he will judge those who remain in uncircumcision, that is, the Gentiles. For he sent them a number of prophets to instruct them upon this subject. And when the time that has been assigned to the earthly kingdom has been accomplished, then will come the purification of souls, because perversity will have ruled over all things. All the powers of the sea will be agitated and will dry up. The firmament will pour out no more rain; the springs will disappear; the rivers will flow no more. . . ."

Similarly apocalyptic perspectives can also be found in the visions of the end of times which occur in the Manichaean writings.[71]

Still another kind of writing is presented to us by No. 30, *A Revelation by Dositheus, or the three Stelae of Seth.* This little work, not more than ten pages long, and without any preamble to indicate its origin whether real or fictitious, is devoted to the transcription of these three "stelae": they are, in fact, three hymns, of which here is a sample: "Let us rejoice, let us rejoice, let us rejoice! We have seen, we have seen, we have seen what truly was in the beginning, what truly was, what was the first eternal, the unbegotten. From thee came forth the eternals and the perfect aeons." The last words are: "This book is that of the Fatherhood [this Father is the Great Seth]. It is the Son who has written it. Father, bless me. I bless thee, Father!"

Is this a purely Sethian treatise? Certainly we have found already, in the *Apocalypse of Zostrian*, an allusion to three stelae left by Seth, which are perhaps the same as those here transcribed.[72] The Manichaean literature supplies us with a no less

[71] Cf. J. Doresse, "L'Apocalypse Manichéenne" in *La Table Ronde*, No. 110, Feb. 1957, pp. 40–47.
[72] Cf. *Manichäische Handschriften der staatlichen Museen Berlin*, Vol. I, *Kephalaia*, pp. 42–3.

suggestive reference, to a writing which may have been similar to our *Revelation by Dositheus*; and which, according to the words of the *Kephalaïon X*, dealt with "the explanation of the fourteen great aeons that Sethel [i.e. Seth] expounded in his prayer", which included the following: "You are glorious, you the fourteen great aeons of the light. . . ."

At first sight the Revelation of Dositheus recalls, by its style, the hymns and the dialogues between master and disciple which occupy a considerable place in the writings of classic Hermetism.[73] No doubt, if the title of this apocryphon had disappeared, one might even have taken it to be an extract from some lost Hermetic treatise, such as those which we shall find, in several cases, fitted in to our Gnostic collection. Basing himself solely upon such details as we had previously made known to him, Professor H. C. Puech has already raised the problem of the possible origin of this text, at the same time pointing out that the Dositheus mentioned by the heresiologists would seem hardly eligible for the patronage of any Gnostic work, notwithstanding a "wholly fabricated" filiation which would make Dositheus into the rival and the master of Simon Magus—the two prophets being, moreover, presented as the leading disciples and successors of John the Baptist.[74] Let us add here that other persons of the name of Dositheus, so little known that several of them might be allowed an equally vague claim upon our text, are so numerous that one loses all hope of a sure identification: Rabbinical sources alone supply ten such names, and we need only open the *Real-Enzyklopädie* of Pauly–Wissowa to be able to add eleven more![75] Thus it is impossible to know whether our Gnostics were

[73] Upon the Hermetic prayers, cf. A. D. Nock and A. J. Festugière, *Hermès Trismégiste*, vol. I, p. 27, note 79; there is an analogous hymn in the Bruce Codex: see Charlotte Baynes, *loc. cit.*, pp. 26–33; in the *Pistis-Sophia*, cf. S. Schmidt and W. Till, *Koptisch-gnostische Schriften* . . . , p. 358, line 15 *et seq.*

[74] Cf. H. C. Puech, *Les Nouveaux écrits gnostiques* . . . , p. 125; Widengren, *The Ascension of the Apostle and the Heavenly Book*, 1950, pp. 49–51, entertains the tradition of a Samaritan Dositheus, founder of a Gnostic sect; p. 48, note 2; he even refers to certain features, which he finds in Heidenheim, *Bibliotheca Samaritana*, vol. II, pp. xxxv–xl, suggesting contact between Gnosticism and certain Samaritan beliefs. One must also refer to the interpretation and the valuable references given by R. McL. Wilson, "Simon, Dositheus and the Dead Sea Scrolls".

[75] *Realenzyklopädie* of Pauly-Wissowa, V, 1605–9.

artificially labelling their Sethian opusculum with the name of the
legendary Dositheus, master of Simon Magus, or whether the
attribution is to some sectary who really existed. Did not Philaster
mention a Dositheus in his catalogue of heresies, immediately
after the Sethians.[76]

As for the actual substance of the Coptic booklet attributed
conjointly to Dositheus and Seth, perhaps we should first of all
remember, in this connection, the predilection of the alchemical,
astrological and Hermetic literatures for themes touching on the
miraculous discovery of secret texts inscribed upon stelae. Fr
Festugière, in his *Revelation of Hermes Trismegistus*,[77] has written
some definitive pages on this subject. As an example of these
romantic myths, let us only mention a late opusculum on the
origins of astrology, which says that Seth, and then Enoch, inscribed their revelations in Hebrew upon tablets of stone[78]—and
a passage of Josephus which credits the family of Seth with the
erection of stelae of brick and stone, the former to resist fire and
the latter to survive flood. It is noteworthy that the Syncellus
takes up this last tradition, no longer attributing it to Seth but
to Hermes.[79]

Upon our No. 41, *Exegesis upon the Soul*—which is not a great
prophetic revelation but a long treatise by some anonymous
doctor—we must not linger too long. One reads in the preamble:
"The Wise have given the soul a feminine name; it is in truth
feminine and virgin [but] it is also male and female." Are not the
ideas evoked by these first words somewhat analogous to the
speculations touched upon by Zosimos in his book *On the letter
Omega*? Indeed, one of the most interesting things about our
Exegesis is that (as we find also in the texts numbered 35 and 40)
various eclectic glosses and references have been inserted by the

[76] Puech, *Les Nouveaux écrits gnostiques* . . . , p. 124, note 6, points out the
somewhat artificial character of the classification thus used by Philaster.
[77] Festugière, *Révélation* . . . , pp. 319–24.
[78] Festugière, *loc. cit.*, p. 334.
[79] Upon these rivalries between the disciples of Hermes and of Seth, and how
the titles of writings were changed from the name of the one prophet to that of
the other, cf. chap. II, p. 107. The passage of the Syncellus is quoted in Scott,
Hermetica, vol. III, p. 391. Cf. J. Doresse, "Hermès et la Gnose" in *Novum
Testamentum*, I, 1956, p. 62.

compiler of the manuscript. Upon occasion he ranges well outside the specifically Gnostic literature to quote either from purely
Biblical works like *Hosea* or the *Psalms*, or from the pagan classics.
He also mentions "the Poet"—Homer—of whom he borrows
certain points from the story of Ulysses and Calypso, and then
passes on without the least embarrassment to the sorrows of
Israel during the captivity in Egypt. Nor need we be surprised
at this mixture. We have only to open the *Philosophumena* at the
passage about the Naassenes to find that they too made use of the
Odyssey, borrowing from it, as a theme for mystical commentary, the episode of the Hermes of Cyllene recalling the
souls of the Suitors (*Odyssey*, XXIV, 1–4).[80] Or open the commentary of Eustathius upon this same *Odyssey*, and there we find
—compiled from classic sources—an exegesis of the episode of
Ulysses and Calypso that shows clearly why this story attracted
the attention of the Gnostics. "The allegory presents, in Calypso,
our body, which conceals and encloses, like a shell, the pearl of
the soul: that nymph, indeed, imprisoned the wise Ulysses, even
as man is a prisoner in the flesh. . . . Thus Ulysses had difficulty in leaving Calypso, inasmuch as he was naturally attached
to life. But, by the mediation of Hermes . . . that is to say, of
the Reason, Ulysses regained the philosophic homeland he had
so longed for; that is, the intelligible world [true fatherland of the
soul in the eyes of Platonists.] Similarly he regained Penelope—
Philosophy—after being released and disencumbered from that
Calypso".[81]

It was principally in the second century of our era that Numenius of Apamea (that strange philosopher who tried to combine
Platonism with Iranian, Jewish and Egyptian theories, and to
whom Plato was an "atticizing Moses") developed, as did his

[80] *Philosophumena*, V, 7 and 8. Simon Magus had already made use of the myth
of Circe: cf. *Philosophumena*, VI, 15; cf. J. Carcopino, *Le Mystère d'un symbole
chrétien*, p. 65; Valentinus was clever at re-fabricating pieces in verse to illustrate
his doctrines, by putting together selected lines taken from the Homeric poems:
cf. Jér. Carcopino, *De Pythagore aux Apôtres*, pp. 190–192; the same Valentinus,
by establishing the number of the aeons at thirty, thought thus to equal the
number of the gods in the *Theogony* of Hesiod.
[81] F. Buffière, *Les Mythes d'Homère et la pensée grecque*, 1956, pp. 460ff. We are
following, in part, the translation given in the Notes to this work.

disciple Cronius, similar allegories out of the Homeric texts.[82] In this they were continuing an old Pythagorean tradition.[83] Porphyry in his turn was to amplify these tendencies in his *Nymphs' Grotto*.[84] Thus, by giving place in their myths to some Homeric themes, the Gnostics were simply following the fashion of their times.[85] We now know, from the paintings in the Gnostic vault of the Viale Manzoni in Rome, so instructively analysed by M. Jérome Carcopino, to what an extent the myths of the Odyssey, treated as allegories of the experiences of the soul wandering through the world here below, had been complaisantly adopted by Gnosticism.[86]

Now that we have come to the works that do not claim to be very great prophetic revelations but are more of the nature of commentaries upon them, let us turn to the *Epistle of Eugnostos the Blessed*, of which we have two copies, numbered 3 and 8. We have encountered this Eugnostos once before, as the transcriber of the *Sacred Book of the invisible Great Spirit* or *Gospel of the Egyptians*, attributed as we saw to the authorship of the Great Seth (Nos. 2 and 7). The text now to be discussed is presented as Eugnostos' own work.

The epistle begins in a rather commonplace manner, reminding one of the beginning of the *Letter* of the Gnostic Ptolemy *to Flora*[87] and that of several other treatises we find among our new writings: "Rejoice! All men who have been born since the

---

[82] Cf. Buffière, *loc. cit.*, pp. 413ff. and 464; H. C. Puech, "Numénius d'Apamée et les théologies orientales" in *Mélanges Bidez* . . . , 1934 and *Les Nouveaux écrits gnostiques* . . . , pp. 133–4 (Numenius' doctrine managed to combine Gnostic elements with Platonic and Pythagorean conceptions. . . .) Cf. also Cumont, *Lux Perpetua*, pp. 344–5.

[83] Buffière, *loc. cit.*, part IV; Carcopino, *Le Mystère* . . . , pp. 57–68.

[84] Buffière, *loc. cit.*, pp. 419ff.

[85] Which is already evident from vocabulary: e.g., oblivion; the body likened to the prison of the soul; prison of the flesh; chains, etc. See Buffière, *loc. cit.*, pp. 460 and 465.

[86] Cf. above, pp. 92–3. M. Ch. Picard, "La Grande peinture de l'hypogée funéraire du Viale Manzoni" in the *Comptes rendus de l'Académie des Inscriptions et Belles-Lettres*, 1945, pp. 26–51, has shown how these allegories lived on through the works of Philo, Origen and Augustine, who bequeathed them thus to mediaeval Christianity; and how the episode of Circe thus came into the tympanum of the narthex of the church of Vézelay, which had previously been taken to represent the evangelization of the Cynocephales by the Apostle Thomas.

[87] J. Doresse, "Trois livres gnostiques inédits . . . ", pp. 154–5.

creation of the world until now are dust. Concerning God they have sought [to know] who and what he is: they have never found out. The wisest have indeed, from the order of the universe, guessed at the truth, but without attaining to it. The philosophers, on the whole, have conceived three hypotheses, according to which the world either moves of itself, or else is directed by a Providence, or else again by a Fate. These three conceptions are false; it is another theory that will reveal the God of truth."

Eugnostos then begins to describe the universe as unbegotten. The God of truth is immortal, ineffable, unknowable, without beginning.[88] He is called Father of the universe. He has a likeness which is proper to him, which cannot be seen but by himself. He is altogether intelligence, an ennoïa, a thinking, a reflecting, a reasoning and a power, which are, in their turn, the sources of the universe, all born from the first knowledge—from the prescience—of the Unbegotten.

Many people have been mistaken because they have not conceived the distinction made here: that what is born of destruction is destructible, but what is born of incorruptibility is indestructible.

Let everyone, therefore, consider first the hidden things, and then all those that are apparent, even unto the end: thus will he learn how the Faith in that which has never been manifest appears in that which has been made manifest. Here is a principle of knowledge: The Lord of the universe was not called Father, but Pro-Father, for the Father is the origin of that which is made manifest, whereas the First father (Pro-Father) has no beginning—and Eugnostes here enumerates the attributes of the First father who, devoid of any origin, sees himself as in a mirror. It is this First father who has manifested himself in the guise of Father of himself and Generator of himself, appearances which to him are equal in duration but unequal in power. Thus, he has made manifest a vast number of men engendering of themselves, and these constitute the Generation over which there is no monarchy; the Sons of the unbegotten Father, who trust in him.

[88] Upon the Gnostic definition of the unattainable divinity, cf. Puech, *La Gnose et Le Temps,* pp. 81–3; Sagnard, *Gnose valentinienne . . . .* , pp. 331–3 catalogues the multiple qualifications which make up the description of the "unknowable" god.

Eugnostos now tries to pass from the Infinite to the Unbegotten. In the Infinite appeared the Father produced by himself: he produced an androgynous man whose masculine name is lost to us, but whose feminine name is Sophia-Pansophos. The immortal man creates a great aeon with gods and archangels; it is called God of gods and King of kings; it is Faith in the things which took place thereafter; it possesses an intelligence, an ennoïa, a thinking . . . like the primordial being. This first celestial man, uniting himself with his Sophia, produced a hermaphrodite son, and this son is the first Father who begets, is the Son of Man who is also called Adam of the Light. He in his turn creates an aeon peopled by a multitude of angels who are called the Church of the holy lights. He unites with his Sophia and produces a great bisexual luminary who, under his masculine name, is the Saviour creator of all things, and, under his feminine name, Sophia generator of all, who is also named Pistis. From these two last entities are engendered six other couples of spiritual hermaphrodites who produce seventy-two, and then three hundred and sixty other entities: the patterns upon which these series of beings are modelled being those of eternity, the eras, the years, months and days, whilst the hours and the instants were the models for the archangels and the angels.

For the twelve principal entities that he has created, the Saviour fabricates twelve aeons and twelve angels, six heavens in each aeon and five firmaments in each heaven. All this "is good and perfect". True, the description that Eugnostes gives us of it is somewhat complicated and obscure.

The author finishes by describing the passage from multiplicity to unity. Here he reminds us that the partner of the immortal Man was called Silence, because the greatness of his incorruptibility was achieved in a thought without words. Lastly, he tells us: All these entities were created by the thrones and the royalties in the heavens and in the firmaments. In that place there are neither troubles nor storms. Thus were they completed, the aeons, the heavens and the firmaments, by the immortal Man and Sophia his companion. It is from them that all things, even unto the Chaos, have taken their patterns. The work then closes upon these few lines: "Now, all the things that I have just told thee, I have told them in such manner as thou couldst bear, before the ignorance in thee is enlightened, and as would implant all these things in thee, with a purified joy and knowledge."

Who were the adversaries that our Gnostic doctor had in mind? Who were those who, "wiser" than others, had in his opinion come a little way towards the truth? Or those, again, who had gone astray through not knowing how to discern the fundamental difference between the perishable and the imperishable? Did he thus mean to reply to criticisms directed against the Gnostic dualism by some pagan doctors—those, for instance, of Plotinus or his disciples?[89]

With a few secondary variants, the description he gives of the higher world corresponds with such glimpses as we generally obtain from the heresiologists' notices of the Valentinians, the Barbelognostics, the Ophites and the Sethians (as, e.g., in Irenaeus I, 30), etc. . . . His exposition therefore presents us with no such striking novelties as do the other treatises dealing with subjects hitherto little known to us. Nevertheless, Eugnostos' account has perhaps an advantage in that it specifies to us the myths of which an exposition is missing, and helps us better to understand another book, at the beginning of so important a text as our No. 40. It is even possible, in view of the lack of any title at the beginning of this text No. 40, and of the way in which it explains the genesis and arrangement of the lower world—a topic on the brink of which Eugnostos' exposition stops short— that we have here a writing which was, originally, the continuation of our *Epistle of Eugnostos*.

One proof of the importance our sectaries attached to the letter of Eugnostes is that the jar of Chenoboskion has yielded us two copies of it. Another is that there is also a pirated version in which, under the title of *The Sophia of Jesus* (No. 4), exactly the same material as the *Epistle*—preamble and all!—has been cut up and cunningly put together again in the form of an alleged dialogue between the Christ and his disciples. We will examine this other version later; it too must have been thought highly important, for,

[89] Cf. above chap. i, p. 53.

besides the copy restored to us from Chenoboskion, there is a second Coptic version of this same Sophia in the Gnostic Codex at Berlin. Finally, a fragment of the same work in Greek has been found by Professor Puech in the papyrus of Oxyrhynchus No. 1081. This last proves that the *Sophia of Jesus*—as, doubtless, the majority of our writings—was transcribed into Coptic from the Greek, and that consequently the original *Epistle of Eugnostos* from which it was fabricated, was also in Greek.[90]

One would like a better glimpse of the personality of this spokesman for the Great Seth, Eugnostes, whose name survives attached to works of which, all told, no less than five have reached us! His spiritual name[91] is Eugnostos "the well-known" —why is he not called, more happily, Eugnostês "the good Gnostic"! In taking the surname of "the Agapite" he is professing his affection for his brethren. And his secular name of Goggessos would signify "the Murmurer"—a detail less negligible than it may look at first. The term "murmurers" was in fact that which neighbouring peoples (Syrians, Arabs . . .) commonly applied to devotees of the religion of Zoroaster. This was a reference to one of their distinguishing characteristics: for not only did Zoroastrians *whisper* their long prayers (unlike the other pagan clergy who prayed in a loud voice), but it was also in an actual "murmuring" that they transmitted to their disciples the texts of the sacred books themselves, which were not, until a very late period, committed to writing.[92]

[90] H. C. Puech, Communication to the VIth International Congress of Papyrology, Paris, 1949.

[91] Upon these mystical names, see Carcopino, *Mystère* . . . , pp. 45–6 and 61–2; Hélène Wuilleumier, "Etudes historique sur l'emploi et la signification des signa" in the *Mémoires présentés a l'Académie des Inscriptions et Belles-Lettres*, XIII, 2, pp. 599–695. Persistence of this usage even into mediaeval Manichaeism, H. C. Puech and A. Vaillant, *Le Traité contre les Bogomiles de Cosmas le Prêtre*, 1945, p. 27: Sylvanus who was Constantine, Timotheus who was Gegnesios, etc. . . .

[92] Upon this appellation of "murmurers", see Bidez–Cumont, *loc. cit.*, vol. I, p. 90, note 4; vol. II, p. 112, note 1; 119, note 6; 245 (excerpt O.100 from Prudentius, *Apotheosis*, 494); 285, note 3. Cf. also O. Braun, *Ausgewählte Akten Persischer Märtyrer* (*Bibliothek der Kirchenväter*, XXII, 1915), p. 204, § 20; Fr Nau in the *Revue de L'Histoire des Religions*, vol. XCV, 1927, p. 180; West, *Pahlavi Texts*, vol. I, p. 278, note 1; Chavannes-Pelliot, "Un Traité manichéen . . . ", pp. 181–2.

This unknown personage—this Goggessos—is, up to the present, the only Gnostic doctor who was certainly a historical reality and is also directly known to us through his writings.

Among other great apocalypses and Sethian treatises in our library we have still to mention No. 31, *The Interpretation of the Gnosis*, and then some other works without their titles, or seriously damaged; as is the case with No. 16 which deals with the great luminaries and other beings of the higher world. This last concludes as follows: "These revelations—disclose them not to anyone who is in the flesh, for [he is] disembodied who reveals them to thee!—When, therefore, they had heard these things, the Brethren who belong to the Generation of Life praised them up to the highest heavens. Amen."

To this same category also belong the writings Nos. 13, 17, 18 and the isolated pages catalogued under No. 43. These last come from a work which, among other subjects of very general moral tenor, dealt with the influence of demons upon men's souls. Finally No. 44, in which invocations consisting solely of sequences of vowels are mixed up with speculations about the cosmos, may be—since it contains the term *Symphonia*—a work which, according to Epiphanius (XL, 2), was used by the Archontici: "They make abundant use of that book called *Symphonia*, in which they define the celestial circles to the number of eight or of seven. . . ." Here one must remember, also, those *symphona* which are curious sequences of seven vowel-sounds, each one of which is mystically consecrated to one of the planets, the combination of them being supposed to express the harmony of the celestial spheres.[93]

GNOSTICS DISGUISED AS CHRISTIANS

Together with these revelations and treatises which without any equivocation expound the most original of the Gnostic myths, we find, in the library of our Egyptian sectaries, some writings that are Christian in appearance, but which present the same Gnostic expositions in disguise.

[93] Puech, "Archontiker . . . ", cols. 636–7; Preisendanz, *Akephalos, der kopflose Gott*, 1926, pp. 34–5.

The most characteristic of these is the *Sophia of Jesus* (No. 4), a work of which—as we have already remarked—there is another version in the Berlin Codex, and of which fragments have been recognized by Professor Puech in a papyrus of Oxyrhynchus dating from the third century.[94] This *Sophia* or *Wisdom of Jesus* includes the essential contents of the *Epistle of Eugnostos* cut up in order to provide, for an imaginary dialogue, the replies of Jesus to questions put to him by his disciples. Since this adaptation preserves the text of Eugnostos—most of it word for word—the *Wisdom* was most probably composed after Eugnostos' treatise and not the other way round. Moreover the result reads rather oddly, when we find Jesus, who has just appeared in the form of a great angel, speaking the learned and philosophic language of the preamble to the *Epistle of Eugnostos*. The intention, no doubt, was thus to give the *Epistle* the prestige of a revelation attributed to Christ himself—hardly realizing that it might have the opposite effect so to attach the authority of Christ (however fictitiously) to a writing which many initiates must have known already, and bring it down to the level of a mere letter by a Gnostic master. Nevertheless the *Sophia of Jesus* is, in part, original: a few supplementary pages at the end extend the discussion over some subjects Eugnostos did not touch upon.

Let us summarize, not the actual contents of the work, which we have already analysed in its form as an epistle, but at least the new frame in which they are set.

The book begins with a prologue recalling those of the books of *Pistis-Sophia*. After the Resurrection, the disciples are in Galilee, on the mountain.[95] They question one another in vain about the substance of the universe, the divine economy and providence. Then suddenly Jesus appears to them in the guise of a great angel

---

[94] Cf. note 90.

[95] Among them appears the mysterious Mariamne to whom James the brother of Jesus transmitted the doctrine that the Lord had revealed to him, and that the Naasenes boasted of possessing. (*Philosophumena*, V, 7). The Manichaean writings recovered in Coptic also know of her; some Gnostics mentioned by Celsus (see Origen, *Contra Celsum*, V, 62) refer to her. The first of the Priscillianist treatises mentions her in a context including the names of some Gnostic entities—Armaziel, Ioel, Barbilon (cf. Puech, *Les Nouveaux écrits* . . . , p. 114, note 3). We wonder whether Mariamne identifies with Mary the mother of Jesus or with Mary Magdalene.

of light, and replies to their questions. Philip questions him first
on the subject of the hypostasis of the universe and its economy;
and the Saviour replies to him: "I wish you to know that all men
born since the creation of the world until now are dust. . . ."
Thence onward, the text of Eugnostos flows from his mouth,
punctuated only by the pseudo-questions of the apostles. Two
pages give us, however, a few variants. The Adam-Light receives
the additional names of Christ and of Son of God. Furthermore,
instead of giving us the list of the six pairs of spiritual androgynes
whom the Saviour and Pistis-Sophia have engendered, the
Wisdom of Jesus interpolates a different exposition in reply to the
question of a disciple who desires to know how these higher
entities were able to come down into the cosmos. "The Son of
Man", replies the Christ, "joined with Sophia his companion
and produced a great androgyne light: the masculine name of it is
'Saviour generator of all things'; its feminine name is 'Sophia,
universal genetrix', who by some is called 'Pistis'. All those who
come into the world are sent by the latter, in the manner of a
drop from the kingdom of the Light of the All-Powerful. . . .
As for me, I have come thus from the heavenly places by the will
of the great Light; I have delivered this creation, I have undone
the work of the sepulchre of robbers, I have awakened Adam,
to the end that, through me, this drop which has been sent by the
Sophia may bear abundant fruit, that it may become perfect, that
it may no more lack anything . . . that its sons may be
glorified . . . and that they may ascend towards their Father,
that they may know the works of the masculine light. . . ."
This brief passage may have been taken from some treatise in
which the descent of the Saviour into the lower regions was
mythically elaborated; an example of which is found in the long
versions of the *Secret Book of John* (Nos. 6 and 36).

Although the text of the *Sophia of Jesus* goes on to what was
the end of the writing of Eugnostos, it refrains from copying the
very last lines of the *Epistle* (which would have exposed the
fraud) and replaces them by simply writing: "All these things I
have been telling you, I have told them to you that you may be
illumined by the Light." The *Sophia* continues, after this, for a

few more pages of dialogue, in which are debated such subjects as the descent into the cosmos of the luminous particle which comes to animate and save the creature. To a question of Mary's, "Lord, whence have thy disciples come, whither are they going, and what will they do down there?" [That is the fundamental question from which all Gnostic meditations begin!] the Saviour replies by recalling the error of Sophia who wanted to create by herself without a male partner, so that the Father of the universe had afterwards to spread a veil of separation between the Immortals and this imperfect creation. In the eschatology here outlined, we learn that certain human beings will attain to the place of rest, while some others "will become light in the Spirit of the Silence"; that he who will know the Son of Man in knowledge and in charity will ascend even to the interior of the Ogdoad, that is, into the higher realms.

Here, the Chenoboskion manuscript presents a lacuna which the Berlin Codex enables us to fill: the Saviour recalls the descent into the lower world by which he is coming to deliver the human creature enslaved to the Archons. "I have struck off the chains . . . I have broken down the doors of the Pitiless and humiliated them. . . ." Then he concludes: "I have revealed to you the name of the Perfect and the whole desire of the Mother of the Angels. I came to reveal to you that which exists since the beginning. I came because of the pride of the archigenitôr and his angels, who say, 'We are the gods!' to condemn them by revealing to everyone the God who is above the universe. Trample under foot their sepulchres! Let their yoke be broken, that mine may be exalted?" And here are the last words: "These are the things that the Perfect Saviour revealed to them. From that day onward, the disciples set themselves to preach the gospel of God, incorruptible and eternal. Amen".

Such is this *Sophia of Jesus* which C. Schmidt, when he gave the first account of the contents of the Berlin Codex in which he had found a version of it, proposed—for insufficient reasons—to identify with a work ascribed to Valentinus which had also been entitled *Sophia*.

To the same category of works which, at first purely Gnostic, were later disguised as Christian books, belongs one of the most important writings of our collection—the *Apocryphon* (that is, the *secret Book*) *of John*. Of this the library of Chenoboskion even offers us two different versions. The more concise of the two is our No. 1, of which there is another recension contained in the Gnostic codex in Berlin. The edition of our No. 6 is more elaborated. Moreover, No. 36 (of our Codex X) gives of this developed version of the treatise a text that is much amplified and enriched by personal glosses. Here, in brief, is what this major text contains:

The preamble shows us the apostle John, brother of James, shortly after the Crucifixion, troubled by the brutal and ironic question that has just been flung in his face by a Pharisee named Arimanios, in the Temple: "Where has your Master gone now?" John withdraws to the mountain. His spirit is harassed by various problems: Why was the Christ sent into the world by his Father? Who is his Father? What is the aeon like, to which we are going? But then the heaven opens; out of it shines a vision; a transcendent entity appears, seemingly in the form of a young man, a woman and an old man, and declares to the apostle that it is at once the Father, the Mother and the Son. (Is this, then, the Protennoïa in triple form to which our treatise No. 34 is devoted?) It reveals to John the secrets of the universe, visible and invisible, past and future, so that he may transmit them to the Generation of the Elect.

First of all the primordial being—although invisible and inconceivable—is described at length. He does not participate in all the aeons; he has no duration; he exists calmly and at rest in the Silence. He contemplated his own image in the waves of pure Light that surround him. By the thought (the ennoïa) of this invisible Father, a preliminary creation is made manifest; this is the beginning of the formation of the higher world. This entity is the perfect power Barbelon (*sic*), thought and image of the Father, who makes himself into primordial man and virginal spirit. Thus is produced the first thought of the universe—the pronoïa—which is also an ennoïa. Then, at the request of Barbelon, are successively produced prescience, incorruptibility and life eternal: these are androgynous aeons which, with Barbelon and the first ennoïa, constitute two series of five. After this Barbelon, by gazing intently into the Light, conceives a spark which becomes the only Son—the Monogene—or Christ. He is the god begotten of himself, who is possessed of intelligence, will and word. Through the Christ, there appear the four luminaries, Harmozel, Oroïael, Daueithe and Heleleth—who, each accompanied by other aeons, constitute twelve in all. After them appear, the perfect Man Adam, then his son Seth, and finally the holy Generation of the Spiritual, or Seed of the Great Seth. They are installed in the Aeons of the three first luminaries, and, together with the Autogenes, they bless the Father, the Mother and the Son.

Then is recalled the history of Sophia and of the lower creation of which she had rendered herself guilty. Sophia, contrary to the Spirit, wished to create as the primordial Father did; that is, alone and without the collaboration of a partner. She fails, and gives birth to a monster like a serpent and a lion in appearance, Ialdabaôth—to whom the long version in our collection adds the names of Sacla and of Samael. Ashamed of the abortion she has engendered, Sophia conceals it in a cloud of light, so that none of the celestial powers, except the holy Spirit, also called Mother of the living—Zoë—may see it. Ialdabaôth, who has taken from the Mother a portion of the celestial power, makes himself the demiurge of the world below—of the visible universe. In the regions where he establishes himself he creates, in a flame of fire, his own cosmos. By uniting himself with the ignorance that is in him, he engenders, first, twelve powers—Athôth, Harmas, Galila, Iabel, Adonaïu also called Sabaôth, Cain whom the generations of men call the sun, Abel, Abiressia, Iobel, Harmupiael, Melkharadônin and Belias; the last to reign over the abyss of hell.

Here the long version of the *Secret Book* (No. 36) inserts a curious allusion to the myth of the struggle of the Darkness against the Light, which is not clearly indicated in any other of our writings except the *Paraphrase of Shem*. Ialdabaôth—it says—is an unknowable Darkness. But the Light, when it reached to the Darkness, made the Darkness shine, whilst the Darkness, when it pursued the Light, was no longer either Light or Darkness, but found itself despoiled.

Ialdabaôth—continues our mythographer—set up seven kings (one for each celestial firmament)—over the hebdomad of the heavens, and five others over the abyss, in order to govern them. Filled with generations of archangels and angels, this creation continues until there are angels to the number of 360 (in text No. 1 of the Berlin Codex) or 365 (in the longer version). This creation partly reflects the one we have just recounted above, for here we find listed, Athôth, Eloaïu, Astaphaïos, Iaô, Sabaôth, Adônin, Sabbataïos. . . . All these entities have the heads of fantastic animals. Can we explain this very curious repetition of the list of powers, sometimes differently named? Has there been some confusion of texts? But the treatise itself suggests, incidentally, an explanation of this peculiarity. It mentions that each of these powers of the lower heavens is obliged to have *two* names: to each of them one name was given by its creator the demiurge, and the use of this name has a glorifying and fortifying effect upon it: the other name was assigned by the beings of the higher world; and the effect of this, when it is used, is to reduce the power it designates to obedience, and bring it to weakness and destruction.[96]

Each of these powers finally takes into its service various abstract entities: perfection, prescience, divinity, domination, royalty, jealousy, wisdom, etc. . . .

Seeing his creation completed, and contemplating the angels round about him, Ialdabaôth cries out in his pride: "I am a

[96] This allusion to the two names that govern each power went with the theory that, for example each of the seven planets was associated with both a benevolent spirit and a spirit of disorder. Cf. Reitzenstein, *Poimandres*, p. 52, note 3. This agrees also with what is said in the magical writing called the *Testament of Solomon*, of which chapter XVIII is well translated by W. Gundel, in *Dekane und Dekansternbilder*, Gluckstadt und Hamburg, 1936, pp. 383–5. For each demon that Solomon calls to appear before him and to be exorcized, there is given, besides his proper name, that of the appropriate angel whose name alone suffices to exorcize that demon. Thus, the eighth of the genies invoked by Solomon declares: "I call myself Belbel; I wring the hearts and diaphragms of people. But if I hear 'Kharael, shut up that Belbel', at once I am enfeebled!" The twenty-fifth demon says in his turn: " I call myself Rhyx Anatreth; I send disturbance and fever into the bowels. But as soon as I hear 'Arara Arare', at once I faint away!"

jealous god and there is no other god but me!" But—the writer of these revelations points out—Ialdabaôth discloses by his impudent words that there does exist a divinity superior to his own, for how could he declare himself "jealous" if there were no other god at all?

Then his mother, Sophia, grieving over her disgrace, begins to wander hither and thither. To John, who questions him about this, the Christ—the whole narrative has now been put into his mouth—likens the coming and going of Sophia above the abyss to the Spirit of the Creator moving upon the face of the waters in *Genesis.* But, he adds, and he repeats this whenever the Gnostic myth comes near the Biblical account that he is turning upside down—"Above all, you must never understand that in the sense that Moses said it."

The repentance and the tears of Sophia touch the supreme powers, who answer her prayers. They do not take her back into her higher aeon; they enable her, however, to dwell in the Ennead where she is to remain until she recovers from her fall. The Spirit spreads around her a force taken from its plenitude (its Pleroma), and the spouse of Sophia comes down, at last, to help his companion by giving her a pronoïa—a prescience. At the same time, a voice from heaven replies to Ialdabaôth's blasphemous exclamation and declares that "Man exists, as well as the Son of Man!"— a reply that is not fully understood until one refers to the more developed version of it in our writing No. 40. And thereupon the astonished archontic powers, as they bend over the waters in the depths of the realm of matter, see them illuminated by the image of the celestial First Man. The very foundations of the earth quake at this vision.

Ialdabaôth then says to his powers: "Let us go and create a man in the image of God and in our image, so that his image may supply us with light!" Each of the lower powers then takes as a model one feature of the image that has been revealed from on high, and creates a substance in imitation of the perfect First Man. At the same time they all cry: "Let us call him Adam, so that his name may be a power of light for us!"—and every Archon sets to work. Perfection creates a soul of bone, the Pronoïa makes a soul of nerve-tissue, etc.[97] . . . Thus the innumerable parts of the body are fabricated, each by an appointed power. Last, comes the creation of the passions: and here the long version of the text (No. 36) dwells even longer than do the others on the catalogue of the creative entities, complacently listing their fantastic names, and even then not enough to please the learned compiler, who lets us know there are still others that he omits: "If thou wouldst know them they are written in the *Book of Zoroaster*".

Thus was completed the body of the terrestrial Adam. But neither the seven powers of the lower heavens, nor the 360 or 365 angels could manage to stand it upright. Then was it that, in answer to the prayer of the Mother, who wanted to take back from Ialdabaôth the power she had originally yielded to him, the Father on high sent five of his messengers disguised as angels to the Demiurge. Their mission was to give the latter such advice as would make him divest himself of this power and, at the same time, give life to the as yet inert Adam. "Breathe thy spirit into his mouth, and his body will stand upright." But as soon as Ialdabaôth has acted upon this deceptive advice, the body of Adam becomes not only strong, but resplendent. Thus animated, the earthly man has become superior to those who created him. The powers that fashioned him perceive this; they declare that he is wiser than themselves, and, seized with jealousy they cast Adam into the nether regions. This passage should be compared with a quotation given by Clement of Alexandria in his *Stromateis* II, 8; where, following some writing similar to our *Secret Book*, he mentions the terror that came over the creator-angels at the sight of this being they had just formed, when the latter began to

---

[97] This very scholarly list of the seven bodily elements is undoubtedly of Greek origin. It had been borrowed by Iran: Zaehner, *Zurvan*, p. 162, points to it in the *Zâtsparam*, where each of these parts of the body is fabricated by one of the seven planets. The Manichaeans also knew it (*Kephalaia*, p. 107, lines 29–32). A quotation from the *Apocalypse which is in the name of John*, included in the description of the Audians by Theo. Bar-Konaï, bears upon this subject; his details convince us that the work which the Syriac doctor knew under this title was indeed the same as our *Secret Book of John* (cf. above, chap. I, p. 56); one should refer also to H. C. Puech, "Fragments retrouvés de l'Apocalypse d'Allogène", pp. 938–9); Bar-Konaï affirms that this myth had been borrowed "from the Chaldaeans".

utter words out of all proportion with its first origins—sayings that "came to him from Him who, without letting himself be seen, had planted in him a seed of the substance from on high, and was speaking through him so fearlessly".

Upon this the Mêtrôpatôr—that is, the merciful and beneficent Mother—seized with pity for the power which had been thrown into the psychic and sensitive body of Adam, sent as its saviour a spark, a Thought of light called Zoë. But the Archons, with the four elements (fire, earth, water and wind) which they forge together, build another material body which—says our longer version—is to be "the cavern of the refashioning of the bodies with which they, the brigands, have clothed Man! that is, the bondage of oblivion. Thus did man become mortal; this was the first fall, the first separation. . . ."

The Archons take Adam away and place him far below, in Paradise, the delights of which are bitter and illusory. The Tree "of life" is, in its every detail, made of perversity; soon to be associated with it is the "counterfeiting" spirit designed by the Archons to counteract the spirit descending from on high. But in the Tree of knowledge of good and evil lies hidden also the epinoïa—the Thought, or spark of light, sent by the Mother. "Was it the Serpent who taught Adam to eat of that tree?" asks John. The Saviour answers, with a smile, "The Serpent only taught him the seed of desire, hoping thereby to enslave Adam; but he saw that Adam was not obeying him, because of the thought of light that was in him".

Then the Demiurge wants to take away from Adam the strength that is in him. In terms that are still, in part, those of the Biblical *Genesis*, he causes a deep sleep to fall upon Adam, and tries to take from the body of the first man, out of his side, this thought of light, which however escapes him and he catches only a part of it. But with this he fashions a second creation in the form of a woman, a creation which is made to shine by the spark of light, whilst Adam is recovering from his stupefaction by the Darkness in which he was temporarily immersed. Regaining consciousness, he immediately recognizes her as one of his own kind: "This is bone of my bone. . . ." Soon afterwards, Eve and Adam taste of the Tree and, by its means, of the perfect Gnosis. According to our long version, the first couple are incited to transgress the orders of the Creator by the Saviour himself, who says: "I manifested myself in the form of an eagle,[98] upon the Tree of Knowledge (which tree is the spark sprung from the foreknowledge of the holy Light) in order to teach them, and to uplift them from the abyss of destitution."

Then Ialdabaôth, seeing that they had both become estranged from him, but not at all understanding what a mystery had been enacted, cast them out of the garden. And then, filled with desire at the sight of Eve's radiant beauty beside her husband, he seduced her and begot two sons, one with the face of a bear, who is the just Abel; and the other with the face of a cat, who is the unjust Cain. Lastly, Ialdabaôth implants in Adam the seed of desire, in order that the bond of carnal union should be established, and that, according to the "spirit of counterfeit" created by the Archons to combat the action of the light in every human being, Adam and Eve may reproduce their kind. Seth alone will escape from this curse, and be born from the first couple after the superior pattern of the perfect Generation.

Thus the text already adumbrates the divine plan by which the holy Generation that is to be born of Seth will be progressively awakened from oblivion here below and out of the perversity of the cavern.

At this point is interpolated a more consequent dialogue between the Saviour and John, a dialogue which, both in style

[98] For Plato, before this, the eagle was a symbol of the soul; it was also the messenger of the solar god (Cumont, *Lux Perpetua*, pp. 294-5); but one never finds it anywhere in the Gnostic or related literatures, unless among the Mandaeans—and there in the form of the white eagle captured by Anosh-Uthra when he descends upon Jerusalem (according to the *Ginzâ*, quoted by Tondelli in "Il Mandeismo . . . ", p. 53); Hibil-Ziwa also manifests himself in the form of a white eagle (Lidzbarski, *Johannesbuch* . . . , pp. 235 and 131). Perhaps one could illustrate this passage from the design of an ivory tablet of the fifth century, preserved in the Bargello (see A. Venturi, *Storia dell'Arte Italiana*, I, Milan, 1901, p. 421 and fig. 385; Saxl, *Mithras*, 1931, p. 82 and fig. 182): Adam, according to a symbology applied earlier to Orpheus, is shown, in paradise, surrounded by various animals. He is recumbent, right at the top of the panel, under a tree, in the branches of which is perched an eagle which seems about to speak into the ear of the first man, while the serpent is crawling some distance away, right at the bottom of the picture.

8

and content, recalls some analogous passages in the *Pistis-Sophia*. It is manifestly an interpolation. Will all souls be saved? Where will they go when they leave the body? To which questions the Saviour answers by describing two opposite influences, that of the spirit of life coming from on high, and that of the counterfeiting spirit fashioned by the Archons; whence it is that there are two souls dwelling in man, in varying proportions, from the time of his birth, and they wage war within him with varying success. Even those souls which, upon leaving the body, do not go straight into the places of rest, will pass through cycles which may yet bring them to salvation. Only those who, having had the Gnosis, have then turned away from it too late, will be thrown into hell with the angels of destruction—the infernal angels—and will remain there with them in eternal punishment.[99]

Now the principal text resumes its course. We are told how the Demiurge bound to the sphere of Destiny (i.e. to Time) the powers of heaven, the demons, and men;[100] then how Noah was taught by the Light, but could not get a hearing from the rest of mankind. At the same time the Creator, displeased, decided to destroy this base world. Then Noah and the men of the perfect Generation, instead of withdrawing into an ark, as Moses falsely pretended, were taken into a cloud of light[101] which sheltered them when the waters and the darkness of Ialdabaôth spread over all the earth.

Finally, enlarging upon an episode which the Biblical *Genesis* places before the Flood, the *Secret Book* explains how, the better to ruin mankind, the Demiurge decides to send his angels down to the daughters of men, to beget upon them a perverse posterity. In this the angels fail until they take on the appearances of husbands

---

[99] This theme of the destiny of souls had been treated in the *Phaedo*, 80e–82a; see also the fragment XXIII of *Hermes Trismegistus* (=the *Korê Kosmou*) in the edn. Festugière–Nock, vol. IV, p. 12 and vol. III, p. cc.

[100] Upon the Archons being chained—or flayed, according to Manichaean teachings—cf. Cumont, *Recherches . . .* , pp. 25–7; G. Widengren, *Mesopotamian Elements in Manichaeism . . .* , 1932, pp. 34ff., A. W. Jackson, *Researches in Manichaeism . . .* , 1932, pp. 31 and 39; the Coptic *Kephalaion* LXIX, p. 167. Upon the setting in motion of this heavenly host: Cumont, *Recherches*, p. 37; Jackson, *loc. cit.*, p. 39.

[101] Cf. *I Epistle to Corinthians* X, 1; "All our fathers were under the cloud", which alludes in reality to *Exodus* XIII, 21.

of these women and, moreover, seduce them by gifts of gold, silver, iron and copper and all the techniques relating to them. This passage is inspired by an apocryphal tradition that is found also in the book of *Enoch*. Thus the great angels manage to instil into the daughters of men their own spirit of darkness, with which they gorge themselves before coupling with them.

The revelation ends upon an account of salvation which is not very clearly developed except in the two long editions (Nos. 6 and 36). The text of the short version (No. 1 of the Berlin Codex) transcribes a recension which had been mutilated and corrupted by some earlier copyist. Let us summarize what appears in our texts Nos. 6 and 36—the only intelligible versions. There we have a great description of the celestial Power (which here is the Mêtrôpatôr, the Mother) going to awaken Adam from his immersion in the outer Darkness. The style of this passage gives it something of the lilt of a hymn, in the course of which the Mêtrôpatôr repeats: "I am the riches of the Light; I am the memory of the Pleroma". "I walked", it says, "in the depth of the Darkness, and I persevered until I attained to the middle of the prison, to the foundations of Chaos." At the third of these descents into hell "my countenance shone with the light of the ending of their aeon. I penetrated to the midst of the prison, that is, of the prison of the body, and I said: 'Let him who hears wake up from heavy slumber!' Then Adam wept and shed heavy tears, and then he dried them, saying, 'Who called my name? And from whence comes this hope, while I am in the chains of the prison?' I replied, 'I am the pronoïa of the pure light; I am the thought of the virginal Spirit who re-establishes thee in the realms of glory. Stand up, and remember that it is thyself thou hast heard, and return to thy root. For I am the Merciful! Take refuge from the angels of destruction, from the demons of Chaos and from all who hinder thee, and rouse thyself out of the heavy sleep of the infernal dwelling.' Then I stood upright; I sealed him with the light [and] the water with five seals,[102] so that death

---

[102] Cf. the fragment of a Coptic apocryphon of Deir Balaize quoted above, pp. 88–9. We find the five seals again in the concluding formulas of the *Sacred Book of the invisible Great spirit*. Perhaps they have some connection with the "Five Trees" of the *Pistis-Sophia* (cf. chap. II, note 23).

henceforth should have no power over him." Then the Saviour—whether this is now Jesus or is still the Mother is no longer clear—ends the revelation as follows: "Behold, I am about to go up again into the perfect aeon. I have told thee, for thine own ears, all these things. All this, I have told thee so that thou shouldst write it and pass it on in secret to thy spiritual companions!" That is, indeed, the mystery of the resolute Generation (adds John himself) "which the Saviour has disclosed to me so that I might write it and keep it safely. And then the Saviour said to me: 'Accursed be whosoever betrays these secrets for a gift, whether of food, drink, raiment or any other such thing'." Then—concludes the editor—"as soon as he had communicated this mystery he became invisible, and John went to his fellow disciples and began to repeat to them the words that the Saviour had said".

This writing—the fact is obvious—lacks unity. Of the transformations that this alleged *Secret Book of John* has undergone, we can even see the last adjustments taking place, since our manuscripts provide two different editions (not successive but fairly widely separated) of the same work; and in the more complex of these (in Codex X), we can catch an anonymous commentator "in the act" of adding glosses and new references!

The most ancient element is the description, by a triple-faced heavenly being, of the higher world and of the first moments of the inferior creation. Did this earliest account perhaps stop at Sacla's blasphemous exclamation; or at Sophia's wandering to and fro in her torments of remorse? The text of this part was known to St Irenaeus, in an independent form, before the years 180 to 185, for he then gave a faithful summary of it in Chapter xxix of his treatise against heresies.

A more recent portion, in which the revelation is attributed to Jesus, has added to the above the continuation of the Gnostic genesis, with an outline of the first developments of humanity and the first stages of salvation. Into this second part, moreover, is inserted, not altogether happily, a dialogue between Jesus and John upon the destiny of souls; and this in a style quite different from that of the main body of the work.

Lastly, to the end of the treatise has been tacked on the description of the descent into hell of the celestial power who comes to deliver the first man. This part is not found elsewhere in complete and clear form except in the versions which are the latest—Nos. 6 and 36. Had this portion been recently added? Certainly, by its style, it reminds one of various late Christian descriptions of the descent of Jesus into hell: but, in our writing, the principal part is not allotted to the Christ, but to the celestial Mother—which is a sign of archaism. Did this part, then, really exist before in relatively ancient versions of the *Secret Book of John*? It is difficult to be sure. In fact, neither our text No. 1 nor that of the manuscript in the Berlin Codex contains this passage, but both give, in its place, a few very confused lines: possibly, these may represent the editings of a particular line of manuscripts in which one copyist had spoiled this essential exposition by omissions and errors.

But the most important element—that which, for all its straggling and diverse parts, makes a unity of the *Secret Book of John*—is the fictive dialogue in which, from beginning to end, these fragments have been framed. By fitting them into this form, the compiler has reduced the diverse entities and prophets to whom the most ancient portions of this writing were originally attributed, to the two figures of Christ and the Apostle John. Preamble, conclusion, and the speeches exchanged between John and the Saviour—this framework must be as factitious here as in the *Sophia of Jesus*. Irenaeus knew, in its primitive form, the text which afterwards became the first part of the *Secret Book*. He would have thundered with indignation, of which there would certainly have been echoes in his book, if in the copy that he read, this writing had already been attributed to Jesus in person. Briefly, then, the *Secret Book of John* is not only a compilation of somewhat disparate elements: still more is it a ruin repaired here and there, of which the parts that are unrecognizable today may have come from works that were once of capital importance.

That is why this work is still of a quite special value, derived from the earlier importance of the various primitive writings of which it assembles the remnants. One proof of this is the number of references made by heresiologists to the same myths as those it transcribes. Let us remember above all Chapter xxix of Irenaeus, the extraordinary interest of which was noted by Carl Schmidt in 1896: St Irenaeus follows step by step the account of the myth given in the first part of the *Secret Book of John*; several phrases are even textually the same in both cases. And for the second part of the cosmological exposition, and even of the myth as a whole in its Coptic presentation, we can find less exact but still fairly faithful parallels in Irenaeus' account of the Ophite or Sethian Gnostics (I, xxx). When Epiphanius (in paragraph 3 of his Chapter xxxviii) is refuting the Ophites, it is again a system analogous to that of our Coptic book that he analyses—for which reason his notice merits a brief summary here:

From the supreme aeon—so these Ophites affirmed—other aeons emanated, the lowest of which was Ialdabaôth, whose birth they ascribed to the folly and weakness of his Mother, the supreme Power called Prunicos by some, and by others Sophia. Ialdabaôth, created by her ignorance, dwelt in the lower regions. He engendered seven sons, who established as many heavens. But Ialdabaôth separated himself from the powers that were above him, and concealed those powers from the eyes of his progeny, lest the seven Archons he had produced should know of anything that was superior to himself. These Ophites affirm that Ialdabaôth is identical with the God of Genesis. The seven angels or aeons engendered by him produced man, in the image of Ialdabaôth, slowly and with difficulty. At first this man, crawling over the ground like a worm, could not stand upright;[103] but Prunicos the celestial Mother devised a stratagem against Ialdabaôth which would enable her to regain the power which had been taken from her. She meant to make the power of Ialdabaôth pass into the man, and also to introduce into him the spark which

---

[103] Cf. the same feature of the doctrine of Satornil, p. 19 above. The *Philosophumena*'s account of the Naassenes also includes this detail, to which it assigns a Chaldaean origin: "That", they say, "is the first man that the earth ever produced: he lay without breath, inanimate, without movement, like a sculpture" (V, 7); this image of a carved figure recalls the inert, unintelligent statue in the myth of the Kukaeans (see chap. I, p. 58). In Arab Hermetism, the persistence of this theme is perhaps attested by a writing under the name of Balinus which I quote later, pp. 318ff.

is the soul. After that, they said, this man stood up on his feet and knew the Father, superior to Ialdabaôth, and praised him. Then Ialdabaôth, annoyed that anyone should have known what was higher than himself, gave birth to a virtue shaped like a serpent, who is called his son, and by its means, deceived Eve. . . . At the end of the fifth century the Bishop of Lower Egypt, John of Parallos, attacking some heretical works, among which were some *Teachings of Adam*, also censured a *Preaching of John* which may well have been identical with our *Secret Book*.[104] In the eighth century Theodore Bar-Konaï (as Professor Puech has shown us)[105] not only knew the title of that *Revelation of John* but also some details of myths which may be those of our text. It is true that these scraps of information, bearing upon the most widely-known elements of our Gnostics' cosmogonies, might also have come from some other of the *Books of Allogenes*, also known to the same heresiologist.

Let us, however, recognize that, even if we did not know the popularity that this writing enjoyed for long centuries, we should still have reason, from the very complexity of its structure, to believe in the importance that was attached to it. Only a highly esteemed writing could have deserved the honour of adaptations and deformations intended to keep it in use in spite of the continual evolution of the Gnostic doctrines and, at the same time, to enrich and complete it, and make it a summary of all the essential myths. How one would like to know which of the great prophets of Gnosticism it was—Nicotheus or Zoroaster or who else—in whose name the oldest portion of such a venerated book was first presented!

The contents themselves of this writing would demand a very long commentary. In the present introduction, we can only indicate a few individual features.

The most original portion deals with the creation and destiny of man. Many of the features of this myth, which presents Adam as an image of the microcosm, are to be found in certain Iranian

---

[104] Cf. A. Van Lantschoot, "Fragments coptes d'une homélie de Jean de Parallos."
[105] H. C. Puech, "Fragments retrouvés de l'Apocalypse d'Allogène."

texts: in the *Bundahishn*, in the collection of *Zâtsparam*, as well as in the Manichaean writings.[106] Fully to appreciate the strange pessimism of this account of the inferior creation of man by the perverse Ialdabaôth, we must refer back to the pages of the *Enneads* (II, 9) in which Plotinus, in the name of Hellenic philosophy, thunders against the "absurdities" that he finds in the Gnostics. One should, above all, take as the standard of comparison the very different myth, suffused with a radiant optimism, in which the same creation is depicted by the most important of the Greek Hermetic writings—the *Poimandres*.[107]

First of all, it is the creation of the heavenly Anthropos that is described: "The Nous, father of all beings, who is life and light, made a man like unto himself, of whom he became as fond as of his own child; and indeed he was very beautiful; he reproduced the image of his father, so that in reality it was in his own form that he so delighted. And God gave to him all that he had created." This man, in his turn, wished to create: "He separated from his father and entered into the demiurgic sphere where he had to receive all power: he became conscious of the works created by his brother and his works fell in love with him; each one of them gave him a share in their own hierarchy. Thus, having learnt to know their essence and having set himself to participate in their nature, he wanted to break the periphery of the circles and to know the power of him who is established over the fire." It is then that, from on high, this higher man reveals to

---

[106] An attempt to analyse this myth, from the text of the *Secret Book of John* in the Berlin Codex has lately been made by K. Rudolf, "Ein Grundtyp Gnostischer Urmensch-Adam Spekulation" in the *Zeitschrift f. Religions und Geistesgeschichte*, IX, 1957, pp. 1–20. The misadventures of Eve, pursued by the Creator, occur again in the Gnosticism of Justin; among the Audians (Puech, *Fragments retrouvés*, p. 954 and note 1); among the Manichaeans and as far as to the Bogomiles (Puech and Vaillant, *Le Traité contre les Bogomiles* . . . , p. 339). H. C. Puech refers also to the first Priscillianist treatise of Wurtzburg, Schepps edn., p. 18, l. 30 to p. 19, l. 4. Cf. also the *Adversus omn. haer.* of the pseudo-Tertullian, VIII, p. 275 of the Oehler edn. Upon the correspondence of each of the seven planets with an element of the human body—marrow, bone, flesh, etc. . . . see the texts from the *Bundahishn* and *Zâtsparam* cited by Zaehner, *Zurvan* . . . p. 162, and in G. Widengren, *The Great Vohu Manah and the Apostle of God*, pp. 53–4. As for the passions imprisoned in each bodily element, cf. Chavannes-Pelliot, *loc. cit.*, p. 41 (537).
[107] In Nock-Festugière, *Corpus Hermeticum*, vol. I, pp. 10–11.

the material world that reflection of himself which, according to our Gnostics, is apparently to serve as the pattern on which the Archons will fashion Adam. "He leaned over the assembly [of spheres] of which he had broken the envelope, and exhibited to the lower nature the beauty of the divine form. And she [the lower nature] seeing that he had in him inexhaustible beauty and all the energy of the rulers with the form of God, smiled lovingly, for she had seen, reflected in the water, the splendid form of Man, and his shadow extending over the earth. And he, seeing reflected in the water this form resembling himself, which was appearing in nature, he loved it and desired to dwell there." From this union terrestrial man was to be born. . . . "And thence it is that, unlike all the beings that are on earth, man is twofold; he is mortal by his body, and he is immortal by the essential man."

To describe the predicament of man in this world here below, doomed to suffer at the hands of the evil powers, the *Secret Book of John* makes rather complacent use of a certain set of images. The world is "the cavern"; the body is described as the "prison", or the "tomb" of the soul, which is "in chains" here below. The world is also called the "cave of oblivion", where Adam and his posterity are victims of the "brigands"—namely, the inferior powers of heaven. This Hellenic vocabulary was common form among the most scholarly: from Plato down to the last of the exegetists who in their commentaries ascribed mystical meanings to the Homeric episodes of Ares and Aphrodite, of Circe or the grotto of Nymphs, imagery of this kind was customary.[108]

But a much more original theme, and one which has a wealth of profound meanings, is presented to us in relation to the Tree of Life and all the imagery surrounding the formation of the soul of Adam—namely, that of the spirit called a "counterfeiter". This evil spirit, this second soul subject to the influence of the Archons, of the planets, is put into man by the lower powers on purpose to fight against the heavenly spark which is in him, to drag him into sin, to carnal union and to reproduction. Here we have, indeed, the "adventitious soul"

[108] Cf., above, note 85.

8*

to which the Gnostic Isidorus, son of Basilides, even devoted a special book.[109]

Another originality of our writing is the minuteness with which it describes the two trees of Paradise, particularly the false "tree of life" of the Archons. "Its root is bitter, its branches are all deadly, its shadow is a hatred; falsehood dwells in its leaves, its oil is an unguent of perversity, its fruit is sin; its seed is desire. It grows from darkness; those who taste it receive Amente [hell] for their dwelling, and the darkness is their habitation."[110] The description thus outlined of the trees of Paradise came to be further elaborated in the Manichaean myths, where the struggle between the forces of these two antagonistic trees actually epitomizes—according to some Manichaean writings—the origins of the world. Let us take, for example, the passages quoted by the Patriarch Severus of Antioch from a Manichaean book (whose title he does not mention), in a homily preached against heretics.[111]

According to the myth carefully summed up in this sermon, the Good, also surnamed the Light and the Tree of Life, occupies the regions situated to the East, the West and the North, whilst the Tree of Death, identified with evil and uncreated matter, occupies the "meridional and austral" (sic) regions. And, later on, Severus quotes this actual passage: "The Tree of Death is divided into a great number of trees. War and cruelty are in them; they

[109] Cf., above, p. 23; in the *Pistis-Sophia*, cf. chap. II, p. 72. This doctrine appears in Philo, and among the Essenians; cf. below, p. 297; it also exists in the Iranian texts, see p. 282. For its survival among the Messalians, see Cumont, *Lux Perpetua*, p. 79.

[110] Upon the theme of the two trees which, like that of the spirit of life *v.* the counterfeiting spirit, gives our mythographer further opportunity to elaborate the opposition between the two hostile principles, cf. above, chap. I, note 86 and chap. II, note 23. Perhaps there was some link between these myths and the legends about the origins of the wood of the Cross, which became attached to traditions relating to the Cave of Treasures, and of which the Bogomiles had a special apocryphon. Cf. S. Runciman, *The Medieval Manichee*, 1947.

[111] Cumont and Kugener, *Recherches sur le Manichéisme*, fasc. II, 1912, pp. 103ff.; G. Widengren, *Mesopotamian Elements in Manichaeism*, 1946, chap. IX. See also the description of the trees of death and of life in the Chinese Manichaean treatise published and translated by Chavannes–Pelliot, *loc. cit.*, pp. 64–7 (=[560] –[563]). There it is said of one of the trees of death: "The root of this tree is hatred; its trunk is violence; its branches are irritation; its leaves are aversion; its fruits are division; its taste is tastelessness; its colour is denigration".

are strangers to peace, filled with absolute wickedness, and never bear good fruit. [The Tree of Death] is divided against its fruits and the fruits are divided against the Tree; they are not united with that which has engendered them, but all produce parasites in order to corrupt their locality. They are not subject to that which has produced them, but the whole Tree is evil: it never does any good, but is divided against itself and every one of its parts corrupts the one next to it."

What our writing has to say about the descent of the Mother to the First man imprisoned deep in the place of Darkness, states a theme which recurs in Manichaeism, where the redeeming power is definitely represented by Jesus. In his summary of the Manichaean cosmogony, Theodore Bar-Konaï tells us how "Jesus the Luminous came down to the innocent Adam and awoke him from a sleep of death that he might be saved. . . . Even as when a just man finds a man possessed of a formidable demon and pacifies it by his art, so was it with Adam when this friend found him plunged in a deep sleep, awoke him, set him astir . . . drove away from him the seductive demons and shackled far away from him the powerful female archon. Then Adam examined himself and knew who he was. . . . Jesus showed Adam the Fathers dwelling in the Heights, and his own person exposed to everything, to the teeth of the panther and the tusks of the elephant, devoured by the voracious, gobbled by the gluttonous . . . eaten and imprisoned by all that exists, bound in the stench of the darkness. . . . Jesus made him stand upright and made him taste of the Tree of Life. Then Adam looked and wept: he lifted up his voice like a lion roaring, tore his hair, beat his breast and said: 'Woe, woe to the creator of my body, to him who has bound my soul to it, and to the rebels who have enslaved me!'"[112]

In the *Secret Book* the power who descends into hell three times over in order to save Adam, is not Jesus but the heavenly Mother: undoubtedly this is a sign of archaism, and adds to the interest of our version. This descent of the Mother, of the Saviour, into the lower world is a Gnostic theme which, in various other forms, has already attracted a good deal of study.[113] W. Bousset, among others, recognizes in such episodes a reflection of much more ancient myths: perhaps of the descent of Ishtar into hell, as it is described in Babylonian texts.

Finally, one detail peculiar to our manuscript No. 36 is its reference to a *Book of Zoroaster* which gave a list of the names of many inferior powers governing the various parts of the human body. We have been able to identify several other works, of which the compiler of our Codex X has inserted titles, in the other treatises he transcribed; but here the task is more difficult. The special character of the work alluded to prevents our identifying it with the lost Gnostic apocalypse attributed to Zoroaster and mentioned by Porphyry.[114] We have to search among all the innumerable titles and fragments of forgotten writings ascribed to Zoroaster, dealing with magic, astrology and problems of nature. . . . But even in the meticulous inventory of these that has been drawn up by J. Bidez and Franz Cumont[115] we can find nothing that seems to correspond to the kind of work cited by the Coptic commentator.

THE GOSPELS OF CHRISTIANIZED GNOSTICISM

Besides those writings we have just discussed, which within a quite factitiously Christian framework expound strictly Gnostic revelations, our collection includes several works in which the

[113] Widengren, *Mesopotamian Elements* . . . ; Puech, *Le Manichéisme* . . . , p. 82. It was controversy about such a descent of the Spirit that split the Valentinians into an Italian and an Oriental school, see above, p. 30. According to the *Philosophumena*, when the psychic body of Jesus was baptized, said the 'Italians', "the Logos of the Mother from on high"—of Wisdom—descended in the form of a dove, which called to the psychic element and awakened it from the dead. That was the meaning, they said, of the text "He that raised up Christ from the dead shall also quicken your mortal bodies" (*Epistle to the Romans* VIII, 11). The Oriental school, on the contrary . . . held that the body of the Saviour was spiritual already. The Holy Spirit, "the power of the most High" mentioned in *Luke* I, 35, had shaped it within Mary (cf. Sagnard, *Extraits de Théodote*, p. 6). Upon the Manichaean myth of the creation of the first man and the awakening of Adam, cf. H. C. Puech, "Der Begriff der Erlösung im Manichaismus" in the *Eranos Jahrbuch, 1936* (Zürich, 1937), pp. 229–35.
[114] Cf. p. 156.
[115] Bidez–Cumont, *Les Mages hellénisés* . . . , vol. II, part 1.

most authentic Christianity is associated with some Gnostic ideas which are relegated to a secondary plane.

First of these, let us mention the *Teachings of Silvanus* (No. 29), an abstract treatise attributed to a personage whose identity is not given, though his name recalls that of the companion of Peter and Paul whose name is frequently mentioned in the *Acts* and in the canonical *Epistles*.[116] There can be no question, here, of the Silvanus who was a disciple of the Gnostic heresiarch Audius (and, therefore, a member of a sect known to have used, for centuries, some of the writings also found in our present collection)[117] for that Silvanus dates from the fourth century.

More interesting is the text of No. 19. This is an epistle whose title is missing. It vigorously attacks the Pharisees and Scribes of the Law. "To those who can hear, not with the ears of the body but with those of the heart, I will say: Many have sought the truth but have not been able to find it." (We have met with similar preliminary formulas before at the beginning of the letter of Eugnostos and of our text No. 40). "Because of that, the old leaven of the Pharisees and of the Scribes of the Law had power over them." Further on, we are told that the Scribes belong to the Archon, to the evil Prince of this world, "for no one who finds himself subject to the Law will be able to raise his eyes toward the Truth. It is impossible to serve two masters, for the defilement of the Law is manifest, whilst purity pertains to the light. The Law indeed commands one to take a spouse, to take a wife, to increase and multiply like the waves of the sea. But passion, which is agreeable to souls, binds here below the souls of those who are begotten. . . . For them it is impossible to pass by the Archon of Darkness until they have paid back the last farthing."

Then the Baptism of John is recalled, raising the question of "the power who came to us upon the river of Jordan—a sign which showed that the reign of the carnal generation was ended".

[116] *Acts* XV, 22 and XVIII, 5 (Sylvanus is abbreviated to Silas); *II Corinthians* I, 19; *I Thessalonians* I, 1; *II Thessalonians* I, 1; *I Peter* V, 12.

[117] Cf. Puech, article "Audianer". Later, among the Paulicians of the seventh and eighth centuries, according to Peter of Sicily, the leading doctors took the names of the disciples of Paul as their surnames: thus Constantine became Silvanus, Simeon called himself Titus and Gegnesios renamed himself Timothy. Cf. S. Runciman, *The Medieval Manichee*. . . . , p. 50.

Was the baptism dispensed by John regarded favourably by our exegetist? "The river of Jordan, this, to him, is the strength of the body—that is, the essence of pleasures; and the water of Jordan is the desire for carnal co-habitation." As for John, he is "the archon of the multitude. . . . What is revealed to us by the Son of Man himself, is that we must receive the Word of Truth. . . ." Afterwards the same treatise recalls Paradise and the Temptation: "The serpent was wiser than all the animals in Paradise; he convinced Eve by saying to her: 'The eyes of thy heart will be open on the day when thou wilt eat of the Tree which is in the midst of the garden.'" Then the Serpent was cursed. Later on the author asks himself about the Creator: "Who is this god? At first he was jealous of Adam. . . ." In this exposition of Genesis we find that the text has liberal recourse to the myths of the great Gnostic revelations: Doxomedôn, Harmozel, Daueithe, Heleleth and so on, appear again.

After this remarkable treatise, so regrettably deprived of its title, we turn to the *Dialogue of the Saviour* (No. 5). The part of Codex I in which this appears is unfortunately rather damaged, and the order of the pages of this writing presents some problems. It begins with these words: "The Saviour said to his disciples, 'My brothers, the moment has come for us to lay down our troubles and raise ourselves up into Rest. For he who will rise up into Rest will rest eternally.'" After reminding them that he has opened the ways, until then impassable, that lead from this world to the attainment of light and salvation, the Saviour offers up to the Father an eloquent prayer. Then he expounds to his disciples the tribulations of darkness to which they will be exposed when the time of deliverance is at hand. He enlarges at some length upon the abysses, and upon the flames of the blind Archon— Samael. He recalls the first genesis of this lower world, in reply to a question from Thomas: "What was there before heaven and earth had been produced?" He mentions the Place of Life, in which there is no darkness at all, but which his disciples will not be able to see until they have put off the flesh. "What is it that moves the earth?" asks one of them. "The earth does not move", replies the Saviour, "for if it moved it would fall!" No doubt this dialogue, which becomes more and more closely joined between Jesus and his disciples, is also serving as a pretext for the compiler of the work to quote a great many of the sayings attributed to Jesus—the *logia*—of which we find more complete collections in our *Gospels* of *Philip* and of *Thomas*, which we shall be discussing later. Here are a few more sentences from the *Dialogue*: "Matthew said: 'In what manner will the Little attach itself to the Great?' The Lord replied, 'When you abandon the things that cannot follow you, then you will be at rest!' . . . Judas said: 'Why . . . does one live and die?' And the Lord said: 'He who is born of the Truth does not die; he who is born of Woman dies.' . . . 'Pray in the place where there is no woman. . . . Destroy the works of femininity!'"—says the Saviour again later on. Nevertheless, it is from the mouth of Mary Magdalene—who is supposed to know all things—that we are given the following words: "Sufficient unto each day are its troubles; and the labourer is worthy of his maintenance; and the disciple is like unto his master!"

We now turn again to the *Gospels* of *Philip* (No. 38) and of *Thomas* (No. 37), and to the *Secret Sayings told by the Saviour to Jude-Thomas and recorded by Matthias* (No. 42)—this last also called the *Book of Thomas*. Their titles alone indicate that these three writings must have been of capital importance. They also constitute an actual trilogy; for, if we are to believe a passage in the *Pistis-Sophia*, it was to Philip, Thomas and Matthew (or rather Matthias, as Zahn has justly pointed out)[118] that Jesus confided the task of committing his most precious teachings to writing.

Let us look closer at this tradition, which seems so systematically to ignore the existence of the four canonical Gospels. "When Jesus had finished speaking these words, Philip arose quickly, letting fall to earth the book that he was holding—for it was he who wrote down all that Jesus said and all that he did. Philip stepped forward then and said: 'My Lord, it is to me alone that thou hast entrusted the care of this world, in that I am to write all that we shall say and all that we shall do?' . . . Having heard Philip, Jesus answered him: 'Listen, blessed Philip, that I

---

[118] Zahn, *Geschichte des neutestamentlichen Kanons*, II, pp. 758-9.

may tell thee. It is to thee, as well as to Thomas and to Matthew [Matthias] that I have entrusted, by the first Mystery, the writing of all the things that I shall say and that I shall do, as well as all that you shall see. . . .' Then Mary, going up to Philip, began to speak in her turn: 'Hear now, my Lord, let me speak to thee about the words that thou has just said to Philip: it is thou, Thomas and Matthew [Matthias], you three, to whom it has been given by the First Mystery to write all these sayings about the Kingdom of the Light and to bear witness to them. Listen, then, I interpret that saying to thee. It is that which thy light-power prophesied of old to Moses: 'At the mouth of two witnesses, or at the mouth of three witnesses shall the matter be established.'" (*Deuteronomy* XIX, 15). The three witnesses are Philip, Thomas and Matthew (Matthias).[119] Professor Puech has pointed out, independently, that in the *Sophia of Jesus* Philip, Thomas and Matthew (*sic*) are, with Bartholomew and Mariamne, the only interlocutors of the resurrected Saviour.[120]

The *Gospel of Philip* (No. 38) is in fact simply an epistle, though without stated destination, actually a treatise vaguely directed against some adversaries unnamed. And the author?—one passage alone in this writing is in the name of Philip, and it is also presented as a quotation from him. For the rest, the work seems to be written in the name of some "Hebrew Apostles". It has no precise plan, although from beginning to end the book consists of pretty lofty speculations. It begins upon a somewhat vague theme which reappears later in the work: this is concerned with the development of the race of the Perfect; and the passing from the condition of a "Hebrew" to that of a Christian. Here are the opening lines: "A Hebrew man creates Hebrews, and those who are created in this manner are called 'proselytes'; but a proselyte cannot in his turn make other proselytes. . . ." Elsewhere, the same theme is expressed thus: The Father creates the Son, but the Son cannot, in his turn, engender other Sons. . . .

[119] In W. Till, *Koptisch–Gnostische Schriften* . . . , pp. 44ff.
[120] H. C. Puech, *Les Nouveaux écrits* . . . , pp. 117–18. We may add that Philip perhaps acquired this very special prestige from his having "Christianized" nascent Gnosticism, since it was he (according to *Acts* VIII) who had conferred baptism upon Simon the Samaritain.

Photo: Jean Doresse

THE DEIR ANBA-PALAMUN NEAR THE VILLAGE OF EL-QASR, AND THE MODERN CEMETERY ADJOINING IT

Stretching away into the distance, is the little inland desert where the ascetic Palamun, who was to serve as model to Saint Pachomius, had hollowed out his hermitage. The "monastery" which grew up on the spot and to which the name Palamun remains attached, is today no more than a group of churches, none of which is ancient, and no monks live there.

THE SITE OF ST PACHOMIUS'S PRINCIPAL MONASTERY

To the south of the great walled city of Faou-Gibli (the Phôou of the ancient world) lie fallen some of the numerous pillars which still mark the site of the basilica built by St Pachomius for his principal monastery. In the background, about five miles away to the north, rises the high cliff-face of the Gebel et-Tarif.

Photo: Jean Doresse

THE COPTIC PRIEST DAVID, OF THE
VILLAGE OF ES-SAYYAD

This priest had the opportunity of seeing the manuscripts immediately after they were found, but, knowing only the Coptic language of his liturgy, he could not make out what they were about.

The principal arguments of the exposition which ensues rely upon images, are depicted in parables. God is compared, at length, to a good dyer who blends his colours. The breath of the glass-blower blowing a vase is a simile for the pneuma. The destiny of men is discussed in parallel with that of the ass turning a mill, walking miles and miles but always finding himself, for all his trouble, miserably in the same place. The soul which is in no way united to the Spirit is likened to the isolated man or woman, exposed to the gallant advances of persons destitute of wisdom. A long dissertation is based upon symbols derived from the structure of the Temple, of the holy of holies and the veil through which the high priest alone can pass: this is a simile which had been employed before; its symbolism had already been used to support very different arguments in the Gnostic writings of Theodotus, fragments of which have been preserved for us by Clement of Alexandria.[121]

Some apocryphal Christian traditions also are mixed with this text; for example, that of the tree which Joseph the carpenter planted to grow timber for his trade, but which was finally used to make the Cross. A good many of the phrases used are, in style and spirit, of a marked evangelical character; they are veritably *agrapha*. Were these collected for the *Gospel of Philip* from existing Christian traditions? Or were they actually invented for it? These are among the many mysteries which will only be cleared up slowly, if at all.

The doctrinal content? Let us note in passing a development concerning Mary, the pure Virgin whom no power ever defiled, in spite of the denials of certain objectors whom the author of this treatise attacks. The resurrection of the body is defended at length. But the theme to which this work constantly returns is that of the redeeming action of the sacraments. The Eucharist is thus described: "The cup of prayer; in it there is wine, and in it there is water which is present as though it were blood, over which one gives thanks. It is filled with the Holy Spirit; and this is that of the perfect man. When we drink of it, we receive into

---

[121] Clement of Alexandria, *Extraits de Théodote* (edn. Sagnard), Extr. 27, pp. 112ff. and notes pp. 220ff.

ourselves the perfect man, the living water, a body that we have to put on. . . ." Above all, the baptisms are discussed, the means by which a "Hebrew" can become a Christian. These baptisms are a purification by fire and by water; they constitute an "anointing with light". By their means, man is to receive his heavenly partner, the Spirit; and that mystical union is discussed at length in close parallel with marriage, the union in holy matrimony of earthly couples.[122] By this bond man will be delivered from death, and the lower powers will be unable to capture him. Is this doctrine purely Christian? It reminds one strongly of the passage in the fourth book of the *Pistis-Sophia*, which evokes a vision of a strange eucharistic ritual in which fire and water, the wine and the blood are brought together in much the same way as in the sacraments described by this *Gospel of Philip*.[123] One also thinks of the *seals* of light and of water, believed to effect the redemption of Adam, which are mentioned in the final pages of the *Secret Book of John* and, yet again, of the baptism described in the second part of the *Gospel of the Egyptians*. The account of the Naassenes in the *Philosophumena* also states definitely, and in terms analogous to those found in our text, that the Gnostics had a conception of such rites, by which man is "washed in a living water and anointed with an ineffable ointment".[124]

Discreetly, at first, the presence of Gnosticism in the *Gospel of Philip* progressively reveals itself. The unity of things here below is made by water, earth, wind and light, whilst the unity on

[122] Symbolism of the mystical union among the Pythagoreans: cf. J. Carcopino, *La Basilique pythagoricienne de la Porte Majeure*, pp. 120–1. Among Gnostics other than ours; in the teaching of Valentinus, it is the heavenly nuptials of Sophia and the Saviour—compared with the Husband and the Wife in our Gospel—and the union of the Perfect with the angels who surround the Saviour, when once these elect ones, set free from the psychic elements, have entered into the Pleroma (cf. chap. I, p. 31, and Sagnard, *Gnose valentinienne*, p. 193 and pp. 413–15; and *Extraits de Théodote* 64 and 65). The mystical union also figures in the Gnosticism of Marcos; Irenaeus, I, XIII, 3. Among the Manichaeans and Mandaeans, Widengren, *Mesopotamian Elements* . . . , chap. VIII. Cf. also L. Fendt, *Gnostische Mysterien*, 1922.

[123] Cf. above, p. 75; cf. also the pseudo-eucharist of Marcus, in Leisegang, *La Gnose*, p. 234.

[124] *Philosophumena* V, 7; fuller detail is given in Irenaeus, I, XIII about the baptisms and eucharists of the Marcosians; Leisegang, *loc. cit.*, pp. 233–4.

high is made by faith, hope, charity and gnosis. It is Gnosis which, by means of the sacraments already mentioned, brings freedom to man. Here and there the Archons, too, are mentioned, the "brigands", the middle places where the soul is in danger of losing its way, and, above all, Ekhamôth (the Great Sophia) and Ekhmôth (the Lesser Sophia or Sophia of death). Concerning this last detail, it should be noted that this *Gospel of Philip*, whose speculations upon certain words show clearly that it was written in Greek, also glosses upon several names according to their meaning in "Syrian"—that is, Aramaic—and still more, Hebrew. The distinction it establishes between Ekhamôth and Ekhmôth could not otherwise be understood. Such details confirm what the contents of the work have already indicated—the authentically Judeo-Christian origin of these rare mystical speculations.

Epiphanius, in his notice No. 26, states that he knew a *Gospel of Philip*, then in use, moreover, among the *Egyptian* Gnostics. He quotes a few lines said to be taken from that apocryphon; but this passage does not occur in the text we have just been analysing. We find one formulation which is something like it—without being identical—but only in the *Book of the invisible Great Spirit* or *Gospel of the Egyptians*.

The *Book of Thomas* (No. 42) starts off with these words: "Secret sayings that the Saviour told to Jude–Thomas, and that I myself have written, I, Matthew (=Matthias), who . . . heard them while these two were in conversation. The Saviour, brother of Thomas, said to him . . . Listen; I will tell thee the thought that is in thy heart, how they say that thou art in truth my twin brother and my companion, and how thou knowest who thou art and in what manner thou wast born, and in what manner thou wilt become, as they call thee, my brother. . . ." Upon this Thomas prays the Lord to reveal these secrets to him before his Ascension.

At the end of the book Jesus rebukes sinners and praises those who follow his precepts. To sinners he says: "You have plunged your souls into the water of Darkness; you have taken refuge in your own will. Woe to you, who are in error, who are not upheld by the light of the Sun which beholds and judges the universe while he circles round all those works that the

Enemies have reduced to slavery. You forget also the manner in which the moon looks at bodies! . . . Woe to you who love intimacy with that which is feminine. . . . Woe to you because of the powers of your body! . . . because of the attempts of the perverse demons. Who will water you with a refreshing dew to wipe away from you the multitude of the flames and their burning? Who will make the sun to shine upon you and to dispel the darkness that is within you? . . ." To the blessed ones, he preaches: "Blessed are you, you who are blamed and not at all esteemed, for the love that your Lord has put into you; Blessed are you who weep and are sorrowful . . . for you will be delivered from every bondage, and you will be no more in the flesh, but you will come out of the fetters of oblivion of [this] life; you will be the elect, and you will find a repose [an *anapausis*] leaving trouble and regrets behind you. When you are freed from the pains and afflictions of the body, you will receive repose. . . . And you will be kings with the King, united with him as he will be with you, thenceforward, world without end, Amen."

The last words define this work as "*The Book of Thomas the Athlete*, which he wrote for the Perfect ones".

This treatise may possibly be identical with the *Gospel of Matthias*, a heretical work mentioned by Origen and Eusebius, which again, however, may be a confusion with the *Traditions of Matthias* cited by Clement of Alexandria,[125] a book used by the Nicolaitans and Basilideans.[126] The *Philosophumena* writes that Basilides and his son Isidore pretended that Matthias had left them secret discourses which he himself had received from the Saviour in personal conversations. That agrees perfectly with the beginning of our Coptic text.

As for the special importance assigned to Thomas as the supposed twin brother of the Saviour, let us bear in mind the curious Manichaean tradition that the founder of that church of dualism had received revelations from an angel named at-Taûm in Aramaic—a name which can be pretty exactly translated as "twin".

[125] Puech, *Les Nouveaux écrits* . . . , p. 120, note 3.
[126] Puech, *loc. cit.*, p. 120, note 4.

The Manichaeans identified this "twin" with the holy Spirit. They made use, also, of the apocrypha which bore the name of Thomas. For this reason, M. H. Schaeder has suggested that this angel at-Taûm, the "twin", may have been a legendary figure derived from that of the apostle Thomas[127]—a tempting, but perhaps rather a rash hypothesis.

But the principal text of these three—which is one of the most curious that the jar of Chenoboskion has restored to us—is the *Gospel of Thomas* (No. 37). It was Professor Puech who, when I had made the first fragments of it known to him, recognized that this long Coptic text gives us the exact and integral restoration of a writing of which we had hitherto possessed some fragments in Greek, the real nature of which had been wholly misunderstood. We had here the collection of the "sayings of Jesus", portions of which had been discovered in three papyri of Oxyrhynchus— Nos. 1, 654 and 655. It was owing to some premature rumours about this identification that the more sensational press recently announced, very inaccurately, the discovery of a "fifth Gospel".[128]

Let us give a better idea of the nature and range of this discovery. The fragments recovered in Greek from the Oxyrhynchus papyri (found between 1897 and 1903) had led us to believe in the existence of a venerable collection of the *Logia*— or *Sayings*—of Jesus, collected and preserved outside the canonical traditions, and of which the authenticity remained, of course, entirely problematic. Thanks to Professor Puech, we now know that what we had were simply portions of this highly apocryphal *Gospel of Thomas* of which we have now found the complete text.

This identification led, by the way, to one rather amusing conclusion. The principal Greek fragments of Oxyrhynchus was

---

[127] Puech, *Le Manichéisme*, notes 164 and 165. In the apocryphal *Acts of Thomas*, an unnamed personage actually praises Thomas as the "Twin of Christ, apostle of the Most High, initiated into the secret sayings of Christ and receiver of his secret oracles . . ." (§ 39). Concerning what was known of a *Gospel of Thomas* hitherto, and of its use among the Gnostics and Manichaeans, cf. Alfaric, *Les Écritures manichéennes*, II, pp. 184-6.

[128] These rumours were especially rife when the preparations, in Cairo, for an international committee for publication (Oct. 1956) drew the attention of the press to the possible contents of the new manuscripts.

torn right down the middle. For half a century the experts had been trying to supply the words thus missing, and some of their restorations had come to be considered practically incontestable. The discovery of the whole text in Coptic showed us two things at once—that the Oxyrhynchus page No. 654 contained the actual beginning of the *Gospel of Thomas*; and that none of the attempts made to restore its exact meaning had come anywhere near the truth.[129] We will quote the opening lines:

"Here are the secret words which Jesus the Living spoke, and which Didymus Jude Thomas wrote down.—And he said: Whoever penetrates the meaning of these words will not taste death!—Jesus says: Let him who seeks cease not to seek until he finds: when he finds he will be astonished; and when he is astonished he will wonder, and will reign over the universe!— Jesus says: If those who seek to attract you say to you: 'See, the Kingdom is in heaven!' then the birds of heaven will be there before you. If they say to you: 'It is in the sea!' then the fish will be there before you. But the Kingdom is within you and it is outside of you!—When you know yourselves, then you will be known, and you will know that it is you who are the sons of the living Father. But if you do not know yourselves, then you will be in a state of poverty, and it is you (who will be) the poverty!—Jesus says: Let the old man heavy with days hesitate not to ask the little child of seven days about the Place of Life, and he will live! For it will be seen that many of the first will be last, and they will become a (single thing!)—Jesus says: Know what is before thy face, and what is hidden from you will be revealed to you. For nothing hidden will fail to be revealed!"—Here the Greek text of the Oxyrhynchus papyrus adds the following words, omitted from

[129] H. C. Puech, "Un Logion de Jésus sur bandelette funéraire" in *Bulletin de la Société Ernest Renan*, No. 3, 1 (54, pp. 126-9; also G. Garitte, "Le premier volume de l'édition photographique des manuscrits gnostiques Coptes, et l'Évangile de Thomas" in *Le Muséon*, 70, 1957, pp. 59-73. It should be noted that the translation, in the latter article, of the first part of our *Gospel of Thomas* (which corresponds with the Oxyrhynchus page No. 654) is not—contrary to what has been alleged in some quarters—the first revelation of this Coptic text. In fact, H. C. Puech had already made the exact nature of it known in his communication to the Société Ernest Renan, on 30 January, 1954.

the Coptic version: ". . . there is nothing buried which shall not be raised up"—words to which some special meaning must have been attached, for Professor Puech has found them written on the fragment of a shroud unearthed in that same village of Oxyrhynchus.[130]

Further on in the Coptic writing we find the *logia* contained in the two other Greek fragments of Oxyrhynchus—the leaves that are catalogued under the numbers 1 and 655. The Coptic version coincides with the Greek except in one case; that of one of the finest of the *logia*; here it is, from the Greek: "Jesus said, wherever there are two they are not without God; and wherever there is one only, I say it [to you]: I am with him! Lift the stone and thou wilt find me; cleave the wood; I am there!"

The Coptic gives us the substance of this saying divided into two entirely distinct formulas, which, moreover, we find widely separated one from another in the body of the collection. Here is the one: "Jesus says: There where there are three gods, they are gods. Where there are two, or else one, I am with him!" And here is the other: "Jesus says: I am the light which is on them all. I am the All, and the All has gone out from me and the All has come back to me. Cleave the wood: I am there; lift the stone and thou shalt find me there!"

Let us take, at random, a few other examples—and, this time, of *logia* never published before—from those assembled in this vast collection where, ever and again, it is re-affirmed that he who knows these sentences "will never taste death".

"Jesus said: This heaven will pass away, and the heaven which is above it will pass away; but those who are dead will not live, and those who live will not die!—Today you eat dead things and make them into something living: (but) when you will be in Light, what will you do then? For then you will become two instead of one: and when you become two, what will you do then?"

"Jesus says: The Pharisees and the Scribes have taken the keys of knowledge and hidden them; they have not entered, and neither have they permitted (entry) to those who wished to enter. But you be prudent as serpents and simple as doves!"—

---

[130] See the preceding note.

"Jesus says: A vine shoot was planted outside the Father. It did not grow strong: it will be plucked up from the root and it will perish."—"His disciples said to him: On what day shall rest come to those who are dead, and on what day shall the new world come?—He said to them: This (rest) that you wait for has (already) come, and you have not recognized it!—His disciples said to him: Twenty-four prophets spoke in Israel, and they all spoke through you. He said to them: You have passed over Him who is living in front of your eyes, and have spoken of the dead!"—"Jesus says: He who is near me is near the fire, and he who is far from me is far from the Kingdom".—"Jesus says: The Kingdom of the Father is like a man who wants to kill an important person. In his house he unsheathed the sword and stuck it in the wall to assure himself that his hand would be firm. Then he killed the person."—"Jesus says: When you make the two one, you will become sons of Man and if you say: 'Mountain, move!', it will move."—"His disciples said to him: On what day will the Kingdom come? It will not come when it is expected. No one will say: 'See, it is here!' or: 'Look, it is there!' but the Kingdom of the Father is spread over the earth and men do not see it."

It is to be noted that the sayings, both familiar and strange, that we find here, seem to have awakened innumerable echoes in Christian antiquity. Let us quote a few of these:

The saying: "Let him who seeks cease not to seek . . ." occurs in the fifth of the Miscellanies (*Stromateis*) of Clement of Alexandria. Some words from the same passage: "He who is astonished will reign . . ." are also quoted in the second Miscellany as taken from the *Gospel of the Hebrews*. The saying: " There where are three gods, they are gods. Where there are two, or else one, I am with him!" is developed in the *Exposition of the Concordance of the Gospels* by Ephrem the Syrian.[131] The formula: "You eat dead things and you make them into something living!" was used, according to the *Philosophumena*, in the teaching

---

[131] See *Stromate V*, 14, 97—Resch, *Agrapha*, Leipzig, 1906, Agraphon no. 54, and *Stromate II*, 9, 45. For the reference to Ephrem the Syrian, see the edn. Mösinger, c. 14, p. 165—Resch, Agraphon no. 175.

of the Naassenes, who said: "You who have eaten dead things and done living deeds, what will you do if you eat living things?" The sayings; "The Pharisees and the scribes have taken the keys of knowledge . . ." and "Be prudent as serpents . . ." are found, the former in *Luke* XI, 52, and the latter in *Matthew* X, 16. The expression: "You have passed over him who is living . . . and have spoken of the dead!" is repeated by St Augustine in his *Contra adversarium legis et prophetarum* (II, 4, 14); and he says that he took it from apocryphal and even heretical books. The formula: "He who is near me is near the fire . . ." is exactly reproduced by Origen in his *Homily upon Jeremiah* (XX, 3), and in Didymus of Alexandria's *On Psalm 88.* Finally, what is said about the coming of the Kingdom unnoticed by all those who are waiting for it, recalls the analogous terms in *Matthew* XXIV, 23 and following verses. This search for sentences parallel or identical with these in our *Gospel of Thomas* could be fruitfully pursued much further, even into Manichaean literature.

But what, after all, is it, this *Gospel of Thomas* in which Thomas plays no part, which does no more than piece together, end to end —and without mentioning their origins, or providing any literary framework—these sayings baldly attributed to the Saviour? A work also entitled the *Gospel of Thomas* was used by the Gnostics: Origen mentions it: the *Philosophumena* tells us that the Naassenes used it, too. It may well be that these references are to the text we have recovered in Coptic, for they cite two very recognizable passages. These are, in the one case, the saying: "You who, eating dead things, have done living things, what would you do if you ate living things"—and, in the other case, a passage which approximates to another of the *logia* we have just translated, the one about the Kingdom of Heaven being "within man". It was of this interior Kingdom that the Naassenes' *Gospel according to Thomas* spoke expressly in these terms: "He who seeks me will find me among the children over seven years of age, for it is there, in the fourteenth aeon, that I manifest myself". The passage last quoted proved, by the way, a stone of stumbling to the experts who were trying to make out what this *Gospel of Thomas* could have been; it helped to persuade them that what they were looking for was an apocryphal narrative of the childhood of Jesus. This mistaken idea was apparently confirmed by the fact that there does exist, under this same title of the *Gospel of Thomas*, a very mediocre apocryphon which is a collection of rather naïve legends about the Saviour's boyhood. For this reason, the researches being made for fragments of this *Gospel of Thomas* became obstinately misdirected—excepting those of Grenfell and Hunt, who, to their great credit, guessed the truth and conclusively reassessed the facts by which it was disguised.[132] Hidden in the fragment from Oxyrhynchus No. 654 was the first page of the writing they were trying to find!

The Manichaeans—who, as we have already noted, ascribed a high authority to the apostle Thomas[133]—also made use of this apocryphon. Cyril of Jerusalem pointed out that it was a work that ought not to be accepted by Catholics, for "it comes not from one of the twelve apostles, but from one of the three wicked disciples of Mani". Photius and Peter of Sicily condemned it for similar reasons. The work was rejected as heretical by the second Council of Nicaea, by Leontius of Byzantium and by the pseudo-Gelasius in his list of prohibited works. Alexander of Lycopolis noted that— according to certain Manichaeans—the Christ had come to earth at the age of seven, with his senses already organized; a point which recalls the subject of one of the passages we have just quoted.[134]

As Professor Puech, whom we are following almost in the same words, has shown,[135] this collection of *logia* would seem to be no more than an anthology made from texts disparate both in age and in spirit. What is essential in this compilation goes back to the second half of the second century. Some of the sayings were

[132] Grenfell and Hunt, *New Sayings of Jesus and Fragments of a Lost Gospel* (*Egypt Exploration Fund 1904*), p. 23: these authors were well aware that there was a connection between the *Sayings of Jesus* and the sect of the Naassenes, a link that the *Gospel of Thomas* was to establish (pp. 25–6). While disputing the value of the first damaged lines of the Oxyrhynchus papyrus—lines in which the title of the *Gospel of Thomas* was effectually hidden—it was only after hesitation that they rejected what would have been the correct interpretation.
[133] Cf. above, note 127.
[134] Quoted in Alfaric, *Écritures manichéennes* II, p. 185.
[135] See his communication to the Academy of Inscriptions and Belles-Lettres 24 May 1957.

known to the heresiologists, but it is significant that they quote
them as coming from quite other apocrypha than the *Gospel of
Thomas*—from the *Gospel of the Hebrews*, or the *Gospel of the
Egyptians* (a text different from our Coptic one under the same
name). It may well be, indeed, that all the sayings of which our
text is made up were gleaned right and left from previously-
written apocrypha.

As it has often been observed, some of these sayings echo,
in tone and in spirit, familiar passages in the canonical Gospels:
"Jesus said: He who has [something] in his hand, to him will be
given; but he who has not, what little remains to him will be
taken from him".[136] Reading such texts, which may be regarded
as orthodox, one may even wonder whether the form they
impart to certain sayings of Jesus may not be truer than the form
in which they are preserved in the Gospel tradition. Others, on
the contrary, are of a novel and rather peculiar tendency, of
which here are a few examples:

"Jesus says to his disciples: Compare me, and tell me whom I
am like. Simon Peter says to him: Thou art like a just angel!
Matthew says to him: Thou art like a wise man and a philosopher! Thomas says to him: Master, my tongue cannot find words
to say whom thou art like. Jesus says: I am no longer thy master;
for thou hast drunk, thou art inebriated from the bubbling
spring which is mine and which I sent forth. Then he took him
aside; he said three words to him. And when Thomas came
back to his companions, they asked him: What did Jesus say to
thee? and Thomas answered them: If I tell you (a single) one of
the words he said to me, you will take up stones, and throw them
at me, and fire will come out of the stones and consume you!"

We quote another: "Jesus says: Blessed is the man who existed
before he came into being.—If you become my disciples and
if you hear my words, these stones will serve you.—For you
have here, in Paradise, five trees which change not winter nor summer, whose leaves do not fall: whoever knows them will not taste

[136] Cf. *Luke* XIX, 26; also *Luke* XVIII, 18, and *Mark* IV, 25, then *Matthew*
XIII, 12; note the very variable formulation of this saying as it appears in the
different texts.

death."—"Jesus says: Now, when you see your appearance, you rejoice. But when you see your images which came into being before you, which do not die and do not show themselves, how will you be able to bear such greatness?"

Finally, here is the last *logion* of the collection: "Simon Peter says to them: Let Mary go out from our midst, for women are not worthy of Life! Jesus says: See, I will draw her so as to make her male so that she also may become a living spirit like you males. For every woman who has become male will enter the kingdom of heaven." This doctrine was already attested, among others, by a fragment of the writings of the Gnostic Theodotus, preserved by Clement of Alexandria (fragment XXI, 3)[137] which raises the question of the feminine elements which will become masculine in order to unite themselves with the angels and enter into the Pleroma.[138] Moreover, Professor Puech has been able to trace echoes of this curious text, even among the Cathars at the beginning of the fourteenth century.

Certain Gnostic or Manichaean characteristics are clearly marked in certain parts of the Coptic compilation. It is possible, of course, that there may have been other versions of this *Gospel of Thomas*—the three fragments from Oxyrhynchus are too short for us to make a reliable comparison—which were less heterodox. But the censures pronounced upon it by the Church hardly allow us to suppose so.

Such are the first conclusions we can draw from the three alleged *Gospels* we have found, under the names of *Philip*, *Thomas* and *Matthias*. When it becomes possible to analyse them in a more critical manner, no doubt there will be some fascinating discoveries. In several passages these writings recall more or less clearly what the heresiologists quote from *Gospels* entitled *of the Hebrews*,

[137] The fragment LXXIX also explains that the seed, once it is formed, ceases to be female and becomes male, thus being cured of its weakness and submission to the cosmic powers (cf. edn. Sagnard, pp. 98–101 and 202–3); see also the *Philosophumena* (VI, 30) upon Valentinus and upon the Naassenes, summarized above on p. 47. Similar beliefs were entertained by the Pythagoreans and the Hermetists, q.v. J. Carcopino, *Aspects mystiques de la Rome païenne* (5°; *Sur les traces de l'Hermétisme africain*), p. 284, note 2; and *Le mystère d'un symbole chrétien*, pp. 45 and 61–2.
[138] Cf. above, *Gospel of Philip* quoted, p. 224, and note 122.

of the Ebionites, or *of the Nazarenes*. Those long-lost books dealt, apparently, with the same problems as appear in the three great apocryphal Gospels we have recovered in Coptic. Here let us not forget that the titles borne by our Gnostic writings must not be taken as sure indications of their identity. Such appellations were manifestly changeable; they might even be transferred from one writing to another. As we shall presently see, the *Gospel of the Egyptians* from the Chenoboskion library, in which there are two recensions of it, has nothing to do with the one that the heresiologists had heard of; whilst certain verses quoted by Epiphanius (XXVI, 13) as taken from the *Gospel of Philip*, are completely absent from our *Gospel of Philip*, although the substance of them is approximately reproduced in our *Gospel of the Egyptians*! A passage of Clement of Alexandria (*Stromateis*, I, 9, 45) attributes the following saying to the *Gospel of the Hebrews*: "He who marvels will reign, and he who reigns will have rest"; and, in Book V (14, 96) of the same *Stromateis* Clement even repeats the text in more developed form: "Let him never cease from seeking until he finds; when he finds he will be amazed; and when he has been amazed he will reign; and, having reigned, he will be at rest". But in our *Gospel of Thomas* we again find exactly this passage. In short, it is not so much the titles as the contents of our writings that must be taken as the basis for sound identifications.

The library of Chenoboskion contains eight more treatises which also belong to Christian apocryphal literature. Four are under the name of Peter; three are alleged revelations of James, and lastly there is an *Apocalypse of Paul*.

The *Acts of Peter* (No. 20) that we have here is quite unlike anything hitherto known under that title. The opening lines of the writing are damaged; however, we gather that a strange person has appeared, holding in his left hand "a book cover like unto [?] and, in his right, a branch of the styrax tree. His voice booms heavily as he cries through the streets of the city: Margarites, Margarites! [Pearl, pearl!]—I thought [says Peter] that it was a man of that same city." Peter afterwards addresses this mysterious personage, who tells him that he is named Lithargoël. Lithargoël —if we refer back to the Coptic book on *The Investiture of the*

Archangel Gabriel fictively ascribed to St Stephen[139]— is a great angel, the tenth of a series which begins with Gabriel, and includes the four luminaries Heleleth, Harmozel, Uriel, Daueithael; though he holds in his hands not, as he does here, the book and the branch of styrax, but the nard which is the "the medicine of life for souls". But, in our *Acts of Peter*, it is the Saviour who has put on this angelic appearance and who, thus disguised, calls Peter at once by his name, to the latter's great astonishment. We have here, evidently, one of the rather romantic writings of which so many are known in Christian apocryphal literature.

Let us leave aside the *Apocalypse of Peter* (No. 28), a work which, again, is different from that which we possessed before under that title: we can also pass by the *Epistle of Peter to Philip*[140] (No. 15) and the *Prayer of the Apostle Peter* (No. 49). The writings numbered 10, 11 and 45 are three *Revelations* written under the name of James, all three different. The importance that the Gnostics assigned to this James is no doubt due to his having been regarded, like Thomas, as a brother of the Saviour, and to his being the first bishop of Jerusalem. Eusebius, in his *Ecclesiastical History*, has preserved some fragments of the *Hypotyposes* of Clement (a book otherwise lost to us), and in these we read that the Christ, after his resurrection, manifested himself to James "who was one of those who were regarded as brothers of the Lord", and that Jesus had then "passed on the Gnosis to James the Just, to John and to Peter, who themselves [passed it on] to the other apostles". According to St Jerome (in his *Commentary on the Prophet Micah*, VII, 7), who upon this point refers to the *Gospel of the Hebrews*, James would have been the first to whom Christ appeared after the Resurrection. Incidentally, the *Philosophumena*, in what it says of the Naassenes, summarizes certain teachings which those sectaries presented as "the principal points of the doctrine that James the brother of the Lord had passed on to Mariamnê".[141]

---

[139] This unpublished text is to be found in the Pierpont Morgan manuscript 593=Hamouli XVIII, dating from the ninth century; cf. its p. 79.

[140] Cf. Puech, *Les Nouveaux écrits* . . . , p. 116.

[141] Eusebius, *Ecclesiastical History*, I, 12, 5 and II, 1, 4–5; *Philosophumena*, V, 7, 1; Epiphanius, *Panarion*, LXXVIII, 7; cf. also the status assigned to James in the *Clementines*.

The impressive status which the Gnostics attributed to James is moreover attested in our Chenoboskion writings by a curious *logion* in the *Gospel of Thomas*, where the Saviour replies to the disciples: "Wherever you go, you will turn to James the Just for whose sake Heaven as well as earth was produced." In our *Gospel of the Egyptians*, James the Great is placed upon a level with the supernatural powers put in charge of the great baptisms.

The *Apocalypse of James*, catalogued as No. 10, brings Jesus in person into its preamble: he predicts to James: "Tomorrow they will arrest me. . . ." James replies: "Rabbi . . ." and the dialogue ensues. The revelation is Gnostic enough to mention entities such as Akhamôth, and Sophia. Text No. 11 begins with these words: "These are the sayings which were said by James the Just, at Jerusalem. . . . They were written by Mereim, one of the priests. . . ."

The *Apocalypse of Paul* (No. 9) is different from the *Ascensions of Paul*, of which we have, in Greek, a version of the end of the fourth century, and of which there are numerous adaptations in Latin, Syrian, Coptic, Armenian and Old Slavonic. . . .[142] The general theme of the work remains, however, on the whole, the same as in that which was already known. It deals with the ascents of Paul into the heavens,[143] where he is shown the torments of the inferno and then the radiant dwellings of Paradise—the theme which was one day to become that of the admirable *Divina Commedia*. According to our Coptic work, Paul is caught up from the mountain of Jericho into the higher realms. In the first heaven, he witnesses the interrogation of souls. He passes by angels with frightening faces who, with rods of iron in their hands are driving the damned to their punishment. Higher and higher Paul is led, by the angel who acts as his guide, until he has passed successively through the gates of the seven heavens. In the sixth, Paul sees his companions the apostles coming to welcome him. In the seventh heaven a being who has the appearance of an old man accosts him: "Whither goest thou, blessed Paul,

---

[142] Cf. *Dictionnaire de la Bible*; *Supplément*, vol. I, cols. 528–9.
[143] *II Corinthians* XII, 2; cf. Bidez–Cumont, *loc. cit.*, vol. I, p. 230, note 6.

who hast been elect from thy mother's breast?" Paul consults his angel guide, who, by a sign, invites him to reply to the aged man: "I shall return to the place whence I came . . . , towards the world of mortals, that I may again become a slave in the servitude of Babylon.—But how wilt thou find the strength to separate from me? " asks the old man, who adds: "Look, and see the principalities and the powers!" Then, for Paul, a sign is given. . . .

Must we identify this book with that lost apocryphon, the *Ascension of Paul*, known to Epiphanius as in use among the Cainites and mentioned in his *Against the Heresies* (XXXVIII, 2)? Decidedly not: from what we are told of that writing, it described the apostle's ascent into *three* heavens (showing thereby a legitimate desire for conformity with the passage of *II Corinthians* XII, 2, where Paul mentions the vision he had actually had), and not seven heavens, as in the much more audacious fiction entertained by our Gnostics.[144]

*   *   *

Lastly, we have to mention some of the treatises contained in Codex XIII, the greater part of which is now known as the Jung Codex. This is undoubtedly the latest manuscript in the collection. Nevertheless, its unequal and irregular writing is apparently from the same hand as the splendid calligraphy of Codex X. The change from the one to the other of these writings could be explained by the ageing, or by some illness, of the copyist; the second explanation being the more probable. To realize the possibility of this odd phenomenon, one has only to refer to plate 95 in the volume of photographic reproductions already published by the Coptic Museum: page 47 of Codex X includes several lines of the deformed writing which is the rule in Codex XIII, but its deformities, so exceptional in this beautiful manuscript, presently fade away, and we have again the regular calligraphy of our Codex X. In any case, and although Codex

---

[144] The evolution by which the notion of three heavens developed into that of the seven planetary spheres, enveloped by the sphere of the fixed stars, is indicated in F. Cumont, *Lux Perpetua*, pp. 143-4 and 184-6.

THE MANUSCRIPTS OF CHENOBOSK-ION

On the left are the 23 sheets of Codex XIII, the rest of which escaped the Egyptian authorities and became the "Jung Codex".

CODEX X,
PAGES 32
AND 33

At the top of the
left-hand page is
the end of the
*Secret Book of
John.* Under its
conclusion, with-
out any indication
of title, begins the
*Gospel according to
Thomas.*

(*See Note,
p. 328*)

XIII is shown by the personality of its copyist to be an authentic member of the Chenoboskion library, we must emphasize the fact that the subakhmimic dialect in which it is written distinguishes it radically from the rest of the collection. And this separateness is furthermore evident from its contents: these include a *Discourse to Reginos upon the Resurrection* (No. 47), an anonymous treatise which MM. Puech and Quispel think is attributable to Heracleon (No. 48),[145] and a *Gospel of Truth* (No. 46). Nos. 45 and 49, the *Apocalypse of James* and the *Prayer of the Apostle Peter*, have already been mentioned above.

The *Gospel of Truth* has lately been published by MM. Puech and Quispel with an extremely careful translation by M. Malinine. We must remember that the six pages of manuscript missing from this publication are in the collection that went to the Coptic Museum.[146] In spite of its title, the text is simply that of a treatise: it names no author, no addressee; it invokes no great prophet, and no saviour other than Jesus is mentioned in it. Moreover, one finds here none of the multiple names of aeons or luminaries, or allusions to the myths of Sophia and the evil demiurge which characterize the principal writings from Chenoboskion. The references upon which this exegetist most clearly relies are, wisely enough, those of the Holy Scriptures; particularly the Johannine Apocalypse and the *Epistle to the Hebrews*. The text is full of bad rhetoric while otherwise particularly empty —although this *Gospel of Truth* pretends to be "a good news that will be a joy to those for whom the Father, through the Word [that is, the Saviour], has vouchsafed the Gnosis". Whoever has this Gnosis, it affirms, takes what is his and restores it to himself. By Gnosis, a man knows "whence he has come and whither he is going". The Christ is presented as the revealer of "the living Book of the living"; a truth of which one must spell out every

---

[145] Cf. *Evangelium Veritatis*: Jung Codex, edited by M. Malinine, H. C. Puech and G. Quispel, 1956. *Introduction*.

[146] These are reproduced in the photographic edition of Pahor Labib, *Coptic Gnostic Papyri . . .* , vol. I. It must be said that these pages are reproduced in a disorder which it is hard to justify, seeing that the original pagination is in most cases clearly shown at the top of each page. Moreover, it looks as though these leaves have been considerably damaged or even torn since I made the first inventory.

9

letter. It was error and ignorance that rebelled against the Saviour and caused him to be nailed to the Cross. Salvation is represented here as the response to a Call coming from below, like an awakening out of deep sleep. . . . Here and there, however, are passages that make one feel that behind the writing there is a meditation—all too abstract—upon a myth which is never imparted to us in its own terms, but which, judging by certain details, must have been a cosmogony analogous to those disclosed in other Gnostic treatises. Matter, we are told, was set in motion and shaped by error trying to imitate the truth, and this error tried to attract to itself the beings of the intermediate world. The cosmic universe owed its development to the ignorance of the highest God, to anxiety, terror and forgetfulness; but the Pleroma went in search of the elect into these abysses, and that by means of the Gnosis, by the revelation of Jesus and of the Cross. The presence of such elements explains why the work was included by the sectaries of Chenoboskion in their library.

Its origin—the editors cautiously suggest—may perhaps be traceable to the Gnostic Valentinus; but if this work was really representative of him we should have to admit that he was a pretty poor writer! However, in Irenaeus' *Adversus Haereses* (III, 11, 9) written between the years 180 and 185, we read that, "As for the disciples of Valentinus, without let or restraint by the slightest shame, they boast, while showing their writings, of having in their possession more Gospels than are actually in existence. They have even had the impudence to entitle *Gospel of Truth*, a work recently made up by themselves; which in no way agrees with the Gospels of the Apostles. So not even the Gospel itself escapes the blasphemies of these people. . . ." With less precision, the pseudo-Tertullian writes, in Chapter IV of his treatise *Against the Heresies*, that Valentinus, "beside our Gospels possesses another of his own". But these phrases of Irenaeus and the pseudo-Tertullian lead us to suppose that this *Gospel* of Valentinus pretended, by its form and content, to rivalry with the Canonical Gospels, which could not be said of the Coptic writing found under the title of *Gospel of Truth*. It must be admitted, under these conditions, that there is strictly speaking only one argument that may justify identification of this newly-found writing with Valentinus's *Gospel of Truth*—that is, that the vocabulary and ideas of the Coptic *Gospel of Truth* are, as its present editors have underlined,[147] in accord with what we know of the Valentinian Gnosticism.[148]

HERMES TRISMEGISTUS AS AN ALLY OF GNOSTICISM

Lastly, we come to a class of writings that one would hardly have expected to find in a Gnostic library. This consists of the texts which, in some cases, reveal to us a teaching intermediate between Gnosticism and Hermetism, whilst others belong properly to Hermetic literature.[149]

We have mentioned, earlier in the present book, the curious character of the most authentic of the links that connect the two teachings (albeit very superficially)—namely, the *Apocalypse of Dositheus* (No. 30). As for the properly Hermetic writings of this category, they are—significantly—grouped together, five of them, in Codex VI—which was one of the most in use, as we can see from the portions of feathers slipped in between the leaves to mark certain places in the book.

[147] *Evangelium Veritatis*, p. xii.

[148] Let us add that, even if the *Gospel of Truth* in our Coptic collection be descended from an authentic work under this title assigned to Valentinus, it would still be rash to treat it as a true and reliable transcription of that work. Let us not forget that in every case where it has been possible to compare our Coptic texts (which are of the fourth and fifth centuries) with information about more ancient versions of them, it is manifest that each new transcription was taken as an opportunity for alterations, additions and glosses, even for the joining-together of different works, which may have profoundly modified the substance in order to bring it into accord with the beliefs peculiar to our Egyptian sectaries. One need only take, for examples, the case of the *Secret Book of John*, with its two versions different from one another and different also from the most ancient version analysed by Irenaeus (I,xxix); and the manner in which the *Sophia of Jesus* and the *Hypostasis* of *the Archons* were fabricated, the former from the *Epistle of Eugnostos* and the latter from what we have in text No. 40; or, again, count up the glosses and interpolations with which the compiler of our Codex X has enriched the texts that he transcribed—to realize the shifting character, changing from century to century, of Gnostic literature. It is improbable—it would be a miracle—if this *Gospel of Truth*, from *the latest of all* the Chenoboskion manuscripts—even though it were originally modelled on a work of that name ascribed to Valentinus—should have escaped distortion by these avatars, any more than the other writings in our collection.

[149] J. Doresse, "Hermès et la Gnose."

The text of No. 21 is entitled *Authentic discourse* (meaning, rather, "authoritative") *of Hermes to Tat*, a title which should be compared with those of works in the corpus of the Greek Hermetic writings: *Logos Katholikos, Hieros Logos, Logos Apokryphos* —Universal Discourse, Sacred Discourse, Hidden Discourse (these are the Greek treatises IIA, III, XIII). Typically Hermetic in its style, the Coptic work does contain, however, allusions of a Gnostic tendency—for instance, about the creation of the Archons.

The next writing (No. 22) is entitled *The Sense of Understanding, The Thought of the Great Power*. This title recalls the first lines of an extract from a Hermetic book preserved in the florilegium of Stobaeus (now indicated by the number XVIII),[150] where the same words occur together—*noêma, pronoïa, aïsthêsis.* Let us also remember the sub-title *Upon Thought and Sensation*, borne by the IXth treatise of the Greek corpus.

The Coptic text begins thus: "Since we have received a teaching in this place, let us uplift ourselves first to the things that have been said to us, and we shall find this—that he said that he who was treated [?] with violence absolutely, the same is glorified justly. Was it not even so that they outraged him? . . ." The theme is then specified in these words: "We say then, now, since he said that the one who does violence and the one who does justice, both of them possess one force, how can he have said that the Word of the soul is an image without a model?" This rather mysterious preamble is indeed in a style modelled upon that of the Greek Hermetic treatises, were it only for the way in which it refers in a few words to some previous discussions, upon the theme of which the dialogue then starts off in a new direction. In this case the Coptic exposition alludes to a theme discussed before in some discourse which the Chenoboskion library has not preserved for us. (Nor does the formula "an image without a model, the Word of the soul" occur again in any of the Hermetic treatises or fragments of them preserved in Greek.) From this point of departure the discussion goes on to a new subject—the primitive creation of forms, models and natures. The last words

[150] *Hermès Trismégiste*, vol. III, ed. Nock and Festugière, 1954, pp. ciii–cvi and 80–81.

are about the god who takes care of his creatures "in the manner of the cultivator who gives nourishment every day to his produce". This recalls other allusions to the labourer, the "good sower of life", a favourite personage in the Hermetic parables.[151] Treatise No. 23 has no title. This in its turn appears to be the continuation of a previous instruction. Hermes Trismegistus—the Noûs—here explains to his "son" the mysteries of the Hebdomad, of the Ogdoad and of the Ennead[152]—subjects rarely touched upon in the Greek Hermetic writings. Finally, this revelation is saluted with a hymn (ending in a sequence of vowels): "Lord give to us a wisdom drawn from thy power which reaches even unto us, that we may show forth the teaching of the Ogdoad and the Ennead". The substance of the treatise recalls certain passages of the *Poimandres* and of the Greek Hermetic treatise No. XIII.

Writing No. 25 also has no definite title. It very evidently provides a sequel to text No. 23 just mentioned, from which it is separated, in the Coptic manuscript, by the transcription of a purely Gnostic revelation. It concludes with a passage which was already known long before the discovery of our Coptic writings —the prayer which comes at the end of the Latin *Asclepius*, and is to be found also in a Greek magical document—the *Mimaut* papyrus.[153]

But the content itself of our treatise No. 25 has nothing in common with the *Asclepius*. As we have indicated, it takes up the theme of the Hermetic text that precedes it: "I have told thee, my son, that I am the Noûs. I have seen that speech is impotent to

[151] J. Doresse, "Hermès et la Gnose," pp. 59–60.
[152] The Hebdomad corresponds to the lower heavens of the material world: the Ogdoad is the higher world: cf. *Corpus Hermeticum*, ed. Nock and Festugière, vol. I, p. 25, note 64; vol. II, p. 216, note 66: it is the divinity, the celestial kingdom, also called by the Gnostics the heavenly Jerusalem (cf. for example, Sagnard, *Gnose valentinienne*, p. 509). As for the word "Ennead", we do not find this in any Hermetic treatises we have up to the present: it must refer to the Kingdom of the highest entities established above the Ogdoad which itself surrounds and dominates the seven material heavens; Reitzenstein, *Poimandres*, p. 54, compares this notion with certain of the Egyptian cosmogonies which describe nine primitive divinities, one being that of the original creator who engendered the eight others.
[153] Festugière and Nock give this, in a note, in *Corpus Hermeticum*, vol. II, p. 216. Upon the prayer, cf. J. Carcopino, *L'Hermétisme africain* . . . , p. 289.

reveal these things, for the entire Ogdoad, my son, and the soul that is in it, and the angels, sing the hymn in silence." This exposition is intermingled with prayers: "Thee I invoke, thou who dost govern the sovereign power, thou whose word is creative of light and whose sayings are immortal, eternal and immutable."

This treatise—the fourth of the evidently coherent series which we have now under consideration[154]—would seem, at the same time, to bring us to the peroration that concludes them as a whole. It ends, in fact, not only with the prayer we have mentioned but also, just before that, with last exhortations from Hermes to his disciple. The text of what he has just revealed is to be written upon tablets of jasper, defended by eight guardians (four with heads of frogs and four with heads of cats), and protected by a stone. The operation is to take place under astronomical conjunctions, which are given in rather over-simplified form, and—like certain celestial positions mentioned in the *Pistis-Sophia*[155]—derive from an old Chaldaean astrological system.[156] The Trismegistus concludes by dictating a solemn warning, to be written into the text, lest any impious readers should divulge this revelation, use it for maleficent purposes, or try to use it in opposition to the course of Fate. Those who make use of it—says the text—ought to walk according to the law of God, never transgressing it, but piously asking God for wisdom and Gnosis. It is thus, by degrees, that the adepts will enter into the way of immortality, and will attain to a conception of the Ogdoad, which in its turn, reveals the Ennead. The disciples repeat the oath "by the heaven and the earth, fire and water, the seven ousiarchs,[157] the creator spirit, the god who engenders and he who is born of himself and those who have begotten him, that they may guard the things that Hermes has told". Those who

---

[154] The texts Nos. 21, 22, 23 and 25.

[155] C. Schmidt and W. Till, *Koptisch-Gnostische Schriften*, pp. 238–41.

[156] Cf. above, p. 75 and note 35 of this chapter; and, below, p. 271.

[157] The *ousiarchs*, who head this list of all the powers up to the highest, are the rulers of the "essence" or of matter—the rulers of the planets. The term was never encountered till now except in the *Asclepius*, § 19 (cf. *Corpus Hermeticum*, vol. II, p. 375, note 157): this detail is a sign of Iranian influence. The *Asclepius* states that the seven spheres have, as ousiarchs, "that which is named fortune and Heimermene".

broke this oath would be exposed to the wrath of all the powers enumerated—powers which, be it observed, seem to belong more to Gnostic mythology than to Hermetic doctrine. These solemn promises are sealed, as we have seen, by the prayer already known to us in Latin at the end of the *Asclepius* and, in Greek, in the magico-Gnostic papyrus *Mimaut*. After this orison, to which no doubt a special efficacy was attributed, the treatise terminates with the same concluding formula which serves also to close the *Asclepius*: "When they had pronounced this prayer, they embraced one another and went to take pure nourishment in which there had never been blood."

As for text No. 26, it alone—or almost alone—of those in the Chenoboskion library, gives us a writing which we knew before in a less archaic form: but let us first give an analysis of it.

It begins with these sentences: "If thou wouldst see, indeed, the accomplishment of this mystery and the image of this miracle, consider the manner in which carnal union is effected by the male and by the woman. When the former attains to the supreme moment, and when the seed springs forth, at that moment the woman receives the strength of the male, while the male receives the strength of the woman. . . . It is because of this that the mystery of carnal union is practised in secret, so that the conjunction of natures should not be degraded through being seen of the multitude who would despise that work. . . ."

Pious men are few in number, continues our book. Created after the gods, composed of (both) divine and mortal nature, man tends towards the supreme powers. Like them, he too has created in his own image, by fashioning the statues that he worships.

But now, from the mouth of the Trismegistus, we are given a description of the future of the world: "Knowest thou not, Asclepius, that Egypt is the image of heaven, or better still, the dwelling of heaven and of all the powers that are in heaven? . . . Our earth is the temple of the world." Nevertheless "a day is coming when it will appear that the Egyptians have served the divinity in vain, and all their pious worship will become sterile. Indeed all divinity will leave Egypt and take refuge in

heaven . . . for the foreigners will invade Egypt and will
dominate her." Then the Egyptians will be prevented from
worshipping the divinity, and even subjected to torture. The
country will no longer be filled with temples but with tombs.
"And thou, O river, a day will come when thou wilt overflow
with blood instead of water, and when the bodies of the dead
will be piled higher than thy banks." And yet, when that day
comes, they will weep less for one who dies than for anyone who
is still living, having no longer anything of Egypt except the
language. On that day "all that I have taught to you—to you, Tat,
Asclepios and Ammon—all will be accounted as vanity". Even
the physical universe will subside in disorder: this will be the old
age of the world, marked with these three seals—"Atheism, dis-
honour and unreason". Then the divinity will complete the ruin
of this universe by some calamity, before giving it back its first
beauty and restoring all things for a new cycle, so that, in the end,
the gods "will be re-established in a town that will be upon the
borders of Egypt".

After having developed this apocalypse, the treatise enlarges
upon the immortal and the mortal: what is death and, above all,
what is the heavenly judgment of souls? "Listen, O Asclepios,
there is a great demon whom the supreme God has assigned to be
the guardian, and to judge the souls, of men. God established him
in the midst of the air, between earth and heaven: when the soul
goes forth from the body, Fate obliges her to meet this demon:
he then turns her round and examines the manner in which she
has behaved in her life."[158] These eschatological perspectives are
developed at length; and then the text ends.

What we have in this Coptic writing corresponds to a lengthy
portion (from the middle of § 21 to the end of § 29) of an authentic Hermetic writing which, up to the present, had reached us
only in the form of a Latin adaptation—the *Asclepius*, wrongly
attributed to Apuleius.[159] Our Coptic text is more restrained than
the Latin version. If we compare them, it seems that most of the

[158] Cf. above, chap. II, pp. 72–73 upon the judgment of the soul as described
in the *Pistis-Sophia*.
[159] Cf. *Corpus Hermeticum*, vol. II, pp. 59ff. Its existence is attested at the beginning of the fourth century by quotations from it in Lactantius. The Latin

additions that enrich the version of the pseudo-Apuleius are artificial embellishments, or rhetorical elaborations.[160] Moreover, such passages as that upon carnal union with which our Coptic version begins, have been considerably edulcorated in the Latin.

Let us remark, by the way, that the famous "revelation"— "Knowest thou not, Asclepios, that Egypt is the image of heaven . . . ?" with its fictive prophecy of the barbarization of the country by foreigners billeting themselves upon it, and then of the ultimate re-establishment of the order of the gods— offers us the last example of a kind of writing which had been recurrently practised in pharaonic literature from the earliest ages. It had quite a weakness for the elaboration of such pseudo-prophecies retracing, after each period of national misfortune, the conventional picture of a universal disorder, and of the abandonment of Egypt by the gods, and ending with this announcement that, eventually, some sovereign would come, bringing salvation.[161] Naturally, writings of this kind were composed after the enthronement of the fictitiously predicted "saviour".

Let us pass over the various literary problems raised by a comparison between our texts and those of the Greek Hermetic corpus and the Latin Asclepius. As our Coptic compiler has no wish to hide from us, in the note he has inserted between texts 25 and 26, we are only dealing with extracts. The Nos. 21, 22, 23 and 25, which constitute a sequence, must have been the principal parts of that "first treatise" that he says he has copied into this Codex.

When these texts can be analysed more thoroughly, the question will be, above all, whether the Gnostic entities mentioned

version which has come down to us existed in St Augustine's day; he made use of it in the *City of God*. The erroneous attribution of this work to Apuleius began in the ninth century. Fragments of the Greek original have also been preserved by, among others, Johannes Lydus (sixth century).

[160] Our Coptic text comes nearer to some fragments preserved by Johannes Lydus, for example, that of § 28 of the *Asclepius*, (quoted in the *Corpus Hermeticum*, vol. II, p. 334), than to the Latin version.

[161] J. Doresse, "Apocalypses égyptiennes" in *La Table Ronde*, No. 110, Feb. 1957, more particularly pp. 29-35. Cf. the translations of hieroglyphic texts given in Erman, *Die Literatur der Aegypter*, 1923, pp. 122ff.; see also G. Posener, *Littérature et politique dans l'Égypte de la XIIème dynastie*, 1956.

9*

here, in writings which would otherwise seem to conform well enough to the regular teaching of Hermetism, really belonged to the first versions of these works; or whether, on the other hand, they were imported into them by one of our sectaries, who modified the texts in accordance with his own beliefs.

What remains so remarkable is the presence of these Hermetic writings in a library of which all the rest is essentially Gnostic.[162] Moreover, the gloss of the Gnostic compiler—"This is the first discourse that I have copied for you. But there are many others that have come into my hands: I have not transcribed them, thinking that they have already reached you. . . ."—greatly heightens the interest of its presence in this collection. What it shows is that there was in circulation in Upper Egypt, in the second half of the fourth century (the period of our Codex X), a far more important collection of Hermetic treatises, already translated from Greek into Sahidic Coptic,[163] and destined, no doubt, for use by sectaries more or less related to those of Chenoboskion.

The intentional juxtaposition of Hermetic writings and Gnostic treatises shows that some interchange was then going on between the two schools of doctrine. Here, living once again before our eyes, is that syncretic movement which associated the Gnostic prophets not only to the Hermes of Cyllene, but also to the more learned Hermes of the Greek mystical treatises. This is precisely the blend of ideas whose occurrence at that epoch had been suggested, but not satisfactorily proved, by the little treatise of Zosimos the alchemist *Upon the Letter Omega*; in which myths derived from the writings of Zoroaster, some of those of Nicotheus "the hidden" and of the Jewish Gnosis, are treated upon the same footing as writings *On the Natures* and *On Immateriality*, which are imputed to the authority of the Trismegistus.

[162] From the point of view of Hermetic literature itself, it should be emphasized that these writings bring us texts not only unpublished, but also attested by manuscripts going back nearly as far as to the epoch in which the treatises of learned Hermetism were composed (cf. J. Carcopino, *L'Hermétisme africain*, pp. 290-1), from which epoch dates also that magical papyrus *Mimaut* which preserves a Greek text of the prayer that concludes our text No. 25, and which appears again at the end of the Latin version of the *Asclepius* (cf. Carcopino, *loc. cit.*, p. 289, note 3).

[163] Cf. J. Doresse, "Hermès et la Gnose," pp. 58-9.

CHAPTER VI

THE SETHIANS ACCORDING TO THEIR WRITINGS

MY examination of these Coptic writings was—I must repeat—unequal and incomplete. It is certain that when once they become completely accessible, they will be found to be much more eloquent and infinitely richer than can be gathered from my rather hurried notes.

Already, however, the yield from them is considerable; firstly because of their number. No ancient library as rich as this had been found before. The interest of the new manuscripts is enhanced by the homogeneity of the writings they contain, their undoubted unity: most of them belong to the same religious body; they complement one another. Some of them refer to this or that other work included in the same collection. Here, then, it is practically certain that we possess an authentic sacred library. The interest of the new texts is further heightened by their diversity: they depict the same Gnostic myths under the most varied forms: moreover, the great sacred revelations are intermingled with commentaries, sacramental rubrics, prayers, and polemical epistles against adversaries. They are even accompanied by some works from alien groups—Valentinian or Hermetist, in whom our sectaries were interested. Such an assemblage is full of life.

With this library at hand, it at last becomes possible to judge the relative values of the abundant reports upon the Gnostics which the heresiologists have left us and to make fuller use of the best of them. One has only to glance through the new writings to recognize, for instance, the reliability of such an account as that given in the *Philosophumena*—a value already presumed by M. Filliozat—for it is now clear that the texts it summarizes are authentically Gnostic.[1] We can also confirm the accuracy of *some*

[1] Cf. chap. I, note 26.

of the accounts of Epiphanius and the slapdash but pretty realistic character of the information we have from Theodore Bar-Konaï. On the other hand, we are put somewhat upon our guard about what we were told of the great heretical teachers, not one of whom makes any explicit appearance in the writings from Chenoboskion.

In return for reassuring us about the dependability of the heresiologists, the new Coptic books themselves gain in prestige by confrontation with the literature of their adversaries: it is noteworthy, for example, that the principal myths restored to us by the new Gnostic texts are in conformity with what their hostile critics said of the *earliest* Gnosticism. Thus Irenaeus bears witness to the existence, before the year 180, of a writing which constitutes the first part of the *Secret Book of John*; the pseudo-Hippolytus, too, provides us with a guarantee of the early existence of our *Paraphrase of Seth* and of several other apocrypha; Porphyry knew very well the books that we have under the names of *Zoroaster, Zostrian, Messos* and "*Allogenes*". Finally, all this confirms our belief that the majority of our Coptic books were translations from the Greek—even though some of them complacently refer to Hebrew to tell us that Ariael signifies "the Lion of God" or to speculate upon Arbathiao, Ekhmôth and Ekhamôth. At the same time, we recognize that the texts of Codex X have been enriched with glosses and commentaries which, for their part, are very unlikely to be of earlier date than that of the Coptic scribe of this actual manuscript.

What was the sect that owned these manuscripts? Firstly, are we dealing with a group of importance? For it is of course possible that a little group of well-to-do initiates provided themselves with this fine collection of manuscripts. It is manifest, however, that such a fine library could only have been amassed thanks to the activities of many copyists, who were working not only in the place where the library was constituted: we have proof of this, in the personal annotation of the scribe who contributes the Hermetic anthology in our manuscript No. VI[2]: and the whole collection of considerably varied works were written at dates

---

[2] Cf. here, pp. 142 and 248, and J. Doresse, "Hermès et la Gnose," pp. 58-9.

ranging over more than a century. This suggests that there was indeed an actual Gnostic church, maintaining relations with groups situated in other regions.

Nothing in these documents leads us to suppose that the Gnostics in question were addicted to licentious rites: one finds oneself almost disappointed at this, so freely had the heresiologists given us to understand that mysteries of that description were common practice in the principal sects! From the contents of the writings we can pretty well catalogue their owners. The presence of Barbelô among the higher powers; the fact that so many of the books are labelled with the name of Seth; that we find among them a *Supreme Allogenes,* and that they include a *Paraphrase of Shem* (also called *of Seth*)—show that the sect was Sethian.[3] Epiphanius, moreover, tells us that this sect still existed in Egypt at that epoch; he remembers having met some of its adepts there himself. He also tells us that it was well on the way to extinction, which would agree well enough with the fact that our library (whose latest manuscripts date from the end of the fourth century) was buried when some of the books were still practically new. One might, no doubt, think also of the Ophites or of the Naassenes; our Coptic writings do indeed include the *Gospel of the Egyptians* and the *Gospel of Thomas* to which those sects had recourse. One might also wonder whether one had to do with Archontici or Barbelognostics. . . . But it would be useless to try to be more precise; we know from the heresiologists that the sects borrowed from one another without the slightest compunction—and here we have tangible proof of it. Besides, the enemies of Gnosticisim no doubt tended to multiply to excess, in their collections, the various appellations which in different countries were applied to sects in reality very similar to one another.

It is a striking fact that this collection of Coptic books would fairly exactly represent, on the one hand, the anonymous Gnostics mentioned by Porphyry, and, on the other, the repertory of apocrypha utilized by the pseudo-Zosimos in his treatise *On the*

---

[3] It was by chance alone, however, that our Sethian Gnostics happened to live near the town of Shenesit—"the acacias of Seth": see chap. IV, p. 129.

Letter Omega. This guarantees that the collection we have comprises the texts that were most universally current among the sects. We may even consider, if we compare the titles of the rediscovered works with those listed by the heresiologists, that we have nearly all the literature that the ancient enemies of the Gnostics had heard of. What titles are still lacking? Doubtless the *Great Revelation* of Simon Magus; the *Apocalypse of Nicotheus*, the celestial visions of *Marsanes and Martiades*; those of *Phosilampes*; the *Gospel of Eve*, the *Apocalypse of Abraham*; the prophecies that Basilides attributed to *Barcabbas* and to *Barcoph*; the *Baruch* of Justin. . . . But let us not be insatiable! Neither should we forget that our mass of manuscripts still holds a number of writings of manifestly important content upon which it has not yet been possible to replace the right titles. Probably we may yet come to recognize, little by little, some of the famous texts that are still missing. It may be, too, that some of these long-sought writings are disguised under titles different from those we know them by: have we not already recognized the *Book of Nôrea* under the title of the *Hypostasis of the Archons*? The *Revelation of Nicotheus* is perhaps—who knows?—the very book which has been adapted and disfigured to make the essential part of The *Secret Book of John*. It has, in any case, now become certain that only a minute examination of the *Gospels* of *Philip*, *Thomas* and *Matthias*, and of the *Gospel of the Egyptians*, which we have in Coptic, will enable us to decide their nature with certainty, because the references to these texts by the heresiologists are confused, or even erroneous. Let us therefore take confidence in our Gnostics, who, better placed than we are now to select these writings in which they took even keener interest than we do, chose the fifty-odd books that we have before us: and let us also take into account, in compensation for any works we still lack, the fact that we are discovering other works whose existence had long been totally unknown, so that we had never expected to find them.

The leading characteristics of this literature? An outstanding one is the bewildering variety of the ideas and systems it expounds. This want of coherence in its mythology was one of the greatest weaknesses of Gnosticism. Eusebius, in his *Ecclesiastical History*

(IV, 7), makes much of this; Irenaeus, in his treatise against heresies (I, XI, 1) goes so far as to say that when two or three sectaries are together, none of them can express himself in the same way as the others, but each one explains different things, using a different terminology. We have seen plenty of this inconsistency, not only in the discrepancies between their numerous revelations, but in the fact that they borrow from one another, in defiance of all logic, mythical elements that are contradictory or incompatible; and that these writings are presented without scruple under a multiplicity of titles; and that they even go so far as to modify the morals they draw to suit the taste of this or that sect. Hence the *Epistle of Eugnostos* turns into the *Sophia of Jesus*, and a number of bits and pieces are built up into a complete work like the *Secret Book of John*. Not one of our texts can even begin to be the subject of a definite interpretation until we are either assured of its unity or can estimate how many pieces of different origins were strung together to compose it. And then how are we to account for such fantasies? Perhaps by assuming that they were not always transmitted by writing, but were communicated—as was the Zoroastrian literature for a long while during the same centuries—by an oral tradition which rendered them indefinitely and excessively pliable.

The authors of these works—many of which were built up by progressive stages—remain practically unknown to us. In this respect we must note that Gnosticism is in contrast with Manichaeism which presented its writings openly under the names of Mani and his authentic disciples. Gnostic literature systematically disguised its origins under impressive fictitious names, which is equivalent to anonymity—a weakness it shared, alas! with Hermetic literature. Apart from the names of Dositheus and Silvanus, which perhaps correspond to real individuals, our sectaries introduce us to no personality at all except Eugnostos-Goggessos, the author and compiler of sacred writings which he, too, composes, sometimes, in the name of the Great Seth! As a general rule, the Gnostic treatises are attributed to Zostrian, Zoroaster, Messos, Adam, Eve, Seth, Shem and other "Allogenes". Some of the writings entitled with such great names may, perhaps, have been Gnostic adaptations from earlier apocryphal literature: others, particularly those headed with the names of Seth and other "Allogenes", must have been products of Gnosticism itself. By its use of such names, this religion meant to assign a higher origin to the books that it used. Moreover, the Gnostics must have been sincerely convinced of the celestial origin of the revelations written by their own prophets: we have read that their greatest masters—Simon, Menander—regarded themselves as authentic incarnations of the supreme powers, so that they could not express themselves otherwise than in the names of the Enlighteners who spoke through their mouths. This procedure, however, takes on an uglier aspect when our heretics try to introduce a factitious Christianity into their doctrines by forging, for this purpose, spurious Gospels dubbed with the names of James, John, Thomas, Philip and Matthias, and even by putting some of their revelations into the mouth of the Saviour. Such a teacher as Basilides was not above making up a compilation of this kind.

The setting in which these myths are fictitiously revealed is of a no less fantastic character. We are told that the composition of the great apocalypses dates from the earliest times, and that they were preserved under the guardianship of fantastic powers in inaccessible, particularly holy and mysterious places. Of such is the mountain of Charax upon which the sun never rises, the hiding-place of the *Book of the invisible Great Spirit*.[4] As we had read before in the *Pistis-Sophia*, the *Books of Jêou* were dictated to Enoch in Paradise and hidden upon Mount Ararat. The revelations which are decked out with Christian allusions are, for their part, localized around the Temple of Jerusalem, the Mount of Olives, the Mount of Galilee, the Mountain of Jericho and the Jordan. And in the course of these diverse revelations other, not less significant places are mentioned—the mountain from which the power (?) named Saldaô reigns[5]; the mountain of Seir where Noah built the Ark[6]; and, finally, Sodom and Gomorrha whose

---

[4] Cf. chap. v, notes 27 and 58 and, below, note 9.

[5] Or rather, the mountain of Seldaô (?); cf. chap. II, note 35.

[6] According to the *Hypostasis of the Archons* or *Book of Nôrea*. Concerning this mountain of Seir (or Shyr), see chap. v, notes 27 and 58.

names, far from being associated with the maledictions of the Old Testament, here denote the earthly dwelling-places of the perfect seed of the Great Seth.[7] As for the name of Egypt, this also comes into our texts, where it takes on a particular symbolic meaning; it denotes the base matter in which the soul is imprisoned (reminding us that, for the Jewish soul, Egypt represents "the house of bondage"), as it does in the Hymn of the Pearl in the *Acts of Thomas*; and also in the teaching of the Naassenes as it is summarized in the *Philosophumena*.[8]

These details of a mythical geography may seem of only secondary importance: nevertheless, we must try to trace their origins in tradition and history.

One has to reckon, first of all, with a real geographical setting; to recover the elements of which one has to collect all that can be known of the distribution of the Baptist sects—such, for instance, as the Sampseans and the Osseans—who were established in the Nabatene, and Ituraea, in the land of Moab—especially on the banks of the Arnon. One must take account of the area in which Mandaeanism developed.[9] Nor can one neglect the fact that Mani was originally of Babylon, and that a Kantaean such as Papa the master of Battaï came from the same districts of Gaukaï to the east of Ctesiphon. One has then to reassemble all the elements of the mythical geography continually implied in our texts. There we find legends anterior to Gnosticism—those, for instance, which attributed a sacred character to Mount Hermon, the supposed residence of the children of Seth at the beginning of human existence.[10] We must not fail to reckon with some invaluable traditions preserved by the Mandaeans alone. One of their writings, recently published, is the *Haran Gawaïta*, in which we find that Mandaeism knew essentially the *same* mythical geography as that of the Gnostics and of the traditions relating to the Magi, except that the Mandaeans' version omitted the figure of Zoroaster, replacing it by those of their legendary prophets Anôsh-Uthra and Yôhannâ. When their nation began—says the

---

[7] Cf. below, pp. 298-9. [8] Cf. chap. I, note 120.
[9] Upon Gaukaï, place of origin of Papa the Kantaean and of Mani, cf. H. C. Puech, *Le Manichéisme* . . . , note 144.
[10] Cf. chap. I, note 97.

Haran Gawaïta—60,000 Mandaeans were established by a king named Ardavân in the land of the Medes, in which is the White Mountain (that is, the Mountain of Lights so widely renowned that it figures even in Indian mythology!). Upon this mountain Anôsh-Uthra carried on the mysterious guidance and instruction of the child Yôhannâ—of John the Baptist. There, also, Anôsh-Uthra instituted seven Guardians, whom he afterwards established at seven places in Mesopotamia. Then Anôsh caused Babylon to be ruled by the line of Ardavân, who developed Mandaeanism in that country, but was at last overthrown by another dynasty—that of the Sassanids.

Even to this day the Mandaeans regard the great White Mountain of Syr as the most sacred spot in the world. They situate it at the northern extremity of the inhabited world: just behind it are the Mataraha—that is, the gates of the Light watched over by the celestial powers whose function it is to welcome there the souls of the dead. The only waters that are white—which means, purifying—are those of rivers which, like the Jordan—the name of which means "descent"—also flow in that direction, down from the Septentrion towards the south.[11] All these strange myths, we shall find, shed some light upon the obscure allusions preserved in original Gnostic writings—for example, those at the end of the anonymous treatise in the Bruce Codex, or in the second part of the Gospel of the Egyptians, where again we are told about mysterious places held by certain Guardians.

As well as the names of the great prophets to whom the Gnostics chose to ascribe their revelations, these places, then, have their meanings. They show the mythical settings, some of them already hallowed by traditions earlier than the Gnostic, with which our sectaries meant, very consciously, to surround their beliefs.

[11] Cf. Drower, The Mandaeans, pp. 5–6 and 261–3; cf. also on p. 419 of the same work, its index s.v. Tura d Maddai; Drower, The Haran Gawaïta and the Baptism of Hibil-Ziwa, Citta del Vaticano, 1953; Widengren, Stand und Aufgaben der Iranischen Religionsgeschichte (Extract from Numen, vols. I and II, Leiden 1955, pp. [121]–[122] and [130]–[131]; Tondelli, " Il Mandeismo e le origini cristiane," p. 65; Furlani, Peccati e peccatori presso i Mandei, 1950, p. 315; Lars-Ivar Ringbom, Graltempel und Paradies, Stockholm, 1951. Cf. finally the Book of John (edn. Lidzbarski), p. 116, and the Ginzâ (edn. Lidzbarski), pp. 302, 362 and 380 (where the mountain is called Tarwân).

Meanwhile, we may well wonder for what precise reason all these various writings claimed the protection of secrecy, absolutely and in principle. Why all those concluding maledictions, menacing anyone who might unduly disclose them? One answer is that mystical literatures have generally made spectacular professions of being hidden. In a good many cases the secrecy has been bogus. Take, for instance, in Treatise XVI, 2, of the Hermetic *Corpus*, this sentence: "O king . . . guard this discourse safely against all translation, lest such great mysteries should ever come to be known by the Greeks!"—a quite ludicrous recommendation, considering that the treatise in question had never been written in any other language than Greek! No doubt these "revelations" gained, from their supposed secrecy, a hold over the initiates which the open communication of the same writings would not have secured. In a similar fashion, the monstrous lion-headed statue of the Mithraic Aïôn, which might have looked merely comical in the light of day, was revealed only in the gloom of a cell, where the worshipper had but a glimpse of it—in the lurid glimmer of flames made to issue from its jaws of stone— through a crack in the wall.[12] And one must admit that these writings we have discovered, if their contemporaries could have discussed them quite openly, might well have betrayed a mediocrity that would have robbed them of all prestige.

Nevertheless, it is certain that, among the Gnostics, determination to keep their writings secret went far beyond being a mere fiction: their enemies evidently took great pains to obtain knowledge of some of their writings, and, very often, could do so only from imperfect and indirect information. Moreover, in our texts, we can see that the definitive title of the *Apocalypse of Zostrian*, which would identify it as a revelation of *Zoroaster*, has been written in a cryptogram, for the further concealment, from anyone who might chance to have sight of the manuscript, of the authority to which it is ascribed. We may compare this fact with the case of a Hebrew text dealing with certain astrological subjects, which was found in Cave No. 4 of Qumrân: that treatise is, in part, written from left to right—the opposite

[12] Franz Cumont, *Monuments des Mystères de Mithra*, vol. I, 1899, p. 81.

direction to that of normal Hebrew script—on purpose to make it very difficult reading for anyone not practised in that sort of mental acrobatics![13]

We have still to discover what it was, of all the complex elements brought together in Gnostic writings, that constituted, in Gnostic eyes, the authentic and paramount mystery. There were, first—as we have seen—the *names* of some of the Enlighteners to whom they owed such great revelations. In the myths themselves, it was evidently not the astrological conceptions that they wanted to guard from indiscreet disclosures, for these were known to everybody: nor was it the sacramental formulas, precious though they might be; for in this secret literature they only appear in a very limited number of texts. We must therefore suppose that what the faithful were guarding so jealously were the descriptions of the higher world; the names of the entities to be found there; the image, and the mission, of the Saviour; the anti-Biblical interpretation of *Genesis* and of the Mosaic Law; the revelation of what they held to be the esoteric meaning of Christianity; and, finally, their announcement to the faithful follower of the higher nature within himself, and of the means by which he could attain salvation.

All the qualities we have thus far verified in Gnostic writings invest them with a certain ambiguity of character—and this shows itself as much on the plane of literary art as of doctrinal exposition. It is indeed astonishing that texts such as these, which at times are animated—as in certain hymns—by a fine afflatus, winged with startling images; and whose mystical value remains undeniable, could have encaged their splendours in such a mass of particularly clumsy apocryphal fables, and enumerations of countless entities, each more incredible than the last.

Having now summarized some of the new texts in sufficient detail, it would be rather needless to enter here upon another systematic examination of the finer shades of distinction that they develop between the great Gnostic mythologies. Let us, however, emphasize a few general features.

The contents of the Chenoboskion writings differ notably from

[13] J. T. Milik, *Dix ans de découvertes dans le désert de Juda*, 1957, pp. 78–9.

those of the *Books of Pistis-Sophia* and the two *Books of Jêou* which we possessed before, and which are marked by characteristics very near to Manichaeism.[14]

Now, for the points upon which the Coptic apocrypha from Chenoboskion have done most to open our eyes, the first is concerned with what one may call—to use the Manichaean terminology which is not at all out of place in this connection—the *Primal Moment* in the history of the universe; that in which the primitive Principles come face to face before the beginning of the Creation. Texts of which, until now, we had only had glimpses, had led us to wonder whether Gnosticism did not regard the formation of the lower world as simply the result of the fall of a being of Light, whose passion had provoked the insurgence of matter (as, indeed, appears to be the case in some of our new writings)—or whether there really was, in this doctrine, a dualism analogous to that of the Manichaeans, as was suggested by such indirect knowledge as we had about the teaching fictively ascribed to Simon of Samaria, and, still more, about that of Basilides.

This question is answered to admiration by the *Paraphrase of Shem*, for—confirming the same explanation that the *Philosophumena* attributed to the Sethians—it describes the primordial powers as two opposing elements: Light and Darkness, between which, moreover, there is a third *root*: Wind, or Spirit. Remarkably enough, this myth is in full agreement with the doctrine that Basilides had mentioned, according to the *Acts of Archelaüs*, and that the *Great Revelation* of Simon had developed (according to the *Philosophumena*) by specifying that the intermediary principle had issued from the two others. All this proves that such a belief was fairly early established in Gnosticism, if not from its beginning. At the same time it fits in closely with the explanation we have in, for instance, the beginning of the *Bundahishn*. These correspondences bring out all the meaning of the fact that Gnostic apocrypha—such as were known to Plotinus and his disciples, and used by the pseudo-Zosimos, and of which our collection, too, preserves good examples—were attributed to Zoroaster and other Magi with whom Seth and his own were afterwards, in great

---

[14] Cf. chap. II above, pp. 79–80.

measure, identified. But how this doctrine of the three primordial roots could have been harmonized with the exposition of the formation of the higher world by successive pairs of emanations— such as we find in the *Book of the invisible Great Spirit*, in the *Epistle of Eugnostos* and in the first part of the *Secret Book of John*, which all abstain from any mention of these primordial principles —that is still not clearly apparent.

Another notable feature is that the figure of the god who creates the lower world is the subject, in our texts, of two different doctrines. Here we encounter, sometimes, the monstrous figure of Ialdabaôth alone, and sometimes, competing with him, the figure of his son Sabaôth. Ialdabaôth, ignorant and perverse, identified with Sacla, Samael, Ariael, with the devil . . . , manifests himself in every way as the enemy of the designs of the world of light. He is a lion-faced and serpent-bodied being; which approximates him to the "Chnubis" on the supposedly "Gnostic" engraved gems,[15] and, still more, to the composite figure of the Mithraic Aïôn. In fact, like the latter leontocephalic personage, he too is master of the seven heavens, and can therefore be similarly identified with Kronos–Saturn—who is already assimilated in Hellenic thought to Chronos—that is, to Time, the master of fatality.

Yet, in expositions such as those in the *Hypostasis of the Archons* and our text No. 40 we find, coupled with him, the figure of Sabaôth his son, "better and wiser than he", who is converted to the divine plans of the Light and who, for that reason, is installed by Sophia in charge of the seven heavens, in place of Ialdabaôth who is cast down into Chaos. God of the created world, deprived of foreknowledge, but a good god all the same, Sabaôth now receives the throne and the chariot, surrounded by armies of angels, which Jewish mysticism assigned to the Lord. This ascent of Sabaôth to the summit of the heavens, whence Ialdabaôth has fallen, is rather like the accession of Zeus to the supreme divinity in place of Kronos. And it even corresponds, more exactly, to a certain Chaldaean astrological teaching according

---

[15] C. Bonner, *Studies in Magical Amulets*, pp. 54ff. and Plates IV–V. This figure was supposed to be a protection against stomach troubles; and C. Bonner would reduce it to its medical significance alone. I have developed its mythological meaning in an unpublished paper read at the Institute of Egypt in December 1951.

to which each of the planets reigned for the space of a thousand years, so that the antique world found itself under the domination of Zeus, who had just supplanted the first of the planets, Kronos.

Wherever our writings comment upon *Genesis*, in order to give it an interpretation that is the reverse of the accepted meaning— to the point of directly accusing Moses of error[16]—one detail remains obscure: the part played by the serpent. For their anti-Biblicism, consistently applied, should surely exalt the Serpent, who is the revealer of Gnosis to Adam, into a figure of the Saviour. We remember being told that the *Books of Jêou* were revealed to Enoch by the Christ, speaking from "the tree of knowledge and the tree of life in the Paradise of Adam".[17] Yet if we compare, for example, the parallel versions of the *Secret Book of John* one with the other, they are far from being clear upon this point. Our Gnostics did not dare entirely to divest the reptile of his perversity of character. And there is nothing here to help explain what the cult of the serpent could have meant to the sect of the Naassenes, or Ophites—a group related to the sect from which our writings come.

Upon the creation of the first man and of his consort; upon their expulsion from Paradise; and then upon the destinies of the different classes of human beings up to the Deluge, our Coptic writings furnish remarkably rich and precise information. They show few divergences in this part of their mythology. One notes, however, that text No. 40—in which we have also the unexpected intervention of Erôs—is infinitely more instructive than the others about the topography of Paradise, the nature of its trees and their meanings. We notice, again, that our texts are not absolutely in accord about the number and the variety of the defilements to which Eve is subjected by the Archons. They are more in agreement in the particulars they furnish about the nature of the counterfeiting Spirit fabricated by the powers from below in order to make man stumble, and about the different ways in which this parasitic soul is connected with Spirit of a higher

[16] In the *Secret Book of John*; cf. above, pp. 204 and 208.
[17] Cf. p. 73.

origin. At the end of this account of the earliest Biblical ages we meet—in two of the writings—with the important myth of Nôrea, which hitherto had been mentioned only—and too briefly—by Epiphanius.

The account of the salvation brought to mankind is subjected to different interpretations: in some cases the leading part is assigned to the Mother; in others to the Saviour. We even find, in a composite text such as the *Secret Book of John*, that the saving action seems to be performed sometimes by the one and sometimes by the other, quite inconsistently.

As for the writings that claim to be authorized by the Christ and his disciples (excluding from the second of these two classes of apocrypha those in which the figure of Christ has merely been painted over the mythic personage of the Great Seth), they conform with the rest, in that their doctrines do not contradict the Revelations ascribed to Zoroaster, Zostrian, Seth and the other Enlighteners. But they do not go so far as to mix their teaching with that of other writings in the collection from which Christianity is practically absent; and these apocrypha dealing with Christian themes appear to be of later date.

Can one feel, in the multiple system thus expounded to us, the influence of one or another of the great Gnostic teachers? Taking as our standard of reference the reports of the heresiologists upon the leaders of the various schools, the teaching of this particular sect would seem to resemble, above all, that of Basilides. That heresiarch would certainly not have scorned to make use of apocryphal literature of the kind found in our Egyptian jar, since he himself composed (or arranged?) prophecies under the names of Barcabbas and Barcoph which had a certain success among some of the sects—e.g., the Nicolaitans and the great Gnostics. Like our initiates of Chenoboskion, he had recourse to the *Gospel of Matthias*; he is said also to have personally composed a pseudo-Gospel made up of *Sayings of Jesus*[18]—which makes one think, by the way, of our Coptic *Gospel of Thomas*. But above all, it was Basilides who was credited with the most accurate

[18] Cf. Origen, *Homily on Luke*, I, a; Ambrose, *Comment. in Luc. Prooem.*, cf. also Leisegang, *loc. cit.*, p. 140.

knowledge of the Persian doctrine of the primordial principles.[19]
At the head of the created world, he placed both Ialdabaôth and his
son Sabaôth, expressly said to be "much wiser than his father"
And lastly, it is to Basilides and his son Isidore that the speculations
On the Additional Soul—namely, the spirit of counterfeit—are
attributed.

However, the fact that our Coptic writings enlarge upon so
many of the subjects that were known to have been treated by
Basilides does not prove that they borrowed these from him:
we must rather suppose that Basilides himself had known, and
found already very much alive, the same body of myths and
beliefs with which our Coptic sectaries were enlightening less
ancient days.

* * *

Can we venture to say whence it was that Gnosticism, such as it
appears in our writings, derived the most original and most
constant of its doctrines?

Our Coptic texts never make the slightest *direct* allusion to the
Greek philosophers or to their doctrines. Nor is there the least
suggestion of that veneration of images of Plato, Pythagoras or
Orpheus, which the heresiologists ascribed to some sectaries.[20]

[19] Cf. the passage in the *Acta Archelai* quoted above on pp. 20–1 and our
Paraphrase of Shem, confirmed by the summary of it in the *Philosophumena*.
Comparison of these elements with the text of the *Bundahishn* seems conclusive
enough. Bousset had previously pointed out the Iranian character of the passage
about the three principles contained in the *Acts of Archelaüs*; G. Quispel, in his
"L'Homme gnostique; la doctrine de Basilide" in the *Eranos Jahrbuch*, 1948,
pp. 92–4, took him rather harshly to task by saying: "M. Bousset tries quite
recklessly to find the Iranian dualism in Gnostic texts . . . needless to say,
these fantasies have no historical value." Today, it is to the venturesome hypotheses of M. Quispel that these compliments could be more fittingly returned.
And one can but admire the insight—sometimes admittedly a little audacious—
of M. Bousset who, going beyond the actual terms of the still scanty documentation at his disposal, seized so correctly upon the origins of certain myths.
We have remarked before upon the number of Gnostic treatises in which this
theme appears—that of the two principles, separated by the "void", the "spirit"
—and we have also pointed out that the same doctrine underlies §§ 2 and 14 of the
Latin *Asclepius*, where no one seemed yet to have noticed it. Cf. above chap. v,
pp. 150ff. and note 9, and also chap. I, note 124.
[20] Thus Marcellinus and the Carpocratians had painted icons, sometimes
enriched with gold or silver, of the Christ (the features having been drawn by
Pontius Pilate!), of Pythagoras, of Plato and yet others: see Epiphanius, *Heresy*
XXVII, 6.

However, the Hellenic origin of various conceptions is undeniable. Platonism had certainly produced, as it were in outline, some of the themes we find in Gnostic mythology. If we open the *Phaedrus*, the *Timaeus* or the *Phaedo* . . . we are already reading how the accidental fall of the soul cast it out of the supra-sensible world into the materiality of the body, and how the fallen soul still retained, here below, like a secret treasure, memories of the absolute realities it had contemplated at its beginning. The *Republic*, in the episode of Er the Armenian, which amounts to a veritable apocalypse, elaborates the myth of the reincarnation of souls in the bodies of men or of animals: this takes place in a heaven where there are the "ways of the right" which lead upward, and the "ways of the left" leading downward; and where the spirits, before returning to our world, go to drink the waters of Lethe.

Stoicism, also, brought with it a whole philosophical and mystical baggage which did much to inspire our Gnostics. But more striking still is the use made by some of our writings (the latest of the collection, it is true) to the many allegorical commentaries upon the poems of Homer and the *Theogony* of Hesiod —Gnostic recourse to which, at a still earlier date, is attested by notices in the *Philosophumena* and now so happily confirmed by the funerary paintings of the Viale Manzoni; but of which direct literary proofs were lacking until now.

Other relations with classical mythology are less clearly indicated. The *Philosophumena* ascribes to the Naassenes, Peratae, Sethians and others a number of references to the Greek Mysteries, by means of which these Gnostics tried to commentate a teaching which was itself derived from Christianity. In the new writings there are few features—though admittedly some—that might suggest recourse to the Mysteries. But right at the beginning there may have been links with classical mythology. Sophia's struggle against the Archons does evoke the idea of Athena at war with the Titans: Ialdabaôth, dethroned and replaced by Sabaôth, makes us think of Kronos, who prevented his children from ascending towards the light but was at last supplanted by Zeus. And Ialdabaôth again reminds us of the Jupiter against whom

Prometheus rebels. But it is of Prometheus himself that we are reminded by Ialdabaôth's creation of man—of that Prometheus who fashions the first human beings and gives them the gift of fire which he has stolen from the divine powers! True, these parallels, which the modern reader can discover for himself, would hardly seem to have appealed to the authors of our texts; for the learned commentator of Codex X is the only one who has drawn attention to such things—in his remarks on the possible relations between Noah and Deucalion and between Nôrea and Pyrrha.

The only other points significant in this connection are a few incidental details obscurely suggestive of Orphic and Pythagorean influences. First, there is the meaning consistently attached to "the ways of the Right" which we know earlier upon the golden lamellae of the Greek initiates; there is also the part assigned to the Serpent as the most spiritual of animals; and then again—in our writing No. 40—the description of the Tree of Life as a white cypress growing near to a source of Life, surely a reflection of the perpetual fountain near to which stands that other white cypress at the entrance to Hades, according to the Orphic lamellae. Finally, there is the extraordinary part that this same writing No. 40 assigns to Erôs![21] Yet no comparisons of this kind are attempted, with the sole exception of the erudite gloss of Codex X, pointing out the possible connection between Noah and Deucalion, Nôrea and Pyrrha. Perhaps, all things considered, we must take care not to over-estimate the importance of the Hellenic elements in Gnostic mythology.

The skeletal structure of this mythology is of quite another origin. The belief in two opposite principles separated by a third element; the mystical vision of the throne and heavenly chariot of the Creator; the persistent references to *Genesis*, the meaning of which is tortured to yield a novel conception of the inferior world as something evil, and the appeal to envoys or saviours coming down from heaven to awaken Adam—these are the essential fundamentals without which the Gnostic doctrine could not have existed. The original conception of Time within which these

---

[21] Cf. J. Carcopino, *La basilique pythagoricienne de la Porte Majeure*, Paris, 1927, pp. 155, 309-10, 314; and M. J. Lagrange, *L'Orphisme*, Paris, 1937, p. 138.

myths are unfolded is—as Professor Puech has shown—intimately involved with their deeper meaning, but there is nothing Hellenic about it. In short, this is all foreign to Hellenism.[22] It was afterwards that Greek logic came in to give body to these themes, and educe a more comprehensive meaning from them. Greek thought did this the more easily, perhaps, because it found here some of the oriental imagery upon which it had been nourished in its own infancy. But the recourse of Gnosticism to classical thought only modified, in secondary ways, the primitive mythical structure that the new religion had built up. And as for the effects of the Homeric allegorical exegeses, one can only say that these are features which strike one rather as academic accretions. The great visionaries of the early days of the Gnostic movement, even when their mother tongue was Aramaic, generally wrote in Greek: they accordingly decked out their expositions with rhetoric, philosophy or with classical allegories, hardly noticing whether this might modify what was more fundamental. They were only concerned to get a better hearing from the people of their time, who, without exception, had learnt to speak and understand this language when studying the Greek authors in their school-days.

From astrology, Gnosticism derived something much more concrete. Arising in the centuries before our era, from sources as much Chaldaean as Egyptian,[23] astrology had attained a very considerable importance. Infiltrating the different religions one after another, accommodating their myths to its own teachings, it established, by a process of superficial assimilations, a fictive unity between them. Just as we now accept the general laws of modern physics, people then agreed that the course of the world and the lives of beings were under the influences of the heavenly bodies, from which they had no escape. They also assumed, in accord with a connection which, in this case, derived especially

---

[22] We may here refer to the protests of Plotinus against their notion that the world, both terrestrial and celestial, was evil; cf. also W. Bousset, *Kyrios Christos*, 1926, chap. VI.

[23] Cf. Cumont, *Religions orientales*, 4th edn., pp. 117ff.; Boll–Bezold, *Sternglaube und Sterndeutung*, IVte Auflage, 1931, chap. VI; Cumont *L'Égypte des astrologues*, 1937.

from Chaldaean astrology, that after death the soul reascended into heaven to live there among the divine stars, escaping at last from Fate and Time. Some believed that at this consummation the soul "was drawn up by the rays of the sun and, after passing by the moon, where she was purified, went on to lose herself in the shining star of day".[24] Another theory made the planets exercise their influence upon human beings even before birth; in this view, the souls came down from the heights of heaven towards the earth, passing through all the planetary spheres in succession and receiving, in each one, the dispositions and virtues appropriate to that heavenly body. After death, the souls went back by the same path to their original home, abandoning at each stage of their ascent what they had taken while coming, and only after this purification did they attain to the highest heaven. To pass out of the sphere of one planet into that of the next above it, they had to go through gateways guarded by the Archons who, like sentinels, would give way only to those who had the passwords of which the Gnostics, among others, drew up meticulous lists.[25] The doctrine itself was of Babylonian origin. These astrological beliefs were vouched for by the Stoics and, better still, by neo-Pythagoreans such as Numenius of Apamea.

How we should like to have more knowledge of the intense doctrinal and mystical ferments which, after the age of Alexander the Great, animated the "Chaldaeans schools" of Borsippa, of Sippara of Uruk![26] Under the vivifying influence of Hellenism, new ideas emerged from the antique mythology of Babylonia where, for ages past, the Baals had "led the chorus of the stars, the Zodiacal signs and the planets". In a study that is of capital importance, J. Bidez has retraced all this proliferation of mystical themes which invaded the Greek world as well as the Judaic, Iran and even India.[27]

[24] Cf. Cumont, *Lux Perpetua*, pp. 180–2.
[25] Cumont, *Lux Perpetua*, chaps. VI and VII.
[26] J. Bidez, "Les Ecoles chaldéennes sous Alexandre et les Séleucides", extract from *Mélanges Capart*, Brussels, 1935.
[27] Cf. Bidez, *Ecoles chaldéennes* . . . , p. 46. For the relations with India, see Gundel, in *Bursian's Jahresbericht*, vol. CCXLIII, 1934, pp. 115ff; Gundel, *Dekane und Dekansternbilder* describes carefully the diffusion in all directions, well into the Middle Ages, of some of these astrological doctrines.

The Babylonian religion had previously taught, in its myths, that there was an opposition between the dark lower waters and the divine fire. Some of the Sumerian cosmological ideas made known to us by S. N. Kramer presupposed the existence, between the heavens and the earth, "of a third element they called *lil*—a word of which the nearest meaning would be 'wind', 'air', 'breath', or 'spirit'; its essential characteristics seem to have been . . . movement and expansion".[28] The god Enki, the ruler of Wisdom, reigned over certain vivifying sources, and near by them grew the Tree of Life: the light came from the North towards our terrestrial world: the sun and the moon were ships sailing through the sky. The great myths depicted the divinity—the Mother—descending into hell to Tammuz[29]: there was also an account of the Deluge. A likelihood that these myths may, by their images, have prepared the way for some of the Gnostic myths is suggested by, for example, a famous medallion of bronze in the De Clercq collection.[30] On the obverse of this talisman there are three rows of the most fantastic creatures. Right at the bottom, a creature with a human body and a monstrous head, holding serpents in his hands, is kneeling upon a boat, which is sailing over the waters of an abyss. Right at the top are aligned seven Archons, with human bodies and animal heads, and over each of these is an astral or stellar symbol. At the top of the disc, standing out in relief, appears a leonine head—that of Nergal, god of the inferno: and, on turning the talisman over, one finds his whole body on the reverse side, with its monstrous wings and clawed feet—an image worthy to be the demiurge of any of our Coptic cosmogonies!

Earlier, perhaps, than the days of the Magi, these beliefs gave rise to a cult of Time, the generator of all things; master of the celestial revolutions with all their subdivisions into centuries, years, months, days, etc. . . . A kind of anthropomorphism

---

[28] S. N. Kramer, *L'histoire commence à Sumer*, Paris, 1957, chap. XII, p. 119.

[29] Cf. Widengren, *The great Vohu Manah and the Apostle of God*, 1945; *Mesopotamian Elements in Manichaeism*, 1946; *The King and the Tree of Life in Near Eastern Religion*, 1951.

[30] Reproduced, for example, in Contenau, *Manuel d'archéologie orientale*, I, 1927, p. 251.

arose, drawing parallels between the structure of the universe and that of man, conceiving the one as the magnified image of the other—macrocosm and microcosm. It was probably from this same source that a strange conception was entertained by the Manichaeans, and probably by Gnostics also, which the traveller Cosmas, in the sixth century of our era, described as follows: the earth was conceived as a rectangular parallelepiped enclosed by walls of crystal, above which three domes rose one above another, representing the three heavens of ancient Chaldaea.

After the time of Alexander, Bêrôssos, a priest of Bel-Marduk, left his country, established himself at Cos and made the Babylonian mythology known to the Greeks.[31] Others of his compatriots followed his example and a century later one of these, Critodemus, wrote that, having long wandered over seas and over deserts, he had at last, thanks to the gods, attained to a haven of refuge where he had found rest; by which romantic fiction he was announcing, at the same time, higher truths and a way of immortality, in which Bidez has recognized the expression of a Gnosis of liberation.[32]

It was to the mystical glory of that country's name that Julian the Theurgist entitled his famous *Chaldaean Oracles*—the sacred book of a sect which, in its fire-worship, came near to that of the Persian Magi, but whose other imaginations about the divine realms make up a phantasmagoria closely related to Gnosticism.[33]

How could Gnosticism not have taken much and received much from these myths; and from this country, which was soon to export the most powerful and comprehensive of all its expressions—Manichaeism?

It is true that the astrological doctrines imbedded in Gnostic mythology and anthropology are, in great part, theories that were commonly accepted throughout the Greco-Roman world. But here they take on a special emphasis, and acquire some features which relate them very definitely to oriental origins.

One thing we have found, in all that we have seen of Gnosti-

---

[31] Bidez, *Écoles chaldéennes*, pp. 48ff.
[32] *Ibid.*, pp. 83–5.
[33] Cf. chap. II above, note 89; and Cumont, *Lux Perpetua*, pp. 361–5.

cism, is that the mythical powers which do not belong to the heavens of the higher universe become identified with this or that constellation of the *visible* heavens. Sabaôth reigns over the Pole; his throne is situated in the constellation of the Chariot; close to him is the Serpent; the Dragon is neighbour to the Great Bear "at the great commencement of the heavens"; Ialdabaôth is identified with Saturn, and his Archons are the other planets. The writings of certain sects—the Naassenes and Peratae—must have been full of details, even more so than the texts we now possess, which would enable a Gnostic, simply by looking up into the dome of night, to recognize in movement above him many of the powers that are mentioned in this mythology, but to which we can no longer assign an exact astronomical identity.

What a number of symbols, indeed, were revealed to the initiate simply by contemplation of the heavens, whose inhabitants and whose very movements were reduplicated in the physical and spiritual nature of man! The point which was nearest to the world of Light, hidden from all eyes, could be no other than the Pole, around which the obedient spheres were revolving; standing relatively low towards the horizon, it pointed to the North. It was in that direction, at the confines of the terrestrial world, that there was a holy mountain from whence the great revelations came; and from thence alone came the benefic waters. Far to the South, on the other hand, lay the kingdom out of which the Darkness was propagated. Eastward, on the right hand, the stars dawned and went upward; westward they descended and set below the horizon. Below the sphere of the stars moved the seven Archons, the perverse planets, although some Gnostics, and the Manichaeans, excepted from these the ships of the Sun and of the Moon (which the Pythagoreans, earlier still, regarded as the Isles of the Blest). They believed that these two benefic powers were in charge of the reascent of the light scattered throughout the material heavens and here below; so these luminaries were replaced, in order to keep the number of malefic planets up to seven, by the head and tail of the Dragon—that fictive monster to whom they attributed the disappearances of the sun and moon during eclipses. Among the stars the

Gnostics still believed they could see in profile that Virgin of Light who is described in the Book of *Revelation* (XII), crowned with the constellations and with the moon under her feet, and threatened by the dragon with seven heads. Flashes of lightning represented the light of which the Archons, after being seduced, were being violently dispossessed. And the phases of the Moon showed, at its waxing, that it was being filled with the light it had collected; while at its waning, it was sending that light back towards the higher world.[34]

And yet, in the last of the *Books of Pistis-Sophia*, and also in one of our Coptic Hermetic writings—No. 25—we find some references to celestial conjunctions which raise doubts about the astronomical knowledge of the Gnostics; they are so peculiarly fantastic. But in reality, these few fictitious celestial positions derive from an old Chaldaean astrological system, purely mythical, and were already contradicted by the more scientific theories of the Hellenic world; they were retained doubtless for religious reasons. According to that system, the heavenly bodies were distributed among seven *aiônes*—one may say, seven cycles—in such a way that each of these had to reign, in its turn, for one millennium.[35] This theory was sufficiently widely diffused to appear in a certain number of Greek and Latin authors; to be found also in Bardesanes, and, still more, among the Mandaeans. And it is this system which explains equally well for two of our writings—the *Hypostasis of the Archons* and the treatise

[34] Upon the supreme status of Sabaôth, comparable to that of Zeus, cf. Cumont, *Lux Perpetua*, p. 87. Upon his Throne (i.e. space) cf. Zaehner, *Zurvan*, p. 202. Upon the four cardinal points, cf. above, chap. v, note 50; see also H. C. Puech, *Le Manichéisme*, note 294; Festugière, *La Révélation d'Hermès Trismégiste*, vol. I, p. 269; Zaehner, *loc. cit.*, pp. 147ff.; Widengren, *Mesopotamian elements* . . . , p. 39; and, finally, the following texts: *Ginzâ* (edn. Lidsbarski), pp. 280–2 (=*Ginzâ of the Right* VII); *Preface* (arabic) *to the Council of Nicaea*, in Mansi, *Coll. Concil.*, II, 1057–8. Upon light and water coming from the North: Cumont, *Recherches* . . . , p. 164; Tondelli, *loc. cit.*, p. 60. For replacement of the Sun and Moon in the number of the seven planets by the Dragon's head and tail, supposed to produce eclipses; Puech, *Manichéisme*, note 321; De Menasce, *Shkand gumânîk Vichâr*, Fribourg, 1945, p. 47; and the Coptic *Kephalaïon* LXIX, pp. 168–9. Cf., again, upon these notions as a whole, Pr. Alfaric, *Les Écritures manichéennes*, vol. I, 1918, pp. 35–41.

[35] Cf. *Catalogus Codic. Astrolog. Graecorum*, vol. IV, pp. 113–14, and 183–4; vol. V, fasc. 2, pp. 130–6; cf. also Cumont, *Monuments des Mystères de Mithra*, vol. I, p. 35 and p. 157, note 1.

10

No. 40—the theme of the replacement of Ialdabaôth–Kronos by Sabaôth–Zeus. Did our Gnosticism derive any ideas from Egypt itself? Here we touch upon one of the most mysterious of problems. Our writings do not explicitly acknowledge any Egyptian element, nor even mention the name of Egypt except as the symbol of accursed matter.[36] Of the innumerable prophets upon whose revelations Greco-Roman Egypt plumed itself, none are mentioned in our writings—with the exception of Hermes. Nevertheless, when the new Gnostic texts as a whole become available, we shall have to go more thoroughly into this question of some residual borrowings from Egypt. The cosmogonies known to the pharaonic religion were in fact very various. Some of them described the formation of divine Ogdoads—of Enneads, by including the primordial god.[37] In other cases, the creation is ascribed to the *heart* and to the *tongue*, which in this context very exactly represent the thought and the word.[38] The arched body of the goddess Nut, representing the sky, prefigures that episode in the Gnostic cosmologies where Sophia, striving to extricate herself from the abyss of matter into which she has fallen, creates the firmament in a similar manner. Some of the "Geneses" briefly

[36] See above, chap. I, note 120.
[37] Cf. K. Sethe, "Amun und die acht Urgötter von Hermopolis" in the *Abhandlungen der Preussischen Akad. der Wissenschaften*, 1929, No. 4; J. Vandier, *La Religion égyptienne*, 1944, pp. 61–2.
[38] Cf. H. Junker, "Die Götterlehre von Memphis (*Schabaka inschrift*)", *Abhandlungen der Preussischen Akad. der Wissenschaften*, 1939, No. 23, 1940; J. Vandier, *op. cit.*, pp. 62–3 ; Brugsch, *Die Aegyptologie*, 1891, p. 166. The cosmogonic texts of the Ptolemaic epoch which are carved on the little temple of Medinet Habu (consecrated to the primordial gods of Thebes) have not yet been the subject of a methodical publication: one has to depend on the summary analysis made by G. Daressy, *Notice explicative des ruines de Medinet-Habou*, Cairo, 1897, pp. 13–18. Amon-Re, who created himself, is the father of the procreators, who are gods and goddesses. No divinity exists but of his formation, whilst he exists of himself: his aspects are innumerable; he arranged the heavenly bodies. In the beginning he fashioned the universe; he made the light to shine in the darkness, and [he made?] every day and every night. He shone upon the waters, and the earth was in darkness; all the universe was in the liquid abyss: by the light, he produced dryness, and organized everything. At once the father and the mother of the gods, he ordered the return of the sun after each setting [of it]. . . . He made the sky for the cradle of his soul, and the *akhet* [horizon] hides his person. He is the elder eternal . . . preserving his youth throughout the eternity of time, uncreated creator, father of fathers, mother of mothers.

inscribed on the walls of Theban temples resemble fairly closely, in their general outlines, that of the Bible. The creator of the material universe is often described in terms that are equally suggestive of the God of the Old Testament as of the Gnostic Ialdabaôth; and in one papyrus, we read this sentence: "No other god existed before him nor any other god with him when he enunciated his forms . . . nor ever a Father for him who emitted him by saying: It is I who created him." The exclamation: "There is no god but I!" is again repeated in the cosmogony of Hermopolis, passages of which are inscribed on the temple of Petosiris.[39] The story of the Friends of the god Re—of the Merets —a pair of feminine figures who, as early as in the texts of the Pyramids, try to seduce and so ravish away the seed of the gods and of the deceased during their ascension towards the Orient heaven, and with it to enrich their lord and master the sun—this does seem to prefigure the theme of the "seduction of the Archons" by Prunikos, Barbelô, Nôrea, the Virgin of the Light and, again, the third Messenger of Manichaeism.[40] No doubt one could find further parallels between the complex enumeration of souls and spirits which was the Egyptian description of man, and the association of soul, spirit, force and counterfeiting spirit, which was the Gnostic conception of the human being.

After all, the Egyptian religion, too, had been feeling the contemporary influence of the starry beliefs; it was distributing some of its divinities among the stars and heavenly bodies—an operation that came the more easily to it because, since the earliest of pharaonic ages, it had possessed a mystical astrology which— among other things—was enriched by those fantastic figures of *decans* which not only Hellenistic astrology, but all the Middle Ages of the East and the West were to borrow from it.

What was Gnosticism able to derive from this? Such notions, surely, as those of the Peratae, who acknowledged Isis and Osiris as rulers of the hours of the day and of the night, represented

[39] Cf. Al. Moret, *Mystères égyptiennes*, 1927, pp. 120ff., text of the papyrus of Leyden, published by Sir Alan Gardiner in the *Zeitschrift für Aegyptische Sprache*, XLII; G. Lefebvre, *Le Tombeau de Petosiris*, Part I, Cairo, 1924, p. 99.
[40] Cf. Et. Drioton (giving an account of A. De Buck, *The Egyptian coffin texts*, V) in the *Bibliotheca Orientalis* XII, No. 2, March 1955, pp. 61–6.

respectively by the Day Star (Sôthis, i.e. Sirius) and by the constellation of Orion. According to the *Philosophumena*, the Peratae also assimilated Osiris to Sacla—which means to Ialdabaôth.[41] We have already seen how, in consequence of such identification, Gnostics sometimes brought about a highly ambiguous connection between the Egyptian god Seth (Typhon) and the Biblical Seth. Far from being entirely superficial, this connection may well have been facilitated by the fact that certain Egyptian theologies reported by Plutarch (essentially in the *De Iside*, §§ 41 and 49), set up an antithesis between Seth and Osiris, closely analogous to that which the Gnostics developed between Ialdabaôth–Sacla and the divinity of the light. A Greek Hermetic text (the fragment XXV, 8), even suggests that in the Roman epoch, the Egyptian religion arraigned its Gnostics as "sons of Typhon". And, if we pass from the doctrines to the iconography and the rituals, we note a multiplicity of Archons and powers in the original writings of the Coptic Gnostics whose monstrous visages recall the features lent to the constellations and the decans by pharaonic astrology. Moreover, the hell of our Coptic writings retains not only the Egyptian name of *Amente* (that is, the Occident), but also its population of fantastic demons.[42] Finally, the passwords and the seals that our sectaries thought would give their souls safe conduct through the planetary spaces are much the same in spirit as the formulas by which the deceased Egyptian had always had to protect himself, since the days of the Pyramid texts until the latest of the *Books of the Dead*.

[41] Cf. above, chap. v, note 30. Another god besides Osiris has been compared to Ialdabaôth: a red agate of the Roman period found at Memphis invokes, in Greek, the Egyptian god of Leontopolis—Mahes the lion-faced—in terms reminiscent enough of our monstrous demiurge: "Hear my prayer, thou who dwellest in Leontopolis, installed in the holy sanctuary, darting the lightnings and thundering, lord of the Darkness and the winds, in whose hand lies the celestial fate of eternal nature . . . thou, god most glorious of leonine form! . . ." Cf. Preisigke, *Sammelbuch griech. Urkunden aus Aegypten*, No. 5620, with remarks by Spiegelberg.

[42] Cf. above, chap. I, note 11. In the eschatology of the *Pistis-Sophia* there also appears Baïnkhôôkh, that is, Ba-en-Kekou, the "soul of the Darkness", who comes out of the Egyptian *Book of the Dead* to take his place among the angels and aeons of this inferno, which keeps its Egyptian name Amente; cf. Th. Hopfner, "Der Religiongeschichtliche Gehalt des grossen demotischen Zauberpapyrus" in *Archiv Orientalni*, VII, 1935, pp. 114-15.

However, in all this there is no proof of Egyptian influence upon the basic conceptions of Gnostic mythology.

And what of the relations of Gnosticism with Hermetism? The mystical treatises of Hermetism which are known as "learned" (in distinction from the many minor works on astrology, magic, alchemy etc., similarly given under the name of Hermes Trismegistus) possibly date back to the second century of our era, for in the third they were widely influential.[43] What they consist of is, in effect, a kind of Gnosticism, but pagan, and essentially philosophic in its inspiration although it chooses to give itself an Egyptian appearance; and one feels that it owes much to certain oriental myths. A good many of these treatises have never come down to us, or remain only in fragments. Eighteen of them remain complete, almost in their original Greek form, and constitute the *Corpus Hermeticum*, at the end of which is added a Latin adaptation of another treatise of the same nature—the *Asclepius*, the very same treatise of which a partial version in Coptic has turned up in the Chenoboskion library.[44] The dogmas attested by these nineteen writings and by the various fragments, although still fluid, are more stable than those of our Gnostics. They are expounded much more by abstract reasoning than in the form of cosmogonies, geneses or evocations of prophets living at the dawn of human history. Above all, they know nothing of the demoniac figures or the perverse demiurge depicted by Biblical Gnosticism.

The Hermetic treatises—whether epistles or apocalyptic revelations—present themselves essentially in the form of dialogues: although more perfect from the points of view of style and of thought they show, in this and other ways, features in common with our Gnostic literature. The treatise No. XIII— *On regeneration and the rule of silence*—recounts the teaching received by Tat from Hermes "upon the Mountain", a detail which suggests Sinai and the Tables of the Law, but still more the mystic mountain of the Zoroastrian revelations. At the beginning of the

[43] Upon the date of the Hermetic treatises, see J. Carcopino, "L'Hermétisme africain" in *Aspects mystiques de la Rome païenne*, pp. 286-7 and 291.

[44] Cf. above, pp. 245ff.

Poimandres the narrator describes how the Nous appeared to him as a being of immense stature, from whom he received visions and revelations.

One cannot, from only one of the treatises of this *Corpus*, gain an accurate notion of the features which approximate Hermetism to Gnosticism. But let us take the *Poimandres*, of which I have just summarized a passage to compare it with the creation of Adam as described in the *Secret Book of John*; for the former is the text which, on the whole as in its details, comes nearest to the teachings of our Gnostics.

The *Poimandres* begins, then, with this fantastic apparition of the Intellect—the Nous—revealing to the anonymous narrator (the names of Hermes and his disciples appear nowhere in the text) a vision of the Light on high and the Darkness below, the latter being coiled into spirals like a serpent. From this frightful darkness, which is in transformation, is created the moist abyss out of which Fire arises. A holy Word then descends from the Light and covers up the lower, inferior nature, whilst from below the fire flames up over the waters.[45]

Then the Noûs, whose name is Poimandres, explains to the narrator the meaning of this vision of the two primordial principles and of the conflict, or rather the confusion, taking place between them. Thus it is explained to us how, out of the Light, out of the supreme Noûs, there came forth the Word his Son; and how Noûs the Father, who is androgyne, and life and light, then created a second Noûs who is the Demiurge, god of fire and of wind; and how this Demiurge formed the seven rulers of the planetary circles, the masters of Fate. Through the association of the Word with the Demiurge, the seven circles were made to revolve, and their rotation, producing the lower elements, caused the birth of the various animals. It was then—according to the

[45] Thus the *Poimandres* manifests that same dualism which we find in most of the Gnostic myths, more particularly in Basilides and among the Sethians, and which is also connected, through the *Bundahishn*, with Iran. We have also pointed out its discreet appearance in the *Asclepius*, §§ 2 and 14-15. The latter text adds to this a sketch of a very peculiar theme, the essentials of which are to be found in Jewish Gnosticism, among the doctrines of Basilides and the *Books of Jêou*—that of the "retreat" of God from his own omnipresence in the universe, thus leaving a portion of it free for the process of creation.

passage just quoted in reference to the *Secret Book of John*—that the first Noûs created a primordial man in his own image. His own reflection seen in the water and on earth fills this Anthropos with admiration, and this—in a way that recalls the fall of Sophia lured into the abyss by an illusion—decides him to go down into matter, which ensnares him. Thenceforth man is a duality: mortal in his body, immortal in his soul. Nature then gives birth to seven terrestrial men, who are hermaphrodite. The divinity proceeds to separate all the creatures, until then bisexual (animals as well as men), into males and females. That was the beginning of the actual humanity to which we belong.

At death, the material body is abandoned by man. The soul reascends through the planetary circles, restoring at each of the seven zones, like the taking-off of garments, the accidents and passions it had taken on during its descent to the body it was to animate at birth. At the end of this ascension it attains to the Ogdoad and becomes itself one of the powers: it enters into God, and—this is the goal to which Hermetic Gnosis aspires—becomes merged with God.

Description of the first separation between the Light and the Darkness; of the struggle that ensues between the two principles; of the formation of the Word and of the Anthropos by the androgyne Father; of the seduction of a higher being by its image from below which that being wants to rejoin; of its union with nature—with matter[46]; of the generation of a humanity of which the mortal body is associated with the immortal soul . . . —how much the details of this apocalypse remind us, most of them, of those that our Coptic writings describe! Presented in this way, does not Hermetism look very much like a philosophic version of Gnosis, stripped only of its rich and original web of Biblical myths? Does not this give added significance to the fact that our sectaries of Chenoboskion possessed a writing which, entitled with the name of Seth, also resembles in its phraseology and its style some of the Hermetic treatises—a slender link

---

[46] This union of the first man with nature may recall the union between Gayômârt and the earth in the Iranian myth of the *Bundahishn*, XV, 22—see West, *Pahlavi Texts*, vol. I.

278 The Secret Books of the Egyptian Gnostics

between two rival literatures? It was by no means from mere curiosity that our Coptic mystics chose to add to their collection of sacred writings certain books in which doctrines analogous to their own were attributed to Hermes, and which they even put into the same codex with Sethian revelations.

Might this conjunction between Hermetic and Gnostic writings perhaps appear—from the example of it that our sectaries furnish —to be merely an isolated initiative peculiar to the Sethians of Chenoboskion? More probably, it represents what may well have been a pretty general practice in and after the fourth century or even a little earlier. This meeting of Hermes with Seth, Zoroaster and Jesus—an encounter between rival literatures, the one "judaizing" and the other "Egyptianizing"—corresponds, indeed, to the mixture of writings used by the pseudo-Zosimos in his treatise *On the letter Omega*. In his *Book of the Imuth*, which deals with the letter I (he devoted a treatise to every letter of the Greek alphabet!), Zosimos compares some traditions taken from the *Physika* of Hermes with other myths, such as that of the union of the angels with the daughters of men. Perhaps he took these last features from the *Book of Enoch*; but no less possibly from some Gnostic *Genesis*, for—more fortunate than we—he seems to have been well versed in that particular literature.[47]

*　　*　　*

[47] The Greek writings attributed to Zosimos are transcribed and translated in: Berthelot and Ruelle, *Collection des anciens alchimistes grecs*, three vols. 1888; others (including the *Book of Imuth*) which have survived only in the form of Syriac versions or adaptations, are translated in Berthelot, *La chimie au moyen âge*, 1893. We have already mentioned, pp. 81ff., 175, 190, 248, details of the treatise *On the letter Omega* which are typical borrowings from Gnosticism. From the book *On the letter Kappa*, ascribed to this same Zosimos "the Theban", we have gleaned allusions to, among others, the *Book of the Seven Heavens* attributed to Solomon—which describes the water-pots in which the wise king imprisoned the demons. These vessels—seven, in accord with the number of the planets—were carried from Jerusalem to the priests of Egypt. This explains the mysterious "hydria that are in Egypt" mentioned by the Coptic commentator upon our text No. 40 (cf. above, p. 174). In the same treatise Zosimos tells us about the twelve dwellings and of the constellation of the Pleïades which are called "the world of the Thirteen": this feature sheds light on the mention of the Pleïades in the heavenly vision of our *Paraphrase of Shem* (see above, p. 148); it refers to the Thirteenth aeon, higher than the Zodiac, which the soul of the prophet has to traverse, it appears, in its redescent into his sleeping body on earth. (These passages are quoted and commentated, in reference to Berthelot, *Chimie au moyen âge*, by Scott, in vol. IV of his *Hermetica*, 1936, pp. 140-1 and 143.)

One of the profoundest contributions made by our Gnostic myths is to our knowledge of Iranian beliefs.[48]

In the Hellenistic age, the religions of Iran were diffused, under different forms, almost all over the Orient: they had established ramifications especially in Asia Minor, through the Magusaeans.[49] Soon, their influence was also to be manifested in the advent of the Magi to the crib at Bethlehem,[50] as well as in the birth of a new religion, artificially based upon the myth of the Persian god Mithra, whose mysterious sanctuaries appeared all over the Mediterranean world.

Yet Iran, from whence such forces were radiating, was at the same time opening itself to foreign influences. Even earlier, when Babylon had been conquered by Cyrus, the Magi were established all over Mesopotamia; and since then there had been some exchange of their doctrines with the Chaldaeans; they had thus contributed to the making, in this country, of the most brilliant world centre of scientific studies.[51] First Babylonian, then Hellenic and then Judaic conceptions superimposed themselves upon Iranian beliefs, as one can see from the Pahlavi sacred books. The Parsees acknowledge that Shapur I (241–72) had extracts from Greek and Hindu works[52] inserted in their canonical treatises, which were not committed to writing until much later.

When we are comparing these Gnostic texts, handed down from so very eclectic a tradition (not to mention that certain authors distinguish among the Persians as many as three different sects!)[53]—how can we hope to interpret all the parallelisms that

---

[48] Upon the religious literature of Iran, cf. the indications and references in Widengren, *Stand und Aufgaben der Iranischen Relionsgeschichte* (extract from *Numen*) 1955, pp. [58] and [63]. One needs also to refer to the forthcoming studies by J. Duchesne–Guillemin, *Western Response to Zoroaster* (lectures given at Oxford in 1956) and *Dualismus* in the *Reallexikon für Antike und Christentum*.

[49] Cf. Cumont, *Les religions orientales dans le paganisme romain*, chap. v; G. Widengren, *Stand und Aufgaben* . . . , pp. 78–91; Reitzenstein and Schaeder, *Studien zum antiken Syncretismus.*

[50] Cf. Monneret de Villard, *op. cit.*, and Messina, *op. cit.*

[51] Cf. Bidez-Cumont, *op. cit.*, vol. I, pp. 34-8; Cumont, *Textes et Monuments relatifs aux Mystères de Mithra*, vol. I, pp. 8ff. and 14, note 5; G. Messina, *Der Ursprung der Magier* . . . , 1930, pp. 19ff.

[52] Zaehner, *Zurvan*, pp. 10, 139 and 143. Reciprocal influences berween Stoics and Magusaeans; cf. Bidez-Cumont, *op. cit.*, vol. I, pp. 32ff. and 92ff.

[53] Cf. Zaehner, *Zurvan*, p. 58, which refers to Eznik, according to whom some

10*

appear, or decide, in certain cases, whether we are dealing with authentic Iranian traditions which contributed to the formation of Gnosticism or, on the other hand, with late interpolations which in fact were borrowed from the Gnostic teachings by Iran?[54]

It is true that we possess—besides the Iranian literature in the national language to which these reservations apply—one class of writings whose ancient date is perhaps better established. This consists of remnants of mystical or sacred writings that the Magi of Asia Minor—the Magusaeans—composed in Greek. The principal book of this kind, given under the names of Zoroaster, Ostanes and Hystaspes, dates back to the second century of our era.[55] It was these books, perhaps, which did most to prepare the mythical framework in which our Gnosis was coming to birth. How otherwise are we to understand the facts that the Gnostics put the names of Zoroaster, Zostrian and Messos over the revelations that they wanted to invest with the greatest authority —and then that, building a still wider bridge between Iran and their own doctrines, they took the most Iranian of the apocalypses ascribed by the Magusaeans to Zoroaster, and reshaped it to their own liking by putting it under the names of Adam and Seth?

We cannot tell, however, whether the Gnostics wished to regard themselves, more or less fictively, as continuators of the Magusaeans. Perhaps the appellation *Magus*, which tradition attaches to the name of the Gnostic Simon, was not originally meant to indicate the magical practices of which romantic tradition has added so many to that personage's account; but to some openly acknowledged relationship between his doctrine and the Zoroastrian heritage? We lack light on this point. What seems certain is that the traditions which the Gnostics chose to follow came less from authentic Iranians than from that Iranianized Judaism in which Zoroaster was already identified either with Seth, or with Ezechiel, or again with Balaam,[56] or which pretended that Zoroaster had been Abraham's pupil in the art of

among the Persians believed in three principles: the Good, the Just and the Evil; others in two principles, but yet others in seven! The first two of these sects would correspond, respectively, to Zervanism and Mazdaism.

[54] Zaehner, *op. cit.*, chaps. I and II and (on the three "sects"), p. 58.
[55] Bidez–Cumont, *op. cit.*, vol. I, pp. 153–7.
[56] Because of the prophecy that the Book of *Numbers* (XXIV, 17) puts into the mouth of Balaam, " . . . there shall come a star out of Jacob. . . ."

astrology.⁵⁷ This Judeo-Iranian tradition is well known: it produced in writing, under the name of Hystaspes, *Oracles* predicting the end of the world, preceded—and this brought them under the ban of the Imperial authorities—by the fall of the Roman power!⁵⁸ We note, by the way, that our Gnostics seem not to have known these last predictions: since the time of Augustus it had been forbidden to possess or to read them under pain of death; and this would hardly have encouraged the sects to keep them in their libraries, whose secrecy, despite all precautions, was liable some day to be violated.

Let us recall—without enquiring too curiously how this Gnosis came by them—the most indubitably Iranian elements that appear in our Sethian books. First, there is the theme of the three primordial "roots"—as Iran conceived it and in such terms as we find it in the *Bundahishn*.⁵⁹ This is the notion of the highest god, without beginning or end; and that of the supreme Tetrad; that of the all-powerful Wisdom.⁶⁰ There is the horrific silhouette of Ialdabaôth, lion-headed and serpent-bodied—so near to the Mithraic statues of the Aïôn,⁶¹ and also to Ahriman and the spirits

⁵⁷ Cf. Bidez–Cumont, *op. cit.*, vol. I, pp. 41ff.

⁵⁸ Cf. Bidez–Cumont, *op. cit.*, vol. I, pp. 217–18 and vol. II, p. 362, note 3; Messina, *op. cit.*, p. 75.

⁵⁹ Cf. above, chap. I, note 124 and pp. 150ff. To the expressions of this dualism enriched with the intermediary principle found in our texts, let us add, besides the references to the *Poimandres* and the *Asclepius*, the verses of the *Thebaid* of Statius (IV, 515) which allude to a "triple universe" and perhaps express the same notion. Bidez and Cumont comment upon these in *Les Mages hellénisés*, vol. I, pp. 225ff. Note also that the idea of the higher god, distinct from the Demiurge and unknowable, is mentioned in the Clementine *Recognitions* (cf. Bidez–Cumont, *op. cit.*, vol. I, pp. 228–9).

⁶⁰ The supreme god: cf. Widengren, *Stand und Aufgaben* . . . , p. (115); the Wisdom: Widengren, *The Great Vohu Manah* . . . , p. 57; Zaehner, *The Teachings of the Magi*, 1956, chap. VI, and, in the same author's *Zurvan*, pp. 132, 199, 208 and *passim* on the Tetrad. In the same book, chap. IX, particularly pp. 224 and 228–9; the two principles and the three times, in Mazdaism; H. S. Nyberg, "Questions de cosmogonie et de cosmologie mazdéennes, II" in *Journal Asiatique*, CCXIX, 1931, pp. 29–31 (cf. H. C. Puech, *Le Manichéisme* . . . , p. 159).

⁶¹ Upon Ialdabaôth and the Archons, cf. Bidez–Cumont, *op. cit.*, vol. II, p. 281 and note 1: comparison with Ahriman and his evil spirits, rivals of the good god. Cf. also J. Duchesne-Guillemin, "Ahriman et le Dieu suprême dans les mystères de Mithra" in *Numen*, 1955; Widengren, *Mesopotamian Elements in Manichaeism*, chap. II; Junker, "Die Iranischen Quellen der Hellenistischen Aionvorstellung" in *Vorträge d.Bibliothek Warburg*, I.S., 165ff. The reservations expressed by Wikander about the Iranian origin of the monstrous figure of Kronos (in his *Études sur les mystères de Mithra* I, 1950, p. 35) are not wholly convincing.

of evil, these too being rivals of the highest God. There is the Zurvanist theory of the "two souls", very like a preliminary sketch for the Gnostic notion of the "counterfeiting spirit", which we shall find again in the teaching of the sectaries of the Dead Sea.[62] There is even a notion of Gnosis, attested in Iranian texts by the explicit recurrence of the questions: Who am I? To whom do I belong? Whence did I come, and where am I coming to?[63] There are not only the figures of saviours born of the seed of Zoroaster (as, among Gnostics, of "the seed of the great Seth") but also, and very clearly, that theme which has been known, since Reitzenstein discerned its main outlines, as the myth of "the Saviour saved"—which is that of a higher light-power who is at work freeing the sparks of his own light, which are dispersed throughout the lower creation.[64] There are, again, many of the facts and many of the images of this salvation; the glorious vesture put on by the Enlighteners at their passage through the heavens, and the description of the celestial goal as a Treasury.[65] Finally—and even more characteristically, there is the geographical setting itself in which these revelations occur; for our apocrypha situate the most mystic and secret spot in the universe on the dark shores of the eastern ocean, on that Mountain of Lights in which is the Cave of the Magi.[66]

[62] Cf. above, pp. 23, 72, 215 and, further on, p. 297.

[63] Cf. Widengren, "Der Iranische Hintergrund der Gnosis" in *Zeitschrift für Religions- und Geistesgeschichte*, IV, 1952, pp. 103–4; and H. C. Puech, *La Gnose et le Temps*, p. 100 and note 59; *Schkand-Gumânîk Vichâr*, X, 2–11, p. 114 in the edn. of J. de Menasce, Fribourg, 1945—and the reference to the *Pand-Nâmâk i Zartûsht* quoted by de Menasce in his foregoing publication, p. 120.

[64] This myth arises from the belief in a parallelism between the macrocosm and the microcosm; the divine Spirit on high rediscovers itself scattered among men and throughout the cosmos: at the same time an analogous relationship emerges between the heavenly primordial Man and the Messenger who, assuming the function of Saviour, is a being in whom divine and human qualities are combined. Cf. Widengren, *The Great Vohu Manah and the Apostle of God*, p. 7. Upon the successions of royalties and of celestial envoys, cf. Bidez–Cumont, *op. cit.*, vol. I, pp. 217–22 and vol. II, pp. 364–76; Messina, *I Magi* . . . , pp. 74–82.

[65] Cf. Widengren, *The Great Vohu Manah* . . . , pp. 54–5, 60, 71–2, 76ff., 84ff.; p. 89. Widengren quotes the following from the *Zâtsparam* XXI, 8: "Then I saw Vohu Manah . . . under the aspect of a man . . . he had put on, and was wearing, a garment that was like silk, which was not made in pieces and had no seams at all; for its substance was the light, and his stature was nine times that of Zarathustra."

[66] Cf. chap. v, note 24.

To show how naturally mythical notions, practically the same in essentials as those of our Gnostics, could arise in the Iranian mind, I would like to offer a rather amusing piece of evidence. There is a Pahlavi writing of the second half of the ninth century —the *Shkand Gûmânîk Vichâr*, or "Explanation which destroys all doubt"—which is an excellent example of the controversies with Judaism familiarly carried on for more than a thousand years. Its author sets out to refute the myth expounded at the beginning of *Genesis*—that key-text for all Gnostic exegetists. In doing so, he shows in the most spontaneous manner how an Iranian would interpret the Biblical myth. Exactly like our sectaries—just like the *Secret Book of John* which takes even Moses to task on a charge of falsehood—our Parsee is horrified at the description of the primordial dark waters, with the Spirit of God moving over them. This picture of the Creator, far from seeming divine to him, strikes him as monstrous, and the arguments he brings against it are almost the same as those of the Coptic books against Ialdabaôth: "It is evident that he [i.e., God] was not luminous, because when he saw the light he admired it, for he had never seen it before" (*Genesis* I, 4; "And God saw that the light was good"). Besides, the author insists, this Creator "having his place and his dwelling in the darkness and in the black waters and never having seen light before—how could he see that light, and whence came his divinity? . . . And if his root and his dwelling were in the darkness, how could he look light in the face?" This is precisely the accusation—of ignorance of the true light-radiant divinity who was superior to himself—that Gnosticism brought against the Creator of this base world. Why—the Parsee goes on— did this god create Adam and Eve; and why did he then want to keep them in ignorance? Certainly, he adds, "the origin of the science of man upon earth is in the serpent". And then, after having quoted the Biblical sayings which describe the Creator as a "jealous God", the Iranian critic ends by asking "Is this a god—a being who has all these marks and characteristics, to whom the truth is alien and who will not share out his knowledge? . . . But no, this is the devil himself, he who takes his origin from the darkness!" Here, then, is good evidence that the anti-Biblical interpretation of the Old Testament from which Gnosticsm derived one of its essential myths, was that which would quite naturally present itself to an Iranian mind.[67]

Here let us add a few words about the relations which may have existed between Gnosticism and certain Indian doctrines. Since long before the discovery of the Chenoboskion writings this has been a major problem, as much for specialists in Gnosticism as for historians of Indian literature; but no reliable solution has come in sight; and if the one group of doctrines did have some influence upon the other, there has been nothing to show in which direction this took place.

We know that the conquest of Asia by Alexander had opened up the road to India for the Hellenistic world. The Seleucids, from 320 B.C. and as long as Babylon remained their capital city, were on good terms with the Indian princes—Sandracotta, for instance. The Kushana money consisted of coins struck with the images of Herakles, Mithra, Shiva or Buddha, indifferently. But no precise details about the religious and philosophical exchanges of the period between the Orient and the Occident remain discernible for historians. We should need more information about the dominant part played by Iran, whose religious history in these ages remains very little known.

However, it already appears that a comparative study of the doctrines of our Gnostics, and of certain texts of Indian literature also composed about the commencement of our era, promises some discoveries that one could not have hoped for before. Here we can but suggest their possible range. For instance, how could anyone miss the resemblance between the theme of the seduction of the celestial Archons by the Virgin of the Light—a favourite theme with both Gnostics and Manichaeans—and the episode of Vishnu changing himself into a dazzling courtesan, in order to get back from the *asuras* (Titans) the ambrosia they had stolen after the churning of the Sea of Milk? How, above all, could one neglect another extraordinary feature—that, in the mythology of the *Mahabharata*, there is a White Mountain, Svetaparvata, situated in regions beyond the darkness of this world? For here, again, is the Mountain of the Lights, dear to Zoroastrian, Gnostic and Mandaean traditions. And the seven Guardians whom the Mandaeans located precisely there, where the Gnostics also knew them to be, now appear to us—though doubtless the same—in the form of serpents with seven heads![68]

JEWISH AND KABBALISTIC GNOSTICISM

The problem of the relations that there may have been between the Gnostic teachings and Judaism is of no less capital importance.[69] Certain ramifications of the great Gnostic movement were even explicitly believed to have had remote Jewish origins. That is what Hegesippus claimed for them. But the most picturesque tradition of this kind is that which Al Biruni recorded in the eleventh century about some Mandaeans who were descended "from the remaining Jewish tribes who dwelt in Babylonia after the other tribes had left for Jerusalem in the time of Cyrus and Artaxerxes. These tribes, remaining there, adopted a mixture of Magian and Jewish doctrines, like that of the Samaritans in Syria".[70]

For our sects—as we must not forget—the interpretation of the text of the Bible is the real point of departure for their doctrines; indeed their writings sometimes refer to interpretations of words which could have no meaning except in Hebrew or, more often, in Aramaic. Their apocrypha are nourished by images from the

[68] Cf. Senart, *Essai sur la légende de Bouddha*, 2nd edn., 1882, pp. 106–7; Hopkins, "Mythological Aspects of Trees and Mountains in the great Epic" in *Journal of the American Oriental Society*, XXX, 1910, p. 359; and, by the same author, *Epic Mythology* . . . , Strasbourg, 1915, pp. 26, 45 and 105. On the plane of historical records, cf., above, note 27.

[69] The indispensable study is that of G. G. Scholem, *Les grands courants de la mystique juive* (trans. by M. M. Davy), 1950. Among studies of detail, we may cite Graetz, *Gnostizismus und Judenthum*, 1846; A. Buchler, in *Judaïca, Festschrift für Hermann Cohen*, 1912; and the article of the same author in *Monatschrift für Geschichte und Wissenschaft des Judentums*, vol. LXXVI, 1932, pp. 412–56. To the articles enumerated in the Notes that follow let us add: H. J. Schoeps, "Simon Magus in der Haggada" in *Aus frühchristliche Zeit*, pp. 239–54; A. Procope-Walter, "Jao und Seth" in *Archiv. für Religionswissenschaft*, XXX, pp. 34–69; M. Simon, "Sur deux Hérésies juives mentionnées par Justin martyr" in *Revue d'Histoire et de Philosophie religieuses*, XVIII, pp. 54–8.

[70] Cf. E. S. Drower, *The Haran Gawaita* . . . (= *Studi e Testi*, 176), Città del Vaticano, 1953, p. viii.

Books of *Daniel*, of *Enoch*, of the *Ascension of Isaiah* and of the *Jubilees*. Some teachings, like that of Justin in his book of *Baruch*, seem to be founded upon rabbinical speculations. Certain features, with which our apocrypha enrich the story of the creation of Adam and Eve, are to be found in the *Pirqé Rabbi Eli'ezer* and many other treatises. The primordial Adam—the Adam Qadmon —is one of their favourite subjects.[71] The *Haggada* identifies Shem with Melchizedek and accords him a prestige equivalent to that which he has in Gnosticism.[72] A certain Gamaliel (who was perhaps modelled upon a historical personage) is elevated by our Sethians to the rank of a celestial power, watching over the great baptisms and the seals.[73]

Concerning this Hellenistic Judaism one has also to take into account the number of foreign influences that entered into it.[74]

[71] A. Altmann, "The Gnostic Background of the Rabbinic Adam Legend" in *Jewish Quarterly Review*, XXXV, pp. 371-91; Aptowitzer, *Caîn und Abel in d.Haggada*, 1922; Israel Levi, "Le Péché originel dans les anciennes sources juives" in *Annuaire de l'École pratique des Hautes Études*; *Section des Sciences religieuses*, 1907; A. Dupont-Sommer, "Adam 'Père du Monde' dans la Sagesse de Salomon", 10, 1-2, in the *Revue de l'Histoire des Religions*, vol. CXIX, 1939, pp. 182-203; Kraeling, *Anthropos and Son of Man*, 1927; Kurt Rudolph, "Ein grundtyp gnostischer Urmensch-Adam spekulation" in *Zeitschrift für Religions und Geistesgeschichte*, IX, 1957, pp. 1ff.; Scholem, "Die Vorstellung vom Golem" in *Eranos Jahrbuch* XXII, 1953, pp. 235ff.

[72] M. Simon, "Melchisédech dans les polémiques entre Juifs et Chrétiens et dans la légende" in *Revue d'Histoire et de Philosophie religieuses*, 1937, pp. 58-93. The equivalence mentioned here appears in the second century, with Rabbi Ismaël.

[73] In the *Secret Book of the invisible Great Spirit*, Gamaliel is associated with Gabriel, Samlô and Abraxas; the untitled treatise in the Bruce Codex (ed. Baynes, p. 97) names him among the guardians of the aeons with Strempsuchos and Agramas. That Gamaliel may have been a divinized teacher is suggested by his being mentioned together with a Strempsuchos probably identical with the Astrampsychos who comes into the *Philosophumena*'s account of the Perates (V, 13, 8), associated with other celebrated sages—Bumegas, Ostanes, Kurites, Petosiris, Zodarion, Bêrôssos, Zoroaster. Astrampsychos is known elsewhere as an astrologer, originally from Persia or Egypt—more probably Egypt, seeing that the second half of his name includes the name of the crocodile god *Suchos*. A striking fact is that Diogenes Laertius and Suidas put him among the Magi between Ostanes and Gobryas and make him, with Ostanes, the principal successor to Zoroaster. The *Philosophumena* mentions him, somewhat similarly, between Bêrôssos and Zoroaster (cf. Bidez–Cumont, *op. cit.*, vol. II, p. 7; and the article "Astrampsychos" in the *Realenzyklopädie* of Pauly–Wissowa, vol. II, col. 1796).

[74] Cf. the first chaps. of vol. II of S. W. Baron, *Social and Religious History of the Jews*, 1952, and its abundance of notes and summaries.

Of these, must we not give first place to its contacts with Iran?[75] For even after the end of the Exile, many Israelites remained in Media (for example at Ragay and Ecbatana) and in Babylonia (at Nehardea). The Aramaic language was understood as far as the Iranian plateau. The diffusion of the Jewish religion included conversions such as those of Helen of Adiabene and her son Izates in A.D. 44, who were buried later in Jerusalem in the Sepulchres still to be seen there, called the "Tomb of the Kings".

At the same time Judaism was receiving from Iran its myths of salvation and of apocalypse, its eschatology full of archangels, angels and demons, and something of its belief in the enmity between the light and the darkness.[76] For a long time the Hebrew and Pahlavi literatures went on exchanging literary material such as the visions ascribed to certain holy men who had been caught up into heaven.[77] We have already noted how Zoroaster thus became identified with Seth, in a tradition cherished by our Gnostics. They also liked to assimilate him to Balaam, who had foretold the Star of Jacob (*Numbers* XXIV, 15-17). They identified him, again, with Ezechiel, and made him a disciple of Abraham. They even tried to identify him with Nimrod, proud of his renown as an ancient Chaldaean king.[78] It was from all this, and thanks to borrowings from Iranian sources, that there emerged the *Apocalypses of Adam* (one of the principal resources upon which our Gnostics drew) and the abundant, but more orthodox cycle of legends surrounding the multiple variations of the *Cave of Treasures*.

As for Hellenism, its influence is less recognizable, although, against a good deal of reprobation, it was flooding into Jewish culture.[79] The latter responded to this influx by claiming that Moses had been the same person as Musaeus (which would mean

[75] Cf. Messina, *I Magi e Betlemme*, chap. v.

[76] Widengren, *Stand und Aufgaben der Iranische Religionsgeschichte*, 1955, pp. (131), (134).

[77] Cf., for instance, M. Haug, *Ueber das Ardâi Vîrâf nâmeh*, Munich, 1870; it gives the story of a vision of heaven and hell in which there are borrowings from the *Ascension of Isaiah*.

[78] Bidez–Cumont, *op. cit.*, vol. I, pp. 41-9.

[79] Cf. Baron, *Social and Religious History of the Jews*, vol. II, chaps. IX, XII and XIII; Schürer, *Geschichte der Jüdischen Volkes im Zeitalter Jesu Christi*, 3rd edn.; R. Meyer, *Hellenistisches in der rabbinischen Anthropologie*, Stuttgart, 1937.

that Orpheus was but a disciple of that great prophet) and that it was from him that Pythagoras and Plato had derived their doctrines.[80] Do we want proofs of the mixture that this brought about? For one—it looks as though the theme of the casket of the Danaïdes became involved with the visions in a Hebrew *Apocalypse of Isaiah*, one fragment of which has survived.[81] Some images of Hades—for instance the allusion to sinners being hanged, as Homer is, according to the *Catabasis of Pythagoras*, and of analogous torments—passed into the Hebrews' eschatology[82]; and Greek conceptions, although extremely deformed, have insinuated themselves even into one of the greatest of their mystical texts: the *Great Hekhaloth*.[83]

Even the astrological beliefs invaded this branch of Judaism; so much so that it claimed to trace the origins of that star-lore to traditions founded by Enoch, Abraham and others.[84] . . . Thus it was that the Throne and the Chariot of the Lord Sabaôth came to be assigned a place that anyone could see by looking up into the sky: the supreme point of the seven heavens; the Pole around which the hosts of angels and powers—twinkling stars and steady planets—revolved in an obedient and continuous rhythm.[85]

From the assimilation of Zoroaster to Seth, which served as a basis for the beliefs of the sectaries whose writings we have now

[80] Schürer, *op. cit.*, pp. 354ff. and 386ff.; Bidez–Cumont, *op. cit.*, vol. I, p. 41.
[81] Cf. Gaster, in *Journal of the Royal Asiatic Society*, 1893, p. 601.
[82] Cf. *Dictionnaire de la Bible*; *Supplément*, vol. II, col. 409.
[83] Scholem, *Les Grands courants* . . . , p. 376, note 50. We may add, as further borrowings from Hellenism, a physiognomics to which mystical meanings were attached, both among the Essenians (see later, on p. 297) and in orthodox Judaism (Scholem, pp. 61–2 and relevant notes); and we should also mention the speculations on the hidden meanings of numbers. The influence of Pythagoreanism on the Essenians, already known, has been illuminated by, for instance, J. Carcopino, *Le Mystère d'un symbole chrétien*, pp. 53–4.
[84] Upon the influence of Hellenistic astrology on Judaism, see Baron, *op. cit.*, vol. II; and Reitzenstein, *Poïmandres*, pp. 74 and *passim*.
[85] By playing on the initial letter of the name of Sabaôth, the Hebrew could turn the Lord "of Hosts" into Lord "of the Seven" (planets). Cf. Puech's article "Archontiker", col. 642. In Hellenistic astrology we find the planets furnishing themselves with chariots and thrones (cf. Ptolemeus, *Tetrabiblos*, I, 23. Was it these that inspired the images of the throne and chariot of Sabaôth, or were they imitations of the latter?

discovered, must we conclude that our Gnostics, too, derived their traditions from some group that was particularly syncretistic and especially open to Iranian influences, in this very accommodating Judaism? But of this again proof is lacking, though the hypothesis is a very attractive one. Here we must limit ourselves to listing the principal features that connect our Gnostic myths with Judaism. We must note, here, that Jewish mysticism itself had its unmistakable Gnostics—that is, openly heretical believers in dualism; G. Scholem has clearly demonstrated their existence[86]; but this is a subject upon which such an immense literature still remains to be sifted that, without lingering upon the point, we had better look for our connections in Jewish mysticism as a whole, whether it had or had not come directly under Gnostic influences. And to give a more general idea of the relations between the beliefs of our Gnostics and certain themes familiar to Jewish thought, we will refer to the mediaeval evidence: this we have no right to exclude because of its later date; for, after all, even the most ancient writings do not enable us to affirm, in the present state of research, that this or that parallel demonstrates with certainty the existence of a pattern that the Gnostics copied nor, on the contrary, of one that was an import due to Gnostic influence.

An initial phenomenon relating the two literatures is that, just as Gnosticism entitled its apocalypses with the names of Marsanes, Nicotheus "the hidden", Phôsilampes, of Seth and various other "Allogenes"[87], so did Judaism place certain revelations to the account of privileged sages who, following the examples of Enoch and Melchizedek, had gained admission to Paradise—these included Ben Azaï, Ben Zoma, Aher and Rabbi Aqiba.[88] Other Jewish doctors, such as Onias the Just, Hanan and, later, Simeon ben Yohaï, were themselves described as "hidden"

---

[86] Cf. Scholem, *op. cit.*, p. 374, note 24; L. Wallach, "A Jewish Polemic against Gnosticism" in *Journal of Biblical Literature*, LXV, pp. 393–6; Baron, *op. cit.*, vol. II, note 16, pp. 1043–4.

[87] Cf. above (on the intitled treatise in the Bruce Codex), pp. 82–3; the *Paraphrase of Shem*, pp. 147 and 148; the *Treatise on the Triple Epiphany*, p. 181.

[88] According to the treatise *Hagiga*, Scholem, *op. cit.*, p. 65; cf. Peterson, "La libération d'Adam de l'Ἀνάγκη," not forgetting the case of St Paul (II *Corinthians* XII, 2).

before there were any Gnostics.[89] At the same time, one notices
that many of the visions recorded by Judaism suffer from the
same major defect as the Gnostic apocrypha, in that their authors
have chosen to hide their identity behind the names of famous
personages of the past. However, we do know something about
these revelations which, in the case of the Gnostics, eludes us—
that, in many cases—as we are told by, for instance, the *Great
Hekhaloth*—these are visions which the doctor to whom they are
attributed really believed he had had; for which he had prepared
himself by fasting, which he induced at the desired moment by
assuming a certain attitude; and which were recorded just as they
came to him, for he dictated them to scribes installed beside
him.[90]

The most ancient form of the Jewish mysticism was nourished
upon the vision of the divine Throne: towards this the soul of the
seer was uplifted through the celestial spheres, which were
guarded—in accordance with the universal astrology of the
times—by the Archons, who had to be answered with the secret
words, and shown the seals. But here, the revolving spheres are
palaces; they are the *Hekhalôth*, and in the seventh of them
(the highest) is the chariot celebrated in the visions of Ezechiel
and Daniel, that is, the Throne—Merkaba, the primal image of
the Pleroma which contains all the forms of the creation. Among

[89] Onias the Just was (see Josephus, *Ant. Jud.*, XIV, II, 1 and 2) a person beloved
of God who had even had the privilege of obtaining a rainfall which put an end
to a period of drought. During the seditions of the year 65 B.C. he was "hidden".
But the mob found and stoned him. According to R. Goossens, "Onias le Juste,
Messie de la Nouvelle Alliance" (in *La Nouvelle Clio*, No. 7, 1950), this personage
may have been the Teacher of Righteousness of the sect of Qumrân. He is, in any
case, an example of those "just" or "righteous" men who were also described
as "hidden" (Goossens, *op. cit.*, p. 345). In the tradition of the Talmud the title of
"hidden" was similarly given to a later thaumaturgist—Hanan; cf. the treatise
Ta'anith, quoted by Goossens, *loc. cit.* Here we must remember *Enoch* XII, 1:
"And before these things, Enoch was hidden and none of the children of men
knew where he was hidden. . . ." Upon Simeon ben Yohaï, see H. Serouya,
La Kabbale 2nd edn., 1957, p. 44 and S. W. Baron, *op. cit.*, vol. II.

[90] Scholem, *op. cit.*, pp. 62–3 and p. 76. The mystic "has to fast a certain number of days, place his head between his knees, and very softly repeat hymns and
canticles, the text of which we know were traditional. Then, he is drawn into the
inner world and perceives the dwellings, as though he were seeing the seven
palaces with his own eyes. . . ." Scholem compares this posture with that
assumed by Elijah on Mount Carmel.

the most characteristic elements around this Throne is the curtain, the cosmic veil which screens the glory of their Lord from the hosts of angels, as we find it does in the *Book of Enoch*,[91] where it is defined as containing the images of all pre-existing things. This veil—although with another meaning, that of separating the world of light from what is beneath it—appears again among the Coptic Gnostics; and it may be that this was the inspiration of the luminous clouds, in some of their myths, behind which Ialdabaôth hid himself or, indeed, before the Deluge, Noah and his family.[92] As for the divine chariot mentioned before in a line of the anonymous treatise in the Bruce Codex, it is pretty fully described in that glorification of Sabaôth which is one of the essential themes of the *Hypostasis of the Archons*, and of the analogous text to which I have attached the No. 40.[93] As we have seen elsewhere, certain features of this same mysticism appear also in those semi-magical and half-Gnostic texts of prayers put into the mouth of Adam, of which E. Peterson has given us a penetrating analysis.[94] The same ascent into heaven is also implied in the myth of the pseudo-*Mithraic Liturgy*, and this, too, is offered to the glory of the First man.[95] And even the Coptic magical writings usually invoke the powers who, in this same mystical vision, surround the divine Throne.

Some other features of this Judaic Gnosis appear in a writing of almost paradoxical content—the treatise *Shiur Koma* (or "Measure of the Body") which describes the Creator as a fantastic Anthropos. One could compare this with the figure of the supreme Anthropos which is expounded at length in the last writing in the Bruce Codex. Reflections of the same visions have been found in the speculations of Mark the Gnostic.[96]

[91] Scholem, *op. cit.*, p. 85, upon the various entities; among them the seven *middôth* (wisdom, righteousness, justice . . .) who serve before the divine Throne; cf., also *loc. cit.*, p. 87.

[92] Cf. above, chap. v, p. 202 and p. 208. Upon this *cloud* in the magical writings: cf. the Gnostic magical texts quoted on p. 103 and Kropp, *Ausgewählte koptische Zaubertexte*, vol. III, pp. 28-9.

[93] Chap. v above, pp. 163, 167 and 177.

[94] Chap. II above, pp. 107ff.

[95] Cf. above, p. 108 and Scholem, *loc. cit.*, p. 66.

[96] Scholem, *op. cit.*, pp. 76-8 and p. 378, notes 89 and 91; Kropp, *Ausgewählte koptische Zaubertexte*, vol. III, p. 41.

The Jewish mediaeval literature lends itself to more numerous comparisons than do these archaic writings. This is largely because it is derived from ancient traditions, the original form of which is lost. Thus, one oriental source of the theology of the Kabbalists was the *Raza Rabba* or "Great Mystery", a work which has now disappeared, but which had been nourished with Gnostic speculations about the aeons: G. Scholem discovers elements of this in the book *Bahir* which appeared in Provence in the twelfth century.[97]

The thirteenth century saw the composition of the book of the *Zohar*. Scholem has satisfactorily proved that this was derived from the master Moses of Leon. Its doctrine of ten emanations, or *Sephiroth*, proceeding from the hidden and infinite God,[98] is highly reminiscent of the series of abstract powers which are added to the supreme divinity in the mythology of our ancient Gnostics: they are the supreme Crown of God, his Wisdom or his primordial Idea, his Intelligence, his Mercy. . . . With the figure of Moses of Leon is intimately associated that of Joseph Gikatila; so much so that one hesitates to say which of these two Kabbalists was the author of certain texts. Gikatila wrote an opusculum on the *Mystery of the Serpent*, which merits quotation here, so much does it remind us, in some of its features, of the teachings of the Ophites or Naassenes which, however, this doctor cannot have known. Let us borrow G. Scholem's translation[99] of the following passage: "Know that from Isaac have issued thirty-five princes on the left by Edom and by Amalek. Amalek is the head of the primal Serpent; he issued from the Serpent and the Serpent is his chariot. . . . In that place [Rephidim; see *Exodus* XVII] the Serpent and Amalek are found united. . . . Know and believe that the Serpent, at the beginning of creation, was indispensable to the order of the world, so long as he kept his place; and he was a great servant, created to bear the yoke and

---

[97] Scholem, *op. cit.*, p. 88, and the article of the same author "Buch Bahir" in *Encyclopaedia Judaica*, vol. III, cols. 969–79.

[98] The *Sephiroth*, or *Sepher Yetsira*, were the ten primary numbers, in which were comprised all the elements of the world (Scholem, *op. cit.*, pp. 89–90). In the *Zohar*, the *Sephiroth* represent something rather different; the world of spheres (Scholem, *op. cit.*, p. 222).

[99] Scholem, *op. cit.*, p. 409, note 113.

servitude of kingdoms. His *head* reached high above the earth and his *tail* reached down even into Sheol and Abadon,[100] for in all worlds there was a place for him; and he was needed for the ordering of all the chariots, each in its place. And that is the mystery of the Dragon ['Teli'] known to the *Sepher Yetsira* [i.e., the 'Book of the Creation'].[101] It is he who moves the spheres and turns them from the East to the West and from the North to the South. Without him there would have been neither seed nor germination, nor will to produce any created thing. . . . That is the mystery of the tree of knowledge of good and evil. That is why God forbade Adam to touch the tree of knowledge, so long as the good and the evil are linked together. . . . "

Let us remember the *Philosophumena's* account of the Peratae—who were, in fact, a sect of Ophites—and some remarks it lets fall about the great business of the Serpent: "If anyone has favoured sight . . . he will see . . . the beautiful image of the Serpent coiled up at the great commencement of the heavens, and becoming, for all born beings, the principle of all movement; then he will understand that no being . . . is formed without the Serpent."[102]

Some further parallels with the Gnostic myths will be found in the doctrines of the school of Isaac Luria, who lived in the middle of the sixteenth century, and who learned the principles

[100] Cf., among the great Gnostics, the serpent of Darkness, by whom the souls who could not ascend to the Light were swallowed, passed through his body and were cast down into the depths of matter. Abadon is the angel of the abyss; cf. the Book of *Revelation* IX, 11.

[101] The Dragon (Teli) has an important place in the myths of the *Sepher Yetsira* (composed between the third and fourth centuries); cf. A. Epstein, "Recherches sur le Sefer Yetsira" in *Revue des Études juives*, XXVIII, 1894, pp. 63–4. Upon the Gnostic elements contained in the S.Y., cf. Graetz, *op. cit.* The dragon (already alluded to in *Job* XXVI, 13) governs the world and personifies its axis: thus we are dealing with an image of maximum amplitude, of the constellation of the Dragon, neighbour to the Great Bear, and whose star *alpha* marked the Pole until the decline of the antique world. Under the name of 'Aθάλια the dragon Teli passed into Greek astrology: cf. the *Catalogus Codicum Astrologorum Graecorum*, V, fasc. 2, pp. 131ff.; VII, pp. 123ff, p. 245, Note 5, p. 246; VIII, fasc. I, pp. 194–6; cf. also G. Furlani, "Tre trattati astrologici siriaci sulle eclissi solare e lunare" in *Atti d.Accademia Nazionale dei Lincei*, Anno CCCXLIV, 1947, ser. ottava: *Rendiconti Classe di Sc. morali . . .*, vol. II, fascicolo 11–12 (Rome 1948), pp. 569–606; cf. also above, chap. II, our notes 12 and 15.

[102] *Philosophumena*, V, 16.

of the Kabbala in Egypt. Without, perhaps, going so far as to an absolute dualism, his cosmology does assume the real existence of evil in a kingdom of its own: it admits the fall of the portions of the light of the Pleroma down into the lowest depths. One very curious feature of his doctrine is what he calls *tsimtsum*, by which word he means a "withdrawal": this is the notion that the created universe could not have existed, had not God, infinite and therefore everywhere present, withdrawn himself—vacating a portion of himself, in which creation could then take place. In this space—since a creation could not be made out of nothing—he had, however, left a residue of his divine light; the *reshimu* from which the creation was to emerge. Isaac Luria compares this *reshimu* to the oil or wine that still clings to a vessel from which one has poured out the contents. Now, Scholem has been able to show that this doctrine has a quite exact parallel in what the *Philosophumena* writes about the teaching of Basilides[103]; there it is said, of this residue of the Spirit: "When one has put a delicate perfume into a vase, one may empty that vase with the greatest care, but the odour still remains after the perfume has been decanted . . . and the vase retains the odour even though it contains no more of the perfume. Thus it is with the Holy Spirit, separated from and deprived of the Sonhood (from which it came forth): it keeps within itself, so to speak, the virtue of the perfume. . . ." Better still, an allusion to this same notion of withdrawal—of the *tsimtsum*—occurs in the *Books of Jêou*, where it is said that all the primordial spaces with their Paternities came into existence because of this little idea that God had left behind him in space . . . when he had withdrawn into himself.[104]

Of course it is possible that themes of this order (and we have mentioned but a few), which are found in the mediaeval writings of Jewish mysticism and even in the more ancient texts, were inspired by the teachings of the same Gnostics who were combated by the Christian heresiologists. Yet these motives seem so

---

[103] *Philosophumena*, VII, 22; cf. Scholem, *loc. cit.*, pp. 278–72.

[104] *Books of Jêou*, translation by C. Schmidt–W. Till. Cf. Scholem, *op. cit.*, pp. 387–82. The same notion recurs in § 15 of the *Asclepius*: "Locum autem dico in quo sint omnia: neque enim haec omnia esse potuisse (omnibus enim rebus, quae fuerint, praecavendum est loco)."

much in accord with other features of authentically Jewish thought which the Gnostics did not know—thought which, for its own own part, is almost totally ignorant of any dualistic conception of the universe—that one is tempted to believe that it was the Gnostic sects who received a great part of their theories from Judaism. Moreover, we have found, thanks to the very exact analyses of Peterson,[105] that certain mystical themes, connected with the freeing of Adam from Fate, were developed quite apart from Gnosticism, and may go back to more ancient origins. Undoubtedly, the doctrines inherited by our sectaries are anti-biblical: but those who elaborated them could have done so only after long mystical speculation upon the Old Testament—the *Torah* and the *Psalms* in particular—and that probably in Hebrew. The special case of the Sethians is still clearer in this respect: Judaism was not without certain traditions about the Sons of God (*Genesis* VI, 2 and 4) who were thought to be the children of Seth and to have lived, at first, upon Mount Hermon.[106]

THE GNOSTICS AND THE SECTARIES OF QUMRÂN

The problem of the relations of our Gnostics, first with Judaism, and then with Christianity, is resolvable into this more particular question—what relations could there have been between the sects among whom our writings were originally conceived, and the Jewish pre-Christian sects—or the Judeo-Christian ones? The heresiologists insist upon placing the diverse groups of our Gnostics at the top of a genealogical tree, the trunk of which is formed by a number of Jewish groups—Baptist, Samaritan and Judeo-Christian. . . . But on this subject our new writings remain dumb. A Dositheus declares himself, but only as the transcriber of prayers revealed to him by the Great Seth under conditions that throw no light upon his identity. We also find texts headed with the name of the Apostle James to whom, according to Hegesippus, the Saviour had imparted the secrets of Gnosis; and other revelations elaborate reflections upon the

---

[105] Cf. above, p. 109.
[106] Cf. Grünbaum, "Beitrage zur vergleichende Mythologie aus der Haggada" in *Zeitschrift d.Deutsch. Morgenl. Gesellsch.*, 1877, p. 247.

Jordan, and on baptisms; but these constitute a class of writings manifestly distinct from those that most explicitly describe what one would call Gnostic mythology.

By absolutely direct evidence, there is only one pre-Christian sect that we know much about—the sect whose manuscripts have been found near the Dead Sea. But this—as it happens—was a specially representative group, and it played a highly important part in history. Several authors have already raised the question of what relations may have existed between these "Essenians" and the Gnostics: but they were poorly equipped to answer it while they had only such inadequate documentation as was available before our discovery. That is why the definitions of Gnosticism which they used as criteria were not always correct enough; and their conclusions have been mostly negative.[107] However, some interesting facts have emerged: and we are now able to affirm a vague parallel between our Gnostics and the people of Qumrân, not because of the fact that these Essenians associated their Judaic beliefs with Hellenic-Pythagorean inspirations, as we know they did, or from their faith, their discipline of life and their dress.[108] Nor is it because the sectaries of Qumrân made use of the *Books of Enoch* and of the *Jubilees*, nor that they possessed a commentary on *Genesis*—incidentally, this was taken to be a Book of Lamech![109]—which proves to be of little note from a doctrinal point of view. Rather, it is because they regarded a part of the teaching that they passed on as strictly secret. Was it, then, a kind of Gnosis? "Thou hast made me the authorized interpreter of profound mysteries", proclaims their teacher, "Thou hast given me the understanding of thy faith and the knowledge of thy wonderful secrets!" (*Hymns*, 11, 13 and VII, 26). And then, two

---

[107] Cf. R. McL. Wilson, "Simon, Dositheus and the Dead Sea Scrolls" in *Zeitschrift für Religions- und Geistesgeschichte*, IX, 1957, pp. 21–30; for a "negative" opinion, see H. J. Schoeps, "Das gnostische Judentum in den Dead Sea Scrolls" in the same *Zeitschrift* . . . , VI, 1954, pp. 276–9.

[108] Cf. above, note 83.

[109] N. Avigad and Y. Yadin, *A Genesis apocryphon* . . . , 1956. We notice, among the texts (often very fragmentary) still in course of publication, some apocalyptic or messianic writings; a description of the *New Jerusalem*, a Book of Mysteries; they seem to contain nothing of a Gnostic tendency: see "Le travail d'édition des fragments manuscrits de Qumrân" in *Revue Biblique*, 1956, pp. 49ff.

cryptographic alphabets have been identified in the manuscripts from Cave 4. One book, which was meant to remain secret, develops some astrological conceptions, more original than those usually found in this kind of literature that knew no frontiers.[110] In accordance with the morphology of individuals[111] born under this or that sign of the Zodiac, this treatise claims to compute how many men can belong to the world of the Spirits of Light and how many belong to the spirits of the Darkness. Such theories were by no means unknown among our Coptic Gnostics: the *Pistis-Sophia* describes at some length the mysterious seals imprinted by decans upon the hands, the skull, and the rest of the human body during its formation.

In addition, the Qumrân people knew the doctrine of the "two spirits".[112] In their *Manual of Discipline* these "children of light"—as they called themselves—were told that when God created man to rule over the world, he gave him two spirits; one, the spirit of truth, and the other the spirit of perversity. "The origin of the Truth is in the Source of Light, and that of Perversity is in the Abyss of Darkness. All those who practise righteousness are under the domination of the Prince of Light and walk in the ways of the Light, while those who practise perversity are under the domination of the Angel of Darkness and walk in the way of Darkness."[113]

But could there have been any historical relations between the sect that lived on the shores of the Dead Sea and the mysterious founders of our Gnosticism?

[110] See J. T. Milik, *Dix ans de découvertes dans le désert de Juda*, pp. 78–9.
[111] Cf. Scholem, *loc. cit.*, pp. 61 and 62 and the relevant notes.
[112] Upon the theory of the two spirits, and its Iranian origin: see J. Duchesne–Guillemin, "Le Zervanisme et les manuscrits de la mer Morte" in *Indo-Iranian Journal*, I, 1957, pp. 96–9—an article which has the interest of attesting, in the first place, the Zurvanist origin of this doctrine. On the same subject: H. Michaud, "Un mythe zervaniste dans un des manuscrits de Qumrân" in *Vetus Testamentum*, 1955; Dupont-Sommer, "L'Instruction sur les deux Esprits" in *Revue de l'Histoire des Religions*, 1952; K. G. Kuhn, "Die Sektenschrift und die Iranische Religion" in *Zeitschr. f. Theol. und Kirche*, 1952. For recent bibliography on this subject: J. Van Der Ploeg, "Les manuscrits trouvés depuis 1947 dans le désert de Juda" in *Jaarbericht No.* 14, *Ex Oriente Lux*, 1955–6, pp. 101–2. We have pointed out, above, this theory of the two souls in Basilides and other Gnostics—pp. 23, 72, 215, 282. It is also to be found in Philo, *Questiones in Exodum*, I, 23.
[113] *Manual of Discipline*, III, 13; IV, 26.

The extinction of the group at Qumrân after A.D. 70 is an acknowledged fact. We have been wondering what became of the sectaries afterwards; and competent authors have suggested that those who did not return to orthodox Judaism may have swelled the ranks of the first Christians or of the Gnostics.[114] Can we find, in the writings we are now reading in Coptic versions, any indication that the initiates who wrote the originals may have had some links with the Qumrân group? One text—and only one—does appear, in this connection, to be susceptible of an interesting interpretation. This is the *Sacred Book of the invisible Great Spirit,* or *Gospel of the Egyptians,* which alludes to the powers sent from on high to this earth for the dispensation, to the Perfect, of the great baptisms that will assure their salvation: these are, the incorruptible Logogene; Jesus the Living, and, thirdly, a prophet named as "he in whom the Great Seth has clothed himself". With these revealers of the Gnosis are associated, moreover, the "Great Leaders", who are the Apostle James the Great and another named Theopemptos. The passage that must be quoted here is about the great Seth, or rather—as we shall recognize—the anonymous prophet indicated as his incarnation.

The text tells us that: "The great Seth came and brought his seed, and sowed it in the aeons that have been engendered and of which the number is the number of Sodom. Some say: 'Sodom is the dwelling place of the great Seth, which [or: who?] is Gomorrha.'[115] And others say: 'The great Seth took the seed of Gomorrha, and he has transplanted it to the second place which has been called Sodom!'"

---

[114] The influence of the Essenians upon the Sampsaeans is attested by Epiphanius, *Panarion*, XIX, 2. Elkesaï also had inherited their teachings; Essenian elements appear in his works. For possible relations between the Essenians and other sects, see J. Thomas, *Le mouvement baptiste en Palestine et en Syrie*; H. Grégoire, "Note sur les survivances chrétiennes des Esséniens et des sectes apparentées" in *La Nouvelle Clio*, I–II, pp. 354–9.

[115] This expression "the number of Sodom" suggests that the first lines of this passage refer to some speculation about the numerical values of the letters forming the word "Sodom"—values which, added up, would correspond to the number of "the aeons that have been engendered"; doubtless it is in the same way that we must explain the allusion to Gomorrha in the sentence "Sodom is the dwelling place of the great Seth, which [or: who?] is Gomorrha". But should we look for the solution of this in the Greek forms of the names, or in the Aramaic?

At first sight, seeing the rather mysterious context in which these sentences occur, one might think they were concerned—as are the preceding pages of the same writing—with the continuation of a cosmogony of the higher worlds, where there can be no question of anything but spiritual, immaterial entities outside our mundane history. But here two facts are to be reckoned with: first, that "the *seed* of Seth" is an expression which denotes precisely the race of the elect—that is, the sectaries themselves. Secondly, the mention of Sodom and Gomorrha —which cannot be regarded as simply mythical, unless we take it to be an antibiblical gesture like the glorification of Cain, Esau etc., by some of the extremer sects mentioned by the heresiologists[116]—seems, here, to be of quite a different nature. For it is notable that the Sethians whose writings we have here were not Gnostics of the kind most violently opposed to the Old Testament, and—even though, on occasion, they reprove the Creator and criticize Moses—they do not revere persons who in the Bible are accursed. It is not, therefore, the episodes which disgraced Sodom and Gomorrha in antiquity (*Genesis* XXVII–XXVIII) that we have to think of here.

One noteworthy fact that is known about the Essenians is that Gomorrha and Sodom were among the places where they had established colonies. All the evidence it has been possible to collect from ancient literature concerning the localities inhabited by the Essenians has by now been fully analysed and evaluated: yet too little attention has been paid to the fact that Qumrân, according to an identification formerly suggested by F. de Saulcy, was Gomorrha. Moreover, according to the evidence of Synesius of Cyrene,[117] Dion Chrysostome (who lived between A.D. 42 and 125) "has also, somewhere, praised the Essenians, who constitute quite a blessed city established near the Dead Sea in the middle region of Palestine, close to Sodom".

These details show us, not only that, at the commencement of our era, Sodom and Gomorrha had acquired a reputation for sanctity owing to the presence of these colonies of ascetics; they

---

[116] Cf., above, chap. I, note 89; chap. II, p. 76 and p. 78.
[117] In Synesius of Cyrene, *Dion*, § 3 (ed. Terzaghi, p. 240).

also indicate that these people were Essenians. Was it this group, or perhaps some other in their neighbourhood, to which the Sethians wished to connect themselves, through the tradition of which our apocryphon takes care to mention two different versions one after another?—a point which suggests that even then, when the *Gospel of the Egyptians* was composed, this tradition was evaporating into legends. The transfer of the seed of the great Seth from Gomorrha, whence he removes and transplants it to Sodom—may not this also signify some resurrection of a group which, after extinction at Qumrân, was then reconstituted further south? To admit such an interpretation—which I suggest only as a hypothesis—would confirm one in the idea that the great Seth mentioned here was, in fact, not the mythical Seth or the son of Adam, but a *real* prophet to whom our group of Gnostics owed its origin and who, following a tradition almost always respected among our initiates as it was by the Jewish mystics, hid his real identity under a greatly celebrated name. Perhaps, when our writings have been fully deciphered, the details they will disclose may permit us more nearly to identify this mysterious personage, and also to find out who were the other great masters of Gnosticism—Theopemptos, Eugnostos—whose figures are still so obscure. It is, in any case, noteworthy that none of the Gnostic doctors whom the heresiologists knew by name makes any appearance in our original writings.

GNOSTICISM AND CHRISTIANITY

One question in particular arises, which is of the highest interest. To what extent can we discover, in our Coptic writings as a whole, some legacy—or at least some echo—from the movements which were competing with Christianity at its beginning? This is a point upon which any assessment of what the new writings will reveal calls for the most delicate judgment: their variety, and the very nature of the subject, demand a minuteness of examination which can hardly be attempted before the texts are fully published.

We know the story of the false messiah, "the Egyptian" who, about A.D. 52-4, assembled four thousand Jews on the Mount of

Olives by pretending that he would cause the walls of the Holy City to crumble down before their eyes; even the *Acts of the Apostles* (XXI, 38) has put this on record. The Jewish historian Josephus himself stigmatized similar impostors who, despite sanguinary reprisals from the Romans, never ceased from stirring up the masses upon pretexts of revolution or of prophetic visions. It is not impossible that the names of "false prophet" and "antichrist", which orthodox Christianity applied to various anonymous adversaries, may in some cases have been directed against such people as those who claimed to be incarnations of the great Seth. The Nicolaitans mentioned in the Book of *Revelation* (II, 6 and 15) may, indeed, have been devotees of the Gnosticism— so similar to what we find in our Coptic writings—which the heresiologists agree in attributing to them.[118] But what are we to make of the various dissidents "given to strange doctrines", to "fables and interminable genealogies", hypocrites objecting to marriage and forbidding the normal uses of food (*I Timothy* IV, 2–3), presumptuous people who were not afraid to "insult the heavenly Glory" and delighted to "riot in the day-time", whom the *Second Epistle of Peter* (II, 17) compares to wells without water, or clouds blown along by a tempest; who promise liberty, adds the Apostle, but are themselves slaves of corruption? The *First Epistle of John* (II, 19) also rebukes these "many anti-christs . . ." who "went out from us but they were not of us"; and the *Epistle of Jude*, directed against Christians who were

---

[118] Upon this question, see the observations of H. C. Puech in *La Gnose et le Temps*, p. 109 and note 77, on the Gnostic idea that we do not have to await the resurrection—the theory that the *Second Epistle to Timothy* denounces, saying that "Hymenaeus and Philetus . . . concerning the truth have erred, saying that the resurrection is past already". H. C. Puech calls attention to this same doctrine in those ancestors of the Gnostic sects Nicolas and Menander. "This Nicolas . . . driven by an alien [diabolical] spirit, was the first to affirm that the resurrection had already come; meaning by 'resurrection' the fact that we believe in Christ and have received baptism; but he denied the resurrection of the body. And several, at his instigation, have founded sects. Among these were all the self-styled Gnostics to whom Hymenaeus and Philetus belonged. . . ." (Hippolytus, *Fragment I* of the *De Resurrectione*, preserved in Syriac, ed. Achelis, p. 251). Upon the similar opinion maintained by Menander, cf. the other references given by H. C. Puech, *loc. cit.* Ignatius of Antioch, the *Shepherd of Hermas* would furnish still further allusions to what were the first forms assumed by Gnosticism at the beginnings of Christianity.

inclined towards licentious practices, denounces those who "have gone in the way of Cain and run greedily after the error of Balaam for reward" (verse 11).

Certainly the Gnostics whose writings we now possess wanted to make Jesus one of their prophets—even the greatest of them. We m ust not forget that the Saviour preached in person, and made numerous converts, in that mysterious country of Samaria in which Dositheus, Simon and Menander were to arise soon afterwards. The notion of the Christ that our Gnostics produced for themselves enters deeply into the visions that they entertained of a world of Light existing before the Creation. Yet it is clear that although—unlike some of the sects we have heard of—they do not exalt Cain, Esau and the other accursed individuals (which would have been openly to contradict the teaching of the Apostles) they were in fact opposing Christianity by proposing a secret interpretation of it which claimed to be esoteric but was in reality distorted and factitious. How could it have been other than false, this exegesis by visionaries who, far from being wholly converted to Christianity, were still trying to force it into the framework of a mythology irreconcilable with it?

There can be no question here of reverting to the hypothesis formerly advanced by certain writers upon the relationship between Christianity and Gnosticism in general. We know the formula by which Harnack described Gnosis—"a radical and premature Hellenization of Christianity, which rejected the Old Testament". In the light of the new manuscripts, this seems to have little foundation. Lietzmann has had rather better luck, in describing it—though this again seems incorrect—as a regression of Christianity towards its origins, an extreme re-orientalization of Christianity.[119] But both these judgments would give first place to the Christian element in the formation of Gnosticism; and the relations of our sectaries with Christian doctrine look rather different. Moreover, what makes them more difficult to estimate is that they present *two different aspects*. Sometimes their revelations are put into the mouths of Zoroaster, Adam and Seth

---

[119] H. C. Puech, "Où en est le problème du Gnosticisme?" pp. 137-9, recapitulates these definitions.

and take no account whatever of the Gospels; at other times they are explicitly claiming to speak in the name of Jesus. But the writings of these two categories, although they refer to one another and endeavour to answer and to supplement each other, do not always seem able to unify their teachings into a homogeneous whole; contradictions remain. One has only to look at certain obvious seams in such composite works, to see the disparity and opposition between these two halves of their doctrine: in the *Secret Book of John*, for instance, the replacement of the Mother (as the bringer of salvation) by the Christ leads certain passages into inextricable confusion.

It cannot be denied that what constituted the primitive basis of our Gnostics' teaching is most likely to have been their collection of revelations of Zoroaster and of Seth, which, originally quite independent of Christianity, enabled them to produce their audacious speculations upon the Old Testament. But the Christian elements, some authentic, the others factitiously contrived in order to join one doctrine to another—when and how were these added to the more ancient writings? For it was from such an admixture, without the least doubt, that Gnosticism truly and definitively arose.

To bring this question to a clear conclusion, and at the same time to obtain from the Chenoboskion manuscripts the many discoveries that they promise, it will be necessary, then, to confront the new Gnostic texts with authentic Christianity from two different points of view.

The content of some of these Coptic writings is of professedly Christian inspiration; some are made up of sayings attributed to Jesus and are more or less in accord with what is reported in the canonical Gospels: but others contain a sacramental doctrine (of baptisms and eucharists), a moral teaching and an eschatology, which are all more or less strange. Some of these books could not have been fabricated by our sectaries, who did no more, at most, than adapt them. From what current of primitive Christianity were those of the former class derived, and how far are their contents legitimate? That is the first problem that must be tackled.

11

We have then to take into consideration—while allowing for all the incidental misinterpretations, variant readings and contradictions—the *whole* complex of ideas represented by this collection of writings, some under the names of ancient prophets, the rest under that of Jesus. For it was, in fact, in simultaneous reference to the *whole* content of this corpus that our sectaries believed they had arrived at a fuller and truer Christianity.

We cannot yet, of course, guess what such a study will reveal, nor can it be undertaken until after the detailed publication of the Coptic texts. But one can already point to a few fairly general and characteristic facts.

Considering the various more or less Christian apocrypha that the Chenoboskion sectaries had in use, it is a striking fact that these lay claim to the authority of certain Apostles but not of others. Nothing is assigned to the three authors of the synoptic Gospels, nor to Paul. These apocrypha are attributed to James (that "brother of the Lord" who had received secret teachings from him, and to whom our writings accord an almost supernatural status), to Thomas, to Philip, to Matthias and to John and Peter. The more original of these writings claim to impart revelations of a higher order, and are properly Gnostic. But the contents of the more ordinary ones scarcely attempt to disown the teachings of the canonical Gospels, and certain elements in them may have come from a fund of traditions that were current before the compilation of the Synoptics, all the more probably because of the fact that our Gnosticism came into being in a period when the canonical Gospels were not yet in general circulation. It now appears, then, that the problems raised by the most important of our apocrypha that are authentically Christian in doctrine will be difficult to resolve. Indeed, comparison of their contents with what are given in patristic literature as quotations from these same *Gospels* of *Thomas, Philip, Matthias* . . . seems to show that the information available to the heresiologists was liable to a good deal of confusion. It will be easier to determine how far the content of our apocrypha reproduces or carries on orthodox doctrines or, on the contrary, is composed of gross falsehoods made up by the heretics in order to propagate speculations of their own. A great deal of light has been shed upon the complexity of this mixture by Professor H. C. Puech in his preliminary study of the *Gospel of Thomas*—that collection of the "sayings of Jesus" which, more than any other of the Chenoboskion writings, may be reasonably supposed to have imbedded in it some vestiges of non-heretical Christian traditions.

From a more general point of view one could already discern, in our new writings, the chief points upon which they will provide opportunity for comparison of Gnosticism with orthodox Christianity. Firstly, a flood of light is thrown upon the strange figure that the Gnostics made of Jesus. By glossing upon the phrase "the Son of Man", our sectaries placed him in the higher world and made him the Son of the primordial Anthropos. For them, his incarnation was fictitious, and so was his crucifixion. Their teaching about the baptisms and the anointings which prepared them for the ascent towards the Light and for mystical union with the higher entities went far beyond any Christian conception and rejoined, perhaps, those of the pagan mysteries. . . . Should we look to the New Testament for points upon which to make these comparisons and connections more precise? We have already noticed the extremity to which simple allusions to the good and the bad trees (*Luke* VI, 43 etc.) were elaborated in the myths of our sectaries.[120] The *Epistle to the Hebrews* develops a symbolic interpretation of the person of Melchizedek, which prefigures the supernatural part that, according to Gnosticism, is to be played by that mysterious king of Salem. In St John, as in Gnosticism, God is Light (*John* I, 1 and *I Epistle of John* I, 5), and the Light shines in Darkness which comprehends it not. St John writes of the thirst for a living water, of a well of water springing up into everlasting life (*John* IV, 13–14 and VII, 37–8); and our heretics, similarly inspired by the sources of life, justice and wisdom in the *Book of Enoch*,[121] imagine a mystic fountain flowing in the celestial realms under the guard of great powers. When he is reporting the words of Jesus to the woman of Samaria:

---

[120] Cf. above, chap. II, note 23 and chap. V, p. 216 and note 111.
[121] *Enoch* XXII, 9; XLVIII, 1; XCVI, 6.

"Ye worship ye know not what; we know what we worship", St John (IV, 22) is expressing the very notion of Gnosis.

A rapid comparison of the new Coptic texts with the teaching of St Paul is even more eloquent. Apart from the *Apocalypse of Paul* which, from the title itself, evidently means to speak in his name, Paul is never openly named in the other treatises or revelations where, nevertheless, the influence of his teaching is shown by a number of implicit quotations! It is curious, too, to find the *Hypostasis of the Archons*, in its preamble, inserting a verse from the *Epistle to the Ephesians* (VI, 12) before beginning the exposition of a mythology which has obviously nothing more to do with Christianity. And this verse is preceded, in the Gnostic text, by these words only: "The Apostle says . . ." Why is not the name of Paul mentioned here? It is not at all from mistrust of the Apostle: if he were mistrusted his exact words would not have been thus borrowed, nor would their origin have been thus mentioned as authoritative. Is it, then, because of special respect for a master whose name it was forbidden to mention although his teaching was particularly revered.[122] One may well think so, for our sectaries kept in their collection a treatise, under the title of the *Teachings of Silvanus* (No. 29), which they meant, no doubt, to attribute to one of the principal colleagues of the Apostle.

One is immediately struck by the fact that the Christianity taught by St Paul—who himself claimed to have had the benefit of heavenly revelations—is yet nearer than that of John, to the speculations of our Gnostics. One could almost believe one had detected Gnosticism in Paul, when he appeals to "the Wisdom of God in a mystery, even the hidden Wisdom which God ordained before the world unto our glory; and which none of the princes [*word for word* 'of the archons'] of this world [*word for word* 'of this aeon'] have known" (*I Corinthians* II, 7–8). One also feels in him

[122] Cf. the importance assigned to St Paul by the Manichaeans: *Kephalaion I*, p. 13, line 19 and onwards (in the *Manichaïsche Handschriften der staatlichen Museen*, Berlin, 1940). We must also remember the prestige of Paul among the Paulicians, who christened their churches with the names of the Churches formerly founded by the Apostle; and assumed, as their own surnames, the names of Paul's companions; cf. S. Runciman, *The Medieval Manichee*.

the accents of an opposition to the Law no less decided than the anti-biblicism that animates our sectaries: it is through the Law that we come by the knowledge of sin (*Romans* III, 20); it is the Law that produces wrath; where there is no Law there is no transgression (*Romans* IV, 15; *Colossians* II, 22); it is from the *curse of the Law* that Christ has redeemed us (*Galatians* III, 13); the commandments of the Law are even described as "*a ministration of death* written and engraven in stones" in opposition to the New Law, "a ministration of the Spirit" (*II Corinthians* III, 7). The Gnostics classify men into three categories: the hylic, the psychic and the spiritual; and Paul admits the two more important of these; he opposes the spiritual to the psychic: "It is sown a psychic body; it is raised up a spiritual body. There is a psychic body, and there is a spiritual body. And so it is written: the first man, Adam, was made a living *soul*; the last man was made a vivifying spirit. Howbeit, that was not first which was spiritual, but that which is psychic; and afterwards that which is spiritual. The first man is of the earth, earthy; the second anthropos comes from heaven" (*I Corinthians* XV, 44-7). And that distinction is applicable to the whole of this humanity of which we are members. God "hath chosen us in him before the foundation of the world, that we should be holy and without blame before him in love; having predestinated us unto the adoption of children by Jesus Christ, to himself, according to the good pleasure of his will" (*Ephesians* I, 4-5). And Paul not only speaks of the Prince of this world—the Prince of Darkness—and his powers; he also uses the opposition between the Darkness and the Light: "For ye were sometimes darkness, but now are ye light in the Lord: walk as children of the light . . ." (*Ephesians* V, 8). Indeed, for the understanding of our Gnostics' teachings, Paul's definition of the Saviour in *Colossians* (I, 15-20) should be cited in full: "Who is the image of the invisible God, the firstborn of every creature: for by him were all things created, that are in heaven, and that are in earth, visible and invisible, whether they be thrones, or dominions, or principalities, or powers: all things were created by him, and for him: and he is the head of the body, the church: who is the beginning, the firstborn from the dead;

that in all things he might have the preeminence. For it pleased the Father that in him should all fulness [*word for word* 'the Pleroma'] dwell. And, having made peace through the blood of his cross, by him to reconcile all things unto himself: by him, I say, whether they be things in earth, or things in heaven." Is it a piece of Gnostic mythology that Paul is expounding here? One could almost believe it, when one reads moreover, elsewhere, that he is professing to reveal the "mystery which hath been hid from ages and from generations, [*word for word* 'from the aeons'] but now is made manifest to his saints, to whom God would make known what is the riches of the glory of this mystery . . ." (*Colossians* I, 26-7).

But we must take care to note that, with Paul, all this leads to conclusions absolutely opposite to those of the Gnostics. This is no Gnosis that he is preaching; what he is exalting is a wisdom and a grace accessible to all, Jews or pagans. The election of the sons of light is explained by him as predestination. The Law of Moses is an evil—yes; but for man, and because man has fallen. Paul denies absolutely that the Creator bears the responsibility for the original sin committed by Eve and Adam. There is no trace of Docetism in his conception of the Christ, whose blood was, in reality, shed upon the Cross. Lastly, as a moralist Paul emphatically upholds the human duty of respect for the body, which the Gnostics so often despise and defile. The speculations of Paul take their departure from the same mystical themes as those of our sectaries; but these are interpreted by him in the opposite sense.

What, then, is the meaning of these undeniable parallelisms that we have found between the subjects discussed by Paul and those developed by our sectaries? Firstly, that in fact the Gnostics we have brought to light evolved their Christianity largely from an interpretation of the New Testament which was their own. And their interpretation, far from being the product of wild imagination, as at first sight one might suppose, must have been the result of exegesis, *literal* to the point of falsification, applied to the smallest details and biased by Kabbalistic speculations. In that way they had formerly interpreted the Old Testament, meticulously extracting from it scriptural evidences for their opposition to the God of *Genesis*. Thus, from the pronouncement of the Lord of the Law: "I am a jealous God",[123] they drew the conclusion that he was a second-class god; for, otherwise, of whom could he be jealous? "I have gotten a man from [with the help of] the Lord", says Eve after the birth of Cain,[124] from which our Gnostics found reason to believe that the Creator himself had seduced Eve and directly begotten from her the first posterity of mankind. And, in reading "For God hath appointed me *another seed instead of Abel*",[125] a saying of Eve about the birth of Seth, they took it to mean that he was of a different generation, superior to Cain and Abel. The extent to which such exegesis was resorted to, even by authentic Christians, can be exemplified from Paul himself, though he uses the method, indeed, with a very different discernment. But here is his comment upon the 18th verse of Psalm LXVIII: "*When he ascended on high, he led captivity captive and he gave gifts to men*. Now that he ascended, what is it but that he also descended first into the lower parts of the earth? He that descended is the same also that ascended up far above all heavens, that he might fill all things." (*Ephesians* IV, 8–9).

Similar methods of interpretation were familiar to Judaism, even before the allegorical method of the Greek commentators on the *Odyssey*, adapted to Biblical studies by a Philo, had come to equip the practitioners of this artifice with inexhaustible resources of symbology, together with a suppleness of dialectic akin to acrobatics.

Only when we have made allowance for their resort to these procedures do we realize that there is much less disagreement than one had thought at first, between the conceptions that our Gnostics deduced from the Old Testament and those they extracted from the New. One can even, in the end, understand how this literalism enabled them to build up a curious Christianity which was, after all, in harmony the main body of Gnostic conceptions, even with those whose presence is not apparent at first sight.

[123] *Isaiah* XLV, 5–6; and XLVI, 9.   [124] *Genesis* IV, 1.
[125] *Genesis* IV, 25.

CHAPTER VII

THE SURVIVAL OF GNOSTICISM: FROM MANICHAEISM TO THE ISLAMIC SECTS

To give an adequate idea of the extent of the Gnostic movement, of the impulses that swept from one end of the Mediterranean to the other, disseminating scriptures and mythologies more or less similar to those of our Upper Egyptian initiates, one would have to recall the human and historical circumstances in which all this came to pass—in Alexandria, Antioch, Jerusalem, Seleucia-Ctesiphon, Edessa. . . . We should have to evoke the life of, for example, that city of Dura-Europos where archaeology has now had the good fortune to discover, side by side, sanctuaries of all the different kinds of public worship of which the Gnostic cults were, in part, an esoteric and syncretic interpretation. There, were found the Mithraeum, the temples of Adonis, of Zeus-Theos, of Gaddae, of Artemis-Nannaïa; a Jewish synagogue with its paintings still well preserved; a Christian chapel. At the other end of the Mediterranean world we should have to extend our pilgrimage into Rome—Rome, where the subsoil conceals sanctuaries no less various and curious in juxtaposition. Above all, our survey would have to include still other groups and sects that I have passed over in silence. It would have to summarize the Gnosis of Bardesanes;[1] to include the Priscillans who spread from Spain to the south of Gaul in the second half of the fourth century;[2] to mention the Messalians (less Gnostic and more Christian, whose belief that a demon dwells in every man continued the Basilidean doctrine of the *two souls* which they afterwards bequeathed to the Bogomils);[3] and also to recall the

---

[1] Cf. Nau, *Bardesane l'astrologue*; Burkitt, *Religion of the Manichees*, pp. 75–9.

[2] The Priscillianist treatises of Wurtzburg, edited by Schepps, in the *Corpus scriptorum ecclesiasticorum latinorum* 18, in 1899 contain allusions to the myths of our Gnostics.

[3] The ancient texts relating to the Messalians are collected and translated in the preamble to the *Liber Graduum*, edited by M. Kmosko in the *Patrologia*

epic of the Paulician sect of Armenia and Asia Minor, which lasted from the eighth to the twelfth century.[4]

Despite its wide diffusion, Gnosticism was bound to suffer the consequences of the triumph of the Church, and gradually to efface itself. We have seen what pains the Christian doctors took to refute the sects and, above all, to suppress the writings by which their doctrines were propagated. Whether to make themselves more persuasive, or the better to escape persecution, the most important of our great apocalypses arrayed themselves in Christian guise: in the *Sophia of Jesus* and the *Secret Book of John*, we have admired striking examples of such camouflage. Thus it was that some portions of Gnostic myths—chiefly of celestial and infernal visions and some legends about Adam and his descendants—were able to survive in several languages, in spite of the many prohibitions that the Church pronounced against them. The sects had a hard life of it. The Borborites—whom Epiphanius and Theodoret knew and catalogued as one of the sects related to those very Gnostics whose writings we have now recovered—were established as far away as Persia: under Justinian II (685–95) they returned from thence into Syria and Armenia.[5] The picturesque accounts of Theodore Bar-Konaï give us glimpses of Gnostics who would seem to have been much like those of Chenoboskion, persisting obstinately into the eighth century, the period in which the Audians re-established themselves and were using the same sacred books. And indeed, under other forms—those of sects whose remote situation or sturdy organization separated or shielded them from the Christian Church—Gnosticism was to survive much longer; though its history remains very obscure. It is chiefly visible in the great movements of the Paulicians, the Bogomils and the Cathars, though it appears in groups of lesser importance: we may mention one that arose near Soissons about 1125 around Clement de Bucy (and which, like

Syriaca; pars prima, vol. III, 1926. An aberrant sect, that of the Satanians, is described by Epiphanius, *Panarion*, heresy LXXX. Upon the demonic soul in every man: Runciman, *Medieval Manichee*; among the Bogomils, Puech and Vaillant, *Le Traité contre les Bogomiles* . . . , p. 200, note 4.

[4] Cf. S. Runciman, *Medieval Manichee*, chap. III.

[5] Cf. Bareille, article "Borboriens" in the *Dictionnaire de Théologie catholique*, vol. II; Runciman, *loc. cit.*, p. 32; Puech and Vaillant, *loc. cit.*, pp. 306–7.

our Gnostics, held procreation to be a disgrace). Another was formed in the vicinity of St Malo about 1140, by Eudes de l'Étoile, who presented himself as an aeon sent down from on high. All these heretics were summarily classed by their contemporaries as Manichaeans, and history has, in part, endorsed these opinions. In many cases, however, a comparison of their doctrines with the newly-found Coptic texts shows that they were authentic inheritors of our ancient Gnostics.[6]

Organized as a church, on strictly hierarchic lines, the Manichaeans[7] were able to spread their very similar beliefs to the eastern limits of Asia as well as to western Europe, where the Albigenses were their last successors. The Manichaeans, a great many of whose writings have been recovered, followed Gnostic practice in attributing their revelations to Zoroaster, to Seth and to Jesus; to whom they added, as prophets, the Buddha and above all, of course, Manes their founder. They intensified the Iranian dualism of which the Gnostics had made use before them; and by re-thinking it in the countries of its origin, revitalized it.

What did this owe to Gnosticism? Surely we cannot take at their face value the observations of Augustine and Cyril of Jerusalem, to the effect that the doctrine of Manes was connected with that of the Ophites. But Franz Cumont has already pointed out all those features by which Manichaeism resembles the doctrines of, for example, Basilides—which, as we have seen, are so near to those of our Gnostics. Basilides had composed a commentary on the canonical Gospels in twenty-four books; and Manes wrote another—the *Living Gospel*—in twenty-two books. The Docetism of the two systems was similar: Basilides taught that the Christ, far from dying upon the Cross, had caused Simon of Cyrene to perish there in his stead: and in Manichaeism, it was

---

[6] Cf. Runciman, *loc. cit.*, pp. 109–10.

[7] Upon Manichaeism, cf. H. C. Puech, " Le Manichéisme" in the *Histoire Générale des Religions*, ed. M. Gorce and R. Mortier (volume devoted to Indo-Iranians . . . Judaism . . .), 1945, pp. 85–116 and 446–9; by the same author, *Le Manichéisme, son fondateur, sa doctrine*, 1949; Burkitt, *Religion of the Manichees*, 1925; Jonas, *loc. cit.*, vol. I, pp. 284–320; Puech and Vaillant, *Le traité contre les Bogomiles* . . . , 1925 includes a fully-developed exposition of the Bogomil doctrines compared with those of other neo-Manichaean movements; cf. Runciman, *Medieval Manichee*, 1949.

the Prince of Darkness himself whom Jesus caused to be nailed writhing upon the gibbet. In regard to the Baptism, at which they thought the Christ had been substituted for the human person of Jesus, Manes and Basilides were in agreement.[8]

Today, the new Coptic writings illustrate both the *authentically Gnostic* character of the Basilidean doctrine and, in more detail, the close dependence of Manichaeism upon that same form of Gnosticism. The myths that Manichaeism transcribed are to be found in many of the revelations in use among our Coptic sectaries. To quote at random—here is the monstrous figure of Ialdabaôth-Sacla;[9] here is the description of the trees of Paradise, one of which becomes the tree of death;[10] of the creation of Adam, member by member, by the Archons, and their vain efforts to vitalize him; here are the successions of enlighteners and saviours including Shem, Seth and Nicotheus; the salvation of souls, effected by a transmigration through the world of the spheres, by the Sun and the Moon and the Virgin of Light, who purify the lights scattered here below and raise them up again into the heavenly Treasury;[11] and, lastly, the account of the final consummation of the universe.[12]

Manichaeism not only drew upon Gnosticism but also upon Christianity: its texts give us the names of the books on which it relied, and—to our surprise!—here are the same writings, given under the names of Thomas, of Philip and Matthias—just those that our sectaries also used. The discovery, in Coptic, of the originals of these hitherto lost writings, enables us to see just how far our Gnostics' literature is representative of the repertory of writings upon which the Manichaeans relied as models. So it was, indeed, from sects analogous to the one whose library was buried

[8] Franz Cumont, "A propos des écritures manichéennes" in the *Revue de l'Histoire des Religions*, LXXXI, 1920, pp. 40–1. Cf. also Cumont, *Recherches . . .*, p. 10, note 3; cf., lastly, our own article "Le Refus de la Croix" in *La Table Ronde*, Dec. 1957.
[9] Cf. above, chap. v, note 30 and H. C. Puech, "Le Prince des Ténèbres et son royaume."
[10] Cf. above, chap. v, pp. 216–17.
[11] Cf. above, chap. ii, note 24.
[12] See H. C. Puech, *Le Manichéisme, son fondateur sa doctrine*, pp. 84–5; J. Doresse, "L'Apocalypse manichéenne" in *La Table Ronde*, No. 110, Feb. 1957, pp. 40–7.

at the foot of the Gebel et-Tarif that the religion of Manes derived its primary elements.

Undoubtedly! See, moreover, how the most legendary of all the traditional origins ascribed to Manichaeism henceforth takes on a precise historical—or at least symbolical—meaning![13] We find it—this malevolent little story—in the *Acts of Archelaüs*, in which Basilides is quoted at such length. Here it is:

A personage named Scythianus—a "Saracen"—whom we may place somewhere in the second century, believed in a kind of Christianity with which he associated the myth of the two opposite principles. He married a slave whom he had redeemed from one of the places of ill-fame that were swarming in Upper Egypt,[14] and she persuaded him to come to live in her native country, the Thebais. There he learned the "wisdom of the Egyptians" (?) and made a disciple named Terebinth to whom he dictated four books—the *Mysteries*, the *Principles*, the *Treasure* and the *Gospel* (titles of known works, attributed to Manes). He then went to Judaea, but died after arriving there. Terebinth then took refuge in Babylonia: he pretended to have been born of a virgin, to have been fed by angels upon the mountains, and that his name was Buddha. His prestige as a prophet earned him the hospitality of a rich widow, at whose house he died, by falling off a roof. The old woman afterwards purchased a child named Corbicius and had him educated: he presumably received from her the four books that Terebinth had had from Scythianus; and, made rich by these revelations, he changed his name, and became known as Manes. . . .

Such is the story in the *Acts of Archelaüs*. It affirms a mythical

---

[13] According to Manes' own account, this is how the doctrine he taught was revealed to him: "Wisdom and good works have always been revealed to the world by the messengers of God. Thus, at one time, they were brought to India by the emissary named Buddha; at another by Zoroaster to Persia, at yet another by Jesus to the West. Lastly this present revelation has come down, this prophecy has been manifested in this greatest age, by me, Manes, messenger from the God of truth in the land of Babylon" (beginning of the *Shâpurakân*, translated by Cumont in *Recherches* . . . , p. 52). Upon the Gnostic and baptist movements with which Manes seems to have been in contact; Puech, *Le Manichéisme, son fondateur, sa doctrine* . . . , p. 70, notes 145–56 and 268–70.

[14] In the town of Hypsele, immediately to the south of Assiut, according to Epiphanius, *Panarion*, LXVI, 2.

relation between Manichaeism and an authentic Gnosticism—a mixture of dualism and Christianity—which an adept had followed in the Thebais; and that is not too much out of line with what we learn from comparison of the Coptic writings of our Sethians with those of the Manichaeans. This novelette would be still more edifying if our Scythianus had been called *Sethianus*— the Sethian. But let us be content with what we are explicitly given!

The baptist sect of the Mandaeans—the so-called Christians of St John—still exists today, though its adherents are few, in Lower Mesopotamia.[15] The formation of the books it has now in use seems to date from a late epoch; and in these numerous writings Gnostic doctrines are mixed with almost pagan myths. This sect does not scruple to set the revealers and prophets of its doctrines —Hibil (Abel), Shitil (Seth), Anosh (Enoch?)—these are the three "Uthra"—and John the Baptist, in opposition to the Old Testament prophets and also to Jesus, whom they represent as a teacher of falsehoods whom Anosh–Uthra denounced to the Jews. Thanks to the new Coptic texts, we shall now be better able to judge how far these Mandaean writings were derived from genuinely Gnostic literature—or whether both currents flowed from a common source.

These Mandaeans of Lower Mesopotamia are also, sometimes, called *Sabians*. The serious inconvenience of applying this name to them is that it may confuse them with a homonymous but quite different sect, devoted to the worship of the planets, which flourished at the height of the Middle Ages, particularly around the city of Harran, a little to the south of Edessa. The Sabians of Upper Mesopotamia spoke the Syriac language. They attracted the special notice of Islamic authors. They recognize as prophets Enoch, assimilated to Idris; Hermes; Seth the son of Adam, whom they identified with the Agathodaïmon of Greek Hermetic

---

[15] Cf. H. C. Puech, "Le Mandéisme" in *Histoire Générale des Religions*, ed. Gorce and Mortier, pp. 67–83 and 444–6; J. Schmitt, article "Mandéisme" in *Dictionnaire de la Bible*, Supplement IV, cols. 758–88; E. S. Drower, *The Mandaeans of Iraq and Iran*, 1937; E. Peterson, "Urchristentum und Mandäismus" in *Zeitschr. f.d. Neutestamentliche Wissenschaft* XXVII, pp. 55–98. Cf. also Widengren, *Stand und Aufgaben* . . . , pp. 120ff.; T. Save-Söderberg, *Studies in the Coptic Manichaean Psalm-book, Prosody, and Mandaean Parallels*, Uppsala, 1949, chap. VI.

literature; and also Asclepius. These are names that remind one well enough of the mixture of mystical literatures that we have found among our ancient Gnostics.

An exposition of the doctrines of these Sabians by El-Khâtibi describes, in the following terms, the descent of the soul and then its return to the spiritual world (we make use of Chwolsohn's translation of this):

"The soul turned, at one time, towards Matter: she fell in love with it, and, burning with desire to experience bodily pleasures, wished no more to be separated from it. Thus the world was born. From that moment the soul forgot herself; she forgot her original dwelling, her true centre, her everlasting life. . . . But God, unwilling to abandon the soul to its degradation with Matter, endowed her with understanding and the faculty of perception—precious gifts which would remind her of her high origin, the spiritual world . . . , which would restore her consciousness of herself, teach her that she was a stranger here below. . . . As soon as the soul has thus been taught by perception and understanding, as soon as she has regained self-consciousness, she longs for the spiritual world as a man exiled in a strange land sighs for his distant homestead. She is convinced that, to regain her original state, she must loose herself from the ties of this world, from carnal concupiscences, from all material things."[16]

We ought also, perhaps, to mention the Yezidis—the Druses—so-called worshippers of the devil, established in the mountains where numbers of Judeo-Christians took refuge in the first centuries of our era. The image of a serpent appears, sculptured upon the portals of their sanctuaries; and their doctrine contains a good deal of Gnosticism.[17] We must at least name the Ahl-i-Haqq, or "men of God" in Western Persia.[18] There are also the

[16] Besides the work of D. Chwolsohn, *Die Ssabier und der Ssabismus*, St Petersburg, 1856, cf. the bibliography to the art. on "al-Sâbi'a" in the *Encyclopédie de l'Islam*. The text we quote from Chwolsohn's translation has been commented upon by Jonas, *Gnosis . . .*, vol. I, pp. 334–5 and by H. C. Puech in *Le Manichéisme . . .*, note 278.

[17] Cf. in the *Encyclopédie de l'Islam*, the article "Yazîdî" and its bibliography. See also the articles by G. Furlani, "L'Antidualismo dei Yezidi" in *Orientalia* XIII, 1944, pp. 266–7, and "Il Pavone e gli 'Utre ribelli presso i Mandei e il Pavone dei Yezidi", S.M.S.R. XXI, 1947–8.

[18] Cf. in the *Encyclopédie de l'Islam*, the article "Ahl-I Hakk".

Bekhtashis, whose founder came from Khorassan in the thirteenth century: the last monastery in the possession of these mystics is at Cairo, where it stands, half-asleep amid gardens on the flank of the white cliffs of Moqattam, at the entrance to an immense cave extending into the mountain, in whose shadows are ranged the sepulchres of saints.[19]

Within Islam itself some of the most important of the Gnostic traditions spread, and have been perpetuated until this day, more especially in the same regions where Gnosticism had originally been able to germinate. Here, it is true, one must make one reservation: a good deal of the mythology about Adam, Seth and Zoroaster . . . which has survived in Islam as well as in a number of oriental Christian legends, is simply taken from apocrypha which have no marked religious tendency and which, if they ever came from Gnosticism, have lost all religious character.

These are stories from, for instance, the cycle of narratives concerned with the Cave of Treasures, from certain Talmudic treatises, from the *Pirqé Rabbi Eli'ezer*, etc. . . .[20] But Islam also retains some remnants of myths which are authentically traceable to Gnostic origins. There are the fantastic places, such as the Mountain of Qâf—the cosmic mountain that the soul must pass over to attain to the Source of Life, near to which Elijah and the mysterious Khezr keep watch.[21] There is also a tradition that Seth was the first man who could be described, in the Syriac language, by the term *ûriyâ*, "master", a word that recalls the Hebrew *'ôr*, "light",[22] and also evokes for us that name Hôrea which is sometimes applied to Nôrea, the mystical sister of Seth in our Coptic writings. Lastly, the myth of the *Ascension of Mahomet* through the heavens very exactly perpetuates one of the favourite themes of our Gnostics. One feels this still more when, in the miniatures with which this work is sometimes illustrated, one sees the prophet passing through the circles of the

[19] See, in the *Encyclopédie de l'Islam*, the article "Báktâshîya".
[20] References in the *Encyclopédie de l'Islam*, article "Adam".
[21] Cf. Henry Corbin, *L'Imagination créatrice dans le soufisme d'Ibn Arabi*, Paris, 1958; p. 48 and plate facing p. 94.
[22] References in the *Encyclopédie de l'Islam*, article "Shîth".

celestial spheres, like our prophet Shem in the *Paraphrase* attributed to him.[23]

In the Islamic world the preservation of such features, and even of more important myths, was notably favoured by the creation of a vast Arab literature of Hermetic inspiration mingled with alchemical, astrological and cosmological myths derived from very various sources.[24] We cannot even outline the history of this Islamized Hermeticism and of its copious literature. The mystical currents that inspired it were joined, for example, by that of Sufism, thanks to the person of Suhrawardi of Aleppo (after 1191) who drew as much from Platonism as from traditions transmitted in the name of Hermes, and of that Agathodaïmôn who was identified with Seth. But it is not to any personality nor to any celebrated work that we will now allude; the text I wish to quote belongs to the most anonymous and the most unblushingly apocryphal kind of Arab Hermetic literature. It is a treatise fictively ascribed to *Balinus*—a name which disguised that of Apollonius of Tyana. This work, which seems to have been composed in Syria in the eleventh century, pretends to record the discovery of a hidden book entitled *The Secret of the Creation and the Knowledge of the principles of things*. On reading it, one perceives that its content is, in reality, attributed to Hermes: right at the end of this writing we find a chapter, of only a few pages "Upon the Creation of Man".[25] Not very long ago Reitzenstein had already divined the special interest of this text, though he had not then at his disposal any terms of comparison so instructive as our writings from Chenoboskion.[26]

It is Hermes, then, who is supposed to sum up this chapter "Upon the Creation of Man". And this is how he reports the genesis of that being, whom he calls Adamânoûs, the Form of Forms:

[23] Cf. Widengren, *Muhammad the Apostle of God and his Ascension*, 1955.
[24] Cf. L. Massignon, *Inventaire de la littérature hermétique arabe*, published as an appendix to Festugière, *La Révélation d'Hermès Trismégiste*, vol. I, 1. Cf. also H. Ritter, "Picatrix, ein Handbuch Hellenistischer Magie" in *Vorträge der Bibliothek Warburg*, 1921; and J. Ruska, *Tabula Smaragdina . . .*, 1926.
[25] Cf. Ruska, "Kazwînî Studien" in *Der Islam*, vol. IV, 1913, pp. 51ff.; the same author's *Tabula Smaragdina*, p. 147; Kraus, *Jabir ibn Hayyan*, II, pp. 270ff.
[26] Reitzenstein related this with the Naassene doctrine, in Reitzenstein-Schaeder, *Studien . . .*, pp. 112–16.

When the heavenly Virgin had come to power, and when the planets, having been set in motion, were all in exaltation with the exception of Saturn; they conceived the idea of a bodily creation in which their spiritual nature could find expression. By this act of will, a powerful spirit was produced, a pure angel named Hâroûs (?) whom the Virgin clothed with power. He descended to earth; he took three hundred and sixty spirits from the forces and from the spiritual essence of the higher heaven, from the seven planets, from the zodiac and from the earth. He assembled and mingled these spirits, to make them into the first man, after a pattern from the highest heaven. This was Adamânoûs, and Hâroûs let the forces of the Archons flow into him. Thus formed, Adamânoûs was without blemish, but he was still like an animal: he understood nothing, knew nothing; and could not speak. Then Hâroûs heightened his efforts right up to the stars that were withholding understanding, thought and speech, until they allowed these emanations to flow into him.

When this first terrestrial man had been completely created, he raised his eyes towards Hâroûs: that angel was an immense creature who could reach with his hands to each of the planets or to any sign of the zodiac. Adamânoûs, upon seeing him, was filled with admiration—although the first man himself was colossal enough, since he could take hold of the clouds and could hear the sound made by the rotation of the spheres and the motions of the stars. But while the man was thus rapt in contemplation, the angelic creator touched him on the side and, by that gesture, created Haivânoûs, a feminine form that he placed beside Adamânoûs. The sight of his companion filled man with pleasure: he turned away from the contemplation of Hâroûs, and he and Haivânoûs procreated many men. Then Hâroûs taught him a language—does this mean Syriac?

Saturn had seen this creation taking place under the authorization of the heavenly Virgin; and his desire was to destroy both macrocosm and microcosm. But Hâroûs, out of the highest heaven, brought down three powers who chained up the power of the perverse planet. At the same time the evil spirits were bound to the four corners of the macrocosm: it is when they are writhing in their bonds that the earth quakes. Hâroûs afterwards took three hundred and sixty spiritual natures from the planets and from the zodiac to make them into all the kinds of animals and insects: in the first place, he made the useful creatures and then, from the scraps left over, he made the harmful ones; after which he led them all before the first man and gave him instructions about them. . . . Each animal was intimately related with one of the stars. At last Hâroûs announced to Adamânoûs that he was about to return to the highest heaven. "People the earth with thy descendants", he said, "and hand down to them the arts that I have taught thee." Then the first man and the first woman united to procreate fourteen children—seven sets of twins, each pair consisting of a boy and a girl. The planets shared in endowing these children with their respective natures and colours, whilst Hâroûs divided the seven regions of the globe between them—the seven climates.

The writing thus disguised under the name of Hermes and then dressed up again in the authority of "Balinus" is the misrepresentation of a mixture of cosmogonic elements, Hermetic, Iranian and Judaizing—or, more likely, Gnostic, although different from what our Coptic writings disclose. Here we do recognize, however, certain features such as the weakness of Adam immediately after his creation; according to the Sethians he was unable to stand upright when the Archons had moulded him to shape; here he is unable to think or to speak when Hâroûs has perfected his body. We recognize also the evil, destructive part assigned to Saturn—that is, to Ialdabaoth. But who, exactly, is the Virgin at the beginning of this creation and who is this Hâroûs who plays the part of the demiurge? These are questions that only the eventual discovery of a new cosmology inspired by Gnosticism is likely to elucidate.

Seth—as we have seen—is known in Islam, and usually assimilated to Agathodaïmôn, who is one of the great figures of Hermetic literature. The prophetic prestige with which the Gnostics endowed him, he still possesses, especially in the traditions of various Shi'ite groups, therefore chiefly in Mesopotamia or in Iran. In these particular doctrines the survival of

Gnostic themes is ubiquitous and seems immense; but it is a subject that would demand reference to a mass of mystical texts to which, as yet, only specialists have access. How can one indicate the outstanding sects and names? I am able to deal with this literature only in a very incompetent and summary fashion; and will do no more than cite, by way of example, a few points in the beliefs of one of the most important movements—the well-known sect of the Isma'ilites. Their doctrine is genuinely Gnostic.[27] But does it go back to our Gnostics of antiquity? Not only do these sectaries regard Adam as the first of the prophets; they also make Abraham the head of the generation of the Perfect, to which Zoroaster belonged. One of their writings, which dates from about the year 1300, announces that at the resurrection Melchizedek will come as a judge, and that he will then reveal the divine mysteries which the prophets have kept secret during the entire period in which humanity was subject to the religious law. The author of another treatise, of the fifteenth century, adds that Melchizedek is identical with Seth.[28]

Thus the fact is established that Manichaeism, the doctrine which lived on well into the Middle Ages and spread from the extremities of Asia to those of Europe, whose indirect influences still made themselves felt in the Ethiopian Christianity of the fifteenth century, has not been the only survival from Gnosticism nor even the most enduring. For Gnosis has perpetuated itself in forms that are more subtle, but present throughout the Mohammedan East—that is, in the very world where Gnosticism was born. One need hardly be surprised at this. We may add that a historian of the religion and letters of the Mohammedan Middle East would undoubtedly find there, in many centuries, the same complex spiritual currents which, flowing from the Iranian regions, from Mesopotamia, Syria and Palestine carried

[27] Cf. this article "Ismâ'ilîya" in the *Encyclopédie de l'Islam*; and, above all, as introduction to the numerous texts edited and prefaced by Henry Corbin, his study, "De la Gnose antique à la Gnose ismaélienne" in *Convegno di Scienze morali, storiche e filologiche*, May–June 1956; Accademia Nazionale dei Lincei, Fondazione Al. Volta, Rome, 1957, pp. 105ff.

[28] G. Vajda, "Melchisédech dans la mythologie ismaélienne" in the *Journal Asiatique* CCXXXIV, 1943–5, pp. 173ff.

towards the Mediterranean all the diverse elements which united to become Gnosticism.

Is this to say that Gnosticism has survived in the Orient until this day, but has had no revivals in the Occident since the time when the Albigensian movement was extirpated? That would be an exaggeration. For certainly some speculations about Adam and his descendants have lingered on here and there. One can indeed see their reappearance in the preoccupations of the eighteenth century when, after the outbreak of controversies over the reliability of the Bible as history,[29] some people were worried about the disagreements between parts of the Old Testament and, in that connection, about the moral meaning of original sin and the legitimacy of the curse pronounced upon Adam and his posterity, after the first man had been expelled from Eden.

Among the Hermetists fairly precise traditions remained well enough known. At first sight one might think some of these were traceable to the ancient Gnostics; but they came more simply by way of the alchemical literature—Byzantine or Arab—or, thanks to the exegeses of Zosimos, of Olympiodorus and other mystics, from the echoes of certain apocryphal traditions. Some, too, were conserved in Jewish Kabbalistic sources of relatively easy access. In these ways there developed, in our Western world, from the fourteenth to the eighteenth century essentially, an extensive alchemical iconography which illustrates some definitely Gnostic and Hermetic themes.[30] And thus, undoubtedly, were handed down the semi-Gnostic themes that were used by a Martinez de Pasqually in his theurgy.[31] The same is true, also, of the fantasies of a Vintras. Moreover, the dualism that lies at the root of Gnosticism, of its symbols and images, is a sentiment that can awaken in certain souls without their having necessarily received

[29] Cf. Paul Hazard, *Lan Pensée européenne au XVIIIème siècle*, vol. I, p. 105; vol. II, pp. 49 and 133ff. (English trans., *European Thought in the Eighteenth Century*, London, 1954).

[30] Cf. C. G. Jung, *Psychology and Alchemy*, vol. XII of that author's Collected Works, London 1953; especially valuable for its rich array of illustrations.

[31] R. Le Forestier, *La Franc-Maçonnerie occultiste au XVIIIème siècle et l'ordre des Élus Coens*, 1928.

any such tradition whatever. The German romantics—Novalis especially[32]—and the French romantics to a lesser degree (with the exception of Gérard de Nerval), furnish ample proof of this; and one cannot pretend that they were really reviving a Gnosticism that they had never known. The most authentic Gnosticism is, in fact—and today we have access to it—that which is to be found in the long-lost writings that the sands of Egypt have at last happily restored to us.

[32] Cf. Maryla Falk, *I "Misteri" di Novalis*, Naples, 1938.

EPILOGUE

THUS it was that I was able to gain the knowledge of a number of extraordinary Gnostic writings; and, more fortunate (or was it less so?) than Epiphanius, I did not even have to withstand the charms of the beautiful heretics of Upper Egypt. One earthen pot suddenly enriched us with more than forty writings we can decipher, and that we shall be able, when they are published, to study at leisure.

Of all that I have read of these texts—inspired by the ardour of the Orient, its afflictions and its droughts, by the very sight of its nocturnal skies so much more eloquent than ours—I have given a description that is hurried, yet accurate in so far as was possible for me to examine them. I have preferred to give, before my description of what the new discovery contains, a survey of our previous knowledge of this subject of Gnosticism. In that first part of the book I have tried to give due prominence to the remarkable results which our eminent scholars, before these Chenoboskion writings were available, were able to obtain from a documentation still so poor in reliable elements and so rich in misleading and disappointing information. From the new documents we shall obtain not only verification of things which, by those means, we already had glimpses of: a whole religious universe, hitherto only suspected, is beginning to swim into our ken.

From the new texts, Gnosticism becomes a good deal better definable, as the product of a powerful incursion of the great Iranian myths into Jewish mysticism, which was itself nourished by both Greek and Chaldaean philosophical and mystical influences. Thus it was that, from prophets whose identity was carefully concealed, a body of sacred literature grew up under the two imputed authorities of Zoroaster and Seth. Was Christianity only coming to birth, or was it already born, when the first stages of this synthesis took place? Perhaps the sects through

324

whom this genesis was effected assumed attitudes of rivalry towards it? But it was Christianity which acted upon *them*: it invaded Gnosticism and, very soon, found itself there incorporated, but also deformed and, as it were, astray in a land of strange gods. Did this seething mixture (of which a Valentinus and a Basilides were, when all is said, the most moderate of interpreters) tend to the weakening of Gnosticism? Or did it, on the other hand, provide Gnosticism with reasons for leading a parasitic life wherever the religion of Christ was progressing, and thereby enable it to outgrow its Oriental limitations and spread to the ends of the Mediterranean world? The case of Manichaeism, which pushed to the most radical conclusions a mixture of several official religions and of Christianity, with its own Gnostic dogmas, has shown what strength may come from such an alliance. Nevertheless, it is probably that what is most authentic in the Sethian religion, in the Judaized dualism which is the essence of it, is also what survives most obstinately in the lands where it was born—those lands where Islam also came into existence. And it is in highly heterodox Islamic quarters that Gnostic themes have managed to survive until today; perhaps reverting there to their original structure.

Thus considered, Gnosticism reveals itself less as a cloudy doctrine, whose literature is a veritable museum of errors, and more as the creation of anonymous seers, visionaries ardently meditating upon a specific mythology, endlessly educing from it images of hell and heaven which attain to the grandiose; and also lamenting over their exile in the depths of matter, in hymns of a sincerity and beauty—and here I am thinking, equally, of those of the Manichaeans—which are profoundly moving.

Lastly—since the new texts, by a happy chance, arrive together with those from the Dead Sea to give a little more life to our mental picture of some of those centuries which saw the birth and development of Christianity—will they modify, in any way, what we think of the religion taught in the New Testament?

Certainly, when we turn back to the Gospels and the Epistles after a thorough reading of the Gnostic writings, we might feel some momentary qualms at the remembrance of certain rather strange interpretations that our sectaries put upon the same texts, the same sayings. They are, in some cases, not without seductive power. Which is the truth? Was not Christianity itself, at the first, more like Gnosticism? Yet, very soon, before the luminous simplicity of the great Gospels, before the clear and profound thought of Paul, and even before the visions of the Johannine Apocalypse, one is struck by the difference between the two teachings. To read, first, the Gnostic writings, and then to take up the New Testament again is an experience that is well worth while. One soon feels, after reopening the greatest books of authentic Christianity, that here are to be found treasures of life yet more abundant than we had formerly realized. We feel again the incomparable superiority of these texts, with their images and their meanings accessible to all. We marvel that the Gnostic schools were able so long to compete with them, and we can understand why the sectaries preferred, face to face with this religion, to keep their own dogmas secret and hide themselves in the dark.

NOTES ON PLATES 5 AND 11

Plate 5: The Coptic manuscript of the Pistis-Sophia *(Codex Askewianus) open at page 143 (facing p. 126)*

The text shown is that of a passage in the second part of the *Books of the Saviour* (see p. 72 of the present book). Jesus is replying to questions from his disciples concerning the constitution of the human soul, and the judgments and transmigrations to which souls will be subjected after death. Jesus is answering a question raised by Mary, about the treatment of any believer who, having previously "received the mysteries", has forgotten and transgressed them and is now penitent. She has asked whether the brethren ought again to communicate to him the "mysteries" he had received before, or simply to give him the sacraments of a degree higher than that to which he had attained. . . .

" . . . Let thy brethren communicate to him the Mystery which is higher than that which he has already received! They are to accept his repentance and to forgive his sins: the latter, indeed, because he has received [mysteries] a second time; and those others [?] because he has surpassed them. Indeed, it is not this [the highest mystery he had received before sinning] that will hearken and will pardon his sins; but it is the Mystery higher than that which he had yet received which will forgive his sins. Nevertheless, in a case where this brother had received three mysteries in the two Regions, or in the third Region from within, before he turned away and transgressed, in that case no Mystery of those from up on high, any more than those that are below them, will be able to hearken and help in his repentance, except the Mystery of the First Mystery and the Mysteries of the Ineffable: it is these last [alone] that will hearken and will accept his repentance."

"Mary again asked: 'My Lord, if a man has received up to two or even three Mysteries in the two Regions or even in the third [Region], and if this man has not transgressed but dwells uprightly and without hypocrisy in the faith . . . ? The Saviour answered and said: All the men who have received the mysteries in the second and in the third Region and who have nowise transgressed, but are dwelling still, without hypocrisy, in the faith, to such as these it is lawful to take part in the mysteries in what Region they will, from the very first to the last, because they have not transgressed.' Mary went on: 'My Lord, if a man who had known the divinity and who had taken part in the Mysteries of the Light, has turned aside to transgression, has committed iniquity and has not come at all to repentance; if, on the other hand, a man has never found the divinity and has not known it, and is therefore a sinner and also impious—then, when both of these men die, which of the two will receive the greater punishment?'"

Plate 11: Codex X, pages 32 and 33 (facing p. 239)

At the top of the left-hand page is the end of the text of the longer version of the *Secret Book of John* (cf. here, pp. 201ff.)

(The Saviour has just told John that those who divulge the contents of this sacred book in return for some gift or reward will be cursed.)
"He [Jesus] communicated these things to him in a mystery, then immediately He disappeared from before him. Then [John] went to his companions and recited to them what the Saviour had said to him. Jesus Christ! Amen!"

THE SECRET BOOK ACCORDING TO JOHN

Under this conclusion, without any indication of title, begins the *Gospel according to Thomas* (cf. here, pp. 227ff. and Appendix II). For the translation of these pages, see vv. 1–8, pp. 355–7.

Appendix I

THE TEACHING
OF SIMON MAGUS IN THE
CHENOBOSKION
MANUSCRIPTS

AFTER further examination of some pages which I had previously been able to transcribe from the *Treatise on the Triple Epiphany* (No. 34) and the work entitled *The Sense of Understanding* . . . (No. 22), I am better able to recognize the interest and importance —surely of the highest order—of these two writings.

I have briefly described (in pp. 181–2) what is now restored to us by a few remaining leaves (vestiges of Codex IX) of this *Treatise on the Triple Epiphany, on the Prôtennoïa of Threefold Form*, which is also called a *Sacred Scripture composed by the Father in a perfect Gnosis*. Allow me now to give a more detailed analysis of these fragments. What we have here is a cosmogenic exposition, in which the Great Luminaries appear. Here, too, we encounter the mysterious heavenly Virgin called Mirôthea, whom we met before in our *Book of the invisible Great Spirit or Gospel of the Egyptians*. We also find again the ever-changing face of the evil demiurge, master of hell and of Chaos, named Sacla, Samael, Ialdabaôth. All this, it is true, differs hardly at all from what we are told by most of the Sethian revelations restored to us by the Chenoboskion library. But as we continue our reading of this work, we are soon struck by certain exhortations by the mysterious figure, prophetic or divine, to whom these various revelations are now being attributed. Only listen to it!—this entity describing itself in terms which are generally so vague: "I am the Voice that manifests itself beyond my thinking. . . .

It is I whom they call the Thought of the Invisible. . .! I am the Word, unique, ineffable, immaculate, immense, inconceivable; this is a hidden light, which yields a fruit of life, springing from a living water beyond the invisible source. . . . I have sent forth an appeal, to the ears of those who know me. I have called you to enter again into the supreme and perfect Light. You shall enter into this [Light], and there you shall receive Glory from the hands of those who glorify; those who are appointed to give thrones shall give you thrones; you shall receive robes from those who give robes and, by those who baptize, you shall be baptized. . . . I hide myself in each individual: within them I manifest myself; and every thought has desired me while seeking for me because it is I who have given to the universe its image. . . ." Then another voice evokes the revelations which, from this higher being, have gone throughout the universe: "He has manifested the Infinites . . .; he has revealed those that it is difficult to interpret and that are hidden; he has preached concerning those who dwell in the Silence with the First Thought; he has manifested himself to those who are in the Darkness; he has given instruction concerning himself to those who are in the depths; to those who dwell in the secret Treasuries he has spoken of the ineffable mysteries, and all of them have become Sons of the Light!"

Without doubt, the divine apocalyptist whom this writing puts up to speak first and foremost, and who is echoed by the voice of a prophet—this must be the supreme Power himself, if we are to judge of it by the following words: "And the Word which was produced from my Thought became three monads; the Father, the Mother and the Son, voices that dwell in a sensibility having within it a word, possessing all glory and having three masculinities, three femininities, three powers and three names which are in this wise: three ☐ ☐ ☐, which are quadrangles in the secrecy and the silence. . . ."

As for the prophet who, in his turn, repeats these teachings just as he has received them from the supreme Power and then comments upon them at length, it appears that this is the great Seth himself. Here he comes, very soon, to finish this revelation; he is about to give up being the visionary who is transcribing this apocryphon for the elect! Already he is alluding to his prospective ascension to the zenith of the heavens and higher yet—towards the world into which, later on, he will draw the elect. "As for me, I have put on [the person]of Jesus. I have brought him out of the bitter tree [i.e., matter] and have established him in the dwelling of his Father. And the watchers did not recognize me, for I am an imperceptible, I and my Seed which belongs to me: this same I shall establish in its holy Light on high, in the Silence unattainable! Amen."

As for the writing entitled *The Sense of Understanding, the Thought of the Great Power*, we have already noted, in a few words (p. 242), its essential characteristics. This work belongs to the series of "Hermetic treatises", transcribed in Theban Coptic, of which a scribe made a concise anthology for the library of our sectaries. His own vocabulary suggests an authentic relationship with some portions of the Greek Hermetic *corpus*, such as the IXth treatise, or the fragment XVIII of the florilegium of Stobaeus.

But this text, by its title, its philosophical vocabulary and its abstract content, connects itself closely with certain pages of the *Treatise on the Triple Epiphany*. Must we then suppose that *The Sense of Understanding . . .* an alleged treatise of Hermes, may really be the work of Gnostics such as the Sethians?—or, on the contrary, that the *Treatise on the Triple Epiphany* drew freely from the source of standard Hermetism? The same problem presented itself to us before in the *Apocalypse of Dositheus* (No. 30; see p. 188), ostensibly taken from the "three stelae of the great Seth", but whose style and content may well pass for Hermetic!

A third solution, however, ought to be considered. Let us refer back to the expositions of the teaching of Simon Magus, such as that presented in the *Philosophumena* (see pp. 15–19 above) and in particular to the summary of the *Great Revelation* or *Revelation of the Voice and of the Name proceeding from the Great Power*, which is attributed to Simon. We shall be struck by the strange likeness that is apparent between the ideas that are developed in the Simonian doctrine on the one hand, and, on the other, in our treatises *On the Triple Epiphany* and *on the Thought of the Great*

Power. We even find—and this especially in the case of *The Triple Epiphany*—a good many expressions that are identical.

Let us go no further for the moment! A more thorough examination of our Coptic fragments will enable us to judge whether the *Treatise on the Triple Epiphany* can really be identified with the *Great Revelation* which the *Philosophumena* summarizes and attributes to Simon. (If so, it would prove anew how fully and directly the *Philosophumena* drew upon the most authentic and important Gnostic scriptures.) In any case, it is established henceforward that, in its treatises 34 and 22, the Chenoboskion library has restored to us texts of a very notable value: two writings that refer back to the "Simonian" Gnosticism derived, either authentically or apocryphally, from the teachings of Simon Magus! And with these two writings we must doubtless connect that *Apocalypse of Dositheus,* of equally unsettling content, which, by taking on this name of Dositheus, no doubt laid claim to the authorship of Simon Magus' master and rival (see p. 15). Finally, we must not forget that analogies with the doctrines traditionally ascribed to Simon appear again in the great cosmogony of the *Paraphrase of Shem* (see pp. 149ff.) and even in our *Book of the invisible Great Spirit* or *Gospel of the Egyptians.*

Our possession of these writings, and the possibility of analysing the relations between their doctrines and those expounded, on the one hand, in other Gnostic works, and on the other, in various treatises claiming the authority of Hermes—this will enable us to tackle big problems: very difficult ones, certainly, but until now they could not even have been stated! To what degree of authenticity could they pretend, these Simonian teachings described in the *Philosophumena* and, apparently, developed in our Coptic writings? To what extent can the particular kind of Gnosticism that was thus named after Dositheus and Simon have been one of the models, or even one of the origins, of the Sethian Gnosticism? How, and at what stage of its development, and by exchanges tending in which direction, did the latter establish those curious relations with Hermetism which these newly-found writings disclose? These are questions with far-reaching consequences: one feels eager to become better able to deal with them.

THE GOSPEL
ACCORDING TO THOMAS

OR

THE SECRET WORDS OF JESUS

From the Coptic

Originally translated into French, with Introduction and Notes,
by Jean Doresse,
and now rendered into English from the French
by the Rev. Leonard Johnston, L.S.S.,
in collaboration with Jean Doresse

INTRODUCTION [1]

THE Coptic text of the *Gospel according to Thomas* is contained in
the longest and most beautiful of all the manuscripts emanating
from Chenoboskion, Codex X, in which this text occupies pages
32 to 51. The writing of this codex seems to date from the second
half of the fourth century. In addition to the *Gospel*, it contains
various important Gnostic treatises—such as the *Secret Book of
John*, the *Hypostasis of the Archons*, and a similar work which
bears no title; and finally, an *Exegesis on the Soul*. On the other

---

[1] In view of its extraordinary importance, the publishers have decided to give
the translation of the *Gospel according to Thomas* as an appendix to the present
volume, although it is in fact less markedly Gnostic than the other documents
from Chenoboskion. This short introduction was specially written by the author
for this purpose; on certain points, it repeats or even corrects what has been said
briefly in the body of the book, pp. 227–35. It may be mentioned that the author
has already published in French an edition of the *Gospel according to Thomas* with
a more detailed introduction and commentary.

hand, it also contains other apocrypha such as the *Gospel of Philip* and the *Book of Thomas*.

Our work begins with these words: "Here are the secret words which Jesus the Living spoke and which were written down by Didymus Jude Thomas". The title, in accordance with a fairly common practice, is given at the end of the work, on the last line: *The Gospel according to Thomas*.

The work is made up of about a hundred and twenty sayings and incidents attributed to the Saviour: "Jesus says...". These are given one after the other with no attempt to link them together by means of a narrative. How then can the term "gospel" be used to describe such a collection?

We must remember that today we take our idea of what a gospel is from Matthew, Mark, Luke, John and apocryphal works which resemble these; and therefore use the word to indicate some form of biography of Jesus. But this is an unjustified restriction of the meaning of the term. It means "the good news", and therefore does not indicate a narrative but the spiritual substance of the preaching of Jesus. And in that sense, it fits perfectly didactic works or collections like the *Gospel according to Thomas*.

"THE GOSPEL ACCORDING TO THOMAS" IN TRADITION

Is there any trace of this Gospel in ancient Christian literature? Can it be more closely identified? In other words, what would the simple title *Gospel according to Thomas* mean to a historian before the discovery of this Coptic work?

First of all, there was the Greek apocryphal work whose more exact title was *The Gospel of Thomas the Israelite Philosopher*. Many copies of this existed; but it was quite different from our present work. It narrated fictitious incidents from our Lord's childhood, naïve little stories which later on became scattered among other "Infancy Gospels", and won great popularity in the West even up to the Middle Ages. It is here that we find the anecdote of the birds modelled by Jesus on the Sabbath and brought to life by him; or the story of the schoolmaster who tried to teach Jesus the letters of the alphabet and was most humiliatingly put in his place by his pupil. This *Gospel of Thomas the Israelite* may be fairly early in origin; certain elements in it seem to be mentioned by St Irenaeus about the year 180, and even by the *Epistle of the Apostles*, an apocryphal work which dates from between 140 and 170.

But from the middle of the seventeenth century historians were led to believe that besides this work there existed another which bore a similar title—simply *Gospel according to Thomas*—but which, they thought, was completely heretical. They were led to this belief by certain references in patristic literature. Origen, a little after the year 233; Eusebius of Caesarea in 326; Philip Sidetes about 430; all mention the name of this apocryphal work. Some of them, such as Cyril of Jerusalem about 348, speak of it as being used by the Manichaeans; they even accuse the latter of having created it in its entirety—but this is a fable, since the work must have existed long before the origin of Manichaeism.

Unfortunately, there was only one quotation to give any clue about the nature of this lost work. It was contained in the *Philosophumena*, a treatise against heresies attributed to Hippolytus of Rome, dating from the beginning of the third century. According to this work, the Naassenes (the same as the celebrated Ophites who were supposed to venerate the "serpent") spoke about a man's nature which was "at once hidden and revealed", which was "the Kingdom of heaven which we seek and which is inside man". In the gospel entitled *according to Thomas*, the Naassenes spoke explicitly of the Kingdom in these words: "He who seeks me will find me among children aged seven years and over; for after being hidden, in the fourteenth eon I manifested myself in them!" This quotation, with its reference to "children of seven years", made some modern critics think that this lost work must have been a fanciful account of the Infancy of the Saviour, like the gospel of *Thomas the Israelite* already known.

Besides this single direct quotation, there was certain indirect evidence about the nature of the book. Both Christian and Gnostic authors agree in linking it with two other lost "gospels", that of Matthias and that of Philip. According to certain Gnostics, Thomas, Philip and Matthias were the "three witnesses" to whom Jesus after his resurrection entrusted the care of collecting and transcribing his authentic teachings. The Church used Matthew, Mark and Luke; the heretics carefully refrained from using these Synoptics, and the apocryphal gospels of Thomas, Philip and Matthias took their place.

Let us now compare this data with the *Gospel according to Thomas* as it is found at Chenoboskion.

Before we even open the text, we notice that its position in the collection associates it with Philip and Matthias. For the same Codex X contains a *Gospel of Philip*, and a *Book of Thomas* which is explicitly attributed to Matthias. It is hard to believe that this is a mere coincidence; especially since the contents of this *Book of Thomas* fit the description of the lost *Gospel of Matthias*—according to Codex X, the former is a collection of sacred words revealed to Thomas and written by Matthias; whereas, according to the *Philosophumena* (VII, 20), the *Gospel of Matthias* used by the heretics Basilides and his son Isidore contained "the secret doctrines which the Saviour revealed to this Apostle [Matthias] in private discourse".

If now we turn to the text of this newly found Coptic work, we read in § 4: "Let the old man heavy with days hasten to ask the little child of seven days about the place of Life, and he will live. . . ." This recalls fairly closely the text of the *Gospel according to Thomas* commented on by the Naassenes (according to the *Philosophumena* quoted above). The quotation is only approximate; but it carries more weight when we examine more carefully the other Naassene texts given in the *Philosophumena;* for comparing these now with our *Gospel according to Thomas*, we can recognize many other quotations from it, although without any reference to their source.

We may turn next to the abundant Manichaean literature, the "Kephalaia" or "chapters" of Mani, their psalms, etc. Scattered up and down these writings we find, with pleasure and surprise, a fair number of quotations which clearly come from our present work. This means that the work we have in our hands is in all probability that which Cyril of Jerusalem and others condemned because of the use made of it by such heretics.

THE GREEK WORDS OF JESUS

The *Gospel according to Thomas* from Codex X of Chenoboskion is not, however, the first sign of this lost work that the modern world has had. Without knowing it, we had much more extensive fragments of it than the single quotation given by the *Philosophumena*. These were to be found in three strips of Greek manuscripts dating from the third or fourth century, which came from Upper Egypt, from the site on which once stood the large and prosperous city of Oxyrhynchus. Searchers have methodically gone over the soil of this site and have brought to light by the thousand remnants of all sorts of texts, private writings or literary works. The three Greek fragments we referred to are Oxyrhynchus papyrus I, 1 (discovered in 1897), and papyri IV, 654 and IV, 655 (discovered in 1903). These fragments are in fact no more than strips of three different manuscripts. The most important of them, number 655, is no more than the vertical half of a column of text, of which the other half had unfortunately disappeared. Nevertheless, from the moment of their discovery these scraps attracted the greatest interest; for they appeared to present us with a number of sentences or parables spoken by Jesus, though in such a mutilated form as to be almost incomprehensible. The list of studies which these *logia* gave rise to, from the time of their discovery to the present day, is considerable. New Testament scholars conjectured that these three fragments formed part of a single collection of words of Jesus which had been handed down by tradition independently of the canonical gospels, and which had been lost for centuries. Today we are in a position to say that they were right in thinking that they formed part of a single collection, but wide of the mark in their identification of the character of this collection.

The discovery of the complete text of the *Gospel according to Thomas* now enables us to identify the Greek collection of *logia*. The discovery is due to M. H. C. Puech. In July, 1952, I sent him a copy of part of the *Gospel*, including the beginning; he recognized that it was exactly the text which the Greek Oxyrhynchus papyrus 654 presented in a mutilated form. It was in 1954 that he pointed this out. In 1956, when the entire text of the Coptic work was divulged, he was able without further difficulty to verify the complete parallels to the Greek fragments of Oxyrhynchus I and 655. At the same time he was able to restore the exact sense of the Greek fragments by comparison with the unbroken Coptic text, filling in the gaps which philologists (including some eminent names) had previously filled in wrongly by the use of their imaginations. The restored Greek text is given as a footnote to our translation of the Coptic text.

Finally, M. H. C. Puech had the further good fortune to recognize another quotation, a single sentence of the Greek version of our *Gospel according to Thomas*. This was found on a strip of linen, part of a shroud, also from Oxyrhynchus.

Thus, thanks to the text which I myself found and identified in 1948, and thanks to M. Puech's remarks on that text, almost complete darkness gave way to total clarity concerning these most important problems. For indeed, the consequences of this discovery are remarkable. For the past fifty years, the Greek fragments from Oxyrhynchus had led scholars to suppose that a collection of "words" of Jesus, *logia*, existed, which was extrinsic to the tradition of the canonical gospels, but which may well belong to a primitive source. Now we are in possession of the Coptic edition of the *complete* work, in which these words are to be found. Now, this work—going under the name of Thomas—is one of the most ancient and precious apocrypha known. The three Greek fragments and the brief quotation on the shroud bear eloquent witness to the popularity and authority which it enjoyed in antiquity—and give us a further guarantee of its interest to us.

THOMAS

This collection of words of Jesus is put under the authority of St Thomas. How far do the contents support this claim?

The *incipit* of the collection credits Thomas (designated by the triple name of "Didymus Jude Thomas") with the composition of the work. But on the other hand, Thomas is mentioned in the work only once, in § 14. It is true that the part there attributed to him is quite important—the equivalent of that played by St Peter in the canonical gospels' account of the "confession" at Caesarea

Philippi (*Matt.* XVI, 13-20, *Mark* VIII, 27-30). But nothing else in the body of the *Gospel* bears the slightest reference to him. How then are we to explain the fact that it was attributed to him? Is it a simple fiction?

The origin of this fact is to be sought in the strong tradition which attributes to Thomas the rôle of special confidant of the Saviour and heir to his most secret teachings. This tradition is expressed even more clearly in the *Book of Thomas* supposedly written by Matthias, which figures in the same Coptic manuscript. This apocryphon makes Thomas the original source of its teaching; the Apostle (there called "Jude Thomas") is presented as the "twin brother" of the Saviour, and recipient of his hidden doctrines: "The Saviour, brother of Thomas, said to him: Hear! I will reveal to thee what thou thinkest in thy heart: how they say that thou art truly my twin and my companion, how they call thee my brother. . . ."

Traces of the same tradition are found also outside the newly found documents. In the canonical gospels, Thomas hardly appears except in St John (and it may be noted that several passages of the *Gospel according to Thomas* are reminiscent of John's doctrine). Even in the fourth gospel, he appears only in a few incidents, of which the best known is that concerning his lack of faith, when he wishes to touch the body of the Risen Saviour (XX, 24-9). In that text, he is also surnamed "Didymus"; and Didymus in Greek has the same literal sense of "twin" as the name Thomas has in Aramaic: "Thomas who is called Didymus . . ." (*John* XI, 16; XX, 24; XXI, 2). And it is from this repeated use of the name "twin" that the apocryphal tradition was born which made Thomas the brother and confidant of Jesus! The development of these legends can be traced in a few words.

As we know, the ancient church historians mentioned Thomas as having preached the gospel to the Parthians and in Persia. It was said that he was buried at Edessa. From the fourth century, the chronicle credits him in more legendary fashion with the evangelization of "India"—although this term may denote more simply just Central Asia. Crowds of pilgrims then come to venerate his supposed tomb at Edessa—almost as many as for Jerusalem; and from there, the historical figure of Thomas disappears more and more into a cloud of extravagant fables.

Now, this precise district (round Edessa) seems to have given rise to swarms of various kinds of apocryphal works; and on the subject of Thomas, it is remarkable that they seem to spring from the same tradition as that found in the *incipit* of our Coptic gospel and more clearly still in our *Book of Thomas*. For example, they call him by the same peculiar and repetitive name, "Didymus Jude Thomas". He is already given the double name of "Jude Thomas" by authors as closely linked to Edessa as Tatian, Ephraem, the fictitious correspondence of Abgar king of Edessa with Jesus, or the *Doctrine of the Apostles*. In the apocryphal *Acta* devoted to him (and which were written at Edessa, in Syriac, in the third century), he is also currently called "Jude Thomas", and, in the first chapter, also "Jude Thomas Didymus". Further, in Chapter 39 of these apocryphal *Acts of Thomas*, we find the phrase: "Twin of Christ, apostle of the Most-High, thou who art also initiated into the hidden teaching of Christ and hast received his secret words!": which corresponds exactly to the claims made by our *Gospel according to Thomas* and by our *Book of Thomas written by Matthias*. Moreover, these same *Acta* contain a precise reference to a characteristic passage of the new *Gospel*—the three words which the Saviour said to the Apostle and which he could not reveal (cf. § 14 of the translation).

There was, then, a special tradition that Thomas, the twin of Christ, privileged to touch the divine body of the Risen Lord with his hand (so that right up to the Middle Ages his tomb was that of "Thomas of the ever-living hand"!), was privileged also to receive the secret revelations of the Saviour. And it would appear that our gospel, by claiming Thomas as its author and by quoting in § 14 the special rôle he plays, has tried to take advantage of this tradition. And, equally clearly, it appears that the centre of this tradition was the city of Edessa—mysterious and powerful city, which for long claimed to guard the body of the Apostle in the splendid sepulchre it had raised for him. There, all these legends reached full development, and from there they spread to the rest of the Christian world.

CONTENTS OF THE GOSPEL

Each of the hundred and eighteen (or hundred and nineteen if we include the *incipit*) words of Jesus found in the *Gospel* forms an independent saying, and there seems to have been no attempt at methodical grouping. Most of them begin with the formula: "Jesus says", or "Jesus said". Also, certain phrases recur like a refrain: "He who has ears to hear, let him hear!"; "He who will hear these words (or: who knows these things) will not taste death!" But that is the only unifying factor, the only suggestion of literary structure in the book.

The same lack of cohesion characterizes the contents. Some of the sayings are situated during our Lord's earthly life, others can only be attributed to the Risen Lord. Again, some of the sayings can be understood as they stand, but there are many which could only be understood in the light of some context which is not given. Some sentences are simply allusions to incidents which are briefly suggested; others seem to be the continuation of a previous teaching which is not given here. Such sayings cannot easily be understood by a reader who is not familiar with the life of our Lord as it is given in the canonical gospels, or even as it might have been read in some ancient apocrypha which are now lost. But side by side with such omissions, we find repetition of the same teaching, or even of the same saying, accompanied by a different interpretation. Occasionally, also, some sayings seem to deal with the same subject, or develop progressively a definite theme; but that is not a general rule, for one could also point to a disconcerting lack of continuity; certain elements found together in the canonical gospels are here found in widely separate contexts.

However, once we have noted this lack of unity in the *Gospel*, one may then recognize the fact that the contents can be grouped in the following categories.

First there are the sayings, parables and incidents which were already known to us from the canonical gospels. For details, see the Index at the end of this volume, which gives the parallels in the form of tables. It will be seen that most of the parallels in this category are with *Matthew* and *Luke*; there are almost no parallels with *Mark*, and the parallels with *John*, though fairly numerous, are found only in short formulas. Some of these passages are given in almost the same form that they have in the New Testament (§§ 9, 23, 25, 39, 40, 46, 67, 69, 77, 90, 111 . . .). Others are more concise (31, 41, 62, 93, 94, 103 . . .). Others are longer and more diffuse, sometimes linking together sentences which are found separately in the New Testament (18, 37, 38, 44, 51, 52, 68, 80, 100 . . .). In other cases again, homogeneous matter of the canonical gospels is here split into different verses (10 and 17; 69 and 70 . . .).

Sometimes the *Gospel according to Thomas* uses the words of the New Testament, but attaches a different teaching to it (1, 11, and 115, 13, 35, 66, 72, 82, 96, 110). Sometimes it gives the same sort of teaching, and attaches it to sentences, parables or dialogues which are similar in style to those found in the New Testament but not actually found there (8, 14, 15, 24, 29, 78, 101, 102, 106, 113). And finally there are passages which both in style and doctrine are radically different from the orthodox teaching (7, 12, 19, 22, 27, 33, 55, 64, 65, 79, 88, 89, 112, 118).

So much for the relationship between the *Gospel according to Thomas* and the canonical gospels. Let us turn now to its relationship to other early Christian literature. For some of the passages which differ from the New Testament were already known to us, being recognizable in occasional quotations or references in Christian works or heretical writings.

Some of the writings in which these parallels are found give a precise reference to their source. It is remarkable that only in one case (cf. § 4) is this source the *Gospel according to Thomas*. In other cases the source is given as the *Gospel of the Hebrews*, or the *Traditions of Matthias* (cf. 1 and 108), or the *Gospel of the Egyptians* (cf. 27, 42 and 65).

But for the most part these works carry no reference and give no other hint which could have allowed us to guess their connection with our *Gospel according to Thomas* before its recent discovery. This is particularly true of certain apocrypha and Gnostic and Manichaean literature. It is only now that we have the complete text in our hands that we can see the relationship with the various so-called *Acta* of Thomas, Peter, Philip, John or Andrew; the Naassene writings summarized by the *Philosophumena* (cf. our §§ 2, 3, 4, 12, 14, 20, 27); authentic Gnostic works such as the *Gospel of Truth* (cf. our 81) or the *Gospel of Philip* also found at Chenoboskion (cf. our 20) or the *Pistis Sophia* (here, 1, 28, 95); and finally the Manichaean books such as the *Kephalaia* or the *Psalter* which are also found in Coptic (cf. our 4, 5, 43, 60, 88).

These copious references attest the connection between our *Gospel* and other orthodox or heretical literature of the first Christian centuries. The connection will be of two kinds, though it is not as yet always possible to distinguish the two in practice: in some cases our *Gospel* has borrowed from earlier texts; or, more frequently, it was itself abundantly quoted and used by ecclesiastical writers.

The material contained in the *Gospel*, then, varies considerably: some of it is identical with the canonical gospels, some entirely different both in form and in spirit. The relationship between the different categories is a problem of some complexity; but it seems probable that they correspond to different layers of material which were successively juxtaposed in the composition of the present work. This is suggested, for example, by the fact that it sometimes gives not one single form of certain sayings, but two or sometimes even three variations of them, different in form, meaning and even in doctrine. Usually these repetitions are quite independent; no effort has been made to correlate them (cf. §§ 61 and 84: 44 and 106: etc.). But in §§ 77, 78 and 79 we have a triplet which is particularly significant, not only because of the close juxtaposition of variants but also because they display a clear progression in meaning. Number 77 corresponds simply to the text of *Matt.* IX, 37-8 and *Luke* X, 2 (the harvest is great and the labourers few). Number 78 is not found in the canonical gospels but is quoted by Origen in his *Contra Celsum* as having been used by the Naassene Gnostics. Number 79, then, has a certain similarity in structure to the others, and is similar in meaning to the immediately preceding 78; but the metaphor it uses and the teaching it contains make it quite different from the gospel text used by 77. In these three verses we undoubtedly have a characteristic example

12*

of the way in which our *Gospel according to Thomas* was composed. The author, or rather the successive authors, gleaned from the canonical gospels certain texts which met with their approval; to these they added other sentences which the New Testament had not conserved but which tradition still attributed to Jesus; and finally they presumed to add certain formulas invented on the model of the previous sayings but which were designed to popularize the doctrines of the compilers.

THE DOCTRINE OF THE GOSPEL

Let us now try to draw up a brief catalogue of the main ideas in the *Gospel*.

The opening words of the book define its doctrine as the secret revelation given by the Saviour to his disciples (§§ 43 and 48), or even divulged by him in virtue of a higher necessity (§§ 14 and 96). This definition may seem to be contradicted by the fact that much of the material was already well known through the canonical gospels[1]: but it must be taken into account that these quotations are here found in a new context which gives them a new sense—a "hidden" sense.

As far as the divine nature is concerned, it is to be noted that the figures of the Father and the Son are almost identified (§§ 16 and 55): while the Holy Spirit is mentioned only once (49). Jesus, "he who was not born of woman" (16), is also frequently called "Jesus the Living". Could it also perhaps be Jesus who is referred to under the appearance of "the child of seven days" (4)? He is also the historical Jesus who appears in several incidents taken from the gospels (36, 44, 65, 76, 82, 83, 90, 103, 104, 105, 108); he is the "lamb" (64); but above all he is the Risen Lord, omniscient, invisible (42), who is outside this world (29), but is also in any place where there are two or even one of his followers. He is in fact everywhere: in the wood, in the stone (81, cf. 35 in the Greek); though these may also allegorically represent the Cross and the Tomb. If his passion and death are referred to, it is only

---

[1] Unless of course our collection of " Secret Words of Jesus " goes back to a period when the synoptic gospels themselves were not as yet widely circulated. But when we come to date these writings it will be seen that such a hypothesis is hardly worth serious consideration.

through symbols (69, 70) which conceal their crudely physical character; his Incarnation, and his descent into the body (the "corpse") are mentioned, but only as incidents out of the past. The world above—the world of Light—is referred to frequently by allusions to the primordial forms and images which are hidden there (87, 88). The presence of certain beings belonging to the world on high is quite characteristic: these are referred to as "the five trees of Paradise"—trees of the Garden of Eden first, but also abstract entities, the first emanations from the world on high which are reproduced in the saints and the elect (22). This detail of the *Gospel according to Thomas* is the first example known of a theory which later becomes extremely important in certain Gnostic systems and especially in Manichaeism. Another reference to the world above is found in certain "places" where Jesus is found (29 and 71); or "the Place of Life" (4, 63); or in the rôle attributed to James "the Just" and the church, "for whose sake heaven as well as earth was produced" (13).

How are the disciples connected with this world on high? The disciples, the elect, or rather (to use a term well-attested in our work) the "monakhoi" or "solitaries" (17, 54, 65, 79) have attained "unity" or "solitude" by surmounting divisions and opposing contraries, and, like the Saviour himself, belong to the flesh and this world below only on a transitory basis. They come from the Father, whose "sons" they are (55); they belong to the world of Light. They carry within them the sign which is "a movement and a rest" (54 and 55). They will return to this world; according to ideas inherited from Plato, they will pass from the vision of images here below to the contemplation of the models, the breathtaking "images" which exist on high with the Father (87 and 88).

The majority of the teachings which the *Gospel* addresses to these Perfect ones are at the same time those which are most closely akin to the teaching of the canonical gospels; they deal with the Kingdom and its "riches", compared with which the flesh and this world below are only "poverty" and "deprivation". That is the subject of those sayings which usually take the form of parables mysteriously defining the Kingdom (1, 3, 9, 11, 23, 25, 38, 40, 62,

77, 86, 100, 101, 107, 113, 115). Jesus himself said of this Kingdom that it was really present though invisible, and that it was "outside you" and especially "inside you" (a phrase from which the Naassene Gnostics took their inspiration).

But how does one reach the Treasure, that is to say the "riches", Life, the Kingdom? The moral, ascetic or mystical sayings are directed to this end. There are first of all certain principles of knowledge: "Know what is before you. . . . Know Him who is before you. . . . Know yourselves, and what is hidden will be revealed to you. . . . Cease not to seek and you will find!" (3, 5, 96, 112). This discovery will bring admiration; and admiration (a Platonic notion from the *Theaetetus*) will lead to complete knowledge and by it, to the royalty promised to the elect (1). Thus you will attain contemplation and the possession of what "eye has never seen and what ear has never heard. . . ." (18): that is, the Kingdom and its "riches" which will deliver you from "poverty" and the "corpse".

With that are associated moral precepts: reject material goods (41, 67, 73 . . .) and the flesh (a garment to be "trampled on", 24, 42); strip yourselves bare; reject father and mother and every bond of this world (60, 105); neglect even circumcision, which is useless (58). Finally, detach yourself from everything feminine (83); for even feminine beings must become male if they are to enter the Kingdom (118). In this way you will reach the fullness, the unity of the elect. How is that done? By union with each other and union within oneself: where there are three of you, there let the perfect Church spring up; where there are two of you, be in mutual peace; and finally, within yourselves, let perfect unity take the place of primitive dissociation and "division" (35, 53, 65, 110, 118): in other words, let the "outside" become as the "inside", the "upper" like the "lower", the male like the female; let the first become last and the last first: in short, let there be reunion of opposites and complete reversal of everything, of all values cosmic and human. This great theme is repeated tenaciously and often in almost identical terms by some later apocrypha such as the so-called *Acts of Peter* (cf. Chapter 38) and *Acts of Philip* (Chapter 139).

THE DATE OF THE GOSPEL

It is not impossible to date the *Gospel* with relative accuracy. We have seen that it is prior to the *Acts of Thomas* (beginning or middle of the third century?) and various other *Acts* equally ancient. It is likewise prior to the *Philosophumena* of pseudo-Hippolytus (beginning of the third century), which quotes it explicitly once and refers to it without naming it in several other places. But earlier than that no trace of it can be found.

Nevertheless, it is striking that some of the formulas collected in the *Gospel* were known to ecclesiastical literature from the second half of the second century, and even, in one case, from the middle of the century; though it is not known if these sayings were at that time collected together under the title of the *Gospel according to Thomas*.

To go back any further, we would have to be content with calculating the age, not of the work as a whole, but of certain of its more important elements. And to do so would mean dealing with the very difficult problem of the relationship between the para-evangelical texts of this *Gospel* and those of the synoptic gospels. Until this detailed comparison has been made, any conclusion would certainly be premature. But a certain number of facts can be noted. In the first place, it is possible that certain texts may have been simply repeated from the synoptic gospels, at least as regards their substance if not in literal form. But texts which are not found in the New Testament or which are variations of synoptic texts may be authentic remains of an independent tradition which the canonical gospels discarded. We are already approaching hazardous hypotheses, but it may be possible to suppose that certain parts of our *Gospel* were genuinely made up of remnants of a lost collection of words of Jesus; and that these were remoulded and enriched with radically apocryphal elements, and finally presented under the name of the apostle Thomas! But it is better not to be led too far into such speculations. We may limit ourselves to the prudent conclusion that the *Gospel according to Thomas* may well contain elements which are prior to the composition of the synoptic gospels and independent of them; but that the verbal identity with some of the canonical parables makes it probable that it is later than the synoptic gospels, at least in its present form.

Moreover, as we have seen, some passages of the *Gospel* were known and quoted by early Christian writers, as belonging to the gospels *of the Egyptians* or *of the Hebrews* or *of Matthias*. It is difficult to imagine that these writers were guilty of error in these precise cases. In that case we must admit that the *Gospel according to Thomas* borrowed these phrases from other apocryphal works which are now unfortunately lost. This does not mean that it is in the same category as them; it will be later than they are, but in immediate contact with them. It will therefore be a sort of "intermediary" work, through which a more or less substantial part of their teaching was more actively disseminated and transmitted to later times. As we have seen, certain apocryphal *Acts* and heretical works in particular owe their inspiration to it.

It is less easy to form a hypothesis concerning the possible geographical origin of the work, especially as it is a complex of material from so many different sources. However, the quite characteristic mystical ideas it expounds would certainly connect it with Syrian Christianity, the main centre of which was Edessa; it was here also that Thomas, whose name is placed at the head of this collection of "words of Jesus", was most zealously venerated.

THE ORTHODOXY OF THE GOSPEL

Cyril of Jerusalem asserted that the *Gospel of Thomas* was a Manichaean writing; this is out of the question, since the work is well attested before the rise of Manichaeism. Nor can one accept the statement of the *Philosophumena* that it is a Naassene composition. In its Coptic edition, the work does contain certain Gnostic additions or corrections; but the work as a whole contains elements which are scarcely consonant with Gnosticism. There is, for example, the allusion to the resurrection of the body, in §5 of the Greek edition—no doubt this is suppressed in the Coptic edition because it so blatantly scandalized the Gnostics who used the work.

Nevertheless, it would be an exaggeration to say that the orthodoxy of the work is beyond doubt. There are a certain number of original doctrines. Some of these are simply the result of too literal interpretation of certain ideas already present in the synoptic gospels or in St John or St Paul. But others cannot be so explained, and it is precisely these which give the collection its peculiar individuality—though even here it may be true that these are the result of later additions or correction of a more moderate original. These ideas are subtle and striking, skilfully inserted into this mosaic of texts in such a way as to influence the meaning of the context and thus of the work as a whole. The ideas in question are philosophical and mystical notions inherited from hellenic philosophy and particularly from Platonism. Examples are numerous: the theory of pre-existing images or ideas which existed before men or other creatures came into being (87, 88); the rôle attributed to admiration as a step towards knowledge (1); the contempt for the body looked on as a "corpse", just as it is a "prison" or "tomb" in Plato (61, 84); and in the same order of ideas, the exhortation to strip oneself of one's "garments" (42); the notion of androgyny associated with perfection (27, 118); and—no doubt as a consequence of the last—the belief that perfection demands the separation and reunion of contraries (that the male and female should become one, the first last, that the elect should attain "solitude" or "unity").

No doubt the *Gospel according to Thomas* is not the only work in early Christian literature to profess such doctrines in the name of Jesus; it reminds us of the very close relationship there was between Christianity and the best in Greek philosophy. From the little we know of it, the *Traditions of Matthias* seem to have been inspired by the same Platonic spirit; and the *Acts of Peter* and *Acts of Philip* contain echoes of the same teaching. This explains why our *Gospel* was so favoured by certain heretics and especially certain Gnostics. It gave them scope for a certain type of exegesis which would enable them to mix Christian theology with the teachings of Greek philosophy and with certain mystical commentaries which works like Homer and Hesiod had already been subjected to. And it was through these heretics that certain teachings of the *Gospel according to Thomas* were perpetuated late into the Middle Ages; we find echoes of one such curious doctrine, that of § 118, even in the medieval Catharists.

It is indeed remarkable to find philosophical ideas of this nature expressed in such an early Christian writing (for it is beyond doubt that it is early). But these ideas cannot be called 'heretical'. Traces of them are found in St John, St Paul, and above all in the *Epistle to the Hebrews*. They are expressed even more clearly in other ancient Christian literature—for example in the so-called *Second Epistle of Clement*, the earliest known homily. It was natural enough that Greek thought should be used in this way (or to put it more precisely, that the growing Christian Church and Hellenism should meet in this fashion). True, from the fourth century onwards it might be condemned by one or other of the oriental bishops (even though these same bishops may at the same time be engaged in eagerly tracking down the mystical teachings of Iamblichus or Porphyry). But that did not hinder the Latin Church of the Middle Ages from collecting these valuable traditions, and according Platonism a favoured place in its philosophical and mystical systems: a place which it retained till the end of the twelfth century, when it began to give way to Aristotelianism. And even after that time, the Byzantine Church gave the Greek sages a place side by side with the Biblical prophets. Plato was even to be represented (if we are to believe the instructions given to the painters of the school of Athos) with a scroll in his hand inscribed with the words—very similar to those found in the *Gospel according to Thomas*—"The old is new and the new is old: the Father is in the Son, and the Son in the Father: unity is divided into three, and the Trinity remakes Unity!"

THE VALUE OF THE GOSPEL

For the historian, the discovery of this work represents an immense step forward in our knowledge of primitive Christian literature hitherto known only in scattered remnants. Certainly, it would have been an even greater advantage to have found the *Gospel of the Hebrews* or the *Gospel according to the Egyptians* quoted briefly by so many Christian writers. Nevertheless, we are even a step closer to them, given the fact that the *Gospel according to Thomas* is connected with them. Moreover, we have seen that this *Gospel* is attested at the beginning of the third century; this means that it belongs to at least the end of the second century; and even if in its present form it goes back no earlier, at least a great part of its contents must come directly from the middle of the second century and probably even earlier. But this takes us back to a time when the New Testament writings had not yet completely replaced the living tradition; and this collection will contain much information about the literary form in which the teaching of Jesus circulated and the interpretation given to it in authentic Christian circles at that time. It will certainly be indispensable to turn to the parallel witness of the *Gospel according to Thomas*—however ambiguous it may be—for any critical work on many passages of the canonical gospels. Eminent scholars have already begun the work of trying to discern how much of these sayings really goes back to a tradition which the canonical gospels ignored, and which may therefore correspond more or less exactly to teachings of Christ which would otherwise have been forgotten. This is not a rash or foolhardy suggestion. Modern scholars will have to raise certain important questions (though they may not be able to find the answers): but in doing so they are doing no more than Origen, so many centuries before; he also wondered—and that precisely because of a sentence which figures in our *Gospel*, § 86—whether a saying of this kind might not possibly go back to Jesus himself: "Has that been attributed to the Saviour fictitiously; is it a quotation from memory inaccurately recalled; or was it indeed spoken by Jesus?" Jerome also considered that there may be some genuine gold in this "mud" of apocrypha; and St Augustine was prepared to admit that such forgeries could contain some truth.

This is an important suggestion, then; and it is a perfectly legitimate one. We know that the canonical gospels themselves were composed from words of Jesus which had not previously been set in order, and which had been handed down by some tradition which is now lost sight of. We know that there did exist at least one collection of words of our Lord collected from various sources. We know that Papias, about 140, composed five books (now lost) *On the Interpretation of the Logia of the Lord*, and made a collection of these *logia* as part of the preparation for his great work. It is said, further, that the Gnostics Basilides and Isidore claimed to have used a collection which went back to the apostle Matthias, and which is supposed to have been particularly close to certain passages of *Luke* (as indeed is our gospel attributed to Thomas). It would indeed be interesting to know how closely our *Gospel according to Thomas* may be related to one or other of these collections; whether the relationship is direct or indirect; and what traces of authentic tradition each of them contains.

Finally, as concerns the actual substance of the teaching given here, the reader must of course remember that it is not a "fifth" gospel (we have already pointed out the absurdity of this description) : it is, as it stands, only an apocryphal work to which no real authority can be attributed, and even its very composition is artificial. But bearing this in mind, it is still possible to read this collection and in doing so to be brought into direct and moving contact with a very ancient form of Christianity. It was a form of Christianity which was profoundly influenced by Hellenic philosophy and excessively subtle in its conceptions; but at the same time it was extremely demanding in its ideals and in some ways strangely anticipated the finest flights of mysticism of the Latin Middle Ages. Sometimes also we will find in it, veiled in the mysterious language of parables, an original and precise interpretation of passages of the canonical gospels which has appeared obscure to us.

It is a complex, attractive and in some ways really splendid work. What manner of men brought it into being? They must have been men of burning faith; their beliefs had been systematically worked out; they were deeply stirred and illuminated by the new faith. There is no denying the wealth of philosophy contained in their work; the thought is not a naïve repetition, it is subtle and ambitious speculation; and not the least astonishing aspect of it is that it should have been able to find expression, as it does here, with so much art by means of such simple and concise imagery.

PRELIMINARY NOTE

THE translation given here is as literal as possible. This means that in certain places, where the sense is obscure or ambiguous, a word-for-word rendering has been given. For a more precise interpretation, the reader may refer to the notes.

The division into paragraphs has been adopted simply for reasons of convenience, and is not found in the Coptic manuscript. A suggestion of such a division, however, is found in the Greek papyrus Oxyrhynchus 654, which contains the beginning of this work. Here, dashes between the lines, or coronis (>) at the end of certain phrases mark the transition from one "word" to the next. In general, I have taken the formula "Jesus says", or "Jesus said", to mark the beginning of an independent paragraph. This formula is sometimes omitted at the beginning of sentences which are clearly distinct (cf. for example § 32, where the Coptic omits the formula "Jesus says", which is however present in the Greek version); in these cases I have followed the subdivision which the sense of the text seems to require. But in some passages where several sentences in succession seem to be connected together, I have not marked any division so as not to risk breaking up a coherent whole. In any case, our numbering makes no claim to be definitive.

At the bottom of the page, underneath the translation of the Coptic version, I have given a translation of the three sections found in the Greek version of the Oxyrhynchus papyrus (cf. the description of these given above, Introduction, pp. 337–8). The gaps in these fragments have been filled in only where the parallel Coptic text enabled this to be done with certainty. In addition to these parallels, for § 5 I have added the sentence written in Greek on the shroud from Oxyrhnychus mentioned above (Introduction, p. 338).

The signs used in this translation have been reduced to the minimum:

... : meaning completely obscure;
...? or (?): meaning uncertain;

[. . .]   : gap in the text;
⟨   ⟩   : words added by the translator which are not in the
              text; also, translator's remarks;
(p. 32) etc.: pages of the manuscript.

TRANSLATION

(p. 32, l. 10)   Here are the secret words which Jesus the Living spoke, and which Didymus Jude Thomas wrote down.

And he said: "Whoever penetrates the meaning of these words will not taste death!"

1. Jesus says: "Let him who seeks cease not to seek until he finds: when he finds he will be astonished; and when he is astonished he will wonder, and will reign over the universe!"

2. Jesus says: "If those who seek to attract you say to you: 'See, the Kingdom is in heaven!' then the birds of heaven will be there before you. If they say to you: 'It is in the sea!' then the fish will be there before you. But the kingdom is within you and it is outside of you!"

3. "When you know yourselves, then you will be (p. 33) known, and you will know that it is you who are the sons of the living Father. But if you do not know yourselves, then you will be in a state of poverty, and it is you ⟨who will be⟩ the poverty!"

Oxyrhynchus Papyrus 654:

Here are the [secret] words which Jesus the Living spoke an[d which were transcribed by Didymus Jude] Thomas. And he said: ["Whoever penetrates the mea]ning of these words will not taste [death!"]

1. [Jesus says:] "Let him who see[ks] cease not [to seek until he] finds: when he finds, [he will wonder; and when he wond]ers, he will reign, and [reigning, he will have r]est!"

2. Je[sus] says: ["If those] who seek to attract you [say to you: 'See,] the Kingdom [is] in hea[ven, then] the birds of hea[ven will be there before you. If they say: 'It] is under the earth!' [then] the fishes of the sea [will be there be]fore you. And the Kingd[om of heaven] is within you! [He who? . . .] knows this will find [. . ."]

3. ["When] you know yourselves, [then you will know that] it is you who are [the sons] of the [living] Father. [But if you do not] know yourselves, then [. . .] and it is you ⟨who will be⟩ the poverty!"

4. Jesus says: "Let the old man heavy with days hesitate not to ask the little child of seven days about the Place of Life, and he will live! For it will be seen that many of the first will be last, and they will become a ⟨single thing!"⟩

5. Jesus says: "Know what is before your face, and what is hidden from you will be revealed to you. For nothing hidden will fail to be revealed!"

6. His disciples asked and said to him: "Do you want us to fast? How shall we pray, how shall we give alms, what rules concerning eating shall we follow?" Jesus says: "Tell no lie, and whatever you hate, do not do: for all these things are manifest to the face of heaven; nothing hidden will fail to be revealed, and nothing disguised will fail before long to be made public!"

7. Jesus says: "Blessed is the lion which a man eats so that the lion becomes a man. But cursed is the man whom a lion eats so that the man becomes a lion!"

Oxyr. Papyrus 654 (cont.):

4. [Jesus says:] "The ma[n heavy with da]ys will not hesitate to ask the little [child of seven da]ys about the Place of [Life! For you will] see that many of the fi[rst] will be [last, and] the last first, and [that they will] be [a ⟨single thing!"⟩]

5. Jesus says: ["Know what is be]fore your face, and [what is hidden] from you will be revealed [to you. For there] is [nothing] hidden which [will] not be revealed, nor ⟨anything⟩ buried which [will not be raised up!"]

6. [His disciples] asked [and] say to him: "How shall we fa[st and how shall we pr]ay, and how [. . .], and what rules shall [we] follow [concerning eating?"] Jesus says: [". . .] do not [. . .] of truth [. . .] hidden [. . ."]

7. [. . . Ble]ssed is [. . .]
End of the Fragment

Fragment from a shroud from Oxyrhynchus: Greek inscription:

5. Jesus says: "There is nothing buried which shall not be raised up ✠"

8. Then he says: "A man is like a skilled fisherman who cast his net into the sea. He brought it up out of the sea full of little fishes, and among them the skilled fisherman found one that was big and excellent. He threw all the little fishes back (p. 34) into the sea; without hesitating he chose the big fish. He who has ears to hear, let him hear!"

9. Jesus says: "See, the sower went out. He filled his hand and scattered ⟨the seed.⟩ Some fell on the path: birds came and gathered them. Others fell on rocky ground: they found no means of taking root in the soil and did not send up ears of corn. Others fell among thorns; ⟨these⟩ stifled the grain, and the worm ate the ⟨seed.⟩ Others fell on good soil, and this ⟨portion⟩ produced an excellent crop: it gave as much as sixty-fold, and ⟨even⟩ a hundred and twenty-fold!"

10. Jesus says: "I have cast a fire onto the world, and see, I watch over it until it blazes up!"

11. Jesus says: "This heaven will pass away, and the heaven which is above it will pass: but those who are dead will not live, and those who live will not die!"

12. "Today you eat dead things and make them into something living: ⟨but⟩ when you will be in Light, what will you do then? For then you will become two instead of one; and when you become two, what will you do then?"

13. The disciples say to Jesus: "We know that Thou wilt leave us: who will ⟨then⟩ be the great⟨est⟩ over us?" Jesus says to them: "Wherever you go, you will turn to James the Just, for whose sake heaven as well as earth was produced."

14. Jesus says to his disciples: "Compare me, and tell me whom I am like." Simon Peter says to him: "Thou art like a just angel!" Matthew says to him: (p. 35) "Thou art like a wise man and a philosopher!" Thomas says to him: "Master, my tongue cannot find words to say whom thou art like." Jesus says: "I am no longer thy master; for thou hast drunk, thou art inebriated from the bubbling spring which is mine and which I sent forth." Then he took him aside; he said three words to him. And when Thomas came back to his companions, they asked him: "What did Jesus say to thee?" And Thomas answered them: "If I tell you⟨a single⟩

one of the words he said to me, you will take up stones and throw them at me, and fire will come out of the stones and consume you!"

15. Jesus says to them: "When you fast, you will beget sin for yourselves; when you pray, you will be condemned; when you give alms, you will do evil to your souls! ⟨But⟩ when you enter any land and travel over the country, when you are welcomed eat what is put before you; those who are ill in those places, heal them. For what enters into your mouth will not defile you, but what comes out of your mouth, it is that which will defile you!"

16. Jesus says: "When you see Him who has not been born of woman, bow down face to the earth and adore Him: He is your father!"

17. Jesus says: "Men indeed think I have come to bring peace to the world. But they do not know that I have come to bring to the world discord, fire, sword, war. Indeed, if there are five ⟨people⟩ in (p. 36) a house, they will become three against two and two against three—father against son and son against father—and they will be lifted up, being solitaries."

18. Jesus says: "I will give you what eye has never seen, and what ear has never heard, and what hand has never touched, and what has never entered into the heart of man."

19. The disciples say to Jesus: "Tell us what our end will be." Jesus says: "Have you then deciphered the beginning, that you ask about the end? For where the beginning is, there shall be the end. Blessed is the man who reaches the beginning; he will know the end, and will not taste death!"

20. Jesus says: "Blessed is the man who existed before he came into being!"

21. "If you become my disciples and if you hear my words, these stones will serve you."

22. "For you have there, in Paradise, five trees which change not winter nor summer, whose leaves do not fall: whoever knows them will not taste death!"

23. The disciples say to Jesus: "Tell us what the Kingdom of heaven is like!" He says to them: "It is like a grain of mustard: it is smaller than all the ⟨other⟩ seeds, but when it falls on ploughed

land it produces a big stalk and becomes a shelter for the birds of heaven."

24. Mary says to Jesus: "Who are your disciples like?" He says to her: "They are like (p. 37) little children who have made their way into a field that does not belong to them. When the owners of the field come, they will say: 'Get out of our field!' They ⟨then⟩ will give up the field to these ⟨people⟩ and let them have their field back again."

25. "That is why I tell you this: If the master of the house knows that the thief is coming, he will watch before he comes and will not allow him to force an entry into his royal house to carry off its furniture. You, then, be on the watch against the world. Gird your loins with great energy, so that the brigands do not find any way of reaching you; for they will find any place you fail to watch."

26. "Let there be among you ⟨such⟩ a prudent man: when the fruit arrived, quickly, sickle in hand, he went and harvested it. He who has ears to hear, let him hear!"

27. Jesus saw some children who were taking the breast: he said to his disciples: "These little ones who suck are like those who enter the Kingdom." They said to him: "If we are little, shall we enter the Kingdom?" Jesus says to them: "When you make the two ⟨become⟩ one, and when you make the inside like the outside and the outside like the inside, and the upper like the lower! And if you make the male and the female one, so that the male is no longer male and the female no longer female, and when you put eyes in the place of an eye, and a hand in the place of a hand, and a foot in the place of a foot, and an image in the place of an image, then you will enter [the Kingdom!"]

28. (p. 38) Jesus says: "I will choose you, one from a thousand and two from ten thousand, and those ⟨whom I have chosen⟩ will be lifted up, being one!"

29. His disciples say to him: "Instruct us about the place where thou art, for we must know about it!" He says to them: "He who has ears, let him hear! If a light exists inside a luminous one, then it gives light to the whole world; but if it does not give light, ⟨it means that it is⟩ a darkness."

30. Jesus says: "Love thy brother like thy soul; watch over him like the apple of thine eye."

31. Jesus says: "The straw that is in thy brother's eye, thou seest; but the beam that is in thine own eye, thou seest not! When thou hast cast out the beam that is in thine own eye, then thou wilt see to cast out the straw from thy brother's eye."

32. "If you do not fast from the world, you will not find the Kingdom. If you do not make the Sabbath the ⟨true⟩ Sabbath, you will not see the Father."

33. Jesus says: "I stood in the midst of the world, and in the flesh I manifested myself to them. I found them all drunk; I found none athirst among them. And my soul was afflicted for the children of men. Because they are blind in their heart and do not see, because they have come into the world empty, ⟨that is why⟩ they seek still to go out from the world empty. But let someone come who will correct them! Then, when they have slept off their wine, they will repent."

34. Jesus says: "If the flesh was produced for the sake of the spirit, it is a miracle. But if the spirit ⟨was produced⟩ for the sake of the body, it is a miracle of a miracle." But for myself (?), I marvel (p. 39) at that because the [... of] this (?) great wealth has dwelt in this poverty.

35. Jesus says: "There where there are three gods, they are gods. Where there are two, or ⟨else⟩ one, I am with him!"

36. Jesus says: "A prophet is not accepted in his ⟨own⟩ city, and a doctor does not heal those who know him."

Oxyr. Papyrus I:

31. ....] then thou wilt see to cast out the straw that is thy brother's eye."

32. Jesus says: "If you do not fast from the world, you will not find the Kingdom of God. And if you do not make the Sabbath the ⟨true⟩ Sabbath, you will not see the Father."

34. ....] the poverty."

35. Jesus says: "Where there are [two (?) they are] not without God, and where there is one, I say ⟨to you⟩, I am with him. Raise the stone, and there thou wilt find me; split the wood: I am even there!" (*cf.* § 81 *of the Coptic version*).

37. Jesus says: "A city built on a high mountain, and which is strong, it is not possible that it should fall, and it cannot be hidden!"

38. Jesus says: "What thou hearest with thine ear, and the other ear, proclaim from the roof-tops! For no-one lights a lamp and puts it under a bushel or in a hidden place: but he puts it on the lamp-stand so that all who come in or go out should see the light."

39. Jesus says: "If a blind man leads another blind man, both of them fall into a ditch."

40. Jesus says: "It is not possible for someone to enter the house of a strong man and do him violence if he has not tied his hands: ⟨only⟩ then will he plunder his house."

41. Jesus says: "Have no care, from morning to evening and from evening to morning, about what you shall put on."

42. His disciples say to him: "On what day wilt thou appear to us, and what day shall we see thee?" Jesus says: "When you strip yourselves without being ashamed, when you take off your clothes and lay them at your feet like little children and trample on them! Then [you will become] (p. 40) children of Him who is living, and you will have no more fear."

Oxyr. Papyrus 1 (conclusion):

36. Jesus says: "A prophet is not acceptable in his own country, and a doctor does not heal those who know him!"

37. Jesus says: "A city built on the summit of a high mountain, and fortified, can neither fall nor be hidden."

38. Jesus says: "You hear with one of your ears [. . .

Oxyr. Papyrus 655:

41. . . .] from morning to [evening and] from evening [to mor]ning, nor for [yo]ur [food] that you shall ea[t, nor for your] cloth[ing] that you shall put on. [You are mu]ch super[ior] to the lilies which grow and do [not sp]in. If you have a garment, what do you la[ck?] Who can add to your height? He himself will give you your clothing!"

42. His disciples say to him: "When wilt thou appear to us, and when shall we see thee?" He says ⟨to them:⟩ "When you strip yourselves and are not ashamed [. . .

43. Jesus says: "You have desired many times to hear these words which I say to you, but you could not find anyone else from whom to hear them. The days will come when you will seek me, and when you will not find me."

44. Jesus says: "The Pharisees and the scribes have taken the keys of knowledge and hidden them: they have not entered, and neither have they permitted ⟨entry⟩ to those who wished to enter. But you, be prudent as serpents and simple as doves!"

45. Jesus says: "A vine shoot was planted outside the Father. It did not grow strong: it will be plucked up from the root and it will perish."

46. Jesus says: "To him who has in his hand, ⟨more⟩ will be given. But from him who has not, ⟨even⟩ the little he has will be taken away!"

47. Jesus says: "You must be ⟨as⟩ passers-by!"

48. His disciples said to him: "Who art thou, who tellest us these things?" "By the things that I tell you, do you not recognise who I am? But you yourselves have become like the Jews: they like the tree and detest the fruit, they like the fruit and detest the tree!"

49. Jesus says: "He who has blasphemed the Father will be forgiven, and he who has blasphemed the Son will be forgiven: but he who has blasphemed the Holy Spirit will not be forgiven either on earth or in heaven."

50. Jesus says: "Grapes are not gathered from thistles, and figs are not gathered from thorns: they do not give fruit! [. . . a] good man brings out of his barn (p. 41) what is good, but a wicked man brings out of his wicked barn—which is in his heart—evil⟨things⟩, and from them he sows evil, because ⟨they are⟩ evil ⟨things that⟩ he brings out of the abundance of his heart."

Oxyr. Papyrus 655:

43. (*only a few letters of this passage remain*).

44. [. . . have] taken [the key] of [knowledge ⟨gnosis⟩ and have] hidden [it:] they [have not] entered; [and those who wished] to enter, [they] have not [. . .

51. Jesus says: "From Adam to John the Baptist, among those who have been born of women, there is none greater than John the Baptist! But for fear that the eyes ⟨of such a one⟩ should be lost I have said: He who among you shall be the small⟨est⟩ shall know the Kingdom and be higher than John!"

52. Jesus says: "It is not possible for a man to ride two horses, nor to draw two bows. And it is not possible for a servant to serve two masters: otherwise he will honour the one and the other will treat him harshly! Never does a man drink old wine and desire at the same instant to drink new wine; new wine is not poured into old wine-skins, in case they should burst, and old wine is not poured into new wine-skins, in case it should be spoiled. An old piece of cloth is not sown onto a new garment, for a tear would result."

53. Jesus says: "If two people are with each other in peace in the same house, they will say to the mountain: 'Move!' and it will move."

54. Jesus says: "Blessed are the solitary and the elect, for you will find the Kingdom! Because you have issued from it, you will return to it again."

55. Jesus says: "If people ask you: "Where have you come from?" tell them: 'We have come from the Light, from the place where the Light is produced [. . .] outside itself ⟨or: of it-self?⟩. It [. . . (p. 42) . . .] until they show (?) [. . .] their image.' If someone says to you: 'What are you?' say: 'We are the sons and we are the elect of the living Father.' If ⟨people⟩ ask you: 'What sign of your Father is in you?' tell them: 'It is a movement and a rest.' "

56. His disciples said to him: "On what day shall rest come to those who are dead, and on what day shall the new world come?" He said to them: "This ⟨rest⟩ that you wait for has ⟨already⟩ come, and you have not recognised it."

57. His disciples said to him: "Twenty-four prophets spoke in Israel, and they all spoke through you!" He said to them: "You have passed over Him who is living in front of your eyes, and have spoken of the dead!"

58. His disciples said to him: "Is circumcision useful or not?"

He said to them: "If it was useful, their father would beget them from their mother ⟨already⟩ circumcised. But ⟨only⟩ the true circumcision in the spirit gives all profit!"

59. Jesus says: "Blessed are the poor, for the Kingdom of heaven is yours!"

60. Jesus says: "He who does not hate his father and mother cannot be my disciple; and if he does not hate his brother and sister and does not take up his cross like me, he will not become worthy of me!"

61. Jesus says: "He who has known the world has fallen into a corpse; and he who has fallen into a corpse, the world is not worthy of him!"

62. Jesus says: "The Kingdom of the Father is like a man who has [good] seed ⟨in his field.⟩ By night his enemy came (p. 43) and sowed tares over the seed which is good. ⟨But⟩ this man did not allow them ⟨his servants⟩ to pluck up the tares, 'for fear', he told them, 'that in going to take away the tares, you carry off the wheat with it. But on the harvest day the tares will be recognisable; they will be taken away and burnt.'"

63. Jesus says: "Blessed is the man who has laboured; he has found Life!"

64. Jesus says: "Seek to see Him who is living, while you are living; rather than to die and to seek to see Him ⟨only⟩ when you can no longer see Him!"

Just then a Samaritan was going into Judea carrying a lamb. He ⟨=Jesus⟩ said to His disciples: "What ⟨will⟩ this man ⟨do⟩ with the lamb?" They answered: "He will kill it and eat it!" But he said to them: "He will not eat it as long as it is still alive, but only if he kills it and it becomes a corpse" They said to him: "In no other way will he hurt it!" ⟨Then⟩ he said to them: "You yourselves, then, seek a place of rest so that you do not become corpses and are eaten!"

65. Jesus says: "Two will lie down there on one bed: one will die, the other will live."

Salome says: "Who art thou, man; from whom hast thou ⟨come forth,⟩ that thou shouldst lie on my couch and eat at my table?" Jesus says to her: "I am he who has been brought into being by Him who is equal ⟨to me:⟩ I have been given what belongs to my Father!"—"I am thy disciple!"

Because of that, I say this: When ⟨a person⟩ finds himself solitary, he will be full of light; but when he finds himself divided, he will be full of darkness.

66. Jesus says: "When I tell my mysteries to [. . . (p. 44) . . .] mystery: [what] your right hand does, let your left hand not know ⟨that⟩ it does it."

67. Jesus says: "There was a rich man who had many possessions. He said ⟨to himself:⟩ 'I will use my wealth to sow my field, to plant, to fill my barn with harvest, so that need will not touch me.' Such were the things that he thought in his heart. But during that night, he died. He who has ears to hear, let him hear!"

68. Jesus says: "A man had guests. When he had prepared the feast, he sent his servant to call these guests. He went to the first and said to him: 'My master invites thee!' ⟨The other⟩ replied: 'I am due to receive some money from some merchants; they are coming to see me this evening and I am going to give them orders. I ask to be excused from the feast.' ⟨The servant⟩ went to another and said to him: 'My master has invited thee.' ⟨He⟩ said to him: 'I have bought a house and I am needed for the day: I am not free.' He went to another and said to him: 'My master invites thee!' ⟨He⟩ replied: 'My friend is being married and I am giving a feast ⟨for him⟩. I will not come; I ask to be excused from the feast!' He went to another and said to him: 'My master invites thee!' ⟨He⟩ said to him: 'I have bought a field (?) and I have not yet been to receive the revenue ⟨from it⟩. I will not be coming; I ask to be excused from the feast!' The servant returned and said to his master: 'Those whom you invited to the feast have excused themselves.' The master said to his servant: 'Go out into the streets and those whom you find, bring in to dine.' The buyers and mer[chants will not enter] into the places of my Father."

69. (p. 45) He said: "An [important] man had a vineyard which he gave to cultivators so that they should work it and he should receive the fruit from them. He sent his servant so that the cultivators should give him the fruit of the vineyard: ⟨but⟩ they

seized his servant, beat him and almost killed him. The servant came back and told this to his master. His master said ⟨to himself⟩ 'Perhaps he did not recognize them?' He sent another servant: the cultivators beat this one also. Then the master sent his son: he said to himself: 'No doubt they will respect my child?' But when they realized that this was the heir to the vineyard, these cultivators seized him and killed him. He who has ears let him hear!"

70. Jesus says: "Would that thou couldst tell me about the stone which the builders have rejected! It is that one, the cornerstone."

71. Jesus says: "He who knows the All, but has failed to know himself, has failed completely to know, ⟨or: to find⟩ the Place!"

72. Jesus says: "Blessed are you when you are hated and persecuted; but they will not find a position in that place to which they shall pursue you!"

73. Jesus says: "Blessed are those who are persecuted in their hearts. They are those who have known (?) the Father in truth! Blessed are those who are hungry, because they will satisfy their bellies to ⟨their⟩ content!"

74. Jesus says: "When you have something left to share among you, what you possess will save you. But if you cannot share [among you], that which you have not among you, that[...?... will ...] you.

75. Jesus says: "I will [. . .] and no one will be able [. . . (p. 46) . . .]

76. [Someone (?) said] to him: "Speak to my brothers, that they may share with me my father's possessions!" He answered him: "Man, who made me a sharer?" He turned to his disciples and said to them: "Let me not be a sharer!"

77. Jesus says: "The harvest is great but the labourers are few. Pray the Lord to send labourers for the harvest."

78. He said: "Lord, many are round the opening but nobody in the well!"

79. Jesus says: "Many stand outside at the door, but it is only the solitaries who will enter into the bridal chamber."

80. Jesus says: "The Kingdom of the Father is like a man, a merchant, who has a burden and found a pearl. This merchant

is a wise man: he sold the bundle and bought the pearl alone. You also seek his treasure which does not perish, which lasts, into which the moth does not enter to consume and ⟨where⟩ the worm does not destroy."

81. Jesus says: "I am the light which is on them all. I am the All, and the All has gone out from me and the All has come back to me. Cleave the wood: I am there; lift the stone and thou shalt find me there!"[1]

82. Jesus says: "Why did you go out into the country-side? ⟨Was it⟩ to see a reed shaken [by] the wind, and to see a m[an with soft] garments clothing him? [But they are in the dwelling-places of] kings and your great ones, (p. 47) those whom [soft garments] clothe, and they do not know the truth!"

83. In the crowd a woman says to him: "Blessed is the womb which bore thee and the breast which fed thee!" He said to her: "Blessed are those who have heard the word of the Father and keep it! In truth, days are coming when you will say: Happy is the womb that has not brought forth and those breasts which have not given suck!"

84. Jesus says: "He who has known the world has fallen into the body, and he who has fallen into the body, the world is not worthy of him."

85. Jesus says: "Let him who has become rich reign, and let him who has strength refrain ⟨from using it⟩!"

86. Jesus says: "He who is near me is near the fire, and he who is far from me is far from the Kingdom."

87. Jesus says: "Images are visible to man, but the light which is in them is hidden. In the image of the light of the Father, it ⟨this light⟩ will be revealed, and his image will be veiled by his light."

88. Jesus says: "Now, when you see your appearance, you rejoice. But when you see your images which came into being before you, which do not die and do not show themselves, how will you be able to bear such greatness?"

89. Adam was produced by a great power and a great wealth; but he did not receive (?) [. . .] worthy (?) of you, for he was

---

[1] Cf. above, § 35, in the Greek version of *Oxyr. Papyrus* 1.

not worthy [to (?)] be preserved from [being subject (?)] to death."

90. Jesus says: "[The foxes] (p. 48) [have holes] and the birds have [their] nests but the Son of Man has no place to lay his head and rest."

91. He said, he, Jesus: "The body which depends on a body is unfortunate, and the soul which depends on these two is unfortunate!"

92. Jesus says: "The angels and prophets are coming to you; they will give you the things that belong to you. You, give them what you possess, and say: 'When will they come and take what is theirs?'"

93. Jesus says: "Why do you wash the outside of the cup, and do not think that he who made the inside made the outside also?"

94. Jesus says: "Come to me, for my yoke is excellent and my authority is sweet, and you will find rest for yourselves!"

95. They said to him: "Tell us who thou art that we may believe in thee." He said to them: "You examine the appearance of heaven and earth, but He who is in front of you you do not recognise, and this moment you know not how to examine!"

96. Jesus says: "Seek and you will find! But the things you have asked me about during these days and which I have not told you up till now, I now want to tell you, so that you will not have to seek them any longer."

97. "Give not that which is holy to dogs, in case they throw it onto the dunghill; and cast not pearls to swine, for fear that they should make it [. . .]

98. Jesus [says:] "He who seeks will find, [and to whomever wishes to enter (?)] it will be opened."

99. [Jesus says: "If (?)] you have money (p. 49), do not lend it at interest, but [. . .] who (?) will not take them from him."

100. Jesus says: "The Kingdom of the Father is like a woman who put a little yeast [into three] measures of flour and made some big loaves with it. He who has ears let him hear!"

101. Jesus says: "The Kingdom of the Father is like a woman who takes a vessel of flour and sets out on a long road. The handle of the vessel broke: the flour spilled out on the road behind her

without her knowing it and stopping it. When she arrived at the house she put the vessel down and found it was empty."

102. "The Kingdom of the Father is like a man who wants to kill an important person. In his house he unsheathed the sword and stuck it in the wall to assure himself that his hand would be firm. Then he killed the person."

103. The disciples said to him: "Thy brethren and thy mother are there outside." He said to them: "You and (?) those (?) who do the will of my Father, they are my brethren and my mother; it is they who will enter the Kingdom of my Father."

104. They showed Jesus a piece of money and said to him: "The people who belong to Caesar ask us for taxes." He said to them: "Give to Caesar what is Caesar's, give to God what is God's, and what is mine give me!"

105. "He who has not, like me, detested his father and his mother cannot be my disciple; and he who has loved h[is father a]nd his mother as much as he loves me cannot be my disciple. My mother, indeed, has [. . . (p. 50) . . .] because in truth she gave me life."

106. Jesus says: "Cursed are they, the Pharisees, because they are like a dog which has lain in the cattle manger, but will neither eat ⟨ the food there ⟩ nor allow the oxen to eat it."

107. Jesus says: "Blessed is the man who knows [where] the robbers are going to enter, so that he watches, he gathers his [. . .] and girds his loins before they enter."

108. They said [to him:] "Come, let us pray and fast today!" Jesus says: "What then is the sin that I have committed, or in what have I been at fault? But when the bridegroom comes out of the bridal chamber, then they must fast and pray!"

109. Jesus says: "He who knows father and mother shall he be called: 'Son of a harlot!' "?

110. Jesus says: "When you make the two one, you will become sons of Man and if you say: 'Mountain, move!', it will move."

111. Jesus says: "The Kingdom is like a shepherd who has a hundred sheep. One of them, the biggest, went astray. He left the ninety-nine others and looked for this single ⟨ sheep ⟩ until he

found it. After taking this trouble, he said to the sheep: 'I love you more than the ninety-nine ⟨others⟩!' "

112. Jesus says: "He who drinks from my mouth will become like me. As for me, I will become what he is, and what is hidden will be revealed to him."

113. Jesus says: "The Kingdom is like a man who [has] a [hidden] treasure in his field and does not know it. He did not [find it before] he died, and he left his [property to his] son who did not know it ⟨either⟩. He took (p. 51) the field, sold it, and the man who bought it went to till it: [he found] the treasure, and he began to lend at interest to those [whom he] wanted (?).

114. Jesus says: "He who has found the world and become rich, let him renounce the world!"

115. Jesus says: "The heavens and the earth will open (?) before you, and he who lives by Him who is living will not see death", because (?) Jesus says this: "He who keeps to himself alone, the world is not worthy of him."

116. Jesus says: "Cursed is the flesh that depends on the soul, and cursed is the soul that depends on the flesh!"

117. His disciples said to him: "On what day will the Kingdom come?" "It will not come when it is expected. No one will say: 'See, it is here!' or: 'Look, it is there!' but the Kingdom of the Father is spread over the earth and men do not see it."

118. Simon Peter says to them: "Let Mary go out from our midst, for women are not worthy of life!" Jesus says: "See, I will draw her so as to make her male so that she also may become a living spirit like you males. For every woman who has become male will enter the Kingdom of heaven."

NOTES

The numbers refer to the paragraphs of the translation.

6. "nothing hidden will fail to be revealed" no doubt refers to hidden virtues such as those mentioned by Jesus: they are preferable to ostentatious practices of piety, and will one day be made public.

7. For the end of this sentence, the Coptic reads literally: ". . . so that the lion becomes a man"; but it seems most probable that the correct meaning is as given in the translation.

No doubt the lion here represents human passions, or more precisely, the lying spirit of evil. This is suggested by a passage from a Coptic Manichaean Psalm (CCLVII): "This lion which is within me, which defiles me at every moment, I have strangled it and cast it out of my soul. . . ."

12. The first part of this paragraph is quoted and commented on by the *Philosophumena* (V, 8, 31). According to this work, the Naassenes explained it as follows: "If you have eaten dead things and made them living things, what then will you do when you eat living things? These *living things* are rational beings, intelligences, men—pearls which the great Being without form has cast into the work of here below!"

The second part seems to contradict the stress on unity found elsewhere in this work (cf. 27, 28, 110). The solution would appear to lie in the fact that the duality is in fact an aspect of the unity; for the state of "being two" is a synthesis of opposites—male and female, upper and lower, etc. (cf. 27). The sense therefore would appear to be as follows: "In that state where every pair of opposites is united in perfect unity, any increase ('eating') will be assimilated to that unity—even more perfectly than physical eating transforms dead matter into the living substance of the eater."

14. The reply of Thomas to Jesus is in Coptic literally: "Master, to whom thou art like, my face fails utterly to grasp!"—Because Thomas realizes already that Jesus is beyond compare, Jesus tells him that he has already drunk of the fount of divine wisdom and does not need to be taught by him.

15. According to a concept already referred to in 6, fasting, prayer and almsdeeds were the three degrees of active faith, almsdeeds being the highest. Nevertheless, here as in 6, these pious practices seem to be rejected as almost useless and as inferior to the internal dispositions of the soul. In a formula which is so abrupt as to appear rather harsh, this paragraph

underlines the opposition between the regard for these traditional practices and the gospel precept: "Eat what is put before you. . . . That which enters your mouth does not defile you. . . ."

17. ". . . lifted up, being solitaries": that is, elevated to the state of being solitaries.

The teaching: "I have not come to bring peace . . . but the sword" was explained in a similar way by the Sethian Gnostics (according to the *Philosophumena* V, 21); they taught that all bodies, inert or living, of this lower world had to have their basic elements separated from each other if they were to rise to the higher world. Elsewhere in the *Gospel according to Thomas* we find other developments of this doctrine according to which the way of perfection demands solitude, separation, the breaking of the bonds of this lower world: "He who does not hate father and mother cannot be my disciple; and if he does not leave brother and sister he will not become worthy of me. . . ." (cf. §§ 60 and 105; also, 28, 65 and Introduction, p. 346).

19. Cf. the *Gospel of Truth* (Codex XIII, pp. 37-8): "Indeed the Father knows the beginning of all as well as their end. . . . Now the end consists in contemplating that which is hidden. And that which is hidden is the Father, from whom came the Beginning. . . ." Cf. also, in the New Testament, *Apoc.* I, 8, "I am the Alpha and the Omega, the beginning and the end . . ."

20. Cf. the *Gospel of Philip* (Coptic text of Codex X of Chenoboskion) where this formula also appears; and St Irenaeus, who quotes it under the form: "Happy is He who was before becoming man." And in the New Testament, *John* VIII, 58: "Before Abraham was, I am."

22. The five trees, according to the doctrine of oriental Gnosticism and especially Manichaeism, are primordial superior entities; they are usually enumerated as follows: Spirit, Thought, Reflection, Intellect and Reason.

24. ". . . give up the field to these"; literally, "strip themselves before them". For the comparison with "little children",

cf. below, 27, and *Matt.* XVIII, 3: "Unless you be converted and become as little children..." But our text takes this as an exhortation not only to return to the innocence of children, but also to invert all those values—cosmic, human and moral—which have been established since the fall of the first man.

25. "be on the watch against the world": literally, "Be vigilant face to the world." "for they will find any place...": literally, "for the defect that you would have wished to guard against, they will find it in spite of that!"

27. "...eyes in the place of an eye, etc.": It is possible that the last words of this paragraph contain a rather vague reference to an idea that Plotinus develops in his *Enneads* III, 2, 3. They should then be understood: "When you make eyes become strictly eyes; the hand play the part of a hand; the foot confine itself to the function of a foot; and images (that is to say the divine models of the things and beings of this world) have their true value as images—then you will enter the Kingdom."

29. "for we must know about it": literally, "for necessity obliges us to question thee on its subject".

The connection between the question and Jesus' answer is not certain. Probably it should be understood: "This is a subject which you could not fail to know, if you really have the Light within you!"

Or better, "the place where thou art" may be intended to refer to God Himself; in Hebrew God is often referred to by the paraphrase *Maqom*, which means "the Place". In this case, the disciples will be asking him how close he is to the Godhead, and Jesus replies, alluding to himself, that the light which he sends into the world is the proof that the divine Light is present in him.

Part of the ambiguity of the latter half of the paragraph arises from the fact that in Coptic the words "light" and "luminous one" are of the same gender, so that the following pronoun could be either it (the light), or he (the luminous one).

34. The words: "But for myself . . ." seem to be an observation of the compiler, following on Jesus' words. The meaning is: "I am amazed that this great wealth which is the Spirit has come down to dwell in this poverty which is the body!"

35. For the sense of the formula: "Where there are three gods . . ." (proper to the Coptic version), cf. perhaps *John* X, 34: "Is it not written that, 'I have said, You are gods?' If he calls those gods to whom the word of God came . . ." Or perhaps cf. 1 *John* V, 7–8.

The sentence as a whole seems to take as its starting point the same idea as *Matt.* XVIII, 20: "Where there are two or three gathered together, there am I in their midst." But the development is rather different: "Where there is one alone, Jesus is with him. If two who are together become one, then Jesus is with them, and it is an even greater marvel. But if three are gathered together in like manner, then they are the perfect Church, and they attain divinity!"

38. "What you hear with the ear and with the other ear" is equivalent to: "What you hear with both ears."

45. "outside the Father": the elect are in the Kingdom and live "in the Father"; while the wicked are "outside the Father".

51. "for fear that the eyes . . .": the Coptic is very obscure, thus making it prudent to leave this word-for-word translation. One may conjecture the following sense: "It is only to avoid scandalizing and hurting some humble soul that I said: He who is smallest among you shall be higher than John!"

55. On the light from above, that is to say, the supreme divinity, see 81, 87, 88 and Introduction, p. 345. "Movement and rest" is an allusion to notions which classical Greek philosophy discussed frequently, interpreting them in various ways. Cf., for example, Plato's *Parmenides*, 138b–139b.

61. Cf. 84. A being which comes from on high, from the world of images, and experiences the world, has by this very fact undergone a fall; it has entered a material body which is at once its prison, its corpse, its tomb (ideas familiar to Platonic

philosophy): it has "fallen into a corpse". But he who did not refuse this fall, but accepted it and accepted submission to death (that is to say, Jesus), will escape from the corpse!

64. This is one of those passages which seem to represent extracts from works which are no longer known to us, conserved in a form too concise to be directly intelligible. Doubtless it must be understood: "He will not eat the living lamb—he must kill it first and make it a corpse." The disciples reply: "But if he kills it, the man cannot do the lamb any other harm!"

This dialogue recalls a notion found in the apocryphal *II Epistle of Clement*: "The Lord said indeed: You shall be as lambs in the midst of wolves! Peter replied: And if the wolves rend the lambs? And Jesus said to Peter: After their death, the lambs have nothing further to fear from the wolves. You also, fear not those who kill you and cannot then make you suffer anything further. But fear him who after your death has power to cast your soul and your body into the gehenna of fire! Know then . . . that the promise of Christ is great . . . as also the Repose of the Kingdom . . .!"

65. The main part of this paragraph is taken from some apocryphal gospel (perhaps the *Gospel of the Egyptians*?). It centres on Salome's question to Jesus: "Who art thou? Where have you come from, to sit on my couch and eat at my table?" (the couch of course being the place where they reclined at table). Then, this reference to the *couch* probably led to the artificial addition at the beginning of the sentence, of the passage: "Two will lie down on one bed . . ." The next step was an addition by the editor (another example of such a commentary introduced by the editor is found in 115): from the association of these two texts, he tried to bring out the idea that duality is the source of death and darkness, while unity—isolation, solitariness—leads to light and life. Thus the phrase: "Because of that . . ." no doubt introduces the editor's comment: "Because of those two sayings ('Two will lie down . . .' and 'Salome says . . .'), I give you the following teaching. . . ."

13*

66. The missing portion cannot be restored; but judging from the remaining parallel, one might judge the sense to have been: "When I tell my mysteries to one person, I do not tell these same mysteries to another."

69. "Perhaps he did not recognize them?" is the word-for-word rendering of the Coptic; but the sense is clearly: "Perhaps they did not recognize him."

70. "... tell me about the stone ...": could also be understood: "which is the stone ..."

71. "... but has failed to know himself, etc.": literally: "... who has need only of himself, has need of all the Place!"
    For "the Place", see note on § 29: here again, and perhaps also in the following, the Place is a paraphrase for God, like the Hebrew *Maqom*.

72. The Place to which you are pursued is no doubt the same place as that mentioned in the preceding paragraph, that is to say, the Kingdom (the presence of God), which the wicked will not enter.

78. That is, many people stand round the mouth of the well, but no one draws water from it.

80. "has a burden": this seems to mean "his luggage"—i.e., he is on a journey, when he finds a pearl of great price.
    "his treasure": either the Father's, or a treasure like that of the merchant.

81. Cf. the Gnostic *Gospel of Truth* (Codex XIII of Chenoboskion, p. 17): "The All has been in search of Him from whom he came forth; and the All was within him, unseizable, unthinkable!" One might also mention the *Acts of Peter*, Chapter XXXIX: "Thou art the All, and the All is in thee, and thou art! And there is nothing else that exists, except thou alone!" The same allusion is found in *Col.* III, 11: "Christ is all and in all."

84. Cf. 61 above.

85. This saying can be elucidated by §114. It will mean: "He who has acquired the interior riches of the Kingdom, let him comport himself royally (i.e. generously); and he who has a power, let him renounce the use of it!"

86. The Kingdom is the divine presence, which is often compared with fire in the Bible (cf. *Ezech.* I, 27-8, etc.).
87. The doctrine of images is of Platonic origin; they are the models or primordial unattainable ideas, which exist in the mind of God. Here, however, it is the images which are visible, while the light which is within them is invisible. It becomes visible, however, through the Father's light, while his image remains veiled by his light.—This paragraph seems to be connected with the following.
88. "how will you be able to bear such greatness?": literally, "what greatness will you support?"
89. The sense of the missing passage seems to be: "Great as Adam was, he was not as great as you, for . . ."
91. No doubt this is to be explained by *Luke* IX, 57-60 and *Matt.* VIII, 21-2: "Let the dead bury their dead." In this case, "the body which depends on a body" is a living person who, through care for earthly obligations, wishes to bury his dead person. "The soul which depends on these two" is the soul of such a person, a living body depending on a dead body.
92. Perhaps this means: "Have more care to give to heaven than to receive from it, for you receive from the angels and prophets the spiritual food you need." Cf. *Matt.* X, 8: "Freely have you received—freely give."
101. The Kingdom arrives—or is lost—without being noticed; like a woman who loses her flour without realizing it.
102. Cf. *Luke* XIV, 31: the parable of the king who takes into account the strength of his troops before making war.
115. "because . . .": introduces an explanation or conclusion of one of the editors of the *Gospel of Thomas*; cf. 65. He draws a comparison between the person who lives by "Him who is living" (the Risen Jesus) and the person who has achieved solitude and unity.

INDEX OF REFERENCES TO THE
CANONICAL GOSPELS

AN index of references to the canonical Gospels is obviously a necessity in a work like the present. But further, although it does not claim to be absolutely precise, it will cast some light on the structure of these "Words of Jesus". Some parts of the collection will be seen to be almost completely original, others to be more or less homogeneous groups of matter allied to that which is found also in the canonical Gospels.

It will be seen at a glance that the main parallels are with *Matthew* and *Luke*. Even more specifically, most of the references we have picked out concern *Matthew*, Chapters V–VII (the Sermon on the Mount): Ch. XIII (the Parables of the Kingdom); Chs. XVIII–XIX (teachings concerning the life of the community); Ch. XXIV (eschatalogical discourse); *Luke*, Chs. VIII–XIII (Parables and missionary discourse to the disciples); and finally *Mark* IV (Parables) and IX (community life).

Different type distinguishes the different kinds of parallel or analogy:

XXIV, 43–44: where there is almost perfect identity between our text and that of the Gospel;

V, 10–11: where there is certainly a parallel but not complete identity;

VII, 7–8: where there is only a certain analogy;

[XI, 9–10]
[IX, 27]
[VII, 7–8] the same kinds of type enclosed in square brackets indicates that the above relationship—complete parallel, partial parallel, analogy—is found but only in part of the paragraph of our text;

* an asterisk indicates purely oratorical formulas (such as: "He who hears these words will not taste death!" or: "He who has ears to hear let him hear!") which recur throughout the text like a refrain.

THOMAS	MATTHEW	LUKE	MARK	JOHN
Incipit	[*XVI, 28]	[*IX, 27]	[*IX, 1]	[*VIII, 51]
1	[VII, 8]	[XI, 9-10]		
2				
3	[XXIV, 26-28]	[XVII, 20-24]	[XIII, 5 and 21-23]	
4	[*XVIII, 1-4; *XIX, 30; *XX, 16]	[*IX, 46-48; *XIII, 30]	[*IX, 35; *X, 31]	
5	[*X, 26]	[*VIII, 17; *XII, 2]	[*IV, 22]	
6	[VI, 1-18] [*X, 26]	[XI, 1] [*VIII, 17; *XII, 2]	[*IV, 22]	
7				
8	XIII, 47-50 + [*XIII, 9]	[VIII, 9]	[*IV, 9 and 23]	[VIII, 51]
9	XIII, 4-9	VIII, 5-8	IV, 3-9	
10		XII, 49		
11	[V, 18-19?]; [XVI, 28]; [XXIV, 34-35]	[IX, 27]; [XXI, 32-33]; XVI, 17	[IX, 1]; [XIII, 30-31]	
12	[XVIII, 1]	[IX, 46], [XXII, 24]	[IX, 33-34]	
13	[XVI, 13-20]	[IX, 18-21]	[VIII, 27-30]	
14	[X, 8]; [XV, 11]	[X, 7-9]	[VII, 15]	
15				XIV, 8-9
16	X, 34-36	XII, 51-53		
17				
18				
19	[*XVI, 28]	[*IX, 27]	[*IX, 1]	[I, 1 + 4]; [*VIII, 51]; cf. VIII, 57-58
20				
21				
22	[*XVI, 28]	[*IX, 27]	[*IX, 1]	[*VIII, 51]
23	XIII, 31-32	XIII, 18-19	IV, 30-32	

Thomas	Matthew	Luke	Mark	John
24 25 26 27 28 29	XXIV, 43–44 [*XIII, 9]	XII, 39–40 + XII, 35 [*VIII, 9]	XIII, 33–37 [*IV, 9 and 23]	[VII, 34–35] [XII, 26]
30 31 32 33 34	[*XIII, 9] [VI, 22–23] VII, 3–5	[*VIII, 9] [XI, 33–36] VI, 41–42	[*IV, 9 and 23]	
35 36 37 38	[XVIII, 20] [XIII, 57] V, 14 [X, 27 + V, 15]	IV, 24 [VIII, 16 and XII, 3] [XI, 33 sq.] VI, 39 XI, 21 [XII, 22 sq.]	[VI, 4] [IV, 21] III, 27	X, 35 [IV, 44]
39 40 41 42 43	XV, 14 XII, 29 VI, 25 sq.			[VII, 34–36; VIII, 21; XIII, 33; XVI, 16]
§ 44 § 45 § 46	XXIII, 13 + X, 16 VII, 19; III, 7; cf. XXI, 19–21 XIII, 12; XXV, 29	[XI, 52] XIII, 6–9; III, 9 VIII, 18; XIX, 26	cf. XI, 13–14 IV, 25	XV, 5–6

THOMAS	MATTHEW	LUKE	MARK	JOHN
47	[VII, 16-20] [XII, 33]			[VIII, 25]
48	XII, 31-32	XII, 10	III, 28-29	
49	VII, 16-18 + XII, 33-35	[V, 44]		
50	XI, 11	VII, 28		
51	[VI, 24 + IX, 16-17]	[XVI, 13 + V, 36-39]	[II, 21-22]	
52	XVIII, 19 + XVII, 20 and XXI, 21; cf. V, 9	[XVII, 6]		
53				
54		XVII, 20-21		
55	V, 3	VI, 20		
56	X, 37-38; XIX, 29	XIV, 26-27; XVIII, 29	X, 29	
57	XIII, 24-30			
58				
59				
60	[XVIII, 12-14?]	[XV, 4-6?]		
61	[XXIV, 40]	[XVII, 34]		
62	[VI, 3]			
63	[*XIII, 9]	XII, 16-20 [*VIII, 9]	[*IV, 9 + *IV, 23]	
64	XXII, 1-14	XIV, 16-24		
65	XXI, 33-46 [+ *XIII, 9]	XX, 9-19 [+ *VIII, 9]	XII, 1-12 [+ *IV, 9; IV, 23]	
66				
67				
68				
69				
70				
71	XXI, 42-43	XX, 17-18	XII, 10	

THOMAS	MATTHEW	LUKE	MARK	JOHN
72	[V, 10]	[VI, 22]		
73	V, 10-11 + V, 6	VI, 21-22		
74				
75				
76	IX, 37-38	XII, 13-14		
77		X, 2		I, 1-4
78		[XII, 33-44]		
79	[XXII, 14]			
80	XIII, 45-46 + VI, 19-20	VII, 24-25	[XIII, 17]	
81		XI, 27-28 + XXIII, 29		
82	XI, 7-8	[XXI, 23]		
83	[XXIV, 19]			
84				
85				
86				
87				
88				
89				
90	VIII, 20	IX, 58		
91	VIII, 21-22	IX, 59-60		
92				
93	XXIII, 25-26	XI, 39-40		
94	XI, 28-30			
95	XVI, 1 and XVI, 2-3	XI, 16 + XII, 54-56	VIII, 11	
96	[VII, 7-8]	[XI, 9-10]		
97	VII, 6			VIII, 25

THOMAS	MATTHEW	LUKE	MARK	JOHN
98	VII, 7–8	XI, 9–10		
99				
100	XIII, 33 + *XIII, 9	XIII, 20–21 + *VIII, 9	[*IV, 9; 23]	
101		XIV, 31		
102				
103	XII, 46–50	VIII, 19–21	III, 31–35	
104	XXII, 17–21 [X, 37]	XX, 22–25	XII, 14–17	
105	cf. XXIII, 13	[XIV, 26–27]		
106		cf. XI, 52		
107	XXIV, 43–44 [IX, 14–15]	XII, 35, and 39–40 [V, 33–34]	[II, 18–19]	
108	[XVIII, 19 + XXI, 21; XVII, 20]			
109	XVIII, 12–13	XV, 4–6		
110	[XIII, 44]			
111	[V, 18–19?]; [XVI, 28]; [XXIV, 34–35]	[IX, 27]; [XXI, 32–33]	[IX, 1]; [XIII, 30–31]	[VIII, 51]
112				
113				
114				
115				
116				
117	[XXIV, 3]; XXIV, 23–26	XVII, 20–21; [XXI, 7]	[XIII, 4–21]	
118				

INDEX

INDEX

A complete list of the Chenoboskion MSS. is given on pp. 142–5. In the index each work will be found under its own title, which is printed in italic capitals.
N.B. Some works from Chenoboskion, e.g. *ACTS OF PETER*, have a title identical with that of a quite different work, known to us previously, e.g. *Acts of Peter*.

Abadon, 293n.
  in Gikatila, 293
Abel:
  in a Gnostic fragment, 89
  inferior brother of Seth, in Gnostic belief, 158
  in *HYPOSTASIS*, etc., 160
  in Kantaean teaching, 59
  in Ophite teaching, 39, 39n.
  in *SECRET BOOK*, etc. (Cod. X), the man, 207
  a power, 202
  in Valentinianism, 32
Aberamenthô, = Jesus, 74
  a statue of, 105
Abgar, fictitious correspondence of, with Jesus, 340
Abhandlungen der Preussischen Akademie der Wissenschaften, 272n.
Abraham:
  a teacher of Zoroaster in Jewish belief, 280–1, 281n.
  and in Chenoboskion MSS., 287
  effigy of reverenced by Alexander Severus, 11
  in Isma'ilite belief, 321
  in Jewish belief, an astrologer, 288
  in Ophite teaching, 39–40
  in teaching of John of Apamea, 57–8
Abrasax in Jêou the painter, 105
  in *SACRED BOOK OF THE INVISIBLE SPIRIT*, 178
Abraxas, creator-archon in Basilides' teaching, 23
  depicted on gems, 93
  in *APOCALYPSE OF ADAM*, etc., 182
  in *SACRED BOOK OF INVISIBLE SPIRIT*, 286n.
Abu'l Faraj, *see* Gregory bar-Hebraeus
Académie des Inscriptions et Beaux Arts:
  first Chenoboskion find reported to, xii
  first two finds reported to, 119
  Miss Dattari's MSS. reported to, 122
  report on the *GOSPEL OF THOMAS* to, 126, 126n.
Accademia Nazionale dei Lincei:
  Atti. Memorie della Classe di Scienze morali, 73n., 74n., 155n., 293n.

Accademia Nazionale die Lincei (cont.):
  Fondazione Al. Volta, Atti dei Convegni, 177n., 321n.
  Quaderno, 94n.
Achelis, ed., Hippolytus, *De resurrectione*, 301n.
Acts of Andrew, 343
Acts of Andrew and Matthias, 175n.
Acts of Archelaus, an anti-Manichaean treatise, 7
  on Basilides' *Commentary*, 20, 20n., 21
  on Basilides' Three Principles, 21, 259, 263n.
  on origin of Manichaeism, 7, 314
Acts of John, 22n., 28n., 95, 95n., 343
ACTS OF PETER:
  a new work, 146
  described, 235
  discussed, 235–6
  in author's classification, 143
Acts of Peter, not Gnostic, 87
  on Simon's death, 16–17
  relationship of, to *GOSPEL OF THOMAS*, 343, 346, 349, 376
Acts of Philip, 343, 346, 349
Acts of Pilate (Gospel of Nicodemus), 95, 95n.
Acts of the Apostles:
  on Simon Magus, 1, 15–16, 222n.
  on the Egyptian false messiah, 301
  Silas in, = Sylvanus (?), 219, 219n.
Acts of Thomas, 95, 95n.
  "Hymn of the Pearl", 49n., 95, 255
Acts (Acta) of Thomas, 73n., 95, 227n., 340, 343, 347
Adam:
  alchemical interpretation of, 101n.
  and Eve, in Chenoboskion MSS. and *Pirqé Rabbi Eli'ezer*, 286
  depicted in tomb of the Aurelii, 92
  apocryphal books attributed to, 41, 97n., 115
  apocryphal literature about, 47n.
  article in *Encyclopédie de l'Islam*, 317n.
  as depicted on an ivory, 207n.
  as father of Norea, 163
  Cave of, 161n.
  father of Seth, revelations of are pre-Gnostic, 184, 184n.

Adam (*cont.*):
father of Seth, replaced by Seth in *Books of Adam*, 185
freed from Fate, a more ancient concept than Gnosticism (?), 295
his fatherhood of Seth superior to that of Cain, etc., 158
prayers attributed to, 107, 291
in apocryphal books, gives account of creation of man, 96
in Audius' teaching, 56, 57
in Battai's teaching, 60
in *Book of Mysteries*, prophesied advent of Christ, 183
in *Book of the Cave*, etc., 184
in Chenoboskion MSS., as the first man, 261
in Clement, *Stromateis*, 205-6
in a Falasha book, creation of, 97
in a Gnostic fragment, 89
in *GOSPEL OF THOMAS*, 363, 367, 377
in *HYPOSTASIS*, etc., 160
in Isma'ilite belief, 321
in Judaism, in Rabbinical literature, 109
in Judaeo-Gnostic rituals, 105
in Justin's teaching, 34, 34n., 35
in Manichaeism, 217, 218n.
myth of creation of, derived by Manichaeans from Gnostics, 313
in Marcionism, 25
in Mimaut papyrus, 108
in Naassene teaching, 49
in Ophite teaching, 38-9
in *REVELATION OF ADAM*, etc., 182, 183
in *REVELATION ON PISTIS SOPHIA*, 169, 175
in St Paul, 307
in Satornil's teaching, 19
in *SECRET BOOK*, etc., Cod. X, 202, 204, 205, 206, 207, 209, 215, 217, 224
Iranian parallels for, 213-14
Hellenic vocabulary to describe predicament of, 215
compared with *Poimandres*, 276
in *SOPHIA*, etc., 199
in Syriac *Chronicle*, 185
in the *Mithraic Liturgy*, 108
in Theodore's answer, 136
in the pseudo-Zosimos, 100-1, 175
Hebrew myths of, in, 99
in *TREATISE ON BAPTISM OF JOHN*, 220
Adam of the Light in Eugnostos, 194
Adam Qadmon, 286, 286n.
Adam-Light in *Bruce Codex*, pt.2, 82
in *REVELATION ON PISTIS SOPHIA*, 168
in *SOPHIA*, etc., 199

Adamânoûs, in Balinus, 318, 319, 320
Adamas, see Sabaôth the Adamas
the Tyrant, in *Pistis-Sophia*, 67
Adamas-light, in *SACRED BOOK OF THE . . . GREAT SPIRIT*, 178
Adelphius, a sectary in Porphyry, 10, 156
"Adepts of the Mother", 12, 14n.
Admetus in Perataean teaching, 51
Admiration, in *GOSPEL OF THOMAS*, 346, 349, 355
Adonai in Audius' teaching, 56
Adonaios in Ophite teaching, 38
Adonaïu (Sabaôth) in *SECRET BOOK*, etc., Cod. X, 202
in Cod. Berol., 203
Aeolus in Peratic teaching, 51
Aeon:
in Gnosticism, meaning of, 14n.
in a Gnostic prayer, 108
in Ophite teaching, 40
in St Paul, 306
Mithraic, 260
statues of, 257, 281
Thirteenth in *Pistis-Sophia*, 66, 69, 71
Aeons:
in Audius' teaching, 56, 56n.
in Basilides' teaching, 21
in Bruce Codex, pt.2, 82, 83, 84, 85
in Kukean teaching, 58
in *Pistis-Sophia*, the Twelve, 66, 67, 69, 71
in St Paul, 308
in *SECRET BOOK*, etc., Cod. X, 202
in Simon's teaching, 17
in Valentinianism, 27, 29, 32n.
seven, 271
Aeschylus, *Danaids*, on Eros, 176, 176n.
Aetius, Bishop, 46
Against the Hystera, a Cainite book, 36
A genuine discourse by Sophe, etc., an alchemical work, 106
Agapios of Membidj, his evidence for *Allogeneous books*, 158
Agathodaimon, = Seth in Sabianism, 315
in Islam in general, 320
Agramas, in *Bruce Codex*, pt.2, 83, 286n.
Agrippa Castor, *Elenchos*, against Basilides, 7, 20, 20n.
Aher, had been to Paradise, 289
Ahl-i-Hagg and Gnosticism, 316, 316n.
"Ahl-I Hakk", article in encyclopaedia, 316n.
Ahmad Bey Kamal, transl., *Livre des perles enfouies . . .*, 132n.
Ahriman, 154
in Bundahishn, 152n, 153
influence of on Ialdabaôth, 281, 281n.
Ahura-Mazda, 79n.

Index

Aïleu, in *PARAPHRASE OF SHEM*, 148
Aïôn(es), *see* Aeon(s)
Air, intermediate principle in Sumerian belief, 268
= Fatality, in certain prayers, 109
Void =, in Hellenistic writings, 153-4
Akephalos, = Osiris-Onnophris in Jêou the painter, 105
= Seth, in magic, 104, 104n.
Akhamôth, *see* Intention
Akhmim, philosophers from, 135-6
Alchemy:
Alchemical literature, and Gnosticism, 103
and Hermetism, 99, 99n.
influence of Judaism and of Egyptian beliefs on, 107
Olympiodorus' influence in mediaeval, 101n.
Alcibiades of Apamea, sect of, 13
Alexander, effigy of, 11
of Libya, in Porphyry, 10, 156
of Lycopolis, referred to *GOSPEL OF THOMAS* (?), 232
Polyhistor, *Aigyptiaka*, 129, 129n.
Severus, 11
Alexandria, a Gnostic centre, 12
Basilides at, 20
destruction of Serapeum, 138
John of Apamea at, 57
Valentinus at, 26
Alfaric, P., *Les Écritures manichéennes*, 20n., 26n., 155n., 227n., 232n., 271n.
Zoroastre avant l'Avesta, 155n.
Ali Ayub, Minister of Public Instruction, 123
All, The, in *GOSPEL OF THOMAS*, 229, 366, 367, 376
in Marcus' teaching, 33
in St Paul and elsewhere, 376
Allogene, in Porphyry, 10, 156
= Seth, 157-8
Allogeneous books (Books of the Strangers):
cited by heresiologists, 158
identifiable with some Chenoboskion MSS., 158-9
SACRED BOOK OF THE ... GREAT SPIRIT is one of the, 180
Allogenes:
apocalypse of, mentioned in Porphyry, 10
in Plotinus, 101
in Theodore Bar-Konaï, 56, 57
source of his knowledge, 213
used by Archontici, 46
by Sethians, 45, 46
Almond, as symbol, 92
Almsdeeds in *GOSPEL OF THOMAS*, 371

Altmann, A., "The Gnostic background of the Rabbinic Adam legend", 286n.
Amann, article on Naassenes, 48n.
"Ophites", 37n.
Ambrose, *Comment. in Luc. Prooem.*, 262n.
Amélineau, *Notice sur le papyrus gnostique Bruce, Texte et traduction*, 77, 77n.
Amelius wrote against Zostrian, in Porphyry, 10, 102, 156
against Zostrian and Zoroaster (?) in Porphyry, 157n.
Amente:
an Egyptian word, 274, 274n.
in *SACRED BOOK OF THE ... GREAT SPIRIT*, 178
in *SECRET BOOK, etc.*, Cod. X, 216
in *TRIPLE DISCOURSE, etc.*, 181
Ammon in *HERMETIC TREATISE (26)*, 246
Amoias, in *PARAPHRASE OF SHEM*, 148
Amon-Re, in Medinet Habu inscription, 272n.
Anâhita, goddess, 80n.
Analecta Gregoriana, 27n.
Anatolia, Orphic bowl from (?), 90
Andreas-Henning, *Mitteliranische Manichaica*, 49n.
Androgyny associated with perfection, in *GOSPEL OF THOMAS*, 349
Anesas, High Priest, 100
Angels, creation of, in *REVELATION ON PISTIS SOPHIA*, 169
Anicetus, Pope, 36
Annuaire de l'École pratique des Hautes Études. Section des sciences religieuses, 286n.
Anôsh-Uthra, Mandaean prophet, 110n., 255, 256, 315
in *Ginzâ*, 207n.
Anthropos, an, as Creator in *Shiur Koma*, 291
in *Bruce Codex*, 81
shows Jewish influence (?), 291
in *Poimandres*, 214, 277
Ophite, 65
Antioch, Audians around, 56
Axionicus at, 31n.
Gnosticism in, 12, 13
Menander at, 19
Satornil at, 19
Antinopolis, St Pachomius imprisoned in, 130
Anz, "Zur Frage nach dem Ursprung des Gnostizismus", 3, 3n.
Apatôres in *Pistis-Sophia*, 65
Apelles, 25
attacked by Rhodon, 7

Aphredôn in *Bruce Codex*, pt.2, 82, 84
Apocalypse . . ., see also Revelation . . .
Apocalypse of Abraham, 45, 45n., 56
still undiscovered, 252
APOCALYPSE (REVELATION) OF ADAM TO HIS SON SETH:
described, 182–3
discussed, 183–7
in author's classification, 142
Sethian *REVELATION,* Cod. VI, similar to, 187
Apocalypse of Adam:
mentioned by Epiphanius, = *APOCALYPSE OF ADAM TO SETH* (?), 183
works of this name are of Judaeo-Iranian origin, 287
Apocalypse of Allogene:
cited by heresiologists, 158
mentioned in Porphyry, 53, 157, 158
= *SUPREME ALLOGENE* (?), 158
APOCALYPSE OF DOSITHEUS, see REVELATION, etc.,
Apocalypse of Gorgorios, 98n.
Apocalypse of Hystaspes, 184n.
Apocalypse of Isaiah, contains Danaïdes myth, 288, 288n.
APOCALYPSE OF JAMES:
in Cod. III, (10):
described, 237
discussed, 236–7
in author's classification, 142
in Cod. III, (11):
described, 237
discussed, 236–7
in author's classification, 142
in Cod. XIII, 239
discussed, 236–7
in author's classification, 145
Apocalypse of Nicotheus:
mentioned in Porphyry, 157n.
perhaps = *SECRET BOOK OF JOHN,* 252
refuted by Porphyry's followers, 86
still undiscovered, 252
APOCALYPSE OF PAUL:
described, 237–8
discussed, 238
in author's classification, 142
a new work, 146
Apocalypse of St Paul, 36n, 96, 96n.
APOCALYPSE OF PETER, a new work, 236
in author's classification, 144
Apocalypse of Zoroaster, in Plotinus and his followers, 101
mentioned in Porphyry, 157n.
Apocalypse of Zoroaster and Zostrian, in Porphyry, 125, 157n.

APOCALYPSE OF ZOSTRIAN, see DISCOURSE, etc.
Apocalypse of Zostrian, in Plotinus, 101
mentioned in Porphyry, 157n.
mentions stelae of Seth, 187
Apocalypse which is in the name of John, = *SECRET BOOK, etc.,* 205n.
Apocalypses, usually pseudonymous, 289, 290
APOCRYPHON OF JOHN, see SECRET BOOK OF JOHN
Apollonius of Tyana, = Balinus (?), 318
effigy of, 11
survival of Adam legend in Balinus MS., 185n.
Aptowitzer, *Cain and Abel in d. Haggada,* 286n.
Apuleius, not author of *Asclepius,* 246, 247n.
Aqiba, Rabbi, had been to Paradise, 289
Aquilinus, a sectary in Porphyry, 10, 156
Arab Antiquities, Department of, 124
Arabia, Audians in, 55
Arabic Museum, 124
Arara Arare, in *Testament of Solomon,* 203n.
Arbathiaô, in Jêou the painter, 105
Archaeology, 122n.
Archangelike, = *Book of Archangels, etc.,* 171, 172, 172n., 174
cited in *REVELATION ON PISTIS SOPHIA,* 166
Archigenitôr, in *Sophia, etc.,* 200
Archiv für Religionswissenschaft, 285n.
Archiv orientalní, 274n.
Archon, the, among Epiphanius' Gnostics, 8
in Audius' teaching, 57
in *REVELATION OF ADAM, etc.,* 182
(of Darkness), in *TREATISE ON BAPTISM OF JOHN,* 219
of the Occident and Orient, in *SETHITE REVELATION,* Cod. VI, 187
Samael, in *DIALOGUE OF THE SAVIOUR,* 220
Archons:
and Adam, myth of, derived by Manichaeans from Gnostics, 313
flayed, in Manichaeism, 149n., 208n.
Norea's revolt against, in Epiphanius, 163
her seduction of, in Epiphanius, 43, 163–4
similar to Egyptian decans, 274
on Sumerian medallion, 268
seduction of, in Manichaeism, 15n., 74n.
and Gnosticism, 161n.

Archons (*cont.*):
in *AUTHENTIC DISCOURSE*, *etc.*, 242
in Babylonian astrology, 267
in Balinus, 319
in Basilides' teaching, 22
of Fatality, in *Books of the Saviour*, 72
in Codex Askewianus, pt.2, 74
in Gnostic belief, 111
= planets in Gnosticism, 270
in *GOSPEL OF PHILIP*, 225
in the *Great Treatise*, 78, 80
in *HYPOSTASIS*, *etc.*, 160
in Nicolaitan teaching, 14–15
in Ophite belief (Epiphanius), 212 (Irenaeus), 38, 40
in *PARAPHRASE OF SHEM*, 149
in *Pistis-Sophia*, 69
in pseudo-Zosimos, 101n.
in *REVELATION ON PISTIS SOPHIA*, 169
in St Paul, 306
in Satornil's teachings, 19
in *SECRET BOOK*, *etc.*, Cod. X, 206, 207, 208, 215, 216
in *SOPHIA*, *etc.*, 200
in Valentinus' teaching, 31
Archontici, 45–6, 45n.
connected with Chenoboskion MSS. (?), 251
HYPOSTASIS, *etc.*, one of their books, 164
in Porphyry, 55n.
of unspeakable practices (?), 79 n.
teaching of, on Seth (Epiphanius), 150
close to Peratae, 50
their literature alluded to by heresiologists, 158
used Marsianes', etc., *Revelation*, 86
use term "Symphonia" (Epiphanius), 197
Ardavân King, in Mandaean myth, 256
Ariael, = Ialdabaôth, 162n., *ill.* 162
in Chenoboskion MSS., 260
in *REVELATION ON PISTIS SOPHIA*, 166, 175
Ariel, ruler of the winds, in Perataean teaching, 51
Arimanios, in *SECRET BOOK OF JOHN*, 201
Aristophanes, *Birds*, 176n.
Aristotle, icon of, 23
influence of, on Christianity, 350
pseudo-*Lapidary*, 180n.
Arles, statue of Chronos at, 94
Armaziel, in *Priscillianist treatise*, 198n.
Armenia, Borborites in, 311
spread of Gnosticism into, 13
Armenius, 102n.

Arnobius:
Adversus gentes, 102n.
on mysteries of Sabazius, 44
on Zoroaster grandson of Zostrian, 156n.
on Zostrian, 156
Arzdruni, Thomas, on Shem, 155n.
Ascension of Isaiah:
a book of the Archontici, 46
contains similarities to *REVELATION ON PISTIS SOPHIA*, 176, 177n.
influential in Gnosticism, 286
MS. at Louvain, 141
Satan in, 162n.
source of a vision in *Ârdâi Vîrâf nameh*, 287n.
Ascension of Paul, is different from the *APOCALYPSE*, *etc.*, 237, 238
used by Cainites (Epiphanius), 36, 238
Asceticism, in *GOSPEL OF THOMAS*, 346
Asclepios, cult of, as source of Ophite reverence for serpent (?), 44
Asclepius, a prophet, in Sabianism, 316
Asclepius:
contains material similar to Chenoboskion MSS., 143, 275
discussed, 246–7, 246n.–247n.
dualism in, 276n.
in *HERMETIC TREATISE* (*26*), 245, 246, 247
ousiarchs in, 244n.
prayer from, in *HERMETIC TREATISE* (*25*), 243, 245, 248n.
Three Principles in, 263, 281n.
Void in, 152n.
withdrawal of God in, 294n.
Asellus, mystic name, 92
Asia Minor, Marcus' Valentinianism in, 13
Askew, Dr, 64
Ass-headed Seth, 105
Typhon, 104
Assiut, 89
Astaphaïos, in *SECRET BOOK*, *etc.*, as supplemented by Cod. Berol., 203
in Ophite teaching, 38
Astrampsychos, article in *Realenzyklopädie*, 286n.
in Peratean belief (*Philosophoumena*) and elsewhere, 286n.
Astrology, 4
and Hermetism, 99, 99n.
Chaldaean, 12, 50
on reign of planets, 260–1
old system of, influenced Gnosticism, 271–2
Chaldaean system of, in *HERMETIC TREATISE* (*25*), 244
a treatise on, in Dead Sea Scrolls, 297

Astrology (*cont.*):
    Egyptian and in Egypt, 107, 273
    Gnostic, on rule of successive planets,
        164n.
    influence on Gnosticism, 266–7, 271–2
    in Codex Askewianus, 75
    in *Great Treatise* related to system in
        Codex Askewianus, 79
    in Judaism, 288, 288n.
    influence of Judaism and of Egyptian
        beliefs on, 107
    in Peratean teaching, 50
    in *Pistis-Sophia*, 68
    status of in ancient world, 10–11
    Ialdabaôth in, 93
Athalia, = Teli, 293n.
Athanasius, St, *Festal letter XXXIX*, 135
Athena identified with Simon's Helen, 16
Athôth, in *SECRET BOOK, etc.*, Cod. X,
    202
    in Cod. Berol., 203
Audians, 45, 55–7, 55n.
    belief about Eve, 214n.
    literature alluded to by heresiologists,
        158
    re-established in eighth century, 311
    Theodore Bar-Konaï's description of,
        205n.
Audius, 55, 56–7
Apocalypse of Abraham, 56
Apocalypse of John, 56
Apocalypse of the Strangers, 57
Book of Strangers, 56
Book of Requests, 56–7
    only book in fact by, 57
    taught Silvanus, 219
Audollent, A., *Defixionum tabellae*, 106n.
Augustine, St, *City of God*, quotes *Ascle-
    pius*, 246n., 247n.
    Contra adversarium legis, ek., contains a
        logion, 231
    Contra Faustum, 74n., 152n.
    De natura boni, 74n.
    Quaest. ex utroque test. mixtim, 47n.
    Homeric allegory in, 192n.
    on apocrypha, 351
    said Manes was influenced by Ophites,
        312
Aurelii, tomb of, in Rome, 92–3, 92n.,
    93n., 94
Aus frühchristliche Zeit, 16n., 285n.
Authades in *Pistis-Sophia*, 69, 71, 74n.
*"AUTHENTIC" DISCOURSE OF
    HERMES TO TAT*, in author's
    classification, 143
    discussed, 242, 247
Autogenes, in *SECRET BOOK, etc.*,
    Cod. X, 202
Autopatôr in *Bruce Codex*, pt.2, 84

Avesta, influenced Gnosticism, 2
    on Mount of the Lord, 161n.
    source of the Gnostic revelations of
        Adam, 184
    verbal similarity of Gnostic book to, 79n.
    void as Third Principle in, 154, 154n.
Avigad, N., and Yadin, Y., *A Genesis
    apocryhpon*, 296n.
Awakened Sea in Kukean teaching, 58
Awakening, in *GOSPEL OF TRUTH*,
    240
Axionicos, 31, 31n.

Babylon, and Mani, 255
Babylonia, Israelites in after the Exile, 287
    origin of Gnosticism, Islam, etc., in, 110
Babylonian influence on Iranian beliefs,
    279
    origin of a theory of planetary influence,
        267
Bacchus, worshipped at Rome, 90
Ba-en-Kekou, in *Book of the Dead*, 274n.
Bahir, Gnostic influence in, 292, 292n.
Bâhit, stone, 180n.
Bainkhôôkh, in *Pistis-Sophia*, 274
"Báktâshîya", encyclopaedia article, 317n.
Balaam, 280n.
    = Zoroaster, in Gnosticism, 280
    in Chenoboskion MSS., 287
    Zoroaster =, in myth of Saoshyant, 184
Balinus. *Secret of Creation, etc.*, 318–20
    on Adam's prophecies, 185n.
    on creation of man, 212n.
Baptism:
    from the Source, in *SACRED BOOK
        OF THE . . . GREAT SPIRIT*, 179
    in Gnosticism, 224, 224n.
    in *GOSPEL OF PHILIP*, 224
    of the First Oblation, in titleless portion
        of *Codex Askewianus*, 75
Barbeliotes, 41
Barbelô:
    compared with the Drop, 147n.
    with the Tetrad, 33n.
    derivation of name, 81n.
    Egyptian parallel to, 273
    in Barbelognostic belief, 37
    in *Pistis-Sophia*, 66, 113
    in *SUPREME ALLOGENE*, 157
    in the *Revelations of Zostrian and
        Zoroaster*, 157
    in the teachings of the Gnostic Sect
        (Epiphanius), 43, 44
    in titleless portion of *Codex Askewianus*,
        75
    = Monad in *Bruce Codex*, 81n.
    seduced Archons (Epiphanius), 164,
        164n.

Barbelô (*cont.*):
the celestial mother in Nicolaitan teaching, 14–15, 14n.
Barbelognostics, 14n.
connected with Chenoboskion MSS (?), 251
some beliefs similar to *EUGNOSTOS*, 195
(= The Gnostic Sect), in Irenaeus, 36–7, 37n., 86
in *Secret Book of John*, 86
Barbelôn, in *SECRET BOOK*, *etc.*, Cod. X, 201–2
the Mother, in *SACRED BOOK OF THE . . . GREAT SPIRIT*, 178
Barbelos mentioned by St Jerome, 5
Barbilon, in Priscillianist treatise, 198n.
Barcabbas, 20, 41
Barcabbas and Barcoph, prophecies of, still undiscovered, 252
Barcoph, 20
Bardenhewer, O., *Patrologie, III*, 8n.
Bardesanes (Bardaisan) of Edessa, 31, 31n.
Gnosis of, part of the background of Gnosticism, 310, 310n.
St Ephraim's refutation of, 24n.
taught Seven Aeons, 271
Three Principles, 151, 151n.
Bareille, "Borboriens", 311n.
Bargello, an ivory in, 207n.
Bar-Hebraeus on John of Apamea, 57
Baron, S. W., *Social and religious history of the Jews*, 286n., 287n., 288n., 289n., 290n.
Barpharanges, in *Bruce Codex*, pt.2, 85, 85n.
Barrès, *Le Mystère en pleine lumière*, 2, 2n.
Cahiers, XIV, 2n.
Bartholomew, Apostle, not author of the *Book of the Resurrection of Christ*, 95
importance of, in *SOPHIA OF JESUS*, 222
Baruch, angel and tree of Life, in Justin's teaching (*Philosophumena*), 34–5
the prophet, 33n.
Zoroaster =, in myth of Saoshyant, 184
Basilides:
Agrippa Castor's book against, 7
claimed Matthias had left him secret discourses (*Philosphumena*), 226, 336, 352
disciples of believed in reincarnation, 113n.
dualism in, 276n.
Gnostic character of shown by Chenoboskion MSS., 313
his disciples used *Traditions of Matthias*, 226
his sect assembled Chenoboskion MSS. (?), 262

Basilides (*cont*):
in *Acts of Archelaus*, 314
in the history of Gnosticism, 12, 26
facts known about, 262–3
influenced by Persian doctrines and Manichaeism, 7
listed in Hegesippus (Eusebius), 7
mentioned by St Jerome, 5
mentions prophecies of Barcabbas, etc., 252
Barcabbas, 41
on the baptism and crucifixion of Jesus, 113n.
on the soul, 72
quoted by Clement, 5
Three Principles, 151, 259
teachings of, 20–3
origin of (?), 36
close to Manichaeism, 312–13
withdrawal of God from omnipresence (*Philosophumena*), 276n.,
compared with Luria's teaching, 294, 294n.
writings of, 20, 22, 115
put a Christian disguise on, 254
Battai, 59–61
Baynes, C., *A Coptic Gnostic treatise contained in the Codex Brucianus*, 77n., 80, 80n., 81n., 84n., 85n., 189n., 286n.
Behemoth, in *Book of Noah*, 97n.
Beihefte zur Zeitschrifte für die neutestamentl. Wissenschaft, 27n.
Bektashis, 317, 317n.
Belbel, in *Testament of Solomon*, 203n.
Belias, in *SECRET BOOK*, *etc.*, Cod. X, 202
Ben Azaï and Ben Zoma, had been to Paradise, 289
Bendinelli, G., "Il monumento sepolcrale degli Aureli", 92n.
Berbali, a form of Barbelô, 14n.
Berlin Museum, publication of Gnostic MS. by, xiv.
Berossus (Berose) spread Babylonian mythology among Greeks, 269
in Peratean belief (*Philosophumena*), 286n.
Berthelot, *La Chimie au Moyen-âge*, 171n., 278n.
Berthelot and Ruelle, *Collection des alchemistes grec*, 101n., 278n.
Bethkhaduda, 97n.
Bezold, *Die Schatzhöle*, 47n., 97n., 184n.
Bible in demotic (?), 105–6
Biblical texts basis of Gnosticism, 285–6
Bibliotheca Orientalis, 273n.
Bibliothek der Kirchenväter, 196n.
Bibliothèque des philosophes chimistes, 101n.

Bidez, J., "Les Écoles chaldéennes sous
    Alexandre et les Séleucides", 267,
    267n., 269n.
article on coverlet of Heaven, 149n.
La Vie de l'empéreur Julien, 4n.
on Critodemus, 269, 269n.
Bidez, J. and Cumont, F., *Les Mages
    hellenisés*, 10n., 20n., 33n., 97n., 102,
    102n., 151n., 152n., 153, 153n., 156n.,
    184n., 185n., 186n., 187n., 196n., 218,
    218n., 237n., 279n., 280n., 281n., 282n.,
    286n., 287n., 288n.
Biruni, Al, on Jewish origin of certain
    Mandaeans, 285
Bodies, in St Paul, 307
Bodleian Library, *Bruce Codex* in, 77
Bodmer papyrus, II, 141
    III, 128n.
Body:
    contempt for, in *GOSPEL OF
        THOMAS*, 349
    respect for in St Paul, 308
    the parts of the, creation of, 204–5, 205n.
    correspondence of planets to, 214n.
    in *SECRET BOOK, etc.*, 218
Bogomils:
    and wood of the Cross, 216n.
    belief about Eve, 214n.
    belief in Three Principles, 151, 151n.
    inheritors of Gnosticism, 311
    on St Michael and Satan, 96n.
Boll, F. J., "Finsternisse", 73n.
    and Bezold, C., *Sternglaube und Stern-
        deutung*, 266n.
Bonner, C., *Studies in magical amulets*, 23n.,
    52n., 74n., 85n., 93n., 162n., 260n.
Bonnet, *Reallexikon der ägyptischen Reli-
    gionsgeschichte*, 104n.
Book of Archangels by Moses the Prophet,171,
    172, 172n., 174n.
Book of Baruch, on phoenixes, 173, 173n.
Book of buried Pearls . . ., 132
Book of Foreigners (=*Apocalypse of Allo-
    gene*) in Syriac, 158
Book of John, Mandaean, 98
    attributed to Shem, 155
    for Lidsbarski's edition, *see* Lidsbarski
Book of Moses, 107
Book of Mysteries, on Adam and Christ, 183
Book of Noah, on the desert Duidain, 97n.
BOOK OF NOREA, *see HYPOSTASIS
    OF THE ARCHONS*
Book of Norea, divine throne in, and *REV-
    ELATION OF PISTIS SOPHIA*, 177
    mentioned in *REVELATION ON
        PISTIS SOPHIA*, 166
    references to in later works in Cod. X, 170
    evidence for identification of with
        HYPOSTASIS, etc., 163–4

Book of Pistis-Sophia:
    see also *Books of the Saviour: Pistis-
        Sophia MS.*
    bibliography, 65n.
    general description of, 67–71
    Second book, general description of, 71
    abolition of fatality in, 111
    astrological system in, 244
    close to Bruce Codex, 79–80
    comparison of, with *HERMETIC
        TREATISE (26)*, 246n.
    contains a similar hymn to that in
        REVELATION OF DOSITHEUS,
        189
    cosmology of, 71–2
    eschatology of, 274n.
    eucharistic ritual in, 224
    fantastic astronomy in second book of,
        271
    Harnack believed to be *Little Interroga-
        tions of Mary*, 73
    Jewish (Biblical) and Egyptian elements
        in, 106
    less valuable than Chenoboskion MSS.,
        117
    mentions *Books of Jêou*, 77
    more Manichaean than Chenoboskion
        MSS., 258–9
    on Ialdabaôth, 176n.–177n.
    on importance of Philip, Thomas and
        Matthew, 221–2
    on Jesus, 113n.
    on the adventitious soul, 216n.
    on the Perfect one, 109
    on the seals on the parts of the body
        compared with a Dead Sea work, 297
    on Three Phases, 113n.
    parallels with *GOSPEL OF THOMAS*,
        343
    parts of, resemble *SECRET BOOK*,
        etc., 208
    prologue of *SOPHIA, etc.*, resembles,
        198
    quotation from, 327–8
    related to *Bundahishn*, 152n.
    similar to *HYPOSTASIS, etc.*, 159
    the Five Trees in, 209n.
    Virgin of Light in, seduces Archons,
        164n.
Book of Requests, 57
Book of Solomon in *REVELATION ON
    PISTIS SOPHIA*, 167
    identity (?), 170–1
Book of Souls, Mandaean, 98
Book of the baptism of Hibil-Ziwa, Man-
    daean, 98
Book of the Cave, partly Sethian (?), 184n.
    revealed by Adam, 184
    similarities to, in Syriac *Chronicle*, 185

Book of the Chiefs of the Town . . . related to *Schema of* . . . *Heimarmene* (?), 174, 176n.
on Eros (*Philosophumena*), 176n.
Book of the Dead, passwords in, 274
Ba-en-Kekou reappears in *Pistis-Sophia*, 274n.
Book of the Great Treatise, etc., see Bruce Codex
Book of the Investiture of the Archangel Michael, 96n.
Book of the Jubilees, influential in Gnosticism, 286
on Shem, 154
used by Dead Sea sect, 296
Book of the living, in GOSPEL OF TRUTH, 239
Book of the Resurrection of Christ, 95, 95n.
Book of the Secrets of Enoch, on phoenixes, etc., 172–3, 173n.
on Khalkhydras, 173–4, 173n.
Book of the Seven Heavens (Seven Heavens), 172, 174
in pseudo-Zozimos, 278n.
Book of the Signs of the Zodiac, Mandaean, 98
BOOK OF THOMAS, *etc.*, in author's classification, 145
described, 225–6
discussed, 221–2, 234–5, 252, 336, 340
Book of Wisdom, ascent of man in, 109, 109n.
Book of Zoroaster, in Porphyry, 156
referred to in SECRET BOOK, *etc.*, Cod. X, 205, 218
Book of Zostrian, in Porphyry, 156
Books of Adam, Mandaean, 183
Books of the Great Treatise = Books of Jéou, 77
hidden on Ararat, 254
in *Books of the Saviour*, 73, 77
more Manichaean than Chenoboskion MSS., 259
revealed by Christ (= Serpent), 261
withdrawal of God from omnipresence in, 276n., 294, 294n.
Books of the Saviour, A part of, 72–3
Books of Jéou mentioned in, 77
quotation from, 327–8
Books of the Strangers, see Allogeneous books
Borborites, 311, 311n.
Borgia leaflet, 96n.–97n.
Bornkamm, *Mythos und Legende in den apokryphen Thomasakten*, 95n.
Borsippa, Chaldaean teacher, 267
Bousset, W., "Gnosticism", 10n.
Hauptprobleme der Gnosis, 3, 3n., 13n., 14n., 24n., 55n., 152n.
Kyrios Christos, 266n.

Bousset, W., on Babylonian (?) influence in a Gnostic theme, 218
on Iranian influence in Gnosticism, 114
in *Acta Archelai*, 263n.
Brahmans, in *Philosophumena*, 6
Braun, O., *Ausgewählte Akten persischer Märtyrer*, 196n.
Breath, the Sethian third principle (*Philosophumena*), 150–1
Briareus, in Peratean teaching, 51
British Museum, *Codex Askewianus* in, 65
various other Coptic MSS. in, 88n., 96n.
Bruce, James, explorer, 76
Bruce Codex, 76–7
bibliography of, 77n.
compared with Mandaean myth, 256
contains hymn analogous to REVELATION OF DOSITHEUS, 189n.
contains names found in SACRED BOOK OF THE . . . GREAT SPIRIT, 179
and similar doctrines, 180
Gamaliel, etc., in, 286n.
Great Treatise, etc., = *Books of Jéou*, 77–9, 289n.
close to *Pistis-Sophia*, unlike other Gnostic works, 79–80
has Sethian characteristics, 184
Nicotheus in, 86, 99, 159
Pt. 2 without a title, 80–6
Anthropos in, 291
related to Chaldaean oracles, 102
Chariot in, 291
provenance unknown, 136
value of relative to Chenoboskion MSS., 117
Brugsch, *Die Aegyptologie*, 272n.
Bryaxis, statue of Serapis by, 138
Bucher, P., "Les commencements des Psaumes LI à XCIII. Inscription d'une tombe . . .", 132n.
Buchler, A., article in *Judaica*, 285n.
article in *Monatschrift für Geschichte . . . des Judentums*, 285n.
Buddha in Manes, *Shâpurakân*, 314n.
Buddhism, a similarity of, to Gnosticism, 113
Budge, A. E. W., *Coptic Apocrypha in the dialect of Upper Egypt*, 95n., 96n.
Coptic martyrdoms in the dialect of Upper Egypt, 98n.
Miscellaneous Coptic texts in the dialect of Upper Egypt, 96n.
Buffière, F., *Les Mythes d'Homère et la pensée grecque*, 35n., 191n., 192n.
Bulletin de la Cl. des Lettres . . . Académie royale de Belgique, 122n., 128n.
Bulletin de l'Institut d'Égypte, 122n.

Bulletin de l'Institut français d'Archéologie orientale du Caire, 42n., 104n., 132n.
Bulletin de la Société E. Renan, 126n., 228n.
Bulletin of the Byzantine Institute, 125n.
Bumegas in Peratean belief (Philosophumena), 286n.
Bundahishn:
  correspondence of planets with parts of the body, in, 214n.
  doctrine of Three Principles in, 259, 263n., 281
  dualism in, 276n.
  Gayomârt in, 277n.
  myth in, compared with Gnostic belief, 152–3, 152n.
  on Adam, 214
  on the Virgin of Light, 80n.
Bunsen, Hippolyt and his Age, 50n.
Burkitt, Religion of the Manichees, 310n., 312n.
Bursians Jahresbericht, 267n.

C.S.C.O., 118n., 128n.
Cahiers, 2n.
Cain:
  a Gnostic belief about in Theodore of Tabennisi, 135
  a prophet of the Cainites (Irenaeus), 36
  in a Gnostic fragment, 89
  in Gnostic belief, 112
  in HYPOSTASIS, etc., 160
  in Ophite teaching, 39, 39n.
  in SECRET BOOK, etc., Cod. X, 207
  in Valentinianism, 32
  inferior brother of Seth, in Chenoboskion MSS., 158
Cain, the sun, in SECRET BOOK, etc., Cod. X, 202
Cainites:
  Epiphanius on, 45
  use Ascension of Paul, 238
  and Gospel of Eve, 187n.
  Irenaeus on, 36
Cairo, Anti-Rabies Institute, 129
  Bektashi monastery at, 317
  Codex Berolensis bought in, 86
  Coptic Museum, see Coptic Museum
  French Institute of Archaeology, 116
  peasants knew MSS. taken to, 133
Call, to salvation in GOSPEL OF TRUTH, 240
Calmet, D., Dissertation sur Melchisédéch; Commentaire littéral aux Epîtres de S. Paul, 47n.
Caphar-Barusha, Peter the Archontic at, 46
Capparetia, birthplace of Menander, the Gnostic, 12, 19

Carcopino, J., Aspects mystiques de la Rome païenne (Sur les traces de l'hermétisme africain), 234n., 243n., 248n., 275n.
  La Basilique pythagoricienne de la Porte Majeure, 224n., 265n.
  De Pythagore aux Apôtres, 91n., 92n., 93n., 191n.
  on the tomb of the Aurelii, 92, 93n., 192
  Études d'histoire chrétienne, 90n.
  Le Mystère d'un symbole chrétien, 91n., 191n., 192n., 196n., 234n., 288n.
Carpocrates:
  origin of teaching of (?), 36
  teachings of reached Rome, 12
  his sect, 23, 41
  believed in reincarnation, 113n.
  listed in Hegesippus, 7
  lived in Alexandria, 12
Carpocratians, reverenced icons of Pythagoras, etc. (Epiphanius), 263n.
Carystia, home of Celbes, 50, 50n.
Catabasis of Pythagoras, eschatology of, 288
Catacombs, in Rome, 91
Catalogus Codicum Astrolog. Graecorum, 73n., 271n., 293n.
Cathars:
  inheritors of Gnosticism, 311
  on female becoming male, 234
  a parallel of, in GOSPEL OF THOMAS, 349
  on St Michael and Satan, 96n.
Cave of the Magi in Iranian myth, 282
Cave of Treasures, 47n., 96
  of mixed Jewish and Iranian origin, 287
Cave of Treasures and Wood of the Cross, 216n.
Cave of Treasures of the Life of the Silence in Syriac Chronicle, 186
Ceccheli, Monumenti Cristiano-eretici di Roma, 92, 92n.
Cedrenus, 47n.
Celbes of Carystia, 50, 50n.
Celestial Man, in REVELATION ON PISTIS SOPHIA, 167
Celsus, 6–7, 9
  his attack on Christianity far-fetched, 62–3
  on false prophets, 18, 18n.
  on Ophite Diagram, 37, 174
  refers to Mariamne, 198n.
Cerdon, teacher of Marcion, 12, 24
Cerfaux, L., article on Hermetism, 99n.
  "Gnose préchrétienne, etc.", 1n., 3
  "La Gnose simonienne", 16n.
Cerinthus, 12
Chaldaean element in Naassene belief about creation of man, 212
  elements in Audius' teaching, 56
  influence on Iran, 279

Chaldaean Oracles, see Julian the Theurgist
Cham, 20, 20n.
Chaos, in *EUGNOSTOS*, 194
in Hesiod, 175
in *HYPOSTASIS, etc.*, 162
in *Pistis-Sophia*, 69, 70, 71
in *REVELATION ON PISTIS SOPHIA*, 165, 167, 168, 170, 175
in *SACRED BOOK OF THE . . . GREAT SPIRIT*, 178
in *SECRET BOOK, etc.*, Cod. X, 209
in *TRIPLE DISCOURSE, etc.*, 181
Charax, Mountain of, 180, 180n., 254
Chariot:
= Chariot of the Lord Sabaôth in Judaism, 288
origin, 288n.
constellation of, 165
= Propator, in magical prayer, 108, 177n.
in Ezechiel, 177
in Gnosticism, 291
Charles, R. H., on Duidaïn, 97n.
The Apocrypha and Pseudepigrapha of the Old Testament, 173n.
Chavannes, E. and Pelliot, P., "Un Traité manichéen retrouvé en Chine", 158n., 196n., 214n., 216n.
Chenoboskion, description of site, 130–3
history of the town, 129–30
Chenoboskion MSS.:
texts in, listed, 142–5
(a) *Discovery and acquisition:*
discovery of, rumours of manner of, 128
result of author's investigations into, xi–xii, 133–5
most MSS. acquired by Egyptian government, xiii
one MS. acquired by Coptic Museum, xii
one MS. acquired by Jung foundation, xiii
more items to be discovered at Chenoboskion (?), 127–8
[For further details of the acquisition, *see* Coptic Museum]
(b) *External characteristics:*
description of handwriting of, 141
description of the MSS., 137
palaeographic dating of, 138–9, 141
state and dimensions of, 140
(c) *Internal characteristics, etc.:*
and their origin, 308–9
assembled by followers of Basilides (?), 262
attitude to Christianity varies, 302–3
coherence of the collection, 137–8
copyist's words quoted, 143, 145

Chenoboskion MSS. *(cont.)*:
(c) *Internal characteristics, etc.* (cont.):
differ from *Pistis-Sophia* and *Books of Jéou*, 258–9
how first assembled (?), 250–1
include versions of items also found in Cod. Berol., 87, 88
language of, 137, 137n., 138
probable sect of the collectors, 151
show belief in constellations, etc., as mythical powers, 270–1
influence of doctrine of seven aïônes, 271–2
shown to be a representative collection, 251–2
source of doctrines in, 263
Hellenic, 264–5
fundamentals are oriental, 265–6
astrological, 266–7
Sumerian, 268
and later Babylonian, 268–9
influence of Christianity, 300 *et seq.*
peculiarity of the Christian characteristics shown in, 304–8
Dead Sea sect, 296–300
Egyptian beliefs, 272–5
Hermetic beliefs, 277–8
Indian beliefs, 284–5
Iranian beliefs, 279, 281–4
Judaism, 285–95
Simonianism, 331, 332
texts classified by sects, 146
(d) *The individual Codices:*
Codex I–XIII, inventoried, 142–5
Codex I, size of, 140
Codex VI, dialect of, 138
Hermetic works in, 241
scribe of, 250
Codex VIII, dialect of, 137, 138
palaeography of, 141
Codex X, palaeography of, 141n., 238
beauty of, 333
compilation of, 170
date of, 248
glosses, etc., in, 241n., 250, 265
Codex XIII, palaeography of, 138, 139, 141, 141n., 238, 239
a part of the Jung Codex, 145, 238
dialect of, 239
size of, 140
(e) *Evaluation and study:*
committee for publication of, 227n.
extent to which studied by author, xiv
and by others, xv
extent to which used so far, 125–7
importance for Hermetic literature, 248n.

Chenoboskion MSS. (*cont.*):
  (*e*) *Evaluation and study* (cont.)*:*
    importance of certainty about proven-
      ance of, 136
    importance of the find, 249
    in judging heresiologists, 249–50
      and vice versa, 250
    new knowledge from, 259 *et seq.*
    show Basilides was a true Gnostic,
      313
    the Gnostic character of Manichae-
      ism, 313, 315
      and of Mandaeanism, 315
    significance of, xv–xvii, 324–6
Cheops = Sophe, *Discourse*, 106
Cherubim, in *Arkhangelike*, 174
Chester-Beatty collection, 141
Child of the Word, in Zoroastrian
  prophecy, 186
Chnubis, on gems, 93, 260
Christ, *see* Jesus Christ
Christianity, xvi, 1n.
  and Gnosticism, 300–9
  source of Gnosticism in (?), 110
  a pre-Synoptic, source of Gnosticism,
    304–5
  distinguished from Gnosticism, 325–6
  danger of Gnosticism to, realized, 12
  Gnosticism attacked by, 9
    and suppressed, 1
  and Gnosticism, attacked by Celsus, 7
  and Gnosticism in Matter's view, 2
  and Manichaeism, 313
  concept of time in, 111
  in some Chenoboskion MSS., 218 *et
    seq.*
  pseudo-Zosimos influenced by, 100n.
  Yazuqeans influenced by, 61
Chronicle, Syriac in Zuqnîn monastery, on
  the Magi, 185
Chronique d'Égypte, 116n.
Chronos, = Ialdabaôth, 94
  in pseudo-Zosimos, 100
Chrysostom, pseudo-, *Unfinished commentary on St Matthew*, refers to *Writing
  by Seth*, 185
Church, The, in *GOSPEL OF THOMAS*,
  345
  in Ophite teaching, 37
  in Valentinianism, 27
Church, the imperishable, in *SACRED
  BOOK OF THE . . . GREAT
  SPIRIT*, 178
  the perfect, in *GOSPEL OF THOMAS*,
  346, 374
Church of the holy lights in *EUGNOS-
  TOS*, 194
Chwolsohn, D., *Die Ssabier und der
  Ssabismus*, 316, 316n.

Citroen Mission, 121n.
Cleanthes on Hercules, 35n.
Clement of Alexandria:
  cites *Traditions of Matthias*, 226
  First Epistle, on the Phoenix, 172n.
  Hypotyposes on importance of James
    (Eusebius), 236
  quotes Basilides, Valentinus, 5
  quotes Eastern Valentinians, 31
  quotes Theodotus, 5, 5n.
  on male and female, 234, 234n.
  simile of the ass turning a mill, 223,
    223n.
  Second Epistle, parallels in, with
    GOSPEL OF THOMAS, 350, 375
  Stromateis quotes Gnostic myth of
    creation of Adam, 205–6
  quotes a logion from *Gospel of
    Hebrews*, known to us from
    GOSPEL OF THOMAS, 230,
    230n., 235
  on Zoroastrian books, 156n.
  preserves *Comm. on Parchor* on Isidore,
    20n.
Clement de Bucy, a neo-Gnostic, 311–12
Clementine, pseudo-, literature, 47n.
  Recognitions on God and Demiurge,
    281n.
  and *Homilies*, on Simon and Dositheus,
    15, 15n.
Clementines, on James, 236n.
Cleobius, in Hegesippus' list, 7
Cleopatra, in Perataean teaching, 51
Cloud, symbolism of, 291, 291n.
Coddians, 41
Codex Askewianus, 65
  *See also Pistis-Sophia MS.; Books of
    Pistis-Sophia; Books of The Saviour*
Codex Berolensis, 86–8, 86n., 87n.
  a variant from Chenoboskion version,
    203, 209, 211
  contains material found also in Cheno-
    boskion MSS., 126, 146, 177
  contains *SECRET BOOK OF JOHN*,
    Cod. I, 201
  contains *SOPHIA OF JESUS*, 196, 198,
    200, 214n.
  fills lacuna in Chenoboskion version,
    147n., 200
  palaeography and dating of, 141
  published in 1955, 127n.
Commandments of the Sabbath, 97
Commission des Fouilles Archéologiques,
  122
*Comptes rendus de l'Académie des Inscriptions
  et Belles-Lettres*, 89n., 92n., 118n., 119n.,
  122n., 192n.
Constellations, etc., in Egyptian belief,
  273–4

Contenau, *Manuel d'archéologie orientale*, 268n.
Coptic language, 64n.
 dialects, 137n.
Coptic Museum, Cairo:
 description of, 116
 allowed first acquisition to be used by Berlin Museum, xiv
 began publication of first acquisition, xiv, 123
 importance of acquiring Miss Dattari's MSS. for, 121
 these MSS. sent to, in 1952, 124
 these MSS. include pages from Jung Codex, 137, 145, 239
 publication committee set up by, in 1956, 124
 retained some (Chenoboskion) MSS. for purchase, xii, 117
 acquisition reported to press in 1948, 119
 so prices of other parts rose, 120
 these MSS. similar to Eid's MS., 118
 these MSS. of, have been exactly summarized, 127
 state and contents of, 142–5
Coptic Studies in honour of W. E. Crum, 54n., 125n., 139n., 157n., 172n.
Corbicius, Manes' previous name (*Acts of Archelaus*), 314
Corbin, H., "De la Gnose antique à la Gnose ismaélienne", 177n., 321n.
L'Imagination créatrice dans le soufisme d'Ibn Arabi, 317n.
Corpus Hermeticum, see Nock, etc.
Corpus scriptorum ecclesiasticorum latinorum, 310n.
Cos, Berossus at, 269
Cosmas the Traveller, on Manichaean belief about shape of the earth, 269
Cosmocrator in Valentinianism, 29
Cosmogony:
 Audian, 56–7
 Balinus, of, 319–20
 Barbelognostic, 36–7
 Basilides, of, 21–2, 23
 Battai, of, 60
 Borgia leaflet, of, 97n.
 Bruce Codex, pt. 2, of, 81, 82
 Egyptian, 272–3, 272n.
 Genesis, of, attacked in *Shkand Gûmânîk Vichâr*, 283
 Gnostic, general, 61–2, 65
  clarified by Chenoboskion MSS., 259–60
 GOSPEL OF TRUTH, of, 240
 John of Apamea, of, 57
 Justin's, 34
 Kukean, 58–9

Cosmogony (*cont.*):
 Marcionism, of, 25–6, 50n.
 Nicolaitan, 14–15, 21n.
 Ophite, 37–40
 Orphic, in Aristophanes, 176n.
 PARAPHRASE OF SHEM, in, 148, 149
 Perataean, 50–1
 Pistis-Sophia, in, 71
 SACRED BOOK OF THE INVISIBLE SPIRIT, in, 177–8
 SECRET BOOK, etc., Cod. X, in, 201–2
 Sethian, 50n., 52–3
 Simon's, 17–18, 21n., 50n.
Cosmology:
 Sumerian, 268
 TRIPLE DISCOURSE, in, 181
 Valentinus', 27–30
Counterfeiter in Basilides' teaching, 263
 in Chenoboskion MSS., 261
 in Gnosticism and elsewhere, 282, 282n.
 in *SECRET BOOK*, etc., Cod. X, 206, 207, 208, 215
 in *SETHIAN REVELATION*, Cod. VI, 187
 see also Souls, two, theory of
Creator:
 an Anthropos in *Shiur Koma*, 291
 in a Falasha book, 97
 in *SECRET BOOK*, etc., Cod. X, 207, 208
 in *TREATISE ON BAPTISM OF JOHN*, 220
 not responsible for original sin, in St Paul, 308
Critodemus the Babylonian, 269
Cronius, disciple of Numenius, 192
Cross, Coptic, 138, 139, 139n.
 in *Acts of John*, 95
 in Battai's teaching, 60
 in *GOSPEL OF THOMAS* (?), 344
 in *GOSPEL OF TRUTH*, 240
 (Limit) in Aurelii tomb, 92
 (Limit) in Valentinianism, 28, 81n.
 (Stauros) in Bruce Codex, pt.2, 81
 wood for the, in *GOSPEL OF PHILIP*, 223
 wood of, in Bogomile belief, 216n.
Crown of God in *Zohar*, 292
Crum, W. E., *Catalogue of the Coptic Manuscripts in the British Museum*, 88n.
Cryptogram of title of *REVELATIONS OF ZOSTRIAN*, 156–7, 157n., 257
Cryptographic alphabets in Dead Sea Scrolls, 297
Cullman, O., *Le Problème littéraire des écrits pseudo-clémentins*, 12n.

400 Index

Cumont, F., "À propos des écritures manichéennes", 313n.
L'Égypte des astrologues, 266n.
Lux Perpetua, 12n., 43n., 103n., 177n., 192n., 207n., 216n., 238n., 267n., 269n., 271n.
Monuments des mystères de Mithra, 257n., 271n.
on *Mithraic Liturgy*, 108n.
Recherches sur le Manichéisme, I, 15n., 69n., 74n., 80n., 149n., 152n., 162n.–3n., 164n., 208n., 271n., 313n., 314n.
Les Religions orientales dans le paganisme romain, 4th ed., 12n., 90n., 94, 94n., 266n., 279n.
Textes et monuments rélatifs aux mystères de Mithra, 279n.
on resemblance of Manichaeism to Basilides' teaching, 312
Cumont and Kugener, *Recherches sur le Manichéisme*, II, 152n., 216n.
Cyclic view of creation, in *HERMETIC TREATISE (26)*. 246
Cyprus, Valentinus in, 12, 26
Cyril of Jerusalem, on *GOSPEL OF THOMAS*, 232, 335, 348
said Manes was influenced by Ophites, 312

Daden in the teachings of the Gnostic sect, 43
Damascus, Audians around, 56
Danaïdes myth in *Apocalypse of Isaiah*, 288, 288n.
Daniel, influential in Gnosticism, 286
chariot in, 290
Dante:
Divina Commedia, 36n.
and *Apocalypse of Paul*, 237
Daressy, G., "Indicateur topographique du *Livre des perles enfouies*", 132n.
Notice explicative des ruines de Medinet Habu, 272n.
Darkness:
Abyss of and Angel of, in Dead Sea Scrolls, 297
in *BOOK OF THOMAS*, 225
in Bruce Codex, pt.2, 84
in *Bundahishn*, 153
in certain magical prayers, 109
in Iranian myth, 154
in Manichaeism, 152
in Nicolaitan teaching, 14
in *Poimandres*, 276, 277
in *REVELATION ON PISTIS SOPHIA*, 165, 166, 167, 169
in St Paul, 307

Darkness (*cont.*):
in *SECRET BOOK, etc.*, Cod. X, 152, 202–3, 206, 209, 217
in Sethian teaching (*Philosophumena*), 53
one of the Three Principles, 52, 150–1, 259
in the *PARAPHRASE OF SHEM*, 147–8
in *TRIPLE DISCOURSE, etc.*, 181, 330
Spirits of, in Dead Sea Scrolls, 297
Darmesteter, *Zend Avesta*, 154, 154n.
Dattari, Miss (a cultured personage), 120, 121, 122, 123, 124, 137
Daueithel in *Investiture of the Archangel Gabriel*, 236
Daueithe in Bruce Codex, pt.2, 85
in magical, etc., texts, 103
Daughter of Light, in *Acts of Thomas*, 95
Daveithe, in *SACRED BOOK OF THE INVISIBLE GREAT SPIRIT*, 178
in *SECRET BOOK, etc.*, Cod. X, 202
in *TREATISE ON BAPTISM OF JOHN*, 220
David, the Prophet, in *Pistis-Sophia*, 20
Dead Sea Scrolls, xi
and Gnosticism, 15n.
astrological text from, written backwards, 257–8
counterfeiter in, 282, 282n.
preserved in jars, 134n.
Teacher of Righteousness = Onias the Just (?), 290n.
Dead Sea Sect, originated Gnosticism (?), 298–300
parallels with Gnostics, 296–7
Death, power of, in *REVELATION OF ADAM, etc.*, 182
Debarim Rabbah, 175n.
De Buck, A., *The Egyptian coffin texts*, 273n.
De Clercq collection, medallion in, 268, 268n.
Deir anba-Palamun, 131, 133
Deir Bala'izah, Coptic fragments from, 88–9, 209n.
Deir el-Malak, 131, 133, 134
Delatte, A., *Anecdota Graeca*, 171n.
Demiurge, 51n.
Barbelognostic, 37
in Clementine *Recognitions*, 281n.
in *HYPOSTASIS, etc.*, 160
in Plotinus' attack on Gnosticism, 54
in *Poimandres*, 276
in *SECRET BOOK, etc.*, Cod. X, 205, 206, 208
in the Gnostic sect, 41, 42n.
Ophite, 38, 39, 40
Valentinian, 29, 30, 31
Demon of the air, in a Gnostic prayer, 108

Demostratus of Lydia, in Porphyry, 10, 156
Dendera, temple, 130
Derdekea in *PARAPHRASE OF SHEM*, 147, 150
derivation of name, 147n.
Destiny in *Avesta*, 154
Destructive Spirit, in *Bundahishn*, 153
Deuteronomy, quoted in *Pistis-Sophia*, 222
Diagram, an Ophite book, 37, 73n.
preserved in Origen, *Contra Celso*, 7
related to *Schema of* . . . *Heimarmene* (?), 174
DIALOGUE OF THE SAVIOUR, in author's classification, 142
description, 220-1
Dictionnaire de la Bible, 1n., 45n., 48n., 97n., 99n., 184n., 185n., 237n., 288n., 315n.
Dictionnaire de Théologie catholique, 37n., 311n.
Didymus in Perataean teaching, 51
of Alexandria, *On psalm 88*, contains a *Logion*, 231
the Blind wrote against heretics, 7
Didymus Jude Thomas, *see* Thomas, St
Dînânukht, husband of Nuraïta, in Mandaean belief, 155, 164
Diogenes Laertius on Astrampsychos, 286n.
Dion Chrysostom, on location of Essenes (Synesius), 299, 299n.
Dionysic orgies, 44
Dionysos, pseudo-, the Areopagite, 68n.
Diospolis Parva, 129, 133
DISCOURSE OF TRUTH BY ZOS-TRIAN, etc.:
briefly described, 157
dated by reference in Porphyry, 250
Porphyry's reference discussed, 156n., 157n.
identified with Zostrian, *Upon Nature*, 156-7
in author's classification, 142
DISCOURSE OF ZOROASTER, see DISCOURSE OF TRUTH BY ZOSTRIAN, etc.
DISCOURSE TO REGINOS, etc., 239
in author's classification, 145
in the second discovery, 118
Diwan Abatur, a Mandaean book, 98
Doctrine of the Apostles, 340
Domedôn-Doxomedôn, in *SACRED BOOK OF THE* . . . *GREAT SPIRIT*, 178
Dominations, in *Arkhangelike*, 174
in *REVELATION ON PISTIS SOPHIA*, 169
Donkey-headed archon, 79
god, 42n.

Doresse, J.:
"A Gnostic Library from Upper Egypt", 122n.
and first discovery, 116-17
and further MSS., 120, 122, 123, 124
and second discovery, 118-19, 118n.
"Apocalypses égyptiennes", 247n.
at Chenoboskion, 128, 133-4
"Barrès et l'Orient", 2n.
Chnoubis, figure d'un dieu gnostique, 93n., 260n.
"Douze volumes dans une jarre", 122n.
first mission in Egypt, 116
helped Prof. Puech, 126
helped Prof. Till, 125
"Hermès et la Gnose: À propos de l'Asclépius copte", 85n., 125n., 140n., 190n., 241n., 243n., 248n., 250n.
his own use of the discovery, 125
his work plagiarized by some, 126-7
inventory by, 139, 140
unique, 122
"L'Apocalypse manichéenne", 188n., 313n.
L'Empire du Prêtre-Jean, II: L'Éthiopie médiévale, 22n., 98n.
"Le Refus de la Croix; Gnostiques et Manichéens", 22n., 50n., 313n.
"Le Roman d'une grande découverte", 122n.
"Les Apocalypses de Zoroastre, de Zostrien, de Nicothée . . .", 125n., 157n.
"Les Gnostiques d'Égypte", 122n.
"Nouveaux aperçus historiques sur les gnostiques coptes: Ophites et Séthiens", 122n.
"Nouveaux documents gnostiques coptes découverts en Haute-Égypte", 122n.
"Recherches d'archéologie copte: les monastères de Moyenne-Égypte", 89n.
"Sur les traces des papyrus gnostiques", 128n.
"Togo Mina", 116n.
"Trois livres gnostiques inédits", 119n., 125n., 177n., 192n.
"Une bibliothèque gnostique copte . . ." (Brussels), 122n.
"Une bibliothèque gnostique copte" (Paris), 122n., 140n.
"Un Rituel magique des Gnostiques d'Egypte", 74n.
and Togo Mina, "La Bibliothèque de Chénoboskion", 122n.
and Togo Mina, "Nouveaux textes gnostiques coptes . . .", 118n., 122n.

Dositheans, 61, 61n.
Dositheus:
 a real person (?), 15n., 190, 253
 identity of author of *Revelation by
  Dositheus,* 189–90, 332
 master of Simon (?), 15, 189, 189n.,
  190
 not connected with Dositheans, 61n.
 sect of, in Hegesippus' list, 7
Dosthaeans, 61
Doxomedôn in *DISCOURSE OF
  TRUTH, etc.,* 157
 in *TREATISE ON BAPTISM OF
  JOHN,* 220
Dragon:
 Constellation of, 51n.
 (Teli) in Jewish belief, 293, 293n.
 Head and Tail of, in Manichaean
  belief, 74n.
Draguet, R., *Les Pères du desert,* 129n.
Dream of Scipio, different from Gnostic
  visions, 150n.
Drioton, E., Director-General of Service
  of Antiquities, xii, 117, 121, 122
 account of De Buck's book, 273n.
Drop, The, in *SOPHIA OF JESUS,*
  147n.
Drower, E. S., *The Haran Gawaïta and the
  baptism of Hibil-Ziwa,* 256, 285n.
 The Mandaeans of Iraq and Iran, 49n.,
  74n., 256n., 315n.
Druses and Gnosticism, 316
Dualism:
 in *GOSPEL OF THOMAS,* 371, 375
 in names, 203, 203n.
 in *Poimandres,* Gnosticism, etc., 276n.
 not exclusively Gnostic, 322–3
Duchesne-Guillemin, J., "Ahriman et le
  Dieu suprême dans les mystères de
  Mithra", 281n.
 "Dualismus", 279n.
 "Le Zervanisme et les manuscrits de la
  mer Morte", 297n.
 Western response to Zoroaster, 279n.
Dudael, 97n.
Dudaļem, 97, 97n.
Duidaïn, desert, 97n.
Dulaurier, 65n.
Dunstan of Samaria, 15n.
Dupont-Sommer, A., "Adam Père du
  Monde dans la Sagesse de Salomon",
  109n., 286n.
 "L'Instruction sur les deux Esprits",
  297n.
Dura-Europos, evidence of syncretism in,
  310
Dussaud, R., 120
Dwellings of Angels, in the Borgia leaflet,
  97n.

Eagle:
 symbolism of, 207, 207n.
 not Gnostic, 207n.
Earth, in a Falasha book, 97
Easter, heretical views of Audius on, 55
Ebionite (?) tomb in Rome, 91
Ebionites as ancestors of a Gnostic sect, 7
Ebonkh, apa, 130
Ecclesiasticus, MS. of, at Louvain, 141
Eclecticism, fourth century, 278
Eden, in a Falasha book, 97
 (Israel) in Justin's teaching, 34, 35
Edessa:
 Audians around, 56
 burial place of and centre of cult of
  St Thomas, 339–40
 GOSPEL OF THOMAS written in (?),
  348
Egypt:
 as symbol of matter, 49, 49n., 255
 development of Gnosticism in, 12, 13
 Sethians in, 45
 Luria studied in, 294
 origin of Gnosticism, Islam, etc., in (?),
  110
 reason for amount of Gnostic material
  discovered in, 64
 the image of heaven, in *HERMETIC
  TREATISE (26),* 245, 247
 woe prophesied to, 245–6, 247
 modern, government attitude towards
  owners of antiquities, 121
Egypt Exploration fund, 232n.
Egyptian and Judaean elements, mixture
  of, in Gnosticism, 105–6, 106n.
 influence on Chenoboskion MSS., 272–5
 on Gnosticism, 104
 the, a false messiah, 300–1
Eid, Albert, former holder of Jung Codex,
  118, 119, 123, 126, 145
Eighth Book of Moses, 171
Eitrem, S., *Papyri Osloenses,* 74n., 105n.
Ekhamôth and Ekhmôth in *GOSPEL OF
  PHILIP,* 225
Eleazar, High Priest, 100
Eleïnos, in Bruce Codex, pt.2, 85
Elenchos, see Philosophumena
Eleusis, mysteries of, 2, 48
Eleutheropolis, 46
Elijah, in Islamic belief, 317
 posture of, on Carmel, 290n.
Elilaios, in the teachings of the Gnostic
  sect, 43
Elkesaï, influenced by Essenes, 298n.
 of same family as Martos, 46
Elkesaites, as ancestors of a Gnostic sect,
  7
 reinforced Gnostics, 13
Eloaios in Ophite teaching, 38

Eloaïu, in *SECRET BOOK*, etc., Cod. Berol., 203
Elohim, in Audius' teaching, 56
  in Justin's teaching, 34, 35
Elorkaios, in *PARAPHRASE OF SHEM*, 148
Encratites, heretics, 7
Encyclopaedia Britannica, 10n.
Encyclopaedia Judaica, 292n.
Encyclopédie de l'Islam, 316n., 317n., 321n.
End of the world, in *SETHIAN REVEL-ATION*, Cod. VI, 188
Enemy, The, crucified, 22
Enki, in Sumerian belief, 268
Enlightners, Iranian, 282
  of Gnosticism, in *APOCALYPSE OF ADAM*, etc., 182, 183
Ennead, 243n.
  Egyptian, 272
  in Bruce Codex, pt.2, 82
  in *HERMETIC TREATISE* (23), 243; and (25), 244
  in *SECRET BOOK*, etc., Cod. X, 204
Enoch:
  an astrologer, in Jewish belief, 288
  and stelae, in myth, 190
  hidden, in *Enoch*, 290n.
  in Sabianism, 315
  in Theodore's answer, 136
  literature attributed to, plagiarized, 107
  wrote *Books of Jéou* according to *Books of the Saviour*, 73, 254
Enoch, Book of:
  Angels before the Throne in, 291, 291n.
  ascent to Paradise in, 109
  contains similarities to *REVELATION ON PISTIS SOPHIA*, 176
  Dudael in, 97n.
  Enoch in, hidden, 290n.
  fragments of *Book of Noah* in, 97n.
  influential in Gnosticism, 286
  on origin of metal-work, 209
  on the Perfect, 109
  serpents in, and Khalkhydras in *Book of Secrets of Enoch*, 173
  source of Gnostic concept of a fountain, 305, 305n.
  used by Dead Sea sect, 296
  used by pseudo-Zosimos (?), 278
Ephesus, church of, 13
Ephraem, uses form "Jude Thomas", 340
Ephraim, St, on Audians, 56
  on the Kukeans, 58
  St Ephraim's prose refutations of Mani, Marcion and Bardaisan, 24n.
Ephrem the Syrian, *Exposition of the Concordance of the Gospels*, contains a Logion, 230, 230n.

Epicureanism, 11
Epinoïa of the light, in *TRIPLE DIS-COURSE*, etc., 181
Epiphanius, St:
  (*Adversus Haereses*) on Melchizedekians, 46–7, 46n., 47n., 154
  on Sabaôth, 164
  and Irenaeus, attitude of compared with that of *Philosophumena*, 47
  and Peter the Archontic, 46
  mentions myth of Norea, 262
  mentions *Revelations of Marsianes*, etc., 159
  on Archontici, unspeakable, 79n.
  and Severians, 46
  and Seth, 150
  "symphonia" as used by, 197
  on Audians, 55–6
  on Borborites, 311
  on Cainites, 36, 45, 45n.
  (*Contra Haereses*) Cainite use of *Ascension of Paul*, 238
  on Carpocrates, 23
  on Ebionites, 91
  on Gnostics, 15
  on Gnostic sects, 40
  on *Little Interrogations of Mary*, 73
  on Nazarenes, 91
  on Nicolas, 13–14
  and Nicolaitans, 41
  on Ophites, 44, 49
  on Seth's ascension, 158
  on Sethian identification of Christ and Seth, 187
  on the Gnostic Sect, 41, 42, 43, 73n.
  on Sethians, 45, 251
  on the seduction of the Archons, 163–4
  Panarion, 7–9, 8n., 57n., 236n.
  influence of Essenes on Sampsaeans, 298n.
  on Satanians, 311n.
  on Scythianus' slave, 314n.
  quoted Ptolemeus, 26–7
  quotes Cainite *Gospel of Eve*, 187n.
  quotes a *Gospel of Philip*, 181, 225
  which is like *SACRED BOOK OF THE . . . GREAT SPIRIT*, 235
  refuted Marcionism, 25
  refuted Ophite doctrines similar to those in *SECRET BOOK*, etc., Cod. X, 212
  reliability of shown by Chenoboskion MSS., 250
Epiphanius, son of Carpocrates, 23–4
EPISTLE, in Codex V:
  in author's classification, 143
  mentioned, 197
Epistle of the Apostles refers to *Gospel of Thomas* (?), 335

EPISTLE OF EUGNOSTOS:
  described, 192–5
  discussed, 195–7, 260
  in author's classification, 142
  parallels with *TREATISE ON BAP-
    TISM OF JOHN*, 219
  source of *SOPHIA OF JESUS*, 125,
    195, 198, 199, 241n.
Epistle of the Foundation, 22
EPISTLE OF PETER TO PHILIP, 236
  in author's classification, 142
Epistle of Rehoboam (Key to Hydromancy), =
  Book of Solomon (?), 170–1
Epititiôkh, the Virgin, in *SACRED
  BOOK OF THE* . . . *GREAT SPIRIT*,
  178
Epstein, A., "Recherches sur le Sefer
  Yetsira", 293n.
Er the Armenian, in the *Republic*, 156,
  264
Zoroaster=, (Arnobius), 154n., 156
Eranos Jahrbuch, 3n., 14n., 90n., 110n.,
  218n., 263n., 286n.
Erman, *Die Literatur der Aegypter*, 247n.
Eros, Creator of the world, 76n.
  in *Book of the Chiefs, etc. (Philosophu-
    mena)*, 176n.
  in Hesiod, 176
  in *REVELATION ON PISTIS
    SOPHIA*, 168, 175–6
Esaldaiô, 85n.
Esau, a prophet of the Cainites, 36
Eschakleo (=Ialdabaôth), in popular
  Hermetism, 162n.
Eschatology:
  of *Books of the Saviour*, 72, 176
  of Chaldaean astrology, 267
  of Flavia Sophe's epitaph, 89
  Gnostic, 293n.
  of the Gnostic Sect, 43–4
  of the *Gospel of Mary*, 88
  of the *Great Treatise*, 78, 79
  Hellenistic influence on Jewish, 288,
    288n.
  of *HERMETIC TREATISE (26)*, 246
    compared with *Pistis-Sophia*, 246n.
  Manichaean derived from Gnostic, 313
  of *Pistis-Sophia*, 274n., 327
  of *Poimandres*, 277
  of *REVELATION ON PISTIS
    SOPHIA*, 169–70
  of *SECRET BOOK, etc.*, 208, 210
  of *SOPHIA, etc.*, 200
  Valentinian, 30, 31
Es-Sayyâd, 130, 131, 134
Essenes:
  influenced Sampsaeans (Epiphanius),
    298n.
  on adventitious soul, 216n.

Essenes (*cont.*):
  originated Gnosticism (?), 7, 298–300
    or grew up under similar circum-
      stances (?), 15
  parallels with Gnostics, 296–7
  physionomics influenced by Greek
    thought, 288n.
  Pythagorean influence on, 288n.
  use of trowel symbol, 91, 91n.
Ethiopia, in Naassene symbolism, 49
Ethiopian evangelistaries, 22n.
Études carmélitaines, 80n., 162n.
Eucharist, in *GOSPEL OF PHILIP*,
  223–4
Euchites, three primordial Principles in
  teaching of, 151, 151n.
Eudes de l'Étoile, a neo-Gnostic, 312
Eugnostos, transcriber of *SACRED
  BOOK OF THE* . . . *GREAT
  SPIRIT*, 180, 192
  author of the *EPISTLE, etc.*, 192, 196
  a real person, 253
  but identity unknown, 300
EUGNOSTOS, see EPISTLE OF
  EUGNOSTOS
Euno, in Perataean teaching, 51
Euphrates the Perataean, 50, 50n.
  mentioned by Battai, 60
Euripides, *Melanippus*, 90
Eusebius:
  Ecclesiastical History, 5, 5n., 7, 7n., 46n.
  on Agrippa Castor, 20n.
  on Basilides, 20
  on Dositheus, 15n.
  on the variety of Gnostic systems,
    252–3
  quotes Clement *Hypotyposes*, 236,
    236n.
  mentions *GOSPEL OF MATTHIAS*,
    226
  on Nicolas, 13
  on Origen, 35n.
  refers to *GOSPEL OF THOMAS*, 335
Eusebius of Mt Ararat, 96n.
Eustathius, on *Odyssey*, 191
Eutactes, one of the Archontici, 46
Eutychius, 47n.
Evangelium veritatis: Jung Codex, 126n.,
  239n., 241n.
Eve:
  alchemical interpretation of, 101n.
  Gnostic belief about in Theodore of
    Tabennisi, 135
  in *Acts of Thomas*, 73n.
  in *APOCALYPSE OF ADAM, etc.*, 182
  in Audius' teaching, 56–7
  in Chenoboskion MSS., 261
  in *HYPOSTASIS, etc.*, 160, 161
  in Justin's teaching, 34

Index

Eve (cont.):
in Ophite belief, 38–9
(Epiphanius), 213
in *REVELATION ON PISTIS SOPHIA*, 168, 169
in *SECRET BOOK*, etc., 206–7
in *TREATISE ON BAPTISM OF JOHN*, 220
in various beliefs, 214n.
origin of Gnostic myth of seduction, 309
= Pandora, in pseudo–Zosimos, 101
Seth her son by a superior birth to that of Cain, etc., 158
Evil in Battai's teaching, 60
in Gnosticism, 112
Evilat, in Naassene symbolism, 49
Evodius, *De fide*, 22, 74n.
Ex Oriente Lux, 297n.
Exclusiveness, lack of in St Paul, 308
EXEGESIS UPON THE SOUL:
discussed, 190–2
in author's classification, 144
notes in, similar to those in *REVELATION ON PISTIS SOPHIA*, 170
Exodus, referred to in Gikatila, 292
Ezechiel:
Zoroaster = , 280
in Chenoboskion MSS., 287
Ezechiel, Chester-Beatty MS., 141
divine presence as fire, 377
vision of Chariot, 165, 177, 290
Eznik of Kolb, and his *De deo* (*Against the sects*), 24n., 25–6, 279n.
refuted Marcionism, 25

Fabricius, *Codex pseudepigraphus*, 171n.
Falashas, sacred books of, 97–8
Falk, M., *I "Misteri" di Novalis*, 323n.
Fasting, in *GOSPEL OF THOMAS*, 371
Fatality:
= Air, in two magical prayers, 109, 154
Gnostic (?), in pseudo–Zosimos, 101
(Heimarmene), in *Asclepius*, 244n.
Hermetic in pseudo–Zosimos, 100
in Gnostic belief, 111
in Mithraism, 154
in the *Mithraic Liturgy*, 108
sphere of, in *Pistis-Sophia*, 66, 67, 68
in titleless portion of Codex Askewianus, 75
Fate:
Adam freed from, a pre-Gnostic concept, 295
Gnostic (?) in pseudo–Zosimos, 101
Hermetic in pseudo–Zosimos, 100
in certain Gnostic prayers, 107, 108

Fate (cont.):
in Chaldaean astrology, 267
in Gnostic belief, 111
in *HERMETIC TREATISE* (25), 244
in *HERMETIC TREATISE* (26), 246
in *Pistis-Sophia*, 68
masters of, in *Poimandres*, 276
(= Time) in *SECRET BOOK*, etc., 208
Void = , in Hellenistic writings, 153–4
Father, in Barbelognostic belief, 37
in Borgia leaflet, 96n., 97n.
in *DIALOGUE OF THE SAVIOUR*, 220
in *EUGNOSTOS*, 193, 194
in Gnosticism, 61
in *GOSPEL OF PHILIP*, 222
in *GOSPEL OF THOMAS*, 228, 230, 344, 345, 355, 360, 362, 363, 365, 366, 369, 374
in *GOSPEL OF TRUTH*, 239, 372
in Ophite belief (Epiphanius), 44, 213
(Irenaeus), 38
in *PARAPHRASE OF SHEM*, 149
in Perataean teaching, 50, 51
in *Poimandres*, 276, 277
in *REVELATION OF DOSITHEUS*, 188
in *REVELATION ON PISTIS SOPHIA*, 169
in "Rossi", 103
in *SACRED BOOK OF THE . . . GREAT SPIRIT*, 178
in St Paul, 308
in *SECRET BOOK*, etc., 201, 202, 205
in *SOPHIA*, etc., 199, 200
in Theban inscriptions, 273
in *TRIPLE DISCOURSE*, etc., 181, 330, 331
Majesty of the, in Syriac *Chronicle*, 185
of the Universe, in Bruce Codex, 81, 81n., 82, 84, 85
in Naassene symbolism, 92
Plato's view of, according to Christian iconographers, 350
the everlasting, in *SACRED BOOK OF THE . . . GREAT SPIRIT*, 178
(The Good), in Justin's teaching, 34, 35
Father of Fathers, Amon-Re was, 272n.
Father of Greatness, in Battai's teaching, 60
in Manicheism, 152
in teaching of John of Apamea, 57
Fathers in the Heights, Manichaean, 217
Faye, E. de, 3
Gnostiques et Gnosticisme, 4n., 24n.
Fayum, Coptic Manichaean MSS. of, 86n., 119–20
Fendt, *Gnostische Mysterien*, 114n., 115n., 224n.

Festugière, O. P., *Révélation d'Hermès Trismégiste*, 6, 6n., 14n., 99n., 100n., 107, 107n., 108n., 150n., 162n., 164n., 170n., 171n., 190, 190n., 242n., 271n., 318n.
and Nock, *Corpus hermeticum, see* Nock, etc.
Figaro, Le, 91n.
Filliozat, J., "Les Doctrines des Brahmanes d'après saint Hippolyte", 6, 6n., 249
Fire, in *Poimandres*, 276
Flaubert, *Tentation de saint Antoine*, 2
Flavia Sophe, epitaph of, 89, 89n.
Flugel, *Mani*, 152n.
Foerster, W., "Von Valentin zu Herakleon", 27n.
Force, The, in Basilide's teaching, 22
Fragmenta histor. Graec., 129n.
FRAGMENTS ON COSMOS, Cod. XII, briefly described, 197
in author's classification, 145
FRAGMENTS ON DEMONS, etc., Cod. XI, in author's classification, 145 mentioned, 197
French Institute of Archaeology, Cairo, 116
Frey, J. B., "Abraham, Apocalypse of", 45n.
"Adam (apocrypha)", 97n., 185n.
article in *Dictionnaire de la Bible*, 184n.
Friedländer, M., *Der vorchristliche Gnosis*, 4n.
Furlani, G., "Il Pavone e gli altri ribelli presso i Mandei e il Pavone dei Yezedi", 316n.
"I pianeti e lo zodiaco nella religione dei Mandei", 74n., 155n.
"L'Antidualismo dei Yezedi", 316n.
Peccati i peccatori presso i Mandei, 256n.
"Tre trattati astrologici siriaci sugli eclissi solari e lunari", 73n., 293n.

Gabriel, in *Investiture, etc.*, 236
in *Pistis-Sophia*, 71, 113n.
in *SACRED BOOK OF INVISIBLE SPIRIT*, 178, 286n.
Galila, in *SECRET BOOK, etc.*, Cod. X, 202
Galileans as ancestors of a Gnostic sect, 7
Gamaliel in *APOCALYPSE OF ADAM*, etc., 182
in Bruce Codex, pt. 2, 83
in Chenoboskion MSS. and elsewhere, 286, 286n.
in *SACRED BOOK OF THE . . . GREAT SPIRIT*, 178
Gandillac, M. de, *Œuvres complètes du pseudo-Denys l'Aréopagite*, 68n.

Gardiner, Sir A., published Leyden papyrus, 273n.
Garitte, G., "Le premier volume de l'édition photographique des manuscrits gnostiques coptes et de l'Évangile de Thomas", 228n.
Gaspar the Mage, 161n.
Gaster, article in *Journal of R. Asiatic Society*, 288n.
Gaukaï, and Mani, etc., 255, 255n.
Gaul, Valentinianism in, 13
Gayet, 2
Gayomârt, in *Bundahishn*, 277n.
Gebel et-Tarif, 128, 130, 131, 134
Geiger, on Dudael, 97n.
Gelasius, pseudo-, on *GOSPEL OF THOMAS*, 232
Gemmut, in *Books of the Saviour*, 73
Gems, Gnostic, 52n., 74, 74n., 85n., 93
Generation:
of Life, in *REVELATION*, Cod. V, 197
of the Elect, in *SECRET BOOK, etc.*, Cod. X, 201
of the Spiritual, in *SECRET BOOK, etc.*, Cod. X, 202
the Great, in *APOCALYPSE OF ADAM, etc.*, 182
the perfect, in *SECRET BOOK, etc.*, Cod. X, 207, 208, 210
without a King, in *EUGNOSTOS*, 193
in *REVELATION ON PISTIS SOPHIA*, 169
Genesis, 37n., 49n., 104, 104n., 299
account of Creation reflected in *HYPOSTASIS, etc.*, 160
but Flood story different, 160-1
cosmogony of attacked by *Shkand Gûmânîk Vichâr*, 283-4
Gnostic view of, 62
discovery of a codex containing part of, 128n.
in *SECRET BOOK, etc.*, Cod. X, 204, 206
influence of on Medinet Habu cosmogony, 106n.
Land of Nod in, not Duidaïn, 97n.
mention of Seir in, 161n.
on birth of Melchizedek, 46
on the Sons of God, 295
Satornil claimed to correct, 19
source of Gnostic belief about Cain's father, 39n.
texts from, as starting point for Gnosticism, 309, 309n.
view of, in Chenoboskion MSS., 261
Gentiles, in *SETHIAN REVELATION*, Cod. VI, 188
Geography of myth, based on reality, 255
Iranian and Gnostic parallels in, 282

Geon, in Naassene symbolism, 49

George, Syncellus, *Chronographia*, on Seth's ascension, 158, 158n.
on Hermes and stelae, 190, 190n.

German Academy to publish Cod. Berol., 117, 125, 125n.

Gide, A., *Carnets d'Égypte*, 131

Gikatila, Joseph, *Mystery of the Serpent*, 292

Gilgit, discovery at, 121n.

Ginzâ, a Mandaean book, 98, 207n.
see also Lidsbarski

Ginzâ of the right-hand, 61

Ginza Rba, a revelation of Adam, 183

Gitta, 12, 15

Glory, in *TRIPLE DISCOURSE*, 330

Glykas, 47n.

Gnosis (as illumination),
of the God of Truth, in *APOCALYPSE OF ADAM, etc.*, 182
depicted in tomb of the Aurelii, 92
in Bruce Codex, pt.2, 81
in Clement's *Hypotyposes*, 236
in the Gnostic Sect, as means of salvation, 43, 44, 113
in *GOSPEL OF PHILIP*, 225
in *GOSPEL OF THOMAS*, 229, 231
in *GOSPEL OF TRUTH*, 239, 240
in *HERMETIC TREATISE* (25), 244
Hermetism self-defined as a, 99n.
in Iranian belief, 282, 282n.
in Ophite teaching, as means of salvation, 44
in *PARAPHRASE OF SHEM*, as means of salvation, 149
in *SECRET BOOK, etc.*, as damnation to those who backslide, 208
the perfect, 207
the means of perfection in Valentinianism, 29, 30

Gnostic gems, 52n., 74, 74n., 85n., 93

Gnostic Sect, The, 23, 41–4
= Barbelognostics, 36–7, 37n.

Gnosticism: Gnosis, as a system:
definition of, 1, 1n.
general nature of, ix, xvi–xvii
(i) *History*:
background of, 310
decay of, 311
difficulty of study of, 61
partly caused by unreliability of hostile evidence, 62–3
and lack of authentic texts, 63
early history, Puech's views on, 12–13
early history, 13 *et seq.*
Eastern sects, 14
its flourishing, 11
"Gnostics", the term used by Naassenes, 48

Gnosticism: Gnosis, as a system (*cont.*):
(i) *History* (*cont.*):
its flourishing, 11
later legacy of, 321–2
problems of history of, 114–15
sects listed, 7
survival of in the West, 311–12
the beginnings, 10
[The following refer to sects and teachers in their historical setting. Further references will be found under their individual names:]
Archontici, 45–6
Basilides, 20–3
Cainites, 45
Carpocrates, 23–4
Justin, 33–5
later sects, 35 *et seq.*
lesser sects, 46–7
Marcionism was Gnostic, 24–6
Nicolaitans, 13–15
Ophites, 37–40
Satornil, 19–20
Sethians, 45
The Gnostic Sect, 41–4
the later Ophites, 44
sects as described in *Philosophumena*, 47 *et seq.*
Naassenes, 47–50
Peratae, 50–1
Sethians, 52–3
sects as described by Plotinus, 53–4
by Theodor Bar-Konai and others, 55 *et seq.*
Audians, 55–7
John of Apamaea, 57–8
Kukeans, 58–9
Kantaeans and Battai, 59–61
Simon, 15–18
Valentinianism, 18–19, 27–33
(ii) *Hostile writings as evidence*:
see also supra (i) *History*
Acts of Archelaus, 7
Celsus, 7
Clement, 5
Epiphanius, 7–9
Eusebius, 7
Hegesippus, 5
in general, 4–5
Irenaeus, 5
Jerome, 5
Justin, 5
Lucian, 6
Origen, 6
Philosophumena, 6
Plotinus, 9–10
Porphyry, 10
Tertullian, 5
unreliability of, 62–3

Gnosticism: Gnosis, as a system (*cont.*):
  (iii) *Gnostic and related writings, etc., as evidence:*
    see also Chenoboskion MSS. and under the titles of the individual works
    Bruce Codex, 77–86
    Codex Berolensis, 86–8
    lack of authentic texts until Chenoboskion, 63
    monuments and paintings, 89–94
    Pistis-Sophia, 64
      general doctrine of, 65–7
      Books of the Saviour, 72–3
      the *Books*, 67–71
        and their teaching, 71–2
      remainder, 73–6
    related literature, 94–109
    various fragments, 88–9
  (iv) *Modern study:*
    Anz, 3
    Barrès, 2
    became fashionable in nineteenth century, 2
    Bousset, 3
    Cerfaux, 3
    de Faye, 3
    Flaubert, 2
    Gayet, 2
    growth of knowledge about connected movements, 3–4
    Harnack, 3
    Horn, 2
    Jonas, 3
    Lewald, 2
    Matter, 2
    Mosheim, 1–2
    Puech, 3
    Puech on early history of, 12–13
    Reitzenstein, 3
  (v) *Writings, nature of the Gnostic:*
    books still undiscovered, 252
    secrecy concerning, 257
      purpose of, 258
    use of a Christian disguise, 254
    use of *GOSPEL OF THOMAS*, 227n.
    use of Homeric allegory, 192
    use of pseudonyms, 253–4
    various apocrypha attributed to Zoroaster because of doctrine of Three Principles, 259–60
  (vi) *Doctrines:*
    astronomy, mistaken, 271–2
    constellations identified with mythical powers, 270
    cosmogony from Three Principles, 259–60
    demiurge, 112
    lack of uniformity in, 252–3
    evil, 112

Gnosticism: Gnosis, as a system (*cont.*):
  (vi) *Doctrines* (cont.):
    gnosis, 113
    God and the world, opposed, 111
    main doctrines, 61–2, 110–15
    mythical geography of influenced by Mandaeans, 256
    resurrection, 301n.
    Saviour, 112
    sophia, 113
    Three Phases, 113n., 114
    time, 111, 112, 113
  (vii) *Relations with other religions:*
    Gnosticism:
      and Christianity, 300–9
        various theories as to relationship, 302
      Gnostics distorted Christianity, 302
        gave their works a Christian camouflage, 311
        used a pre-Synoptic Christianity, 304–5
      and Islam, 317–22
      and Mandaeanism, 315
        shared a mythical geography, 225–6
      and Manichaeism, 312–15, 314n.
      and Sabianism, 315–16
      and the Yezidis, 316, 316n.
      interrelations with Hermetism shown by Chenoboskion MSS., 248
      influence of Hermetism on, 275, 277–8
        Indian beliefs, 284–5
        Iranian beliefs, 279–84
        Jewish, 289
      Jewish influence on, 285–95
      originated from Dead Sea Sect (?), 298–300
      parallels with Essenes, 296–7
Gobryas in Suidas, etc., 286n.
God:
  a Hermetic view of, in pseudo-Zosimos, 100
  above the universe, in *SOPHIA, etc.*, 200
  and Eve in Audius' teaching, 56–7
  and the soul, in Sabianism, 316
  in Clementine *Recognitions*, 281n.
  in *GOSPEL OF PHILIP*, 223
  in *GOSPEL OF THOMAS*, 229, 369
  in *GOSPEL OF TRUTH*, 240
  in *HERMETIC TREATISE* (25), 244
  in *HERMETIC TREATISE* (26), 246
  in Kukean teaching, 58
  in *Pistis-Sophia*, 65
  in *Poimandres*, 215, 277
  in St Paul, 307
  in *Zohar*, 292

God (*cont.*):
is Light, in St John, 305
of gods, in *EUGNOSTOS*, 194
of the lower world, two different beliefs about, in Chenoboskion MSS., 260
of the Silence, in *SACRED BOOK OF THE . . . GREAT SPIRIT*, 180
of truth, in *EUGNOSTOS*, 193
origin of Gnostics' concept of an inferior, 309
retreat of, from His omnipresence, 276n., 294, 294n.
the everlasting, in *APOCALYPSE OF ADAM*, etc., 182
the higher, in *HYPOSTASIS*, etc., 159
the supreme, in Bruce Codex, 81
the supreme, in Chenoboskion MSS., of Iranian origin, 281
the supreme, in Gnosticism, 111
the supreme, in *SUPREME ALLO-GENE*, 328-9
Goggessos, transcriber of *SACRED BOOK OF THE . . . GREAT SPIRIT*, 180
a real person, 197, 253
significance of the name, 196
Gomorrah, home of the perfect, 254-5
in *SACRED BOOK OF THE IN-VISIBLE . . . SPIRIT*, 298, 298n., 299, 300
Good, in Battai's teaching, 60
Goossens, R., "Onias le Juste, Messie de la Nouvelle Alliance", 290n.
Gorce, M. and Mortier, R., eds., *Histoire générale des religions*, 312n., 315n.
Gorgorios, author of Falasha apocalypse, 97-8
Gorthynian sect, 15
Gospel, characteristics of a, 334
Gospel of the Ebionites, as quoted by heresiologists resembles *GOSPEL OF THOMAS*, 235
GOSPEL OF THE EGYPTIANS, see *SACRED BOOK OF THE IN-VISIBLE GREAT SPIRIT*
Gospel of the Egyptians, 48n., 350
described by Epiphanius, 235
quoted as source of logia known to us in *GOSPEL OF THOMAS*, 233, 342
mentioned in *Philosophumena*, etc., 48, 85n.
is not *SACRED BOOK OF THE INVISIBLE . . . SPIRIT*, 180-1
relationship of, to *GOSPEL OF THOMAS*, 348
Gospel of Eve, a book of the Gnostic Sect, 42, 187n.
still undiscovered, 252

Gospel of the Hebrews, 350
in Jerome, *Micah*, 236
quoted as source of Logia known to us in *GOSPEL OF THOMAS*, 233, 234, 235, 342
quoted in Clement, 230
relationship of, to *GOSPEL OF THOMAS*, 348
Gospel of Judas, used by Cainites, 36
of Judas Didymas (?), 36n.
Gospel of Mary, 87, 88
publication, 87n.
GOSPEL OF MATTHIAS, see *BOOK OF THOMAS*
Gospel of Matthias, = *GOSPEL OF THOMAS* (?), 336
believed to be connected with *GOSPEL OF THOMAS*, 335
mentioned in Origen, Eusebius, 226
relationship of, to *GOSPEL OF THOMAS*, 348
Gospel of the Nazarenes, in heresiologists resembles *GOSPEL OF THOMAS*, 235
Gospel of Nicodemus, 95, 95n.
Gospel of Perfection, of the Gnostic Sect, 42
GOSPEL OF PHILIP, described, 222-3, 224-5
discussed, 221-2, 223-4, 225, 234-5, 234n., 252, 336, 343, 372
in author's classification, 144
Gospel of Philip, believed to be connected with *GOSPEL OF THOMAS*, 335
in Epiphanius, partly corresponds with *SACRED BOOK OF THE . . . GREAT SPIRIT*, 181, 225, 235
used by the Gnostic Sect, 42
GOSPEL OF THOMAS (with *LOGIA IESU*):
belongs to a group of writings purporting to be written by Philip, Thomas and Matthew, 221-2
COMPLETE TRANSLATION OF, 335-70
contents described and relationship with New Testament, etc., discussed, 341-4, 347-8, 351-2
index of references in, to canonical Gospels, 379-83
dating of, 347-8
described and discussed, 231-5, 334 *et seq.*, 352
discussion of attribution to Thomas, 338-40
historical value of, 350-1
importance of James in, 237
in author's classification, 144
notes on the text, 370-7

GOSPEL OF THOMAS (with LOGIA
IESU) (cont.):
  orthodoxy of, 348–50
  parallels in other literature to the Logia,
    230–1
  position in codex associates it with
    Philip and Matthias, 336
  previously known in part from Oxy-
    rhynchus fragments of Logia, 226–9,
    227n., 228n., 337–8
  unpublished Logia from, 229–30
  Puech's work on the Logia, 126, 126n.,
    305, 337–8
  provides an authentic tradition, alterna-
    tive to the synoptic gospels (?), 351
    quoted, 228, 229, 233–4, 237
  referred to by Origen, etc., 335–6
  resembles St John's teaching, 339
  study of, will throw light on lost
    writings, 252
  teachings of, 344–6
  works of the same title, 231–2, 334
  written in Edessa (?), 348
Gospel of Thomas, 48, 48n.
  early references to, 335
  work mentioned by Origen and in
    Philosophumena is GOSPEL OF
    THOMAS, 231
  on Jesus' childhood, 232, 334–5
GOSPEL OF TRUTH, described, 239–
  240
  discussed, 126, 126n., 240–1, 241n., 343,
    372, 376
  in author's classification, 145
  in second discovery, 118
Gospels, the canonical:
  Basilides' commentaries on, 20
  index of references to, in GOSPEL OF
    THOMAS, 379–83
  relationship of, to GOSPEL OF
    THOMAS, 347–8, 349
  warning in against false prophets, 18
Gothaios, leader of a Gnostic sect, 7
Götze, A., "Die Schatzhöhle. Ueberlie-
  ferung und Quelle", 184n.
Governors, the two Great, in Pistis-Sophia,
  66
Graber, A. and Nordenfalk, C., La
  Peinture romane, 80n.
Grace, in SACRED BOOK OF THE
  . . . GREAT SPIRIT, 178
Graetz, Gnostizismus und Judentum, 285n.,
  293n.
Great Book, Mandaean, 98
Great Hekhaloth, Greek influence on, 288
  method of composition, 290, 290n.
Great Treatise according to the Mystery, see
  Bruce Codex
Grebaut, S., 47n.

Gregoire, H., "Note sur les survivances
  chrétiennes des Esséniens et des sectes
  apparentées", 298n.
Gregory bar-Hebraeus, his evidence for
  Allogeneous books, 158
Gregory of Nazianzus, supposititious work
  of, 96n.
Grelot, P., "La Géographie mythique
  d'Henoch", 97n.
Grenfell and Hunt, New sayings of Jesus and
  fragments of a Lost Gospel, on GOSPEL
  OF THOMAS, 232, 232n.
Griffith, F. Ll. and Thompson, H.,
  Demotic magical papyrus of London and
  Leiden, 74n.
Gruenbaum, "Beiträge zur vergleichende
  Mythologie aus der Haggada", 39n.,
  295n.
Guardian of the Great Light in Pistis-
  Sophia, 66
Guardians, Mandaean and Gnostic, 256
Gundophar, King, = Gaspar, 161n.
  in Acts of Thomas, 95
Guentch-Ogloueff, M., "Noms propres
  imprécatoires", 42n., 104n.
Gundel, W., Dekaner und Dekansternbilder,
  171n., 203n., 267n.
  article in Bursians Jahresbericht, 267n.
Gurha (statue) in Kukean teaching, 58–9

Habib, disciple of John of Apamea, 58
Hackin, Jos., at Gilgit, 121n.
Hades, Jewish concept of, influenced by
  Greek, 288
Hadrian, Emperor, 12
Haggada, 39n.
  identifies Shem with Melchizedek, 154,
    286
Hagiga, 289n.
Haivânoûs in Balinus, 319
Hammer, J. de., Mémoire sur deux coffrets
  gnostiques du moyen âge, 90n.
Hamouli MS., XVIII, 96n., 236n.
  XIX, 96n.
Hamra-Dûm, 118, 128, 131, 133, 134
Hanan, 289, 290n.
Haran Gawaïta, Mandaean, 98, 255–6, 256n.
Harmas, in SECRET BOOK, etc., Cod. X,
  202
Harmozel, in Bruce Codex, pt.2, 85
  in Investiture of the Archangel Gabriel,
    236
  in magical, etc., texts, 103
  in SACRED BOOK OF THE . . .
    GREAT SPIRIT, 178
  in SECRET BOOK, etc., Cod. X, 202
  in TREATISE ON BAPTISM OF
    JOHN, 220

Harmupiael, in *SECRET BOOK, etc.,*
Cod. X, 202
Harnack, A. von, his view of Gnosticism,
3, 302
Marcion, 24n.
Neue Studien zu Marcion, 24n.
on *Books of Pistis-Sophia,* 73
Hâroûs, in Balinus, 319-20
Harran, Sabians lived around, 315
Harris, J. R., 70n.
Haug, M., *Ueber das Ardâi Vîrâf nâmeh,*
287n.
Hazard, P., *European Thought in the
Eighteenth Century,* 322n.
Heads of the town up to the aether, a
Perataean book, 50
Heavens, opening of, 74n.
in *Pistis-Sophia,* of Egyptian origin, 106
Hebdomad, 243n.
in *HERMETIC TREATISE (23),* 243
in Ophite teaching, 38
in Valentinianism, 29
not in *Pistis-Sophia,* 66
Hebrew proselytes, in *GOSPEL OF
PHILIP,* 222
Heeg, *Catalogus astrologorum Graecorum,*
170, 170n.
Hegesippus claimed Jewish origin for
Gnosticism, 285
quoted by Eusebius, 5, 5n., 7
on beginnings of Gnosticism, 15
Heidenheim, *Bibliotheca Samaritana,* 189n.
Heimarmene, *see* Fatality
Hekhaloth, in Jewish mysticism, 180n., 290
in Rabbinical literature, 177
Heleleth, angel:
in Bruce Codex, pt.2, 85
in *HYPOSTASIS, etc.,* 161
in *Investiture of the Archangel Gabriel,* 236
in magical, etc., texts, 103
in *SACRED BOOK OF THE . . .
GREAT SPIRIT,* 178
in *SECRET BOOK, etc.,* Cod. X, 202
in *TREATISE ON BAPTISM OF
JOHN,* 220
Helen, companion of Simon:
in Simon's teaching, 16, 17
seduced Archons (Epiphanius), 164,
164n.
Helen of Adiabene, a Jewish proselyte,
287n.
Helenê, = Selenê, in Dositheus' teaching, 15
Helios, = Fatality in Mithraism, 154
prayer to, 108
Hellen, in Perataean teaching, 51
Hellenism, concept of time in, 111
Hellenistic influence on Judaism, 287-8
Hemerobaptists, as ancestors of a Gnostic
sect, 7

Heracleon, disciple of Valentinus, 26, 30-1
TREATISE (48) by (?), 239, 239n.
Hennecke, E., *Neutestamentliche Apokryphen,* 2nd ed., 87n.
3rd ed., 139n.
Heraclitus, on Hercules, 35n.
Hercules, in Justin's teaching, 34-5
in other allegories, 35n.
Heresiologists:
accurate on Nicolaitans (?), 301
description of Valentinians by, resembles
EUGNOSTOS, 195
not always accurate, 304
on *Gospel of the Egyptians,* 181
refer to *Allogeneous Books,* 157-8, 180
Hermaphrodite, in *REVELATION ON
PISTIS SOPHIA,* 168
Hermes:
and Seth, 190, 190n.
frequent occurrence of name in Roman
catacombs, 91-2
in Bruce Codex, pt. 2 (?), 84
in *On regeneration, etc.,* 275
in Sabianism, 315
in Syncellus, 190
of Cyllene, among Ebionites, etc., 91-2
in Naassene teaching, 48, 91-2
On the Immaterial, in pseudo-Zosimos,
100
only Egyptian prophet mentioned in
Chenoboskion MSS., 272
Physika in pseudo-Zosimos, 278
supposititious author of *Balinus, Secret,
etc.,* 318
The Wing in a magical text, 107
THOUGHT OF GREAT POWER
attributed to, 331
Hermes Trismegistus:
see also Poimandres
in *HERMETIC TREATISE (23),* 243
(25), 244
(26), 245
is plagiarized, 107
literature attributed to, described, 99
HERMETIC TREATISE (23), 243, 247
in author's classification, 143
HERMETIC TREATISE (25), 243-5,
247, 271
in author's classification, 143
HERMETIC TREATISE (26), described,
245-6
discussed, 246-7, 246n.
in author's classification, 143
Hermeticism:
and Gnosticism, interrelated, 3, 4, 55n.
belief in Eschakleo, 162n.
Berbali in, 14n.
close interrelations with Gnosticism
shown by Chenoboskion MSS., 248

Index

Hermeticism (*cont.*):
described, 275–7
in Chenoboskion MSS., 241 *et seq.*
in Islam, 318–20
in *REVELATION OF DOSITHEUS*, 189, 331
in *TRIPLE DISCOURSE*, 331
influence of, on Gnosticism, 275, 277–8
modern not directly Gnostic, 322
popular, close to Gnosticism but pure
unconnected with Gnosticism, 99
secrecy in, 257
writings of, typical titles of, 242
pseudonymous, 253
Hermetists, belief about seed, 234n.
Hermon, Mount, and children of Seth, 39n., 255
Hermopolis, temple of Petosiris:
cosmogony of, 273
Psalms, inscriptions containing, at, 106n.
Herzfeld, *Archaeological history of Iran*, 161n.
Herzog-Haupt, 37n.
Hesephekh, in *SACRED BOOK OF THE . . . GREAT SPIRIT*, 178
Hesiod, *Theogony*:
allegorization of, in Chenoboskion MSS., 264
and Valentinus, 191n.
mystical commentaries on, 349
on Chaos, 175, 176
on Eros, 176
quoted by the pseudo-Zosimos, 99
Hibil-Ziwa, Mandaean, 207n.
Hierabiblos, in *REVELATION ON PISTIS SOPHIA*, 169
identity (?), 171
Hierakas on Melchizedek, 47
Hierosolymus, 42n.
Hippolytus, *De resurrectione*, 301n.
pseudo-, reference in, dates *PARAPHRASE OF SETH*, 250
on Justin, 33
Hippolytus of Rome, not author of *Philosophumena*, 3, 6
Refutatio omnium haeresium, 6n.
Holy Spirit, in *GOSPEL OF PHILIP*, in Eucharist, 223
in *GOSPEL OF THOMAS*, 344, 362
in *HYPOSTASIS*, etc., 161
in Luria, 294
Manichaean, identified with At-Taûm, 227
in *Pistis-Sophia*, 113n.
in *REVELATION ON PISTIS SOPHIA*, 167
in *SECRET BOOK*, etc., Cod. X, 202
in Valentinianism, 28, 218n.

Homer:
Christian allegorization of *Odyssey*, 192n.
Eustathius' commentary, on *Odyssey*, 191
Gnostic use of *Odyssey*, 93, 192, 349
icon of, 12
in *Catabasis of Pythagoras*, 288
in Numenius, 192
Naassene use of *Odyssey* (*Philosophumena*), 48, 191
note in *EXEGESIS*, etc., on *Odyssey*, 191
poems allegorically interpreted, 11, 215
in Chenoboskion MSS., 264
not fundamental to the MSS., 266
quoted by pseudo-Zosimos, 99
Valentinus' use of, 191n.
Hopfner, T., "Der religionsgeschichtliche Gehalt des grossen demotischen Zauberpapyrus", 274n.
Hopkins, *Epic mythology*, 285n.
"Mythological aspects of trees and mountains in the great Epic", 285n.
Horaios in Ophite teaching, 38
Hôrea, = Nôrea, 45, 163
meaning of name (?), 317
see also Nôrea
Horn, J., *Ueber die biblische Gnosis*, 2, 2n.
Horner, G., *Pistis-Sophia*, English translation, 65n.
Horus and Seth, 104
Hosea, in note in *EXEGESIS*, etc., 191
Hû (Diospolis Parva), 129
Hydria, 169, 171, 172–4, 172n.
Hymen, cloud of, in *PARAPHRASE OF SHEM*, 148
explanation of, 149
Hymenaeus, in *II Timothy*, etc., 301n.
"Hymn of the Pearl", *Acts of Thomas*, 49n., 95, 255
Hymns, from Dead Sea Scrolls, 296
HYPOSTASIS OF THE ARCHONS (BOOK OF NÔREA):
in author's classification, 144
described, 159–63
discussed, 163
divine throne in, compared with that in *REVELATION ON PISTIS SOPHIA*, 177
fabricated from *REVELATION ON PISTIS SOPHIA*, 241n.
Noah built ark on Seir, 254
quotation from St Paul in, 306
importance of Sabaôth in, 291
the supplanting of Ialdaôth by Sabaôth, 260
explained by doctrine of successive aîônes, 271–2
to be compared with *REVELATION ON PISTIS SOPHIA*, 165

Hypsele, Scythianus' slave at, 314n.
Hystaspe, in Tabari, 155n.
Hystaspes, books attributed to, 4, 102, 280
 Oracles, Judeo-Iranian, banned by the
 Empire, 281

Iabel, in SECRET BOOK, etc., Cod. X,
 202
Iabraôth, in titleless portion of Codex
 Askewianus, 75
Iahweh Sabaôth, 12
Ialdabaôth:
 derivation of name, 163n.
 and Ahriman, 281, 281n.
 and man paralleled by Zeus and
  Prometheus, 264–5
 and Mithraic Aïôn, 281
 and Sabaôth paralleled by Kronos and
  Zeus, 264
 = Ariael, 162n., ill. 162
 (Ariael and Samael) in REVELATION
  ON PISTIS SOPHIA, 166, 167–8,
  174–5, 271–2
 = Chnubis (?), 93
 in a cloud, Jewish origin of (?), 291
 in a fragment, 88
 in Basilides' teaching, 263
 in Gnosticism, 162n.
 = planet Saturn, 270
 in Nicolaitan teaching, 14
 in Ophite belief (Epiphanius), 44, 212,
  213, 214
 (Irenaeus), 38, 39, 40
 in Pistis-Sophia, 1, 69, 70, 176n.–177n.
 in the Gnostic Sect, 41, 42n., 43
 (?) in tomb of Aurelii, 92
 Mahes, comparable with, 274n.
 = Sacla, 51n.
 Sacla comparable with Seth and Osiris
  (Plutarch), 274
 = Sacla, derived by Manichaeans from
  Gnostics, 313
 (= Sacla, etc.) in Chenoboskion MSS.,
  260
 (Sacla, Samael) in SECRET BOOK,
  etc. Cod. X and Cod. Berol., 152,
  202–4, 205, 207, 208
 (= Samael) in HYPOSTASIS, etc.,
  162–3, 271–2
 (Samael) in TRIPLE DISCOURSE,
  etc., 181, 329
 = Saturn, 164n.
 similarity of Egyptian Father to, 273
 statue of (?) in Rome, 94
Iamblichus, 4
Iaô, in Jêou the painter, 105
 in Ophite teaching, 38
 in Rabbinical literature, 109

Iaô (cont.):
 in SECRET BOOK, etc., Cod. Berol., 203
 in the teachings of the Gnostic Sect, 43
 Little, the Good, in Pistis-Sophia, 66
 on gems, 93
 Iaô-Sabaôth, in magical, etc., texts, 103
 Ibraôth, in First Book of Pistis-Sophia, 177n.
Ideas, theory of, in GOSPEL OF
  THOMAS, 345, 349, 373
Idris, = Enoch in Sabianism, 315
Iessea Mazarea . . ., in SACRED BOOK
  OF THE . . . GREAT SPIRIT, 179
Iesseus [ ] Mazareus . . ., in APOCA-
  LYPSE OF ADAM, etc., 183, 184
Ignatius of Antioch, 301n.
Immortals, in REVELATION ON
  PISTIS SOPHIA, 165
 in SOPHIA, etc., 200
Imprimérie Nationale, Paris, 123
Incantations, used by Gnostics, 54
India, beliefs from, in Gnosticism, 284–5
 origin of Gnosticism, etc., in, 110
 relations with the West, 284
Indivisible, in Bruce Codex, pt.2, 83
Indo-Iranian Journal, 297n.
Infinite in EUGNOSTOS, 194
Infinites, the, in TRIPLE DISCOURSE,
  330
Innocentii, sect, in Rome, 91
Institute of Egypt, 119
Intelligence, in Audius' teaching, 56
 in Valentinianism, 27, 28
 of God, in Zohar, 292
Intention (Akhamôth), in APOCALYPSE
  OF JAMES (10), 237
 of the Wisdom in Valentinianism, 28,
  29, 30
INTERPRETATION OF THE GNOSIS,
  dialect of, 138
 in author's classification, 144
 mentioned, 197
Interrogations of Mary, a book of the
  Gnostic sect, 41, 57n.
Iobel, in SECRET BOOK, etc., Cod. X, 202
Ioel, in Priscillianist treatise, 198n.
Iouël in Bruce Codex, pt.2, 82
 the Virgin, in SACRED BOOK OF
  THE . . . GREAT SPIRIT, 178
Investiture of the Archangel Gabriel, 235–6
Invisible, The, see Propatôr
Iranian belief(s):
 described, 279–81
 exemplified in Chenoboskion MSS.,
  281–4
 in adventitious soul (two spirits), 216,
  297n.
 in celestial ascents, literature of, 150n.
 in creation of parts of body by planets,
  205n.

Iranian belief(s) (*cont.*):
 influence of, on Basilides, 262–3, 263n.
 knowledge of extended by Chenoboskion, 279
Iranian elements in certain prayers, 109
Iranian influence, in Chenoboskion MSS.,
  279, 281–4
 in *HERMETIC TREATISE* (*25*), 244n.
 on Gnosticism, 102, 114, 152–3
 on Judaism, 287
Irenaeus, St, 61
 attitude of compared with that of
  Philosophumena, 47n.
 on Basilides, 21, 21n., 23
 on Barbelognostics (*History*), 86
 on *Book of Norea* (*Adversus haereses*), 163
 on Cainites, 36
 on Carpocrates, 23
 on Gnosticism, 18–19, 19n., 81n.
 on Gnostic morality (*Adversus haereses*),
  112, 112n.
 on lack of uniformity in sectaries' views
  (*Adversus haereses*), 253
 on Marcos' mystical union, 224n.
  on Marcos' rites, 33
  on Marcosian baptism, 224n.
 on Ophites, 26n., 36, 37–40, 44
 on Ophites and Sethians, close to
  SECRET BOOK, etc., Cod. X, 212
 on Simon, 16, 17
 on the Gnostic Sect (Barbelognostics),
  36–7
 on the Valentinians, 18–19, 26n.
  and their Gospel of Truth (*Adversus
   haereses*), 240
 on Valentinus (*Adversus haereses*), 27,
  30, 31
 parody of Valentinus, 32, 32n.
 on various Gnostic sects' beliefs similar
  to *EUGNOSTOS*, 195
 opposes doctrines of *SECRET BOOK*,
  etc., 127
 proves earliness of *SECRET BOOK OF
  JOHN* (*Contra haereses*), 250
 summarizes part of *SECRET BOOK*,
  etc., 210, 211, 212, 241n.
 quotation in, similar to *GOSPEL OF
  THOMAS*, 372
 refers to *Gospel of Thomas* (?), 335
 The so-called Gnosis unmasked, etc., 5
Isaiah the Prophet in *Pistis-Sophia*, 68
Isaiah, 29, 29n., 38n., 68, 68n., 149, 309,
 309n.
Ishmaelites, confuse Seth, Shem, etc., 155
Ishtar, descent of into hell, 218n.
Isidore, son of Basilides:
 claimed Matthias had left him secret
  discourses (*Philosophumena*), 226, 336,
  352

Isidore, son of Basilides (*cont.*):
 On the adventitious soul, 23
  by Basilides as well, 263
 teachings of, 20n.
  on the additional soul, 72, 216
 writings of, 20
Isis, in Egyptian belief, 51n., 104
 = Euno, in Peratean belief, 51
 and Osiris, in Peratean belief, 273–4
 worshipped at Rome, 90
Islam, and Gnosticism, 110, 317–22
 and Hermetism, 318–20
Islam, Der, 318n.
Ismaël, Rabbi, first to identify Shem with
 Melchizedek, 286n.
Isma'ilites, Gnostic in origin, 321
"Ismâ'ilîya", 321n.
Isoauel, in *SACRED BOOK OF THE
 . . . GREAT SPIRIT*, 179
Israel, the firstborn, in *REVELATION
 ON PISTIS SOPHIA*, 167
Ituraea, home of baptist sects, 255
Izates, a Jewish proselyte, 287

J.T.S., 88n.
Jaarbericht. Ex Oriente Lux, 297n.
Jackson, A. W., *Researches in Manichaeism*,
 208n.
Jâmâsp, son of Fashd, 155n.
James, M. R., *The Apocryphal New Testament*, 16n., 28n., 48n., 95n., 96n., 175n.
James, St, the Apostle:
 as brother of Jesus in Naassene belief
  (*Philosophumena*), 198n.
 believed to be a brother of Jesus, 48, 236
 in *APOCALYPSE OF JAMES* (*10*) and
  (*11*), 237
 in *GOSPEL OF THOMAS*, 237, 345,
  357
 in *SACRED BOOK OF THE . . .
  GREAT SPIRIT*, 237
 in tomb of the Aurelii, 93
 reverenced by Ebionites, etc., and
  Gnostics, 91
 some Chenoboskion MSS. attributed to,
  304
James the Great, strategus, in *SACRED
 BOOK OF THE . . . GREAT SPIRIT*,
 179
Jars as MSS. container, 134n.
Jealousy in *REVELATION ON PISTIS
 SOPHIA*, 165
Jêou, in *Books of the Saviour*, 73
 in *Pistis-Sophia*, 66, 69, 71, 177n.
 in the *Great Treatise*, 77
 in titleless portion of Codex Askewianus, 75
 the Painter, stele of, 105

Jeremiah, mentions MSS. in a jar, 134
Jerome, St, *Ad Evagrium*, 47n.
  Commentary on Micah, 236
  Contra Vigilantius, 5, 5n., 14n.
  on Basilides, 23
  on apocrypha, 351
Jerusalem:
  the heavenly, 48
    in Bruce Codex, pt.2, 84
    in tomb of the Aurelii, 93
    = Ogdoad, 243n.
  town of, Tomb of the Kings at, 287n.
Jesus Christ, ix
  = Aberamenthô, a statue of, 105
  Adam prophesied advent of, in *Book of Mysteries*, 183
  and Saoshyant in the Magi writings, 102
  and the Jordan, 49
  as redeemer in Manichaean belief, 217
  at end of Codex Askewianus, 76
  childhood of described in a *Gospel of Thomas*, 232
  compared to Ophiouchus, 50n.
  crucifixion, in Basilides' teaching, 22, 22n.
  crucifixion in Manichaean belief, 22
  early collections of logia of, 351–2
  entrusted Philip, etc., with teachings (*Pistis-Sophia*), 221–2
  icons, etc., of, 11, 12, 23
  (?) in a fragment, 89
  in *Acts of John*, 95
  in *Acts of Thomas*, 95, 340
  in *APOCALYPSE OF JAMES (10)*, 237
  in *BOOK OF THOMAS*, 225, 339
  in *Books of the Saviour*, 72, 73
  in Bruce Codex, pt.2, 85
  in Chenoboskion MSS., 305
  in Gnosticism, 111, 113, 113n.
  in Justin's teaching, 35
  in Mandaean teaching, 110n.
  in Manes, *Shâpurakân*, 314n.
  in Manichaeism, 102
  in Marcionism, 24, 25, 26
  in Naassene teaching, 48
  in Ophite teaching, 37, 40
  in *Pistis-Sophia*, 67, 68, 69, 70, 71, 327, 328
  in St Paul's works not Docetic, 308
  in *SOPHIA*, etc., 198–200
    (Adam—Light) in *SOPHIA*, etc., 199
  in the *Great Treatise*, 77, 78, 79
  in the teachings of the Gnostic Sect, 43
  in titleless portion of Codex Askewianus, 74, 75
  in *TRIPLE DISCOURSE*, etc., 181, 331
  in Valentinianism, 28, 29, 30, 31, 218n.
  in Yazuqean teaching, 61
  James a brother of, 236–7

Jesus Christ (*cont.*):
  logia of in *DIALOGUE OF SAVIOUR*, 221
  logia of, in Origen, 343, 351
  Manichaean belief that He came to earth at age of seven, 232
  Manichaean view of His baptism, 113n.
  mentioned by Satornil, 19n.
  preached in Samaria, later to become birthplace of Gnostics, 302
  problem of the Logia solved by Chenoboskion MSS., xiv
  (Saviour) discourse of, handed on by Matthias (*Philosophumena*), 226, 336
  in *ACTS OF PETER*, 236
  in *DIALOGUE OF THE SAVIOUR*, 220–1
  in *Gospel of Matthias (Philosophumena)*, 336
  in *GOSPEL OF THOMAS*, 228, 229, 230, 231, 233, 237, 344–5, 346, 351, 355 *et seq.*, 371 *et seq.*
  in *GOSPEL OF TRUTH*, 239, 240
  in Kukean teaching, 59
  in *SECRET BOOK*, etc., Cod. X, 201, 202, 204, 206, 207, 208, 210, 211, 303, 328
  sayings of, Basilides' collection of, 20
  = Seth, 45
  in Sethian teaching (Epiphanius), 187
  = Serpent in *Books of Jêou*, 261
  Shem=, in *PARAPHRASE OF SHEM*, 149
  special relationship of Thomas, etc., to, in Gnosticism, 335–6
  the assayer, in Bruce Codex, pt.2, 82
  the Christ, in *REVELATION ON PISTIS SOPHIA*, 167
  the great Christ, in *SACRED BOOK OF THE INVISIBLE . . . SPIRIT*, 178
  the Living, in *SACRED BOOK OF THE INVISIBLE . . . SPIRIT*, 298
  Thomas, a brother of, 225, 226, 339–40
    Manichaean parallel, 226–7, 227n.
  writings ascribed to, among Chenoboskion MSS., 262
Jewish elements in *REVELATION ON PISTIS SOPHIA*, 176–7
  mysticism, chariot image in, 83
  myths in pseudo–Zosimos, 99
Jewish Quarterly Review, 286n.
Jews, believed to have a donkey-headed god, 42n.
Job, 293n.
Johannes Lydus, quotes Greek *Asclepius*, 247n.
John, disciple of John of Apamea, 58
John of Apamea, 57–8
  The Foundations, 58

John of Parallos, 9
  denounced a *Teachings of Adam*, 183, 213
  and a *Preaching of John* (= *SECRET BOOK, etc.?*), 213
  put St Michael books on Index, 96n.
John Rylands collection, Coptic letter in, 141
John, St:
  (i)
  Christians of, *see* Mandaeans
  depicted in tomb of the Aurelii, 93
  in a fragment, 89
  in Clement, *Hypotyposes*, 236
  in *SECRET BOOK, etc.*, Cod. X, 201, 204, 206, 207, 210, 328
  in *TREATISE ON THE BAPTISM, etc.*, 212–20
  influence of, on *Odes of Solomon*, 70n.
  not author of St Michael book, 96n.
  (ii)
  I Epistle:
    antichrists = Gnostic teachers (?), 301
    Light in, 305
  (iii)
  Gospel of:
    Coptic MS. of, 141
    part of, in recently discovered Papyrus Bodmer III, 128n.
    Greek MS. of, Papyrus Bodmer II, 141
    Light in, 305
    notion of Gnosis in, 306–7
    resembles *GOSPEL OF THOMAS*, 339, 342, 349, 350, 372, 374
    Thomas in, 339
  (iv)
  Revelation of:
    compared with *GOSPEL OF THOMAS*, 372
    on Virgin of Light, 271
    refers to Nicolas, 13
    REVELATION OF PISTIS SOPHIA compared with, 167
    Samael in, 177n.
    source of part of *GOSPEL OF TRUTH*, 239
    Virgin in *REVELATION OF ADAM, etc.*, compared with, 183
John the Baptist, 15
  in *GOSPEL OF THOMAS*, 363
  in Ophite teaching, 40
  teacher of Dositheus, etc., 189
  Yôhannâ (Mandaean) = , 256
Johnson, Rev. L., translator, 333
Jonas, H.:
  Gnosis und Spätantiker Geist, etc., I, 3, 3n., 16n., 37n., 47n., 50n., 52n., 68n., 95n., 112, 112n., 151n., 157n., 312n., 316n.
  II, 3, 3n.

Jordan, as a symbol, 48–9, 49n.
Joseph, in *GOSPEL OF PHILIP*, 223
  in *Pistis-Sophia*, 70–1
Josephus, *Antiqu. Judaeorum*, 290n.
  on false messiahs, 301
  on Seth, 190
Joshua, 49, 68n.
Journal Asiatique, 155n., 158n., 281n.
Journal of Biblical Literature, 289n.
Journal of Ecclesiastical History, 87n.
Journal of the American Oriental Society, 285n.
Journal of the Royal Asiatic Society, 288n.
Judaeus, 42n.
Judaica. Festschrift für Hermann Cohen, 285n.
Judaism, a belief of, that teachers were caught up to heaven, 108–9
  influence of, on Gnosticism and the Chenoboskion MSS., 285–6, 295
  Hellenistic influences on, 11, 287–8
  influence of, on "Rossi", 103
  influence of, on Yazuqeans, 61
  Iranian influences on, 287
  mixed with Egyptian elements, 105–6, 106n.
  parallels of, with early Gnostic literature, 289–91
  mediaeval Jewish literature and Gnosticism, 292–5
  related to Gnosticism (?), 110
Judas, in *DIALOGUE OF THE SAVIOUR*, 221
Jude, Epistle of, 301–2
Jude-Thomas, connected with Edessa, 340
  in *BOOK OF THOMAS*, 225, 339
  in *GOSPEL OF THOMAS*, 228
  see also Thomas, St
Jüdische Zeitschrift, 97n.
Julian the Theurgist, *Chaldaean oracles*, 4
  bibliography of, 103n.
  close to Gnosticism, 269
  influenced by Gnosticism (?), 103
  on the membrane dividing the fires, 149n.
  related to Bruce Codex, pt.2, 85–6, 102
Jung, C. G., *Psychological types*, 52n.
  Psychology and Alchemy, 322n.
Jung Codex:
  a part of Codex XIII, 137, 145
  description and contents of, 238–9
  dialect of, 137, 239
  edition of, 126, 239n.
  see also Eid, A.
Jung Institute, Zürich, xiii–xiv, 123, 145
Junker, H., "Die Götterlehre von Memphis", (*Schabaka inschrift*), 272n.
  "Die Iranischen Quellen der hellenistischen Aionvorstellung", 281n.
Just ones, The, in Bruce Codex, pt.2, 82, 84

Justice, in *REVELATION ON PISTIS SOPHIA*, 168
Justin, St, 80n.
    Apology, 28n.
    Baruch founded on rabbinical speculations, 286
    teachings of, in *Baruch*, 33–5
    still undiscovered, 252
    Syntagma, 5, 5n.
    on Eve, 214n.

Kronoš, of Iranian origin (?), 281n.
Kropp, A. M., *Ausgewählte Koptische Zaubertexte*, 85n., 103n., 291n.
Kuh-i-Khwâga, cave of Adam at (?), 161
Kuhn, K. G., "Die Sektenschrift und die iranische Religion", 297n.
Kukeans, 58–9
    myth of creation of man, 212n.
Kurites in Peratean belief (*Philosophumena*), 286n.

Kabbala, 2
Marcus' numerology similar to that of, 33
Kahle, P., *Bala'izah*, 88n.
Kalapataurôth in *Books of the Saviour*, 73
Kantaeans, 59–61, 59n.
Kashqar, Bishop of, 7
Kasser, R., ed., *Papyrus Bodmer III*, 128n.
Kaukaban, 46
Kaulakau in Naassene teachings, 49
Kelkheak and Kelkhea, in *PARAPHRASE OF SHEM*, 148
Kem-âtef, 93
Kemi, 132n.
Kephalaia (*Kephalaion*), 80n., 162n., 188n., 189, 205n., 208n., 271n., 306n., 336, 343
Key to Hydromancy, = *Epistle of Rehoboam*, 170
Khalkhydras, in *Book of the Secrets of Enoch*, 172–4
Kharael, in *Testament of Solomon*, 203n.
Khâtibi, el-, on Sabian myth of soul, 316, 316n.
Khesr, in Islamic belief, 317
Khnum of Elephantis, 93
Kingdom, in Clement, *II Epistle*, 375
    in *GOSPEL OF THOMAS*, 228, 230, 231, 345, 346, 355, 358, 359, 360, 363, 364, 366, 367, 368, 369, 370, 373, 374, 376, 377
    of Light, in *Pistis-Sophia*, 222
    in the *Great Treatise*, 79
Kings, II, 68n.
Kmosko, M., ed., *Liber Graduum*, 310n.
Knowledge, principles of, in *GOSPEL OF THOMAS*, 346
Kohut, on Duidaïn, 97n.
Korah, a prophet of the Cainites, 36
Kore kosmou, 208n.
Kosmopoiia, 14n., 162n.
Kraeling, *Anthropos and Son of Man*, 286n.
Krafft, J. G., *De haeresi Audianorum*, 55n.
Kramer, S. N., *L'Histoire commence à Sumer*, 268, 268n.
Kraus, *Jabir ibn Hayyan*, 318n.
Kroll, W., *De oraculis Chaldaicis*, 103n.
    Collection of Chaldaean Oracles, 86n.

Labib, P., *Coptic Gnostic Papyri in the Coptic Museum*, 122n., 239n.
    Director of the Coptic Museum, 124
Labriolle, P. de, *La Réaction paienne*, 42n., 62n.
Lactantius, *De ave phoenice*, 172n., 173
    Inst., 70n.
    quotes Asclepius, 246n.
Ladamês the Great, 131–2
Lagrange, M. J., *L'Orphisme*, 265n.
Lambert of St Omer, *Liber Floridus*, 80n.
Lampetians, 57
Lantschoot, A. van, "À propos du *Physiologus*", 172n.
"Fragments coptes d'une homélie de Jean de Parallos", 9n., 96n., 183n., 213n.
Lapidary of Aristotle, 180n.
Last Supper, in tomb of the Aurelii, 93
Law, in *TREATISE ON BAPTISM OF JOHN*, 219
    opposition to, in St Paul compared with Gnostic anti-biblicism, 306–7, 308
Lebreton, J., *Histoire de l'Église*, 19n.
    Histoire du dogme de la Trinité, 4n.
Lefebvre, G., *Le Tombeau de Petosiris*, 106n., 273n.
Le Forestier, R., *La Franc-Maçonnerie occultiste au XVIIIème siècle et l'ordre des Élus Coens*, 322n.
Lefort, L. Th., *Les Pères apostoliques en copte*, 118n.
"Les premiers monastères pachomiens", 130, 130n.
    transl., *Les Vies coptes de Saint Pachôme ...*, 129n., 135, 135n., 136, 136n.
Left, Place of the, in *Pistis-Sophia*, 66
Left and Right, in Ophite belief,
    in *Pistis-Sophia*, 66–7
    in Valentinianism, 30
Leisegang, H., *La Gnose*, 10n., 14n., 23n., 33n., 43n., 65, 65n., 66, 66n., 73n., 224n., 262n.
    on the Orphic (?) bowl, 90, 90n.
Leontius of Byzantium, on *Gospel of Thomas*, 232
Leontopolis, Mahes, god of, 274n.

Leptis Magna, 11
Leslau, W., *Falasha anthology*, 98n.
Leusiboras, mentioned by St Jerome, 5
Levi, in *Gospel of Mary*, 88
Levi, I., "Le Péché originel dans les anciennes sources juives", 286n.
Leviathan in the *Diagram*, 73n.
Levitical sect, 14
Lewald, *Commentatio ad historiam religionum veterum illustrandum pertinens de doctrina gnostica*, 2, 2n.
Lewy, H., *Chaldaean Oracles and Theurgy*, 86n., 103n.
Leyden, *Kosmopoiia* in a papyrus at, 162
papyrus of, published, 273n.
Liber Graduum, 310n.
Licentiousness, none in Chenoboskion MSS., 251
Lidzbarski, ed., *Ginzâ*, 155n., 164n., 256n., 271n.
ed., *Das Johannesbuch der Mandäer*, 155n., 164n., 207n., 256n.
see also Book of John
Liechtenhan, R., "Ophiten", 37n.
Sophia of Jesus (Cod. Berol.) translated by, in part, 87n.
Lietzmann, his view of Gnosticism, 302
Life everlasting, in *SACRED BOOK OF THE ... GREAT SPIRIT*, 178
in Satornil's teaching, 19
in Valentinianism, 27
the, in *GOSPEL OF THOMAS*, 233, 364
Life of Adam and Eve, 45n.
Light:
and Darkness in the Magi writings, 102
army of the, in Zoroastrian prophecy, 186
collected by the moon, a Gnostic belief, 271
freeing of sparks of, in Iranian belief, 282, 282n.
God is, in St John, 305
in *Book of Great Treatise, etc.*, 79, 80
in Bruce Codex, pt.2, 83, 84
in *Bundahishn*, 152, 153
in certain Gnostic prayers, 109
in Codex Askewianus, 80
in *GOSPEL OF THOMAS*, 357, 359, 363, 367, 373, 374
in Iranian myth, 154
in Manicheism, 152
in *Pistis-Sophia*, 66, 67, 69, 70, 71
in *Poimandres*, 276, 277
in pseudo-Zosimos, 101
in *REVELATION ON PISTIS SOPHIA*, 169
in St Paul, 307
in *SECRET BOOK, etc.*, Cod. X, 152, 201, 202–3, 207, 208, 209

Light (*cont.*):
in *SOPHIA, etc.*, 147n., 199
in the *PARAPHRASE OF SHEM*, 147–8
in *TRIPLE DISCOURSE*, 330, 331
Iranian belief about holiness of shown from *Shkand Gûmânîk Vichâr*, 283
myth of collection of, derived by Manichaeans from Gnostics, 313
of the All-Powerful, in *SOPHIA, etc.*, 199
one of the Three Principles of the Sethians (*Philosophumena*), 52, 150–1, 259
Prince of, Source of and Spirits of, in Dead Sea Scrolls, 297
sons of, elected, in St Paul, 308
in *TRIPLE DISCOURSE*, 330
The, in Manicheism, 216
world of, in *GOSPEL OF THOMAS*, 345
Lights, Mountain of, in mythology, 256
Limit, in Battai's teaching, 60
in Valentinianism, 28, 31, 81n.
the, in tomb of the Aurelii, 92
Linus, 53
Lion as a symbol in *GOSPEL OF THOMAS* and elsewhere, 371
Lithargoël, in *ACTS OF PETER, etc.*, 235–6
Lipsius, R. A., *Die Quellenkritik des Epiphanius*, 8n.
Little, the, and the Great, in *DIALOGUE OF THE SAVIOUR*, 221
Little Interrogations of Mary, 73
Livre des perles enfouies ..., 132, 132n.
LOGIA JESOU, see GOSPEL OF THOMAS
Logia, early collections of, 351–2
Grenfell knew were connected with Naassenes, 232
Naassene explanation of a logion in *GOSPEL OF THOMAS* (*Philosophumena*), 371
new, from *GOSPEL OF THOMAS*, 237, 229–30
ancient allusions to, 230–1
Oxyrhynchus fragments are from *GOSPEL OF THOMAS*, 227, 228, 228n., 229, 232, 232n., 234, 337–8
emendations to, proved wrong, 227–8, 338
quoted in Origen, 343, 351
Logogene, in *SECRET BOOK OF THE INVISIBLE ... SPIRIT*, 298
Logos of the Mother, in Valentinianism, 218n.
Lord, The, in Porphyry, 86
Lord God in Battai's teaching, 60

Lord of Glory, in Bruce Codex, pt.2, 84
Lot, wife of, in Theodore's answer, 136
Louvain, MS.9 and MS.12, 141
Lucian, *Alexander or the false prophet*, 6
Luke, St:
  disregarded by Gnostics, 336
  no Chenoboskion MS. attributed to, 304
  Gospel of, 20, 24, 41, 67n., 68n., 80n., 233n., 305
  close to Basilides' collection of Logia, 352
  contains a Logion, 231
  parallels with *GOSPEL OF THOMAS*, 341, 343, 352, 377, 378
Luminaries, Great in *TRIPLE DISCOURSE*, etc., 181, 329
Luria, Isaac, 293–4
Luxor, 128, 130
  author at, 119
Lycos valley, original home of Gnosticism, 12
Lyons, Valentinianism in, 13

McCown, *The Testament of Solomon*, 171n.
Macrocosm and microcosm, origin of belief in, 268–9
Magi, 102
  in *Book of the Cave*, etc., 184
  in Christian belief, 184
  in Syriac *Chronicle*, 185 ι
  Iranian, 279
  traditions of, mythical geography of, 161n.
  shared with Gnosticism, etc., 255
Magical literature, 4
  and Gnosticism, 103, 105
  and Hermetism, 99, 99n.
  Hermes, *On the immaterial* is against, 100
  influence of Judaism and of Egyptian thought on, 107
Magical prayers:
  Chariot in, 291
  fatality in, 154
Magusaeans, 279, 279n., 280
Mahabharata, a White Mountain in, 284–5
Mahes, similar to Ialdabaôth, 274n.
Mahomet, ascension of, a myth of Gnostic origin, 317–18, 317n.
Malinine, M., introduction by, to *Gospel of Truth* (*Evang. Ver.*), 239
Malinine, M., Puech, H. C., and Quispel, G., eds., *Evangelium Veritatis*, 126n., 239n., 241n.
Male, E., *L'Art réligieux en France au XIII siècle*, 1n.

Man:
  creation of, in Balinus, 319
  in Borgia leaflet, 96n.
  in Bruce Codex, pt.2, 83
  in *EUGNOSTOS*, 194
  in *HYPOSTASIS*, etc., 159
  in Ophite belief (Epiphanius), 212–13
    and elsewhere, 212n.
  in Valentinianism, 29–30
  ascent of, in Gnosticism, 108
  categorization of, in Gnosticism and in St Paul, 307
  in certain Gnostic prayers, 107
  in *Poimandres*, 214, 215
  in *REVELATION OF ADAM*, etc., 182
  in *SACRED BOOK OF THE . . . GREAT SPIRIT*, 178–9
  in *SECRET BOOK*, etc., Cod. X, 202, 204, 206, 215, 217
  primordial, and the Messenger, in Iranian belief, 282n.
  in Valentinianism, 27
  Son of, in Naassene teachings, 49
  the, in *REVELATION ON PISTIS SOPHIA*, 168
  The First, in Ophite belief (Irenaeus), 37, 38, 40
  The Perfect, in Sethian teaching, 53
Manchester Guardian, report in, xiii
Mandaeanism, 34
  Adam important in, 183
Mandaean(s):
  and Gnosticism, 315
  confusion of, 61
  shared a mythical geography, 255
  of Gnostic derivation, 98, 99
  and Kantaeans, 59n.
  anti-Christian, 110, 110n.
  belief about Shem, 155
  belief in ships of the sun, etc., 74n.
  sacred books of, 98
  books of, allude to Yazuqaeans, 61
  certain Mandaeans of Jewish origin (A Biruni), 285
  doctrine of seven aïônes, 271
  eagle in, 207n.
  Mountain of Lights and an Indian parallel, 285
  mystical union in, 224n.
  myth of Nuraïta (Norea), 164
  Seven Guardians and Indian parallel, 285
  and time, 111–12
Manes, 4
  as depicted in *Acts of Archelaus*, 7
  death of, 49n.
  early history of (*Acts of Archelaus*), 314 (*Shâpurakân*), 314n.
  Gaukaï, place of origin of, 255n.

Manes (*cont.*):
  influenced by Bardesan's Gnosticism, 31n.
  influenced by Mesopotamian baptists, 98
  influenced by Ophites (Augustine, etc.), 312
  mentioned by St Jerome, 5
  revelation by at-Taûm to, 226–7
  St Ephraim's refutation of, 24n.
  the *Mysteries*, etc., attributed in *Acts of Archelaus* to Terebinth, 314
  see also, Kephalaia
Manetho, on Moses, 105
Mani, *see* Manes
Manichaean MSS. of Fayum, 86n., 119–20
  exact provenance of unknown, 136
Manichaeism, xvi–xvii, 3
  and Battai, 59,60
  and Christianity, 9, 313
  and Gnosticism, 312–15, 314n.
    confusion of, 61
  and Kantaeans, 59, 59n.
  attacked in *Acts of Archelaus*, 7
  beginning of suppression of, 13
  GOSPEL OF THOMAS, in fact, written before rise of, 348
    used in, 227n., 232, 335
  influence of, in GOSPEL OF THOMAS, 234
  importance of St Paul in, 306n.
  influence of, in *Acts of Thomas*, 95
  influence of, in *Great Treatise*, 80
  influence of in *Pistis-Sophia*, etc., 259
  Mountain of Lights in, and Indian parallel, 284–5
  neo-Gnostics classed as followers of, 312
  of Gnostic derivation, 98
  origin of (*Acts of Archelaus*), 314
    (*Shâpurakân*), 314n.
  parallels in, to the Christian "Coming of the Kingdom", 213n.
  Third Messenger in, and Egyptian belief, 273
  Three Phases in the cosmology of, found also in Gnosticism, 113n., 114
  work by Nicotheus mentioned in, 86, 86n., 159
  writings of, 4
    not pseudonymous, 253
  Beliefs in Manichaeism:
    about end of world, 188
    about importance of St Thomas, 232
    about Mariamne, 198n.
    about St Michael and Satan, 96n.
    about Seth, 188–9
    about Shem, 154–5
    about souls, 69n.
    about time, 112
    about Trees of Paradise, 216

Manichaeism (*cont.*):
  Beliefs in Manichaeism (cont.):
    creation of parts of body by planets, 205n.
    in Sacla, 162n.–3n.
    in Two Principles, 152
    in Virgin of Light, 80n.
    Jesus Christ as redeemer, 217
    Jesus Christ came to the earth at age of seven, 232
    man's luminous nature alien (=allogeneous), 158n.
    mystical union, 224n.
    on Adam, 214, 218n.
    on baptism of Jesus Christ, 113n.
    on Eve, 214n.
    on shape of earth (Cosmas), 269
    planets evil, sun and moon good, 270
    root, as a symbol, 147n.
    seduction of the Archons by Norea, 161n., 164, 164n.
      by crew of ships of sun, etc., 74n.
    sky made of Archons' skins, 149n.
    that Adam bore witness to the advent of Christ, 183
    tree symbolism, 80n., 147n.
    whispered prayers, 196n.
Manichäische Handschriften der staatlichen Museen Berlin, 188n., 306n.
Manilius, *Astronomica*, 44
Mansi, *Coll. Concil.*, 271n.
Manual of Discipline of Dead Sea Sect, 297, 297n.
Marcellina, in Rome, 12
Marcellinus, reverenced icons of Pythagoras, etc. (Epiphanius), 263n.
Marcianus, a heretic, 46
Marcion, 24
  his Foreign God compared with Allogeneous Seth, 158
  in Rome, 12–13
  sources for, 24n.
  three primordial Principles in teaching of, 151
  various opponents of, 7
Marcionism, 24–6
Marcionite influence on *Commandments of the Sabbath*, 97
Marcus, inspired by Barbelô and the Tetrad, 147n.
  mystical union and baptism in teaching of (Irenaeus), 224n.
  pupil of Valentinus, 32
  teaching of, 33
  spread of, 13
Mariamne, 48
  in Naassene belief (*Philosophumena*), 236
  in tomb of Aurelii, 92

Mariamne (*cont.*):
   in *SOPHIA, etc.*, 198n., 222
   identity (?), 198n.
Mariès, L., *Le "De deo" d'Eznik de Kolb connu sous le nom de "Contre les sectes"*, 24n.
Mark, St:
   Gospel of, 67n., 68n., 233n., 339
   disregarded by Gnostics, 336
   no parallels with GOSPEL OF THOMAS, 342
      except certain parables, etc., 378
   no Chenoboskion MS. attributed to, 304
Mark the Gnostic, Jewish influence in, 291
Marmarô and Marmarôth in "Rossi", 103
Marsanes, caught up to heaven, 109
   in Bruce Codex, pt.2, 82, 86
   our ignorance of, 114
Marsanes and Martiades:
   the celestial visions (revelations) of, 46, 46n., 86
   still undiscovered, 159, 252
Martana, a prophetess, 46
Martiades, caught up to heaven, 109
   see also supra: Marsanes and Martiades
Martinez de Pasquales, derived his ideas from alchemists, 322, 322n.
Martos, a prophetess, 46
Mary, in GOSPEL OF THOMAS, 234, 359, 370
   in *Pistis-Sophia*, 68, 69, 70, 222, 327, 328
   in *SOPHIA, etc.*, 198
   (Magdalene?), 88
   Magdalene, in DIALOGUE OF THE SAVIOUR, 221
      in *Pistis-Sophia*, 71
      Mariamne = (?), 198n.
   the mother of Jesus, in Valentinianism, 30–1, 218n.
      Mariamne = (?), 198n.
   the Virgin in GOSPEL OF PHILIP, 223
Masbutheans as ancestors of a Gnostic sect, 7
Mashya, 46n.
Mashyanê, 46n.
Maspero, J., *Histoire des Patriarches d'Alexandrie*, 139n.
Massignon, L., "Inventaire de la littérature hermétique arabe", 318n.
Mataraha, in Mandaean myth, 256
Matrimony, as a symbol, in GOSPEL OF PHILIP, 224
   elsewhere, 224n.
Matter, in *Acts of Thomas*, 95
   in Gnosticism, 62, 113
   in Marcionism, 25
   in Ophite teaching, 38
   in Peratean teaching, 50, 51
   in *Pistis-Sophia*, 66
   in Sabianism, 316

Matter, *Histoire critique du Gnosticisme*, 2
Matthew, St:
   and Basilides, 20
   disregarded by Gnostics, 336
   Gospel of, 67n., 68n., 373, 374, 377, 378
   a source of the Five Trees, 80n.
   cited, 339
   contains a logion, 231, 233n.
   in *Books of the Saviour*, 72
   in DIALOGUE OF THE SAVIOUR, 221
   importance of in *Pistis-Sophia*, 221, 222
   in *SOPHIA, etc.*, 222
   in GOSPEL OF THOMAS, 233, 341, 343, 357
   in tomb of the Aurelii, 93
Matthew, St (Matthias):
   importance of, in Gnosticism, 335–6
   in *Pistis-Sophia*, 221, 222
   in *SOPHIA OF JESUS*, 222
   in BOOK OF THOMAS, 225
   in tomb of the Aurelii, 93
   secret discourses of, left to Basilides, etc. (?) (*Philosophumena*), 226, 336, 352
   no Chenoboskion MS. attributed to, 304
Mazdaism, 280n., 281n.
   combats between celestial spirits in, 177n.
Medea in Peratean teaching, 51
Media, Israelites in, after the Exile, 287
Medinet Habu, Temple at, 106n.
   texts from, 272n.
Mélanges Bidez . . ., 192n.
Mélanges Capart, 267n.
Mélanges de Ghellinck, 89n.
Mélanges Franz Cumont, 39n., 57n.
Melkharadonin, in SECRET BOOK, etc., Cod. X, 202
Melchizedek, 46
   as Seth, 47
   in a fragment, 89
   in Ishmaelite belief, 155
   in Isma'ilite belief, 321, 321n.
   in myth of Saoshyant, 184
   in *Pistis-Sophia*, 66, 69
   in St Paul, 305
   in teaching of John of Apamea, 57, 58
   Shem = , in Haggada, 154, 154n., 286
   similarity of Bruce and Askew Codices on, 80
   (= Zorokothora) in the *Great Treatise*, 79
Melchizedekians in Epiphanius, 154
Mémoires présentés à l'Académie des Inscriptions, etc., 196n.
Memorie. Pontifical Academy of Archaeology, 92n.
Memphis, agate of Mahes found at, 274n.

Menander, leader of a Gnostic sect, 7, 19, 20
  from Capparetia, 12
  on the resurrection of the dead, 301n.
  regarded himself as a divine incarnation, 254
Menasce, J. de, *Schkand-gumânîk Vichâr*, 271n., 282n., 284n.
Mereim, in *APOCALYPSE OF JAMES* (11), 237
Merkaba, in Jewish mysticism, 177, 290
Mesites in *Bundahishn*, 152n.
Mesopotamia Audians in, 56
  Mandaeans in, 98, 315
  Manichaeism in, 98
  spread of Gnosticism into, 13
Mesos, revelation of, mentioned by Porphyry, 10, 53, 156
Mesotes, cloud of, in *PARAPHRASE OF SHEM*, 148
Messalians, 310, 310n.–311n.
  believed in adventitious soul, 216n., 310
Messenger, = Saviour in Iranian belief, 282n.
  third, Manichaean, paralleled in Egyptian belief, 273
Messiah, the false, 300–1
Messina, G., *Der Ursprung der Magier*, 279n., 281n.
  I Magi a Betlemme e una predizione di Zoroastro, 155n., 156n., 161n., 184n., 279n., 282n., 287n.
Messos, Gnostic use of name shows Magusaean influence, 280
  in *REVELATION OF MESSOS*, 157
Metal-work, myth of origin of, 209
Metempsychosis, in Simon's teaching, 16
Mêtropatôr, in *SECRET BOOK*, etc., Cod. X, 206, 209
  in Valentinianism, 29
Meyer, R., *Hellenistisches in der rabbinischen Anthropologie*, 287n.
Michael, St, Coptic works on, 96n.
  in *Pistis-Sophia*, 71
Michael the Syrian, *Chronicle*, on Battai, 60–1
Michaud, H., "Un mythe zervaniste dans un des manuscrits de Qumrân", 297n.
Microcosm and macrocosm, parallelism of and light-collecting myth, 282n.
Migne, *Patrologia graeca*, 47n., 68n.
  Patrologia latina, 47n.
Mikheus and Mikhar, in *APOCALYPSE OF ADAM*, etc., 182
  in Bruce Codex, pt.2, 85
  and Mikhea, in *SACRED BOOK OF THE INVISIBLE . . . SPIRIT*, 179
Milik, J. T., *Dix ans de découvertes dans le désert de Juda*, 258n., 297n.

Mimaut papyrus:
  Asclepius prayer in, 108, 243, 245, 248n.
  also found in Chenoboskion MS., 143
Mina, Togo, Director of the Coptic Museum:
  and Miss Dattari's MSS., xiii, 121, 122
  and author alone knew full history, xiv
  and the first discovery, xii, 116–17
  and the second discovery, xii, 118, 118n., 119
  "Le Papyrus gnostique du Musée copte", xv, 118n., 119n.
  death, 123
  obituary, 116n.
Minucius Felix, *Octavius*, 42n.
Mirôthea, in *SACRED BOOK OF THE . . . GREAT SPIRIT*, 178
  in *TRIPLE DISCOURSE*, etc., 181, 329
Miscellanea Giovanni Mercati, I (*Studi e testi*, 121), 9n., 183n.
Mithra, corresponds to Third Principle in Zoroastrian writings, 154
  = Fatality, 154
  in *Bundahishn*, 152n.
Mithraic Liturgy:
  Adam glorified in, 291
  and supposititious author of, 108
  ascent into heaven in, 291
  Helios (Mithra) as intermediate principle in, 154
  not Mithraic, 108n., 291
Mithraism, of Iranian origin, 279
  spread of, in Roman world, 11
  statue of the Aïôn in, 257
Mnesinous in *APOCALYPSE OF ADAM*, etc., 182
  in *SACRED BOOK OF THE . . . GREAT SPIRIT*, 179
Modestus, against Marcion, 7
Monad (*Sacred book*), 171
Monad, in Bruce Codex, 81
  = Barbelô, 81n.
Monasteries of Central Egypt, 89n.
Monatschrift für Geschichte und Wissenschaft des Judentums, 285n.
Monde, Le, xii, 232n.
Monneret de Villard, U., *Le Leggende orientali sui Magi evangelici*, 97n., 102n., 156n., 157n., 161n., 184n., 185n., 186n., 279n.
Monogene (Only-begotten) in Bruce Codex, pt.2, 81, 81n., 82–3
  in *SECRET BOOK*, etc., Cod. X, 202
Montet, P., *Le Drame d'Avaris. Essai sur la pénétration des Sémites en Égypte*, 42n., 104n.
Monumenti antichi, 92n.

Moon, as a collector of light, 271
  in Bruce and Askew codices, 80
  in *Pistis-Sophia*, 69
  ships of, in *Pistis-Sophia* and Egyptian belief, 106
Moret, A., *Mystères egyptiennes*, 273n.
Moses:
  blinded Samael, in Jewish tradition, 175, 175n.
  in *Book of Archangels*, 171
  in Manetho, 105
  in *Monad*, 171
  in *Pistis-Sophia*, 222
  = Musaeus, in Jewish belief, 287–8
  Pythagoras, etc., learnt from, in Jewish belief, 288
  supposed author of apocalyptic book, 45
  was wrong about Noah, according to *SECRET BOOK, etc.*, Cod. X, 208, 261, 261n.
Moses of Khorene, on Shem, 155n.
Moses of Leon, *Zohar*, 292, 292n.
Mosheim, *Institutiones historiae Christianae majores*, 1–2
Mösniger, ed. of Ephrem, 230n.
Mother:
  absence of, in teaching of John of Apamea, 58
  in Archontici's teaching, 150
  in Gnosticism, 62
  (Plotinus), 54
  in Ophite belief (Epiphanius), 44, 212
  in *PARAPHRASE OF SHEM*, 150
  in *SACRED BOOK OF THE . . . GREAT SPIRIT*, 178
  in *SECRET BOOK, etc.*, Cod. X, 201, 202, 205, 206, 209, 210, 211
  as saviour, 303
  discussed, 217–18
  of the Living, 202
  in Sumerian belief, 268
  in *TRIPLE DISCOURSE*, 330
  in Valentinianism, 29
  of heaven, Sethian (Epiphanius), 187
  of Life, in Kukean teaching, 58, 59
  of the Angels, in *SOPHIA, etc.*, 200
  of the Living, in Gnosticism, 48
  in *HYPOSTASIS, etc.*, 160
  in Ophite belief (Irenaeus), 37, 38, 40
  the Great, mysteries of, 48
  the Supreme, taught Seth, an attested belief, 158
  universal, in Bruce Codex, pt.2, 82, 84
Mountain, Hermetic and Zoroastrian, 275
  of Lights, in Iranian myth, 282, 285
  Indian parallel, 284
  of Victories (of the Lord), 161n.
Movement and rest, in *GOSPEL OF THOMAS* and elsewhere, 363, 374

Müller, C. D. G., *Die alte koptische Predigt*, 96n.
Musaeus, 53
  = Moses, in Jewish belief, 287–8
Musanios, in Bruce Codex, pt.2, 84
Musanus, wrote against the Encratites, 7
Muséon, Le, 130n., 228n.
Mustapha Amer, Dr, Director of Service of Antiquities, 124
Mysteries, Greek, 2
  influence of, on Gnosticism (*Philosophumena*), 264
  used by Naassenes, 48
Mystery, the, in *Pistis-Sophia*, 327, 328
  of the Ineffable, in *Pistis-Sophia*, 71
  the First, in *Pistis-Sophia*, 65

Naas the serpent, in Justin's teaching, 34, 35
Naassenes, ix
  general description of, in *Philosophumena*, 47–50, 47n.
  and serpent, unexplained by Chenoboskion MSS., 261
  and the Kingdom inside, 346
  baptism among (*Philosophumena*), 224, 224n.
  belief of about James (*Philosophumena*), 198n., 236
  belief of, in creation of man (*Philosophumena*), 212n.
  connected with Chenoboskion MSS. (?), 251
  evidence for connecting with *GOSPEL OF THOMAS* (*Philosophumena*), 335, 336, 343
  (Origen), 343
  explanation by, of a logion in *GOSPEL OF THOMAS* (*Philosophumena*), 371
  fond of astronomical identification of mythical powers, 270
  Grenfell knew used Logia, 232n.
  "Hermes is the Word" (*Philosophumena*), 84
  influence of, in Balinus (?), 318n.
  knew a certain logion (*Philosophumena*), 230–1
  on masculine women (*Philosophumena*), 48, 234
  the Gnostics attacked by Plotinus were (?), 55n.
  unknown to Gikatila, 292
  used a *Gospel of Egyptians* (*Philosophumena*), 180–1
  used a *Gospel of Thomas* (*Philosophumena*), 231
  used almond symbol, 92
  used Egypt as symbol of matter (*Philosophumena*), 254
  used *Odyssey* (*Philosophumena*), 191

Nabatene, home of baptist sects, 255
Naga Hamadi, 128, 129, 130
Names, two, for certain entities, 203, 203n.
Naples, Borgia collection at, 96n.
Nau, F., *Bardesane l'astrologue*, 310
  article by, 196n.
Nauck, 176n.
Nazarene (?) tomb in Rome, 91
Nazareans, 13
  as ancestors of a Gnostic sect, 7
Neo-platonists, 2, 4
Nergal, on Sumerian medallion, 268
Nerval, 322
Nhuraïta, *see* Nuraïta
Nicaea, Council of and Audius, 55
  Second Council of, rejected *GOSPEL OF THOMAS*, 232
Nicolaitans:
  believed myth of seductions of the Archons (Epiphanius), 163–4
  descriptions of in *Book of Revelation* and in heresiologists tally, 301
  teachings of, 14–15
  Three Primordial Principles in teachings of (*Philosophumena*), 151
  used *Traditions of Matthias* (Clement), 226
Nicolas, the deacon, a founder of Gnosticism, 13–14, 15, 18, 35, 36
  in Hippolytus, 301n.
Nicomachus on Hercules, 35n.
Nicotheus:
  as enlightener in Manichaeism, 86n.
  caught up to heaven, 109
  in Bruce Codex, pt.2, 86
  on the Monogene, in Bruce Codex, pt. 2, 82
  our ignorance of, 114
  taken over from Gnosticism, 313
  Revelation of, is authentically Gnostic, 115
    mentioned by Porphyry as confuted by Plotinus, 10, 53, 99, 156
    mentioned in Manichaean books, 86
    referred to in pseudo-Zosimos, 99, 100, 101
    still undiscovered, 159
Nimrod, Zoroaster=, in Chenoboskion MSS., 287
  in myth of Saoshyant, 184
Noah:
  and Deucalion, in Cod. X, 265
  and Norea and the Ark in Gnosticism, 163
  and Norea in Gnosticism, 164
  and Norea in Mandaean belief, 164
  built Ark on Seir (*HYPOSTASIS, etc.*), 254
  in a cloud, Jewish origin of (?), 291
  in a Gnostic fragment, 89

Noah (*cont.*):
  in *Book of Jubilees*, 154
  in *HYPOSTASIS, etc.*, 160–1
  in Mandaean belief, 155
  in Ophite teaching, 39
  in *REVELATION OF ADAM, etc.*, 182
  in *SECRET BOOK, etc.*, Cod. X, 208
  in *SETHIAN REVELATION*, Cod. VI, 187
  in Syriac *Chronicle*, 185
  in the teachings of the Gnostic Sect, 42, 43n.
Nock, A. D. and Festugière, A. J., *Corpus hermeticum*, 152n., 189n., 208n., 214n., 242, 243, 243n., 244n., 246n., 247n., 257, 274, 275, 331
Nod, Land of, not Duidaïn, 97n.
Nokrashi Pasha, Prime Minister, assassinated, 123
Nôrea:
  and Pyrrha in Cod. X, 265
  as Horea, 45
  Egyptian parallel to, 273
  = Horea, in *HYPOSTASIS, etc.*, 161, 161n.
  in Ophite teaching, 39
  in the teachings of the Gnostic Sect, 42, 43, 43n.
  myth of, 163
    knowledge of, enlarged by Chenoboskion MSS., 262
    seduced Archons, 164n.
    in Epiphanius, 164
    wife of Seth, = the Mandaean Nuraïtha, 155, 164
Noûs, in Basilides' teaching, 21, 22
  in *HERMETIC TREATISE (23)*, and (*25*), 243
  in *Poimandres*, 214, 276, 277
Nourelle Clio, La, 122n., 140n., 290n., 298n.
Nouvelles littéraires, Les, 122n.
Novalis, 323
Novum Testamentum, I, 85n., 125n., 140n., 190n.
Numbers, 280n., 287
Numen, 256n., 281n.
Numenius of Apamea, 191–2, 192n.
  adopted an astrological eschatology, 267
Numerology, in Marcus' teaching, 33, 33n.
Nuraïtha, = Nôrea in Mandaean myth, 155, 164
Nut, myth of, similar to that of Sophia, 272
Nyberg, N. S., "Questions de cosmogonie et de cosmologie mazdéennes", 281n.

Obscurity, in *REVELATION ON PISTIS SOPHIA*, 165
Odeberg, *Introduction to 3. Enoch*, 109n.

Odes of Solomon, 70n.
  in *Pistis-Sophia*, 70
Oehler, ed. of pseudo-Tertullian, 214n.
Ogdoad, 243n.
  in Basilides' teaching, 23
  in Egyptian belief, 272
  in *HERMETIC TREATISE* (*23*), 243
    (*25*), 243, 244
  in Ophite belief, 38
  in *Poimandres*, 277
  in *REVELATION ON PISTIS
    SOPHIA*, 167, 168, 169
  in *SOPHIA, etc.*, 200
  in Valentinianism, 27, 29
  not in *Pistis-Sophia*, 69
Ogdoads, in *SACRED BOOK OF THE
    . . . GREAT SPIRIT*, 178
Ohrmazd, 154
  in *Bundahishn*, 152–3, 152n.
Old man, in *APOCALYPSE OF PAUL*,
    237–8
Old Testament, in Coptic, 106n.
  in Gnostic belief, 112
  Iranian and Gnostic hostility to, 283–4
  translated into Greek, 100, 100n.
Olympias, in Peratean teaching, 51
Olympiodorus of Alexandria, commentary
    on Zosimos, 101n.
Omega, the letter, in pseudo-Zosimos,
    100
Omophore, = Sacla (?), 163n.
On regeneration and the rule of silence, 275
On the generation of Mary, a book of the
    Gnostic Sect, 41
One becomes two; in *GOSPEL OF
    THOMAS*, 230
Onias the Just, 289, 290n.
Ophiouchus, constellation, 44
  Christ compared to, 50n.
Ophites, 12, 36, 37–40, 45
  a bowl of the (?), 90
  and serpent, unexplained by Cheno-
    boskion MSS., 261
  and Valentinianism, 26n.
  as described by Epiphanius, 44
  as described in *Philosophumena*, 66–7
  attacked by Celsus, 9
  belief that Samael was blind (Theodore
    Bar-konai), 175n.
  believed in the Anthropos, 65
  connected with Chenoboskion MSS. (?),
    251
  doctrines of, similar to *EUGNOSTOS*,
    195
  doctrines of, similar to those in *SECRET
    BOOK, etc.*, Cod. X (Irenaeus and
    Epiphanius), 212–13
  influenced Manes (Augustine, etc.), 312
  literature of, 7

Ophites (*cont.*):
  Peratae a sect of, 51, 293
  physiological allegory of (Epiphanius),
    49
  sources, 37n.
  unknown to Gikatila, 292
  used *Book of Norea* (= *HYPOSTASIS,
    etc.*), 163
  used *Diagram* (Celsus), 174
Orbe, A., *En aurora de la exegesís del IV
    Evangelio*, 27n.
  Los Primeros herejes ante la persecucion,
    22n., 27n., 50n.
Oriael, in Bruce Codex, pt.2, 85
Orientalia, 49n., 316n.
Origen, *Commentary upon the Gospel of St
    John*, 6
  Against Celsus (Contra Celsum), 6, 7, 9,
    18n., 198n.
  quotes a logion known to us in
    GOSPEL OF THOMAS, 343
  Homily on Luke, 262n.
  Homily upon Jeremiah, contains a logion,
    231
  Homeric allegory in, 192n.
  mentions a *Gospel of Matthias*, 226
  mentions a *Gospel of Thomas* (i.e.
    GOSPEL OF THOMAS), 231, 335
  on Hercules, 35n.
  wondered about the authenticity of
    another logion known to us in
    GOSPEL OF THOMAS, 351
Orion (= Osiris) in Peratean doctrine, 274
Oroïael, in magical, etc., texts, 103
  in *SACRED BOOK OF THE . . .
    GREAT SPIRIT*, 178
  in *SECRET BOOK, etc.*, Cod. X, 202
Orpheus, *Bacchics*, 53
  effigy of, 11
  symbology of applied to Adam, 207n.
Orphic (?) bowl, 90, 90n.
Orphism, 2
  in Aristophanes, 176n.
  in Chenoboskion MSS., 265
Osiris and Seth, 104, 104n.
  –Onnophris, in Jêou the painter, 105
  = Sacla, 162n.
  (= Sacla) in Peratean doctrine (*Philo-
    sophumena*), 51, 274
Osseans, as ancestors of a Gnostic sect, 7,
    255
Ostanes, books attributed to, 4, 102, 280
  in Peratean belief (*Philosophumena*),
    286n.
  in Suidas, etc., 286n.
Ostia, statue of Chronos from, 94
Ouroboros, 73n.
Ousiarchs, 244n.
  in *HERMETIC TREATISE* (*25*), 244

Oxyrhynchos, papyri from, 87
  fragments of a collection of logia among, 227–8, 228n., 229, 232, 232n., 234, 337–8
  fragment of *SOPHIA*, etc., among, 196, 198
  papyrus, 1
    translated, 360–1
  papyrus 654 paragraphed (?), 353
    translated, 355–6
  papyrus 655 translated, 362
  shroud fragment from, 229, 338, 356

Pachomius, St, 129–30, 129n., 132, 135
Palamun, teacher of St Pachomius, 130, 131, 132
Palestine, Audians in, 55
  Marcionites in, 25
Pand-Nâmâk i Zartusht, 282n.
Pandora, = Eve, in pseudo-Zosimos, 101
Papa the Kantaean, 255, 255n.
Papias, *On the interpretation of logia*, 351
Paradise, a man caught up to, in *II Corinthians*, 109
  ascension into, in Rabbinical literature, 108
  in a Gnostic fragment, 89
Paraphrase of Seth, described in *Philosophumena*, 52, 154
  = *PARAPHRASE OF SHEM* (*Philosophumena*), 150
PARAPHRASE OF SHEM (*SECOND TREATISE OF THE GREAT SETH*):
  attribution of, 289n.
  compared with *Bundahishn*, 152–3
  dated by reference in pseudo-Hippolytus, 250
  described in *Philosophumena*, 150–1
  has Three Principles, a Gnostic belief, 151
    unlike *REVELATION ON PISTIS SOPHIA*, 175
  in author's classification, 143
  Pleiades in, 278n.
  SECOND TREATISE, etc., concluding title of, 149
  shares with *SECRET BOOK*, etc., Cod. X, myth of Light and Darkness, 202
  Shem or Seth (?), 154–5
  Simonian analogies in, 332
  summarized, 146–50
  Zoroastrian elements, in, 153–4
Parchor, 20, 20n.
Passwords, Gnostic, for ascending souls, 267
  Egyptian and Gnostic, 274
Patrologia syriaca, 310n.–311n.

Paul, St:
  Colossians, 307, 308, 376
  I Corinthians, 208n., 306
  II Corinthians, 109, 219, 219n., 237n., 238, 289n., 307
  Ephesians, 307
    contains example of literal exegesis, 309
    quoted in *HYPOSTASIS*, etc., 159, 306
  Epistles, warnings in, against false prophets, 18
  Galatians, 24, 307
  great influence of, 306
  Hebrews, Melchizedek in, 47, 47n., 305
    source of part of *GOSPEL OF TRUTH*, 239
    source of some ideas in *GOSPEL OF THOMAS* (?), 350
  icon of, 12
  ideas present in, developed in *GOSPEL OF THOMAS*, 349
  importance of among Manichaeans, 306n.
  among Paulicians, 306n.
  in *APOCALYPSE OF PAUL*, 237–8
  in Marcionist teaching, 26
  names of his disciples taken by Paulicians, 219n.
  no Chenoboskion MS. attributed to, 304 except *APOCALYPSE*, etc., 306
  Romans, 218n., 307
  seems near Gnosticism, 306–8
    but is not, 308
  I, II, Thessalonians, 219, 219n.
Paulicians and Gnosticism, 311, 311n.
  importance of St Paul among, 306n.
  took names of St Paul's disciples, 219n.
Pauly-Wissowa, *Realenzyklopädie der classischen Altertumswissenschaft*, 73n., 189, 189n., 286n.
Pearl, symbolism of, in *Acts of Thomas*, 95
Pelliot, P., at Ten Huang, 121n.
Peratae:
  an Ophite sect, 51, 293
  belief in the Serpent (*Philosophumena*), 51, 293
  identified astronomical objects with mystical powers, 51, 270, 293
  in *Philosophumena*, 47, 50–1
  origin of name, 51n.
  on Eros (*Philosophumena*), 176n.
  on Isis and Osiris, 273–4
  three primordial Principles in teaching of, 50, 151
  use *Book of the Chiefs*, etc. (*Philosophumena*), 50, 174
Perfect one in *Pistis-Sophia*, 109
  in Rabbinical literature, 109

Perfect, The, 80n.
  descended from Seth and Nôrea, 163
  generation of, in Isma'ilite belief, 321
  (imperishable generation) in *REVELA-
    TION OF ADAM, etc.*, 182–3
  in *BOOK OF THOMAS*, 226
  in Bruce Codex, pt.2, 84, 85
  in *GOSPEL OF PHILIP*, 222
  in *GOSPEL OF THOMAS*, 345
  in Naassene teaching, 48
  in Ophite teaching, 39, 40
  in *PARAPHRASE OF SHEM*, 149
  in *Pistis-Sophia*, 67, 71
  in *REVELATION ON PISTIS
    SOPHIA*, 166, 169
  in *SACRED BOOK OF THE IN-
    VISIBLE . . . SPIRIT*, 298
  in *SOPHIA, etc.*, 200
  in the Gnostic sect, 43
  in *TRIPLE DISCOURSE, etc.*, 181
  in Valentinus' teaching, 224n.
  (incorruptible generation = Gnostics),
    161, 161n.
  (incorruptible generation), in *SACRED
    BOOK OF THE INVISIBLE . . .
    SPIRIT*, 178, 179
  Seth the first of, in Sethian teaching,
    45
Pergamus, church of, 13
Peroz, King, 59, 60
Persia, Borborites in, 311
  Marcionites in, 25
  origin of Gnosticism, Islam, etc., in (?),
    110
Persian theories of good and evil, 21
Peter, of the Archontici, 45–6
Peter, St, *II Epistle* of, 301
  in *ACTS OF PETER*, 235, 236
  in Clement, *Hypotyposes*, 236
  in *Gospel of Mary*, 88
  in *GOSPEL OF THOMAS*, 233, 234,
    357
Peter of Sicily, ' on *GOSPEL OF
    THOMAS*, 232
  on Paulicians, 219n.
Peterson, E., "La Libération d'Adam
    d' 'Ανάγκη', 107, 107n., 108, 109,
    109n., 154, 154n., 164, 164n., 177n.,
    289n.; 291, 295
  "Urchristentum und Mandäismus",
    315n.
Petosiris, inscription from temple of, 106n.,
    273, 273n.
  in Peratean belief (*Philosophumena*),
    286n.
Pettazoni, R., "La figura monstruosa del
    Tempo nella Religione mitriaca", 94n.
Phallicism, in Gnosticism, 35n.
  in Sethian and Orphic teaching, 53

Pharisees, in *GOSPEL OF THOMAS*,
    229, 231, 362, 369
  in *TREATISE ON BAPTISM OF
    JOHN*, 219
Phbôu, 129n.
Pherecydes, 20n.
Phibionites, 14, 41
Philaster, *De haer.*, 47n.
  on a Dositheus, 190, 190n.
  writings of, 7
Philetus, in *II Timothy, etc.*, 301n.
Philip of Gortyna, book against Marcion, 7
Philip, of the *GOSPEL OF PHILIP*, 222
Philip, St, the Apostle, met Simon (*Acts*),
    15, 16, 222n.
  importance of in Gnosticism, 222n.,
    335–6
  in *Pistis-Sophia*, 68
  importance of, 221–2
  in *SOPHIA, etc.*, 199
  importance of, 222
Philip Sidetes, refers to *GOSPEL OF
    THOMAS*, 335
Philo, 2
  Homeric allegory in, 11, 192n.
  in *Quaestiones in Exodum*, 297n.
  on adventitious soul, 216n.
  similarities of, to Gnosticism, 11
Philocomus, writings of, 10
  in Porphyry, 156
Philosophumena, 13n., 61
  accuracy of shown by Chenoboskion
    MSS., 249
  Christ and Ophiouchus compared in,
    50n.
  compared with Epiphanius and Irenaeus,
    47
  criticism of, 6
  discovery of, 3
  editions of, 6n.
  on Basilides, 21, 21n., 336
    and Isidore and the secret discourses of
      Matthias, 226
    his view of the creation of the demi-
      urge, 23
    on the withdrawal of God, 294, 294n.
  on eclecticism of Gnosticism, 99
  on Esaldaiô, 85n.
  on *Gospel of Matthias*, 336
  on Homeric, etc., allegorization in
    Gnosticism, 264
  on influence of the Mysteries on
    Gnosticism, 90, 264
  on Isidore, 336
  on Justin, 33, 35
  on later Valentinianism, 30–1
  quotes logia, 230–1, 335, 336
  on Marcus, 33
  on Naassenes, 47–50, 335

Philosophumena (cont.) :
gives Naassene explanation of a logion, 371
Hermes of Cyllene in Naassene belief, 91–2, 92n.
Hermes Trismegistus in Naassene belief, 84, 84n.
Naassene belief about creation of man, 212n.
Naassenes used Egypt as a symbol of matter, 255
Naassenes used a *Gospel of Egyptians*, 180–1
a *Gospel of Thomas*, 231
on Naassene baptism, 224, 224n.
on Naassene syncretism, 176
on Naassenes' use of *Odyssey*, 191, 191n.
on Naassenes' view of James, 198n., 236, 236n.
on Naassenes' view of masculine women, 48, 234
on *Odyssey* in Gnosticism, 93
on Ophites, 66–7
on *Paraphrase of Seth*, 150, 152n., 154
on Peratae, 47, 50–1, 104n.
on Peratean belief in Eros, 176n.
about Osiris, 274
about the Serpent, 293, 293n.
Peratean sages, 286n.
on Satornil, 19–20, 19n.
on Sethians, 47, 52–3, 52n.
on Sethian belief in the need to separate out the base elements, 372
on Sethian belief in Three Principles, 259
on Simon, 16, 17–18, 17n.
Great Revelation, 332
Three Principles in, 259
on the split in Valentinianism, 218n.
on Valentinianism, 27
on Valentinus, cosmogony of, 27
on masculine women, 48, 234
quoted, ix
quotes *GOSPEL OF THOMAS*, 335, 336, 347
statement in, that Naassenes composed *GOSPEL OF THOMAS* cannot be true, 348
summarizes *Book of the Chiefs, etc.*, 174
summarizes Naassene literature, 343
Philotesia, Paul Kleinert zum LXX Geburtstag gebracht, 37n.
Phison, in Naassene symbolism, 49
Phoenix, in *REVELATION ON PISTIS SOPHIA*, 169
and elsewhere, 171–4
references to in Christian literature, 172n.
Phôs, meaning of Greek word, 101n.
= Adam, in pseudo-Zosimos, 101

Phôsilampes, on the Monogene, in Bruce Codex, pt.2, 83
our ignorance of, 114
works by, still undiscovered, 159, 252
Photius, condemned *GOSPEL OF THOMAS*, 232
Phrygian origin of almond symbol, 92
Physiologus, 172n.
Physionomics, Judaeo-Hellenistic, 288n.
Picard, C., "La Grande peinture de l'hypogée funéraire du Viale Manzoni", 92n., 192n.
Pierpont Morgan MS.593, 96n., 236n.
Pirqé Rabbi Eli'ezer, 154n.
parallels Gnostic account of Adam and Eve, 286
Pistis, in *EUGNOSTOS*, 194
in *SOPHIA, etc.*, 199
= Sophia, in *HYPOSTASIS, etc.*, 161
Pistis-Sophia in *Pistis-Sophia*, 69, 70
Pistis-Sophia (Book of), see *Book of Pistis-Sophia*
Pistis-Sophia MS. (Codex Askewianus):
brief bibliography, 65n.
discussion of arrangement of, 76
final part of, 75–6
Gnostic beliefs as background to summary of the MS., 65–7
Harnack's view on, 73
history of, 64–5
provenance unknown, 136
titleless part of, 73–5, 79
see also Book of Pistis-Sophia; Books of the Saviour
Place of Life, in *DIALOGUE OF THE SAVIOUR*, 220
in *GOSPEL OF THOMAS*, 345, 356
Place of the Just, in *Pistis-Sophia*, 66
of the Midst, in *Pistis-Sophia*, 71
of the Rulers of Destiny, in *Pistis-Sophia*, 71
of the sons of the love of the truth, in *PARAPHRASE OF SHEM*, 149
the, in Hebrew, is God, cf. *GOSPEL OF THOMAS*, 373, 376
Places of the Right, in *Pistis-Sophia*, 71
Planets, a Babylonian theory of the influence of, 267
correspondence of, to parts of body, 214n.
reign of, in Chaldaean belief, 260–1
seven powers of, in magical, etc., texts, 103
Plato, 2
derived his doctrine from Moses, according to Jewish belief, 288
icon of, 23, 350
influence of, on mediaeval Christianity, 350
Parmenides, on movement and rest, 374

Plato (*cont.*):
Phaedo, on the destiny of souls, 208n.
Republic, Er and his vision, 154n., 156, 264
some Chenoboskion doctrines derived from, 264
source of teaching, on ideas in *GOSPEL OF THOMAS*, 345, 377
on soul in *GOSPEL OF THOMAS*, 374–5
statement about Father and Son attributed to, by Christian iconographers, 350
Theaetetus, source of theory of Admiration in *GOSPEL OF THOMAS*, 346
Timaeus, source of Gnostic concept of the Limit, 28n.
used eagle as symbol of soul, 207n.
Valentinus influenced by, 26
wide influence of, on *GOSPEL OF THOMAS*, 349
Pleiades:
in *PARAPHRASE OF SHEM*, 148, 278n.
explanation of, 148n.–149n.
in pseudo-Zosimos, 278n.
Pleroma, 234
in Archontici's teaching, 150
in Bruce Codex, pt.2, 81, 82, 84
in *GOSPEL OF TRUTH*, 240
Jewish Throne, compared with, 177
in *Pistis-Sophia*, 69
in St Paul, 308
in *SECRET BOOK, etc.*, Cod. X, 204, 209
in tomb of the Aurelii, 92
in Valentinianism, 19, 27, 28, 29, 31
in Valentinus' teaching, 224n.
Plesithea, in *SACRED BOOK OF THE ... GREAT SPIRIT*, 178
Ploeg, J. van der, "Les manuscrits trouvés depuis 1947 dans le désert de Juda", 297n.
Plotinus:
answered in *EUGNOSTOS*, (?), 195
believed in a good universe, 111
and opposed belief in an evil world, 266n.
Enneads, mentions sectaries, 156
on Gnostics, 9–10, 9n., 10n., 53–4, 54n., 214
referred to in *GOSPEL OF THOMAS* (?), 373
Nicotheus attacked by (Porphyry), 10, 53, 99
note on Porphyry's *Life of*, 125n.
on Zoroaster, etc., 101
works refuted by his school still undiscovered, 159

Plutarch, *De facie in orbe lunae*, 69n.
De Iside, 42n., 104, 152n., 274
Pneuma, the cloud of the, in *PARAPHRASE OF SHEM*, 148
Pognon, ed., *Book of Scholia*, by Theodore Bar-Konai, 175n.
Inscriptions mandaites des coupes de Khouabir, 46n., 57n., 58n., 59n.
Poimandres, = Nous in *Poimandres*, 276
Poimandres:
Creation in, compared with *SECRET BOOK, etc.*, 276–7, 276n.
creation of man in, 214–15
similar to *HERMETIC TREATISE (23)*, 243
Three Principles in, 281n.
see also Archangelike, etc.
Pole Star, 51n.
in a Gnostic prayer, 108
Porphyry:
cites *APOCALYPSE OF ALLOGENE*, 158
Life of Plotinus, 10
excursus on part of, 125n.
mention of apocalypses in, 156
textual question on title of apocalypse(s), 157n.
mentions work by Nicotheus, 159
Nymphs' Grotto, 192
on Gnostics, 53, 55n.
on Zoroaster, etc., 102, 218
Philosophy of the Oracles, 86, 86n.
references in, date some Chenoboskion MSS., 250
the Chenoboskion MSS. correspond closely to his titles, 251
Portal of Life, in *Pistis-Sophia*, 66
Posener, G., *Littérature et politique dans l'Egypte de la XIIème dynastie*, 247n.
Posture, as a help to vision, 290, 290n.
Power:
The, in Simon's teaching, 17
in Satornil's teaching, 19
The Supreme, in Ophite belief (Epiphanius), 212
in *TRIPLE DISCOURSE*, 330
Powers, in *Arkhangelike*, 174
in *REVELATION ON PISTIS SOPHIA*, 168
Praedestinatus, 47n.
Prayer, in *GOSPEL OF THOMAS*, 371
PRAYER OF THE APOSTLE PETER, 236, 239
in author's classification, 145
Preface to the Council of Nicaea, 271n.
Preisendanz, K., *Akephalos, der kopflose Gott*, 104n., 197n.
Papyrusfunde und Papyrusforschung, 134n.

Preisigke, *Sammelbuch griech. Urkunden aus Aegypten*, 274n.

Pretextat, catacombs of, 90

Preuschen, 45n.

Die Apokryphen gnostischen Adamschriften aus dem Armenischen übersetzt . . ., 184n.

Priapus, in Justin's teaching, 35

Prince, The, in teachings of the Gnostic sect, 43

Prince of Darkness, in St Paul, 307

Principles, Three primordial:
in Gnosticism, 151
in Hellenistic writings, 153
in Iranian belief, 152–3, 152n.

Principles, two only in Manicheism, 152, 152n.

Priscillans, and Gnosticism, 310, 310n.

Priscillianist treatise, of Wartzburg, 198n., 214n., 310n.

Proclus, *In Rempublicam*, 154n.

Procope-Walter, A., "Jao und Seth", 285n.

Prodicos, in Clement of Alexandria, 156n.

Prometheus, similar myth in Gnosticism, 264–5

Pronoïa, a, in *REVELATION ON PISTIS SOPHIA*, 168
in *SECRET BOOK, etc.*, Cod. X, 204–5

Propatôr (Pro-father), in Bruce Codex, pt.2, 84
in *EUGNOSTOS*, 193
in Judaeo-Gnostic invocations, 164–5
(= Sabaôth) in magical prayer, 108, 177n.
the Invisible, in *Pistis-Sophia*, 66, 69
in Valentinianism, 27, 28, 30

Protennoïa, of *TRIPLE DISCOURSE, etc.*, in *SECRET BOOK, etc.*, Cod. X, 201

Proto-archon, in *HYPOSTASIS, etc.*, 160

Protogenitor, in Bruce Codex, pt.2, 84

Prounikos, a name of Barbelô, 15
in Ophite belief (Epiphanius), 212
myth of, similar to that of Friends of Re, 273
seduced Archons, 164n.

Prudentius, *Apotheosis*, 196

Psalms, in hieroglyphics, 106n.
in note in *EXEGESIS, etc.*, 191
in Pauline exegesis, 309
in *Pistis-Sophia*, 70
influence of, on Chenoboskion MSS., 295
origin of belief about Shem, 47n.
some painted on wall near Hamra Dûm, 132, 132n.

Psalms of Solomon, 34n., 80n.

Psalter, the Manichaean, 343, 371

Ptolemaic Books, in Greek, 106

Ptolemies, libraries of, 100

Ptolemy, disciple of Valentinus, 30–1
Epistle to Flora, 26–7, 27n.
resembles *EUGNOSTOS*, 192
son of Arsinoe, in Perataean teaching, 51
Tétrabible, 288n.

Puech, H. C.:
and report of first discovery, xii
"Archontiker", 45n., 46n., 157n., 197n., 288n.
article in *Le Monde* on *GOSPEL OF THOMAS*, 232–3, 232n.
attributes *TREATISE (48)* to Heracleon, 239, 239n.
"Audianer", 55n., 157n., 219n.
Communication to the VI International Congress of Papyrology, 87n., 196, 196n., 198
contribution to Hennecke, *Neutest. Apokr.*, 139n.
deduced nature of *Allogeneous books*, 158
"Der Begriff der Erlösung im Manichäismus", 218n.
Der vorchristliche Gnosis, 4n.
established that logia were from *GOSPEL OF THOMAS*, 126, 126n., 305, 337–8
"Fragments retrouvés de l'Apocalypse d'Allogène", 39n., 57n., 150n., 158n., 205n., 213, 213n., 214n.
helped publish second discovery, 318n.
his classification of Chenoboskion MSS., 139
his use of Chenoboskion MSS. for explanation of the logia, xiv
La Gnose et le temps, 3n., 12n., 36n., 42n., 68n., 110, 110n., 111, 111n., 112n., 113n., 114, 162n., 187n., 193n., 266, 282n., 301n.
"Le Mandéisme", 315n.
"Le Manichéisme", 312n.
Le Manichéisme, son fondateur, sa doctrine, 30n., 66n., 69n., 74n., 80n., 86n., 112n., 113n., 147n., 152n., 218n., 227n., 255n., 271n., 281n., 312n., 313n., 314n., 316n.
"Le Prince des Tenèbres", 80n., 162n., 313n.
"Les nouveaux écrits gnostiques . . .", 54n., 57n., 139n., 157n., 189, 189n., 190n., 192n., 198n., 222n., 236n.
"Numenius d'Apamée et les théologies orientales", 192n.
on female becoming male among Cathars, 234
on the *SOPHIA OF JESUS*, 87, 222

Puech, H. C. (*cont.*):
"Où en est le problème du Gnosticisme", 3, 3n., 4n., 12n., 19n., 27n., 302n.
summary of, 12–13
preliminary study on GOSPEL OF THOMAS, 305
recognized GOSPEL OF THOMAS, 126, 227, 228n.
report by, to the Académie des Inscriptions, 119
told of first discovery by author, 117
"Un logion de Jésus sur une bandelette funéraire", 126n., 228n., 229
writings by, plagiarized, xv
and J. Doresse, "Les nouveaux écrits gnostiques . . .", 118n., 119n.
and Quispel, published *Gospel of Truth*, 239
and Vaillant, A., *Le Traité contre les Bogomiles de Cosmas le prêtre*, 96n., 151n., 196n., 214n., 311n., 312n.
Purgatory, Mandaean, 98
Pyrrha, wife of Deucalion, in the teachings of the Gnostic sect, 43, 43n.
Pythagoras, 33n.
derived doctrine from Moses, according to Jewish belief, 288
icon of, 12, 23
influence of his teaching on Valentinus, 26
Pythagoreanism:
belief about seed, in, 234n.
belief that Sun and Moon were Isles of the Blest, 270
in Chenoboskion MSS., 265
influence of, on Essenes, 288n.
mystical union in, 224n.
use of Homeric allegory in, 192
use of trowel symbol in, 91, 91n.

Qâf, Mountain of, in Islamic belief, is of Gnostic origin, 317
Qenah, 130
Qolastâ, a Mandaean book, 98
Quispel, G., attributes TREATISE (*48*) to Heracleon, 239, 239n.
criticism of his hypotheses, 263n.
"Die Reue des Schöpfers", 127n.
"L'Homme gnostique; la doctrine de Basilide", 263n.
"La Lettre de Ptolémée à Flora", 27n.
"L'Inscription funéraire de Flavia Sophe", 89n.
"The Original doctrine of Valentine", 27n.
Qumrân, = Gomorrha (?), 298–300
works from, *see* Dead Sea Scrolls

"Race without king", in Naassene belief, 50
Races of man, in Valentinianism, 29, 31, 32
Raza Rabba, Gnostic influence in, 292
Re, Friends of, myth of, similar to that of Prounikos, 273
Reallexikon für Antike und Christentum, 45n., 55n., 279n.
Recherches des sciences réligieuses, 16n.
Recognitions, *see* Clementine, pseudo-, *Recognitions*
Recollection, in Gnosticism, 113
Recurrence, in Gnosticism, 113
Reflection, in Basilides' teaching, 22
Regions, in *Pistis-Sophia*, 327, 328
Reincarnation, in Gnosticism, 112–13, 113n.
in Manichaeism, 113
Reitzenstein, R.:
and Schaeder, *Studien zum antiken Synkretismus aus Iran und Griechenland*, 37n., 46n., 47n., 103, 103n., 150n., 279n., 318, 318n.
Das mandäische Buch des Herrn der Grösse . . ., 59n.
on Iranian influence, 114
on myth of Saviour saved, 282
Poimandres, 3, 18n., 47n., 55n., 99n., 100n., 105n., 106n., 170, 170n., 171, 171n., 172n., 174n., 203n., 243n., 288n.
Repose of the kingdom, in Clement, *II Epistle*, 375
Resch, *Agrapha*, 230n.
Rest, in DIALOGUE OF THE SAVIOUR, 220
Resurrection, Gnostics believed it had to be waited for, 301n.
Retreat of God, *see* Withdrawal, etc.
REVELATION, in Cod. IV:
in author's classification, 142
mentioned, 197
REVELATION OF ADAM TO HIS SON SETH, *see* APOCALYPSE OF ADAM, etc.
REVELATION OF ALLOGENE, *see* SUPREME ALLOGENE
REVELATION OF DOSITHEUS (THREE STELAE OF SETH):
described, 188
discussed, 188–90, 241, 331, 332
in author's classification, 144
part of, compared with REVELATIONS OF ZOSTRIAN, etc., 157
REVELATION OF JAMES, *see* APOCALYPSE, etc.
Revelation of John, Audaean book (Theodore Bar-Konai), 56

REVELATION OF MESSOS:
described, 157
in author's classification, 144
referred to, by Porphyry, 156
dated by reference in Porphyry, 250
REVELATION OF NICOTHEUS, see
APOCALYPSE, etc.
REVELATION OF SETH (Cod. V):
briefly described, 197
in author's classification, 142
REVELATION ON PISTIS SOPHIA:
described, 165–70
discussed, 170–7
in author's classification, 144
a continuation of *EUGNOSTOS* (?),
195
a parallel in, with *TREATISE ON
BAPTISM OF JOHN*, 219
importance of Eros in, 265
importance of Sabaôth in, 291
informative about Paradise, 261
Orphic influence on view of Paradise in,
265
Sabaôth's supplanting of Ialdabaôth in,
260, 271–2
source of *HYPOSTASIS*, etc., 241n.
system of *HYPOSTASIS*, etc., similar,
159
Revelations of Marsanes, etc., see Marsanes,
etc.
REVELATIONS OF ZOSTRIAN, etc.,
see *DISCOURSE OF TRUTH*, etc.
Révillout, E., on Bruce Codex, 77
Revue biblique, 16n., 97n., 107n., 296n.
Revue d'histoire et de philosophie religieuses,
154n., 285n., 286n.
Revue de l'histoire des religions, 6n., 109n.,
196n., 286n., 297n., 313n.
Revue de l'Orient chrétien, 47n.
Revue de l'Université de Bruxelles, 3n.
Revue de philologie, 149n.
Revue des études arméniennes, 24n.
Revue des études juives, 293n.
Rheinhardt, Dr, 86
Rhodon, book against Apelles, etc., 7
Rhyx Anatreth, in *Testament of Solomon*,
203n.
Right, ways of, an Orphic concept, 265
Right and left in Gnosticism, 14n.
Ringbom, L. I., *Graltempel und Paradies*,
256n.
Ritter, H., "Picatrix, ein Handbuch
hellenistischer Magie", 318n.
Roeder, G., *Bronzefiguren*, 105n.
Roman world, mystical religion in, 11
Rome, development of Gnosticism in, 12
Marcionites in, 25
near-Gnostic and Gnostic cults in,
evidence of monuments, 90–4

Rome *(cont.)*:
tomb paintings in Viale Manzoni, 192,
264
Valentinus in, 26
Root, as Manichaean symbol, 147n.
in *PARAPHRASE OF SHEM*, 147
Rossi, editor and text, 103n.
Rotation of the spheres, 68, 68n.
Royalty in Audius' teaching, 56
Rudolph, K., "Ein Grundtyp gnostischer
Urmensch-Adam Spekulation", 34n.,
214n., 286n.
Ruelle, ed., *Sacred book of Hermes*, 171
Rufin, *History*, 139n.
Runciman, S., *The Mediaeval Manichee*,
216n., 219n., 306n., 311n., 312n.
Ruska, J., *Das Steinbuch des Aristoteles*, 180n.
"Kaswînî Studien", 318n.
Tabula smaragdina, 318n.

S.M.S.R., 316n.
Sabalân, Adam's cave at (?), 161n.
Sabaôth:
(Adonaïu) in *SECRET BOOK*, etc.,
Cod. X, 202
comparable to Zeus, 271n.
Discourse by, 106
in *Ascension of Isaiah*, 176–7, 177n.
in Basilides' teaching, 263
in *Book of Enoch*, etc., 176–7
in Chenoboskion MSS., 260
in Epiphanius, 164
in *HYPOSTASIS*, etc., 163
and *REVELATION ON PISTIS
SOPHIA*, 271–2
importance of, 291
in Jêou, the painter, 105
in Nicolaitan teaching, 14
in *Pistis-Sophia*, 113n., 176n.–177n.
in *REVELATION ON PISTIS
SOPHIA*, 166–7, 168
and *HYPOSTASIS*, etc., 271–2
in *SECRET BOOK*, etc., Cod. Berol.,
203
in the teachings of the Gnostic sect, 43,
44
= Jupiter, 164n.
Jewish anagram of, 288n.
Little, the good, in *Pistis-Sophia*, 66
Lord, Throne, etc., of, in Jewish star
lore, 288
on his throne and Propatôr identified,
108
rules the Pole in Gnosticism, 270
Sabazius = , worshipped at Rome, 90
the Adamas, in titleless portion of Codex
Askewianus, 74–5
in the *Great Treatise*, 78

Sabaôth (*cont.*):
  the Good, in *Pistis-Sophia*, 66, 68, 69
  in titleless portion of Codex Askew-
    ianus, 75
  the Great, in Ophite teaching, 38
  the little, the Good, in titleless portion of
    Codex Askewianus, 75
Sabazios:
  devotees of, banished from Rome, 12
  mysteries of, 44
  mystics of, 43n.
  (= Sabaôth), worshipped at Rome, 90
Sabbataïos, in *SECRET BOOK, etc.*, Cod.
  Berol, 203
"Sâbi'a, al-", 316n.
Sabians of Upper Mesopotamia, influenced
  by Gnosticism, 315–16
Sacla, 51n., 85n.
  = Ialdabaôth, 162n.
  in *HYPOSTASIS, etc.*, 163
  (Ialdabaôth) in *SECRET BOOK, etc.*,
    Cod. X, 202, 210
  Ialdabaôth = Seth the god, 104n.
  in Chenoboskion MSS., 260
  in *SACRED BOOK OF THE . . .
    GREAT SPIRIT*, 178–9
  in the teachings of the Gnostic sect, 43
  in *TRIPLE DISCOURSE, etc.*, 181, 329
  = Omophore, 163n.
  = Osiris in Peratean teaching (*Philo-
    sophumena*), 51, 274
Sacred Book, The, see *Hierabiblos*; see also
  Monad
Sacred Book of Hermes to Asclepius, 171
*SACRED BOOK OF THE INVISIBLE
  GREAT SPIRIT*, or *GOSPEL OF
  THE EGYPTIANS*:
  described, 177–80
  discussed, 180–1
  in author's classification, 142
  author's work on, 125
  baptism in, and *GOSPEL OF PHILIP*,
    224
  contains myths similar to those described
    by Irenaeus, 127
  creation by pairs of emanations in, 260
  "Five Seals" of, cf. *SECRET BOOK,
    etc.*, Cod. X, 209n.
  Gamaliel, etc., in, 286n.
  Gospel of Philip (Epiphanius) related to,
    225, 235
  Guardians in, paralleled by Mandaean
    belief, 256
  has Sethian characteristics, 184
  has Simonian characteristics, 332
  hidden in Mt. Charax, 254
  importance of James in, 237
  in first discovery, 117
  needs much further study, 252

*SACRED BOOK OF THE INVISIBLE
  GREAT SPIRIT* (*cont.*):
  not the *Gospel of the Egyptians* known to
    the heresiologists, 253
  passage in, shows Dead Sea sect is
    ancestor of Gnosticism (?), 298–300
  source of part of *GOSPEL OF
    THOMAS* (?), 375
Sadducees, sect of, founded by Dositheus,
  15
Sages, names of, in titles of Gnostic and
  Hebrew works, 289
Sagnard, *Extraits de Théodote*, 218n., 223n.,
  224n., 234n.
  *La gnose valentinienne et le témoignage de
    St Irenée*, 6n., 14n., 27n., 28n., 30n.,
    31n., 32n., 33n., 86n., 193n., 224n.,
    243n.
St Malo, neo-Gnostics at, 312
Saldaô, = Seldaô (?), 254
Salome, in *GOSPEL OF THOMAS*, 364,
  375
Salvation, in Chenoboskion MSS., 262
  in *GOSPEL OF TRUTH*, 240
Samael, = Ialdabaôth, 162n.
  (Ialdabaôth) in *Book of Enoch, etc.*,
    176–7
  (Ialdabaôth) in *HYPOSTASIS, etc.*, 162
  (Ialdabaôth) in *REVELATION ON
    PISTIS SOPHIA*, 166, 174–5
  (Ialdabaôth) in *SECRET BOOK, etc.*,
    Cod. X, 202
  (Ialdabaôth) in *TRIPLE DISCOURSE*,
    etc., 181, 329
  in *Ascension of Isaiah*, 177n.
  in Chenoboskion MSS., 260
  in *DIALOGUE OF THE SAVIOUR*,
    220
  in *HYPOSTASIS, etc.*, 160
  in Jewish tradition, 175, 175n.
  in *Revelation of St John*, 177n.
Samaria, Christ preached in, and it later
  became the birthplace of Gnostics, 302
  early home of Gnosticism, 12, 15
Samaritan sect, 15, 15n.
  ancestors of a Gnostic sect, 7
Samlô, in *APOCALYPSE OF ADAM*,
  etc., 182
  in *SACRED BOOK OF THE IN-
    VISIBLE . . . SPIRIT*, 178, 286n.
Samos, Epiphanius honoured in, 24
Samothrace, mysteries of, 2
Sampseans, a baptist sect, as ancestors of a
  Gnostic sect, 7
  adored Martos, etc., 46
  influenced by Essenes (Epiphanius), 298n.
  influenced mythical geography of
    Gnostics, 255
Saoshyant, and Jesus, 102, 184

Satan, fall of, in Coptic homilies, 96
Ialdabaôth =, 162n.
substituted by St Michael in Mani-
chaeism, 96n.
Satan (_Études carmélitaines_), 80n., 162n.
Satanians, in Epiphanius, 311n.
Satornil, leader of a Gnostic sect, 7, 12
teachings of, 19–20, 19n., 212n.
Saturn, in Balinus, 319
Saulasau, in Naassene teachings, 49
Saulcy, F. de, suggested Qumrân =
Gomorrha, 299
Save-Soderberg, T., _Studies in the Coptic
Manichaean Psalm-book prosody and
Mandaean parallels_, 315n.
Saviour:
advent of, in Syriac _Chronicle_, 185
in _ACTS OF PETER_, 236
in _BOOK OF THOMAS_, 225, 226
in _DIALOGUE_, etc., 220–1
in Gnosticism, 112, 113, 282
in _GOSPEL OF THOMAS_, 228, 229,
230, 231
in oriental Valentinianism, 218n.
in St Paul, 307–8
in _SECRET BOOK_, etc., Cod. X, 206,
207, 208, 210, 211, 217
in _SOPHIA_, etc., 199, 200
in Zoroastrian prophecies, 186
(Jesus) in _GOSPEL OF TRUTH_, 239,
240
marriage of, in Valentinus' teaching,
224n.
(Messenger) in Iranian belief, 282n.
son of Adam of the Light, in _EUG-
NOSTOS_, 194
Saviours, Iranian and Gnostic, 282
pre-Gnostic belief in a succession of, 184
successive, in _APOCALYPSE OF
ADAM_, etc., 183
Saxl, _Mithras_, 207n.
Sayings of Jesus, see Logia
Schaeder, M. H., 227
Schaeffer, C. F. A., 120
Schema of the Celestial Heimarmene, in
_REVELATION ON PISTIS
SOPHIA_, 167
identity (?), 174
Schepps, ed., _Priscillianist treatises_, 214n.,
310n.
Schmid, J. M., _Des Wardapet Eznik von
Kolb " Wider die Sekten"_, 24n.
Schmidt, C.:
and the Manichaean MSS. of Fayum, 120
"Ein vorirenäisches gnostisches Origi-
nalwerk ...", 86n.
"Gnostische Schriften in koptischer
Sprache aus dem Codex Brucianus",
77n.

Schmidt, C. (_cont._):
"Irenäus und seine Quelle in _Adv.
Haeres._", 37n., 86n.
on _Codex Berolensis_, 86–7, 86n., 87n.
on Irenaeus' account of Gnostic cosmology, 212
on _SECRET BOOK OF JOHN_, 126–7
on _SOPHIA_, etc., 200
Philotesia, 81n.
Pistis-Sophia, with a German translation,
65n., 87n.
"Plotinus stelling zum Gnostizimus",
55n.
and Polotsky, J., _Ein Mani-Fund in
Aegypten_, 86n.
and Till, W., _Die gnostischen Schriften
des koptischen Papyrus Berolinensis 8502_,
125n., 147n., 189n., 244n., 294n.
Schmitt, J., "Mandéisme", 315n.
Schoeps, H. J., "Das gnostische Judentum
in den Dead Sea Scrolls", 296n.
"Simon Magus in der Haggada", 16n.,
285n.
Scholem, G., "Buch Bahir", 292n.
Les Grands courants de la mystique juive,
109n., 177, 177n., 285n., 288n., 289,
289n., 290n., 291n., 292, 292n., 294,
294n., 297n.
"Die Vorstellung vom Golem", 286n.
Schott, S., _Bücher und Sprüche gegen den
Gott Seth_, 104n.
Schuerer, _Geschichte der Jüdischen Volkes im
Zeitalter Jesu Christi_, 3rd edn., 287n.,
288n.
Schuhl, P. M., _Essai sur la formation de la
pensée grecque_, 176n.
Schwartze, M. G., _Pistis-Sophia_; A Latin
translation, 65n.
Scott, W., _Hermetica_, 149n., 172n., 190n.,
278n.
Scribes, in _GOSPEL OF THOMAS_, 229,
231
in _TREATISE ON BAPTISM OF
JOHN_, 219
Scriptura nomine Seth, 96–7
in pseudo-Chrysostom, 185
Scythianus, in _Acts of Archelaus_, 314
Sea of Light, in Kukean teaching, 58
Seals, Five, 209, 209n.
in _SECRET BOOK_, etc., 224
_SECOND TREATISE OF THE GREAT
SETH, see PARAPHRASE OF SHEM_
Secrecy, in Gnosticism, Hermetism, Mith-
raism, Dead Sea sect, 257–8
in Gnosticism and Dead Sea Sect, 296
SECRET BOOK OF JOHN:
a Gnostic book in a Christian disguise,
311
= _Apocalypse of Nicotheus_ (?), 252

SECRET BOOK OF JOHN (cont.):
creation by pairs of emanations, 260
dated in part by Irenaeus, 250
in first discovery, 117
Light and Darkness in, 151–2
myth of Adam compared with
    Poimandres, 276
notes in, similar to those in *REVELA-
    TION ON PISTIS SOPHIA*, 170
book lists in, also similar, 174
parallel in *Shkand Gûmânîk Vichâr*, 283
Saviour (Christ) or Mother, in, 262
several versions of, 126, 201, 241n.
the Serpent in, 261, 261n.
two parts inconsistent (Mother-Christ),
    303
in Cod. Berol., 87, 88, 126, 201, 211
discovered recently, 37, 37n.
part of, described, 209
sources, 87n.
in Codices I and IV, in author's classifi-
    cation, 142
described, 201, 209–10. 211
discussed, 210
source of passage in *SOPHIA, etc.*,
    199
in Codex X, in author's classification,
    144
described, 201–10
discussed, 205n., 210, 224, 328
illustrated, 239
translation of passage illustrated, 328
unique passage in this version, 218
*SECRET SAYINGS TOLD BY THE
SAVIOUR, etc., see BOOK OF
THOMAS*
Secundus, 24
Seed, becomes male, in Theodotus, 234
Seed, of Life, in a Zoroastrian prophecy,
    186
Seed of the Great Seth, in *SECRET
BOOK, etc.*, Cod. X, 202
Seir, in Edom, 161n.
location of, 161n., 180n.
Mountain of Victories to E. of, in
    Syriac *Chronicle*, 186
Mountain, where Noah built the Ark
    (*HYPOSTASIS, etc.*), 161, 254, 254n.
White Mountain of, Mandaean, 256
Seldaô, Mountain, Saldaô a mistake for,
    254, 254n.
in Bruce Codex, pt.2, 85, 85n.
in *SACRED BOOK OF THE . . .
    GREAT SPIRIT*, 179
Selenê = Helene, in Dositheus' teaching, 15
Sellaô, wrongly, for Seldaô, 85n.
Selmelkhe, in Bruce Codex, pt.2, 85
Senart, *Essai sur la légende de Bouddha*, 2nd
    ed., 285n.

*SENSE OF UNDERSTANDING, see
THOUGHT OF THE GREAT
POWER*
Sensibility, in *SACRED BOOK OF THE
. . . GREAT SPIRIT*, 178
Sephir Yetsira, 292n., 293, 293n.
Sephiroth, in Jewish belief, 292, 292n.
Septimus Severus, 11
Serapeum, destruction of, 138
Seraphion of Thmuis, 7
Serapion, library of the temple of, 100
Serapion of Antioch, 46
Serapis, inscriptions to, near Cheno-
    boskion, 132
some worshippers of, turned to Christi-
    anity, 139
Serouya, H., *La Kabbale*, 290n.
Serpent:
among Yezedis, 316
Demon, in *Books of the Saviour*, 73
of the Gnostic sect, 43
= Dragon, 73n.
Constellation of, 51, 51n., 73n.
in Gikatila, 292–3
in *HYPOSTASIS, etc.*, 160
in Orphism, 265
in Peratean belief (*Philosophumena*), 293,
    293n.
in *REVELATION ON PISTIS
    SOPHIA*, 168
in *SECRET BOOK, etc.*, Cod. X, 206
in *TREATISE ON BAPTISM OF
    JOHN*, 220
of Darkness in Gnosticism, 293n.
role of, among Naassenes and Ophites,
    not explained by Chenoboskion MSS.,
    261
son of Sabaôth (Epiphanius), 164
The, in Aurelii tomb, 92
The, in Ophite teaching, 38, 39
    and elsewhere, 44–5
The, in Sethian teaching, 52–3
The, venerated by some Gnostics, 112
view of, in Chenoboskion MSS., 261
Sesenges-Barpharanges, 85n.
Sessenggenpharaggen, in *SACRED
BOOK OF THE . . . GREAT SPIRIT*,
    179
Seth:
and his books, in Syriac *Chronicle*, 185
and stelae, in Josephus, etc., 190
Apocalypse of, used by the Gnostic sect, 41
Archontici's teaching on, 150
as a Gnostic prophet, 39n.
as author of *TRIPLE DISCOURSE*,
    181, 330–1
as brother of Nôrea, 163
caught up to heaven, 109
evidence for this, 158

Seth (*cont.*):
  children of, in Judaism, 295, 295n.
  on Mt. Hermon, 255
  his birth, in Gnostic cosmogony, 158
  in *APOCALYPSE OF ADAM TO
    SETH*, 182, 183
  in *Book of the Cave*, etc., 184
  in Gnosticism, 104–5, 104n., 274
  Nôrea, wife of, in Gnosticism, 155
  origin of Gnostics' respect for, 309
  in Ishmaelite belief, 155
  in Islamic belief, 317, 320
  in Jêou the painter, 105
  in *Kephalaia*, 189
  in magical, etc., texts, 104, 106
  derived by Manichaeans from Gnostics,
    313
  in Ophite teaching, 39
  in *REVELATION OF DOSITHEUS*,
    157, 188
  in Sabianism, 315
  in *SACRED BOOK OF THE IN-
    VISIBLE . . . SPIRIT*, 179, 298, 300
  SACRED BOOK, etc., written by, 180
  incarnated as a teacher, in *SACRED
    BOOK*, etc., 298, 300
  in *SECRET BOOK*, etc., Cod. X, 202,
    207
  in Sethian belief (Epiphanius), 45
    = Christ, 87
  in Valentinianism, 32
  local cult of at Chenoboskion (?), 129
  replaced by Melchizedek in some sects,
    46–7
  seed of, 255
    and seed of Zoroaster, 282
    in *SACRED BOOK*, etc., 178, 179,
      298, 299, 300
    in *TRIPLE DISCOURSE*, 331
  (Setheus) in *Revelations of Zostrian and
    Zoroaster*, 157
  in the teachings of the Gnostic sect, 43
    = Shem, in *PARAPHRASE OF SHEM*,
      154
  some myths ascribed to, identical with
    the Zoroastrian, 187
  sometimes identified with Melchizedek
    in Isma'ilite belief, 321, 321n.
  son of Adam, = Allogene, 157–8, 159
    and Zoroaster in the Magi writings, 102
    confused with the god in Gnostic-
      ism (?), 104–5, 274
    in *Gospel of Nicodemus*, 95
    = Setheus in Bruce Codex, 81, 81n.,
      82, 83, 84
  –Osiris, in Plutarch, comparable with
    Ialdabaôth–Sacla, 274
  the three Stelae of, 188
  unimportant in *HYPOSTASIS*, etc., 160

Seth (*cont.*):
  works attributed to, 45, 97, 190
    plagiarized, 107, 190n.
  Zoroaster = , 280
    = Zoroaster in Chenoboskion MSS.,
      287, 288
Seth, the Egyptian god, 42n., 104
  bibliography of, 104n.
Sethe, K., "Amun und die acht Urgötter
  von Hermopolis", 272n.
Sethel, = Seth, 189
Setheus, the Earth-Shaker, = Seth, 81n.
  see also Seth
Sethi, an Egyptian dynasty, 104
SETHIAN REVELATION:
  in Codex VI, in author's classification, 143
    described, 187–8
  in Codex IX, in author's classification,
    144
Sethians:
  Archontici a subdivision of, 46, 46n.
  assembled Chenoboskion MSS., 251
  attitude, to Old Testament, 299
  believed in need of separation of basic
    elements, 372
  believed in Three Principles, 259
  Book of Cave, originated from, 184n.
  characteristic spiritual entities of, 184
  doctrines of, similar to those in *SECRET
    BOOK*, etc., Cod. X, 212
  doctrines similar to *EUGNOSTOS*, 195
  in Philaster, 190
  in *Philosophumena*, 47, 52–3, 150
  in Porphyry, 55n.
  influenced by Hermetism, 332
  influenced by Simonianism, 332
  literature of, alluded to by heresiologists,
    157–8
  nearly extinct in Epiphanius' time, 251
  physiological allegory of, 49
  related to Borborites (Epiphanius, etc.),
    311
  sect described by Irenaeus was appar-
    ently, 36
  sects related to, 53
  Seth = Christ among (Epiphanius), 187
  used *Book of Nôrea*, 163
Seth–Typhon, text from cult of (?), 107–9
  in Judaeo-Gnostic rituals, 105
Seven aïônes, 271
  Guardians, Indian parallel to the, 285
Seven Heavens, (*Book of the*), 172, 174
Seven middôth before the Throne, 291n.
  planets, Sabaôth Lord of, in Jewish
    belief, 288n.
  powers, in a fragment, 88
  principles, in Iranian belief, 280n.
  rulers, in *Poimandres*, 276
  spheres, development of notion, 238n.

Index

437

Severians, 46
Severus of Antioch, on Manichaean belief
   in Trees of Paradise, 216–17
Sex, in Naassene teaching, 50
   in Nicolas' teaching, 13
   in Phibionite teaching, 43
   in Satornil's teaching, 20
   in Simon's teaching, 16
   licentiousness of some sects, 62, 115
Sexual union, as a symbol in *HERMETIC
   TREATISE (26)*, 245, 247
Shapur I, inserted Greek and Hindu
   extracts in Iranian books, 279, 279n.
Shem:
   as Melchizedek, 46–7
   sources, 47n.
   ascension of, prototype of Mahomet's,
      318
   derived by Manichaeans from Gnostics,
      313
   in *APOCALYPSE OF ADAM, etc.*, 182
   in Armenian tradition, 155n.
   in *Book of Jubilees*, 154
   in Ishmaelite belief, 155
   in Manichaean belief, 154–5
   in myth of Saoshyant, 184
   in *PARAPHRASE OF SHEM*, 147, 148,
      149
      = Jesus Christ, 149
      (Sêem) = Seth, 154
   in Tabarî, 155n.
      149
   Mandaean belief on, 515
      = Melchizedek, in *Haggada*, 154, 286
   son of Nôrea in Gnostic belief, 164
Shenesit (= Chenoboskion), 129, 251n.
Shepherd, the Good, in tomb of the
   Aurelii, 92
Shepherd of Hermes, 118n., 301n.
Shi'ites reverence Seth, 320–1
"Shîth", 317n.
Shiur Koma, 291
Shkand-Gumânîk Vichâr, 271n., 282n.,
   283–4, 284n.
Shum-Kushta, Mandaean name for Shem,
   155
Shyr, *see* Seir
Sibylline Oracles on Shem, 155n.
Silas, in *Acts*, 219n.
Silence:
   cloud of, in *PARAPHRASE OF SHEM*,
      148
   in a fragment, 89
   in Bruce Codex, pt.2, 81
   in *EUGNOSTOS*, 194
   in Marcus' teaching, 33
   in *SACRED BOOK OF THE . . .
      GREAT SPIRIT*, 178
   in *SECRET BOOK, etc.*, Cod. X, 201

Silence *(cont.)*:
   in *TRIPLE DISCOURSE, etc.*, 181,
      330, 331
   in Valentinianism, 27
The, in Simon's teaching, 17
Silences, in Bruce Codex, pt.2, and
   Chaldaean Oracles, 85–6
Silvanus the Audian, 55, 219
   a real person (?), 253
Silvanus of *TEACHINGS OF SIL-
   VANUS*, the companion of St Paul,
   306
   mentioned in *Acts*, etc. (?), 219, 219n.
   not the Audian, 219
Simeon ben Yohaï, 289, 290n.
Simon, M., "Melchisédech dans la
   polémique entre Juifs et Chrétiens et
   dans la légende", 154n., 286n.
   "Sur deux hérésies juives mentionnées
   par Justin martyr", 285n.
Simon of Cyrene, crucified in place of
   Jesus, 113n.
   in Basilides' teaching, 22
Simon Magus, the Samaritan from Gitta,
   12, 15
   baptized by Philip, 222n.
   death of, 16–17
   disciples of, 19, 20
      believed myth of seduction of the
      Archons, 163–4
      believed in reincarnation, 113n.
   founder of Gnosticism, 15–16, 35
   Great Revelation still undiscovered, 252
      taught Three Principles (*Philosoph-
      umena*), 259
   has acquired legendary characteristics, 13
   in *Acts*, 1, 15, 222n.
   leader of a sect, 7, 26
   meaning of "Magus", 280
   mediaeval legends and iconography, 1
   on Circe, 191n.
   regarded himself as a divine incarnation,
      254
   taught by a Dositheus, 15, 189, 190
   teachings of, 16
      in *GREAT REVELATION*, 17–18
      similarity of *TRIPLE DISCOURSE*
      and *THOUGHT OF GREAT
      POWER* to, 331–2
      of other Chenoboskion MSS. to, 332
   sources for, 16n.
   three primordial Principles in teaching
      of, 151
Simon, St, monastery of, 57
Sinope, Bishop of, father of Marcion, 13
Sippara of Uruk, a Chaldaean teacher, 267
Sirius (= Sôthis), 274
*Sitzungsberichte der Heidelberger Akademie,
   Philos.-Hist. Klas.*, 184n.

Sitzungsberichte d. Kgl. preussischen Akademie d. Wissenschaft, 86n.

Sobhy, G., 117

Socrates, *History*, 139n.

Sodom, home of the perfect, 254-5
in *SACRED BOOK OF THE IN-VISIBLE . . . SPIRIT*, 298, 298n., 299, 300

Sodomites, the, 36
in Gnostic belief, 112

Soissons, neo-Gnostics at, 311

Solitaries, in *GOSPEL OF THOMAS*, 345, 358, 363, 372

Solmis, in the *Revelations of Zostrian and Zoroaster*, 157

Solomon, King, as author of magical books, 170, 171n., 172
Book of the Seven Heavens, in pseudo-Zosimos, 278n.
exorciser of demons, in *Testament of Solomon*, 203n.
imprisoned demons, 172, 172n., 173, 174, 278n.
Testament, see Testament of Solomon

Solomon of Basra, knew Zoroastrian prophecies of a saviour, 186
The Book of the Bee, 47n.

Son, in Borgia leaflet, 97n.
in Bruce Codex, 81
in *GOSPEL OF PHILIP*, 222
in *GOSPEL OF THOMAS*, 343, 362
in Perataean teaching, 50, 51
in *REVELATION OF DOSITHEUS*, 188
in *SACRED BOOK OF THE . . . GREAT SPIRIT*, 178
in *SECRET BOOK*, etc., Cod. X, 201, 202
in *TRIPLE DISCOURSE*, 330
Plato's view of, according to Christian iconographers, 350

Son of God (Adam-Light), in *SOPHIA* etc., 199
Hermetic, in pseudo-Zosimos, 100

Son of Man:
a, in *GOSPEL OF THOMAS*, 230, 368
in *EUGNOSTOS*, 194
in *SACRED BOOK OF THE . . . GREAT SPIRIT*, 178
in *SECRET BOOK*, etc., Cod. X, 204
in *SOPHIA*, etc., 199, 200
in *TREATISE ON BAPTISM OF JOHN*, 220

Son of the Light, in Battai's teaching, 60

Sonhood, in Luria, 294

Sons of God, in *Genesis*, 295

Sons of Man, in *GOSPEL OF THOMAS*, 369

Sons of the Light, *see* Light

Sons of the Unbegotten Father, in *EUGNOSTOS*, 193

Sophe, = Cheops, *Discourse*, 106

Sophia, see Wisdom

SOPHIA OF JESUS:
described, 198-200
discussed, 198, 200
in author's classification, 142
a Gnostic work in Christian camouflage, 311
a version of *EUGNOSTOS*, 125, 195, 196, 198, 241n.
author's work on, 125
Greek original of part of, from Oxyrhynchos, 87, 196
myths in resemble Irenaeus' description, 127
Philip, etc., only interlocutors of the resurrected Saviour, 222
refers to the Drop, 147n.

Sophia of Jesus, another version, in Cod. Berol., 87, 88, 196, 198
sources, 87n.

Sôthis (Sirius), = Isis in Peratean doctrine, 274
= Venus, related to Isis, 51n.

Soul:
adventitious, belief in, in various religions and sects, 216n.
Basilides' and Isidore's teaching on, 23, 54n., 72
in *SECRET BOOK*, etc., 215-16
Isidore's teaching on, 23, 215-16
Egyptian teaching on, paralleled Gnostic (?), 273
in *Acts of Thomas*, 95
in Gnostic belief, 112
migration of, in *Great Treatise*, 80
Sabian myth of the fall of, 316
teaching on, among sects related to Sethians, 53-4, 54n.-55n.
in *Books of the Saviour*, 72
in *Pistis-Sophia*, 69

Souls, two, doctrine of, among Messalians and Bogomils, 310, 311n.
two, theory of, in Dead Sea sect and elsewhere, 297, 297n.

Source of Life, in Islamic belief, 317

Sozomen, *History*, 139n.

Space, in *Bundahishn*, 152

Spheres, arrangement of, in *Pistis-Sophia*, 71

Spiegelberg, on Preisigke, 274n.

Spirit:
(Breath, Wind) the third, intermediate, principle of the Sethians, 52, 150, 259
descent of, in Valentinian schools, 218n.
Great, in *SACRED BOOK OF THE GREAT SPIRIT*, 178, 179
Holy, *see* Holy Spirit

Spirit (*cont.*):
in *GOSPEL OF PHILIP*, 223, 224
in *PARAPHRASE OF SHEM*, 147, 148
intermediate principle in Sumerian belief, 268
primordial, in Nicolaitan teaching, 14
the, in *SECRET BOOK, etc.*, Cod. X, 204
the virginal, in *SECRET BOOK, etc.*, Cod. X, 209
Spirit of the All, in Simon's teaching, 17
Spirit of the Father of the Truth, in *HYPOSTASIS, etc.*, 159
Spirit of the Silence, in *SOPHIA, etc.*, 200
Spirits, of Light, in Dead Sea Scrolls, 297
of the All-Powerful, in "Rossi", 103
of the Power, in Borgia leaflet, 97n.
two, theory of, in Dead Sea sect and elsewhere, 297, 297n.
Spiritual body, in St Paul, 307
Statius, *Thebaid*, on triple universe, 281n.
Stein, *Philo und der Midrash*, 154n.
Stein, Sir A., at Ten Huang, 121n.
Stephen of Byzantium, 129n.
Stephen, St, *Investiture of the Archangel Gabriel*, 235–6
Stobaeus, *Florilegium*, Hermetic fragment in, 242
THOUGHT OF THE GREAT POWER related to (?), 331
Stoicism, adopted a Babylonian astrological eschatology, 267
source of some doctrines in Chenoboskion MSS., 264
Stoics and Magusaeans, 279n.
on Hercules, 35n.
Stratiotici, 14, 41
Strempsuchos, in Bruce Codex, pt.2, 83, 286n.
our ignorance of, 114
Strophaeos, in *PARAPHRASE OF SHEM*, 148
Studi e testi, 9n., 183n., 256, 285n.
Suchos, crocodile god, and Astrampsychos, 286n.
Suez Canal, the hostilities over, 124
Sufism, influenced Islamic Hermetism, 318
Suhrawardi of Aleppo, 318
Suidas, on Astrampsychos, 286n.
Sun, in Bruce and Askew codices, 80
in Egyptian belief, 273
ships of, in Egyptian belief, 106
in *Pistis-Sophia*, 69
ships of, in *Pistis-Sophia*, 106
Sun-god and Seth, 104
SUPREME ALLOGENES:
dated by reference in Porphyry, 250
discussed, 157–9
in author's classification, 144
mentioned by Porphyry, 156

Sutekh, 42n.
Svetaparvata, in *Mahabharata*, 284
Symphonia, of the Archontici, 46, 46n.
Symphonia, term used in Cod. XII and by Archontici, 197
Syncellus, *see* George, Syncellus
Synesius of Cyrene, *Dion* on location of Essenes, 299, 299n.
Syr, *see* Seir
Syria, Borborites in, 311
in Naassene symbolism, 49
Marcionites in, 25
original home of Gnosticism, 12
Orphic bowl from (?), 90
Syrian gods, in Rome, 94

Ta'anith, 290n.
Tabarî, 155n.
Tabennisi, 129n., 135
Table ronde, La, 2n., 22n., 50n., 122n., 188n., 247n., 313n.
Taha Hussein, Minister of Public Instruction, 123
Talmud, 290n.
evidence of, for Bible in demotic, 105
Tammuz, in Sumerian belief, 268
Targum Ierushalemi, 97n.
Taricheas, in the *Great Treatise*, 78
Tartarus, father of Typhon, 104
Tarwân, sacred mountain (*Ginzâ*), 256n.
Tat, in *HERMETIC TREATISE* (26), 246
in *On regeneration, etc.*, 275
Tatian, attacked by Rhodon, 7
used form "Jude Thomas", 340
Taûm, at-, and Manes, 226–7
Taurus, Audians in, 55
Teacher of Righteousneous, Onias was (?), 290n.
Teachings of Adam denounced by John of Parallos, 183
TEACHINGS OF SYLVANUS, discussed, 219, 219n., 306
in author's classification, 144
Te'ezaza Sanbât, 97, 98n.
Teli the Dragon, Jewish, 293, 293n.
Temple, symbolism of, in *GOSPEL OF PHILIP* and in Theodotus, 223
Ten Huang, discoveries at, 121, 121n.
Terebinth, in *Acts of Archelaus*, 314
Tertullian, 5
Adversus Valentinianos, 5n., 18, 18n., 31n., 35n., 45
De anima, 19n.
De idol., 68n.
De praescriptione haereticorum, 5n., 47n.
refutation of Marcion by, 24
pseudo-, *Adversus omnes haereses*, 214n.
on Valentinus, 240
Scorpiace, 5n.

Terzaghi, ed., Synesius, *Dion*, 299n.
Testament of Solomon, 171, 171n., 203n.
Tetrad, compared with the Drop, in *SOPHIA*, etc., 147n.
in Chenoboskion MSS., of Iranian origin, 281, 281n.
in Marcus' teaching, 33, 33n.
Texte und Untersuchungen, 3n., 55n, 77n.
Thebaid, Marcionites in, 25
Theodore Bar-Konai:
Book of Scholia, 46n., 175n.
wrote at end of eighth century, 9
described later Gnostics, 311
his description of *Apocalypse of . . . John* resembles *SECRET BOOK*, etc., 205n., 213
his evidence for *Allogeneous books*, 158
knew of Zoroastrian prophecies of a Saviour, 186
on Audians, 55, 56–7
on John of Apamea, 57–8
on Kantaeans and Battai, 59–61
on Kukeans, 58–9
on Lampetians, 57
on Mandaeans, 61
on Manichaean myth of Jesus redeeming Adam, 217
reliability of, shown by Chenoboskion MSS., 250
Theodore, abbot of Tabennisi:
author of Borgia leaflet (?), 96n.
wrote and spoke against heretics, Gnostics, 135–6
Theodoret, on Borborites, 311
Theodosius of Alexandria, *Eulogium of St Michael*, 96n.
Theodotus, disciple of Valentinus, 26
of the oriental branch, 31
quoted by Clement, 5
on seed becoming male, 234n.
on women becoming male, 234
symbolism of Temple in, 223, 223n.
Theologische Zeitschrift, 127n.
Theopemptos, identity of unknown, 300
in *SACRED BOOK OF THE . . . GREAT SPIRIT*, 179
Thirteen, the word of the, = Pleiades, in pseudo-Zosimos, 278n.
Thirteenth Aeon, in *Pistis-Sophia*, 149n.
Thomas, St:
as a brother of Jesus, 225, 226, 340
in Manichaean belief, 226–7, 227n.
as alien (= Allogeneous), 158
as evangelist of India, etc., 339
attribution of *GOSPEL OF THOMAS* to, 338–40, 355
cult of, around Edessa, 339–40, 348
importance of, in Gnostic belief, 335–6, 339

Thomas, St (*cont.*):
importance of, in Manichaean belief, 232
in *Pistis-Sophia*, 221, 222
in *SOPHIA OF JESUS*, etc., 222
in *BOOK OF THOMAS*, 225, 226, 339
in *DIALOGUE OF THE SAVIOUR*, 220
in *GOSPEL OF THOMAS*, 231, 233, 338, 355, 357, 371
relative importance of, in *Gospel of St John*, 339
Thomas, J., *Le mouvement baptiste en Palestine et en Syrie*, 298n.
Thorndyke, L., *A History of Magic and Experimental Science*, 1n.
Thoth, = Adam, in pseudo-Zosimos, 100, 101
author of Hermes' doctrine, 107
Thought:
First, in Bruce Codex, 81
in Audius' teaching, 56
in *PARAPHRASE OF SHEM*, 147, 148
in *TRIPLE DISCOURSE*, 330
in Valentinianism, 27
the First, in *TRIPLE DISCOURSE*, 330
Thought of Ialdabaôth, in *REVELATION ON PISTIS SOPHIA*, 166
Thought of Light, in *SECRET BOOK*, etc., Cod. X, 206
Thought of the Father, in Gnosticism, 61–2
THOUGHT OF THE GREAT POWER (SENSE OF UNDERSTANDING):
described and discussed, 242–3, 247, 329, 331–2
in author's classification, 143
Thought of the Invisible, in *TRIPLE DISCOURSE*, 330
Three heavens, notion of, became seven spheres, 238n.
Three male Children, in *SACRED BOOK OF THE . . . GREAT SPIRIT*, 178
Three Moments, in *Great Treatise*, 80
Three Phases, 113n., 114
Three Principles:
a doctrine of e.g. *PARAPHRASE OF SHEM*, 259–60, 263n.
in Chenoboskion MSS., of Iranian origin, 281
and elsewhere, 281n.
in Iranian belief, 280n.
in Sumerian belief, 268
not known in *REVELATION ON PISTIS SOPHIA*, 175
THREE STELAE OF SETH, see *REVELATION OF DOSITHEUS*

Three Times, the, in *Pistis-Sophia*, 66
Throne, in Jewish mysticism, 290–1,
   291n.
in Rabbinical literature, 177
Throne of the Lord Sabaôth, in Jewish
   star lore, 288
   origin (?), 288n.
Tigris, in Naassene symbolism, 49
   mentioned by Battai, 60
Till, W., ed., *Die gnostischen Schriften des
   koptischen Papyrus Berolinensis 8502*,
   87n.
helped by author over Codex Berolinensis, 125
Koptische-Gnostische Schriften, 65n., 77n.,
   222n.
published Codex Berolensis, 87, 87n.
"The Gnostic Apokryphon of John",
   87n.
to help publish Chenoboskion MSS.,
   117
translation of *Pistis-Sophia* by, 109n.
Time:
concept of, as a criterion, 110–11, 114
   (Fate=), in *SECRET BOOK, etc.*,
   Cod. X, 208
Gnostic concept of, 111, 112
   unhellenic, 266
   (= Ialdabaôth), 260
in *Avesta*, 154
in Chaldaean astrology, 267
in *HYPOSTASIS, etc.*, 161
Iranian cult of, 268
Timotheus of Alexandria, *Discourse upon
   Abbatôn*, 97, 98n.
Timothy, *I Epistle* to, 301
II Epistle to, 301n.
Titles of Gnostic and Hebrew revelations,
   289, 290
Tondelli, L., "Il Mandeismo e le origini
   cristiane", 49n., 207n., 256n., 271n.
Torah, influence of on Chenoboskion
   MSS., 295
Tour, La, de St Jacques, 74n.
Traditions of Matthias, Gnostic, cited by
   Clement, 226
parallels in, with *GOSPEL OF
   THOMAS*, 349
quoted as source of logia known to us
   from *GOSPEL OF THOMAS*, 342
"Travail d'édition, Le, des fragments de
   Qumrân, 296n.
Treasure, see Ginzâ
Treasure, in *GOSPEL OF THOMAS*,
   346
Treasures, the Sixty, in the *Great Treatise*,
   77
Treasures, etc., Cave of, in Syriac *Chronicle*,
   186

Treasuries, the secret, in *TRIPLE DIS-
   COURSE*, 330
Treasury of Light:
   common to Codex Askewianus and
      Bruce Codex, 79, 80n.
   concept of, derived by Manichaeans
      from Gnostics, 313
   in *Books of the Saviour*, 73
   in *Pistis-Sophia*, 65, 66, 67, 69, 71
   in the *Great Treatise*, 77, 78
   in titleless portion of Codex Askew-
      ianus, 75
   in Zoroastrian prophecy, 186
Treasury, the, in Iranian belief, 282
TREATISE, in Codex XIII, (48), by
   Heracleon (?), 239
   in author's classification, 145
TREATISE, EPISTLE, in Codex V, in
   author's classification, 143
   mentioned, 197
*TREATISE ON BAPTISM OF JOHN,
   etc.*, in Codex V, described, 219–20
   in author's classification, 143
   parallels with *EUGNOSTOS* and
      *REVELATION   ON   PISTIS
      SOPHIA*, 219
*TREATISE ON THE TRIPLE EPI-
   PHANY, see TRIPLE DISCOURSE,
   etc.*
Trebius Iustus, tomb of, 92
Tree of Knowledge, in *Books of the
   Saviour*, 73
Trees, in Gnostic, etc., symbolism, 80n.,
   147n., 345
   in twelfth-century Christian symbolism,
      80n.
   of Paradise, in *GOSPEL OF THOMAS*,
      345, 358
   in Manichaean belief, 216–17, 216n.
   in *SECRET BOOK, etc.*, 216, 216n.
   meaning of, 372
Triad, Hermetic, in pseudo-Zosimos,
   100
TRIPLE DISCOURSE, etc., 289n.
   description, 181, 329–31
   discussed, 331, 332
   in author's classification, 144
Triple-Power, in Bruce Codex, pt.2, 82
   of the Great Archon in *Great Treatise*,
      78
Triple-Powers, in *Pistis-Sophia*, 66
   in titleless portion of Codex Askewianus,
      75
Trowel symbol, 91
Truth, in *DIALOGUE OF THE
   SAVIOUR*, 221
   in *TREATISE ON BAPTISM OF
      JOHN*, 219
   in Valentinianism, 27, 28

Tsimtsum, in Luria, 294
Two in one, in GOSPEL OF THOMAS, 230, 359
Two Principles, in Chenoboskion MSS. and elsewhere, 281n.
in Iranian belief, 280n.
incompatible with Three (?), 260
Typhon, in the Great Treatise, 79
= Seth, in Judaeo-Gnostic rituals, 105
in magic, 104
sons of, = Gnostics (?), 274
Tyre, 16

Ulysses, in Eustathius' commentary, 191
in note in EXEGESIS, etc., 191
in tomb of the Aurelii, 93
Unbegotten, in EUGNOSTOS, 194
Unity, in GOSPEL OF THOMAS, 345, 349, 371, 375
Universe, evil in Gnostic belief, 111
but destined to salvation, 113
Upon the Investiture of St Michael, 96
Uranius, Audian, 55
Uriel, in Investiture of the Archangel Gabriel, 236.
Urkunden des Aegypt. Altertums, 104n.

Vajda, G., "Melchisédech dans la mythologie ismaélienne", 155n., 321n.
Valentinianism, 13, 54n.–55n.
Tertullian on, 18–19, 18n.
Valentinians, belief in the Limit and the Cross, 60n.
doctrines similar to those of EUGNOS-TOS, 195
Gospel of Truth (Irenaeus), 240
Valentinus, author of GOSPEL OF TRUTH (?), 126, 240, 241, 241n.
his use of Homer, 191n.
leader of a Gnostic sect, 7, 12
life of, 26
on masculine women (Philosophumena), 48, 234
possessed a gospel (pseudo-Tertullian), 240
pupils of, 26, 30 et seq.
Secundus was a pupil of, 24
Sophia by, not SOPHIA OF JESUS, 200
split in his sect, 12
split over descent of Spirit, 218n.
teachings of, 27–30, 33
origin of (?), 36
quoted by Clement, 5
sources for, 27n.
used matrimony as a symbol, 224n.
view of Seth in, 39n., 45
works by, 26, 115
wrote a Gospel of Truth, 26

Vandier, J., La Religion égyptienne, 272n.
Vây, 154
in Avesta, 154
in Bundahishn, 153
Vendidad, 80n.
Venturi, A., Storia dell'arte italiana, 207n.
Venus, = Sothis, 51
Vetus Testamentum, 297n.
Vézelay, Circe in church of, 192n.
Vibia, tomb of, 90
Victories, Mountain of, in Syriac Chronicle, 186
Vigilantius, a Gnostic, 5
Vigiliae christianae, 27n., 118n., 119n., 122n., 125n.
Vincent, L., "Le Culte d'Hélène à Samaria", 16n.
Vintras, 322
Virgin:
a, bearing a child, in APOCALYPSE OF ADAM, etc., 183
and child, in a Zoroastrian prophecy, 186
heavenly, in Balinus, 319
in Acts of Thomas, 95
in REVELATION ON PISTIS SOPHIA, 167, 168
in "Rossi", 103
= Sophia (?) in Bruce Codex, pt.2, 84
Virgin of Light:
—Archons and Vishnu—Asuras, 284
Egyptian parallel to, 273
in Books of the Saviour, 73
in Manichaean belief, 80n.
derived from Gnostic, 313
in Pistis-Sophia, 66
seduced Archons, 164n.
similarity of Bruce and Askew codices on, 80
visible in the night sky, a Gnostic belief, 271
Virtue, The, in Ophite teaching, 38–9
in Satornil's teaching, 19
Virtues, the, in Basilides' teachings, 22
Vishnu—Asuras and Virgin of the Light—Archons, 284
Vohu Manah, in Zâtsparam, 282n.
Voice, the, in TRIPLE DISCOURSE, 329
Void, = Air and Fate, in Hellenistic writings, 153–4
in Avesta, 154
in Bundahishn, 152n., 153
Völker, W., Quellen zur geschichte der christlichen Gnosis, 4n., 6n., 7n., 17n., 20n., 33n.
Vorträger der Bibliothek Warburg, 281n., 318n.
Vouaux, L., 16n.

Wallach, L., "A Jewish polemic against Gnosticism", 289n.

Wartzburg, Priscillianist treatises of, 198n., 214n., 310n.

Waters of Life, in Bruce Codex, p.2, 85

Ways of the Midst, in the *Great Treatise*, 79
 in titleless portion of Codex Askewianus, 75

Wellman, *Der Physiologus*, 171n.

West, *Pahlavi texts*, 196n., 277n.

White Mountain, in *Mahabharata*, 284
 in Mandaean myth, 256

Whole, in a Coptic fragment, 89

Widengren, G., *The Ascension of the Apostle and the Heavenly Book*, 189n.
 The Great Vohu Manah and the Apostle of God, 80n., 214n., 268n., 281n., 282n.
 "Der iranische Hintergrund der Gnosis", 95n., 282n.
 The King and the Tree of Life in Near Eastern Religion, 268n.
 Mesopotamian Elements in Manichaeism, 208n., 216n., 218n., 224n., 268n., 271n., 281n.
 Muhammad, the Apostle of God and his Ascension, 158n., 317n.
 Stand und Aufgaben der Iranischen Religionsgeschichte, 256n., 279n., 281n., 287n., 315n.

Wikander, *Études sur les mystères de Mithra*, 281n.

Wilpert, "Le pitture dell'ipogeo ... presso il viale Manzoni ...", 92n.

Wilson, R. McL., "Simon, Dositheus and the Dead Sea Scrolls", 15n., 61n., 189n., 296n.

Wind (= Spirit), one of the Three Sethian principles, 259

Wisdom (Sophia):
 absence of, in teaching of John of Apamea, 58
 aeons of, in Bruce Codex, pt.2, 85
 Egyptian, myth of Nut similar to, 272
 in *Acts of Thomas*, 95
 in *APOCALYPSE OF JAMES* (10), 237
 in Audius' teaching, 56
 in Barbelognostic teaching, 37
 in Chenoboskion MSS., of Iranian origin, 281
 in *EUGNOSTOS*, 194
 in *HYPOSTASIS*, etc., 161-3
 in Judaeo-Gnostic invocations, 165
 in Ophite belief (Epiphanius), 212
 in *PARAPHRASE OF SHEM*, 149
 in *Pistis-Sophia*, 66, 69, 70, 71
 in *SECRET BOOK*, etc., Cod. X, 202, 204, 210
 in *SETHIAN REVELATION*, Cod. VI, 187

Wisdom (Sophia) (*cont.*):
 in Simon's teaching, 17
 in *SOPHIA*, etc., 199, 200
 in tomb of Aurelii, 92
 in Valentinianism, 27-9, 30, 31, 32
 Logos of, in Valentinianism, 218n.
 marriage of, in Valentinus' teaching, 224n.
 of God, in St Paul, 306
 in *Zohar*, 292
 parallel of Anthropos in *Poimandres*, 277
 (*Pistis-Sophia*), in *REVELATION ON PISTIS SOPHIA*, 165-8, 169, 175
 Prounikos, Egyptian parallel of, 273
 in Ophite belief (Irenaeus), 38, 39, 40
 (Sophia), in a Gnostic fragment, 88
 in a Gnostic prayer, 108
 in Gnostic belief, 113
 struggle against Archons paralleled by Athena and Titans, 264
 (Sophia Pansophos) in *EUGNOSTOS*, 194
 (the Great and the Little) in *GOSPEL OF PHILIP*, 225
 = Virgin in Bruce Codex, pt. 2 (?), 84

Withdrawal of God, in Luria, Basilides, and *Books of Jêou*, 294

Woman, the First, in Ophite belief, 37

Womb, in Sethian teaching, 52-3
 in the *Mithraic Liturgy*, 108
 symbolism of, 52, 52n.

Wombs, in Bruce Codex, pt. 2, and *Chaldaean Oracles*, 85-6

Women, as Gnostic proselytizers (Epiphanius), 8-9
 rendered male, in *GOSPEL OF THOMAS* and elsewhere, 234

Word, the, in Barbelognostic teaching, 37
 in Basilides' teaching, 22
 in Bruce Codex, pt.2, 81, 84
 equivalent to Monogene, 81n.
 in Naassene belief, 48
 in Peratean teaching, 50
 in *Poimandres*, 276
 in Sethian teaching, 52-3
 in *TRIPLE DISCOURSE*, 330
 in Valentinianism, 27
 of the soul, in *THOUGHT OF THE GREAT POWER*, 242
 of Truth, in *TREATISE ON BAPTISM OF JOHN*, 220
 (= Saviour) in *GOSPEL OF TRUTH*, 239

World of Light, in Kukean teaching, 58
 in *Pistis-Sophia*, see Treasury of Light

Writing put under the name of Seth, see Scriptura, etc.

Wuilleumier, H., "Études historiques sur l'emploi et la signification des signa", 196n.

Wunsch, R., *Sethianische Verflüchungstafeln aus Rom*, 106n.

Yazdani or Yaswani, = Battai, 61
"Yazîdî", 316n.
Yazuqeans, 61
Yezdegerd II, 59
Yezedis, and Gnosticism, 316, 316n.
Yôhannâ, in Mandaean belief, 255, 256

Zacchaeans, 41
Zachaeus, disciple of John of Apamea, 58
Zacharias, 41–2, 41n.
Zaehner, R. C., *The Teachings of the Magi*, 281n.
  Zurvan, a Zoroastrian dilemma, 151n., 152n., 205n., 214n., 271n., 279n., 280n., 281n.
Zahn, *Geschichte des neutestamentlichen Kanons*, 221, 221n.
Zaradusht, Zarathustra, *see* Zoroaster
Zâtsparam, on Adam, 214
  parts of body fabricated by, and correspond with, planets in, 205n., 214n.
  Vohu Manah in, 282n.
Zeal, in Audius' teaching, 56
Zeasar, in Naassene teachings, 49
Zeitschrift d. Deutsche Morgenl. Gesellsch., 39n., 295n.
Zeitschrift für Aegyptische Sprache, 273n.
Zeitschrift für die Neutestamentliche Wissenschaft, 87n., 315n.
Zeitschrift für Religions- und Geistesgeschichte, 15n., 34n., 95n., 214n., 282n., 286n., 296n.
Zeitschrift für Theologie und Kirche, 297n.
Zend Avesta, *see Avesta*
Zervan, = Shem, 155n.
Zeus, identified with Simon, 16
  in pseudo-Zosimos, 101
  in titleless portion of Codex Askewianus, 75
Zodarion, in Peratean belief (*Philosophumena*), 286n.
Zodiac, in *Pistis-Sophia*, 66, 67, 71
  in Zosimos, Syriac version, 149n.
Zoë, in *HYPOSTASIS*, *etc.*, 162–3
  in *REVELATION ON PISTIS SOPHIA*, 167, 168, 169
  in *SECRET BOOK*, *etc.*, Cod. X, 202, 206
Zoëga, *Catalogus codicum copticorum*, 96n.

Zogenethles, in Bruce Codex, pt.2, 85
Zohar, 292, 292n.
Zoroaster:
  and Anâhita, 80n.
  Apocalypse of, mentioned in Porphyry, 10, 53, 156, 218
  author of prophecies of a saviour (Theodore Bar-Konaï, etc.), 186–7
  Baruch compared with, 33n.
  = Baruch in myth of Saoshyant, 184
  books attributed to, 4, 115, 154, 280
  = Cham, 20n.
  = Er, in Arnobius, 156
  Gnostic use of name shows Magusaean influence, 280
  identified with Seth, etc., 280
  in Chenoboskion MSS., equals Balaam, Ezechiel and Nimrod, 287
  equals Seth, 287, 288
  in Manes, *Shâpurakân*, 314n.
  in Manichaeism, 102
  in Peratean belief (*Philosophumena*), 286n.
  in pseudo-Zosimos, 100, 101
  in Suidas, etc., 286n.
  in Tabari, 155n.
  myths about, 102
    some identical with those ascribed to Seth, 187
  seed of, and seed of Seth, 282
  Upon nature, 154n.
  writings attributed to contain substance of the revelations of Adam, 184
  (Zarathustra) in *Zâtsparam*, 282n.
Zoroaster, grandson of Zostrian, 156n.
Zoroastrianism, as a source for Gnosticism, 2
  influenced Basilides, 7
  Mountain in, and Indian parallel, 285
Zoroastrians, whispered their prayers, 196
Zorokothora (= Meldizedek), in the *Great Treatise*, 79
Zosimos, pseudo-:
  On the letter Imuth, 278n.
    mentions Hermes, *Physika*, 278
  On the letter Kappa, 278n.
  treatises of, 148n.–149n.
  Upon action, the commentary on, 101n.
  Upon the letter Omega, 99, 100n.
    quotations from, 100–1
    Chenoboskion MSS. fairly represented in titles mentioned, in, 251–2
    eclecticism of, 278, 278n.
    on Adam, 175
    references to other works in, 170
    shows syncretism, 248
    similar to *EXEGESIS ON THE SOUL*, 190
    work by Nicotheus mentioned in, 159

Zosimos, pseudo- (*cont.*):
 Upon the letter Omega (*cont.*):
  work by Solomon mentioned in, 172,
   172n.
Zostrian, ancestor of Zoroaster, 101–2,
 102n.
 apocalypse of, mentioned in Porphyry,
  10, 53, 156
 books attributed to, 115
 Gnostic use of name shows Magusaean
  influence, 280

Zostrian (*cont.*):
 in Arnobius, 156
 Upon nature, 156
  identified with DISCOURSE OF
   ZOROASTER, 156
Zürich, Jung Institute, *see* Jung Institute
Zuqnîn monastery, *Chronicle* in the,
 185
Zura, disciple of John of Apamea,
 58
Zurvanism, 280n.